Public Speaking in Canada

Building Competency in Stages

Sherry Devereaux Ferguson

OXFORD
UNIVERSITY PRESS

OXFORD
UNIVERSITY PRESS

8 Sampson Mews, Suite 204, Don Mills, Ontario M3C 0H5
www.oupcanada.com

Oxford University Press is a department of the University of Oxford.
It furthers the University's objective of excellence in research, scholarship,
and education by publishing worldwide in

Oxford   New York

Auckland   Cape Town   Dar es Salaam   Hong Kong   Karachi
Kuala Lumpur   Madrid   Melbourne   Mexico City   Nairobi
New Delhi   Shanghai   Taipei   Toronto

With offices in

Argentina   Austria   Brazil   Chile   Czech Republic   France   Greece
Guatemala   Hungary   Italy   Japan   Poland   Portugal   Singapore
South Korea   Switzerland   Thailand   Turkey   Ukraine   Vietnam

Oxford is a trade mark of Oxford University Press
in the UK and in certain other countries

Published in Canada
by Oxford University Press

Copyright © Oxford University Press Canada 2006

The moral rights of the author have been asserted

Database right Oxford University Press (maker)

First published 2006

Library and Archives Canada Cataloguing in Publication

Ferguson, Sherry Devereaux

Public speaking in Canada : building competency in stages / Sherry
Devereaux Ferguson.

Includes bibliographical references and index.
ISBN-13: 978-0-19-542008-1
ISBN-10: 0-19-542008-X

1. Public speaking – Textbooks. I. Title.
PN4121.F47 2006   808.5'1   C2005-906898-13

5 6 7 – 14 13 12

Cover Design: Brett Miller
Cover Image: © stockbyte/business objectives

This book is printed on permanent (acid-free) paper ∞.
Printed in Canada

Contents

Acknowledgements   ix

Preface   xi

1   Public Speaking in the Age of Accountability: A Critical Model   1

Learning Objectives   1
The Birth of Critical Society in Canada   2
Trends in the Environment   3
A Critical Model for Public Speaking   12
Conclusion   18
Questions for Discussion   19

2   Communication Apprehensiveness: Learning to Cope with Anxiety   20

Suggested Assignment: Assessing and Coping with Anxiety   20
Learning Objectives   20
Situational Anxiety and Public Speaking   21
Causes of Communication Apprehension   24
Physical Manifestations of Communication Anxiety   27
Coping Strategies   28
Conclusion   36
Questions for Discussion   37

3   Listening with a Purpose   38

Suggested Assignment: Hearing, Perceiving, and Processing Information   38
Learning Objectives   38
Purposeful Listening   39
Influence of Perception on Message Reception   41
Reciprocal Responsibilities of Listeners and Speakers   52
Conclusion   54
Questions for Discussion   56

4   Acquiring the Basic Skills: The Speech of Introduction   57

Suggested Assignment: The Speech of Introduction   57
Learning Objectives   57
Step 1: Getting Started   58
Step 2: Getting Organized   60
Step 3: Writing an Introduction   67
Step 4: Developing the Body of the Speech   75

Step 5: Connecting Your Thoughts   75
Step 6: Closing with a Memorable Thought   77
Step 7: Practising and Delivering the Speech   79
Conclusion   86
Questions for Discussion   86

5   Researching, Analyzing, and Adapting to Your Audience   88

Suggested Assignment: The Speech of Welcome   88
Learning Objectives   88
Researching and Analyzing Your Audience: Creating Useful Profiles   89
Analyzing Your Speaking Environment   95
Adapting to Your Audience   96
Taking Ethical and Critical Concerns into Consideration   111
Conclusion   112
Questions for Discussion   113
Appendix: Sample Speeches of Welcome   113

6   Putting Principles of Delivery into Practice   115

Suggested Assignment: The Impromptu Speech   115
Learning Objectives   115
Preparing an Impromptu Speech   116
Building Credibility through Delivery   118
Meeting Technical Challenges   135
Setting Realistic Goals   135
Putting the Significance of Delivery into Perspective   137
Conclusion   138
Questions for Discussion   138
Appendix: Selected Videos on Public Speaking, Available in Canadian
    Libraries   139

7   Visual Aids and Software Presentations   140

Learning Objectives   140
Purposes of Visual Supports   140
General Principles   141
Different Kinds of Visual Supports   143
Presenting Statistics in Visual Formats   148
PowerPoint and Other Computer-Generated Presentations   152
Questions for Discussion   157
Appendix: PowerPoint Presentation   158

8   Researching and Supporting Your Ideas: The Informative Speech   163

Suggested Assignment: Preparing the Informative Speech   163
Learning Objectives   163

Different Types of Informative Speeches   164
Step 1: Choosing Your Topic   165
Step 2: Framing Your Purpose Statement   166
Step 3: Writing Your Thesis Statement   166
Step 4: Researching Your Speech   167
Step 5: Identifying Points of Possible Confusion   175
Step 6: Choosing an Organizational Pattern   175
Step 7: Developing an Outline   181
Step 8: Writing a Preview Statement   182
Step 9: Writing Your Introduction   182
Step 10: Developing Your Outline with Supporting Materials   191
Step 11: Linking the Parts of the Speech   201
Step 12: Adding Interest with Visual Aids   202
Step: 13: Concluding the Speech   203
Conclusion   204
Questions for Discussion   204
Appendix: Sample Student Informative Speeches   204

9   Ethos, Logos, and Pathos in Persuasive Discourse   209

Suggested Assignment: A Debate Involving Minority Voices   209
Learning Objectives   209
Ethos as a Persuasive Strategy   210
Pathos as a Persuasive Strategy   222
Logos as a Persuasive Strategy   224
Conclusion   227
Questions for Discussion   228

10   Speeches to Convince, Stimulate, or Actuate   229

Suggested Assignment: Preparing a Persuasive Speech   229
Learning Objectives   229
Step 1: Selecting Your Topic   230
Step 2: Framing a Tentative Position Statement   235
Step 3: Translating Your Position Statement into a Thesis Statement   236
Step 4: Researching Your Audience   236
Step 5: Defining Your General Purpose   236
Step 6: Framing a Desired Outcome   237
Step 7: Matching Audiences with Organizational Patterns   238
Step 8: Writing Your Introduction   248
Step 9: Supporting Your Ideas   252
Step 10: Choosing Evocative Language   253
Step 11: Adapting Your Materials to Your Audience   264
Step 12: Linking Your Ideas   268
Step 13: Writing Your Conclusion   268
Step 14: Delivering Your Speech   269
Step 15: Responding to Questions   270

Questions for Discussion   270
Appendix: Sample Student Persuasion Speeches   271

11   The Language of Propaganda   280

Suggested Assignment: Engaging in a Coffee Shop Discussion on Ethics   280
Learning Objectives   280
Defining Propaganda   280
The Toolbox of the Propagandist   284
Fallacies in Reasoning   292
Problems with Statistics   297
The Critical Communication Model as a Basis for Assessing the Ethics of
    Communication   299
Conclusion   299
Questions for Discussion   300

12   Speaking in Social Contexts: The Social Occasion Speech   301

Suggested Assignment: Preparing a Social Occasion Speech   301
Learning Objectives   301
Types of Social Occasion Speeches   302
The Use of Humour   307
Conclusion   310
Questions for Discussion   311
Appendix: Sample Student Special Occasion Speeches   311

13   Speaking in Classroom Contexts: Team Presentation   321

Suggested Assignment: Making a Team Presentation   321
Learning Objectives   321
Choosing a Theme   324
Setting Teaching and Learning Objectives   324
Deciding on an Agenda of Learning Activities   325
Managing Group Dynamics   339
Delivering the Presentation   341
Questions for Discussion   348

14   Speaking in Political and Business Contexts: Goodwill and Other Special Purpose Speeches   350

Suggested Assignment: Preparing a Special Purpose Speech   350
Learning Objectives   350
Political Contexts   351
Business Contexts   359
Delivering the Manuscript Speech   365

Conclusion   366
Questions for Discussion   366

15   Professional Speechwriting   367

Suggested Assignment: Preparing a Ghost-written Speech   367
Learning Objectives   367
Steps in Producing a Ghost-written Speech   368
Techniques for Preparing a Manuscript for Delivery   379
Relinquishing Ownership   381
Evaluating Your Efforts   382
Employment Opportunities as a Freelance Writer   385
The Debate over the Ethics of Ghost Writing   387
Conclusion   390
Questions for Discussion   391

16   The Nature and Function of Rhetorical Criticism   392

Suggested Assignment: Preparing a Rhetorical Analysis   392
Learning Objectives   392
Speaker Motives   393
Environment   393
Audience   399
Speaker   400
Message   403
Outcomes   404
Cost of Achieving Outcomes   404
Questions for Discussion   404
Appendix: Sample Rhetorical Analysis   405

Appendix: A Selection of Speeches   409

Dr Martin Luther King Jr: Lincoln Memorial, Washington, DC,
   28 August 1963   409
Prime Minister Joe Clark: Eulogy for John G. Diefenbaker, Saskatoon,
   22 August 1979   411
Prime Minister Pierre Elliott Trudeau: Paul Sauvé Arena, Montreal,
   14 May 1980   412
Prime Minister Kim Campbell: Canada Day, Vancouver, 1 July 1993   417
Earl Charles Spencer: Eulogy for Diana Princess of Wales, Westminster Abbey,
   London, 6 September 1997   417
Governor-General Adrienne Clarkson: Eulogy for Canada's Unknown Soldier,
   Ottawa, 28 May 2000   419
Dr Leslie Tutty: 11th Anniversary Memorial Service for Montreal Massacre,
   Calgary, 6 December 2000   421
Prime Minister Jean Chrétien: Ottawa Central Mosque, Ottawa,
   21 September 2001   422

Patrick Brazeau, Vice-Chief, Congress of Aboriginal Peoples: Native Women's
Association of Canada, Ottawa, 22 March 2004   422
Senator Vivienne Poy: Zonta Club, Hong Kong, 24 November 2004   424

Notes   427

Index   445

Acknowledgements

I am grateful to many people for their professional and personal support. Beginning with the *professional*, I would like to express my gratitude to members of the Oxford team. I would like to thank David Stover, Vice-President and Director of the Higher Education Division at Oxford University Press Canada, for his unwavering support for this project and his ongoing responsiveness to questions and concerns. Clifford Newman, appointed to oversee the review process and market research, was a thoroughly delightful correspondent—consistently positive, cheerful, and helpful. I was sorry when his role in the project came to an end. Another positive contact within the Toronto office has been managing editor Phyllis Wilson, who has steered the development of the project—responding to questions and putting me, as required, in touch with other members of the Oxford team. I also had the pleasure of working with Marta Tomins, consulting editor for Oxford. I have appreciated Marta's professionalism, personable way of dealing with authors, and patience. At the same time, I have profited from her gentle nudges at moments when my enthusiasm for spending long hours at the computer was flagging. Thank you, David, Cliff, Phyllis, Marta, and other members of the Oxford team, including Jessica Coffey (permissions) and Lisa Rahn (marketing).

I am also grateful to two sets of reviewers, who recommended the project and helped to guide its direction at the proposal and draft stages of the book: Thank you for your time and thoughtful comments. I have incorporated a number of your suggestions and given serious consideration to all of them.

I very much appreciate the generosity of authors, public figures, and personalities who have allowed me to use their work without fee—James McCroskey and Earl Charles Spencer, as well as many others whose speeches appear in the book. I would also like to thank colleagues and friends Juline Ranger, Laura Peck, and Brian Creamer for contributing 'tips from professionals'. Thanks to Garrett Patterson for sharing a speech schedule.

Other contributors, listed in the credits section of this book, include former and present students and members of Toastmaster clubs, who took the time to share their experiences. Even if I was not able to use all of your contributions, I appreciated your sharing them with me. Thanks to Erika Adams and Bruno Lepage for taking time to help with the final look of the PowerPoint presentation and to Maristela Carrera for contributing some of the pictures of Brazil.

On a personal *and* professional level, I would like to thank Gill Ferguson, who produced almost all of the photographs that appear in the book. Since Gill lives in London, England, we have corresponded at all hours of the day and night. The highest-ranked contributor to the Nikon challenges for 2005, Gill has added immeasurable value to the book. My daughter Alexandra Hendriks also made an important contribution to this project. A former instructor of speech and Ph.D. from the University of Arizona, Ali created the test bank for use by instructors. She also helped with creating some of the line and bar graphs in the book. My youngest daughter, Cameron Ferguson, who worked part-time as a graphic artist for the CBC in earlier years, contributed the cartoon figures for the communication model. I thank Bruno Lepage, son in spirit, for rescuing me when I became absolutely befuddled, unable to figure out how to complete some action on the computer. Without his intervention, the book would be missing some necessary diagrams. Thanks to Joe Ferguson for taking the time to draw a map of Brazil and to Desirée Devereaux and others for sharing their speech experiences. I also appreciate the use of two photographs by George Smith and Jules Leduc.

On a strictly *personal* level, I would like to acknowledge the love and support of my husband Stewart Ferguson and mother Maureen Devereaux. On a daily basis, I draw strength from their presence in my life. And finally, even though my son Eric has not participated in this project, he is often in my thoughts, as are my six little grandchildren—Ella, Émilie, Erica, Morgan, Solan, and William.

Preface

I have been involved in the study or teaching of speech for almost a half-century; so in career terms, this book is long overdue. Two of my friends in graduate school at Indiana University wrote their first speech books (now well-established in the market) several decades before me. For that reason, I cannot boast a book that is into its sixth or seventh edition. Obviously, there are disadvantages to coming so late into a fairly saturated market, populated by so many credible academics.

There are, however, also advantages. One advantage is lack of commitment to the past—the opportunity to begin with a fresh perspective, rather than making incremental changes over a number of years. As some well-publicized cases have demonstrated, problems can arise if people undergo too many cosmetic surgeries. The same is true for books!

A second advantage is the opportunity to synthesize knowledge gained over the course of a career—to bring a lifetime of experiences to bear on the project. This book will be very different from the one that I would have written in the early 1970s. And even as I have worked on the project, I have continued to question prior assumptions about what works best in an undergraduate speech class.

When I engaged in early talks with Oxford representatives about this project, one informed me that—given the enormous resources that go into producing an introductory book and the number of well-established books on the market—they did not want to add another book to the market unless I could offer a novel approach. Since the teaching of public speaking relies on classical principles, that request would seem to be a difficult one. But over the years, I have struggled with certain dilemmas in teaching the introductory speech course—dilemmas that I know others also confront. In this book, I have tried to overcome some of these problems. The following discussion describes nine characteristics of the book that make it appealing to instructors of the undergraduate speech course. The approach is assignment-based, additive, flexible, comprehensive, innovative, user-friendly, substantial, current, and Canadian.

First, the approach is *assignment-based*. A brief survey of the Internet reveals that large numbers of instructors (probably the majority) adopt assignment-based approaches in teaching the undergraduate speech course. This book responds, as others do not, to the important need to recognize how most instructors actually teach the undergraduate speech course. This book aims to make their job easier.

When using existing books on the market, instructors confront the difficult decision as to which materials to cover first. The dilemma arises because the authors have adopted a 'topic-focused' rather than 'assignment-focused' organizational scheme. For some 50 years or more, the typical introductory speech book has been organized around discrete subject areas such as knowing your audience, conducting research, developing your outline, supporting your ideas, and presenting the speech. In other words, each chapter addresses a different step in the public-speaking process. To cover all of the steps, you must read the entire book. To make matters yet more confused, the discussions of different types of speeches (informative, persuasive, social occasion, and other), which form the basis for the speaking assignments, appear in yet another chapter, often positioned at the end of the textbook.

Yet every area of speech theory and practice is relevant to the preparation of the first speeches; theoretically, then, students should have completed all of the readings before they present the first speech. Of course, that is an impossible expectation. So how does one time order chapters of often equal importance, such as communication apprehension, audience adaptation, research techniques, organizational formats, attention-getting devices, language, delivery, ethics, and listening styles? Authors of speech books have provided no answer to this question, and different authors choose different sequences for presenting their ideas. But whatever order they select, the same dilemma exists for the instructor of speech. Where to begin when so much is relevant to the first speaking assignments?

As a consequence of the above organizational choices, instructors have to piece together their reading assignments, assigning bits and pieces of different chapters. The process of putting together an outline for courses is time-consuming and frustrating for the beginning teacher of speech. The adoption of a new book requires that the instructor engage in another patchwork exercise.

To deal with the issue of time sequence, instructors often delay assignments such as informative speaking until late in the term, leaving little time for other major speaking assignments. Others generate their own materials as booklets or handouts, which they distribute or place on the Web. Many choose not to use textbooks.

An assignment-based approach eliminates these kinds of problems. Each chapter presents the information and skills required to fulfill the assignment that accompanies that chapter. The instructor does not need to go beyond that chapter when assigning readings. The student does not need to read the entire book to prepare the early speaking assignments. And this approach mimics the one used by most instructors.

An increasing number of colleges and universities are putting their courses on-line. The structure of the present book is more appropriate for on-line courses than any other speech text presently on the market. The assignment-based modular nature of the approach works well with WebCT and blackboard applications.

Second, this book assumes that *an additive approach works best*. Each new assignment allows the student to apply principles learned earlier in the course, but also to acquire new knowledge and skills. The chapter overview, which follows, demonstrates the way in which this book encourages the student to build competency in stages.

Chapters 1–3 suggest introductory exercises that allow students to consider their ethical obligations as speakers, confront their public-speaking fears, and come to a better understanding of how listeners process information and share responsibility for the success of a speech event.

By Chapter 4, the students become involved in their first speaking assignment—the speech of introduction. This chapter suggests steps to follow in creating a speech of introduction. The assignment introduces students to the basics—writing an introduction, thesis and preview statements, transitions, and conclusions. The chapter also discusses common organizational schemes that apply to a speech of introduction. The focus in terms of theory is on the use of attention-getting devices.

Chapter 5 provides the opportunity for students to apply principles of audience research, analysis, and adaptation in a speech of welcome. After conducting research on their classmates, the students prepare welcoming comments for a fictitious event. An impromptu speaking assignment in Chapter 6 enables the students to put aside content issues long enough to focus on principles of delivery. The instructor can tape and replay videos of the speaking performances, focusing on verbal and non-verbal elements of delivery.

Chapter 7 includes material on visual aids and PowerPoint or other software presentations. This chapter (the only one that does not include a suggested assignment) supports the material in Chapters 4, 8, 10, 13, and 14. A demonstration or informative speaking assignment, discussed in Chapter 8, asks the students to engage in research, choose appropriate organizational schemes, make effective use of visual aids, and speak extemporaneously from note cards. Chapter 9 asks students to choose sides in a debate involving policy issues of relevance to minority populations. In assuming the voice of minority groups or members of the establishment, the students are able to put their newly acquired knowledge of source credibility into practice, as well as to demonstrate their ability to use logic and reasoning in arguing their points of view.

Chapter 10 introduces the student to purposes of persuasive speaking and schemes of organization that apply to this genre of speaking. The chapter leads the student through the process of writing and delivering a persuasive speech. Like earlier assignments, the persuasive speech assignment requires the students to engage in research, adapt ideas to their audiences, select the best organizational formats, and use sound logic and reasoning. However, the assignment also asks the students to use various linguistic devices in appealing to the emotions of their audiences. The students are expected to use repetition, metaphors, analogies, antithesis, and other linguistic devices in this speech. The nature of the assignment requires that the students memorize large segments of their speeches, even if they use note cards in delivering them.

No discussion of persuasive speaking would be complete without a consideration of ethics. Although every chapter of the book asks the students to look at ethical questions related to speechmaking, Chapter 11 asks the students to meet for an in-depth 'coffee shop' discussion. In some informal setting, the students discuss the boundaries of ethical communication; instances where speakers have crossed these boundaries; and examples of fallacies in reasoning, improper use of statistics, and the implications of applying the critical communication model described in Chapter 1.

Chapter 12 expects the students to prepare and deliver a social occasion speech (wedding toast, roast, tribute, or other special occasion speech). A number of these genres present the opportunity for speakers to practise incorporating humour into their speeches. If the students choose to use humour, however, they must follow the ethical guidelines described in this chapter. The speeches should also reflect the best practices of the chosen genre.

Large increases in college and university enrolments have created the necessity for instructors to require team (rather than individual) presentations. Chapter 13 prepares students for those assignments by asking them to create and deliver a team presentation using PowerPoint. This presentation should engage the audience in a variety of learning activities, reflecting educational theories addressed in the chapter. Chapter 14 discusses the basic ingredients in different kinds of business and political presentations. Students have the opportunity to apply principles acquired earlier in the course when preparing and delivering these talks.

Chapter 15 asks the students to prepare a manuscript speech for delivery by a second party (local politician, bureaucrat, or business person). An organizational member should be prepared to work with the novice speechwriter and offer feedback at the end of the process.

Finally, Chapter 16 looks at the major components in a rhetorical analysis. The last assignment in the book asks students to attend a live speech event, which they use as a basis for their analysis. Alternatively, the students can analyze a videotaped speech or work from a speech script. This assignment allows the students to pull together many of the theories learned in the course. The chapter also returns the students to the critical communication model featured in Chapter 1.

In conclusion, an additive approach ensures that students will not feel intimidated by having to acquire all of the information at one time. Instructors, for their part, can place a focus on different elements as the course progresses; and the grading of speech assignments can reflect the expanding knowledge and skills base of the students. So delivery, for example, will probably receive less emphasis in the early speeches, more emphasis in the later speeches, after the students have benefited from instructor and peer feedback and readings.

Third, the approach is *flexible*. Chapters 1–11 introduce the student to the basic principles of speechmaking, with each new chapter adding layers of information. Chapters 12–16 offer information of a supplemental nature, which will be of interest to specific audiences. Since the book includes 16 chapters, most instructors will pick and choose assignments from the book. An instructor in a speechwriting course, for example, might decide to omit the chapters on delivery and team presentations but require the chapters on ghostwriting and rhetorical analysis. The instructor of a speech course populated by business or engineering students might place more emphasis on assignments such as team presentations, project proposals, and related subject matter. A continuing education instructor may want to focus on the kinds of speech situations commonly encountered by the particular mix of adult students in the class. The range of content in the book allows the instructor to pick and choose from a variety of concepts, including some assignments and omitting others.

The approach also assumes that some instructors will want to substitute favourite assignments for those suggested in this text. So long as the assignment demonstrates principles discussed in the chapter, no problem should arise from the substitution. An instructor of speech in a fashion design program, for example, may want to require a process demonstration for the informative speaking assignment but substitute a sales talk for the more conventional persuasive speech assignment. The structure of the book lends itself to easy substitutions or adaptations of assignments.

The coverage is *comprehensive*. Many concepts discussed in the book are standard to every public-speaking text. People have studied the psychology of audiences and the canons of speech since the days of Aristotle. Speech is the oldest of arts and a fast-developing science. Any book that omitted the important learnings, acquired over centuries, would be seriously deficient. Consequently, I have included lengthy discussions of informative, persuasive, social occasion, and business and political genres. This book addresses standard subject areas such as communication apprehension and stresses the importance of audience adaptation. Speech instructors have indicated, in surveys, that speech textbooks should include an emphasis on both topics. This book also responds to a demand for in-depth discussions of support materials (source credibility, emotional and logical supports). Throughout the book, I talk about the importance of taking cultural considerations into account in adapting to audiences. In essence, all of the basics appear in this book. The coverage is comprehensive.

The book comes with a number of supplementary materials, including discussion questions at the end of each chapter, an appendix with memorable speeches by historical and contemporary figures, a test bank, an activity manual for instructors, and references within the chapters to on-line and other resources.

In addition, the approach is *innovative*, incorporating a number of features not included in other speech textbooks. The assignment-based and additive approach of the book is certainly novel. However, other features are equally innovative. The critical communication model, appearing in the first chapter, includes an ethical component, not captured in other speech models. While every speech text openly recognizes the importance of ethical considerations, I do not know of any that incorporate this component into their models. The model also includes a number of environmental variables, unique to this book. The book draws upon a large number of contemporary examples to illustrate the dilemmas faced by speakers in today's environment.

The book also includes such novel assignments as a coffee-shop discussion on ethics and a speech of welcome. The speech of welcome enables students to focus, early in the course, on the audience-centred nature of public speaking. The assignment also allows them to put audience adaptation theories into practice. A number of the points raised in the discussion on PowerPoint presentations are also not offered in other books.

A chapter on ghost-writing draws on the experiences of the author, involved for 10 years in writing speeches for federal ministers and executives. Other books do not include this topic, even though the majority of professional communicators must engage in ghostwriting at some point in their careers. In fact, the large majority of professional communicators do far more writing of speeches for others and coaching than delivering speeches.

Another novel feature of the book is the inclusion of a chapter on rhetorical analysis. Many instructors ask their students to attend and analyze a live public-speaking event as one of their speaking assignments. Others request that the students analyze a videotaped performance or the script of a speech. Yet no other introductory textbook discusses the basics of how to put together a rhetorical analysis. Usually, this material appears in a second- or third-year course (or even a graduate course) that is specific to rhetorical analysis. While the discussion on rhetorical analysis in Chapter 16 is not as sophisticated as these upper-level discussions, the students have access in this book to a basic approach for undertaking the assignment. A sample rhetorical analysis accompanies the chapter.

I have aimed for a book that is *user-friendly*, with an abundance of examples, tips from professionals, sample student speeches, and visuals. Lecture time is limited in speech courses, and instructors tend to use the class time to focus on skills acquisition. So students must acquire most of the theory through readings, undertaken outside of class. For that reason, I have tried to achieve a 'student-friendly' style of writing. I have also tried, in the book, to anticipate a number of the questions that I find myself answering year after year for students.

At the same time that I have aimed for a student-friendly book, I have tried to offer content that is *substantial and current*. Some public-speaking texts are so elementary (compared to their peer texts in psychology, sociology, engineering, and other disciplines) that the discrepancy becomes painfully apparent, and our students complain (in their words) that we are 'dumbing down' the content. This book seeks to achieve readability without sacrificing substance.

And that leads to a final and very important point. The book offers a *Canadian perspective*, including numerous examples that reflect the experiences of our students. They will be able to relate easily to the examples and other Canadian content. At the same time, I recognize that we live in a larger world than Canada, and I include more limited discussion of examples and speeches from the United States and Britain.

In memory of my father
Aden Nelson Devereaux

I miss you.

CHAPTER ONE

Public Speaking in the Age of Accountability

A Critical Model

Learning Objectives
- To learn more about the birth of critical society.
- To understand influential trends in the environment.
- To become acquainted with the Critical Communication Model (CCM).

Guerrilla artists redraw ads, replacing the faces of Gap models with hollow skulls. They reconstruct an Obsession perfume ad to show a bulimic model leaning over a toilet bowl. Participants in a 'Reclaim the Streets' campaign stop cars and hold parties on blocked roads to protest the loss of public space. With the rise of globalization, a growing number of political and social activists use civil disobedience to make their voices heard. These anti-corporate movements are 'global, anarchic and chaotic, like the Internet . . . [they use] to organize.'[1]

Canadians, who have become increasingly critical and outspoken in the early years of the twenty-first century, number among these activists. The World Values survey confirmed this growing tendency of Canadians to question authority and protest offensive policies and activities.[2] In fact, the survey suggested that we are the 'most protest-oriented of all the national samples',[3] causing some government leaders to feel under siege. Canadian youth join and sometimes lead representatives of other countries in campaigns against globalization, the stockpiling of nuclear weapons, and military engagement. Activism on the Internet is a strong and growing global trend.

Public speakers enter an existing climate larger than the auditorium in which they speak. This environment has *political*, *social*, *cultural*, *economic*, and *technological* dimensions, as well as *rhetorical conventions*, that shape how people respond to public discourse. Speakers must understand not only the profile of the immediate occasion and audience, but also the prevailing climate of the day. In 2006, that understanding requires an acknowledgement of the fact that we live in an age of accountability.

Thus, this first chapter takes a *macro* perspective, looking at the 'big picture' within which contemporary speech events occur. Other chapters in the book examine public

speaking from the *micro* perspective—looking at audience, speaker, and listener variables.

In the following discussion, we will examine the birth of critical society in Canada, as well as trends in the political, economic, cultural, legal, technological, social, and rhetorical environment. I also propose a critical model for public speaking (see Figure 1.2).

The Birth of Critical Society in Canada

Canada has strong critical traditions in academia and a thriving popular theatre that draws its inspiration from the Theatre of the Oppressed, a movement associated with Augusto Boal. Using the techniques of Boal, groups such as the Catalyst Theatre and Peace Theatre (Alberta), Headlines Theatre (Vancouver), Theatre Sans Détour (Quebec), and Mixed Company and KYTES (Ontario) have made their mark on the cultural scene. Until quite recently, communication studies in Canada have had an almost myopic focus on the threat to cultural and political sovereignty from outside influences (most notably, from the United States).

With the publication of *The Manufacturing of Consent* (1988), Noam Chomsky and Edward S. Herman became the apostles of this new critical age. Arguing that elitist economic interests have replaced public interests, Chomsky and Herman decry the size, profit orientation, wealth, and concentrated ownership of a handful of media giants. They point to the dependency of mass media on advertising as their primary source of income and on government, business, and 'experts' as the dominant sources of information.[4] These dependencies, they claim, create a bias that supports financial interests.

The next major influence in the construction of critical society came in the person of Canadian Naomi Klein, the daughter of activist filmmaker Bonnie Klein. Bonnie Klein made her mark in the 1970s with the highly controversial anti-pornography film *Not a Love*

Photo Gill Ferguson

Story. Following in the footsteps of her mother, Naomi Klein became a something of a cult figure in the 1990s with the publication of *No Logo*, a powerful discourse against the branding of North America by large corporations.[5] While not everyone agrees with Klein's anarchist stance on some issues, few would dispute that her book has helped to shape a more cynical and critical society—a society that trusts less and asks more questions. Klein has been a major force in the international anti-globalization movement.

Growing activism and commitment to social justice are evident in many spheres of Canadian life. In October 2000, women staged marches in Quebec and elsewhere in Canada against poverty and violence towards women. At the same time that women have organized to gain a louder and more powerful voice, fathers' rights groups have increased in numbers and strength. Some grandparents also have organized to demand visitation rights with estranged grandchildren; and, as a group, seniors have moved from the sidelines to the front lines of political life. Inputting key words such as *advocacy* and *protest* into search engines brings up a surprising number of sites dedicated to seniors' issues and efforts, including a 'Fax the Feds' Web site. Government departments that publish telephone numbers for inquiries and complaints know that the largest number of calls typically come from seniors.

The 'Raging Grannies'—a group of activist seniors in Victoria, British Columbia—have captured headlines for their creative approaches to environmental activism:

> They sing outrageous songs to familiar tunes, dress in outlandish costumes and relentlessly protest the presence of American warships and submarines armed with nuclear weapons in our waters, the presence of a nuclear weapons guidance system on Winchelsea Island off Nanoose, the continuing and intensifying involvement of Canada in a military strategy they believe is wrong.[6]

Trends in the Environment

The following discussion examines trends in the political, economic, cultural, technological, social, and rhetorical environments within which contemporary speakers raise their voices.

Increasing Cynicism in the Political Sphere

Recent polls have shown the emergence of an increasingly skeptical and distrusting public. The Toronto Centre for Ethical Orientation, for example, found that close to

90 per cent of people surveyed said that they have lost trust in private businesses and government institutions. Among other complaints, the public resents the proliferation of voice-mail systems and electronic transactions, which have replaced the personal element in interactions with businesses and institutions. Nine out of 10 Canadians also agree that trust is on the decline globally.[7]

In an unprecedented and dramatic way, the Canadian public dismissed the Progressive Conservatives in 1993. Justice Minister Kim Campbell had inherited the position of Prime Minister from Brian Mulroney, but she could not secure the position. In the 1993 election, the Progressive Conservative Party set a historical precedent by losing all but two seats. This election virtually eliminated the party from the political map, and the Bloc Québécois and Reform Party came to occupy the historical place of the Progressive Conservatives in the House of Commons.

In 2001, the Office of the Auditor General of Canada (OAG) unleashed a storm that continues to threaten the viability of the Liberal Party and the credibility of top federal government officials. Headed by Auditor General Sheila Fraser, a team of auditors uncovered a number of weaknesses in the accounting and spending practices of the Liberal government, then in power under Jean Chrétien. Fraser claimed that the Chrétien government had mismanaged hundreds of millions of dollars between 1997 and 2001 and, in so doing, had betrayed the public trust. The allegations led to 36 separate investigations by the RCMP.

An angry public responded to the crisis of confidence in the summer of 2004 by electing a minority Liberal government, thus stripping the ability of leader Paul Martin to act without the agreement of opposition parties. Since the opposition included a mix of representatives holding strong regional views, including Bloc Québécois politicians, the weakened mandate threatened the survival of the new government—and the coherence of Canada. In November 2005, the government fell.

Increasing activism in Canadian society is often, but not necessarily, liberal in orientation. The 2004 federal election showed a growth in the strength of conservative and separatist forces, as compared with the 1993 election. Based on the outcomes of a conference held in Calgary in May 1996, University of Calgary professor David Taras concluded that a growing number of journalists have abandoned a position of neutrality. He said that Canadian journalists increasingly are taking an activist—albeit sometimes corporatist—perspective on issues.[8] The outcry against malfeasance on the part of public figures comes from all political spheres and finds its way into the public discourse.

Increasing Activism in the Economic Sphere

Under the leadership of Maude Barlow and others, Canadians have taken front-line positions in anti-globalization protests at Seattle (1999 World Trade Organization meetings), Quebec City (2001 Organization of American States Summit of the Americas), and Kananaskis, Alberta (2002 G-8 summit). These protests cover a wide range of issues:

> The growing trend toward anti-globalization activism is directed, first, against 'big business'—multinational corporate power—and, second, against 'big money'—global agreements on economic growth. Allegations of exploitive labour and human-rights abuses reach back to the mid-1990s when a number of corporations producing major brand name products, such as Nike sneakers, Gap jeans, and

Starbucks coffee, were accused of union-busting, sweatshop working conditions, and child labour practices on a global scale. Among other well-known multinationals, McDonald's, Monsanto, and Shell Oil were indicted for similar faults. The litany of castigation ranges across a broad spectrum, including paying low wages, offering minimal health benefits, depleting old-growth and rain forests, using unsafe pesticides, bio-engineering agriculture crops, violating animal rights, and colluding with violent and repressive regimes. Activists, however, are divided in their anti-globalization position. The larger segment supports restructuring corporations to reflect accountability and transparency; the smaller segment, while also supporting these objectives, actively promotes the total demise of global structures including the WTO [World Trade Organization]. Anarchist activists and some environmentalists fall in the latter category.[9]

Protests against the activities of large multinational corporations have increased dramatically in number and volume since the beginning of the 1990s. Watchdogs such as the Corporate Library track the annual salary increases of Fortune 500 CEOs,[10] and 'culture jammers' subvert advertisements to send anti-corporatist messages. Corporate leaders and politicians face the necessity to respond to these criticisms publicly—to tailor their discourse to the questions of their shareholders and constituents. Many of the topics explored by student speakers concern these same issues.

Photo Gill Ferguson

Increasing Activism in the Legal Sphere

We are living in an age of class action suits and legal accountability. Class action suits are brought to the courts by one or more individuals, who represent a larger group of people with a grievance against a company. A growing number of legal firms specialize in class action lawsuits.

Prominent employers sued in recent years include such diverse businesses as Coca-Cola, Wal-Mart, Home Depot, Bell Canada, Rogers, Telus, and Ford Motors. Plaintiffs have named government departments such as Veterans Affairs as defendants in other class action lawsuits. Charges filed against these employers range from claims of racial and gender discrimination to failure of employers to pay overtime to workers. Other lawsuits allege misrepresentation of policies and services or illegal seizure of funds.

In a much publicized case, McDonald's was sued for serving coffee so hot that it burned a customer who spilled the coffee in her lap. Vioxx was withdrawn from the medical market in the fall of 2000 after some studies revealed that prolonged use of the drug doubles the risk of heart attacks, strokes, and blood clots in users. By October 2004, a Quebec consumers' group had announced its decision to ask the courts to consider a case against Merck Frosst, the manufacturer of Vioxx.

The tobacco industry continues to be a prime target for class action suits, with another recent filing against Imperial Tobacco in British Columbia. Class action suits over environmental issues also proliferate. Automobile insurance premiums have sky-rocketed as a consequence of large settlements and payments to victims of accidents, to the point that many people can no longer afford to drive their own automobiles.

Issues such as same-sex marriage and the privatization of health care have perforated our legal landscape in recent years. In a historic decision on 12 July 2002, the Ontario divisional court recognized the 14 January 2001 marriages of gay couple Kevin Bourassa and Joe Varnell and lesbian couple Anne and Elaine Vautour. After a ruling by the Ontario Court of Appeal on 10 June 2003, the province made legal history by registering the earliest gay and lesbian marriages.[11] Similar actions soon followed in British Columbia, Quebec, and Yukon, as Canada's Supreme Court took the matter under consideration. On 19 July 2005, Canada's Parliament removed the issue from the courts by legalizing same-sex marriages.

These legal issues inspire much of our most contentious public discourse. Speakers have always had to consider the legal implications of their words. In the current environment, they must be especially cautious. Careful research and adequate documentation are critical in preparing to speak in public.

Increasing Diversity in the Cultural Environment

A number of changes have occurred in the demographics of Canada. Unlike countries that have closed their doors to large-scale immigration, Canada continues to encourage an influx of immigrants from all over the world. The viability of the country's social safety net depends on replacement of a rapidly aging population. By 2001, the number of Canadians born outside of the country—18.4 per cent—had reached its highest level since 1931.

Until 1960, most immigrants arrived from Europe and the United States. In recent years, however, the majority have come from Asia (including the Middle East), Africa, and the Caribbean. A threefold increase in visible minorities (excluding Aboriginals) has occurred in Canada since 1981. Almost three-quarters of new immigrants locate in the large metropolitan centres of Toronto, Montreal, and Vancouver.[12]

Canada prides itself on its mosaic (as opposed to melting pot) character. A 2002 study by Communications Canada found that 85 per cent of Canadians cite multiculturalism as an important Canadian value. In the same survey, 83 per cent of Canadians agreed that Canada is tolerant of religious and cultural differences, and 78 per cent said that Canada is open to immigration.[13] In an earlier Environics survey, 76 per cent of Canadians agreed that immigration has a positive impact on our economy; and they gave a seventh-place ranking to multiculturalism/tolerance as an important Canadian value.[14]

Unlike the deteriorating situation in many countries marked by ethnic and religious conflicts, these surveys reveal an increasingly tolerant population—even in light of concerns raised by the events of 11 September 2001. In the five-year period leading to 2004, the number of foreign students studying in Canada increased by 60 per cent.[15]

Linguistic diversity also characterizes Canadians. According to the 2001 census, approximately 17.5 million Canadians are anglophones; close to 7 million are francophones; and more than 5 million are allophones, who speak neither French nor English as a first language.[16] The three largest language groups among the Aboriginal population are Cree, Inuktituk, and Ojibway. Ethnic Canadians list more than 100 different languages as their mother tongues. The largest increases between 1996 and 2001 occurred in language groups from Asia and the Middle East: Chinese, Punjabi, Arabic, Urdu, Tagalog, Tamil, Dravidian, Pashto, and Konkani.

Other changes are also occurring in the social portrait of Canada. The number of students enrolled in university has increased dramatically. Statistics Canada reported the highest increases in a decade in university enrolments in 2001–2, and the average university class included significantly more women than men. The female university population numbered a record 510,000, compared to 377,000 males. In disciplines such as communication and psychology, the ratio is even more dramatic. Although men still outnumber women in fields such as engineering and architecture, the number of women studying in these fields has increased by 50 per cent over the past five years.[17]

The changing nature of our cultural mosaic has implications for the makeup of Canadian audiences. Audiences are increasingly multicultural. Their values and experiences may sometimes differ from those of indigenous Canadians, especially in their first years in the country. The account of a young student illustrates this point:

> My parents Ruth and Kurt Chuop met in the midst of a Cambodian genocide, a time when all sense of humanity seemed to have vanished. Yet in this sea of despair and destruction, they were each other's anchors. They were hopeful that, when the war ended, they could start a new life together. Although Canada was a foreign land to them, they instinctively knew that if they worked hard enough, nothing would be impossible. As you can probably guess, that was before they had four children. My poor naive parents! They had no idea that raising children in Canada would be a little different from raising children in the Cambodian countryside. I can remember the first time that I approached my mother about dating. She looked at me in shock and stated that good Cambodian girls never date. They marry good Cambodian men chosen by their parents. Ahh, arranged marriages. Yeah, this wasn't going to work. Needless to say, my parents abandoned the idea pretty quickly amidst our forceful protests.[18]

As speakers, we must appreciate the changing nature of our audiences. And we must show respect for the cultural differences and the varying perspectives on dating, marriage, and other social and political issues.

Changes in Technological Environments

In today's wired world, speakers have many different audiences, often scattered through the community or dispersed around the province, country, or globe. Some are present in the immediate speaking environment, but many are not visible to the speaker. The auditorium may have a seating capacity of 300 persons; but television, radio, and the Web do not respect such limitations. In the case of a political speech, many advocacy groups, politicians, bureaucrats, and members of the general public may listen to the speech on the radio, observe the speech on television, or read excerpts from the speech on the Internet or in a newspaper. A speaker may have no idea of the range of his audience or its numbers. As one person noted in colourful language:

> The speakers of today's online community sit in wired caves, sometimes clothed in only their underwear, using Adobe Photoshop (a popular graphics editing program) and cryptic computer language codes to convey their character to the receivers of the message: the web surfing public. Not only is the speaker him or herself now invisible to the audience, but we, as the audience, cannot even be certain that the speaker is limited to a single person. Such constructs of character have led, in extremes, to the 'big brother' feelings of paranoia. . . . After all, how can we trust that which we not only cannot see, but also that for which we cannot determine a number of speakers?[19]

As new technologies proliferate, more extensive collections of speeches become available in audio and video formats. The ready availability of these archived speeches promotes the necessity for authenticity. Speakers can no longer craft one message for Toronto audiences and another for Winnipeg audiences. As speeches become accessible on the Internet, people can verify the stances of speakers on various issues. This potential for authentication means that speakers have little incentive to lie or deceive their publics. Recognizing this new environment, organizations (especially governments) have placed an increasing stress on consistency in messaging.

Changes in Social Environments

We are living in less formal days than many of the speakers we study in history books, films, and videos. That lack of formality intrudes into all aspects of our social interactions, including speechmaking. When I was growing up, everyone wore formal black attire to funerals, just as women wore hats to Easter church services; and no one ever wore white shoes with a black or navy dress. Very specific conventions governed the dress of both men and women, and different occasions called for different kinds of dress. Such expectations persist in enclaves of the culture, but they are no longer generalized. Today one should not be too surprised to see some people dressed in shorts or jeans at memorial services or funerals.

Rules of social engagement have also changed in other ways. An increasing number of people are choosing interactive media, watching reality shows that encourage their participation, and listening to radio and television talk shows that solicit their feedback. If hockey and soccer fans want to get on the field with the players, it should not be surprising in today's environment. On a recent visit to New Orleans, I noticed that many of the establishments on Bourbon Street no longer feature paid entertainment. They rely on tourists and students to climb on the stage, join the musicians, and become part of the act.

While some would argue that television has created a culture of passive observers who expect only to be entertained,[20] I would say that this view may reflect the previous decade, but not this decade. The success of reality shows such as *The Apprentice, Survivor, I Want to Be a Hilton*, and *Hell's Kitchen* suggests that viewing audiences seek shows that engage them. They watch the shows, in part, to figure out who will emerge as victor or survivor. The same is true of many of the forensic crime shows such as *CSI*

Miami, where the audiences follow the trail of evidence to see where it leads. Television shows such as *Canadian Idol* require that audiences select the final winners of the competition. *The Bachelor* and *The Amazing Race* demand that the audiences figure out who will remain at the end of the show. Almost every kind of contemporary programming, from *the fifth estate* to *Fear Factor*, allows opportunities for feedback and the acquisition of additional information on subjects of interest to the audience.

In the same way, speakers are finding that their audiences do not want to be passive observers, witnessing events in which they have no role to play. They want to be involved and engaged.[21] Some cultures employ specific techniques in public speaking that allow for high levels of audience participation. One example is Kenya, where audiences are not just spectators. They are 'participants coming together to construct a shared communal meaning'.[22] A common speech strategy is to leave the ends of sentences unfinished, waiting for an audience response. Many African-American preachers use this same technique.

Changes in Rhetorical Conventions

Like the social traditions that govern dress, the rules governing the display of emotion in public speaking have undergone transformation. A short journey to eighteenth-century France and nineteenth-century Britain and North America allows a glimpse of how speaking styles have changed over the years. In Britain, orators such as Richard Sheridan sometimes fainted in mid-delivery of their speeches—a calculated action that conveyed their emotional attachment to the subject of their speeches. In France, the chaotic days of the French Revolution produced a master orator, Maximilien Robespierre. In highly emotional and ritualized speeches, Robespierre declared his personal sufferings and his anticipated place in martyrdom. He used elaborate gestures and dressed in a flamboyant style. Female members of his audience, in anticipation of the climactic moments of the speech, would hold their handkerchiefs in waiting, poised to weep upon cue from the speaker.[23]

Box 1.1 Excerpt from a Nineteenth-Century Book on Elocution

When the pupil has got the habit of holding his hand and arm properly, he may be taught to move it. In this motion he must be careful to keep the arm from the body. He must neither draw the elbow backwards, nor suffer it to approach to the side, but while the hand and lower joint of the arm are curving towards the shoulder, the whole arm, with the elbow, forming nearly an angle of a square, should move upwards from the shoulder, in the same position as when gracefully taking off the hat; that is, with the elbow extended from the side, and the upper joint of the arm nearly on a line with the shoulder; and forming an angle of a square with the body; . . . —this motion of the arm will naturally bring the hand, with the palm, downwards, into a horizontal position, and when it approaches to the head, the arm should, with a jerk, be suddenly straightened into its first position, at the very moment the emphatical word is pronounced. This coincidence of the hand and voice, will greatly enforce the pronunciation; and, if they keep time, they will be in tune, as it were, to each other; and to force and energy, add harmony and variety.

Source: John Walker, 'The Elements of Gesture', in William Scott, *Scott's New Lessons in Reading and Writing* (Philadelphia: A. Walker, 1816), 16.

In nineteenth-century North America, students studied the art of elocution in classrooms, and the more affluent received private tutoring. The textbooks of the day gave explicit instructions on how to express various emotions through voice, movement, and gestures. Speakers sought to mimic the mannerisms of great and noble men.[24] Works such as John Walker's 'The Elements of Gesture' and Gilbert Austin's *Chironomia* set the standard for instruction (see Box 1.1).[25] A hand to the brow, an extended arm, a broad sweeping movement—each gesture carried an explicit meaning to the audience. The speakers learned how to apply the stylized gestures to memorized passages, not unlike the rote exercises practised by schoolboys in the Roman Empire or the declamations of the Hellenistic period in Greece.[26] Audiences of the day rewarded this highly theatrical style of delivery with rapt attention and accolades.

In the late 1800s, a movement called Chautauqua developed. Initially, the movement involved the development of community programs, first on Lake Chautauqua in New York and later in other locations. The community events featured a series of speakers, who lectured on a wide diversity of religious, cultural, scientific, and political topics. As the movement matured in the early 1900s, speakers began to move from location to location on the 'Chautauqua circuit'. Programs typically lasted from three to seven days. At the peak of the movement in the mid-1920s, lecturers on the circuit were speaking to more than 45 million people in more than 10,000 communities in 45 states.[27] Over time, a variety of entertainers (magicians, actors and actresses, and opera singers) joined the group of tent performers; however, the core event continued to be the public speakers:

> Lecturers were the backbone of Chautauqua. Every topic from current events to travel to human interest to comic storytelling could be heard on the Circuits. Chautauqua would swell by the thousands to see William Jennings Bryan, the most popular of all Chautauqua attractions. Until his death in 1925 his populist, temperance, evangelical, and crusading message could be heard on Circuits across the country. Another popular reformer, Maud Ballington Booth, the 'Little Mother of the Prisons,' could bring her audiences to tears with her description of prison life and her call to reform. In a more humorous vein, author Opie Read's homespun philosophy and stories made him an enduring presence on the platform.[28]

The lectures could last for hours, and families saw the events as a form of entertainment.

The American Chautauqua company Ellison-White set up operations in Calgary in 1917, and the movement flourished from there until 1935. The company sent speakers to 148 Canadian towns in the four western provinces in 1917 and to 294 towns in 1918. Although the Chautauqua phenomenon experienced its greatest popularity in western Canada, two circuits were operating in Ontario by 1926. An American company known as Swathmore Chautauqua served over 50 towns in the Maritimes and Newfoundland. Some independent Chautauquas also operated in locations such as Niagara Falls, Toronto, and London. The movement was popular until the early 1930s, when the Great Depression combined with the influence of automobiles and radio to spell the death of the Chautauqua circuits.[29]

At the same time that the Chautauqua movement was flourishing, students studied the art of elocution in classrooms and delivered memorized speeches as a form of entertainment at school events. In legislatures and other political settings, it was not unusual for politicians to speak for four or more hours to packed rooms. British parliamentarian Richard Sheridan spoke for four days in the impeachment trial of Warren Hastings.[30] If a politician in Parliament were to speak for several hours in today's environment, we would consider that he was filibustering, an unpopular means of delaying a vote on some bill or policy! In short, prior to the advent of movies and television, audiences had a high tolerance for listening to speakers for extended periods of time—a situation that has changed dramatically.

Modern audiences have different expectations and make different demands on speakers. The media have created a generation of audiences who expect short and provocative speeches, as opposed to long and entertaining speeches. When I write speeches for politicians and bureaucrats, I find that the average time requirement for speeches is 10 to 15 minutes. About 10 years ago, I was asked to write speeches that were 20 minutes in length. When I was growing up in the 1950s, political figures often spoke for 30–45 minutes, considerably shorter than the famed Chautauqua speakers such as William Jennings Bryan but notably longer than their peers in this century. The speeches keep getting shorter and shorter, as attention spans collapse and audiences turn to alternative media for information.

We have moved from an eloquent and emotional past to an informal and conversational present. Unlike the audiences of Sheridan and Robespierre, modern audiences view histrionic and contrived styles of delivery as inappropriate. For the majority of occasions, people expect a warm, conversational, and spontaneous style of delivery—not a grand oratorical happening. Former Prime Minister Jean Chrétien acquired the reputation of being the 'little guy from Shawinigan' who spoke from 'a big heart'; and the late Prime Minister Pierre Trudeau rejected the stereotype of the staid politician. He did pirouettes behind the back of Queen Elizabeth, slid down staircases for effect, and spoke softly and intimately to the television cameras. Among the separatists of Quebec, former Premier René Lévesque projected the same 'real' quality in his public appearances and speech-making, frequently appearing with a cigarette dangling from his mouth. Chrétien did not have the suave sophisticated style of his predecessor Brian Mulroney, and Lévesque did not have the polished eloquence of his compatriot Jacques Parizeau. But the legacies of Chrétien and Lévesque as speakers will be no less than the legacies of Mulroney and Parizeau, because Canadians do not judge speakers on delivery alone. Canadians want to feel a sense of connection with the real person when they choose their leaders. In speakers, they expect the same qualities.

Television has been a dominant influence in moving public address from the formal to the conversational. Most of the time, cameras observe communicators at close range. The gestures or body movements of the actor in a theatre or the classical orator appear exaggerated, affected, or even ludicrous on television. In the vernacular of the theatre, such techniques give the appearance of a 'ham' performance. More appropriate are small and natural gestures and a low-key tone. Also, regardless of the immediate setting in which the communicator is operating, television audiences receive him, in most cases, in the intimate territory of their homes. Such a setting for the transaction favours an intimate style of delivery. Thus, the competent communicator strives for verbal and non-verbal styles suitable for intimate personal space. In the late 1960s, Marshall McLuhan observed that television would require the emergence of a more flexible and casual politician.[31]

In the same way, the *content* and language of the communication must conform to these same criteria.[32] In 1988, Kathleen Jamieson wrote an award-winning book in which she suggested that this new definition of eloquence suggested the need for an increased emphasis on narrative (storytelling), self-disclosure, and visual modes of persuasion.[33]

Even while audiences like to see the 'real' person, they are not always comfortable with strong displays of emotion. They may feel uncomfortable when speakers become too personal. Sally Field learned that lesson in 1984 when she accepted the Academy Award for her role as leading actress in *Places in the Heart*. In a moment of uncontained happiness, she gushed: 'I haven't had an orthodox career, and I've wanted more than anything to have your respect. The first time I didn't feel it, but this time I feel it, and I can't deny the fact that you like me, right now, you like me!' Field's acceptance speech became the object of mockery and cynical commentary. Critics believed that she had gone 'over the top' with this outpouring of emotion.

In 1997, however, audiences reacted differently to an acceptance speech by Cuba Gooding Jr. When Gooding received the award for best supporting actor in *Jerry Maguire*, he shouted, 'I love you! Tom Cruise! I love you, brother! I love you, man! . . . Everybody, I love you. I love you all. Cameron Crowe! James L. Brooks! James L. Brooks, I love you. Everybody who's involved with this, I love you. I love you. Everybody involved.'

Perhaps the difference in the audience reactions to two displays of emotion derived from the fact that Sally Field focused on herself in a very personal way, revealing her insecurities, whereas Cuba Gooding focused on the audience.[34] When speakers are unable to maintain their composure in speaking about a highly personal topic, they can create a situation that is uncomfortable for the audience. On more than a few occasions when giving speeches in class, students have begun to cry while talking about the death of a parent or sibling. The audience does not know how to react in these situations.

Despite the tendency of many contemporary audiences to feel uncomfortable with strong displays of emotion, such displays are allowed—and even expected—when someone experiences a serious loss. On these occasions, audiences anticipate that speakers will display emotion. As Scott Peterson (tried for the murder of his wife Laci Peterson) and other defendants have discovered, audiences will judge them badly if they do not display sufficient emotion in the courtroom and in front of the television cameras. The Russian public criticized Premier Vladimir Putin for his stoic response to the deaths of hostages at Beslan in September 2004. They wanted him to show more emotion.[35]

Finally, changes have also occurred (within certain settings) in the topics deemed appropriate for public consumption. When Ellen DeGeneres 'came out' on her television show *Ellen* in 1997, she soon lost her place on prime-time television. Now she has a new talk show, and all of the major networks carry programs focused on gay or lesbian characters or personalities. *The Vagina Monologues* could not have been performed on university and college campuses 10 years ago.

A Critical Model for Public Speaking

In this transformed society, words are sometimes more important than actions. Critics accused Jean Chrétien and Paul Martin of hiding their involvement in the sponsorship scandal. Entrepreneur and media magnate Martha Stewart was indicted and convicted, not for insider trading, but because she lied about her actions. Former President Bill Clinton was castigated not because he had an affair with Monica Lewinsky, but because he lied about the affair. People today have high expectations of public personalities. They expect transparency and honesty, and they hold the officials to high standards of accountability. These expectations are part of the environment within which speakers function.

In response to the demands for accountability, many organizations increasingly focus on goal-setting and evaluation. The logic goes as follows. You cannot have accountability without evaluation, and you cannot have evaluation without goals. Similarly, you cannot evaluate the ethics of any speaker or speech without examining purpose or intent behind the speech as a starting point. Thus, the components of an ethical communication model include speaker, message, channel, environment (political, technological, social, cultural, economic, and rhetorical), noise, audience choices, speaker choices, outcomes of speech, and ethical bases for judging costs of achieving outcomes. The process is interactive and iterative in nature. That is, a dynamic exchange occurs between speaker and listener, in which they often exchange roles, offering feedback and asking questions. When the lis-

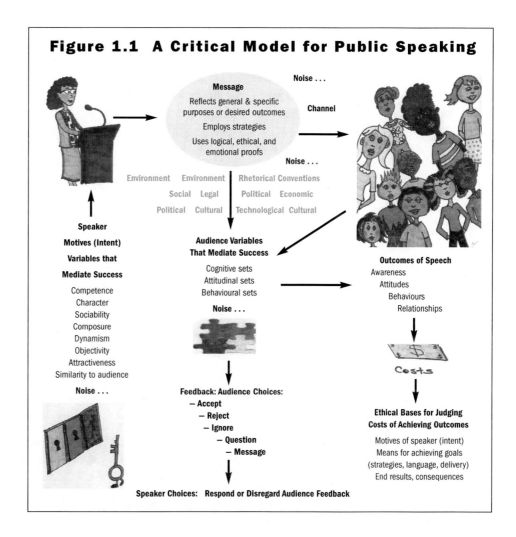

Figure 1.1 A Critical Model for Public Speaking

Message
Reflects general & specific purposes or desired outcomes
Employs strategies
Uses logical, ethical, and emotional proofs

Noise . . .

Channel

Noise . . .

Environment Environment Rhetorical Conventions
Social Legal Political Economic
Political Cultural Technological Cultural

Speaker
Motives (Intent)
Variables that
Mediate Success
Competence
Character
Sociability
Composure
Dynamism
Objectivity
Attractiveness
Similarity to audience
Noise . . .

Audience Variables
That Mediate Success
Cognitive sets
Attitudinal sets
Behavioural sets
Noise . . .

Outcomes of Speech
Awareness
Attitudes
Behaviours
Relationships

Costs

Feedback: Audience Choices:
— Accept
— Reject
— Ignore
— Question
— Message

Ethical Bases for Judging
Costs of Achieving Outcomes
Motives of speaker (intent)
Means for achieving goals
(strategies, language, delivery)
End results, consequences

Speaker Choices: Respond or Disregard Audience Feedback

tener becomes speaker, the process repeats itself. Like other communication models, this one helps to explain communication processes, visually depicts relationships, and assists in identifying possible points of communication breakdown.

Speaker

The speaker, or source of the message, provides the starting point in any model of public speaking. Speakers translate ideas into symbols or language codes. Speakers come in all varieties, from politicians to activists to comedians. They represent the spheres of business, government, private industry, and the voluntary sector. They seek to entertain, inspire, inform, and persuade us.

Speakers have specific purposes in giving speeches. In the most general terms, speech purposes can be to inform, convince, move to action, entertain, or inspire. In more specific terms, speakers may seek to inform about a new border security policy, persuade the audience to accept new screening procedures, entertain the audience with stories about humorous episodes at border crossings, or inspire the audience to pursue some personal goal. Sometimes speakers have motives or purposes in delivering a speech that they do not share with the audience: to repair a damaged image, to encourage the audience to vote for their party in the next election, or to explain their many absences from Parliament.

Because public speakers have intent when they speak—some purpose or set goal—we must include an ethical dimension in the study of public speaking. Most people would argue that we are most responsible when we commit an intentional act. In the court system, we hold people more accountable if they act with purpose and understand the possible consequences of their actions. In the same way, audiences judge messages, at least in part, on the intent of the speaker.

The credibility of any speaker also influences our acceptance of the person's message. When speakers arrive at the podium, they come with baggage. We call this baggage source credibility. The term *source credibility* refers to the perceived intelligence, knowledge, and tangible attainments; sociability; appearance; character and reputation; personality; sincerity; dynamism and composure of a speaker. Numerous studies in persuasion demonstrate that the greater the credibility of a source, the greater the chance that the audience will accept the message of the speaker. Roman orator Cicero stated that audiences take the actions of a person's life into account when they judge a message:

> It contributes much to success in speaking that the morals, principles, conduct, and lives of those who plead causes, and of those for whom they plead, should be such as to merit esteem, and that those of their adversaries should be such as to deserve censure.[36]

Message

A speech is the message delivered by a speaker to an audience—an oral form of communication at some point in time. (I say 'at some point in time' because archived speeches may appear in written format.) Usually speakers have a strategy for achieving their purposes. The strategy may not be obvious to the audience, but a scholar of rhetoric should be able to uncover speech strategies.

A politician may, for example, choose to focus a speech on domestic rather than international concerns if her performance in office has been stronger in the domestic arena. This is a strategic choice that she makes. In another situation, a politician may use extensive appeals to the Canadian value system as a means of achieving his purposes. In seeking support for legislation in favour of same-sex marriage, for example, Prime Minister Paul Martin appealed to two of our most cherished value orientations—tolerance for differences and equality under the law. A second strategy was also necessary, however, since many members of the Liberal caucus and the Conservative Party objected to the legalization of same-sex marriage. To appear moderate and flexible, the Liberals stressed the right of individual churches and pastors to decide whether they would perform these services.

Making matters more complicated, the Martin government had the problem of remaining on good terms with the Bush administration. Since Canada was pushing its legislation at the very moment that Bush was facing pressure to make the same acts unconstitutional in the United States, Canada risked antagonizing its important neighbour to the south. While most Canadians would not have objected to the contrast, the government could not afford to draw strength from a comparison of the two situations at a time when they were trying to rebuild damaged relations with the US. Their speech strategies reflected the complexities in appealing to different audiences—Canadians with varying belief structures and Americans.

Box 1.2 A Question of Ethics

An anti-gay Web site features a picture of Matthew Shepard 'burning in hell'. (Matthew Shepard, a college student in Colorado, was the victim of a hate crime against homosexuals. His death by beating in 1998 received extensive media coverage.) The click of a button allows the Web visitor to hear Matthew 'scream in hell'. Another Web site gives detailed instruction on how to build explosive devices. You learn that two Web site visitors were involved in the Columbine massacre. A group of protestors carry placards with the words 'Down with the government'. A speaker argues that pro-choice advocates are murderers; and the next day, two people die in the bombing of an abortion clinic. A student writes an essay that advocates violence against adherents to the Muslim faith. A Web site carries pornographic images of children, while another hosts images of women who appear to be victims of violent rape. A personal ad, which requests the services of a hit man, appears in a magazine for mercenaries. An organization called Victims for Justice distributes information on former convicts to potential employers and landlords.

The materials contain statements of an inflammatory nature, intended to create fear and hate in the readers. When ex-convicts move into a neighbourhood, VFJ members demonstrate outside their homes, delivering speeches over loudspeakers. They call for neighbourhood dwellers to use whatever means necessary to drive the offenders from their neighbourhood.

What are the limits of free speech? What constitutes hate speech? Images that degrade or words that defile? The perpetration of false information that unfairly depicts some racial, religious, or minority group? Language that inflames or encourages people to take violent action against others? Language that results in deaths or injuries? Should we protect all groups in society, even those who break the law? Should we consider the outcomes of the speech event? What happens when we put limits on the rights of people to speak freely in a democratic society? Do significant differences exist in how we should treat the above cases? What are the implications of censorship? Try to define 'hate speech'.

Speakers use *logical*, *emotional*, and *ethical* proofs to develop their speeches. Logical proofs include evidence, reasoning, and argumentation. Emotional proofs involve psychological appeals to the emotions of the audience. Ethical proofs require the building of source credibility—demonstrating intelligence, character, and goodwill. Although a speaker enters the room with an initial credibility, she can change these perceptions during the course of the speech.

Channel

'Channel' refers to the medium by which a message is transmitted. At the most basic level, the air that carries our messages is a medium. We may also use radio or television signals to convey our messages to larger numbers of people. Speakers can reach audiences through audio and video conferences. An increasing number of communicators are choosing the Internet as a means of reaching audiences. Like other communicators, speakers have an increasingly diverse number of channels, or media, for transmitting their messages. However, the new technologies lower the level of control over what happens to the message. Once the words leave their mouths, speakers have little control over how far or where the words travel. Their messages may appear in whole or in part in a variety of media. A magazine may reprint the entire text of a speech, but chat groups on the Internet or newspapers may select passages out of context for inclusion in their discussions. Television coverage often includes extremely brief 'sound bites' of speeches.

Environment

The environments in which we seek to inform, persuade, motivate, and entertain are too diverse to justify mention. However, in the broadest terms, speechmaking occurs in political, social, economic, cultural, and technological contexts. For the public speaker, rhetorical conventions are part of this context. When critics engage in rhetorical analysis of the type discussed in Chapter 16, they consider all of the above variables. Communication models, however, often fail to elaborate on the contexts in which speakers operate. Yet these contexts frame the speech acts and help us to understand possible reasons that speakers succeed or fail.

Audience

Language symbols become ideas in the minds of listeners, who decode the messages received from speakers. The resulting ideas may or may not be the same as those in the speaker's head. Understanding and acceptance of messages relies on successful negotiation of a number of internal variables in audiences, including cognitive, attitudinal, behavioural, and perceptual sets. The 'noise' generated by these internal factors can pose problems as serious as a loud air-conditioning unit or the discomfort of an overheated room. Both internal and external factors make reception and processing of information difficult.

Listening is hard work, requiring that we hear what someone says; selectively perceive, assimilate, and categorize the information; and finally develop a mental response to the message. We filter out a large part of what we hear every day, especially information that jars with what we already know and accept to be the truth. We perceive selectively, ignoring information that does not conform to our expectations. In today's environment, the challenge faced by many speakers is even greater than in the past. When speakers attempt to reach their audiences by means of radio, television, or the Internet, they compete with a variety of stimuli. The target audience may be preparing a meal, reading a newspaper, or watching a video at the same time that they are listening to the speaker. Multiple media may be operating in the listening space.

Noise

Noise often occurs in the attempt to communicate our ideas and opinions. By *noise*, we mean any form of interference in the communication process. This noise can manifest itself in the speaker, the environment, the channel, or the listener. A speaker may be tired, confused, or unsure of how to communicate her ideas. She may be insecure with a particular audience, and the lack of confidence may cause her to lose her composure or to forget her speech. Listeners may be biased or prejudiced on the topic addressed in the speech. They may also feel tired, overworked, or stressed by some event in their personal lives. These factors may prompt audience members to allow their thoughts to drift in other directions. If someone is hungry, the person will think about food instead of the content of the speech. Cultural misunderstandings can short-circuit the reception process. Audience expectations related to social norms in dress or codes of behaviour can create communication problems. Factors in the external environment—the sounds of traffic, a ringing cellphone or pager, coughing, or whispering among audience members—can also cause an audience to lose focus. A malfunctioning microphone or computer can interrupt the ability of the speaker to convey information. Thus, noise in the environment can be internal (psychological) or external (physical) impediments to communication.

Feedback Options

Ultimately, the listener decides whether to accept, reject, ignore, or question the intent, means, and end results of the speech. In a live situation, audiences provide non-verbal (and sometimes verbal) feedback to the speaker. The term *feedback* refers to the discernible response of a listener to a message. Non-verbal feedback may take the form of a shake of the head, smile, yawn, or nod. The listener may turn away from the speaker or look at her watch. There may be a delay in the processing of verbal information, because many listeners provide their feedback via the Web, e-mails, letters, telephone calls, and personal contact following a speech event.

Outside of a classroom situation, listeners do not feel bound to remain in a speaking environment that does not meet their expectations. Today's audiences do not adhere to the same social conventions as their parents—conventions that required people to stay in their seats and to look interested even when they were bored or tired of listening to the speaker. So the ultimate form of feedback in a speaking situation is to leave. If listeners do not get what they want from a speaker, they have other options, over which they have a much higher measure of control. That is, the vanishing audience members can decide when to acquire the information (morning, afternoon, or evening), how much to acquire (skimming of material versus in-depth research), and from what sources (television, radio, the Internet, magazines, books).

When audiences gather for a formal speech event, they have high expectations. Arriving at most speech events requires a relatively high investment—negotiating traffic, fitting the event into a hectic work and personal schedule, and sacrificing some other activity. Since the costs are high, the benefits must be high.

Speakers, for their part, may choose to respond to—or disregard—listener feedback. If they respond, the loop begins again: speaker-listener-speaker. Speakers may acknowledge the validity of a comment, respond to a question, or ask a question of the audience member who shows non-verbal signs of confusion or upset.

Outcomes of Speech

To evaluate the extent to which they have achieved their purposes, speakers must articulate desired communication outcomes (related to specific or general purposes) in advance of the speaking event. Positive outcomes for speeches could be increased understanding (speeches to inform), positive attitudes (speeches to persuade), action (speeches to motivate), or pleasurable feelings (speeches to entertain). Negative outcomes, however, are equally possible. Acceptance of purpose as part of communication process implies the presence of a results-oriented model.

Ethical Bases for Judging Costs of Achieving Outcomes

In an age of accountability, we must look at results in terms of responsibilities. Audiences judge public figures, in particular, on such ethical criteria as motives and truthfulness (*intent*), the extent to which the message was framed and delivered in an ethical manner (*means*), and the consequences of the speech act (*end*).

As speakers, we must judge the benefits of what we achieve against the costs. In an ethical model, we judge the costs of our rhetorical efforts to ourselves and others. Did we have honourable motives? (*intent*) Did we intend for our words to bring harm to others? (*intent*) Did we tell the truth? (*means*) Were we able to achieve our purposes without loss of integrity? (*means*) Did we incur damage to our reputation or standing in the community? (*end*) Did our words result in physiological or psychological harm to others? (*end*)

For scholars of rhetoric, the inclusion of ethics in a communication model makes complete sense. From the time of Aristotle, Isocrates, Cicero, and Quintilian, rhetoricians have stressed the importance of character and honesty in speaking. The growth of critical society gives new energy to the argument of classical and modern scholars that speakers should truly be 'good men [or good women] with good speech skills.'[37]

Conclusion

The volatility of the Canadian public, their willingness to take a stand on ethical issues, and their strong reactions to perceptions of wrongdoing on the part of government or other public officials have revealed a change in levels of societal tolerance for lying, deception, and irresponsible behaviour by public figures. Public speakers face this same cynical public when they go to the podium. Gone are the days when audiences bow to authority figures or accept words on faith. They expect politicians and other public figures to be able to back up their opinions, to speak with transparency, and to stand behind their words. And if television or radio commentators expose inconsistencies—shifts in position or language—audiences react. While not all of us will become public figures, we confront the same expectations when we speak in public. We must be prepared to speak directly and honestly, to respond to questions, and to translate our words into actions. We are living in an age of accountability.

The chapters that follow address, in detail, the components of the critical communication model—speaker, message, channel, specific environments, and listener. Vignettes, intended to provoke discussion of ethical considerations in public speaking, appear throughout the book.

Questions for Discussion

1. Describe examples of 'noise' in your classroom environment. Consider internal and external distractions with which speakers may have to contend.
2. How many live speech events (outside of the classroom) have you attended in the last year? What prompted you to attend the live events, as opposed to acquiring the information from some other source (media, second-hand accounts, etc.)? Did the speakers meet your expectations? Why or why not?
3. Identify some speech topics that would have been unacceptable until recent years. Identify some speech topics that would still be unacceptable within a classroom setting.
4. Do you agree that we are living in an age of accountability? Give examples to support your reasoning.

CHAPTER TWO

Communication Apprehensiveness

Learning to Cope with Anxiety

Assessing and Coping with Anxiety

Complete a test such as the Personal Report of Communication Apprehension (PRCA-24) to determine your personal level of communication apprehensiveness or the Personal Report of Public Speaking Anxiety (PRPSA) to learn more about your level of speech anxiety. Discuss how you feel when you experience communication anxiety and how you cope with these feelings. Practise exercises such as deep breathing and visualization that can help to reduce speech anxiety.

Learning Objectives
- To understand the nature of speech anxiety.
- To learn the causes of communication anxiety.
- To be able to identify the physical manifestations of anxiety.
- To learn how to cope with speech anxiety.

Leslie was a quiet retiring man, gentle in manner and soft-spoken. But appearances can be deceptive. Leslie suffered from a condition called *social phobia*, a fear of evaluation that creates a state of confusion and anxiety in individuals placed in a social situation. Literally any interpersonal encounter—whether ordering a meal at a restaurant, interacting with a grocery clerk, or responding to a request for directions—created mental havoc in Leslie, causing him to stammer, turn red, and become generally incoherent.

In order to cope with these extreme levels of social anxiety, Leslie planned every communication event. At home with family members, he would sit alone in a corner, practising for possible interpersonal encounters, planning even the laughs that he could insert into the conversation. In a restaurant, he would follow the lead of the first person to order, 'I'll have the same.' Any successful social interaction was a major life accomplishment for Leslie, cause to celebrate by repeating the conversation over and over again once he returned home. His brother once remarked that Leslie's tension was so palpable that it could be felt by everyone in a crowded room.

I suspect that Leslie's case is more extreme than most. However, University of Toronto professor Martin Katzman says that social phobia (or social anxiety disorder) is more common than most people realize, affecting 13 per cent of Canada's population. He goes so far as to say that his work at the Anxiety Disorders Clinic (Centre for Addiction and Mental Health, University of Toronto Medical School) leads him to believe that social phobia is *the* most common anxiety disorder:

> The illness is associated with an intense fear of evaluation in social or performance situations. . . . Among individuals with social phobia, the problem is not only shyness, but also the negative thoughts and feelings that get triggered by their feared situations, which cause them to avoid the situation altogether. Even signing a cheque in front of someone else can be potentially humiliating, because there is the possibility of a nervous shake of the hand. Social phobia is intensely painful and disruptive for those who crack under pressure. Physical symptoms include rapid heart rate, shortness of breath, trembling, and urgency—or failure—to urinate. Other situations commonly feared are public speaking, eating and drinking in a restaurant, and meeting new people. In some cases, the fear escalates to a point where individuals experience panic attacks. . . . For many sufferers of social phobia, what fuels their fears is the desire to be perfect. An array of hypothetical questions floods their minds: What if I say something silly? What if I start sweating? What if I pass out? . . . There are artists who never show their work purely because they are afraid of being evaluated. One question they constantly ask themselves is, 'What if it's not good enough?' Because they avoid social situations, individuals with social phobia live in a diminished world. Many are unable to develop their careers, build long-term relationships and lead full lives. Though they may crave success, students with social phobia might fear rejection so much they'd rather give up applying for school than to risk failure.[1]

Communication apprehensiveness is a large part of the problem experienced by social phobics. Most feared are situations such as public speaking and meeting new people, because they carry the highest threat of evaluation. This chapter will focus on situational anxiety of the type experienced by public speakers, the causes of communication apprehensiveness, physical manifestations, and coping strategies.

Situational Anxiety and Public Speaking

Psychologists differentiate between anxiety associated with particular personality traits (*trait* anxiety) and tension generated by specific situations (*situational* anxiety). While someone with trait anxiety will experience high levels of anxiety in *many different* communication environments, a person with situational anxiety will feel tense *only in certain situations*—public speaking, for example, or job interviews.

Situational anxiety afflicts virtually everyone at some point, including celebrities. When sitcom star Jennifer Aniston won the October 2002 Hollywood Film Award for her starring role in *Friends*, her acceptance speech was less than memorable. Afterwards Aniston explained, 'I understand the whole crying thing now. I forgot the cast! I'm just terrified. I have stage fright unless I have something written for me to say. I couldn't speak. I'm a blithering idiot.'[2] Actor Mel Gibson performed his first school play sitting down, because he was so nervous that his legs would not support his body,[3] and Donny Osmond thought he was going to pass out when he had a panic attack during a 1994 performance.

By the time Kim Basinger won a Golden Globe, Screen Actors' Guild Award, and Oscar for her 1997 role as supporting actress in *L.A. Confidential*, she had acted in 20 major films. But that experience did not prevent her from forgetting her acceptance speech at the March 1998 Academy Award ceremonies. Faced with a lack of words, she simply thanked her director, cast, and crew before concluding: 'I just want to thank everyone I've ever met in my entire life. If anyone has a dream out there, just know that I'm living proof that they do come true. This is for you, Daddy!'[4] And she walked off the stage. As it happened, the audience was highly appreciative of her brevity; and people applauded her show of sincerity and humility in accepting the award.

Box 2.1 A Question of Ethics

Lisa had a deep fear of speaking in any position other than number three. At the end of the first class meeting, she privately informed her speech instructor that she *had* to speak in third position in every assignment. According to Lisa, she had never made a presentation in any other position to that point in her life. The instructor believed that the speech class was an opportunity for the young woman to confront an irrational fear that appeared to cause her great emotional distress. Since the class policy was to allow the students to volunteer for speaker positions, she told Lisa that she would have to open the question of speaking order to the entire group.

When another student requested the third speaking position, Lisa panicked. She firmly informed her classmate that she could not take that position. Believing the request to be unreasonable and reacting with some surprise to the authoritarian tone of the demand, her classmate took a staunch position and refused to change. Lisa was dismayed. Panic-stricken, she continued her efforts to persuade the other student to change speaker position until it was clear that the student would not yield. If you were the instructor in this class, how would you deal with such a situation?

A humorous account of stage fright comes from the experience of British actor Alfred Edward Matthews, who was performing in a West End London production. A pivotal scene required that he answer a telephone on stage. When the telephone rang on cue, Matthews crossed the stage, picked up the receiver, and froze. Realizing that he had forgotten his line, he turned to another actor and said, 'It's for you.'[5]

Lacking the option of such a creative exit from the situation, speakers with stage fright seek other ways to deal with their anxieties. Following the advice of professionals, they may begin by assessing their level of comfort in speaking situations. James C. McCroskey designed the Personal Report of Communication Apprehension (PRCA) to measure more generalized communication anxiety (trait anxiety)[6] and the Personal Report of Public Speaking Anxiety (PRPSA) to measure anxiety specific to public speaking (situational anxiety).[7] The most recent version of the trait anxiety instrument is the PRCA-24. The work of McCroskey and his colleagues at West Virginia University has largely defined the study of communication apprehension since 1970.

Public speaking ranks close to the top of anxiety-producing situations. As noted earlier, Martin Katzman says that fear of public speaking is one of several events most feared by Canadians with social phobia.[8] A 1997 study found that 20 per cent of public-speaking students experience anxiety of a severe nature,[9] and a 2001 Gallup poll found that fear of public speaking ranked second only to fear of snakes among the general population.[10] Earlier polls have generated similar findings, with fear of death occupying a significantly lower ranking than public speaking.[11] Referring to these results, comedian and television actor Jerry Seinfeld once joked, 'Now this means, to the average person, if you have to go to a funeral, you're better off in the casket than doing the eulogy!'[12]

Some communication apprehensives experience the kind of panic described by Katzman, where they have difficulty breathing or continuing. When delivering a speech, one student would bring her child to the front of the classroom with her so that, if she succumbed to panic, the child could lead her from the room. In such situations, the woman experienced extreme difficulty breathing. According to the National Alliance for the Mentally Ill (NAMI), panic disorders of the above variety tend to occur more than twice as often in women as men (4.9 per cent of women as opposed to 1.2 per cent of men).[13] Studies also show that women experience higher levels of communication anxiety, in general, than men.[14]

The problem of succumbing to irrational fears is not restricted to inexperienced speakers. Surveys suggest that 76 per cent of experienced speakers feel anxious prior to reaching the podium.[15] One of my own experiences supports that observation. At the age of 55, I had been speaking and performing in public situations for 40 years. While in school, I had participated actively in competitive debate, interpretive reading, extemporaneous and impromptu speaking, oratory events, and theatrical productions. My professional career had involved teaching speech, theatre, and a broad range of communication courses; and I had been involved in community theatre, as well. I assumed that the shaky hands, the weak knees, and the trembling voice were vestiges of a long abandoned youth. But I was wrong! I learned that, at any point in our lives, we can become a casualty of speech anxiety.

On the occasion in question, I had been asked to speak to a group of program evaluation experts on approaches to evaluating communication programs, a little-researched topic at that time. The audience was large, and I believed that they knew a great deal more about the topic of program evaluation than I knew (*first cause of anxiety*: fearing that others know more than you know). The group was also unfamiliar to me, since they came from another discipline; and the auditorium was filled to capacity (*second cause of anxiety*: large and unfamiliar audience). Moreover, I was in a hectic work period with little time to prepare for the occasion (*third cause of anxiety*: lack of preparedness).

That nervousness escalated to panic when I arrived at the auditorium, 15 minutes before the opening speaker, to find that the overhead projector had been positioned at least 10 feet from the speaker's podium. To make matters worse, the podium and equipment were on two different levels! Because I had planned to use both a manuscript and visuals, I did not know what to do. Too late to ask for changes in the physical setting and too flustered to ask someone else to assist with the visuals, I assumed the role of roadrunner. I dashed from one level to the next as I delivered my speech to a room filled with hundreds of people. I was breathless and exhausted from the tension and unexpected high level of physical exertion. My knees and hands shook uncontrollably, and even while I was speaking, I worried that the negative experience would permanently undermine my self-confidence in speaking situations (*fourth cause of panic*: last-minute arrival and lack of time to adjust to physical environment).

In fact, it did take a few months and several speaking events to recover the sense of security that I had felt prior to this calamitous presentation. Presenting on a subsequent occasion to a group of six colleagues, I experienced the same high level of anxiety that I had felt with the audience of hundreds. Had I stopped speaking at that point, I might have remained an anxious presenter. I chose a different route. And for many people, the decision to withdraw from public speaking or to face another audience is key to overcoming speech anxiety. If you stop speaking when you have had a bad experience, you will never have a good experience.

Causes of Communication Apprehension

In 2003, Paul A. Broughton presented a paper at the National Communication Association convention in Miami, which summarized 20 years of research into the causes of communication apprehension. Broughton based his review on research published in *Communication Education*.[16] Those and other findings help us to understand the kind of anxiety experienced by public speakers.

Box 2.2 We feel more anxious communicating . . .

· In unfamiliar and novel situations
· With strangers or people who seem unlike us
· In situations involving evaluation
· With larger audiences
· In more formal situations
· In a non-native language
· When others have high expectations of our performance

· When we set high personal standards for ourselves
· In situations where we are conspicuous
· In situations where we are ignored
· To people of higher status than ourselves
· After we experience failure.

Unfamiliar and novel situations create anxiety.[17] The situations that cause the highest levels of anxiety are those in which we face the unfamiliar. Actor Antonio Banderas confessed to being terrified to make his Broadway debut in the musical *Nine*. Although a seasoned stage performer in his native Spain, he felt completely intimidated by the idea of performing on the historic stages of New York City. He said, 'You don't even know how you're gonna respond on the stage. You can sing at home, but it's a different deal. You have to go on stage with an orchestra, having to project for two-and-a-half hours in a play.'[18] Banderas worried unnecessarily, because the Outer Critics Circle Broadway/Off-Broadway nominated his production for 12 awards.

To overcome his fear of the unfamiliar, French actor Jean-Louis Barrault hid on the set of the stage play *Volpone* until the director, actors, and stage crew had departed for the night. Then he spent the night, sleeping in Volpone's bed before an imaginary audience, to prepare for the next day's performance.[19]

We experience greater states of anxiety when communicating with strangers than with people we know well.[20] Commonwealth gold medallist swimmer Susie O'Neill said she dreaded being selected for team events because they required talking to people she did not know. Some people stutter and stammer when they communicate with strangers; and children sometimes develop a condition called *selective mutism*, where they stop speaking entirely to avoid situations where they must speak to strangers.

We feel more apprehensive when communicating with people we perceive to be unlike us.[21] We tend to gravitate towards people who are similar to us:

> Individuals seek out, enjoy, understand, want to work and play with, trust, vote for, and marry others with whom they share characteristics they regard as important. These include values, religion, group affiliation, skills, physical attributes, age, language, occupation, social class, nationality, ethnicity, residential location, and most other aspects on which human beings differ.[22]

We are most comfortable with people with similar characteristics, at least in part because such situations present fewer novel elements and unknown features. As speakers in such situations, we can anticipate levels of audience understanding and possible reactions. *Xenophobia* refers to an irrational fear and dislike of people who are different from us. Some people use the term to refer exclusively to racial discrimination; however, the meaning is sufficiently broad to encompass differences of race, gender, culture, sexual orientation, ethnicity, caste, colour, religion, place of birth, linguistic profile, or other distinguishing feature.

We feel heightened states of anxiety in situations involving evaluation.[23] When surveyed in 1993–4 about major sources of stress, a group of competitive gymnasts revealed that fears of negative evaluation, fear of making a mistake, and high expectations of self or others were three major sources of stress. One gymnast said that she felt stress 'when all of these people are watching you, other people who are better than you, judges watching your every move.' Another said, 'I'm afraid I'll mess up and embarrass myself.'[24]

With a touch of humour, Virgin Records founder Richard Branson recounted his reaction to a situation requiring formal evaluation by the audience:

> [Microsoft CEO] Bill Gates invited me to talk to thirty or forty chief executives from around the world. Just before I got up on stage, forms were handed out to everybody, and Gates said, 'It's very important that all of us are tested in our lives. Richard's about to speak and I'd like you all to mark him out of 10.' Now, that intimidated me. . . . I thought I'd gotten out of school thirty-five years ago. I turned to the guy on my right—I think he was the head of Amazon—and said, 'I'll give you a 10 if you give me a 10.'[25]

The fear of evaluation, in some cases, derives from feelings of vulnerability in situations where our fate moves out of our control and into the hands of someone else. The more serious the potential consequences of that loss of control, the more likely we are to feel apprehensive, as in a job interview or custody hearing. The importance attached to making a positive impression affects our level of anxiety.

We feel more anxious in larger and more formal situations.[26] The larger the audience, the greater will be the number of evaluations of the performance. The more formal the situation, the more restrictions and rules apply. However, for some speakers, the reverse is the case. For many years, I was most comfortable with the ambiguity and relative anonymity of large audiences, where I could 'perform' instead of having to connect on a personal level. In essence, I became an actress in the classroom, bouncing about the stage, using all the techniques that I had learned in theatre—broad gestures, large movements, animated voice, and dynamic presence. In the smaller classroom, I had to have a quieter presence and more personal style of presentation. I could not rely on theatrics to hold the attention of my audience.

Close proximity to the audience and the loss of spatial barriers that psychologically separate speaker and audience construct a different dynamic. In a small classroom, you notice every micro-expression that crosses the faces of your audience. In a large auditorium, you do not have this kind of feedback. You only notice if the whispers become a din or rows begin to vacate. The intimacy of small classroom settings throws off many speakers who are used to performing in large formal settings. I have noted, over many years, that some of my most experienced student speakers (e.g., former debaters) are surprised to find that they feel more anxious in the intimacy of a classroom environment.

We feel more nervous when we are communicating in a non-native language. We fear the negative evaluations of those who speak the language more fluently.[27] For anyone who has tried to practise a second language or worked in a bilingual culture such as Canada, this principle seems so obvious as to require little formal authentication.

We feel greater anxiety when others have high expectations of our performance or when we set high personal standards for ourselves.[28] In the competitive figure-skating world, people know that the greatest pressure is always on those who hold last year's medals. The expectations of a repeat award-winning performance can create excruciatingly high levels of anxiety, even among seasoned performers. The daughters and sons of well-known actors and actresses often experience the same feelings. Actress Bridget Fonda suffered from stage fright for the first two years of her career. She attributes her fears to the fact that people associated her name with Peter Fonda (her grandfather) and Jane Fonda (her aunt). The association carried the probability that she would be judged by stricter standards than those applied to other fledgling actresses.[29]

We become more anxious when we think that the audience is disinterested or unresponsive.[30] Speakers look for signs of support and interest. When they do not receive this positive feedback, they may forget their speeches, cease trying to make contact with the audience, or stammer and stutter from nervousness.

We feel greater anxiety in situations where we are conspicuous or in situations where we are totally ignored.[31] One contributor to an Internet forum explained that he is comfortable sitting at a table with a group of 12 or more people; but if he begins to feel that he is on display, he panics. He said that he has dropped classes to avoid oral presentations, and he avoids social situations where he could become the centre of attention. At the other extreme, we become uncomfortable in situations where we are ignored. We wonder why no one will look at us, and we search our minds for reasons to explain the lack of responsiveness. Usually we are most comfortable in situations that involve moderate levels of attention.[32]

We experience greater apprehension when speaking to individuals or groups of higher status than ourselves.[33] These feelings of apprehension often translate into more rigid and tense postures.[34] Once we have transmitted such signals of insecurity and lack of confidence to the audience, we have a harder time gaining their respect and attention.

We experience greater apprehension after we experience failure.[35] After forgetting the words to several songs in a 1967 concert in Central Park in New York City, Barbra Streisand refused to sing in public for 27 years.

We feel more nervous if we anticipate failure. Fear of making a bad impression is the greatest indicator of speech anxiety.[36] At the height of his career, while directing and acting at the National Theatre in London, Sir Lawrence Olivier began to worry that fatigue would cause him to forget his lines; the phobia persisted for five years. One of my own experiences also illustrates how our fears can become self-fulfilling prophecies. I was acting in a college play when the thought struck me that I had never forgotten a line in a play. Moreover, I had never experienced stage fright. As the time approached for that evening's performance, I could not get the thought out of my head. Then I began thinking that I *could* forget a line; and that night, for the first time in four years of acting, I could not concentrate and blanked on one of my lines. After that night, I never felt the same sense of sureness as before the incident.

Physical Manifestations of Communication Anxiety

We can look at signs of communication apprehension (including speech anxiety) in terms of what we as speakers feel, what others see and hear, and what mechanical devices (connected to the body) register. The following are common manifestations of *what we as speakers feel*:

- tightness in the throat and a dry mouth;
- frequent swallowing;
- weak knees;
- shortness of breath;
- cold hands;
- faintness or dizziness;
- sinking feeling in stomach or abdomen;
- inability to focus;
- a sense of confusion and disorganization;
- blankness of mind or blockages of memory;
- difficulty sleeping in the period leading to the communication event.

Rae Tattenbaum, a certified instructor in biofeedback, told the story of a talented mezzo-soprano who came to her for help with concentrating during performances. The young woman explained that she always noticed the tightness of her pantyhose when she was singing, and when that happened, she lost focus: "'My pantyhose,' she told me. "That's what I think about when I'm performing.'"[37]

Others see the avoidance of eye contact, licking of lips, flushed face, awkward posture and unnatural movements, restless pacing, aimless gesturing, fidgeting with objects, shaking hands, and uncontrolled blinking of the eyes.

Others hear an abnormally fast or slow rate of speech, weaker voice, higher pitched voice, breaking or quivering voice, blurred or unclear speech, more slips of the tongue, non-fluencies such 'um' and 'uh', and lack of vocal variety.

Mechanical devices, attached to the body, *detect* increased perspiration, dilation of pupils, faster pulse rate, higher blood pressure, an increase in blood sugar, increased glandular secretions, reduced digestive processes due to the diversion of blood from the stomach and intestines to the brain and muscles, and irregular breathing.

Coping Strategies

Like other successful performers, speakers have to learn to channel nervousness to their benefit. Anxiety generates energy, which seasoned performers harness and use to their advantage. News anchor Walter Cronkite once joked that the difference between a professional and a novice is that the professional has taught his butterflies to fly in formation.[38] Studies demonstrate that students typically report much lower levels of speech anxiety by the end of a public-speaking course.[39] As competency increases, levels of anxiety decrease.[40] Even by the end of the fourth speech, students experience significantly reduced levels of anxiety.[41] Suggestions for coping with speech anxiety appear in the following discussion.

Before the Speech

Select a subject with which you are comfortable. One student chose to give his demonstration speech on how to polish shoes. Afterwards he confessed that his own lack of interest in the topic and the fear of boring his audience caused him to feel extremely nervous. Another student delivered a speech on how to do an Axel, a standard jump in figure skating. Since only a few students had been involved in competitive figure skating, the technical details were tedious and hard for most to understand. At the other end of the spectrum, the figure skaters in the group already knew the material, and the speech rehashed old ideas. A recognition of the situation generated anxiety in the speaker, which could have been avoided by choosing a different topic.

Prepare thoroughly in advance of the speech occasion. If you are concerned about filling the time, forgetting your speech, or not knowing the answer to questions, you are more likely to be nervous. If you are worried that the audience may know more than you about the subject, you need to exert still more effort to feel comfortable with your topic. On the other hand, if you have invested time in your topic, your audience should be able to recognize and respect the effort.

Concentrate in particular on your introduction and conclusion, which you may choose to memorize. Research demonstrates that speaker anxiety diminishes considerably after the first 30 seconds of a presentation.[42] And first impressions do count.

Most of the time, you will not want to memorize the entire speech. Rather, prepare notes from which you can speak. It is easier to find your place in notes than in a manuscript speech.

Find out who will be present at the speech. The unfamiliar is unnerving. If you have researched and adapted your speech to your audience, you will feel less nervous delivering the speech. If you face a hostile audience, you will need to devise strategies for reaching the group. If you know that you are speaking to experts, you should gear your language and presentation style to that level.

Practise delivering and timing your speech so that you do not exceed time limits. Realizing that you are significantly over your time limit can cause you to become anxious and flustered. You may rush to complete the speech and, in the process, leave out important sections that cause the speech to seem disorganized and disjointed. You also risk losing focus and forgetting parts of the speech.

When practising, do not stop until you have reached the end of the speech—even if you forget part of the speech. Learning how to overcome moments of failed memory or to cope with mistakes is part of the process of becoming an accomplished speaker. Do not expect every session to be the same. With extemporaneous speaking, your words will vary somewhat with each practice.

Familiarize yourself with the physical arrangements of the setting in which you will speak and with the equipment. If you have planned to deliver your speech to a small intimate group and you find yourself in an auditorium setting, you may lose your confidence. Be sure that you have tested the equipment and identified problems in advance of the speaking event. Also be certain that the room will hold the same equipment and the same seating arrangement on the day that you are to present. If you suspect that you will have to rearrange furniture, plan to come early or to request necessary changes.

Use visualization techniques to imagine an ideal presentation. Speakers who practise visualization techniques report decreased levels of communication anxiety, and most scholars recognize the value of visualization in producing an optimal performance.[43] The most convincing evidence comes from the athletic world. A survey of Canadian runners reported that 99 per cent use mental imagery to prepare for an important race. They visualize their winning performances, step by step, sometimes for two or three hours at a time.[44] Olympic competitor Curt Clausen voiced the opinions of most athletes when he said, 'The difference between you and the guy next to you is almost completely mental. At the highest level, that's what makes the difference.' Some Olympians say that it accounts for 90 per cent of their success, because the time that separates winners from losers is often seconds.[45]

Visualization helps to make unfamiliar situations more familiar. You anticipate the details of the moment when you will stand before the audience, so that the actual event appears like a rerun of what you imagined as a perfect performance. Canadian sports psychologist Peter Jensen says, 'You can't do things you can't imagine.'[46]

With visualization, you create or recreate an event in your mind, using all of your senses to imagine the experience and including both internal and external perspectives.

Internal imaging involves seeing, feeling, and experiencing an event from the perspective of the participant. Being 'in the body' limits our vision to what we would see as a participant in the event. A baseball player at bat, for example, would be able to see the pitcher and the people on the field; but he would not see the home-plate umpire, the catcher, or the players on the bench. Laurie Graham, winner of five World Cup races in alpine skiing, describes how she takes an internal perspective in her imaging:

All of us use visualization a lot in our sport. You have to know the course one hundred percent; all the bumps, which way the turns go, what the terrain is like, what the snow is like, the optimum line you want to be on, and the optimum position. All that goes in and we watch ourselves in our minds run the course and run it well. If we make a mistake in our mind we rewind, go back and just see ourselves doing it right, from start to finish. Actually I don't watch myself, I visualize it as if I'm running the race; the course is coming at me. There are different ways to visualize. You can go through the course just skiing the gates, so you know where the gates are. But then you have to ski through the course fast, feeling the way you want to ski.[47]

In the case of public speaking, internal imaging involves seeing, hearing, and feeling the sensations from the perspective of the speaker.

When someone takes an external perspective, on the other hand, the person is 'out of the body'. She becomes a spectator, an onlooker. Barbara Underhill, former world champion in pairs figure skating, describes what occurs when you take the external perspective:

> I go up to the top of the rink, above the audience where the ice looks clear. I just look at the ice and trace out our program on the ice in my mind. I'm looking at the ice and seeing us skating the routine and going through every move, tracing it out.[48]

In the case of public speaking, external imaging involves witnessing the event from the perspective of an audience member. The position of observer enables the speaker to see things that she might not perceive from inside the body, and she has less of an emotional connection to the event. The speaker might see herself as confident and erect in posture, smiling, making eye contact with different audience members, using natural easy gestures, and receiving applause as she finishes her speech. Whereas the internal emphasizes the kinesthetic, the external stresses the visual.

Both perspectives are important, although some people prefer one to the other. Gaetan Boucher, double gold medallist in speed skating at the 1984 Olympics, describes how he moves between internal and external perspectives in imaging:

> I always do the same thing. When I go from the warm-up bench to the starting line, I go to the same spot, flex a couple of times, make the hole for my blades where I start, get in position and picture the way I will skate. I try to get inside myself, instead of having a video view. The video view is more visual. You see yourself. If I am inside myself, it is really me that is skating and I do not see myself going around the corner like a video. I am trying to picture from the inside but sometimes I cannot. I usually see myself start the race from the back and then it is like I get closer and follow right behind. Then I see the turn from the side. But then I move back inside myself and I come around the turn, seeing the turn coming.[49]

Suggestions for how to practise visualization vary from one practitioner to another. The following description embodies the principles included in most instructions. To prepare for visualization, some people begin by writing a description of what they want to imagine—that is, their 'perfect performance', including as many details as possible. Visualization should involve all of the senses. Imagine the sound of the fan, the brightness of the lighting, the smell of azaleas outside the window, the sound of papers rustling while you wait for students to put away their notebooks, the smiles on faces of friends, and other details about the speaking environment. Sometimes speakers record this description on an audiotape that they can replay. In preparation for a visualization, some watch videotapes of performers they would like to emulate. Before beginning the first visualization exercise, you should read through the written script or listen to the audiotape. Then prepare for the mental imagery by doing a relaxation exercise.

Once relaxed, imagine a simple experience, such as going to the front of the class-room to speak. Assume an internal perspective in the beginning, visualizing details of the setting and relying on all of your senses to experience the moment. After you have attempted this exercise a few times, add details to the imagery. Imagine a perfect per-formance, from a physiological and emotional perspective. If you see yourself experi-encing some problem, visualize yourself recovering from the situation with grace and confidence. If you experience the sensation of fear or you feel your body tensing in anticipation of some part of the speech, use self-talk and trigger words to quiet your negative emotions. Shut out distracting or negative thoughts and focus on the speech and the audience. Then switch to an external perspective. Ten minutes of practice each day can make a significant difference to performance.

Box 2.3 Coping: Before the Speech

· Choose a topic with which you are comfortable.
· Prepare thoroughly.
· Concentrate on your introduction and conclusion.
· Find out who will be present at the speech.
· Practise delivering and timing your speech.

· Don't stop until you've reached the end of the speech.
· Familiarize yourself with the setting and equipment.
· Use visualization techniques to imagine an ideal presentation.
· Get enough sleep the night before the speech event.

Finally, get enough sleep the night before the speech event. A late night can compromise your ability to think clearly on the day of your speech event.

During the Speech

Dress appropriately and comfortably. Avoid question marks when you choose outfits for a speaking event. You want to be able to concentrate on your speech, not to worry about whether you are dressed appropriately. So if you think that a skirt might be too short or a tie too loud, return them to the closet. If you think you will feel shaky in high heels, choose a better pair of shoes. If you are worried that an outfit could emphasize an attribute that you would rather not share with your audience, then select another item. Choose clothing that allows freedom of movement. You want to feel comfortable when you speak. Much communication anxiety derives from factors related to physical appearance.[50]

No one standard in dress exists, as we will discuss in a later chapter. We have differ-ent personalities and body types. Audiences and speaking occasions vary, and cultural expectations differ. In short, prescriptions are not possible. But you should try to look your best in whatever you wear to a speaking occasion; and after you consider your audience and occasion, you should think *psychological and physical comfort*. If you are unsure about the audience or the occasion, err on the conservative side.

Be on time to deliver the speech. If you are racing to get to the event, you will be emo-tionally fatigued, flustered, and breathless before you begin your speech. In an April 2005 episode of *The Apprentice*, Donald Trump eliminated candidate Angie from the competition after she choked on a presentation. Angie attributed her poor presentation to the tension that she felt after being stuck in New York traffic, unable to arrive at her destination until the last minute, and to an unexpected glitch in her presentation (the loss of a jacket to be worn by a fashion model).

While waiting to speak, tense and relax your hand, leg, and other muscles. Such actions help to rid your body of excess tension created by the rush of adrenaline.

Before beginning to speak, take a couple of deep breaths to relax. One of the most visible signs of nervousness is a fast-paced delivery, accompanied by breathlessness, a higher-pitched voice that is thin rather than full in tone, a failure to pause for emphasis, and garbled and inarticulate speech. Anxiety restricts the chest and throat muscles. A deep breath, on the other hand, will open the airway and send oxygen to your lungs and brain. Sitting straight against the back of your chair, hold your breath for four to five seconds before slowly exhaling. If you can find a private corner, you might also want to do some facial exercises, designed to loosen facial and jaw muscles. The exercise requires you to open your mouth wide and then close tightly.

Athletes often use visualization to relax prior to an event. Race-walker Andrew Hermann says that he imagines a smooth blue liquid running through his body. If that does not work, he proceeds to a second image: 'I picture brown sugar and pouring water over it. I see it dissolve and it makes the tensions dissolve wherever they are.'[51]

When delivering the speech, concentrate on what you are saying instead of how you are saying it; eliminate distractions. If you focus on the ideas in your speech, you will have less time to worry about your shortcomings. Sport psychologists use the term *peak performance* to describe times when athletes are at their personal best. Canadian sport psychologist Peter Jensen says that athletes who have experienced a peak performance describe it in the following way:

> You're focused and relaxed—athletes always say it's as if things are happening in slow motion. They see everything, they anticipate, and yet the time went by very quickly. And that kind of duality . . . where at the end, it changes to, 'Gee, I just got out here, I would have liked to stay out here longer—and yet while I was out there, everything was so slow. I could see everything, I had time for everything, I didn't feel rushed.'[52]

Some athletes describe their peak performances as 'out-of-body' experiences. Others describe the experience as 'being in a cocoon', totally detached from distractions in the environment. Many describe peak performances as being 'in the flow', where the person has a feeling of absolute control, complete confidence, and absorption in the happening.[53] Golfers talk about being 'in the zone'. US Olympic Training Center sport psychologist James Bauman said that numerous studies have confirmed that successful athletes have a higher-than-average capacity to deal with distractions:

> Olympic athletes in particular find ways to remain focused on an event to the exclusion of negative influences such as unruly crowds, inclement weather, even family problems. While the vast majority of us spend lots of time worrying about things we can't control, successful athletes attend primarily to those cues or stimuli that are relevant, or within their control.[54]

Experts say that the focus must always be on the activity being performed. Focusing on someone else's performance just distracts.

While speaking, concentrate on the audience instead of yourself. Look for signals of understanding. If you see your audience drifting or looking uncertain, insert an attention-getting device, ask a question, catch the eye of individuals who appear to be losing interest, or find an alternate way to explain an idea that may have generated confusion. Try not to respond to signs of disinterest by drawing into yourself. Maintain direct eye contact with your audience and focus on friendly faces in the audience if you feel that your confidence is waning. Once you have received positive reinforcement from those audience members, you can try again with those who appear bored or negative.

Deliver the speech with outward signs of confidence and do not verbalize your anxiety. Studies in non-verbal communication have demonstrated that psychologists can experience the feelings of patients by assuming the postures of the patients. If you assume more confident postures, you will feel more confident. Also the audience will feel more comfortable.

If you perceive your status to be lower or your assets less than that of your audience, remember that you may be superior in some other domain. The theory of multiple intelligences, discussed in Chapter 13, focuses on our multi-dimensionality as human beings. So while I may be better at writing or speaking, you may better at art or music. Judge yourself as a whole person in moments when you feel insecure—a person with as much value and as many abilities as anyone sitting in the audience.

If you feel your mouth becoming dry during your presentation, take the time to pause and take a swallow of water. Bring a bottle of water with you to the speaker's stand.

Recognize that even the best speakers make mistakes. No one is perfect. In your practice sessions, plan how to improvise if you get off track. Bring note cards with you even if you think that you will not need the notes. Also realize that your audience will not notice all of the mistakes unless you point them out, and they will accept minor mistakes.[55] You know the speech; they do not know it. Sometimes performers build their reputations on a nightmarish performance. Legendary British comedian Tommy Cooper gained his reputation after his first devastatingly bad performance at the age of 17. He forgot his lines as soon as the curtains parted. He would open his mouth to speak, but no words would come; and he would close his mouth again. The audience responded with rapt attention.

> 'All right,' he thought, 'get on with it.' He got on with it and everything went wrong. His grand finale was the milk bottle trick. 'You have a bottle full of milk,' he told the entranced audience, 'and you put paper over the top. You turn the bottle upside down, and take the paper away. The milk stays in.' With bated breath, the audience watched. He turned the bottle. He paused for effect. He took away the paper. Drenched. All over him. As if he had not done enough already, Mr. Cooper then got stage fright and began working his mouth furiously without any sound coming out. At this point he started to tremble and walked off, perspiring heavily. Once in the wings, he heard the massed cheers of a standing ovation. His future glory was assured.[56]

As one person noted, 'It is quite possible that if Tommy Cooper's tricks had worked, no one would have heard of him.'[57]

If you make a mistake, regain your focus and continue. Golf champion Tiger Woods talked about the importance of regaining focus after you make a mistake: 'My father and I call it *zoning*. If you mis-hit a shot, hit it out of bounds, put it in the water, you have to get your focus back. You've got to start thinking ahead, don't look behind.'[58]

Use visual aids, which shift attention from speaker to speech and give meaningful actions to your hands.[59] Beginning speakers often feel as if they have gained three or four extra appendages. Visual aids offer an activity for your hands and give you a purpose for moving around as you point to, explain, and change your visuals.

If you become aware that you are making uncontrolled and fidgety movements, substitute larger controlled movements that add instead of detract from your speech. Fidgeting sometimes reflects a need to express yourself more naturally and openly. You should always use a presentation mode that seems comfortable to you.[60]

If you begin to doubt the effectiveness of your presentation, shift into positive self-talk (before and during the presentation).[61] Just as listeners have time to think about other topics while they are listening, you have time to take mental side trips during the course of delivering a speech. With this excess time, you may begin to worry that your audience looks bored, inattentive, lethargic, or hostile. When confronted with self-doubts, engage in positive conversation with yourself. Say, for example, 'Okay, I'm doing pretty well. Most people look interested.' 'This next section should be easy to explain.' Or 'I think this next example will get the audience's attention.'

Many Olympic competitors carry on conversations with themselves throughout their competitive events. Sue Holloway, silver medallist in pairs kayaking, described how she focused on positive thoughts in the 1984 Olympics: 'Immediately before the race I was thinking about trying to stay on that edge, just letting myself relax, and doing a lot of positive self-talk about what I was going to do. . . . I was thinking all kinds of positive things, like I could do well, I was going to be good, I was feeling strong, how Alexandra and I had worked so hard, and our boat was fast, and things like that; all positive, trying to feel like I wanted to feel.'[62] Some people use trigger words such as 'smooth and easy', 'let it happen', or 'focus'. Numerous studies have found a positive relationship between self-talk and competitive success. A 1992 study of Olympic gymnasts confirmed that the more positive the self-talk, the higher the chances that an athlete will excel, whereas negative self-talk has the opposite effect on an athlete's success.[63] A 1994 study found that junior tennis players who used self-talk won more points than players who did not.[64]

Recognize that audiences have many different issues and preoccupations and that their reaction to your speech may have absolutely nothing to do with you. When I first began teaching, I interpreted lack of student attention or knitted brows as a personal criticism. I thought that I must be doing something wrong when students looked preoccupied or angry or frustrated—that my lecture was boring, that I had made some statement that offended, or that the students disliked me as an individual. Then I began teaching the first-year course in interpersonal communication, where I asked students to keep journals of their communication experiences. I learned a great deal from those journals, which made for emotional reading. At any given moment, the students were undergoing a vast range of experiences—experiences that had to have an impact on their ability to listen and to perform in the university classroom. During the course of a semester, some had lost close family members to disease or accidents. A number experienced a breakup with a boyfriend or girlfriend. Away from home for the first time, many were terribly lonely; and almost all expressed self-doubt and concern about being evaluated unfavourably by peers. Some students did not have enough to eat, as they were operating on budgets that scarcely paid the tuition and rent. Others did not know where they would get their rent at the end of the month.

In short, I came to realize that nine times out of 10 the student lost in her thoughts or frowning into her books was probably not thinking about my class. More often, she was thinking about a broken relationship, a hospitalized grandparent, or whether she had forgotten to put money in the parking meter. I came to realize that the sleepy-looking young man in the back row might be working double shifts to pay for next semester's tuition.

When speaking, you should not ignore non-verbal signals from listeners. You should always try to capture and maintain the attention of all your listeners. But you should not necessarily assume responsibility for failure. Many internal and external factors influence audience behaviours. What you see as a bored countenance may be the face of a student who studied or worked all night. What you interpret as negativity may be deep sadness or frustration, whose source has nothing to do with your speech. If your presentation is at 7:00 p.m., after your classmates have been in classes since 8:30 a.m., your efforts to hold their attention may not always be successful. Moreover, you should remember that, when people leave the classroom at the end of the period, they are more likely to be thinking about their problems than about your speech. So put matters into perspective—both as you speak and when you engage in self-evaluation after the fact.

Recognize that different cultures react in different ways to speakers. Patterns of eye contact vary greatly, for example, between mainstream and some minority cultures. People of European heritage tend to look at a person while listening and away from the person while speaking. Africans do the opposite, maintaining eye contact while speaking but not while listening. If you are using eye contact as a measure of attentiveness, then you might reach conclusions that are the opposite of the truth.[65] Other listening behaviours can be equally confusing.[66] As a speaker, learning more about cultural differences in audience members can help you to avoid misinterpreting cues that you receive from the audience. We are most comfortable in situations that do not bring surprises.

If you freeze or panic, get past the moment. Early in his figure-skating career, Elvis Stojko placed tenth in school figures at a local competition, seriously diminishing his chances of winning a medal. But instead of perceiving himself as a loser, he simply said, 'Well, that's the figures, oh well. I'll get better with those. But right now, let's get on with this.'[67] He placed second in that competition and went on to become seven-time champion of Canada, three-time world champion, and two-time Olympic silver medallist.

If a student says that he is unable to finish a speech, we talk (as a group) about the situation. Class members share their perceptions with the speaker, as well as the feelings that they have experienced at the podium. On occasion, I offer to alter the speaking environment in some way to help the person to overcome his fears. I usually allow the speaker to select an alternative arrangement, perhaps delivering the speech from behind a table or even sitting on the floor with other students positioned in a circle. On one occasion, the speaker requested that the audience sit on the floor while he spoke from a standing position! Unusual, perhaps, but he was able to finish his speech; and the next

---

Box 2.4 Coping: During and After the Speech

· Dress appropriately and comfortably.

· Be on time to deliver the speech.

· While waiting, tense and relax your hand, leg, and other muscles.

· Before beginning, take a couple of deep breaths.

· Concentrate on what you are saying instead of how you are saying it.

· Concentrate on the audience instead of yourself.

· Deliver the speech with outward signs of confidence.

· Do not verbalize your anxiety.

· If your mouth becomes dry, pause and take a swallow of water.

· Recognize that even the best speakers make mistakes.

· Use visual aids, which shift attention from speaker to speech and give meaningful actions to your hands.

· Substitute larger controlled movements for fidgety uncontrolled ones.

· Shift into positive self-talk if you feel lack of confidence.

· Recognize that seemingly negative responses from the audience may have nothing to do with you.

· If you panic, get past the moment.

· After the speech, put the occasion into perspective by applying the '10-year rule'.

---

time he spoke, he did not request any special seating arrangement. He had conquered his fear.

After the Speech

If you have not performed at your personal best, put the occasion into perspective by applying the '10-year rule'. Ask yourself, 'In 10 years' time, will this event be important?' In all likelihood, no one but you will remember the occasion after a year or two. More important, no one but you will really care. Doing well in a speech is important, but unless we are in the defendant's box at a murder trial, few speeches are life-and-death matters. We should never allow this fear to dominate our professional and personal lives or discourage us from participating fully in life. In fact, some studies suggest that audiences prefer speakers who are less than perfect.[68] Strive to do your best but recognize that a less-than-perfect performance will not usually result in long-term damage to more than your ego or occasionally your wallet (in the case of a failed sale or business transaction). As sports psychologist Peter Jensen noted: 'On a bad day, you might say, "I'll just try this and then I'll re-evaluate myself and see where I'm at."'

Conclusion

Although communicators with trait anxiety may make some progress in a supportive speech environment and should not dismiss the potential value of the experience, introductory speech classes are not the best place to learn coping techniques for severe problems. Social phobics such as Leslie require the help of counsellors who specialize in treating severe social anxiety. The use of techniques such as desensitization, cognitive restructuring, group therapy, and skills training help the person to learn how to cope in social environments. Some psychologists believe in combining medications with these techniques. Obviously, introductory speech classes do not allow for these kinds of intensive therapeutic approaches for dealing with serious social phobias. Speech classes, on the other hand, are the perfect environment for giving people the skills to cope with situational anxiety.

Questions for Discussion

1. Describe any physical or emotional symptoms that you experience when speaking before an audience? Have you ever panicked in these circumstances?
2. Review some of the causes of communication anxiety. Using this list of causes, analyze a situation in which you felt nervous.
3. How do you cope when you experience apprehensiveness associated with public speaking? Before the speech? During the speech? During question period? Can you offer any advice to others?
4. When delivering a speech, what makes you most nervous? Fear of forgetting the speech? Lack of confidence in your knowledge or expertise? Audience reactions to your speech? Discomfort or issues with your dress? The physical environment? Equipment or technology problems? Difficulty in relating to different linguistic or cultural groups? Other?
5. Have you tried visualization as a means of controlling your apprehension? In what context? Preparing for a sports competition? A speaking competition? Other? Did you adopt an in-body or out-of-body approach to the visualization?
6. Describe your most successful speaking experience. Your least successful. What were the characteristics of each situation?

CHAPTER THREE

Listening with a Purpose

Hearing, Perceiving, and Processing Information

The following exercises are designed to demonstrate principles related to perception and listening. Exercise #1 requires volunteers to describe a drawing, which the remainder of the group attempts to reproduce from the verbal account. Alternatively, volunteers may be seated on opposite sides of a cardboard divider. One delivers instructions on how to construct a set of blocks to a second individual, who builds the structure on the basis of her understanding of the instructions. The cardboard divider should be placed so that neither individual can see the structure being built by the other. Subsequently, the instructor leads the larger group in discussion of what happened—what types of information were understood or misconstrued, transmitted accurately or inaccurately, dropped, added, distorted, or sharpened.

Exercise #2 requires sending several members out of the class prior to showing a film with unfamiliar cultural content, then recalling them. Several members of the viewing audience come to the front of the class to describe the contents of the film to those who did not see it. Afterwards, the absentee members offer their understanding of what transpired in the film, based on the accounts of their classmates.

Exercise #3 requires that students describe specific characteristics of someone—a classmate who is asked to leave the room, an unexpected guest, a celebrity, or other individual.

As in the case of Exercise #1, the discussions following Exercises #2 and #3 should be tied to theories of perception and listening.

Learning Objectives
- To identify common listening purposes.
- To understand the influence of perception on message reception.
- To appreciate the reciprocal responsibilities of speakers and listeners.

As a society, we suffer from Attention Deficit Disorder (ADD). When tested immediately after a 10-minute presentation, the average listener hears, comprehends, and remembers only about 50 per cent of the information. After 48 hours, the amount retained has diminished to 25 per cent.[1] In classroom situations, 10 per cent is a common retention rate.[2]

Experts tell us that these poor listening skills carry a price tag in the business world.[3] The Sperry Corporation in New York concluded that, if each one of its 87,000 employees made a $10 mistake each year due to not listening (e.g., taking a wrong number or wrong order), the financial consequences to the company would be close to $1 billion a year.[4] Others tell us that poor listening skills are equally expensive in our personal relationships. As reported in the book *Women and Love*, the number-one complaint of women is that men do not listen; but author Shere Hite says that women are not much better than men at listening.[5]

If we heed these experts, we will view the statistics on retention and recall as highly problematic. But studies of perception lead to a more sophisticated understanding of the numbers. The experience of one man, who regained his sight after 30 years of blindness, illustrates that knowing *what to retain* and *what to discard* is far more important than grasping every detail of our environments. He explained:

> When I could see again, objects literally hurled themselves at me. One of the things a normal person knows from long habit is what not to look at. Things that don't matter, or that confuse, are simply shut out of their seeing minds. I had forgotten this, and tried to see everything at once; consequently I saw almost nothing.[6]

The term *selective perception* refers to the process by which we selectively perceive and retain certain kinds of information, while we ignore or discard other information. Because we are bombarded by approximately 1,600 bits of information a minute, we must disregard a great deal of what we receive. As listeners, the challenge is to retain the significant.

This chapter explores common listening purposes, the influence of perception on message reception, and the reciprocal responsibilities of listeners and speakers in a public-speaking situation. This discussion aims to expand our understanding of the receiver portion of the communication model introduced in Chapter 1.

Purposeful Listening

Our purposes for attending speech events govern how we perceive much of the information we receive from speakers. People attend speech events for many different reasons. Some of the most common relate to acquiring information; connecting with an important person; being inspired personally or professionally; offering support to a speaker or

Photo Gill Ferguson

It's now or never
Come listen to me
I'm very clever
I know everything

Tomorrow will be to late
It's now or never
My word won't wait.

cause through our presence as an audience member; or recognizing the accomplishment of someone who is receiving an award, graduating, or retiring. Because our reasons for attending events are so diverse, the reasons for listening are equally varied. The assumption that we listen predominantly to obtain information is highly flawed. While this purpose may dominate classroom and professional situations, it is less salient as a reason for listening in many other contexts. Even so, making some distinctions among the various kinds of listening can be useful as a means of understanding the complexities of listening.

Deliberative listening involves hearing, understanding, and storing information for later recall, as well as analyzing and drawing conclusions from the information.[7] Anticipating the possibility that we may use the information at a later date, we attempt to receive the message without distortion. Also we evaluate the quality, relevance, and usefulness of the information. The motives for deliberative listening are logical, rational, and critical in nature. The process stresses comprehension and evaluation.

Empathic listening, by way of contrast, means listening to understand the person as well as the message.[8] This kind of listening has an emotional, as well as an intellectual, component. In that sense, empathic listening implies more than comprehension of words and rational meanings. When we listen empathically, we listen to the whole person (verbal and non-verbal aspects of delivery). Mutual respect, support, and trust characterize the process of empathic listening. Some Asian cultures place a greater value on the emotional aspects of listening than do North Americans.[9]

Deliberative listening plays an important role in societies that value free speech. The viability of democracies depends on the ability of citizens to judge the quality of the public and political messages they receive. In an environment where information moves freely, with few restrictions, we must be able to differentiate between fact and opinion, truth and exaggeration. In other situations, however, deliberative listening may be less useful. In many social situations and classrooms, we want to do more than judge the other person. We want to offer encouragement and support to the speaker. We want to build a relationship. In those cases, some blend between deliberative and empathic listening may be most appropriate.

Other listening purposes are more complex in psychological terms. We may go, for example, to hear a speaker who is a noted humanitarian, the winner of a Governor-General's award, or an intellectual of great note. Our purposes for attending the speech may be less to learn than to experience the person, as in the case of attending a speech by the Dalai Lama. Because most people have difficulty with his accent, the Dalai Lama speaks through a translator. But for those who admire the man, being in his presence is sufficient reason to attend the event. Sometimes we may want to occupy the same physical space as an admired political figure or entertainer or to feel a vicarious connection with someone or something bigger than ourselves. We may enjoy telling our family and friends that we attended a lecture by geneticist and environmentalist David Suzuki or a reading by author and actress Anne Marie MacDonald. Many Canadians travelled across the country to be present at the funeral of Pierre Trudeau; others travelled to Rome for the final farewell to Pope John Paul II. Some people want to be part of events that will be written into history books. Others will attend a lecture from a sense of obligation or to show respect and friendship for a colleague. Through our presence, we may express our support for a person, a cause, or a policy. During World War II, the British often risked their lives to attend sell-out performances of public events in support of the war

Photo Gill Ferguson

cause. The freedom riders to the US South in the 1960s took grave risks to attend rallies with charismatic speakers such Martin Luther King Jr.

We may look for inspiration or emotional support from a lecturer. For 22 days and 2,286 miles in 1999, Lance Armstrong cycled across some of the most intimidating terrain in Europe to capture the first of his seven straight Tour de France victories. This remarkable accomplishment did not compare to Armstrong's personal victory two years earlier against the most aggressive form of testicular cancer. After crossing the finish line on the Champs Elysée in Paris, Armstrong offered inspiration to all who face life-threatening illnesses: 'If there's one thing I say to those who use me as their example, it's that if you ever get a second chance in life, you've got to go all the way.'[10] In subsequent years, many cancer patients and their families filled the auditoriums where Lance Armstrong spoke about the importance of personal strength and resolution. The audiences knew the story, but they went to experience the man and to draw emotional support from his words.

Like the audiences of the Chautauqua Circuit, we sometimes attend a speech event to be entertained. We may not plan to spend time in the Arctic, but we may enjoy listening to someone else talk about his adventures in Canada's Far North. We may look for speakers like Jim Carey or Mike Myers, who will make us laugh. Comedians often double as speakers at public events. Part of preparing for a public-speaking event involves recognizing the purposes of audiences in attending the event. The speaker then accepts responsibility for trying to meet those audience goals.

Influence of Perception on Message Reception

What is the nature of perception? How does perception influence communication? How do listeners respond? What other variables affect the ability of listeners to maintain focus in a communication situation? We examine answers to these questions in the following section.

Nature of Perception

Perception is learned and culture-bound, value-laden, holistic, backward-looking, selective, and relative.

Perception Is Learned and Culture-Bound

As infants, we learn to organize information received through senses such as sight, touch, smell, sound, and taste. Consider the everyday learning that occurs with a sense such as sight, which we take so much for granted. The retina of the eye registers an image such as a child eating ice cream. The optic nerve cluster collects the image of the child and transmits it to the brain for processing. Although the retina acts like a camera lens in capturing the image, the optic nerve does not retain any form of organization in transmitting the image. Rather, the bits and pieces of information, which constitute the image, arrive in the brain in a random, chaotic, and completely disorganized fashion. That is, the nerves that carry the thousands of bits of information may not terminate in places adjacent or even close to each other. The individual must learn that a specific nerve terminal in the brain represents a particular point in space. No replication of the image exists until the brain processes and organizes all the bits of information. Visual systems recognize learned patterns among the vast overload of available information.[11]

In a well-known experiment, a researcher constructed some special glasses that not only distorted his vision but also turned the world upside down. He wore the glasses day and night for an extended period of time. By the end of the orientation period, his vision was so good that he was able to fly an airplane and ride a motorcycle while wearing the goggles. At the completion of the experiment, the researcher removed the glasses to find that his world without the glasses had turned upside down. The person had to retrain his brain to organize the incoming information in a way that allowed him to function normally.[12]

Just as we learn sight by experience, we also learn touch by experience. To illustrate the point, ask another person to close his eyes. After he closes his eyes, touch his arm *lightly* with varying combinations of fingers (e.g., three fingers from one hand and two fingers from the second hand), placed simultaneously on the skin. Ask him to tell you how many fingers you have placed on his arm. Repeat the experiment several times. (In order for the experiment to work, all fingers must touch the skin at the same time.) On the first couple of tries, you will not be able to differentiate a total of one from four, five, or more fingers on the skin. After several tries, however, you will learn to discriminate. A person who has learned Braille can discriminate between various combinations of six raised dots, representing the letters of the alphabet, placed about an eighth of an inch apart. In the same way as with sight and touch, people can learn to distinguish between sounds that are initially indistinguishable.[13]

How we perceive taste is also learned. People in some Middle Eastern countries regard the eyes of sheep as a delicacy. Favourites of my Scottish husband are steak and kidney pie and tripe (the stomach lining of cows). Many natives of Louisiana consider alligator to be a delicacy, and some cultures eat grub worms found under rotting logs or

Photo Gill Ferguson

insects coated with chocolate. Unappealing, you say? Well, it is all in the mouth (and nose) of the beholder. Perception is both learned and culture-bound.

Perception Is Backward-Looking

The learned nature of perception means that it is backward-looking in its interpretation of the present. We constantly anticipate the past. Films such as *The Others* are able to succeed in building plot lines based on deception, because audiences have learned perceptual sets about horror films. These sets are based on prior encounters with the conventions of the genre. In *The Others*, Nicole Kidman plays the role of a single mother with two children. Her children's life-threatening allergies to sunlight enable the movie producers to establish a dark, foreboding, and suspenseful setting. The mother and children grow increasingly fearful that they are living in a haunted house with servants whom they suspect to be the living dead. We follow the movie, convinced that we know the familiar plot line. We ignore many signs, such as the failure of the children to respond to sunlight, the ability of the wife to communicate with her obviously dead husband, the historical dress, the archaic speech, the strange mannerisms of those who live in the house, and the interactions between the children and a young boy, whom we suspect to be a spirit presence. In short, we ignore many signs that could have led us to a different conclusion about what was going on. In the end, however, we realize that our perceptions have led us to the wrong assumptions. We have been duped. Yes, the house is haunted; but no, the haunted are not the ones we believe them to be.

These same kinds of deception occur in *Sixth Sense*, where audiences ignore sign after sign that things are not as they perceive them to be. If you watch the film a second time, you see many signs that you did not see on the first viewing. You approach the film from a different perceptual set. Listeners within speech settings fall prey to the same perceptual traps. We interpret new information in the light of past experiences and pre-dispositions. *We see what we expect to see.*

Because much of our perceptual learning occurs when we are young, speakers face a difficult task when they have a limited amount of time (usually no more than 15 or 20 minutes) to influence the knowledge and belief sets of their audiences. Even when listeners are positively disposed to learn something new, by necessity, they use old frameworks and schemes of classification to interpret and file the information. In *The Act of Creation*, Arthur Koestler describes how creative leaps often come from people outside of a particular field of study or in dream states, because they are not constrained by the old conceptual frameworks.[14] The more we know about a subject, the more expertise we acquire, the more difficult it becomes to think 'outside of the box'.

As audience reactions to the films *The Others* and *Sixth Sense* demonstrate, we pick out what we regard to be significant detail in any event and interpret the information in the light of what we already know, believe, and expect to see. In 1915, cartoonist W.E. Hill conceived a well-known optical illusion that demonstrates this principle. Tongue in cheek, Hill titled the drawing 'My Wife & My Mother-in-Law'[15]. Prior expectations will lead you to see either a young woman or an old hag.

Perception Is Selective

Numerous studies of eyewitness accounts also demonstrate the selective nature of perception.[16] Judges and lawyers know that two people may see the same robbery from virtually the same angle and distance, yet disagree on almost every detail of the event. These discrepancies in perception include such basics as the height, weight, eye colour, hair colour, and manner of dress of the robbery suspect. The learned nature of perception leads us to focus on some details and to ignore others. An athlete, for example, might notice the degree of muscularity in the robbery suspect. A fashion designer might notice the dress. A plastic surgeon might make mental

Blythe Hartley and Emilie Heymans of Canada compete in the women's synchronized diving 10-metre platform event during the Athens 2004 Summer Olympic Games. (Photo by Jamie Squire/Getty Images)

notes about the bone structure of the person. *In other words, we see what we know.*

In the 2001 sniping murders that took place around Washington, DC, numerous eyewitnesses described the presence of a white truck or van at the locations of the sniping incidents. For weeks police searched for a white van before apprehending the suspects in a very different kind of automobile. In the end, the 'white van' turned out to be an older model, blue, four-door Chevrolet sedan. On a more humorous note, on 25 June 2004, Mark Allen Patterson walked into the offices of the *Gadsden Times* in Alabama to report that the eyewitness to his robbery (a robbery he had committed) had given incorrect information. He wanted the newspaper to correct their inaccurate reporting of his truck as green (rather than burgundy).[17]

Perception Is Value-Laden

Perception is also value-laden. A study by Leo Postman, Jerome Bruner, and Elliott McGinnies demonstrated that audiences are quicker to perceive information that fits with their existing value orientations.[18] After testing people to identify their values, the researchers flashed the words representing those values on a screen for a brief millisecond. Then they gradually increased the time that words appeared on the screen until all participants in the experiment could recognize the words. The findings follow:

> Those persons with a strong religious value orientation were able to see the word *religion* when it was on the screen for a very brief instant. Others, less religiously oriented, required that the word be on the screen for a longer period before they recognized it. Things that are important to us, those which we value, are the ones we perceive.[19]

In short, *we are most likely to see what we already believe to be the truth.*

Perception Is Relative

A six-foot individual might perceive a 5′5″ suspect as 'short', whereas someone five feet tall might perceive the suspect as 'tall'. Serious consequences can result from such perceptual discrepancies. Kirk Bloodsworth spent eight years in jail (two on death row) before being exonerated for the rape and murder of a nine-year-old girl. Part of his problem stemmed from an inaccurate description. The authorities were looking for a 6′5″ man. In the end, the confessed murderer proved to be only 5′7″ tall.

In the movie *Annie Hall*, the viewer sees Alvin Singer (played by Woody Allen) talking to his psychiatrist on one side of a split screen. The psychiatrist asks about Alvin's relationship with Annie Hall, 'How often do you sleep together?' Alvin replies, 'Hardly ever, maybe three times a week.' On the other side of the split screen, Annie (Diane Keaton) speaks with her counsellor. Asked the same question, Annie responds, 'Constantly, I'd say three times a week.'[20]

We also read signs within a context. The signs acquire meaning, depending on the context that surrounds them. If someone is smoking a cigarette in front of an office building, we assume that the person is smoking tobacco. If someone is holding what appears to be a cigarette in an alleyway, surrounded by homeless people, we assume the person is smoking an illicit drug. The movie *Fahrenheit 911*, directed by Michael Moore, shows President George W. Bush speaking about a serious matter of state. As soon as Bush concludes his statement, the camera opens up to show the President on a golf course, preparing to swing a golf club. Bush says to the interviewer, 'Now watch this shot!' Contextually, his previous comments have acquired a whole new meaning.

As discussed in Chapter 1, public speakers communicate within a larger context that includes social, political, economic, technological, and cultural factors, as well as personal experiences that affect the perceptions of listeners. I regularly deliver Power-Point presentations to federal communication officers on the history of government communications. One of the slides refers to the economic downsizing that took place in the months following the 1993 election of the Chrétien government. The slide says that, during the Chrétien years, 'the money disappeared.' In previous years, everyone knew I was talking about the depressed state of the Canadian economy in the 1990s. But over the past several years, the federal government has had to answer for the misappropriation of millions of dollars under the Liberal government. So when I showed the slide 'the money disappeared' in my most recent presentation, the audience erupted into laughter. The words had assumed a whole new meaning, based on the revised social and political context in which they appeared.

Influence of Perception on Communication

All of the above characteristics of perception influence and interact with each other in the communication situation. In the case of public speaking, we can refer to our perceptual frames as *listening frames*. Media analysts talk a lot about 'framing theory'—a reference to how journalists structure and tell their stories. Framing theory says that journalists put a 'spin' on their reporting of issues. Choices made in the telling of the story influence audience interpretations of what they read and hear.[21] But audiences also have frames within which they receive this information. In a public-speaking situation, these listening frames dictate whether and how we will perceive, understand, accept, and/or act on information. In the context of this discussion, we could define *listening frames* as 'frames of mind or attitudinal sets that allow the entry of certain kinds of information and block other kinds of information.' Communication can fail when we set our listening frames to block information with which we disagree, ignore or discard information that appears to be of little interest or value, or lack the background to process the information.

Disagreement with Information
If a journalist or speaker tells a story using an unacceptable frame, we simply ignore or distort the information to fit our expectations or needs. In line with the backward-looking nature of perception, we rely on past experiences to interpret new information. We also perceive selectively, in a way that is congruent with our values and beliefs. The My Lai massacre of Vietnamese citizens by American troops in 1968 illustrates the kinds of omissions and distortions that can occur when listeners selectively perceive and filter information:

> A war correspondent was present when a hamlet was burned down by the United States Army's First Air Cavalry Division. Inquiry showed that the order from division headquarters to the brigade was 'On no occasion must hamlets be burned down.' The brigade radioed the battalion: 'Do not burn down any hamlets unless you are absolutely convinced that the Vietcong are in them.' The battalion radioed

the infantry company at the scene: 'If you think there are any Vietcong in the hamlet, burn it down.' The company commander radioed his troops: 'Burn down that hamlet.'[22]

The case of US Air Force pilot Major Harry Schmidt, tried in July 2004 for the 'friendly fire' bombing deaths of four Canadian soldiers in Afghanistan, illustrates this same point. Schmidt did not accept the 'hold fire' order that came from the ground because he had already decided that the situation required an aggressive action. His listening frame was set to block all incoming information that did not conform to this attitudinal set.

Our attitudes towards certain kinds of information influence how we configure our listening frames. We set the frames to filter certain kinds of information, much like we set levels of security for filtering spam from our computers. If we set the level of security too high (level 5, for example, instead of level 3), we may miss some of the messages because the program does not recognize the information as significant. Figuratively speaking, the computer program diverts the messages to the spam folder; and we may never know that the messages arrived in the system unless something happens to draw our attention to the inappropriate setting.

Sometimes we allow stereotypes to govern our reception of information. We may silently criticize the speaker, preparing arguments in our heads. Sometimes we react to physical appearance or other status cues, which cause us to dismiss the words of the speaker. Emotionally charged words can trigger a negative response that causes listeners to cut the lines of communication.

Lack of Interest in Topic

Communication can fail if we have no interest in the topic. We may be apathetic about the speaker, the subject matter, or the occasion. We may see no purpose to the speech, or we may be totally bored by the subject. In those situations, we often fake attention or tune out discussions that require too much mental exertion. Some of us become quite good at concealing our lack of attentiveness. I have been complimented for my close listening behaviours on some occasions when I have been mentally absent from the room for extended periods of time. But when someone asks a question, to my embarrassment, I am forced to reveal my 'out-of-body' experience. Most of us share this escapist tendency from time to time, especially in social situations. We have set our listening frames to discard information that has little interest or perceived value. In line with perception theory, we must necessarily ignore a large amount of the information that comes to us each day. We select and filter the information that we perceive to be useful.

Lack of Background to Interpret Information

Sometimes, however, we simply lack the knowledge or experience to recognize patterns. In those situations, the holistic nature of perception leads us to fill in the gaps. I used to show a film called *The Good Times are Killing Me* to my students in Windsor, Ontario. The film depicts the Mardi Gras celebrated by the 'Cajun' population of southwest Louisiana, descendents of the Acadians of Nova Scotia.[23] The Cajuns celebrate a Mardi Gras quite unlike the famous New Orleans Mardi Gras. In the traditional Acadian celebration, masked and costumed men (*les capitaines*) ride on horseback through the countryside and towns, begging for chickens, sausages, rice, vegetables, and other donations. Dressed in black capes and cowboy hats, *les capitaines* carry white flags. A lone individual, accompanied by a band of musicians, sings the haunting Mardi Gras song.

> Mardi Gras runs are not without strict rules of conduct. For example, the authority of *le capitaine* is absolute. He leads the procession and distributes any liquor that is consumed. No member of the colourful band of beggars may enter private property without his permission. He approaches each farmhouse with raised white flag to ask permission from the homeowners for *les Mardi Gras* to enter. If he receives an invitation, he drops or waves the flag to signal the others. They are expected to sing and dance and beg with great energy at homes that are donating to the gumbo.[24]

Before departing, the masked beggars chase down live chickens that they will eventually take back to the villages or towns, where the women will prepare chicken and sausage gumbos for the evening celebration. The dancing and festivities continue at the local dance hall until midnight, the beginning of the Lenten season.

After showing the film to my Windsor students, I asked several of the class members who had viewed the film to describe what they had seen to others who had not viewed the film. I did nothing to prepare the students for the subject matter of the film, as I wanted to demonstrate how we add, drop, and distort information that is incomprehensible within our listening frames. I wanted to illustrate processes such as *levelling* (the elimination of details from a story), *sharpening* (the exaggeration and accentuation of striking features of stories), and *assimilation* (fitting stories to our preconceptions and cultural frameworks). The film was an ideal vehicle for illustrating these points because the content was totally alien to the students. They had no relevant frames within which to fit the events of the film.

Apart from the costumes and the drinking, no familiar cues exist in this film for a group of Canadian university students. No floats, grand balls, or krewes (groups that stage the parades and costumed balls) characterize this rural French Mardi Gras. No throwing of beads or crowning of royalty in $100,000 costumes takes place in locations like Eunice, Basile, and Mamou. Although many of the Acadian customs and food are now a part of the New Orleans scene (and the New Orleans–style Mardi Gras has now invaded Acadiana), it was not the case before the 1980s. Historically, New Orleans had different roots from Acadiana. New Orleans had a Creole population, originally settled by French and Spanish elites, members of the wealthy class. Later the Creole population expanded to included Africans and people of other cultures. The Acadians, on the other hand, were refugees from Canada, peasants forced out of Nova Scotia by the British.

When I asked my students to describe the seemingly bizarre events in the film, they had no context within which to interpret the events. They did not understand why masked men would be riding through the countryside, begging for chickens. They found the wringing of a chicken's neck to be unsettling. Unable to speak French, most Windsor students had no idea of what the Mardi Gras song meant or represented. They did not understand the context or meaning of the celebration. In short, they were totally confused, and their accounts demonstrated how listeners try to make sense of information where they have no relevant frames of reference. The next section describes some of their responses.

How Listeners Respond

How do listeners respond when they have inadequate listening frames to process culturally alien information? What do they retain of the information? What do they add in an effort to make sense of the concepts? What do they ignore when they do not agree with the information or it is so alien that they cannot process it? How do they distort the information to fit their perceptual frames? The following discussion will use the class exercise with the Mardi Gras film as a means of illustrating these points.

Retention in Perceptual Frames

In the class experiment, what was retained? First, the recounting of the events demonstrated the *sharpening* effect in perception.—how listeners tend to retain the most outrageous and sensational details, such as the wringing of the chicken's neck. They also remembered costumed men riding through the countryside or dressing (some in women's clothing) for the festivities.

Additions to Perceptual Frames

Students often embellished the story, adding details that were not present in the film, such as a conversation or reason for some action. They might make up a conversation where the women on farms beg the costumed men to sing a song for them, or they might say that the men were on their way to a masquerade ball. The additions seemed to be attempts to make sense of what they had seen—to find some logical and reasonable explanation for the events they had witnessed (*assimilation* to their cultural expectations). The added details also made the person reporting appear better informed and the story more interesting. The new information often added 'spice' to the story. The students might say, for example, that the women were frightened when the masked men arrived or that the masked men were drinking heavily.

Losses from Perceptual Frames

Overall, the accounts were simplistic and underdeveloped (*levelling* effect), with much lost from the original account. Typically students talked about how the Cajuns like to drink, party, go horseback riding, and chase chickens. Often the students omitted major contextual details such as the music, a pervasive force in the film. Yet context is so important to our understanding and perception of the world. When one student was questioned about the omissions, she said, 'It's strange because I heard the music in my head all of the time that I was recounting the story. I just didn't think to mention it.' A classic article by George A. Miller argued that people can usually recall no more than seven points, 'plus or minus two';[25] some argue that the number may be closer to five than seven.

Distortions of Perceptual Frames

What was distorted? The students changed the story to fit their understanding of the world. When some aspect of the film did not make sense, the person invented an explanation or changed the story line (another example of *assimilation*). They might say, for example, that *les capitaines* were modern-day pirates who rode in bands through the countryside, forcing people to give chickens to them.

An exercise such as this allows one to go inside the head of the listener to see how people deal with culturally alien information. The film's usefulness as a vehicle for teaching derived in part from its weaknesses. The Cajun population of Louisiana loudly protested this depiction of their culture and decried the way in which the filmmakers provided no context for the happenings in the film. One source noted:

> The final version . . . portrayed the Cajuns as a strange tribe of vulgar, hard-partying, drunks, the front-line in a losing battle for cultural and ethnic survival in America. . . . Louis Landreneau is presented dressing as a woman, complete with brassiere and pantyhose, wig and makeup, under the careful supervision of his mother, without explaining that he is preparing for his community's Mardi Gras celebration. The Mardi Gras is eventually presented with no explanation other than the definitions gathered by the fascinated but unenlightened crew from drunken participants.

When working with other kinds of unfamiliar materials (e.g., Inuit folktales), students react in the same ways. They try to explain the folk stories in rational, scientific terms. Dreams become reality in the recounting of the stories. The students winnow down the details so that the narratives reach a very low level of complexity. They distort and exaggerate the most outrageous moments—the moment, for instance, when an Inuk hunter turns into a bearskin. They lose the cultural context for the stories. What the students hear depends greatly on what they already know. When the students attempt to pass the information from one to another, their accounts get shorter and shorter as more and more details disappear. (Box 3.1 summarizes the above discussion.)

Box 3.1 Processing Culturally Alien Information

We tend to retain
 . . . the most outrageous and sensational details.

We tend to add
 . . . embellishments and 'spice' to secure interest.
 . . . logical causes and explanations for events.
 . . . details that make us look more informed.

We tend to drop
 . . . contextual details.

We tend to distort
 . . . storylines that do not fit our cultural experience.

Other Influences on Listening Effectiveness

In addition to perceptual and attitudinal issues, the gap between speaking and listening rates explains some of the difficulties experienced by listeners. Numerous studies have found that listeners can think significantly faster than speakers can speak. Some studies set average information-processing rates at 300 words per minute[26] and speaking rates at 125 words per minute.[27] Other studies identify an even wider gap between the rates at which people listen and speak. They have shown that people can listen effectively at speeds four or five times greater than normal speech.[28] A number of years ago, researchers at the University of Toronto found that blind and partially blind students effectively developed the ability to 'speed listen' to recorded playbacks of their professors' lectures. By increasing the playback speed, they could listen to a 60-minute lecture in 40 minutes. Despite the 'chatterbox' effect, they were able to comprehend the content at this significantly faster rate.[29] Our brains are able to handle information at jet speed, but speakers deliver the information at a locomotive pace. In such a situation, listeners tend to succumb to distractions in their heads and in their physical environments.

Still another variable concerns the physical environment. The furnishings, the acoustics, the lighting, and the general ambience of the setting influence the receptiveness of an audience to the speaker's message. Through choice of colours and furniture, some rooms convey warmth and antiquity, while others transmit coldness and modernity.[30] Classic studies by Abraham Maslow and Robert Mintz found that more positive exchanges occur in 'beautiful' rooms, surroundings that are visually and aesthetically pleasing.[31] Other studies have found that people make harsher judgements of others in uncomfortable settings.[32]

Many characteristics of the physical environment can influence the success of a speaker. The presence of strong perfumes creates an impossible environment for those with allergies or asthma. Other detractors include background noise, overheated or cold rooms, musty or unpleasant smells, sounds of traffic, or music that jars with the personal tastes of listeners. Conversations between audience members also offer competition to speakers. One researcher contends that the average room contains 43 decibels of sound.[33] In unpleasant environments, windows offer a route of escape; and speakers lose listeners to the fall foliage, squirrels scampering in the park, and the muted conversations of passing pedestrians.

The comfort and arrangement of chairs or auditorium seating have an impact on reception of a message. The design of some chairs encourages people to remain in the environment for long periods of time (e.g., seating in lounges), whereas other chairs are designed to become uncomfortable after a few minutes.[34] The unfriendly and uncomfortable seating arrangements in airports encourage people to move into the restaurants and bars. The same principles apply to auditorium and other settings where speech events occur. Audiences, especially older people, may be prone to avoid the discomfort of some physical settings; or they may find it difficult to pay attention in certain settings. Seating that relaxes people too much, of course, can have the equally undesirable effect of putting people to sleep. The presence of barriers also influences communication. To create a sense of immediacy with the audience, speakers often remove physical obstacles such as podiums that separate them physically and psychologically from their listeners.

One influential study, especially relevant to public speaking, looked at the effects of straight-row seating on classroom dynamics.[35] Raymond S. Adams and Bruce J. Biddle observed instruction by 16 teachers in 32 classrooms of first, sixth, and eleventh grade students. The subject matter was varied. Their findings were consistent across all teachers, subjects, and grade levels. The principal finding was the following:

> The main determinant of whether a student was actively and directly engaged in the process of classroom communication was his or her *location*, or place in the setting. In a typical straight-row seating arrangement, the researchers identified an 'action zone' or center of activity where most interaction takes place. This area . . . extends from the front of the room directly up the center line, diminishing in intensity as it moves farther away from the teacher. In this zone are the students to whom the teacher talks. The process is reciprocal, for it is these same students who talk to the teacher.[36]

Later studies confirmed the finding that those in the front row and the centre of the other rows tended to participate the most actively. Other studies have found that overall participation diminishes as you go from the front to the back of the room.[37] Robert Sommer found that the most active participants in seminar rooms sit across from the instructor.[38]

According to James McCroskey and Rod McVetta, the tombstone-like (row-by-row) seating arrangement still characterizes 90 per cent of university classrooms.[39] Some more recent studies have indicated that speakers tend to communicate in a diamond-shaped pattern. All of the studies, past and recent, concur that when listeners fall outside of these communication zones, the level of their engagement diminishes. These studies then have relevance for listeners, who can take specific actions to avoid passivity when sitting in the 'dead zone'. The public speaker, for his part, must take care not to restrict eye contact and body orientation to the 'action zone'.

Reciprocal Responsibilities of Listeners and Speakers

Drawing on the preceding discussion, we can speculate about possible reasons for communication breakdown.

- *First*, meanings reside in people, not in words.
- *Second*, similar backgrounds and experiences enhance the likelihood of successful communication (where we assign the same meanings as those intended by the speaker).
- *Third*, the more frequently we interact, the higher the likelihood that we will develop a common vocabulary and that the words of the speaker will trigger the intended response.
- *Fourth*, the more we speak in specific and concrete (as opposed to general) terms, the greater the likelihood that listeners will understand the true intent of our words.
- *Fifth*, nervousness on the part of the speaker and frustration on the part of the listener decrease the probability of successful communication.
- *Sixth,* when meaning is painful to us, we switch off or distort.
- *Seventh,* when we are sensitive on particular subjects, we may see meaning that does not exist in the words of a speaker. We may be insulted, for example, by a remark not intended personally.
- *Eighth*, feedback usually helps to ensure consensus on meanings.

Understanding these principles can help the speaker to identify and correct possible sources of misunderstanding.

But speakers are not the only ones with a responsibility for communicating ideas. Audiences bear as much responsibility for a successful speaking event as speakers. An early study by Ivey and Hinkle demonstrated the importance of supportive feedback.[40] In this experiment, six participating students began a psychology class in a non-attentive mode. They slouched in their seats, showed no interest in taking notes, and avoided eye contact with the instructor. The instructor, for his part, lectured in a monotone, used no gestures, and paid little or no attention to the students. At a prearranged signal, the students switched from passive to active listening behaviours. They sat up straight in their chairs or leaned forward to show interest in the lecture, engaged in direct eye contact, and took notes. Once the students showed interest in the lecture, the instructor began to gesture; he spoke more rapidly; and the class session became animated. At a second prearranged signal, the students reverted to their passive listening behaviours; and after a painful attempt to regain the interest of the group, the instructor returned to his lacklustre performance.

The point of this story is clear. Through positive and supportive feedback, audiences can encourage speakers to perform optimally. A good audience gives non-verbal feedback by paying close attention to the speech—nodding on occasion, smiling, looking for eye contact with the speaker, leaning slightly forward or otherwise orienting the body towards the speaker. Courteous and attentive audiences put away notes and avoid conversations (spoken or written) while speeches are underway (see Box 3.2).

Box 3.2 How To Be a Good Listener

Tips on Good Listening Attitudes

- Be a selfish listener; think about what you can get from the speech.
- Be open-minded; don't listen with the purpose of finding fault.
- Withhold judgement until the end of the speech; don't stop listening or plan your arguments while the person is still speaking.
- Put yourself in the position of the speaker; ask why the person has this perspective.
- Try to understand what the speaker is saying; focus on main ideas.
- Avoid anticipating what the person is going to say; you may be surprised.
- Be compassionate when the person makes mistakes in delivery; no one is perfect.
- Pay more attention to content than to delivery.
- Pay more attention to ideas than to the way in which they are expressed.
- Block distracting thoughts and noises, which impede listening effectively.
- Avoid stereotyping speakers; don't make assumptions on the basis of ethnicity, sex, age, or other factors.

Tips on Good Listening Behaviours

- Use non-verbal language to encourage the speaker to do his or her best—smiling when appropriate, nodding occasionally, and orienting your body towards the speaker.
- Avoid talking to friends or making distracting noises during the speech.
- Don't read or engage in other work assignments while the person is speaking.
- Don't mumble or leave your seat if you disagree with the speaker; give the person a chance to finish the speech before challenging the ideas.
- Ask questions *after* the speech; don't use frowns and shakes of the head to question while the speech is still in progress.
- Control 'micro expressions', those fleeting looks that last a second but have a long-term impact on speakers.
- If the speaker hesitates, use non-verbal signals to encourage him or her to continue.
- Combine praise with criticism when you comment on the speech.

As speakers, we are most drawn to those audience members who give us highly positive feedback and, at the other extreme, highly negative feedback. We look at the people who are smiling and nodding to gain strength. We make eye contact with those who are giving negative feedback to try to figure out what is wrong and to effect a change in their attitudes. Sometimes, the negative feedback causes us to become nervous and to lose our concentration. If we fail repeatedly to get any response to our efforts, we may tune out that part of the audience to avoid the negative contact.

Verbally, audiences give feedback when they respond to questions by the speaker, ask questions at the end of the speeches, or provide oral or written comments. In a speech class, if the feedback is sufficiently specific and descriptive, speakers can learn a great deal from their peers. In other words, you should never say, 'Great speech!' or 'I hated the speech.' Such comments not only offend (in the latter case), but they also offer no constructive direction for change. Speakers learn nothing from such vague comments.

Feedback should always convey, in a timely and specific fashion, what worked well and what requires improvement. Immediate feedback makes a stronger impression than delayed feedback. Feedback should employ descriptive rather than judgemental language. You could say, for example, 'too much shifting from foot to foot'. That would be descriptive. The same statement, framed in evaluative language, would be 'It's really annoying when you shift from foot to foot.' Useful feedback offers specific directions for change such as 'Try to eliminate some of the lower body movement in your next speech.'

Feedback should focus on the modifiable. Pointing to a lisp or stutter, an unpleasantly nasal voice, or a thick accent serves no purpose. These kinds of problems are best noted in private sessions, at which time instructors can direct the student to appropriate resources such as speech therapists or language departments. Repeated critiques by peers just serve to demoralize, since these kinds of deficiencies require time and expert help to correct.

Limiting individual feedback to the identification of two strengths and two areas for improvement allows listeners to focus on major points. Asking for feedback in the form of numbers is less useful, since standards among novice speakers vary so greatly. Also people use numbers as crutches, allowing them to avoid identifying strengths and diagnosing problems. The importance of requesting strengths, as well as challenges, cannot be overstated.

A supportive atmosphere is essential to learning. In a negatively charged atmosphere, little improvement will take place. In a positive atmosphere, the students establish close friendships, offer support to each other through responsive attitudes and constructive feedback, and learn to better their own speaking and critical listening skills.

Conclusion

At the same time as speakers bear a responsibility to audiences, audiences bear a responsibility to speakers—to pay attention and model supportive behaviours, to listen to the whole message before passing judgement, and to listen to the whole speaker (some speakers have important messages even if their delivery is weak). The audience must judge the truthfulness of the speaker, the accuracy of the message, and the ethics of the presentation.

Listening is hard work, requiring that we hear what someone says; selectively perceive, assimilate, and categorize the information; and finally develop a mental response

---

Box 3.3 A Question of Ethics

The auditorium was filled to capacity with people and the noise of many conversations. The audience of new immigrants was heterogeneous in composition. The purpose of the gathering was to prepare the group for the challenges they would confront in adjusting to a new country. Attendance was compulsory.

Samantha, the event organizer, moved to the speaker's podium, where she called for order. Several guest speakers filed onto the stage, seating themselves behind her. She introduced the first speaker. There was a ripple of applause at the conclusion of the speech. At the conclusion of the second speech, the audience again applauded, less enthusiastically this time. Finally, an attractive, young, and well-dressed woman rose to talk about the challenges of raising children in Canada—about the need to understand and tolerate differences in cultural approaches to such matters as child-rearing and socializing.

By this time, many members of the audience were tired. They yawned and talked quietly among themselves. Many held jobs that required them to rise at five in the morning or earlier. Having been awake for many hours, some resented having to attend an evening event. To make matters worse, a large number spoke English as a second language, which meant they had to pay close attention to understand the speeches. As the evening continued, many did not bother. Some showed signs of upset at the advice offered by the speaker. They interpreted her comments as saying that they should tolerate behaviours in youth that violated their cultural and religious values. Part of their reaction derived from their judgement of the speaker's age and dress. Some thought that she was too young to voice an opinion on child-rearing. Others believed she must be from an environment of privilege, unable to understand their situation.

The speaker reacted to their inattentiveness and unrest by growing more nervous. She stammered and repeated portions of her speech; she referred more often to her notes; her complexion turned a bright red. To those sitting closest to the stage, it was obvious that her hands were shaking uncontrollably. She spoke faster and slurred her words, making it still more difficult for her audience to understand the speech. The audience read these signs as a lack of self-confidence and inadequacy. How does this example reflect some of the principles discussed in this chapter? Who was responsible for the failed speech?

---

to the message. We frequently hear what we expect to hear. We tend to switch off when we do not understand or disagree with an idea. Nervousness and frustration also interfere with our comprehension of messages. Our listening frames are set to filter out a large amount of the information we receive each day. If the filter levels are set too high, we will not hear, comprehend, or retain important information. If they are set too low, however, we will suffer the effects of information overload. If our interest flags at times when listening to a speech, we should remind ourselves that we had a purpose in coming to the event. We should ask ourselves, 'What can I get out of the situation?' Even if the quality of the speech is less than we had anticipated, we may still be able to fulfill our initial purposes in attending the event.

In later chapters I will explore some of the ways in which speakers can overcome these internal and external obstacles to effective listening. We will discuss, for example, how speakers can tie their discussion to existing perceptual frames to facilitate assimilation by the audience, add novel ideas that sharpen the information, use concrete and memorable details to avoid levelling effects, and rely on multiple sensory channels to reach the audience.

Questions for Discussion

1. Close your eyes for a moment. Think about what you recall of your immediate surroundings. Keeping one hand over your lowered eyes, make a few notes about the features in the physical environment that come to the top of your mind. Then look up and compare your notes with those of other members of the class. Note the differences in what you have noticed from what other people have noticed.

2. How do your purposes for listening shift from one situation to another? Give examples.

3. Describe a situation in which you have had little interest in listening. What were the characteristics of the situation? What could have increased your interest in listening?

4. Do you listen more often in a deliberative or empathic fashion? Recount some incident in which you reacted negatively to deliberative listening on the part of your parents, friends, or partner and/or positively to empathic listening.

5. The following adjectives have been used to describe characteristics of perception: culture-bound and value-laden, holistic, backward-looking, relative, and selective. Give examples from you experience to illustrate these characteristics of perception.

6. Does your classroom setting have a positive or negative impact on the listening patterns of your fellow students? Explain.

7. Evaluate the impact of audience behaviours on your speech experiences to this point in time. What kinds of listening and feedback behaviours have made your speaking experiences more pleasant? What kinds of behaviours have made your experiences more difficult or unpleasant? Identify class members who have demonstrated supportive listening behaviours. Evaluate your own listening behaviours. Based on the readings and class discussion, what could you do to become a better listener and to make your classmates feel more comfortable when they are speaking?

8. Describe some dominant stereotypes (e.g., used car salesmen, morticians, professors, hockey players, scientists, accountants, artists, engineers, etc.). How do the stereotypes impede our ability to send and receive messages?

CHAPTER FOUR

Acquiring the Basic Skills

The Speech of Introduction

The Speech of Introduction

The goal of your first speech (2-3 minutes in length) is to introduce yourself to the class. Identify an object that will reveal some important aspect of your personality, values, or experiences. Bring this object with you to class (either the object itself or a visual representation of the object) and use it as a catalyst for talking about yourself. In other words, allow this object to generate a theme that becomes the organizing principle for the speech. Your speech outline (one page long) should conform to the model presented in this chapter. No bibliography is required. The emphasis in evaluating this speech will be on the basics of putting a speech together, including use of attention-getting devices, clear purpose and/or thesis statements, statement of structural progression, clarity of organization, and appropriate linking statements.

Learning Objectives
- To learn how to select a topic and write thesis and purpose statements for a speech of introduction.
- To learn how to get organized, including making an outline and writing a preview statement.
- To learn how to get audience attention in an introduction.
- To discover how to develop the body of the speech.
- To learn to connect ideas and parts of the speech by using transitions.
- To learn to close the speech with a memorable thought.
- To understand the importance of practising the speech, using an extemporaneous style of delivery.

Speeches of introduction are common in workplace, social, and classroom contexts. Within some African cultures, they rank alongside speeches of welcome and appreciation as *the* most common speech given by the average person.[1] In this chapter, we will consider seven steps in preparing a speech of introduction. Those steps include (1) getting started by choosing a theme, deciding on the purpose of the speech, and writing a thesis statement; (2) getting organized by identifying and ordering the main ideas and writing a preview statement; (3) developing an introduction; (4) developing the main body of the speech; (5) using connectives to link ideas and internal summaries to orient listeners; (6) concluding with a memorable thought; and (7) practising the speech, using an extemporaneous mode of delivery.

Step 1: Getting Started

The first step in the speech process involves *choosing a theme, deciding on the purpose of the speech, and writing a thesis statement.*

Choosing a Theme

The process of deciding on a speech topic generally entails library research. With a speech of introduction, however, *you* are the subject of the speech. Therefore, you can skip the research step and begin by selecting some physical object (ring, ticket, hockey skates, old running shoes, T-shirt, mug, or other artifact) as a catalyst for talking about your personality, relationships, interests, or experiences. The ring, ticket, agenda book, or other object allows you to pursue a theme in the speech, rather than just telling us that you have two sisters, a brother, and a cat; you like Italian food; and you are in second year of university. Although these latter points may define you, audiences are bored by such listings. The most interesting speeches of introduction pursue themes; they have a central organizing principle.

Photo Gill Ferguson

A friend noted, for example, that the music collection of her daughter changed with each new relationship. In short, the music seemed to reflect the taste of whoever had the greatest influence on her at a particular point in time. If she were giving a speech, she could talk about how her appreciation of music reflects different phases in her life or relationships.

Among the themes chosen by students for this assignment, one brought a teacup to the front of the class to talk about how her shaking disorder had influenced her life. Another brought a pair of boots and described all of the places that her boots had travelled. She allowed the boots to tell the story. Another student brought a piece of bent metal to explain how the twisted metal reflected characteristics of his personality. One brought a tourist mug, with various images that depicted the environment in which she had grown up. She talked about experiences related to the pictures on the mug.

Objects such as ballet shoes, skates, or a guitar allow you to talk about the influence of dance or skating or music on your life. T-shirts often carry messages about your personality or travels. An agenda book can be used to launch a discussion of organizational abilities or interest in attending certain kinds of events. A plane ticket may represent time spent studying abroad in an exchange program. Other objects represent other passions or causes to which you have contributed. Sometimes passions become obsessions, which (if not too serious) can present an opportunity to add humour to a speech. Audiences enjoy speakers who can laugh about their own shortcomings and foibles. To the extent that you can choose an original theme, you should do so, passing up themes that are likely to be overused.

Deciding on a Purpose

Speeches may be serious and informative or light and entertaining in tone and purpose. General speech purposes include the following: to inform, convince, actuate (move to action), or entertain. Some persuasion speeches seek to inspire or motivate listeners to achieve higher purposes or goals in their lives. Some informative speeches pay tribute to the lives of people who have made some contribution to society. So many more specific purposes reside under the broad purposes of informing, convincing, actuating, and entertaining.

Sometimes speakers have more than one purpose when they deliver a speech. Politicians regularly show up at social occasions to explain their positions on issues, update constituents on what is happening in Parliament or municipal government, and demonstrate that they are accessible and approachable. The topics of these speeches are diverse and ostensibly informative in nature. The primary intent of the politician, however, may be persuasive or motivational in nature: to establish goodwill or obtain votes in the next election. So the distinctions among speech purposes may be less clear in practice than on paper.

In-class speech assignments usually designate a general purpose, but the student decides on the specific purpose of the speech. Examples of specific purposes in speeches to inform could be 'to explain how to get involved in student government' or 'to describe how to conduct a meeting'. If the general purpose is 'to persuade', the specific purpose could be 'to persuade students to adopt healthier lifestyles' or 'to convince people to stop smoking'. If the general purpose is 'to actuate', the specific purpose could be 'to encourage people to give more money to charity'. If the general purpose is 'to entertain', the specific purpose could be 'to give a mock graduation speech designed to entertain'. The outline should include a statement of general and specific purposes for giving a speech.

Framing a Thesis Statement

Every speech should be unified, governed by one central idea that all other points support. This single declarative sentence, or *thesis statement*, should encapsulate everything you want to say. The more carefully you have framed the purpose statement, the easier it will be to articulate the thesis. Examples of thesis statements follow:

- This old sweatshirt and these running shoes have seen some remarkable sights.
- This photograph of Mount Everest tells you where I want to be in five years time.
- My experience with bungee jumping is one that I would not want to repeat.
- This journal reveals how my life changed after I came to university.

Note that the above are not compound statements, with two or more points. Each statement refers to a single idea, which becomes the organizing principle for the speech. Every other statement in the speech must support and develop the thesis statement. If you cannot relate some part of your speech to this thesis statement, the point does not belong in the speech.

Sometimes, you will discover that your thesis statement cannot contain all the points that you wish to make. When that happens, you must rewrite the thesis statement to cover what you intend to say. *The main point of the speech should be clear—to you and to your audience.* The thesis statement gives unity and coherence to your speech.

You will note that some thesis statements suggest speech content of a more informative nature, while others appear to have persuasion or entertainment as their focus. The thesis statement for a speech of introduction should be informative in character.

Step 2: Getting Organized

The organizational process involves three major tasks: *identifying and ordering main points, developing an outline of the points, and writing a preview statement for your introduction.*

Identifying and Ordering Major Points

Next you need to decide on an organizational scheme for the speech. The most common patterns used in speeches of introduction are *chronological, spatial, topical, narrative,* and *comparative*.

Chronological patterns are time-based: first to last, last to first, past to present, present to past, past to future, or future to past. A speech about the worst hotel fires, for example, might employ a time-based form of organization. A chronologically ordered speech on major hotel fires could begin with the Winecoff Hotel in Atlanta, Georgia (*1946*), before proceeding to a description of the Taeyokale Hotel in Seoul, Korea (*1971*); the MGM Grand Hotel and Casino fire in Las Vegas (*1980*); the Dupont Plaza Hotel in San Juan, Puerto Rico (*1986*); and the Manor Hotel in Manila, the Philippines (*2001*).

The *spatial* pattern organizes content according to location or relationship of the parts in space. Often we are talking about some kind of geographical ordering. In the case of a speech on the worst hotel fires, the speaker could talk about catastrophic hotel fires in *Korea*, *Puerto Rico*, the *Philippines*, and the *United States*. Alternatively, the speaker could organize the discussion of hotel fires according to where they began in the buildings. Perhaps some fires began in hotel rooms situated on different levels, others in kitchens or common areas. Like the ordering by regions of the country, this latter form of organization qualifies as spatial ordering.

A *topical* form of organization groups ideas according to some logical ordering of subject matter. Many different patterns of logic are possible. Speaking on the subject of major hotel fires, the speaker could have four major divisions to the speech: (1) *origins* or *causes* of the hotel fires (cigarettes, explosions, faulty wiring); (2) *motivations* behind the fires (accidental or deliberate); (3) *effects* of the fires (numbers of people killed and injured); and/or (4) *follow-up actions* by governments (e.g., new building and fire codes). Note that *causes* and *effects* constitute two (out of many) possibilities for topical ordering of material. If you seek, however, to establish a *relationship* between causes and effects, you have chosen a different organizational scheme, which will be covered in the chapter on persuasion.

The *narrative* form of organization, which is becoming increasingly popular, involves telling a story.[2] If you choose to use this form of organization, you could recount a personal experience with surviving a hotel fire. The experience could be your own or someone else's account.

If you chose to use the *comparative* form of organization, you could compare the actions taken by people who survived major hotel fires with actions taken by those who lost their lives in the fires. The thesis of your speech, in that case, could be: 'People who survive major hotel fires behave differently from those who perish in the smoke and flames.'

You may use one kind of organization for headings (e.g., chronological) and a second (e.g., topical) for subheadings, as demonstrated below:

I. Fire at Winecoff Hotel—1946
   A. Origins
   B. Causes
   C. Effects
II. Fire at Taeyokale Hotel—1971
   A. Origins
   B. Causes
   C. Effects
III. Fire at MGM Grand Hotel and Casino—1980
   A. Origins
   B. Causes
   C. Effects
IV. Fire at Dupont Plaza Hotel—1986
   A. Origins
   B. Causes
   C. Effects
V. Fire at Manor Hotel—2001
   A. Origins
   B. Causes
   C. Effects

The same rules apply to the choice of organizational schemes for speeches of introduction.

Developing an Outline

The next step is to develop an outline. Below is an example of standard outline form taken to the fifth level of detail: first-level headings (I, II, III, etc.), second-level headings (A, B, C, D, etc.), third-level headings (1, 2, 3, etc.), fourth-level headings (a, b, c, d, etc.), and fifth-level headings such as (1), (2), and (3).

I.
   A.
   B.
      1.
      2.
      3.
         a.
         b.
            (1)
            (2)
         c.
         d.
      4.
   C.
II.
   A.
   B.
   C.

Six rules apply to the development of speech outlines.

First, limit the number of subheadings. Three reasons explain this limitation. Every level carries additional details, which require time to develop. Since you do not have time to develop a large number of points in a short speech, you have to limit the number of levels. In addition, too many levels of detail confuse the listener. If a speech proceeds into great detail on one point, the listener can lose her place in the larger structure of the speech. Finally, if you use more than three levels (first-, second-, and third-level headings) in a five-minute speech, you are probably pursuing a tangent at the expense of a more balanced presentation. In a balanced presentation, you give equal time to all major points. You will rarely go to the fifth level of detail in any speech. A 2–3 minute speech of introduction requires no more than two or three levels of detail. Internal summaries and transitional statements help to keep the organization of the speech in the mind of the listener.

Second, do not mix sentences and phrases in an outline. You should not, for example, have a phrase such as 'types of fighter planes' as a heading in your outline and use a sentence such as 'One type of fighter plane is the F-16' for the first sub-point. The first cluster of words 'types of fighter planes' is not a sentence; it is a phrase. To correct the inconsistency, you can change the phrase into a sentence such as 'Several types of fighter planes are common to the US Air Force.' Alternatively, you can change the sentence into a phrase such as 'the F–16 fighter plane'. Either outline format is acceptable (phrase or sentence), but you must be consistent.

Third, standard outline format requires that each level have at least two sub-points. In the event that you have only one sub-point, you should combine that point with the heading that it supports. So if you have only 'A', you should combine 'A' with the Roman numeral that it supports (I, II, III, etc.). If you have only '1', you should combine '1' with the letter that it supports (A, B, C, etc.). If you have only 'a', you should combine 'a' with the number that it supports (1, 2, 3, etc.).

The fourth rule in outlining is to use parallel construction. The ideas that appear at each level or under the same heading should reflect the same organizing principle. If your speech is about rollover risks for various classes of vehicles, the major headings in your discussion could be frontal risk, side risk, and rollover resistance. The next level of headings could identify vehicle types such as sports vehicles (SUVs), vans, and trucks.

You would *not* include the RAV-4 or the Chevrolet Tracker at the same level as SUVs, vans, and trucks. To include the name of a specific SUV in a list of vehicle types would be to violate the organizational principle for that level. If you go to a third level of organization, however, you could include the RAV-4 or Chevrolet Tracker at that level. The following outline illustrates this point.

I. Frontal risk
    A. SUVs
        1. RAV-4
        2. Chevrolet Tracker
    B. Vans
        1. Nissan Quest
        2. Toyota Sienna
    C. Trucks
        1. Chevrolet Silverado
        2. Dodge Ram
II. Side risk
    A. SUVs
        1. RAV-4
        2. Chevrolet Tracker
    B. Vans
        1. Nissan Quest
        2. Toyota Sienna
    C. Trucks
        1. Chevrolet Silverado
        2. Dodge Ram
III. Rollover resistance
    A. SUVs
        1. RAV-4
        2. Chevrolet Tracker
    B. Vans
        1. Nissan Quest
        2. Toyota Sienna

C. Trucks
  1. Chevrolet Silverado
  2. Dodge Ram

The same principle applies to all levels of outlines. A second brief example illustrates this point. In the case of a speech where you talk about exotic pets, you might have *alligators*, *tigers*, and *turtles*. To go to another level of detail in your discussion, you could talk about *different kinds* of alligators (Chinese and American), tigers (Amur, Bengal, Sumatran, South China, and Indochinese), and turtles (desert, painted box, spiny, and others).

The fifth rule requires that you indent each new point and capitalize the first word in every statement or phrase. See the above outline.

The sixth and final rule obliges you to assign only one idea to each point. The following illustrates an inappropriate inclusion of multiple ideas in one statement: 'Accidents result when boaters do not have any kind of operating licence; also they should not be allowed to drink when they are operating a boat.' This statement contains two different ideas. The two statements should appear as separate points, as illustrated in the following outline.

Issues Related to Boating Safety

I. The first issue relates to the importance of being licensed to operate a boat.
   A. Knowing the rules is important.
   B. Demonstrating your suitability to operate a boat is important.
II. The second issue relates to behaving responsibly when operating a boat.
   A. Drinking while operating a boat is dangerous.
   B. Speeding in areas with swimmers is hazardous.
   C. Paying attention to your surroundings can help to prevent accidents.

Boxes 4.1 and 4.2 illustrate the six principles of outlining. The first outline employs full sentences; the second uses phrases.

Box 4.1 Outline Using Sentences

General Purpose: To inform
Specific Purpose: To introduce myself to the class by talking about the role that uniforms have played in my life
Thesis: My name is Sabrina St-Cyr, and this is my life in uniform.
Preview statement: In this speech, I will introduce you to some of the uniforms that reflect my school, work, and extracurricular experiences.

I. Like many of you, I wear a multitude of uniforms—for school, work, and recreational activities.
   A. At one point in my life, I did not buy any new clothes for almost three years.
   B. In many ways, these uniforms have come to represent me as a person.
   C. My name is Sabrina St-Cyr, and this is my life in uniform.

II. My uniforms reflect the activities in my youth and the periods in my life.
   A. At age eight, I joined Brownies and Girl Guides.

Box 4.1 continued

B. When I turned 13, I joined the Air Cadets.
   1. Air Cadets helped to fill a gap in my social life when my friends went different ways after junior high school.
   2. Since my father is in the military, my parents thought this was a good idea.
   3. During my six years in Air Cadets, I earned a number of badges.
      a. This first badge shows the different camps that I attended.
      b. The second represents my status in cadets, where I aged out as a warrant officer.
      c. This next badge means I was a drum major.
      d. I earned the Legion medal, at the end of my fourth year, for outstanding citizenship.
   4. In the uniform of the Air Cadet, I learned leadership and discipline.
C. This next uniform, worn for two and a half years at Wendy's Family Restaurant, represents my entrance into the workforce.
   1. During my time at Wendy's, I was trained in every area except the grill.
   2. On the basis of performance, I got a number of pins.
   3. This experience also represents my passing from child to adult: earning money and having more responsibility.
   4. The experience prepared me for future jobs.
D. My high school uniform reflects my academic side, as well as my experiences in band, badminton, and track and field.
E. After high school and air cadets, I followed the military tradition and joined the reserves.
   1. In the reserves, I am a supply technician.
   2. This past summer, I completed my trade course and participated in a training exercise.
   3. My experiences in supply work have been rewarding.

III. The uniforms that I will wear in the future are still unknown.

Box 4.2 Outline Using Phrases

General Purpose: To inform
Specific Purpose: To introduce myself by talking about the role of uniforms in my life
Thesis: My name is Sabrina St-Cyr, and this is my life in uniform.
Preview statement: In this speech, I will introduce you to some of the uniforms that reflect my school, work, and extracurricular experiences.

I. A multitude of uniforms in our lives—school, work, and recreational activities
   A. Three years without clothing expenses
   B. The meaning of uniforms in our lives
   C. Uniforms as a way of introducing myself

II. Uniforms as a reflection of the activities in my youth and the periods in my life
   A. Brownies and Girl Guides at age 8
   B. Air Cadets at age 13

Box 4.2 continued

1. A way to bridge a gap in my social life
2. A tie to my father's life in the military
3. Badges earned in Air Cadets
   a. The first badge—camps attended
   b. The second badge—my status as a warrant officer
   c. The third badge—my life as a drum major
   d. The Legion medal—a reward for outstanding citizenship
4. Acquisition of discipline and leadership skills

C. My entrance into the workforce at Wendy's Family Restaurant
   1. Training received
   2. Pins awarded for performance
   3. Earning money and having more responsibility
   4. Preparation for future jobs

D. My high school uniform as a reflection of my academic side and my experiences in band, badminton, and track and field

F. Following the military tradition by joining the reserves
   1. Acting as a supply technician
   2. Completing my trade course and participating in a training exercise
   3. Satisfaction gained from a life in the reserves

III. A future of yet unknown uniforms

Writing a Preview Statement

Preview statements, often called statements of structural progression or orientation, announce what you will cover in the speech:

> First, I want to tell you who Bill Peters is. Then I want to tell you why he is important to this organization. Finally, I want to tell you how you can all become a little more like the Bill Peters of this world.

In short speeches, statements of structural progression can be extremely brief. One sentence is sometimes sufficient.

> In this speech, I will address three major points: the dramatic increases in cases of AIDS in some African countries, the lack of resources currently available to combat the spread of AIDS, and the role that Canada can play in halting the march of AIDS across the African continent.

Unlike readers, listeners cannot refer to the previous page or flip ahead to see where the speaker is going. For this reason, it is extremely important to advertise where you are going with a speech. An old adage says: You should tell an audience what you are going to tell them. Then you should tell them. Then you should tell them what you told them.

Step 3: Writing an Introduction

Although this chapter places development of the introduction as the third step in the speech-making process, many speakers prepare their introductions (and conclusions) before organizing and writing the main text of the speech.

While the body of the speech should be logical and clear in its development, the introduction and conclusion should be creative and interesting. Speeches should begin with an attention-getting device, followed by purpose and/or thesis statements and a preview of the organization of the speech. Effective attention strategies ensure that your introduction is memorable. Attention strategies also help the speaker to adapt to the audience. We have already discussed purpose and preview statements. Now we will discuss attention-getting strategies.

Early studies in the psychology of attention identified the average attention span of audiences as ranging between two seconds and one minute—not a long time.[3] Reflecting the conclusions of these early scholars, Walter Dill Scott observed:

> In public address it is seldom that we are able to hold the full and undivided attention for more than a few seconds or a few minutes at best. The hearer's attention is constantly wandering or decreasing in force. He may renew it by personal effort, or else something we say or do may bring back the wandering or waning attention.[4]

The fact that typical speaking rates vary between 100 and 140 words per minute[5] and audiences comprehend at a rate of 300 words per minute explains at least part of the problem.[6] Audiences have much time to contemplate other topics and think about a multitude of subjects—relationships, food, assignments, and responsibilities at work, to mention but a few.

The attention-getting phase of the speech should not be too lengthy. Over many years of writing speeches for others, I learned that it takes about two minutes (sometimes less, depending on rate of speech) for the average speaker to get through one page of typed material (double-spaced, 12-point Times Roman font). So a five-minute speech will be no more than three double-spaced pages in length. Beginning speakers often overestimate what they can cover in five minutes, causing them to run seriously over their allotted time in speeches. For a five-minute speech, a one-paragraph introduction with attention-getting device, thesis statement, and preview statement should consume less than one-half of a page. In a longer speech (15 minutes or about eight pages in length), the introduction could be closer to three-quarters of a page in length and the conclusion could be as much as half a page.

As noted in Chapter 3, the responsibility for holding the attention of audiences lies with both listeners and speakers. This chapter focuses, however, on speakers. The most common attention-getting strategies in speeches of introduction are *immediacy strategies*; *references to the novel*; *suspense and shock techniques*; *linguistic strategies such as use of sensory-*

laden language and quotations; activity, drama, and conflict; and humour. Gimmicks come with a price tag.

Immediacy Techniques

Immediacy techniques close the psychological distance between speaker and audience. In a speech of introduction, the speaker may make a *reference to someone in the audience,* extend a *personal greeting or compliment,* mention *the occasion or surroundings,* mention a *recent event,* share *personal details* (i.e., self-disclose), adopt a *conversational style,* and/or ask a *question.* This chapter focuses on immediacy techniques from the perspective of content. Chapter 6 will discuss the use of immediacy strategies in delivery.

In the following example, the speaker greets her audience, refers to some members by name, compliments the audience on their choice of program topics, and talks about recent events that have had a financial impact on the audience.

> Being introduced by a town crier is a new experience for me. Thank you for your kind—and very vocal—introduction! I am pleased to be with you today at the twentieth annual Tourism Convention. This has not been our best year! Our region has faced a number of crises in recent months, which have caused a decline in the number of visitors. The drought conditions, the forest fires, the high cost of gasoline, and fear of SARS have had an impact on the numbers of people choosing to spend their dollars in this area. But you have all come together to find a long-term solution to our problems. When I see members of so many groups—small businesses, banking institutions, community organizations, municipal associations, environmentalists, and others present—I know that your efforts will be productive, because co-operation breeds results. Bob, Nancy, thank you so much for inviting me to be your keynote speaker. I am honoured for the opportunity to address your organization, and I congratulate you and other committee members for putting together such an interesting program.

Conversational language conveys the impression that a speaker is 'in the moment,' speaking on a one-to-one basis to audience members. The following example comes from a June 2002 speech by Alex Himelfarb, Clerk of the Privy Council and Secretary to the Cabinet:

> I have an excellent, well-written speech in my hands, but it is for another day. I'm just going to talk to you for a few minutes. It's been a crazy few weeks. It's been a crazy few months. It's sort of hard to be a public servant, don't you think? I mean, think about it. September 11th turned everything upside down. It changed everybody's perceptions of the world, of trust in the future, and of trust in government. . . . And of course, we've discovered how volatile and exciting the world of politics is. I was going to say 'Holy shit!' but I know that's exactly what my colleagues at Privy Council were worried about. So I won't say that because it's totally inappropriate. And I want it on the record that I didn't say that.[7]

Another nice example comes from a speech by the Honourable Hilary M. Weston, then Lieutenant-Governor of Ontario:

Having been described in certain circles as 'a lady who lunches', I confess to wondering whether I was wise to be seen having a meal in public at noontime. But, of course, I was delighted to accept your kind invitation, not least because your organization has proven time and again that women know and care as much about the issues of the day as men—and can eat at the same time![8]

References to the familiar also bring a sense of immediacy to the speech. In the following example, Kristen Pidduck begins her speech by talking about a situation with which many students can identify, especially students in a public-speaking course. She also engages in self-disclosure, another immediacy technique:

I would make a bet that at some point or another almost every person in this class has suffered from a case of the shakes. Maybe it happened in a situation such as this one, where you had to stand up and give a talk. Or maybe it was because your blood sugar level was low, or you had not eaten in a while. Maybe you were very tired. I would also bet that, at that time, you became very aware of yourself, your actions, and your fine motor skills. Think of how you felt in those moments. Were you upset because you couldn't pour milk properly? Or you couldn't focus on the words in a book because your hand was shaking? Maybe you had trouble signing your name or writing an essay. Now imagine going through your whole life in this way. You would be surprised by the number of people who do. I do. My name is Kristen Pidduck, and the cup of tea that I am holding represents all of the things that I cannot drink or eat because of my shaking disorder.[9]

Another immediacy strategy entails asking questions of the audience. Sometimes the questions appear at the beginning of the speech. At other times, they are sprinkled throughout the speech. An example follows:

Did you have problems finding affordable housing this semester? Are you eating Kraft dinner and tuna delight because your rent is too high? Do you live with a dripping faucet, knobs that won't stay attached to the doors, and locks that don't work?

When listeners respond to the questions, they become active participants in the speech event. Sometimes speakers ask for a show of hands or a verbal response from their audience. At other times, the questions are rhetorical in nature. By *rhetorical*, I mean that the speaker does not expect the audience to respond in any visible or audible way to the question.

Well-phrased rhetorical questions stimulate the audience to think about—but not to verbalize—the response. 'What was the most difficult decision you ever had to make?' 'If you could—or had to—live the life of someone else, whom would you choose?' 'Do you know the average cost of a university education 20 years ago? Ten years ago?'

The next example of a rhetorical question uses the multiple-choice concept:

Which word best describes the typical Canadian student? A. Tired. B. Frustrated. C. Overcommitted. D. Broke. According to many of the students with whom I have spoken, the appropriate answer may be 'E. All of the above.'

Several criteria apply to the use of rhetorical questions. Rhetorical questions must be acceptable to the audience. They should also be realistic. Many audience members tune out the speaker who asks an unrealistic question such as, 'How many of you would like to earn a million dollars on your spring break?' Finally, the questions should be sufficiently simple that the audience can respond without conducting complex mathematical exercises in their heads. They could probably respond fairly easily, for example, to the question 'How much did you spend last year on DVDs?' But if you asked how much they spent last year on recreation, you would lose them. First, they would have to figure out what you meant by 'recreation'. Then they would have to think about the cost of each item. Finally, they would have to multiply the figures. When speakers ask questions, they should pause long enough for the audience to consider the answer. In this case, for all practical purposes, the speaker might as well sit down after asking the question, because the calculations would consume the class period. Of course, that does not happen. What does happen is that the audience loses interest when they are asked complicated questions.

Additional criteria apply when you expect a show of hands or other visible response to your questions. Ask questions that do not call for embarrassing or incriminating responses. Do not ask, for example, how many students failed to report their summer income, cheated on their last examination, or smoked marijuana.

Speakers sometimes over-rely on questions as an attention-getting strategy in the introduction to speeches. They ask questions when they have not devoted sufficient time to preparation or cannot think of a more interesting or creative way to begin their speeches. Asking questions of the audience is usually not sufficient to capture their interest. The questions should be combined with vivid and concrete description or some other attention-getting strategy. I have heard many boring speeches that included all of the technical elements but lacked lustre and interest.

References to the Novel

Whereas reference to the familiar *gains* attention, reference to the unfamiliar *holds* attention. Speakers must offer novel facts and information if audiences are to see a reason to continue listening after the initial comments. When speakers fail to make this transition from known to unknown, they lose their audiences. The following example illustrates the offering of novel information to an audience:

> Many of you have heard the term 'obsessive compulsive disorder'. In shorthand, the term is OCD. Having a personal acquaintance with OCD, I would like to introduce you to some little-known facts about this potentially crippling psychological disorder. I am able to give you these special insights because I struggle with OCD. People with OCD spend hours fighting the need to clean everything around them. They cringe at the thought that they might touch a door knob or a sink that is inhabited by unseen microbes. Many people with OCD repeat actions, over and over again. For example, they don't check doors once each night. They check them three or four times. They also check gas stoves and other sources of possible danger multiple times before they can feel comfortable that they are safe. Other people with OCD collect useless items—old clothing, magazines, newspapers, and pots and pans. They spend hours going through garbage cans, and they find it almost impos-

sible to sort and give away anything. Some people with OCD are excessively slow in completing tasks because they want to ensure that everything is perfect. I am a 'cleaner' and a 'repeater', and I struggle daily to overcome these compulsions. They do not define me, but they have a huge impact on my life.

Perception studies tell us that intensity and contrast draw our attention. Extremely large and extremely small objects draw our attention, as do objects that stand out as different. In line with theories of perception, we can see that while references to the familiar evoke a context for the discussion, references to the novel add information to that perceptual set.

Suspense and Shock Techniques

The producers of reality shows have mastered the art of building and maintaining suspense. They continually add new twists so that the audience can never be complacent. They perpetually change the rules and dynamics of the game to hold the interest of audiences. On *Survivor* and *The Apprentice*, the producers switch people to different teams to add more conflict and uncertainty. On *For Love or Money*, they change the value of the cheques held by contestants. They bring unexpected guests to the house of *The Bachelor*, and they ask unsuspecting contestants to take lie detector tests on *Who Will Marry My Dad? Big Brother 5* added a 'DNA factor' to the show. Hostess Julie Chen explained the meaning of DNA in this way: 'This year's theme is *Do Not Assume. Project DNA* for short. Nothing is as it seems. Everything is open to interpretation.' In the same way, speakers build to an unanticipated climax, as in the following example:

> I squeezed my mother's hand as tight as I could. The cool metal from the gun pressed against my ear. A woman wearing all white was holding the gun. In a calm and soothing voice, she said to me, 'I am going to count to 3 and then shoot. Ready? 1 . . . 2 . . . 3 . . . BANG!' I let out a loud scream. Then I glanced at the mirror in front of me. That was when I saw the piercing through my right ear.[10]

The public speaker works within a much more constrained time bracket than producers of reality shows. The suspense builds quickly to a climax. When speakers use suspense techniques, they engage the audience by arousing their curiosity or provoking them to question the meaning of a statement. Sometimes the speaker mentions some point to be raised later in the speech, information to be provided, or questions to be answered. If the information or questions hold interest for audiences, they will listen to get answers to the questions.

Box 4.3 A Question of Ethics

Many of the reality shows use shock techniques to capture audience attention. On *Survivor*, for example, the producers replayed an event in which a woman claimed that she was sexually harassed by one of the participants, who was naked at the time. On *Who Will Marry My Dad?* a woman was shown abandoned at a church in full wedding garb. Subsequently, she learned that the daughters of the prospective groom had chosen her for elimination from the show. The programs that feature wife and husband swapping often include highly derogatory comments about participants, retained for their entertainment value. On *My Big Fat Obnoxious Boss* (a spoof on *The Apprentice*) participants were deceived into thinking they were participating in a real competition. In fact, their 'boss' was an actor who asked them to panhandle on the streets of Chicago, lie to people, sleep on pillows stuffed with dollar bills, and eat spam. (They were told the spam was an expensive cuisine.) In short, many reality shows focus on sensational and shocking moments, as well as deceit.

Sometimes speakers also use shock techniques. They write a shocking word on a blackboard, show a disturbing photograph, or select a topic for its shock value. A speaker may show photographs of animals abused in cosmetic testing or graphic images of accident victims. Sometimes they use language that is politically incorrect in an effort to demonstrate the problem of racism or sexism. (Some speakers also use the same kind of attention devices for humorous effect.) They argue that, if they are members of the disadvantaged group, they have the right to call themselves whatever they please.

Should motive be taken into account in judging the ethics of the technique? If the speaker uses one of these shock strategies to shake listeners from an apathetic posture, is he or she justified in using the strategy? What criteria determine whether a shock technique is ethical? Does the end purpose (awareness versus humorous effect) make a difference in judging the ethics? Should members of the same racial or gender group be able to poke fun at themselves?

Speakers also grab our attention when they use statistics or examples that surprise or shock, such as the following: 'More children contract sexually transmitted diseases each year than all the victims of polio in its 11-year epidemic, 1942–53.'[11] A second extended example follows:

> In 1850, you could purchase a slave in the United States for approximately $1,000. In 2005, you can purchase a young girl in Amsterdam or Bangkok for $600. You can purchase an adult slave on the Ivory Coast of Africa for $40. There are more slaves in the early years of this century than in any other period in the history of civilization.[12]

Linguistic Strategies

Highly evocative and sensory-laden language also can gain the audience's attention. In the next example, the speaker describes the environment in sensory terms—sights, sounds, tastes, and smells. By accessing multiple channels of perception, she increases the chances that audiences will note and absorb the information.

> Imagine! It's June. You're on vacation with family and friends. After living off Raman noodles for months, you have saved enough money to reach your destination. Clear blue skies above. You face great iron gates that welcome you to an enchanted castle. You smell cotton candy and hot dogs. Every colour in the rainbow surrounds you in the form of brilliant costumes. You see adventurous rides

that go faster than the speed of light. You hear captivating music and children squealing with excitement. You can almost taste and feel the sticky sweetness of a candied apple. Life can't get better. As you take everything in, you notice something out of the corner of your eye. Suddenly you are overcome with nervousness. All those years of anticipation have finally led to this moment. You try to catch your breath, but you have lost the ability to speak. Your palms are sweating, your knees are shaking, and you are face to face with your dream. You are finally meeting Mickey Mouse.[13]

Quotations are commonly used to get attention in the introductions and conclusions of speeches. Lines from Robert Frost's poems have appeared in many inspirational speeches over the years. A favourite is: 'Two roads diverged in a wood, and I . . . I took the one less traveled by, and that has made all the difference.' John Greenleaf Whittier is another often quoted poet: 'Of all sad words of tongue and pen, the saddest are those "It might have been."' Always cite the source of a quotation. You might say, for example: 'Satchel Paige, famed baseball player from the 1950s, observed, "Work like you don't need the money, love like you've never been hurt, and dance like no one else is watching."'[14]

Some quotations are humorous. In a speech on fast food, for example, one of my students quoted Steve Elbert as saying, 'Fast food is equivalent to pornography, nutritionally speaking.'[15] George Burns appealed to older audiences with jokes such as the following: 'You know you're getting old when you bend over to tie your shoe and think, "What else can I do while I'm down here?"' In a similarly light vein, seemingly ageless baseball player Satchel Paige wryly observed, 'Age is a case of mind over matter. If you don't mind, it don't matter.' Most of the time, the pithy quotation works best; but you will usually need to combine short quotations with other vivid content such as stories, explanations, or other attention strategies. In conclusions, however, quotations can more readily stand on their own.

Activity, Drama, and Conflict

Canadians like hockey, figure skating, soccer matches, and golf. Hundreds of thousands buy lottery tickets every week. At the end of the day, they like to know who has won and who has lost a competition. References to activity, drama, and conflict capture audience attention. In political races, the media quickly narrow the race to a manageable number of contenders (two or three) they can easily follow and depict as winners or losers. They talk about the front-runners and the laggards. They build drama as the race progresses. Once the media have narrowed the field, the public can more easily pick a favourite to follow, as in a sports competition.[16] Audiences like plots that develop quickly. The reality shows must eliminate someone each week to maintain the interest of the audience. The element of competition must be ever-present.

In the same way, speakers hold the interest of audiences by adding conflict and drama to their speeches and maintaining a relatively fast pace in developing story lines. In the next example, speaker Andrew Gowing describes an action-filled experience:

In January of 2000, I learned first hand the dangers of snowmobiling on uncharted terrain. While out for a day of riding, my friend and I decided to abandon the trails and ride through a farmer's field. The choice was not a good one. At the crest of a hill, we came upon a three-foot-high snowdrift. Unable to slow down in time, we hit the drift at 60 kilometres an hour. The jolt threw me into a nearby barbed wire fence. The two cracked ribs, six stitches in my arm, and a badly sprained wrist were enough to convince me that an established trail system is a critical part of snow-mobile safety.[17]

Humour

Many speakers employ humour as a means of 'warming up' the audience, in the same way that comedians warm up studio audiences prior to the taping of television shows. The use of humour in speeches can, however, be risky. Not everyone shares the same sense of what is funny; and used inappropriately, humour can be highly offensive. Some standard rules apply to its use, and speakers would do well to heed the rules. First, speakers should always avoid racist or sexist humour. Second, the joke should be fresh enough to capture the interest of the audience. Third, the joke or humorous experience should be relevant to the topic of the speech and to the audience.

In the following example, the speaker relies on an unexpected twist to achieve humour. The statement begins with a philosophical thought by an unknown author: 'If you love something, set it free. If it comes back, it will always be yours. If it doesn't come back, it was never yours to begin with.'[18] Then the speaker continues with the unexpected: 'But if it sits in your living room, messes up your stuff, eats your food, uses your telephone, takes your money, and doesn't appear to realize that you actually set it free in the first place, you either married it or you gave birth to it.'

In a speech delivered to an APEX symposium in 2002, Alex Himelfarb (Clerk of the Privy Council and Secretary to the Cabinet) poked gentle fun at himself: 'I am bilingual. My body is bilingual. My ears are bilingual. My heart is bilingual. It's just my mouth that lets me down sometimes.' Speakers should take care, however, to observe certain limits with self-deprecating humour. The humour should not depreciate the credibility of the speaker in areas that are critical to acceptance of speech content.

Not everyone is comfortable using humour that employs a punch line. Many people stumble on the punch line or fail to time it properly. Sometimes they confuse the telling of the joke. Traditionally, women have been less comfortable than men with stock jokes, especially in mixed-gender situations.[19] Women often prefer to recount an experience with humorous content as opposed to a joke with a punch line. The following exemplifies that 'softer' approach to humour:

On January 1, 2004, my parents will celebrate their 25th anniversary—a quarter of a century of marriage. To this day, I don't know how they did it. I asked, on one occasion, what their secret was. My dad replied, 'When you've had all you can take, and you can't take it no more, mark an X on the calendar. If things haven't improved by exactly six months from that day, pack your bags and leave. It's over.' My mom smiled. She said that, for her, the answer to their staying together was simple. They had agreed that whoever left first had to take the kids.[20]

Gimmicks

Sometimes speakers use gimmicks such as tearing up dollar bills or bringing live animals to class to capture the attention of their audiences. Gimmicks, however, are always extremely risky; and live animals draw the attention of the audience away from the speaker. I was asked a couple of years ago whether a speaker could bring a rifle to class to demonstrate how to load a rifle. (His hobby was competitive shooting.) Of course, I said 'No.' Given the environment set in place by incidents such as the shooting at a high school in Taber, Alberta, I could only imagine the reaction of the class and the university's security officers to the presence of a gun in the classroom. While the rifle was not a gimmick in the true sense of the term, its effect on the class would have been equivalent to bringing a cobra into the room.

Box 4.4 Speakers Beware!

Be careful when you use live visual aids! I remember one speaker who brought a young, two-foot alligator as a prop. Although it was muzzled, all attention was on the alligator for the five minutes she was speaking; and as a result, nobody really heard her speech. That's visual overkill.

John Busby

Step 4: Developing the Body of the Speech

You have decided on a topic and purpose for the speech; developed an outline of major points that you want to cover; and written an introduction. Your next step is to fill out the speech. You need to develop each of the points in your outline, using concrete and interesting language. A speech of introduction or personal experience will not employ supporting materials such as statistics and expert testimony. The speech will, however, depend on such supports as *personal experiences, examples, stories, quotations,* and *humour.* Later chapters will go into depth on the use of these support materials.

Step 5: Connecting Your Thoughts

Transitions, signposts, and internal summaries ensure that the speech moves easily from one idea to the next. They tie the speech into a coherent whole.

Transitions

Transitions help the listener to follow a speech. Transitions connect thoughts, establishing the relationship between paragraphs or major points in a speech. Examples of transitions can also are *in addition to, also, moreover, however, next, so much for,* and *now.* Transitions can also include longer phrases, such as: 'The next point that we will discuss . . . .'; 'So much for . . . now we will turn to . . . .'; 'Now that we have explored the nature of the problem, we will look at solutions . . . .'; 'This is one part of the problem; the second part is . . . .'; 'We have spent a lot of time talking about the problem, it's time to discuss the solution.' Sometimes transitions serve a secondary function of placing emphasis on certain points: 'The most critical factors to take into account when you choose a new house are. . . .' 'Above all else, you need to understand . . . .' Additional examples of common transitions appear in Box 4.5.

Box 4.5 Common Transitions

Comparison: likewise, in the same way, in relationship to, in comparison with, similarly, in a similar fashion, once more, like, analogous to, just as, in a like manner, comparable to, mimicking, typical of, duplicating, akin to, not unlike

Contrast: Nevertheless, on the contrary, on the one hand . . . on the other hand, but, rather, instead, still, yet, however, despite, by way of contrast, nonetheless, although, even so, notwithstanding, regardless, in spite of, even though

Time: Before, after, in the meantime, during, as soon as, next, at last, first, then, immediately, subsequently, currently, at the same time, usually, to begin with, eventually, meanwhile, recently, once, simultaneously, finally

Emphasis: Most important, above all, in fact, surely, the most striking, indeed, truly, certainly, furthermore, most assuredly, without doubt, most critical, most substantial, in truth, beyond doubt, unquestionably, notably, of course

Location: Near, above, beyond, adjacent to, beneath, in front of, behind, to the left, to the right, opposite, between, below, alongside, away from, bringing up the rear, elsewhere, further from, the far side of, beyond, atop, parallel to

Addition: Moreover, in addition to, once again, also, not only . . . but also, as well as, besides, another, equally important, along with, together with, also, so too, another significant, also under consideration, aggravating

Clarification: For example, for instance, specifically, to illustrate, namely, in particular, such as, stated differently, simply stated, in other words, to demonstrate, the following example, put another way, exemplifying, to clarify, because

Conclusion: As a result, thus, consequently, hence, accordingly, as noted, in my view, in conclusion, in short, briefly, as mentioned earlier, in closing, in summary, in the final analysis, to conclude, therefore, on the whole, all things considered

Concession: Although, granted that, I admit that, naturally, admittedly, certainly, even though, while it may be true, failing that, the worst-case scenario, at any rate, at least, it may appear that, all kidding aside, given that, without doubt

---

Signposts

Signposts are like bookmarks. They are brief statements or questions that position the listener in the speech. Sometimes they are just numbers, as in the following example:

'The first life-altering event in my life was . . . . The second life-altering event was . . . . The third life-altering circumstance happened when . . . .' An alternative way of signposting is to ask questions as you enter each new area of discussion. For example, a speaker may introduce the problem section of a persuasive speech by asking, 'What is the problem?' Once she reaches the solution part of her speech, she asks, 'What can the company do about the problem?' She concludes the speech by asking, 'What can *you* do about the problem?'

Like transitions, signposts act as connectors. However, they also alert the listener to major divisions or headings in the speech. In that sense, they relate back to the statement of structural progression—the preview or orientation statement that appears in the introduction to the speech.

Internal Summaries

Internal summaries also help to ensure the continuity of a speech. Especially important to longer speeches, they remind the audience of the logical progression of the speech. The following example illustrates this point:

In short, understanding figure skating entails learning a whole new vocabulary. Once you understand that vocabulary, you can gain entry to the world of figure-skate judging. As I have explained, however, that experience can be a disillusioning one for many novice skaters and their parents.

Notice that the internal summary, in this instance, is brief. A two- to three-minute speech of introduction may not require an internal summary; the brevity and simplicity of the speech content eliminate the need.

Step 6: Closing with a Memorable Thought

Conclusions should leave audiences with a memorable thought. In a speech of introduction, the speaker can use a *quotation*, *poem*, or *anecdote* that relates closely to the main point of the speech. Alternatively, the speaker can incorporate a moment of *humour* in a speech that is light-hearted. The next example comes from a student speech in which the young woman talked about her addiction to coffee. She concluded her speech with the following statement:

Although I may not be as dark, mysterious, or Italian as my favourite coffee, I'd say that we have more than a few characteristics in common. I like it, need it, and am often wearing it to some degree or another. I guess that some would say I am addicted, but I like to say I've made a life choice. Cappuccino, latte, et moi! Partners for life![21]

Sometimes speakers link their conclusion to the opening thought of the speech. This linkage to the introduction of the speech ties the speech into a neat package. In the introduction to a student speech titled 'Bungee Jumping', Mary Kathryn Roberts talked about the importance of facing your fears:

Everyone has his or her own ideas about the meaning of fear. For some of you, fear may be coming in front of a group and speaking, as I am doing now. For me, fear presented itself in September 2003 in the form of Velcro, awkward harnesses, and a really big rubber band! Last summer I faced my fear. After much trembling, sweating, and giggling, I finally leapt, screamed, and then glowed in the realization that I had done it. I had bungee jumped!

In the conclusion of the speech, the speaker returned to this initial idea. She said:

And I believe that is what life is about: facing your fears, crossing the boundaries that you place upon yourselves. Sure, I may never go bungee jumping again, and I still get shaky atop a ladder. But I can say that I did it. And I will always have this tape of my sloppy, awkward leap to remind me to *just jump*. There is never any regret in taking a safe risk. Just jump.[22]

The conclusions to longer speeches often include summaries of major points, as in the following example:

In the introduction to this speech, I told you that I had made three influential decisions during the course of my skating career. My first decision was to move to Toronto to skate when I was only 15 years old. That decision led to studying under a coach of Olympic fame. The second major decision was to change from singles skating to pairs skating. I met my partner for life when I made that decision. My third decision, which still causes me grief, was to turn professional at the age of 23. Lacking confidence in my ability to compete against younger athletes, I persuaded my partner to retire with me and to join an ice show. Not only did I give up my Olympic dreams, but I asked my partner to do the same. We don't spend a lot of time any more thinking about it, and she doesn't blame me. But if we could turn back the clock, you would see us in Turin, Italy, in 2006. Author and business entrepreneur Joe Karbo once said, 'The only things I regret . . . are the things I didn't do.' Never give up your dreams!

Like introductions, conclusions should not be too lengthy. They should not introduce new material. They should provide closure. In an 8–10 minute speech, the above conclusion is an appropriate length. The conclusion to a five-minute speech should be half the length of the above. The conclusion to a two- to three-minute speech of introduction should be no more than several sentences. When you put together the introduction and conclusion to a speech, they rarely will consume more than 20 per cent of your speaking time. In short speeches, conclusions typically are briefer than introductions. The conclusions of longer speeches include summaries of major points, as in the above example. The conclusions of shorter speeches usually make only brief mention of major points, perhaps incorporated into a single sentence.

A final point about conclusions concerns the tendency of novice speakers to want to thank their audiences for listening to them. At other times, they make apologetic statements such as 'I hope that I haven't taken up too much of your time'; 'I will stop boring you now'; or 'That's it!' As a speaker, you offer something of value to the audience. So listeners should thank you, rather than the reverse. Box 4.6 illustrates the basic structural elements in a speech on elder abuse, but the example excludes the development of the major points.

Box 4.6 Overview of Structural Elements in Speeches

Attention: Thank you. I am pleased to be with you today, speaking on behalf of Elisha Winters, representative for seniors' issues. I am not unique this afternoon in representing the interests of someone absent from this room. Many of us at this meeting are, in one way or another, standing in for someone else. Some of you are here to give a voice to women who have been physically or psychologically battered, often by those they most trusted and loved. Others speak for the children, many of whom have likewise suffered the traumas of family violence. Acting on behalf of Ms Winters, I am here to speak for the seniors—voices that, too often in the past, have not been heard in the noisy corridors of power. *Statement of purpose:* As a spokesperson for seniors, I would like to take the next several minutes to introduce you to some concerns specific to the area of elder abuse. *Thesis sentence:* Elder abuse is a problem to which all of us must pay attention, especially governments. *Preview statement:* I would like to discuss three points in particular that are relevant to a good understanding of this topic. *First,* I would like to acquaint you with what we believe to be a profile of the older victim. *Second,* I would like to suggest what appears to be emerging as a profile of the abuser. *Third,* I would like to focus your attention on what many are finding to be the most critical challenges in dealing with the problem of elder abuse. *Transition:* In considering this last point, we should not forget to look at cultural influences. *Signpost:* Now that you know a little more about the characteristics of the older victim, we can look at the emerging profile of the abuser, my second major point. *Conclusion:* International Women's Day is important because it gives us an opportunity to recognize the fact that violence against women knows no geographical, socio-economic, or cultural differences. The problem is universal. It also knows no age boundaries. In the 1960s, child abuse was an emerging topic. In the 1970s, wife assault began to capture headlines. By the 1990s, the problems of older Canadians were more commonly recognized and discussed. Whether young or old, able or disabled, victims of violence have much in common. And those of us who have gathered today to represent their interests have much to share and learn from each other. The time has come to speak out against violence, to give a voice to those unable or afraid to speak for themselves. We must also learn to listen more carefully and help the victims of violence to find their own voices.

Step 7: Practising and Delivering the Speech

The term 'extemporaneous speaking' refers to a situation where a speaker prepares and practises a speech but limits memorization to the introduction and conclusion.

Note Cards

Typically, the person speaks from $3'' \times 5''$ or $5'' \times 8''$ index cards that contain key words. Sometimes, however, these note cards also include quotations and key passages that the speaker wants to say word for word. Since only the speaker sees the note cards, he can put anything that he wants on the cards. When a speaker chooses to place the entire speech on the cards, however, he runs the risk of being tempted to read the speech. Many students have told me that, no matter how hard they try, they cannot get away from reading speeches that appear in their entirety on note cards. Also it is hard to see the major points on a card if the format is full text. If you lose your place, it is harder to locate it.

For that reason, limit the information on note cards to key points and a few quoted phrases (see Box 4.7). When you speak from key points, you can add ideas at the last minute to your note cards. You may decide, for example, to add a reference to someone in the audience, another person's speech, or some unexpected news. These references add a sense of immediacy to your speech and encourage the audience to feel that you are speaking spontaneously and sincerely.

Box 4.7 Sample Note Cards

(based on speech by Julie Huot)   1of 2

Do you know someone with an invisible disability? I do. We all do. According to statistics, two of us in this class have an invisible disability. What do I mean? Let's start with a few facts.

Stats Canada—over 2 million university students in Canada
University of Ottawa Web site—over 27,000 students
Faculty of Arts—3,800

How many cope with the challenges of an invisible disability?

1 in 10 Canadians
Potentially 200,000 students affected
Translates into 380 students in our faculty

35 per cent of students identified with a learning disability drop out of high school—2X the rate of non-disabled peers

---

Huot   2/2

Three key points:

1) Learning disabilities are often unrecognized and invisible to people not directly affected by it.

2) Students with learning disabilities attending university can succeed with minimum accommodations.

3) To ensure equal access to higher education, society must assign resources to provide for people with learning disabilities.

Definitions:

Learning disabilities—'unusual difficulties with spelling, writing, math, concentration, and memory'

Accommodations—what people with learning disabilities need from the outside world in order to be successful

For example: extra time on an exam, quiet room, access to a computer.

Depending on the length of the speech, two to five cards usually are sufficient. Follow your outline format. Do not include too many words on a single note card and put the key words in a sufficiently large font or handwriting. Some people use colour coding to highlight points that they want to emphasize or have trouble remembering. You should be able to grasp the ideas quickly when you look at the note cards. Printing in all capital letters is harder to read than a mix of lower- and upper-case letters. Numbering the cards ensures that you can find your place if you drop them, as sometimes happens.

Box 4.8 Tips for Using Note Cards

· Use 3″ × 5″ or 5″ × 8″ index cards—never regular paper!
· Write clearly and legibly, large enough to see easily.
· Use mostly key words.
· Write out quotations and statistics; note sources.
· Limit the number of points per card to five or six.

· Highlight or underline hard-to-remember points.
· Avoid using more than five cards.
· Number the cards.
· When you deliver, hold the cards with one hand.
· Maintain eye contact; do not read from cards.

Practise the speech but do not try to repeat the same words each time you deliver the speech. Slight variations in wording give the impression that you are 'in the moment'. Properly delivered, an extemporaneous speech sounds spontaneous even if you have practised the delivery a number of times. The perception of spontaneity arises from the fact that you use somewhat different words each time you deliver the speech. Delivering a speech before your roommate or in front of the mirror improves your chances of success. Studies have found a positive relationship between the quality of a presentation and the amount of time spent preparing, processing, and practising the speech (silently and aloud).[23] See Box 4.9 for tips on how to sound extemporaneous with a well-practised speech.

Speakers should memorize only the introduction and conclusion to speeches. A smooth introduction and memorable conclusion leave a favourable impression on the audience. You should never read from note cards; rather, you should glance at the cards from time to time to remind yourself of the next thought sequence. Maintaining consistent eye contact is critical to a good delivery. Hold the cards in one hand and do not

---

Box 4.9 Practise by Listening

I have a technique for practising my speeches that allows them to sound extemporaneous even though I have practised them. I write out my speech well in advance. Then I record myself reading the speech on one of the little hand recorders. For the week leading to the speech, I never look at notes but simply listen to the speech over and over—sometimes in the car, sometimes in other situations. I do not memorize the speech, but I do become extremely familiar with the material, details, and order of points. The technique works well because it is like listening to yourself deliver a speech flawlessly over and over again. The lack of memorization allows for a natural delivery and a little improvisation upon delivery. Clients marvel at my never using notes—not even to deliver factual content with dates and dollars interspersed. This is not a technique I was ever taught or read about. I got the idea from techniques used in sport where you visualize over and over the perfect performance.

Mary Charleson, Vancouver

play with them while delivering your speech. When you move from one card to the next, look at your audience so that their attention is on you, not the note cards. Never substitute pieces of paper for note cards. The rustling of large pieces of paper distracts the listener, and small scraps of paper look unprofessional.

Visual Aids

Some studies suggest a correspondence between time spent in preparing a visual aid and the overall quality of the speech, including content and delivery.[24] Several cautions apply, however, to the use of visual aids. When showing a three-dimensional object, be sure that audience members can see the object from their seats. When objects are too small, too large, too awkward, or inappropriate to bring to class, you should construct a model or display a photograph of the object. You can enlarge the photograph at a print shop, for example, and mount it on a poster board. Alternatively, you can use an overhead projector, slide projector, or the computer to display the photograph.

Do not circulate objects or photographs among the audience when you are speaking. When you are ready to talk about the object, place it between yourself and the audience. Sometimes speakers place objects at selected points in the room, sufficiently close for the audience to see without straining. At other times, they wait until the conclusion of the speech to display the object at close range or to pass it around the room. Sometimes they place the photocopies, face down, at individual seats and ask that the audience not look at the material until requested. When you have finished using a visual aid, cover or remove it from the view of the audience. Additional discussion on the use of visual aids appears in Chapter 7.

Conclusion

In this chapter, I have considered seven steps to be taken in preparing and practising a speech of introduction. Those steps include *getting started* by choosing a theme, articulating the purpose of the speech, and writing a thesis statement; *getting organized* by identifying and ordering the main ideas and writing a preview statement; *fleshing out* your ideas; *providing connectives* to link ideas and internal summaries to orient listeners; *concluding* with a memorable thought; and *practising* the speech, using an extemporaneous mode of delivery.

The Appendix to this chapter shows different models of organization for the speech of introduction. Sample speech #1 conforms to a *chronological* sequence of development, whereas speech #2 demonstrates a *spatial* pattern. Sample speech #3 illustrates the *topical* pattern of organization, and speech #4 models the popular *narrative* scheme of organization. Sample speech #5 demonstrates the *comparative* pattern of organization. These speeches also depict the most common elements in a speech of introduction— the employment of an effective attention step, thesis statement, preview statement, transitions, signposts, and conclusion.

Questions for Discussion

1. Identify three objects that represent some aspect of your experiences, personality, or values. Explain why you selected these objects. What do they say about you? Why

do you consider them important to someone else's understanding of you? How could you use them to communicate your personality to an audience in a speech of introduction?

2. Think about some of your classes at the university and, without identifying specific professors, talk about what captures your attention in lectures? How do their strategies differ from those of less effective speakers?

3. Identify some celebrity or politician who is good at making audiences feel a sense of immediacy or psychological closeness. Which characteristics of the person's speaking style encourage this reaction?

4. What kind of humour appeals to you? What kind of humour do you find offensive?

5. After giving your speech, what would you say about the feedback that was provided by your peers? What kind of feedback was most helpful? Least helpful? Generate some rules for feedback that will be both respectful and useful.

Appendix: Sample Speeches of Introduction

Speech #1 (Chronological Pattern): Passages

by Alyssa Jacobs

Attention Step:

I squeezed my mother's hand as tight as I could. The cool metal from the gun pressed against my ear. A woman wearing all white was holding the gun. In a calm and soothing voice, she said to me, 'I am going to count to 3 and then shoot. Ready? 1 . . . 2 . . . 3 . . . BANG!' I let out a loud shriek. Then I glanced at the mirror in front of me. That was when I saw the piercing through my right ear. These are the earrings from that day. [Show earrings.]

Thesis Statement (underlined):

My name is Alyssa Jacobs. I am 21 years old, and I have 18 unnecessary holes in my body. <u>My parents would never have fathomed that, after this first encounter with the piercing gun, I would go through a series of stages of piercing various parts of my body, each with symbolic significance.</u>

Preview Statement (to orient audience to organization of speech):

Three acts of piercing, in particular, stand out as marking transition stages in my maturation and in my relationship with my parents: my first earrings, the piercing of my belly button, and my tongue piercing.

Signpost to First Major Point (underlined):

<u>When I had my first piercing</u>, I was only eight years old. But after having my ears pierced, I felt really grown up. My parents' supportive attitudes helped me to feel that I had

entered a new and more mature stage in my life. In my mind, I had moved from childhood into pre-adolescence.

Signpost to Second Major Point (underlined):

<u>The next piercing</u>, which marked my transition to adolescence, occurred when I was 13. This was my belly button period. The man who did the piercing took me into a small room, which was probably a converted closet. If the two of us had wanted to stand up at the same time, it would not have been possible. Afraid of sharing my decision with my parents, I hid the piercing for months. This is the ring from my belly button piercing. [Show ring.]

By the time I went to the doctor for my yearly checkup, months later, the piercing was severely infected. As the doctor was examining it, my mother walked into the room and saw it for the first time. She flipped out and ran out of the office. She wouldn't talk to me for weeks.

That night, when my father came home, my mother was still crying and screaming. My father thought that the whole family had died in a common tragedy. My parents eventually got over their upset, but to this day they can't look at that ring without cringing. My parents' reaction underscored the fact that I had entered my teenage years, and we were negotiating a new relationship.

Signpost to Third Major Point (underlined):

<u>The third piercing came</u> when I was 18. The piercing of

my tongue marked my transition from adolescence to adulthood. [Show piercing.] I had just graduated from high school and was about to start CEGEP. My parents' reaction was calm, considering that I had just put a hole in my tongue. All they said was, 'You've lost your mind.' They had finally accepted that I was grown up and they couldn't stop me from doing what I wished.

I have since taken out my tongue ring, an action that pleases my parents greatly, even though they won't admit it. I have grown out of my 'tongue piercing phase', but I am not quite yet finished with putting holes in my body. My last piercing occurred when I was 20.
Conclusion:

Body piercing has been practised for centuries in many different cultures. Some believe that the practice originated as much as 5,000 years ago. Body piercing is one of the oldest forms of body modification; yet the reasons for piercing the body are as diverse as the cultures from which they come.

In my case, the piercing of each new part of my body came at a time when I was undergoing a transition—from childhood to pre-adolescence, from pre-adolescence to adolescence, from adolescence to adulthood. And each piercing drew a unique reaction from my parents that reinforced the transition that I was undergoing. Eventually I will take out all of the earrings; however, the impressions created in my memories will never disappear.

Speech #2 (Spatial Pattern): Boots

by Heather Montgomery

Last fall I took a three-month journey to a number of different countries. I wanted to learn more about myself—and about other people. I did just that while walking in these boots, and I would like to share those experiences with you.

Just imagine my excitement and anticipation of crossing the Pacific Ocean for the first time to discover a whole new world. Crossing 15 time zones and flying 32,000 miles round trip. And on one part of my trip, I spent time in a place where time doesn't really exist.

The trek that I took to Nepal was the most emotional of my journey. To this day I can still smell the fresh air of the Mount Everest region. Seeing the mountain for the first time from the base camp stunned me. It was so beautiful. It is a scene of so much triumph and tragedy that I couldn't wait to get closer. I walked 194 kilometres in these boots to 17,500 feet above sea level, only to be defeated hours from my goal because I was too ill to continue.

One of the ways I was able to get over that defeat was by reflecting on how far I had come and what I had seen along the way. From the children who knew nothing of the Western world to one night where the air was so clear that I saw more stars than I ever knew existed. I was proud of my accomplishment.

From Nepal, my boots walked me into a hospital in Thailand. My first hospital experience consisted of a one-week stay in Bangkok—alone and afraid. After getting out,

I recovered the only way I knew how. I spent five days in Phuket by the pool sipping strawberry daiquiris!

From there, my boots and I flew to Kuala Lumpur, Malaysia, where I spent a lot of time quietly observing. I made it to the observation deck of the Petronas Towers, where Sean Connery and Catherine Zeta-Jones recently stole billions in their movie *Entrapment*. In Singapore, I reflected on the beauty of the women. I have never seen so many faces of porcelain and grace.

Before I returned home, I had one last adventure. I spent six weeks in Australia, where I ate crocodile and discovered freedom when I jumped out of an airplane at 14,000 feet! I met people who will be my friends for life, as well as the man of my dreams. I also spent Christmas with my best friend of 16 years who had married an Aussie the year before.

Upon my return home, I realized that—out of everything I had experienced—what mattered most was that I had learned something important about myself. I had learned that I had courage I never knew I had—courage to pursue a dream that mattered to me.

My boots still have mud caked to their soles and I'm not going to remove it. The mud has been with me since the start of my journey, and I only collected more as I went. As I continue through life and gain more experience, I think I should gain more mud along the way too.

Speech #3 (Topical Pattern): My Secret Addiction

by Joanna Mennie

My name is Joanna, and I am an addict. When I was 15, my mother (of all people) introduced me to a toxin that has forever changed my life. I grew up a home where my ultimate role model exposed me to her problem and convinced me that living life her way was okay. I can still see it now. There we would sit, mother and daughter, indulging in our family cycle of addiction, drinking cappuccinos and latte. And now, without coffee, I don't know if I could get through a day.

Some of you may be wondering how a generic Tim Horton's double double could really be seen as an artifact that says a lot about me. You should realize, however, that this cup of coffee—as well as many others like it—not only reflects who and what I am, but also gives me the kick that I need to keep being me. In this speech, I will tell you a little about how coffee reflects my personality, the disastrous consequences of not having my daily fix of coffee, and how coffee contributes to my successes.

The erratic energy that we associate with a strong cup of coffee also reflects my active, social, and somewhat scattered nature. In kindergarten, Mrs Fortin named me the tiny little chatterbox, and since then, I've been known to shamefully assume the role of the 'overly drunk girl making a fool out of herself' from time to time.

In a constant state of caffeination, I buzz through life. But when I don't have sufficient levels of caffeine coursing through my veins, the real disasters unfold. Without caffeine, I am often late, sleep-deprived, overly spontaneous, and oblivious to my physical surroundings. On the first day of school, my third year here, I had to call a friend in the morning to ask whether the library was in Morrisett or Montpetit. I also had to ask where these buildings are located on campus.

Another revealing incident occurred at the beginning of my first year in university. Having awakened a little late, I decided to forego my morning coffee and got ready as usual. I gathered my books, got dressed, and strolled out to the bus stop, proud of myself for having made good time. As I entered the bus shelter, two business men, who had been chatting pleasantly, stopped mid-sentence and stared right at me. I assumed that they were creepy and faced the other way. It was only when people, passing by in cars, pointed and laughed that I realized what was going on. There I stood with flawless makeup and straightened hair, my toothbrush hanging out of my mouth, complete with a chin full of toothpaste. And really, how does one recover from such a thing gracefully? I just swallowed, gagged, wiped the toothpaste off my face, and placed my toothbrush in my purse. Now Joanna does not skip her morning coffee!

Beyond kick-starting my day, a little caffeine gives me a boost when it's time to perform. I have always been extremely creative, and I write constantly. Whether it's time to act, deliver a speech, compete at improvisation in front of a screaming crowd, or sing opera for a panel of musical elite, coffee is part of my preparatory ritual.

Though I may not be as dark, mysterious, or Italian as coffee, I'd say that we certainly have more than a few things in common. I like it, need it, and am often wearing it to some degree. I guess my dependence could be seen as an addiction, but I choose to call my relationship with the beverage a life choice—and one of which my mom is proud.

Speech #4 (Narrative Pattern): Blue Bunny—a Piece of Home

by Natalie Kalata

I want you to imagine a market, like the one here in Ottawa—but bigger, with thousands of people shouting, bargaining. Shawls, scarves, and scraps of material are draped on top of large metal poles—an attempt to create a canopy to protect people from the exhausting heat of the sun. Merchants flank both sides of the cobbled, winding road. The air is so thick with the smells of sweat and spices that the only thing keeping you from passing out is your excitement and wonder. Then suddenly sirens go off. A loud booming voice comes over the intercom and says something, but you don't understand the words. Your heart starts to pound. A sinking feeling hits the bottom of your stomach, and you begin to run. Then BANG—an explosion. You hit the ground. When you get back to where you're staying, you grab your stuffed animal or GI Joe or your diary or picture of your family and you hold it tight and you begin to feel better.

'Home is where the heart is', or at least that's what someone famous once said. But what happens if you're away from home? For me, I like to take a piece of home with me wherever I might go. I call him 'Blue Bunny'.

When I was five, my mom remarried—this great big bear of a man whom I now call *Dad*. To anyone else, his six-foot-three, 275-pound stature is slightly intimidating; but when you get to know him, he's as gentle and soft-spirited as a bunny rabbit. And when he won a blue bunny, this stuffed animal, on our first father-daughter adventure, Blue Bunny and I became almost as close as my dad and I. From that point on, Blue Bunny and I became inseparable.

Vegas, Mexico, Israel, Denmark, England, Barbados, Virginia, New York, Muskoka, and Ottawa—Blue Bunny has been there. Blue Bunny has seen the Dead Sea. He has climbed to the top of Mount Masada and watched the sun rise. He has been awakened by gunfire, but he has also heard the soft soothing call of a loon. He has sat in the grid-locked traffic of New York City and ridden through the valleys of Virginia and the mountains of Barbados. He has wandered the streets of Copenhagen and swum among the coral reefs of Cuba.

There is something to be said about things that make you feel at home, no matter your geographic location. Poets have written about the strong appeal of home, and musicians have sung songs about its relentless pull.

Home is very important to me. When I feel scared, nervous, excited, or angry, home is the place I go to feel okay; and when I'm with my blue bunny, I'm home.

Speech #5 (Comparative Pattern): The Shape of My Personality

by Jeff Dillman

In case you are wondering why I would have brought such a strange prop to the podium, I would like to tell you a little about its history and relevance to this speech of introduction.

First its history. My initial contact with this piece of bent metal occurred shortly after I began working at in a bicycle repair shop in the summer of 2002. One day, a customer brought a used bicycle to the store. The rear wheel needed to be replaced. And so I ordered and fitted the new wheel onto the bike. When I returned the bike to its owner, I kept the bent wheel.

Having little to do for parts of every day, I found that the metal offered some source of entertainment. I experimented with twisting and bending it into various shapes. Over the course of the summer, I began to reflect on its qualities and value. In doing so, I saw parallels with some of my own personality, some findings that I would like to share with you today.

Metaphorically, the bent rim has many of the qualities that I like to see in myself: seemingly opaque, yet sometimes you can see right through it; firm yet flexible; unusual looking, but strangely intriguing; kind of slim; generally quiet unless dropped; and originally well-rounded, but now a little screwy.

My experimentation with the rim also symbolizes my more creative instincts. The ability to shape what some might see as a piece of junk into a unique piece of art. The ability to see art in what others might see as a twisted piece of metal. I am a wannabe artist myself.

The rim also demonstrates my enjoyment of simple pleasures. When it comes to having summer jobs, there are few rules that I value. However, I do believe in working hard until you master a task and then gradually relaxing into an easier posture.

I value having a good time. Life is more than just work. And so I have transformed the bent wheel from a tool used only to perform work into a source of amusement and pleasure.

I hope that this strange-looking object has helped you to learn a little bit about me—my interests, quirks, and values.

CHAPTER FIVE

Researching, Analyzing, and Adapting to Your Audience

SUGGESTED ASSIGNMENT

The Speech of Welcome

A welcoming speech (two minutes in length) presents the opportunity to apply principles of audience adaptation. You may welcome a mythical audience to an occasion of your choice. You can approach the assignment in one of two ways. You can imagine that your task is to welcome the audience to the larger speaking event (conference, professional meeting, or social gathering) and to introduce the first speaker at the conclusion of your welcoming comments. Alternatively, you can pretend that *you* are the keynote speaker. In that case, you conclude your welcoming remarks by stating the purpose and thesis of your speech and previewing the organization of your speech. In either case, you assume the role of a fictitious speaker in a fictitious environment. No outline or bibliography is required for this speech. The emphasis in evaluating the speech should be on the extent to which the speech reflects appropriate audience adaptation strategies.

Learning Objectives
- To learn about researching and analyzing your audience.
- To gain knowledge related to analysis of speaking environments.
- To learn strategies for adapting your speech to your audience.
- To learn to take ethical and critical concerns into consideration.

Oprah Winfrey is, without doubt, the diva among television talk show hosts. Her success has brought her enormous wealth and popularity. In October 2002, *Fortune* ranked Oprah number 10 among the world's most powerful women in business. In 2004, she occupied the number-three spot on *Forbes's* top celebrity list. While Oprah's down-to-earth personality, sense of humour, optimistic approach to life, and altruism play a critical role in her appeal to audiences, her success is based on more than her personality. Oprah is a virtuoso in the art of *audience adaptation*—a term that refers to the practice of

Photo Gill Ferguson

taking the values and beliefs, interests, needs, and knowledge levels of an audience into account in the process of communicating with a group.

This chapter explores the concept of audience adaptation by looking at research and analysis techniques and adaptation strategies. Public speaking is audience-centred, not speaker-centred. Definitions of success depend to a significant degree on answering such questions as the following: Did I meet audience expectations and fulfill their needs? Did I make a contribution to their levels of awareness, offering additional knowledge and information? Did I influence their attitudes or behaviours? In other words, did I have an impact? Did my speech make a difference? Too often, novice speakers think almost exclusively in terms of performance. Was my delivery without glitches? Did I maintain my composure? Did I use the right number of hand movements? Did I fidget? The fact is that audiences are willing to overlook presentation flaws if they think that the speaker has recognized and attempted to meet their needs. Understanding your audience is fundamental to meeting their needs. Thus, this chapter considers how to research, analyze, and adapt to your audience. The chapter also considers the need to analyze and take situational variables into account.

Researching and Analyzing Your Audience: Creating Useful Profiles

In a seminal communication model, Wilbur Schramm said that our success as communicators depends, to a great extent, on the degree to which our fields of experience overlap with those of our audience.[1] By *field of experience*, Schramm refers to the totality of what we are at the moment of communication. Since we constantly learn from new experiences, we are never the same at any two moments in time. In accordance with Schramm's ideas (see Figure 5.1), the most effective communication occurs

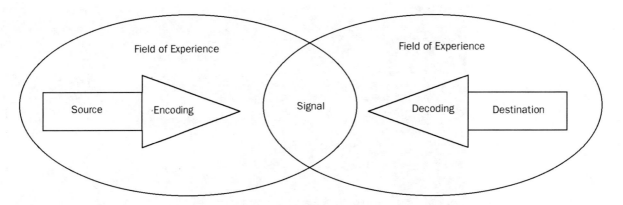

Figure 5.1 Wilbur Schramm's Field of Experience Model

between people who share the same background, language and culture, beliefs, attitudes, and values. That is, we can communicate with others to the extent that we have overlapping fields of experience.

Audience research requires the collection of the following three kinds of information: *demographic*, *psychographic*, and *personality*. This information can come from many different sources. Speakers can contact representatives of host organizations to ask for additional information on the speaking environment, the audience, and planned and past activities of the group. They can conduct research on the Internet (Web pages and references to the organization), request the annual report or publications that describe the operations of the organization, or schedule interviews with members of the group. Some organizations maintain profiles of employees, which they will share with speakers or training directors. Speakers often engage in conversation with audience members prior to the speaking event to learn more about their interests and priorities. Even last-minute information can often be worked into a speech.

Creating a Demographic Profile

As a speaker, the first stage in researching your audience is to seek information that will enable you to construct a *demographic profile* of the audience, taking factors such as age, sex, gender, marital and parental status, race, ethnicity, culture, income, education, and occupation into account. For example, if you are speaking on education reform, you should ask whether you will have school board members, teachers, or students—or a combination of the three groups—in your audience (*occupation*). If you choose to speak against the violent content of some popular song lyrics, you should learn whether your audience will be over 40 or under 20 (*age*) and predominantly men or women (*gender*). A successful speech to inform the audience about black holes in space requires knowing whether the majority of your audience members are astrophysicists, students in an undergraduate astronomy class, or science fiction writers (*education* and *expertise*). Deciding to speak on the rising costs of college tuition to a group of university students requires that you understand their economic situation, such as level of access to bursaries and employment (*income*). A speech on police brutality or the terrorist attacks on the World Trade Center and the Pentagon requires that the speaker be sensitive to demographic variables such as *race* and *ethnicity*.

The *Oprah* show offers a model for studying the fundamental principles of audience adaptation. First, like any good speaker, Oprah Winfrey knows the demographic makeup of her audience. On the basis of audience research, the producers of *Oprah* will have created a profile of television viewers in terms of age, gender, race, occupation, education levels, income, marital and parental status, ethnicity and cultural affiliations, and other variables. (It should not be surprising to learn that the demographics of Oprah's audience are different from those who watch Maury Povich or Ricky Lake.) Armed with knowledge of the demographic characteristics of the viewing audience, the producers of any talk show are able to uncover topics and guests of interest to this audience.

Based on the subject matter of *Oprah*, we should not be surprised that most viewers are women between the ages of 18 and 54.[2] The daytime status of the show suggests that many are 'stay-at-home' moms. Oprah explicitly acknowledges a particular kind of viewer when she makes comments such as, 'Now put down your laundry and pay attention' or 'Give your children some crayons and listen to what Dr Phil has to say.' In the same way, she discusses topics that appeal to women (often mothers) in their early and middle adulthood who are trying to identify what they want from life or seeking to revitalize their marriages. A common theme on *Oprah*, for example, is the importance of taking time away from the children to reflect on one's priorities and to engage in activities that result in self-actualization. Other popular themes include discussions on weight loss, fitness, and makeovers.

A smaller number of the discussion topics are aimed at older women who confront the 'empty nest' syndrome or face a crisis in their marriage or lives—serious illness, loss of a family member or valued friend, employment difficulties, or other catalytic events that cause the person to re-evaluate priorities and make lifestyle adjustments. Although men frequently appear on the show, almost invariably they accompany women, offering support for their wives or partners and explaining their relationship problems from the male perspective. One often suspects that the motivation for appearing on the show has originated with the female partner. The level of language and the topics discussed suggest that most viewers would have at least a high school education. Many would have some university education.

Oprah also demonstrates an awareness of the demographics of her television audience when she selects guests to appear on the show. Women appear more often than men. A number are authors of books and people with higher education such as psychologists, educators, social workers, and other professionals. Many of the celebrity guests reflect the cultural diversity of North American society. Not infrequently, Oprah's guests include individuals with mixed ethnic or cultural heritages. In short, both Oprah and the producers of her show appear to be keenly aware of demographics. For that reason, her show offers an excellent example of audience research, analysis, and adaptation to these groups. Any successful speaker takes similar measures in preparing for the public speaking occasion.

Creating a Psychographic Profile

The term *psychographic* refers to psychological factors such as beliefs, attitudes, and values. This category could also include personality variables. Audience adaptation requires knowledge of these psychological variables, as well as an awareness of the strength with which audience members hold their convictions.

Beliefs

A *belief* is faith in the credibility of some concept or idea. We may believe, for example, that the Liberal Party has better social policies than the Conservative Party, that men have an advantage over women in the workplace, or that the health-care system is in decline. The average person has hundreds of thousands of beliefs about people, politics, health, relationships, and countless other topics. We may believe that private schools are better than public schools, that Canada should stay out of the war in Iraq, or that western Canada is the best region in which to live. Our beliefs may be valid or invalid, supported or unsupported by evidence. A belief does not have to be true for us to accept it.

Attitudes

Clustered together, beliefs constitute attitude sets. An *attitude* is a predisposition to respond in a given way to objects, situations, or people—in other words, to display or act on our beliefs. If we believe, for example, that crime is on the rise, that our children are vulnerable to being kidnapped or molested, and that the government is not spending enough on crime prevention, we may have an attitude of distrust towards the government in power. If we believe that marijuana alleviates pain and that terminal cancer patients should be able to select their drugs of choice, we may have a positive attitude towards the legalization of marijuana for palliative purposes. In other words, a set of related beliefs leads to attitudes, which in turn influence our actions.

Beliefs and attitudes vary greatly across audiences. If a speaker suspects that some beliefs held by an audience are erroneous or ill-founded, she may need to address those misperceptions in order to accomplish her speech purposes. She may need to consider audience attitudes towards her topic. Audiences may be interested or disinterested in any given topic, receptive or unreceptive to the position advocated, and friendly or unfriendly towards the speaker. Sometimes speakers have captive audiences, required by

Photo Gill Ferguson

their employers or professors to attend the speaking occasion. At other times, audience members may go to considerable trouble to attend a speech event. The speaker should take these motivations and perceptions into account. The following chapter will look at examples of audience adaptation strategies that recognize the beliefs and attitudes of audiences.

Values

Whereas people have thousands of attitudes, they have only dozens of values. The term *value* refers to an ideal or moral principle that is at the foundation of our belief structures. Communication Canada conducted a survey in 2002, which asked people to select the social values most important to them on a personal level. The following percentages of people chose these values from lists of paired values: family (79 per cent), respect (66 per cent), peace (65 per cent), freedom (64 per cent), helping others (63 per cent), integrity (58 per cent), safety and security (57 per cent), fairness (56 per cent), co-operation (54 per cent), appreciation of our history and heritage (54 per cent), openness and tolerance (54 per cent), democracy (51 per cent), sharing (51 per cent), caring (51 per cent), community (48 per cent), friendliness (48 per cent), politeness (40 per cent), being inclusive (30 per cent), humility (26 per cent), and individual autonomy (26 per cent).[3]

In a 2001 survey, Environics identified values that rank high in Canadian society. Those values include freedom/choices (59 per cent), beauty/geography; climate/resources (23 per cent), health care/medical system (20 per cent), quality of life (18 per cent), opportunities/economic stability (12 per cent), peaceful/no war (10 per cent), multiculturalism and tolerance (10 per cent), democratic country (8 per cent), people friendly/polite/kind (8 per cent), safety/low crime rate (7 per cent), social programs (7 per cent), international reputation (7 per cent), good country (6 per cent), education system (6 per cent), clean (3 per cent), born here/identity (3 per cent), and bilingual (2 per cent).[4]

How do values relate to beliefs and attitudes? If the CEO of a company accepts the *values* of efficiency, innovation, and competitiveness, he may hold the *belief* that organizations should periodically restructure their processes. These beliefs, in turn, may lead to an *attitude* that supports organizational layoffs in poor economic times or in situations where new hires could increase profit margins. If the same CEO had placed a greater priority on the values of generosity and caring, he might have made different choices. So when speakers appeal to the basic values of audiences, they lay the groundwork for gaining acceptance of their ideas.

Returning to our earlier example, the producers of *Oprah* demonstrate a sound knowledge of the values of those who watch their program, as well as the reference groups with which they identify. It is obvious, for example, that viewers of *Oprah* are (or aspire to be) optimists in their approach to life, adherents to the value that 'the best is yet to be', upwardly mobile, and believers in the values of achievement, self-fulfillment, and independence. Many are likely to place a strong emphasis on spirituality and altruism and to be reasonably liberal in their approach to issues of politics, religion, and race and ethnicity. Family values are close to the top of their list of priorities.

A dominant characteristic of Oprah's audience is their common quest for self-improvement—in their marriages, in personal growth (spiritual and otherwise), in physical health, and in financial security. Whether decorating small spaces in their homes or allocating time to various household responsibilities, they aim to make the maximum use of available resources in the most efficient and effective way. Most members of Oprah's audiences have reached a point in their lives where they have the time and resources to ponder more than survival issues, and they value quality of life. They believe in taking action and assuming personal responsibility for their choices. They care about the environment and the kind of world their children will inherit.

The program content of *Oprah* clearly responds to the values, needs, and interests of these psychographic groups. For example, Oprah introduced 'Dr Phil' to her show to offer psychological advice. Andrew Weil, MD, of the University of Arizona has appeared on multiple occasions to offer counsel on acquiring healthy nutritional habits and achieving physical well-being. Others such as author Maya Angelou offer spiritual advice. An appearance by rock star Bono illustrates Oprah's practice of bringing social and political activists on the show. She has established an 'angel' network, which recognizes extraordinary efforts by ordinary individuals to better the lives of others through altruistic deeds.

As mentioned earlier, values are more stable than beliefs and attitudes, but differences in the priority levels assigned to the values, the numbers of people who subscribe to the values, and the intensity with which people hold the values vary over time and in different cultural contexts.

Needs

The basic needs of people, on the other hand, remain constant across all groups and all periods in time. Abraham Maslow presents a staircase of human needs, beginning with physiological and safety needs and progressing to love, esteem, and ultimately to self-actualization.[5] According to Maslow, humans are able to concentrate on satisfying self-esteem and self-actualization needs only after they have satisfied the three lower-level needs (physiological, security, and love). A starving man may be obsessed by the thought of food; but once fed, he can think about satisfying other needs such as security (finding a safe place to stay) and love (finding a companion and status in his community).

In many regards, the higher-level needs represent luxuries in many developing countries, where people face daily the threat of starvation and inadequate resources to deal with earthquakes or other natural disasters. Those people will be too occupied with finding food for their families, tending to ill or injured children, and maintaining at least rudimentary shelter to think about self-esteem or self-fulfillment. Even in the most affluent countries, relatively few people achieve self-actualization—a state characterized by independent lifestyles, freedom from restraint, and the ability to pursue personal goals. Creativity and curiosity are markers of self-actualizing behaviours. Most often, people satisfy these kinds of interests and goals outside of the workforce, through pursuit of hobbies and other personal interests.

The advertising industry appeals to the range of human needs. Vitamin and food advertisements appeal to the *physiological* needs of audiences. Insurance companies typically appeal to the *security* and *love* needs of people. Advertisements for hair products and makeup usually appeal to *love* and *esteem* needs. Such appeals suggest that the products will improve your looks, job opportunities, and/or your ability to attract a mate. Prestige appeals to *self-esteem* often appear in advertisements for automobiles and designer clothes. Recruitment advertisements for universities and military institutions often play to the *self-actualization* needs of individuals.

In the same way as advertisers, speakers may stress how their information or proposed solutions to problems will help the audience to meet their physiological, security, love, esteem, or self-actualization needs. The section on adaptation strategies gives examples to illustrate this point.

Creating a Personality Profile

Personality factors also mediate the possibility that a speaker can achieve shifts in audience opinion.[6] Some audience members embrace change relatively fast. Others are rigid on every issue, steadfast in maintaining their initial position. Two personality variables in particular have an influence on how people respond to persuasive messages: level of self-esteem and the extent to which the individuals are open- or closed-minded.

Although the creation of an audience profile based on personality attributes is probably unrealistic most of the time, recognition of the existence of these personality types within the audience is important. And occasionally, you may face an audience that fits one of these profiles. An audience of CEOs, for example, is not likely to have esteem issues. People of low self-esteem do not tend to achieve those positions. Other groups are identifiably more open-minded and inclined to accept change than others.

Self-Esteem

Individuals with high self-esteem are more difficult to persuade than individuals with low self-esteem. The former tend to resent highly directive messages and to resist outside pressures. They are more likely to respond to optimistic than pessimistic messages. Low-esteem individuals, on the other hand, are more likely seek the approval of others, pay more attention to pessimistic messages, and feel little ability to influence their situation.[7] People with high levels of anxiety regarding decisions also tend to resist persuasive messages.[8]

Dogmatism

The term *dogmatic* refers to people who are closed-minded.[9] Compared to more open-minded individuals, dogmatics place a high value on trusted sources and have a hard time accepting messages that conflict with their existing beliefs. They tend to be more pessimistic than open-minded individuals, to see problems in a narrow way, and to reject the ideas of those who do not agree with trusted authorities. An open-minded individual, on the other hand, does not believe that authorities absolutely determine policies, and they are willing to consider and accommodate new and more controversial ideas.[10] Nonetheless, it would be inappropriate to divide people into dogmatics and non-dogmatics, as most people fall somewhere between the extremes.

Analyzing Your Speaking Environment

Understanding the particulars of the speaking environment (occasion and place) is also important to a speaker. What is the occasion? Will other speakers precede or follow the speaker? Will the situation be formal or informal? Will a podium be available to the speaker? The speaker needs to know what to expect in terms of the physical environment—for example, the arrangement of the room (auditorium seating or chairs arranged in a circle) and the furniture (movable or bolted to the floor). Will the audience expect to participate in an interactive session, with a lengthy question-and-answer period following the more formal comments by the speaker? Chapter 6 considers how speakers can use the physical environment to create a sense of psychological closeness to their audiences.

Adapting to Your Audience

Speakers adapt to their audiences in many different ways. Some of the most common strategies include choosing an appropriate topic, framing a realistic purpose, and recognizing the audience through a variety of means. The following discussion will consider these adaptation strategies in more depth.

Choosing a Topic and Approach

Knowledge of demographic variables (age, occupation, gender, education, income, and race and ethnicity) and psychographic variables (values, beliefs, and attitudes) can guide the speaker's choice of subject matter and approach. The immediate situation and historical context also influence the acceptability of certain topics.

Some topics are inappropriate with certain audiences and in certain circumstances. A student who gave a demonstration speech to a high school class on how to apply makeup to corpses (she worked for a funeral home) was not considering the feelings of people who are uncomfortable with death. Other topics such as basic dental hygiene (proper ways to brush teeth) are so ordinary or familiar that no one cares about the subject matter.

One student, who worked part-time at McDonald's, delivered a demonstration speech on how to make a Big Mac. Another instructed the class on how to make Kraft macaroni and cheese, which entails boiling water and opening a package. In the first instance, the class could have cared less, as everyone knew what went into a Big Mac. Since the speaker could not divulge the ingredients of the sauce, she had no new information to convey. In the second instance, involving the preparation of Kraft's macaroni and cheese dinner, the choice of topic was an insult to a university level class. The speaker could have made the speech more interesting to the group, however, by talking about variations on the basic recipe—different kinds of ingredients (vegetables, sauces, etc.) that could add flavour and nutrition to the meal. Many university students do eat macaroni and cheese dinners as part of their staple diet. So talking about ways to add variety to the meal, to combine the dish with other complementary courses, or to make macaroni and cheese the featured course in an inexpensive candlelight dinner for friends could have been appropriate. But the speech would have needed to have a creative or innovative twist to capture attention and some novel information (not already known) to maintain that attention.

In previous chapters, we have talked about the concept of immediacy, closing the psychological gap between speaker and audience. This concept also applies to the selection of topics. Issues that are current and vital to the individual are more meaningful than those that are remote in time, place, or likelihood of occurrence. Although we may be concerned about famine in Niger and earthquakes in Japan, we are likely to have

Box 5.1 A Question of Ethics

Michael knew that a number of his classmates were smokers. They often stood outside the school doors, smoking between classes. They also smoked in bars and restaurants. Even though he knew that he might upset the smokers in the class, he believed strongly that no one should smoke on school premises or in other public places. His speech teacher had cautioned that students must adapt their speeches to the class. Michael was not sure what this warning implied. To what extent should he try to adapt his topic to his audience? Should he temper his point of view or offer some excuses for the smokers in the audience? Ethically, what was his obligation? Michael thought that, if he decided to argue against smoking, he could say that he had been a smoker at one time himself. That way, the audience would think that he could identify with their feelings. Also they would assign more credibility to him as a speaker. In actual fact, Michael had never smoked.

Maria planned to deliver a speech with a feminist perspective, focused on ways to protect oneself against sexually transmitted diseases (STDs). She had delivered a similar talk on several occasions to women's groups. Some students objected, however, to the choice of topic on the basis of its being inappropriate for delivery in a speech class. They said that, if Maria were giving the speech in another kind of environment (a sex education class or a talk to young girls), the content might be appropriate. The male members of the audience indicated that they had little interest in the topic. Should Maria disregard these opinions when selecting and developing her talk? Are all topics appropriate for all occasions? Do you agree that another occasion would be more appropriate for delivery of such a talk?

Linda wanted to speak on her phobia, her intense dislike of using public bathroom facilities. She planned to deliver the talk in fulfillment of her after-dinner speaking assignment, which required humorous content.

How do you feel about these speech topics? Does the audience have the right to define point of view and subject matter for a speaker? Should speakers change their topics just because an audience disagrees with the subject matter? To what extent should speakers adapt their speeches to meet audience expectations or biases? Should they ever exaggerate or fabricate expertise and experience to win the audience to their point of view?

stronger feelings when wildfires threaten homes in British Columbia, tornados wreak havoc in Saskatchewan, or crippling winter storms bear down on Newfoundland.

Some topics, however, are too current and too sensitive to discuss in certain time periods and situations. It is important to recognize that the classroom is a captive situation for students. Students do not have the option of staying or leaving, whereas in other circumstances, people can exit the auditorium or room if they object to the subject matter. In the period immediately following 11 September 2001, many Canadians (including members of the country's Muslim community) were shocked and disturbed by an event that they could not begin to understand. In the early days following the attack, before all of the facts were known, Muslim students would have been very uncomfortable listening to a speech that decried the terrorist acts—not because they identified with the terrorists but because they felt vulnerable to attacks themselves. Some racist acts were taking place in isolated parts of the country.

Sometimes speakers have difficulty in handling highly sensitive issues such as racism, or they may find themselves unable to finish speeches with highly painful or emotional content. With topics such as the death of a parent or sibling, for example, the risk that the speaker may lose control is high. So speakers need to think carefully about whether they can manage a topic of this nature. Audiences become uncomfortable when speakers lose control. At the same time, however, speakers should care about their topics. The best speeches come from situations where the speakers feel passionately about their subject matter. So a balance must be achieved. Ultimately, the choice of topics is a highly personal one, for which no one set of criteria exists.

Framing a Realistic Purpose

Similar cautions apply when discussing speech purposes. Some purposes are simply not achievable. If you are speaking to an audience of pig farmers, you are not likely to persuade them to endorse vegetarianism. But you may be able to convince them to take more care in the management of manure and to avoid water and crop contamination—serious problems that pose a threat to water and food supplies.

A speech to persuade members of a conservative church group that they should support same-sex marriage will probably have little impact—or certainly not a positive impact. The large majority of church members will have a stable attitude set, formed over many years and tied to traditional concepts of family and community. Their beliefs will have been reinforced by authority figures within their churches, schools, and political institutions. So confronted with an audience that has articulated strong opposition to liberalization of social policies, the speaker should either choose a different topic or adjust the purpose to a more realistic one—in this instance, perhaps seeking to persuade the audience that they should support legal rights (if not marriage rights) for same-sex couples and condemn acts of intolerance and violence that violate church principles. On the other hand, if you are speaking to a more liberal organization, an achievable purpose could be arguing for the legitimacy of same-sex marriages. The following excerpt from a student speech illustrates how one student recognized the limits of what she could accomplish in her speech:

> I am sure that all of you have heard about the recent controversy surrounding the legalization of same-sex marriages. There has been much discussion of the issues around campus and in the news. I have to admit that it surprises me to learn that there are still people who say that homosexuality is wrong, that it is sinful or immoral. It surprises me, but I am not here to convince anyone to reconsider his or her views. And I am not here to tell you that your views are wrong or outdated. I *am* here to persuade you to look for common ground, where we can all find a place to stand and agree. I believe that common ground is tolerance. We must learn to be tolerant of other people's beliefs and orientations. And even if we do not share the beliefs, we should respect each other for our life choices. Mr Garrison, a character in one of my favourite cartoons, *South Park*, said it best: 'Look, just because you have to tolerate something doesn't mean you have to approve of it! *Tolerate* means that you're putting up with it!' We need to get better at putting up with each other.[11]

Social judgement theory tells us that the initial attitudes of an audience have a significant effect on the speaker's potential to achieve attitudinal or behavioural changes. Listeners have latitudes of acceptance, non-commitment, and rejection. Persuaders are most likely to effect change if they stay within a person's 'latitude of acceptance.' By *lat-*

itude of acceptance, we mean that the position of the persuader is consistent with—and highly favourable to—audience views on the topic. If the arguments of the persuader fall within the audience's latitude of acceptance, the speaker has a good chance of achieving attitudinal or behavioural change.

If the arguments fall into the *latitude of non-commitment* (meaning that audience members neither accept nor reject the ideas), more limited change is possible. Prior to hearing the speech, listeners may lack sufficient information to form an opinion, or they may not care very much about the topic. If the speaker provides the missing information and motivates the audience to think seriously about the subject, listeners may experience attitudinal or behavioural change (In this situation, attitudinal change is more likely than behavioural change.)

But if the position and arguments of the persuader fall into a *latitude of rejection* (meaning that they are highly objectionable to listeners), no change is likely.[12] In fact, negative change may occur. One European experiment, for example, demonstrated that postings of 100 km/hour speed limits on a six-lane highway did more to decrease the speed of travellers than postings of 80 km/hour. In other words, someone accustomed to driving 110 kilometres an hour would be inclined to comply with a speed limit of 100 kilometres an hour. However, the same person would reject a specified limit of 80 kilometres and continue to drive at an unreduced speed of 110 km/hour. Social scientists explained their findings by saying that 80 km/hour fell outside the drivers' latitude of acceptance.[13]

Large latitudes of rejection characterize individuals who feel passionately about a topic. Subjects such as religion, politics, and sex polarize people in this way, where the non-committal zone is very small. Topics of this nature also are tied to our most central beliefs, and, according to Milton Rokeach, we experience little change in beliefs that are at the centre of our value systems.[14]

Recognizing Your Audience

Strategies for recognizing the audience include establishing personal connections, making reference to a shared perspective or common struggle or fate, connecting through reference groups, complimenting the audience on achievements and recognizing their sacrifices, acknowledging audience beliefs and attitudes, recognizing commitment to shared principles and values, talking in terms that are meaningful, using appropriate language, relating to the knowledge levels of the audience, and recognizing multiple audiences.

Establishing Personal Connections
Sometimes speakers thank the people who introduced them or the audience that issued the invitation to speak:

> Thank you for your kind introduction, James. Good to see you again, this time in Vancouver. Not more than six months ago, in Seattle, James and I shared the same platform. And here we are again, on the other side of the border, swapping stories and experiences with another great audience. I am also happy to see other committed colleagues—Lisa Berry, Joan Conner, and Larry Mills. Thank you for inviting me to participate in your event. I hope that this will become an annual exchange.

This speaker could have continued with still further audience identification strategies:

> It seems appropriate for representatives of our two countries to speak on the same platform. Canada and the US have so much in common—Pacific salmon, free trade, and even airwaves. We also share the snowbirds, older Canadians who—like our geese—migrate twice each year between our two countries. So while we all know that a border exists between Washington state and British Columbia, we also know that the strength of our ties is greater than the invisible line that separates us.

Sometimes speakers refer specifically to the comments of preceding speakers. For example, a sales presentation aimed at convincing an audience to purchase a home security system could begin with the following kind of statement:

> I was really interested in John's comment on the high cost of maintaining home security systems. You may be surprised to learn that I absolutely agree with what he had to say. However, he didn't mention one interesting point. He didn't mention the high cost of *not having* home security systems. I would like to share some statistics on break-ins that have occurred in your neighbourhood in recent months.

Sharing a Common Perspective, Struggle, or Fate

Often speakers talk about sharing a common perspective or fate with the audience—the concept of oneness with the audience. Em Griffin uses a Biblical example to illustrate this point.[15] In the Old Testament, Ruth ties her fate to that of her mother-in-law Naomi. She says to Naomi, 'For where you go, I will go, and where you lodge, I will lodge; your people shall be my people, and your god my God.' This concept of identification reflects a well-known communication theory called *dramatism*, associated with theorist Kenneth Burke.[16] In a farewell address to the Canadian Club in December 2001, Hilary M. Weston (former Lieutenant-Governor of Ontario) spoke similarly of the interdependencies that characterize the modern world and of our common fate:

> The globalization of commerce and communications has made us all partners in each other's well-being. If some of the planet is suffering massive poverty, none of us can feel smug in our prosperity. If some of the planet is at war, none of us can expect to remain forever at peace.

In a speech delivered at the Ottawa Central Mosque on 21 September 2001, former Prime Minister Jean Chrétien tells his Muslim audience that he considers them to be part of the family of Canada, and he stands with them against those who would act in retaliation against the perpetrators of violence:[17]

> I know that the days since September 11, 2001, have been ones of great sadness and anxiety for Muslims across Canada.... I wanted to stand by your side today. And to reaffirm to you that Islam has nothing to do with the mass murder that was planned and carried out by the terrorists and their masters....Above all, I want to stand by your side to condemn the acts of intolerance and hatred that have been committed against your community since the attack. Let me say that I turn my

back on the people who have done this. I have no time for them. . . . I say today, once again, that we are all Canadians. We stand together as one against this evil. We grieve together as a family. As one nation we defy the twisted philosophy of the terrorists. And shoulder to shoulder we will pursue the struggle for justice.

At other times, politicians talk about the fact that they would not introduce a policy that would harm some member of their family—their mother, grandmother, or other symbolic individual. In other words, they argue that they stand to profit or gain by the same policies as their audience.

Sometimes speakers use the mother language of the audience to establish a commonality of background and experience with the listeners. When speaking to an audience at Canada's Emerald Ball in 2001, Hilary Weston greeted her Irish audience with the Gallic word *Fáilte*; she concluded her speech with the Irish blessing '*Go raibh maith agaibh, agus Beannacht Dé*.'

In an eloquent speech delivered on 1 November 2001, Assembly of First Nations National Chief Matthew Coon Come urged the Standing Committee on Justice and Human Rights to put a sunset clause into the proposed anti-terrorism Bill C-36. But first, before proceeding to his major arguments, he focused on the psychic ties that bind Canadian Natives with their American neighbours:

> First, I want to convey to you the sense of seriousness that First Nations peoples hold the September 11, 2001 events. This is our homeland. Our Elders refer to it as mother earth, and when anyone harms our mother in whatever form, be it through the destruction of the environment or by the taking of human life that was put here, it hurts us. We feel for the families who senselessly lost their loved ones, for we too have known loss. We have been here for many, many generations and too have known terror in our homelands, but never on the scale recently experienced. Skilled Mohawk Ironworkers helped build those buildings which were destroyed, and, in fact, were the first on the scene to help with rescue attempts. First Nations citizens feel the same fear as other Canadians. Our people travel on both sides of the border because our homelands and our relatives are on both sides. Our ancestors are buried on both sides of the border and we have many friends in the United States. With this unspeakable act the world has changed; our world has changed, and we are prepared to do our part to return to the sense of security that we formerly had.

Connecting through Reference Groups

At other times, speakers adapt to their audiences by pointing to audience members with whom the larger group can identify. In his bid for the leadership of the Liberal Party in June 1984, former Prime Minister John Turner made reference to many occupational groups within Canadian society:

> For the last three months, I have met thousands of people across our country and I have listened to them. Everywhere, I have listened and learned from the miner of Cape Breton, the pork producer from the Quebec Eastern Townships, the new executive employee in the Public Service Commission of Canada in Ottawa, the

young immigrant of Metropolitan Toronto, the wheat producer from Hudson Bay, Saskatchewan, the fisherman from the east coast of Vancouver Island.

His references to the provinces of Nova Scotia, Quebec, Ontario, Saskatchewan, and British Columbia and to the northern territories appealed to regional identifications.

Similarly, to connect with his audience and to indicate his allegiance, federal cabinet minister John McCallum began his 28 April 2005 speech to the Toronto Board of Trade with the following words: 'We all have many identities. I am a politician. A 55-year-old Caucasian male. An Ontarian. But above all these things I am Canadian.'[18]

Sometimes political leaders position representatives of particular groups in the audience (e.g., the widow of a fallen soldier, the representative of a Saskatchewan farmers' association, or a member of a multicultural organization). At some point in the speech, the politician acknowledges the presence of these individuals. In this way, the speaker is able to connect with a much larger group of people—all those who share demographic or other characteristics with the acknowledged audience members. The identifications may be regional, occupational, ethnic, political, or other.

Complimenting the Audience

Where appropriate, a speaker may offer a compliment, as in the following example:

> As an international aid worker and former human rights activist, I am well-acquainted with the work of your group. And I can say, without hesitation, that your most recent interventions have been critical in securing the release of a number of individuals who had been listed as missing.

In October 1996, Matthew Coon Come, then Chief of 12,000 Crees of northern Quebec, spoke at a Canada seminar sponsored by Harvard University. His strategy was to establish common ground while complimenting and thanking his audience:

> Good afternoon. Wachiya. First, I would like to thank Professors Raymond Breton and Henry Lee for inviting me to take part in the Canada Seminar sponsored by the Harvard Center for International Affairs and the Kennedy School of Government. It is an honour and a pleasure to be here. Harvard University, the cities of Cambridge and Boston, and the State of Massachusetts, have a history of committed and timely engagement with human affairs around the world. The record shows that it was that these communities were among the first to take up the torch against apartheid in South Africa. . . . And in the last few years, my people the James Bay Crees called upon the people of Massachusetts and New England to help us in our struggle to prevent the further destruction of our traditional lands by Hydro-Québec. The support we gained from this community in defeating the Great Whale Hydroelectric Project will be remembered for years.[19]

Acknowledging Audience Beliefs and Attitudes

Effective speakers always consider the beliefs and attitudes of their audience when they plan their speeches. They look at the backgrounds and experiences of the audiences to see how they might react to positions held by the speaker. Sometimes they acknowledge the gap that separates speaker from audience. Always they seek common ground that will facilitate communication.

A speech delivered in 1991 by then US President George H. W. Bush is an excellent illustration of how speakers try to adapt their arguments and strategies to their knowledge of audience beliefs and opinions. In his declaration of war against Iraq, Bush recognized that many middle-aged Americans still remembered the long, drawn-out engagement in Vietnam. He realized that many Americans had participated in anti-war protests in the 1960s and early 1970s, denouncing the establishment as morally bankrupt. Others had fled the country to avoid engaging in a war they believed to be indefensible. Many had lost friends and family members in the conflict, and thousands made annual pilgrimages to the Vietnam War memorial in Washington, DC, to pay homage to those who had died in a war that no one really understood.

Now in 1991, the sons and daughters of these former activists were of fighting age. How would they view a president who was ready to lead the country into another conflict? Recognizing the potential resistance of his audience to his basic speech purpose—to declare war to drive Iraqi forces out of Kuwait—Bush attempted to reassure his audience that the conflict would not be long, costly in lives, or ill-supported in logistical terms. At one point, he said:

> This will not be another Vietnam. . . . Our troops will have the best possible support in the entire world, and they will not be asked to fight with one hand tied behind their backs. I'm hopeful that this fighting will not go on for long and that casualties will be held to an absolute minimum.[20]

Understanding that his audience included many who would have protested the military draft policies of the Vietnam War, Bush also stated, 'Ours is an all volunteer force.'

Anticipating that some might remember the poorly trained youths who had barely graduated from high school when they were conscripted to fight in Vietnam, he said that the soldiers who would fight in Iraq had been 'magnificently trained'. In response to the argument that many Americans never really understood why the country had entered the civil war in Vietnam, Bush proclaimed that the troops are 'highly motivated' and that they 'know why they are there.' He also said, 'We're here for more than the price of a gallon of gas'—a pre-emptive response to those who would accuse him of economic motives in declaring the war.

Recognizing Audience Commitment to Shared Principles and Values

When former First Lady (currently Senator) Hillary Clinton rose to speak before the women gathered in Beijing, China, on 5 September 1995, she faced a sympathetic but highly diverse audience. The women at the Fourth UN Conference on Women came from around the globe. They had vastly different backgrounds and experiences and widely diverse social, political, and religious beliefs. So the challenge to find common ground meant that Hillary Clinton had to move to the level of the most basic human experiences to find a meeting place. She adapted to this rhetorical challenge by beginning her speech in the following way:

This is truly a celebration—a celebration of the contributions women make in every aspect of life: in the home, on the job, in their communities, as mothers, wives, sisters, daughters, learners, workers, citizens and leaders. It is also a coming together, much the way women come together every day in every country. We come together in fields and in factories. In village markets and supermarkets. In living rooms and boardrooms. Whether it is while playing with our children in the park, or washing clothes in a river, or taking a break at the office water cooler, we come together and talk about our aspirations and concerns. And time and again, our talk turns to our children and our families. However different we may be, there is far more that unites us than divides us. We share a common future. And we are here to find common ground so that we may help bring new dignity and respect to women and girls all over the world—and in so doing, bring new strength and stability to families as well. By gathering in Beijing, we are focusing world attention on issues that matter most in the lives of women and their families: access to education, health care, jobs, and credit, the chance to enjoy basic legal and human rights and participate fully in the political life of their countries.[21]

Hillary Clinton's examples draw on the values shared by all members of her audience—values such as love of family, freedom, independence, and human dignity.

In the same way, federal Revenue Minister John McCallum made reference to shared values when he addressed the Toronto Board of Trade: 'Politics is about values. Our values define us. Our Canadian identity transcends our regional roots. When we have disagreements, we need to talk about them specifically and resist the temptation of divisive regionalism. The roots have to come together to make a living tree.'

Where diversity is present, speakers must be sensitive to the needs of the various groups. For example, to prepare a speech on the need to lower corporate taxes, you should learn whether representatives of the local small business bureau, industry representatives, or members of an anti-poverty coalition will attend your speech. If you have a mix of the groups in your audience, you may want to acknowledge the diversity but, at the same time, identify underlying values and principles that unite the group.

In the following example, Sarah Johnson recognized—after arriving at the occasion—that the subject of her speech was ill-suited to the values of her audience. She had to make an immediate adjustment to the situation:

I was a member of a progressive speech club with a dynamic membership. In 2000, a club member asked if I would speak at the meeting of another group who wanted to start a similar club. The location was a church, not unusual because churches often give up their basements for free. As it turned out, however, I had been invited to speak at a Baptist church, and my audience was the church congregation. (I figured this out when I walked through the door.) The topic of my planned speech was the story behind the large (very large) tattoo on my back. Not exactly the best topic for a conservative Baptist audience. As you can well imagine, I was pretty nervous. I did not have another speech in my back pocket, and I could not back out because I was the only speaker. Since I knew my material, I was able to improvise, which is what I did for most of my presentation. I still told the story behind the image, but I never mentioned the word *tattoo*. The tattoo image of an infant appealed strongly to the mothers and grandmothers in the audience, and I changed my speech from educational (yet shocking) to a warm and earthy celebration of motherhood. The audience never knew that I had planned a very different speech![22]

Recognizing Audience Needs

In the speech cited ealier, Hillary Clinton appealed to the most basic needs of audiences—physiological, safety, and security (references to health, jobs, and credit), love (references to family and children), esteem (references to dignity and respect), and self-actualization (references to education and personal aspirations). Speakers recognize audience needs when they translate their information into terms that are immediate and meaningful to the audience, as in the following:

> How would you feel if I told you that one out of three of you will be dead in five years time? Scared? Shocked? Incredulous? If I were speaking this morning to a group of adults in Botswana, Africa, my audience would not be shocked or incredulous. Why? Because they live every day with the tragic reality that 36 per cent of their friends and family members will die with the HIV virus. Most will never receive treatment. Their prognosis is terminal.

This technique is a common one used by seasoned speakers. For example, Johanne Gelinas (the Commissioner of Environment and Sustainable Development, Office of the Auditor General) translated her statistics on the threat to the Canada's water supply into the following analogy: 'Livestock operations in Ontario and Quebec generate enough manure to equal the sewage from over 100 million people.'[23] Note that the speaker used a local example, and she generated a comparison designed to shock her audience into awareness of the extreme nature of the threat to their health. Rather than present bare statistics, Gelinas used a comparison to make the numbers more meaningful to her listeners—the essence of good audience adaptation.

In another case, a speaker used the statistics on deaths from cigarette smoking to construct a strong compelling image:

> The toll in human life and suffering is almost unimaginable. . . . If, in the year 2020, we were to stack each person who died a smoking-induced death one atop the other, we could build a column of bodies reaching 180 km into the sky. If we would continue to pack these bodies one atop the other for just one more year, a warning light would have to be placed at the apex of this column to prevent the International Space Station from ploughing into this grotesque metaphor.[24]

Finally, consider one last example. In May 2004, the Canadian Medical Association published a study demonstrating that between 9,250 and 23,750 hospital patients die each year as a result of so-called 'adverse events'—professional jargon for medical mistakes.[25] To make this statistic more meaningful to a class of medical students, the speaker could translate the statistic into the following terms:

In a worst-case scenario, almost 24,000 patients could die in Canadian hospitals this year, victims of medical mistakes. In a good year, only 9,200 patients die at the hands of well-meaning physicians and health-care workers. These statistics come from a study published in the *Canadian Medical Association Journal*. Statistically speaking, a large number of these deaths will occur in our province—perhaps as many as 50,000 over the next 10 years.[26] That means that, at some point in your life, you have probably met—or will meet—at least one of the people who have made such a mistake. Your family physician or a nurse, your professor—people who entered the medical profession because they wanted to help people. It could be that you will work with this person at some point in the future. Unless you maintain the most dedicated vigil, that offending person could be you. We are all human, but our mistakes cost more when we are doctors.

Thus, speakers get our attention when they relate their ideas to basic physiological, safety, belonging, self-esteem, and self-actualization needs. When the examples and statistics reflect situations close at hand, they mean more than examples and statistics that concern remote places and situations. The closer the proximity of the example, the illustration, or the statistic in terms of time, place, and potential impact—the more meaningful the material will be to your audience. Thus, the most meaningful examples will relate to your university, your town, your province, and your country.

Using Appropriate Language

The use of gender-neutral language is important. Terms such as *policeman*, *fisherman*, *chairman*, *manpower*, and *mankind* are offensive to some people. The more politically correct terms are *police officers*, *fishers*, *chairperson* or *the chair*, *human resources*, and *humans* or *humankind*. Substitute *skilled worker* for *tradesman*, *firefighter* for *fireman*, and *letter carrier* for *mailman*. In addressing some audiences, you may want to consider all the connotations of 'girl' or 'lady' and use instead *young woman*. In the same way, *young man* will be preferable to *boy* with some audiences.

Terms such as *older adults* or *seniors* are preferred to *old people*. Since many people (including a number of older Canadians) live in relationships outside of marriage, in situations of uncertainty the reference to *partner* is safer than marital-specific terms such as *husband* or *wife* or *spouse*. Avoid unnecessary descriptors such as *woman* doctor, *lady* lawyer, or *gay* activist.

When referring to people with disabilities, public speakers should avoid the use of terms such as the *handicapped*, the *disabled*, or the *blind*. Instead speakers should say *people with disabilities* or *people who are blind*. Like all of us, people who are blind or deaf prefer to see themselves as people first—people who, like all of us, have certain assets and liabilities. Their disabilities or illnesses do not define their potential. Also, speakers should avoid terms like *wheelchair-bound*, *people suffering from HIV*, or *victims of heart disease*. People with disabilities usually see themselves as coping with their challenges, not bound or handicapped by them. Many overcome remarkable obstacles in their quest to lead independent lives. So they are fighters, not victims. People who are deaf, for example, have their own language; and many consider their communication system to be equal or superior to that of people who communicate with verbal language. They even have their own unique system for expressing humour. They resent being stigmatized by words that imply an inferior status.

The language used to refer to members of minorities must also be politically sensitive. The term *Asian* is preferable to *Oriental*, and reference to a specific national origin such as *Japanese*, *Chinese*, or *Thai* is preferable to *Asian*. Some Canadians prefer the designation *African Canadian* to *black*. However, since many families of African, Asian, and other national origins have been in Canada for generations, not all want to be labelled by the countries of their long-dead ancestors. Over time and among different groups, variations often occur in what is deemed desirable or acceptable. Canadian governments presently use the terms *Aboriginals* or *Natives* to refer to the Inuit and Indian populations of the country. However, some Native peoples prefer to maintain the designation *Indian*.

A controversy has arisen in the United States among some members of the African-American community over the acceptability of language used by rappers and some comedians. What you hear in the media or on CDs should not necessarily be repeated. And members of that community have shifted their preferred names over time from *coloured* to *Negro* to *Afro-American* to *black* to *African American* to *people of colour* (a recent trend among some African Americans). In the same way, many people of Spanish-American descent now ask to be called *Latino* instead of *Hispanic*; and some Latino residents of Texas have coined the term *Tejano*. Canadians do not always concur with Americans, however, in regard to nomenclature. In brief, speaker beware!

Level of language is also important when a speaker attempts to reach audiences of varying backgrounds and education levels. Despite the popular conception that writers and speakers should always avoid jargon and technical language, organizational experience tells us that jargon can be very useful in communicating with others within our own professional culture (legal, medical, or other). Such language is equivalent to shorthand, which makes it easier and faster to communicate in a succinct and clear fashion with those who share the language. But when you attempt to communicate with members of other publics, who do not know the language, you risk being misunderstood.

In the same way, despite its negative connotations, 'bureaucratese' can be effective in communicating within government environments, where diplomacy in communicating is valued and ambiguity provides a safety net for politicians and bureaucrats who fear having their communications publicized. When these same individuals go outside of government to communicate with their constituencies, they must speak a different, more comprehensible language. Speakers who communicate with a lay audience should use direct and conversational language; they should avoid jargon that could alienate or confuse. Bureaucrats and politicians should avoid terms such as *stakeholders*, *target groups*,

---

Box 5.2 The Importance of Clear Terminology

I remember an occasion when a wannabe nurse peppered her speech with a great number of medical terms and acronyms (e.g., TLC, ECG, SMAC, ICU, and the like), none of which the audience understood. While the speaker gained a position of power within the group, she did not follow good speaking practice. It's always better to tell the audience what the terms mean; then everyone is on an even playing field. I can fill your ears with railway engineering terms, which my compatriots would understand, but others would wander away from the conversation with glazed eyes.

John Busby

strategies, and *portfolios* when speaking to lay audiences. They should also avoid overly ornate and pretentious language.

A common technique for adapting to an audience in linguistic terms is to speak in the first-person plural ('we') and the second person ('you'). In the first instance, the speaker pulls the audience into her frame of reference. In the second case, the speaker communicates with the audience in a direct and personal fashion. A speech should also be 'sayable.' That is, the speaker should be able to breathe at regular intervals in the speech. This necessity should be factored into the writing of the speech. Many speech writers talk out loud as they write speeches. If the words do not sound right, cluster properly, or convey a thought in memorable language, they reword the thought. If the cadence and rhythm of the speech are not right, they begin again. *Speech is for the ear, not the eye.* You must tune yourself to the aural dimensions of language when you write a speech. Pretentious language, for example, is often 'unsayable.' Eloquence often resides in simplicity—the nice turn of phrase, the lyrical thought, the compelling analogy.

Relating to the Knowledge Level of the Audience

Correctly diagnosing the level of knowledge held by your audience is critical to audience adaptation. The following example illustrates the experience of Milton Himsl:

> I was to present a two-hour Unix System Administrator's course at the annual users' conference. The course was fully booked, and about 30 people showed up. I was very nervous; so I just introduced myself and then launched right into it. I didn't really make eye contact with anyone until about five minutes into the talk when I was more relaxed. When I finally looked away from my notes, I found one shining-eyed person, hanging onto my every word and another 29 people staring like deer caught in the headlights. I stopped and asked what was wrong. It turned out that 29 of the 30 people didn't know anything about Unix and thought that a System Administrator was the person responsible for the General Ledger activities of the store. I had a class full of accountants![27]

Once the speaker had regained his composure, he asked what the group expected from the seminar and whether they had any specific questions. He knew nothing about accounting or the General Ledger function of the company software, but he offered to note all their questions and to post the answers in the computer lab. As the questions were posed, class members began to share answers and experiences; and the instructor assumed the role of facilitator. He asked the class to move into the computer lab and break into groups so that they could better share their expertise. When he announced that the session was over, only half of the participants looked up from their computers to wave okay. The others were too engrossed in what they were doing to notice. To the instructor's surprise, the feedback at the end of the session was extremely positive. The instructor had managed to adapt to the knowledge level of his audience and to the situation by maintaining a flexible attitude.

Recognizing Multiple Audiences

In today's wired world, speakers have many different audiences, often scattered throughout the community or dispersed around the state, country, or globe. Some are present in the immediate speaking environment, but many are not visible to the speaker. The auditorium may have a seating capacity of 300 persons; but television, radio, and the Web do not respect such limitations. In the case of a political speech, many advocacy groups, politicians, bureaucrats, and members of the general public may be listening to the speech on the radio, observing the speech on television, or reading excerpts from the speech on the Internet or in a newspaper.

Sometimes the audiences are contemporaries of a speaker; at other times, the speaker writes for future generations and remote constituencies. An example would be the June 1964 speech of Nelson Mandela, delivered in a courtroom in Pretoria, South Africa, immediately prior to his sentencing to a lifetime in jail. Facing a possible death sentence, Nelson Mandela delivered a four-hour speech, judged to be the most emotionally gripping of his political career. He concluded with the words:

> During my lifetime I have dedicated myself to the struggle of the African people. I have fought against white domination, and I have fought against black domination. I have cherished the ideal of a democratic and free society in which all persons live together in harmony and with equal opportunities. It is an ideal which I hope to live for and to achieve. But, if needs be, it is an ideal for which I am prepared to die.[28]

Mandela knew that future generations of South Africans and influential leaders in other countries would read his speech and pay attention to the words. At the same time, he knew that the people present in the courtroom that day would probably pay no heed to what he had to say. Nor would they circulate his words to other South African blacks for fear of revolt. The real impact of the speech would be felt over an extended period of time. So Mandela had more than one audience. In many regards, his least important audience was his immediate one, composed of jurors, judge, and spectators in the courtroom. He did not have his true audience—present and future generations of South African blacks or sympathetic leaders and constituencies from other countries—in the courtroom.

Sometimes speakers explicitly acknowledge these more remote audiences—those not present in the auditorium or the bleachers or even in the same historical period. For example, US President John F. Kennedy addressed a number of international, as well as domestic, audiences in his 1961 inaugural address:

> To those old allies whose cultural and spiritual origins we share, we pledge the loyalty of faithful friends. . . . To those new states whom we welcome to the ranks of the free, we pledge our word that one form of colonial control shall not have passed away merely to be replaced by a far more iron tyranny. . . . To those peoples in the huts and villages of half the globe struggling to break the bonds of mass misery, we pledge our best efforts to help them help themselves. . . . To our sister republics south of our border, we offer a special pledge: To convert our good words into good deeds. . . . Let all our neighbors know that we shall join with them to oppose aggression or subversion anywhere in the Americas. And let every other power know that this hemisphere intends to remain the master of its own house. To that world assembly of sovereign states, the United Nations, our last best hope in an age where the instruments of war have far out-paced the instruments of peace, we renew our pledge of support. . . . Finally, to those nations who would make them-

selves our adversary, we offer not a pledge but a request: That both sides begin anew the quest for peace, before the dark powers of destruction unleashed by science engulf all humanity in planned or accidental self-destruction.[29]

In his September 2001 speech to the Muslim community in Ottawa, discussed earlier, Jean Chrétien also addressed two audiences: his immediate audience (to whom he offered solace) and extremists within the remote viewing audience (to whom he offered a warning).

Adapting to the Situation

Strategies for adapting to the situation include making references to the occasion, the location of the speech, and the historical context. Speakers face unique challenges when their speaking environment includes two audiences—the audience present in the auditorium and the television viewing audience. Yet public speakers often face this dilemma, and many politicians and members of Parliament tailor their speeches to appeal to their remote viewers. By adopting a more conversational and personal style of delivery, sprinkled with occasional witticisms, the speakers are able to reach these remote viewers and encourage a feeling of physical and psychological proximity. Pierre Trudeau was a master at using the intimate eye of the television camera to reach Canadians. But this kind of delivery, as we will discuss in the next chapter, may be less suited to members of the immediate audience, who would prefer a more animated style of delivery with greater variations in movement and voice.

References to Occasion and Place

References to occasion and place are a common instrument for audience adaptation. By creating awareness of shared physical and psychological space, speakers bridge the gap that separates them from their audience. The concept of immediacy (discussed in previous chapters) becomes important in this context. The following example illustrates reference to place as a means of audience identification:

> It is always a special pleasure for me when my itinerary takes me to Victoria. The city of gardens and tea rooms. A city that seems, like few others of its size, to enjoy an inner peace, a tranquility that comes with age and knowing who you are. It is a city without an identity crisis. Victoria is a wonderful blending of the old and the new. Is there any other city in Canada with trees as old and grand as Victoria? Gas lanterns and carriages left over from another era. And, as close as the nearby waterfront, structures of iron and steel to remind us that the future is never far away.

Another example follows:

> I am so pleased to be in Toronto for the opening ceremonies of Little Italy week. Thank you, Bill and Amanda, Dr Antonelli and Mayor Con Di Nino, for inviting me to share this occasion with you. One of the things that I always enjoy about your wonderful city is the opportunity to re-experience the true spirit of Canada—its multiculturalism and its history as a country that welcomes all who come to its shores. Standing in this lobby today—with its fountain, its cobblestone

floors, and its wonderful murals—we can all appreciate the part of Canada that is Italy. How much less would Canada be if you had not chosen to make this country your home!

In the above instance, the speaker also uses the reference to place as a means to compliment the audience for their collective contribution to Canada. In his eulogy for former Prime Minister Pierre Trudeau, Joe Clark spoke of the historical setting within which he was delivering his speech:

> If I am to speak personally, I am honoured to be able to pay my final tribute to Pierre Trudeau from the floor of this House of Commons. He was an enigmatic man—tough and kind and cold-blooded and sympathetic. While I never thought that I knew him well, it was here that I knew him best.[30]

Reference to Historical Context

On other occasions, speakers connect with their audiences by beginning with a reference to historical occasion—an occasion shared by both the speaker and the audience. For example, on 17 April 1982, Pierre Elliott Trudeau welcomed the Queen of England and announced the patriation of the Canadian Constitution with the following words:

> Today, at long last, Canada is acquiring full and complete national sovereignty. The Constitution of Canada has come home. The most fundamental law of the land will now be capable of being amended in Canada, without any further recourse to the Parliament of the United Kingdom. In the name of all Canadians, may I say how pleased and honoured we are that Your Majesty and Your Royal Highness have journeyed to Canada to share with us this day of historic achievement.[31]

When, on 15 January 1991, Audrey McLaughlin, leader of the New Democratic Party, spoke against Canadian involvement in the Gulf War, she made a reference to historical date:

> I recall that Martin Luther King, whose birthday is today, once said about Vietnam that the bombs that explode on the foreign battlefield also explode at home. Is there anyone who does not believe that the bombs dropped in the Middle East will not indeed explode in every community in the world?

Strategies for adapting to the situation include making references to the occasion, the location of the speech, and the historical context.

Taking Ethical and Critical Concerns into Consideration

In advance of presentations, news commentators often predict the words and positions of political and celebrity speakers, analyze and interpret their strategies, and offer critiques of their speech content. When audience adaptation or other rhetorical strategies become transparent, they lose their effectiveness. So if television commentators on *The National* or *CBC Newsworld* predict that the Prime Minister will make appeals to the international community in his next address—and he makes those appeals—the audience becomes acutely aware of the rhetorical strategies. If this enhanced awareness leads to the perception that the speaker is attempting to manipulate us, we react accordingly, rejecting the arguments and appeals and resisting movement in the direction urged by the speaker. We become cynical and skeptical.

The environment in which we deliver our speeches is a vastly changed one from earlier in this century, when 'stump' speakers often presented different messages to different audiences as they travelled across the country. Today television and radio stations can—and do—replay the words of public communicators at will, allowing audiences to witness and hear the previous positions and commitments of the speaker. In such a situation, honesty and consistency are not only desirable characteristics for public communicators; they are compulsory.

Audiences want to know that speakers are sincere in their motivations and that they have some personal stake in what they advocate. Audiences expect, in current lingo, a 'connect' between what leaders say and do. Employees call for CEOs and top managers to model the behaviours that they espouse. In the current environment, Canadians question the truthfulness of many top leaders, including top government officials and business leaders. Trust of business and political leaders is at an all-time low.[32]

When audiences believe speakers (or leaders) to be insincere, they move in the opposite direction. In the eyes of the audience, the insincere speaker is the companion of the glib salesperson who talks for money and the slick politician who talks for power and position. So while audience adaptation means recognizing, respecting, and trying to reach your audience, the term does not mean lying to your audience, attempting to influence them by unethical means, or pretending to be someone other than yourself. Critical to long-term credibility is consistency in the messages conveyed to audiences.

Conclusion

Audience adaptation is more than just recognizing individuals in your audience. Adaptation also involves telling your audience why a topic should matter to them and how your solution can help to satisfy their physiological, safety, love, esteem, and self-actualization needs. Audience adaptation is acknowledging the beliefs, opinions, and values of your audience. Television reality shows such as *Survivor* and *Big Brother* illustrate well the importance of understanding how to adapt your message to different audience members. To stay alive in the game—to avoid eviction—survivors must constantly monitor their personal communications and create messages that resonate with the other players. What works with one individual will not necessarily achieve the same results with a second. So the framing of messages and appeals changes as the players seek to persuade the other competitors to keep them in the game. The final vote, which determines the ultimate survivor, comes from the players themselves. So the participants must be constantly aware of individual peer reactions, as well as group alliances that may have formed.

In the same way as the competitors on *Survivor* and the other reality shows, speakers must become familiar with their audience, plan their communications carefully, monitor reactions to their communications, and adjust their strategies as required. In short, they must engage in ongoing audience adaptation. Unlike the TV reality shows, however, audience adaptation does not imply presenting an erroneous picture of your position, compromising your values, or catering to your audience by shifting positions to accommodate the person or the occasion.

The chapters on persuasion will look in more depth at the different kinds of audiences faced by persuasive speakers and the strategies that can be adopted to meet the challenges posed by apathetic, unreceptive, or hostile audiences.

Questions for Discussion

1. Based on the audience analysis assignment in this chapter, brainstorm some topics that might be of interest to your classmates. Obtain feedback from the class on your ideas.
2. Identify demographic characteristics that you share in common with your classmates? In which areas do you differ?
3. Can you think of some topics that might be of more interest to men? Women? Seniors? Lawyers? Musicians? A particular cultural or ethnic group? People in your home town or region of the country?
4. Identify some reference groups to which you belong or aspire. What can someone learn about your values by knowing the reference groups to which you belong? How do these groups help to define you as a member of an audience?
5. Explain how speaking strategies on a topic such as date rape would need to take demographic variables such as gender, age, culture, and marital status into account. How could you make the speech relevant to a group with diverse demographic characteristics?

Appendix: Sample Speeches of Welcome

Speech #1

by Jenn Thomlinson

Take a minute. Sit back in your chairs and imagine this situation. You're one on one with someone—someone you find very attractive, someone who seems to be stimulating you in all the right ways, someone whose eyes say it all up to that climactic moment. Then suddenly, after only three minutes, it's all over and they get up and walk away. Would you be upset? You shouldn't be. 'Why?' you ask. Because this is the only time when three minutes is enough! Welcome, everyone, to the wonderful world of speed dating.

It's good to see such an enthusiastic group, eager to meet the many singles who joined you in tonight's quest for the right partner. For many of you, this is your first acquaintance with this new and unconventional form of dating. So for our newcomers, let me explain the process. Speed dating is a quick form of dating in which the men circulate about the room, spending three to five minutes with each of the women, who will sit at tables for two. On these mini-dates, you will get the chance to become some-

what acquainted with the other person. You will have some basis for deciding if you want to pursue the acquaintance further.

After five minutes is up, a buzzer will signal the end of the date. On the cards provided to each individual, you will check the 'yes' or 'no' box, indicating whether you want to see the person again. The men will proceed to the next table. At the end of the night, we will collect the cards, calculate the matches, and e-mail the contact information of the people with whom you had a positive connection.

I am happy to report that I have looked at the profiles of several audience members, and I am quite certain that we already have some matches in the making. A striking number of you are hockey and soccer fans; so already we're seeing similar interests. Good news for the young women seeking older men, as we have one in the group waiting to talk to you! Another common area of interest was people who enjoy reality TV shows. Look around, singles. The person sitting across the room could be your future signifi-cant other, and he or she is only a mini-date away.

We've all been through the hardships of dates from hell. Perhaps someone drank too much, they said too much, or they were just too much themselves. These are the dates that drag on and on, when you would give anything for them to have ended after five minutes. Worry no longer, friends.

Speed dating has arrived, and Cupid is ready to strike you with his arrow. I know that you are anxious to try your hand at the 'lance-romance' talk, but before we begin, I would like to invite Elizabeth Snowden to say a few words. Lizbeth met her husband at these very tables last year—proof positive that speed dating works. Here to offer words of optimism, please join me in welcoming Lizbeth.

Speech #2

by Mary Kathryn Roberts

Good afternoon. Welcome to the fourth annual Writers Coalition conference and congratulations to each of you for being selected to participate in this four-day event! This auditorium is filled with talented young writers who worked hard to qualify for a place in our workshops. It is an honour to welcome such an impressive pool of talent to our city—participants, workshop facilitators, and guest speakers.

If you will take a moment to look around the room, you will recognize some familiar faces. Margaret Walker has helped to organize the Writers Coalition for the past two years, and we are proud to have her back again. Joining us, as well, are acclaimed novelist Steven Styles and playwright Kenneth Adams. They are here to share their experience

and offer their advice to you. Thank you so much for accepting our invitation, Steven and Kenneth.

The next four days will give all competition winners the opportunity to polish your writing skills in areas of your choice. You will be able to choose from categories such as poetry, novels, short stories, and non-fiction. You will also have a chance to network with our workshop facilitators, seasoned writers who can open doors for you in the profes-sional world of writing.

So over the next few minutes, I will give you a short overview of the workshops, as well as discuss our expecta-tions of you. Today you will be assigned to groups where you will become acquainted with other aspiring young writers. Tomorrow's workshops will proceed as follows. . . .

Speech #3

by Dana Troster

Welcome to the information session on the Students Abroad Program. I would like to extend a big thanks to the university administration for allowing us to talk with you about our program. We are here today because we under-stand that travelling on a student budget can be problem-atic. The Students Abroad Program (SAP) is your chance to take that extended vacation while covering costs of living and adding international work experience to your CV.

With offices around the world, our goal is to help you have a rewarding experience in a country of your choice. You may want to snorkel on the Great Barrier Reef of Aus-tralia or visit the amazing sets of *Lord of the Rings* in New Zealand. As communication students, you may want to learn about the inner workings of the British Broadcast Corporation in England or help advertise the Cannes Film Festival in France. Whatever you are seeking, SAP can help

you to find it. Fifteen per cent of our Canadian participants come from this region.

Travelling can be scary, especially for young adults. Going to a new place with a new language and culture can be confusing. But SAP will assist you with travel and accommodation arrangements. You will be able to travel in a group, where you have the comfort of friends, or you can travel solo, giving you an opportunity to extend your group of acquaintances. No matter your preference, an SAP team will be there to greet you and to assist you in settling into your new community.

At this time, I would like to introduce you to Jerome Newman, our president, who will walk you through the details of the program and answer your questions. Jerome began this program more than 10 years ago, but he is as enthusiastic about its benefits as the day that he registered the first participants. Jerome, you're on.

CHAPTER SIX

Putting Principles of Delivery into Practice

The Impromptu Speech

The assignment is a one-point speech (1–2 minutes) to be prepared and delivered during a class period. As the name suggests, one-point speeches develop one relatively limited idea such as 'Co-op programs help students to get jobs when they graduate'; 'Increases in tuition make it necessary for many students to work full-time'; or 'Video lottery terminals (VLTs) are responsible for many suicides.' Use several examples to develop one point. Avoid thesis statements that would involve developing several points, such as: 'Co-op programs have three major benefits'; 'Rising costs in university education have involved increases in tuition, books, and health fees'; or 'Video lottery terminals (VLTs) contribute to the wealth of provinces and the poverty of many low-income Canadians.'

Possibilities for this impromptu assignment include speaking on a current political or social issue or a quoted remark on some issue. Quotations work well because they are sufficiently broad to allow individuals to bring their own experiences to the topics. Another possibility is to speak about a personal experience such as 'My Most Terrifying Moment' or 'My Most Embarrassing Moment'. Students are allowed 10 minutes to prepare their speeches. Videotaped presentations can be replayed—once without sound and once with sound—focusing first on the nonverbal elements and then on the verbal. The emphasis in marking this assignment will be on delivery (the focus of this chapter), as well as on application of other principles learned to date in the course (the quality of the introduction and conclusion, the statement of purpose, the clarity of the thesis, and the use of attention-getting and audience adaptation strategies).

Learning Objectives
- To learn how to prepare for the impromptu speech.
- To discover how to build credibility through delivery.
- To understand the nature of technical challenges and how to deal with them.
- To set realistic goals for progress in public speaking.
- To put the importance of delivery into context.

An early study by Alan H. Monroe found that people see effective public speaking as synonymous with effective delivery.[1] In this chapter, we will look at strategies for building credibility through delivery, meeting technical challenges, setting realistic goals for progress in public speaking, and putting the importance of delivery into context. The chapter begins with a discussion of how to prepare for an impromptu speech, an assignment that will allow you to put principles of delivery into practice.

Preparing an Impromptu Speech

Preparation for an impromptu speech follows the same path as preparation for other speaking engagements: (1) development of an introduction (including attention strategies and statements of purpose, thesis, and orientation); (2) development of one or more major points (supported by examples, stories, statistics, etc.); and (3) a concluding statement with a brief summary and link back to the opening thought. Sometimes speakers define one or more terms in order to establish a frame of reference for the audience. Common supporting materials in impromptu speeches include personal anecdotes, stories, parables, and examples. Box 6.1 includes tips for preparing an impromptu speech.

Box 6.1 Tips for Preparing an Impromptu Speech

· Think in advance about stories with morals that could apply to many different topics.
· Do not reveal your topic prior to speaking.
· Begin with an attention-getting device.
· Proceed to a thesis statement.

· If the speech has more than one point, offer a preview of major points to be covered.
· Develop major point or points of speech.
· Have a clear, interesting conclusion that ties together the speech.

The term *impromptu speaking* refers to an unexpected speaking occasion, a time when you are forced to think on your feet, without benefit of more than a few minutes of preparation time. Some believe, however, that no speech is truly impromptu because people collect stories in their heads that they use on occasions when they must speak unexpectedly. They also draw on experiences from their past. As F.E. Smith (Lord Birkenhead) once said of former British Prime Minister Winston Churchill, 'Winston has devoted the best years of his life to preparing his impromptu speeches.'

To the extent possible, people tend to avoid impromptu speaking. Faced with the need to perform spontaneously, speakers often use parts of speeches that have worked for them in the past. Some have favourite passages they insert in numerous speeches. (Classical rhetoricians applied the term *commonplaces* to these recycled passages.) Government leaders rarely have only one version of any speech. Their speech writers typically prepare multiple versions of the same speech, adapted to various circumstances and audiences. At other times, speech writers in large organizations prepare *speech modules* (policy statements and examples that anyone in the organization can use). Faced with the need to produce speeches on short notice, speakers paste together relevant points from the speech modules. These modules serve much the same function as the form letters that organizations use to respond to public requests for information.

Photo Gill Ferguson

Communicators also prepare what are called 'Q's and A's' (questions and answers) to ensure that bureaucrats and politicians make as few impromptu remarks as possible. In fact, communicators often quake if their government leaders depart from a set script, because consistency in messaging is extremely important. We live in a time when the media can press a button to replay the words of a politician, government leader, or CEO. Organizations are legally and socially responsible for public statements. So they must take particular care when they speak 'off the cuff.'

When I was in high school, students prepared for impromptu speaking competitions by reading the most recent issues of *Time* magazine and *Newsweek* (quick and easy to digest) and memorizing stories and quotations that they could apply to almost any topic. I recall that a friend, who competed often in such competitions, had a favourite story he adapted to almost every competition. He told a parable of the person who is allowed to visit both hell and heaven. When he visits hell, he sees people sitting at a grand banquet hall. Chained together, the people are unable to eat the wonderful dishes in front of them. When the visitor goes to a second room, he is surprised to see a similar situation, where again people sit at a long banquet table. As in the first instance, chains connect them. In this room, however, the people are eating! They have found a way to partake in the feast by feeding each other. By co-operating, they have learned to survive and enjoy the opportunities that are so close at hand.

At this point, my friend launched into whatever happened to be the main topic of the impromptu speaking assignment. In today's terms, that could be Canada's peace-keeping mission in Afghanistan or the plight of people in New Orleans in the wake of Hurricane Katrina. It could be the domestic crisis involving congested highways or homelessness or lack of co-operation between political parties. The story could lead into a discussion of alienation in cities, unemployment, or the high debt load resulting from university loans. In every case, the moral of co-operation can be applied as a generic concept applicable to the solution of almost any crisis experienced by individuals, institutions, or governments. Experienced speakers rely on these kinds of planned passages to carry them through moments when they must speak 'without preparation'.

Another story that could be adapted to many different speech topics is the following:

When poachers want to capture monkeys, they go about it in a surprisingly simple way. They place bananas or coconuts in a long-necked ceramic vase. The mouth of the vase is sufficiently large for the monkey to insert his paw in an open fashion, but not large enough for the monkey to remove the fruit with a clenched fist. The vase is also too heavy to be carried away by the monkey. Because the monkey refuses to give up the fruit, the poachers are able to walk up to the jar and capture the exhausted monkey without any resistance. Obviously, the fruit is not worth the price that the monkey has to pay with his life. But he steadfastly refuses to relinquish the valued prize. Such are many of the sacrifices that we make in our own lives. We refuse to recognize when we have invested too much in a worthless enterprise, surrendered too much for too little return, or paid the ultimate price for victory. Like the monkey, we become entrapped, overcommitted.

A Web search allowed me to identify the number of different contexts in which people have used this story. Interestingly, the applications ranged from discussions of the Indo-Pakistani conflict to matters pertaining to global economies to the importance of sticking with troubled marriages. The possibilities for the application of this tale are endless.

Most organizational and professional speakers try to avoid truly impromptu speaking situations. But for those who must speak about formal matters in a spontaneous fashion, this impromptu speaking assignment will be helpful. In addition, this speaking assignment allows an almost exclusive focus on delivery, since little time exists for preparation of content.

Building Credibility through Delivery

Studies have found that audiences judge speakers on the basis of the following factors: perceived *composure, dynamism, trustworthiness, sociability, status, competence,* and *objectivity.* Most of these factors include elements on which delivery has an impact.

Composure

North American audiences are more likely to accept the messages of speakers who appear to be *composed.*[2] A recent study uncovered the reason that audiences may feel uncomfortable when speakers make too many mistakes:

> Why is it so annoying to watch someone else make a mistake? Maybe because it affects the same areas of the brain as when a person makes his or her own mistake, Dutch researchers say. Experiments in which volunteers tried a computer task and then watched each other do the same thing showed the brain reacted in a similar way whether the observer made the mistake, or watched someone else make it. . . . For their experiment Hein van Schie and colleagues hooked up 16 men and women to electrodes to measure brain activity and then sat them in front of a display screen with a joystick. The task was simple—to move the joystick in the same direction as certain arrows appearing on the screen. . . . After each trial, the volunteers were told whether they were correct. When people realized they had made an error, a distinctive electrical signal arose from a brain region called the anterior cingulate cortex. The same thing happened when the volunteers watched other volunteers try the experiment and make the occasional mistake.[3]

The Dutch researchers concluded that 'similar neural mechanisms are involved in monitoring one's own actions and the actions of others.'

Controlling Posture and Eliminating Extraneous Movements

Audiences sometimes see external behaviours as manifestations of inner qualities. So if a speaker appears rigid in stance, the audience may conclude that the speaker is also inflexible in her approach to issues. Similarly, audiences see nervous and uncontrolled movements as indicators of lack of confidence.

The nervous and uncertain speaker has a large repertoire of awkward postures and uncontrolled movements upon which to call. Some of the most common postures include slouching against the speaker's stand, leaning against a table or chair, crossing legs, standing with one hip out of place or with feet spaced too widely apart to be natural. The most common uncontrolled movements include rocking back and forth (sometimes back to front, sometimes side to side), kicking a leg, and bobbing the body. Uncontrolled hand and arm movements include tightly clutched hands (in front or behind the body), hands on the hip, a tight grip on the two sides of the speaker's podium, swinging arms, holding or rubbing one arm, touching the hair, flipping the hair, and playing with an object such as a rubber band. Not surprisingly, audiences see increased reliance on these kinds of movements and *manipulators* (the term applied to the massaging, rubbing, or holding of our own bodies) as signs of discomfort.[4]

Outward signs of composure, on the other hand, include upright posture and controlled body movements. The importance of gaining control over extraneous body movements and gestures cannot be overemphasized. The inexperienced speaker will be most comfortable with feet spaced slightly apart, a stance that carries an impression of balance. As the speaker grows more comfortable with the audience and the act of speaking, she may practise taking the occasional step towards one side of the audience or the other. These movements should be purposeful, and the speaker should assume positions that are fixed for a period of time. Pacing is a sign of nervousness, lack of confidence, and indecision or weakness. Any kind of movement should appear motivated, not random or aimless.

In my experience, women face a particular challenge in public speaking. Sometimes women adopt mannerisms that are 'little girl' in nature—twisting a strand of hair, tugging on clothing, hunching their shoulders, or giving kicks of their feet as they speak. I make this observation on the basis of many years of teaching public speaking, as well as attending professional workshops where members of the audience have discounted the views of otherwise competent speakers who demonstrated these mannerisms. Consciously or unconsciously, viewers associate these kinds of gestures with children. While all speakers (male and female) risk loss of credibility, in my experience, the risk is especially high for women and for speakers with a naturally youthful appearance.

Achieving Fluency

Fluent delivery (not stammering, stuttering, or relying on 'mmhs' and 'uhs'), appropriate use of pauses, and appropriate emotional control are also important. Most speakers have verbal crutches on which they rely when they face an uncertain moment in a speech. The speaker might say, 'uh', 'okay', 'um', 'ah', 'you know', 'well', 'whatever', 'ur', 'anyway', or 'like'. The smacking of lips and other noises serve as filler in those moments when the alternative is silence. In reality, moments of silence can build suspense or allow an audience to think about a point the speaker has made. As with other aspects of delivery, the mantra should be, 'Eliminate anything that detracts from the message.' Filler noises intrude, like white sound, into the consciousness of the audience and take the focus away from the speech. The noises also detract from the impression that the speaker is confident and composed. We associate fluency and calm during silence with composure. Studies also demonstrate a relationship between fluency and perceptions of competence.[5]

Taking Control of Silence

Experienced speakers use silence to gain and maintain control over their speaking environments. When they reach the front of the room or the podium, they pause before beginning the speech. They wait for audience members to stop talking, to put down their pens and paper, and to turn their attention to the front. When they ask a rhetorical question of the audience, they pause long enough to allow the audience to respond to the question in their minds. After making a statement with strong emotional impact, experienced speakers wait long enough for the comment to have maximum effect. Sometimes speakers pause before stating a startling fact, waiting for the undivided attention of the group. Just as seasoned speakers pause before beginning their speeches, they also pause after concluding their speeches. They allow the audience time to process the final thought before they vacate the stage or speaker's platform. Inexperienced speakers, on the other hand, rush from one sentence to the next and often complete their last sentence on the way to their seats.

Public speakers, however, are often afraid of silence; and if they forget a point or lose their place, they feel great embarrassment. But the speaker who has lost his place or breath should not hesitate to pause, collect his thoughts, and then continue. Sometimes a drink of water will give a speaker the required time to remember the next point and alleviate the dryness of throat that comes with tension. Pauses also serve other functions, as the later discussion on dynamism will consider.

The easiest way to separate experienced from inexperienced actors and actresses is to examine their use of silence. Actors such as Robert Redford, Richard Gere, and Harrison Ford have mastered the art of silence; and we read strength and power into their dialogues. North American speakers could learn from the Asians, who are comfortable with lapses in speaking: 'The Taoist view is that one who speaks doesn't know, one who knows doesn't speak.'[6] Similarly, strangers gathering for purposes of work in the Apache culture may not break their silence for days.[7]

Controlling Emotional Displays

As discussed in an earlier chapter, North American audiences are usually uncomfortable with high levels of emotionalism in presentations. They typically attempt to control such displays. A few years ago, I led a discussion of media coverage of the Oka, Quebec, crisis—a situation where the Mohawk of Kanesatake mounted an armed protest against the expansion of a municipal golf course onto sacred burial grounds. One of the politicians speaking publicly on the topic was MP Ethel Blondin (now Blondin-Andrew), who represents the Western Arctic riding in the House of Commons. The consensus in the discussion (especially among the men) was that Blondin, a Dene, had destroyed her credibility by displaying excessive emotion before the television cameras. In the eyes of many television viewers, she had appeared close to tears as she delivered her speech. And, in fact, in the days following her speech, some television commentators criticized Blondin for an overly emotional presentation to the House of Commons.

One of the factors that contributed to the impression of extreme emotion was the rising inflection that characterized the ends of her sentences. Combined with a relatively high-pitched voice that often seemed to be breaking, the inflection pattern suggested to English-speaking Canadians that Blondin was close to tears. Although some women believed that the emotional delivery increased the credibility of Blondin along the sincerity dimension, others reacted negatively to the display.

Sometime later I was watching *North of 60*, a CBC drama about Lynx River, a small town in the Northwest Territories. To my surprise, I realized that the inflection of the female Native speakers sounded remarkably close to that of Ethel Blondin. Moreover, the pattern of rising inflection at the ends of sentences did not connote excessive emotion at all. Rather, the pattern characterized the normal discourse of Native speakers living in the Northwest Territories. The perception that Ethel Blondin was close to tears in her delivery to Parliament was probably erroneous. Nonetheless, the lesson to be learned from Blondin's experience remains intact. Mainstream audiences in North America do not like speakers to lose their composure and become overly emotional in a public situation. For that reason, when speakers are unsure that they can speak on a topic without breaking down, they should select another topic.

Dynamism

North American audiences appreciate speakers who are *dynamic*.[8] External signs of dynamism in a speech include energetic movements, gestures, and sufficient volume, emphasis, and variety in the voice. In a public-speaking context, presenters who lean on the podium, lower their heads to speak, talk in low voices, and mumble will not convey the required degree of dynamism. Charisma appears in some discussions as a source credibility factor associated with dynamism and attractiveness.[9]

Making Appropriate Use of Gestures
Within some cultural settings, absence of gestures can convey boredom, blandness of personality, and lack of energy.[10] If you are speaking to an audience of Greeks, Italians, Arabs, South Americans, or Africans, you may find that they will expect you to use broad and animated gestures. Countries such as Japan, on the other hand, expect a minimum of hand gestures in public speaking. A sudden and unanticipated movement of the hand can completely distract a Japanese listener.[11] If animated hand and body movements are part of the culture of your audience, you may want to work towards a more animated mode of delivery. If you are speaking to an audience of Asian businessmen and women, on the other hand, you may want to use more constrained gestures.

The above advice comes, however, with cautions. If you attempt to use gestures that do not match your personality or comfort level, they may appear flamboyant or awkward. Rather than contributing to the sense that you are a dynamic speaker, the gestures may convey the impression that you are insincere. Many beginning speakers are overwhelmed by the number of considerations that they must integrate into their delivery during a speech—voice, posture, volume and enunciation, pronunciation, proper breathing, and not least, control of the speech content. They find it difficult to employ new and unfamiliar gestures in their first speeches. No one answer exists for how many and what gestures you should use in speaking, but the goal should be to strive for a natural and sincere style of delivery. For some speakers, that goal implies using more gestures; for others, it

Photo Gill Ferguson

means fewer. The main criterion is that gestures should not draw attention to themselves. They should complement your speech in the most natural way possible.

Creating a Sense of Dynamism and Immediacy by Engaging the Audience

A politician once told me that when he catches the eye of a member of his audience, the person will look immediately afterwards at the people on either side to see if they have noticed the attention.[12] I checked, on a few occasions, to confirm the validity of his observation. He was right. The fact is that audience members like to be noticed. They want to catch the sweaty towel tossed by a rock performer or the bouquet at a wedding. They want others to see that they have been singled out for attention.

Like the performers in the Broadway musical *Cats*, the speaker can leave the stage and walk among the audience. She can invite audience members onto the stage to participate in the speaking event. She can pass a microphone around the audience and request feedback. She can ask selected members of the audience to engage in some relevant activity. In demonstration speeches, speakers can ask for volunteers from the audience to participate in the demonstration or hand out supplies to selected members of the group so that they can join the speaker in performing some task such as making candles, creating a card for an anniversary, or reading the meaning of a Tarot deck. The speaker can ask the audience to join her in practising a Salsa step, or she can ask for a volunteer willing to receive a back massage. A speaker can ask the audience to close their eyes and imagine a spoken scenario. Creative and dynamic speakers find ways to engage their audiences. Speaking at a graduation exercise at the University College of the Fraser Valley, alternative theatre director David Diamond asked 300 gowned students, faculty, and their families and friends to participate with him in the spontaneous construction of a 'theatrical moment'. Afterwards, he asked 20 audience members to join him on stage to 'complete the image' of graduating.[13]

Conveying Dynamism through Pitch, Inflection, and Rhythm

Every culture uses pitch, inflection, and rhythm to give meaning to speech. The term *pitch* refers to the highness or lowness of the voice, and the term *inflection* refers to changes in pitch. Through pitch and inflection, speakers convey both emotion and energy. When people lack variation in pitch and inflection, we say that they speak in a *monotone* (one level). A monotonous voice is a serious barrier to an effective presentation.[14] Clear, strong vocal presentations convey a sense of dynamism and energy, whereas voices that are weak and thin transmit the opposite impression. Most speakers of English follow an inflection pattern that ends with a lowering of pitch at the end of sentences. Some other cultures have a rising inflection at the ends of sentences.

Rhythm refers to a 'harmonious flow of vocal sounds'[15] or patterns of movement. Speakers often vary their rhythm according to the seriousness of the occasion. To convey seriousness of purpose, for instance, East Indians adopt a 'slow ponderous . . . rhythm and a low pitch.'[16] In general, however, speakers should avoid excessive predictability in speech rhythm. Like the lapping of waves against the shore, predictable patterns of rising and falling speech can lull an audience to sleep. Predictable patterns also can destroy a sense of spontaneity and give the impression that the person is reading the speech. (We tend to fall into patterns when we read out loud.) The speaker who is criticized for falling into a pattern can insert pauses to eliminate the impression of reading or delivering a memorized speech. Pauses interrupt patterns and help speakers to sound more spontaneous.

Even though an animated delivery is preferable for most occasions, speakers should avoid a choppy delivery. Studies demonstrate a relationship between fluency and perceptions of competence.[17] Choppiness in delivery, or the breaking of speech into little bits and pieces, is one of the most common problems among beginning speakers. To avoid choppiness in delivery, an experienced speaker practises the speech aloud, identifying the places to take a break and to breathe, so that the speech does not become fragmented in delivery. Too many breaks, too often, destroy the aesthetic quality of speeches. The strategic placement of pauses, as discussed in another section, allows the speaker to maintain fluency of presentation and to breathe at the right places. The following example illustrates how a speaker can break a passage into readable, but flowing, segments:

> We face a crisis in health care. / We stand at the edge of a precipice / and if we do not take care / we will be in free fall / unable to control where or how we land. / We know that we must find a way to bridge the gap / between what we have and what we need. / However, / we also know that / at present / we lack the resources to make a credible effort.

Conveying Dynamism through Rate and Volume

Audiences attach a higher level of dynamism to individuals who speak in a relatively rapid and animated fashion with sufficient volume. However, the nature of the content; the language skills, cultural expectations, and knowledge of the audience; the occasion;

the personality and linguistic skills of the speaker; and the speaking environment (physical and technical) influence choices regarding both rate and volume of speech.

The nature of the content should have an impact on rate of speech. When you are talking about a concept that is complex and difficult to understand, using technical language, or defining terms, you should speak more slowly. The audience needs time to process more complex information. When you are giving statistics or asking the audience to relate an idea to their own experiences, allow more time for thought. A faster rate of speech, on the other hand, works well with lighter topics. In recounting a story, giving an example, or talking about an idea that can be easily grasped, you can speak more quickly. Public speakers tend to speak more rapidly when they are excited or interested in a topic. Sometimes they speak more rapidly when they build towards a climactic moment in a speech, as happened in Martin Luther King Jr's historic speech, 'I Have a Dream'. King's pace quickened from an average rate of 92 words a minute in the early part of his speech to a rate of approximately 145 words per minute at the climax.[18]

If a speaker addresses a topic about which he feels strongly, he may raise his voice from time to time to show emotional engagement with the topic. People associate loud and rapid speech with strong emotions and high levels of involvement with a topic.[19] But many audiences react negatively to an angry speaker, automatically viewing the person as out of control. Establishing a contrast between softness and loudness in delivery is often the best approach. The most commanding moments in a speech may be the times when the speaker lowers the voice and speaks in soft tones for dramatic effect—to build suspense or to add a more tempered emotional energy to the speech.

The language skills and knowledge level of the audience also influence choices regarding rate of speech and volume. A presenter may speak at a faster rate with audiences who share his linguistic profile; or he may speak louder with some audiences (e.g., Latinos and Arabs) than with others (Japanese and Chinese).[20]

The nature of the occasion also influences choices regarding rate of speech. The greater the sense of occasion, the slower the rate of speech is likely to be. Racing through a eulogy, a state speech, or a declaration of war would be inappropriate. In summary, while a faster-paced speech conveys dynamism and energy, speakers may need to slow their rates to connect with more sombre occasions.

The average rate at which people speak varies between 120 and 150 words per minute,[21] but rates of delivery often reflect the personality of the speaker or the level of confidence that the speaker feels with the language. When I wrote English speeches for cabinet ministers whose first language was French, I wrote shorter speeches because they typically spoke at a slower rate in English than in French. In short, no one rate of speech may be best for every speaker.

Environmental factors (physical and technical) also deserve consideration. The acoustics of the room or auditorium, the lighting, and equipment have an impact on delivery options. Microphones pose special challenges in speaking. When using a microphone, speakers must exercise even greater control over volume to avoid the impression of shouting at the audience. Placing the microphone about two to three inches from the mouth typically works best. Other challenges occur in an auditorium darkened for purposes of delivery. A speaker who is standing in a brightly lit area will not be able to see the audience. In that situation, eye contact becomes virtually impossible. In outdoor settings, echo effects can create havoc for the speaker who does not know how to control for feedback from the amplification system (Box 6.2).

Box 6.2 Whose Voice Is This, I Ask?

The occasion was graduation night. As a teacher of drama and public speaking, I had been charged with presenting honours awards at high school graduation, held in an outdoor stadium. Confidently, I walked to the microphone, ready to deliver my speech. But I was barely into my introduction when I heard a loud, strange voice throwing my words right back at me a few seconds after I said them! I was horrified to realize that the voice echoing over the stadium's public address system was my own. I had never spoken over a public address system in such a large venue before and had no idea such a thing could happen. I was so flustered that I forgot my entire speech and ended up ad libbing the whole thing. To this day, I'm still not sure of what I said, but since the honour graduates did come forward to receive their awards, I assume that I at least called their names. I've never since had to speak in such a situation, but if the need arises, I will definitely be more prepared and will *practise* in the location beforehand.

Desirée Devereaux

Trustworthiness

Speakers can establish trust through eye contact and consistency between verbal and non-verbal elements in delivery.

Creating Trust through Eye Contact

Another important dimension of source credibility is *trustworthiness*, also termed *character* or *safety*.[22] In terms of delivery, the most visible indicator of trustworthiness in North America is the willingness to look someone in the eye. An important factor in source credibility, the maintenance of direct eye contact tells the audience that the speaker is open, honest, and trustworthy. In some cultures, however, direct eye gaze signals a lack of respect for the listener or an aggressive personality. In addition to mainstream North America, the cultures that are most comfortable with direct gaze include the Arab, Latin American, and southern European countries. The Chinese, Japanese, Indians, Pakistanis, and people in Northern Europe look only peripherally (or not at all) at their conversation partners in interpersonal situations.

A speech student, Jamie Hodgins, recounted his experience with cultural differences when he taught a hip-hop workshop in Asia (see Box 6.3). Murray Smith, a teacher and consultant in Brandon, Manitoba, described a similar experience in a very different cultural setting (see Box 6.4).

Box 6.3 Silence in Singapore

Sitting on the plane, I ran through the routines that I would be teaching in a two-week 'hip-hop' workshop, scheduled to begin upon my arrival in Singapore. While I had been teaching 'hip hop' for a long time, I had never ventured so far from home; nor had I ever taught in a cultural environment other than my own. I had no idea what it would be like to instruct students in the tiny country of Singapore. But I soon found out. Amidst nerves and uncertainty, I took the stage to teach my first class. And there they were—a room full of students—so poised, prepared, and expressionless that I felt like a drill sergeant in my own Hip-Hop army! At home, I usually have to spend the first five minutes settling down a rowdy room before giving choreography; but in my class in Singapore, you could have heard a pin drop. Everyone was attentive and focused. The silence was deafening. I didn't know how to interpret it. I was used to separating people who were making a disturbance and calling for quiet. I immediately felt that no one was enjoying himself or herself, and I decided to lighten the mood. My voice got louder, my tone got shriller, and I did not let anyone escape from my most direct eye contact. No change at first. Then slowly I heard a quiet mumble begin to make its way around the room. It sounded like friendly banter. Relieved and happy that the room was finally alive with noise and movement, I increased my level of activity still further. I waved my arms. I jumped about the stage. I used the most animated facial expressions at my disposal. This had to be my best performance ever. Meanwhile, the mumbling grew into a loud rumble, and I could hear nearly every student saying

aiyah. The class ended on this note, after which a student approached me to ask if I knew the meaning of what everyone was saying. Cheerfully, I said that I wasn't sure but I thought that it might be some sort of laughter or acknowledgement. Politely but firmly, she said that I was wrong; and she explained the meaning of the exclamation. *Aiyah* meant 'a universal feeling of surprise and disappointment'! To say the least, I was horribly embarrassed and more than a little anxious for my next class. But a fellow staff member talked me through some 'less North American' techniques, which served me well through the remainder of the two-week workshop. I learned that it is very important to have background knowledge of the culture. While I thought that I was being funny, other people found me offensive. Had I simply taken the time to learn more about the Singapore culture, my first teaching experience in Asia would have gone a lot more smoothly.

Jamie Hodgins

Box 6.4 When Cultures Clash

I taught in an isolated community in northern Manitoba. My class was 15 Cree students studying to become teachers. Having taken public-speaking courses, I was excited to incorporate what I had learned into my teaching. At the beginning of the course, I focused on good voice projection, eye contact, hand and body gestures, as well as audience participation. I thought that my classes were great, as I asked questions that engaged my students to think and interact with the material being presented. One day, however, one of my students asked to see me. I suspected he wanted to tell me how inspired he was to be in the course. Instead, his question confused me. 'Why are you so rude?'

he asked. 'Rude?' I asked in return. He then explained that Crees always lower their eyes as a sign of respect for the person to whom they are speaking. Natives consider both direct eye contact and questions to be extremely aggressive. When a Cree knows you are ready to listen to his or her words, the words will be spoken. To ask questions as to what one is thinking is an invasion of that person's private space. From that day forth, I changed my classroom techniques and became less dependent on my acquired public-speaking expertise.

Murray R. Smith, PhD
Brandon University (retired)

Building Trust through Consistency between Verbal and Non-verbal Behaviours

In speaking, we strive to achieve a fit between what we say and how we say it. When the first President Bush announced allied military action in the Persian Gulf in January 1991, he smiled as he spoke of the declaration of war. Commentators later criticized the President for lack of consistency between the seriousness of the announcement and the manner in which he delivered the speech. George W. Bush has the same tendency as his father to speak about serious subjects with what seems on occasion to be a half-smile or smirk. The effect is diminished credibility in the eyes of those who expect consistency between the verbal and non-verbal elements in delivery.

Fiorello La Guardia, multilingual mayor of New York City (1933–45), was a master at achieving congruency in verbal and non-verbal language. A study of old news reel footage of La Guardia's campaigns found that the body language of La Guardia reflected the language in which he was speaking. Even without sound, researchers could identify the language in which La Guardia was speaking.[23] If La Guardia spoke in Italian, his gestures were broad and expansive; in Yiddish, they were short and choppy. When speaking in English, on the other hand, his gestures were much more constrained, conforming to an American tendency to restrict broad gestures to situations of anger, frustration, excitement, or other intense emotion.

We transmit as much as 93 per cent of our meaning through non-verbal communication.[24] Used effectively, gestures or *illustrators* (i.e., non-verbal acts that accompany speech) reinforce what we say in words.[25] Gestures clarify, reinforce, and add emphasis to points made in our presentations. When confronted with inconsistencies between words and body language, people tend to believe the body language.

Audiences also trust speakers whom they perceive to be similar to them in some way, a trait called *homophily*.[26]

Sociability

Audiences like speakers who are *sociable*. One of the most common ways by which speakers can create the perception of sociability is through immediacy behaviours. *Immediacy behaviour* refers to any effort to create a sense of psychological closeness with the audience. Although originating with the study of teacher–student interactions,[27] the concept holds relevance for public speakers as well.

Immediacy behaviours in delivery include stepping out from behind the lectern in order to bridge the psychological distance between speaker and audience, smiling often, adopting a conversational tone and rate of speech, using natural gestures, and wearing clothing that communicates warmth in colours and design.

Creating a Sense of Immediacy through Conversational Delivery

I learned the importance of *immediacy* in speaking at the age of 17 when my debate partner and I had reached the next-to-last round of a debate competition. We were both experienced speakers, accomplished at delivering in a fast staccato style. We were accustomed to meeting each argument raised by the opposition in a cold, analytical fashion before proceeding without pause to the next point. Logic was our forté. But on the day that we met Amy, I learned a valuable lesson. Amy was a member of the opposing team; and when she rose to speak, everyone listened. She smiled at the judge and at my partner and me. She paused before beginning her speech to be certain that she had the attention of the audience. Then she spoke in a friendly and personal fashion. Her unhurried and sociable way of speaking surprised me. (You have to be a speed listener to keep up with most debaters, and the typical North American debater sounds pretty upset and angry. As late as the 1950s, however, speaking at a rapid rate may have been the best way to persuade.[28])

Amy was a different kind of speaker. She spoke in a warm and conversational way, explaining each point in some detail, unlike the usual scattergun approach. And even though she covered far fewer points than we had covered, the audience knew what she had said when she finished. She created a sense of immediacy with her audience by smiling, maintaining a relatively relaxed posture, and proceeding at a slower pace than the typical debater. She left her position behind the speaker's podium to stand closer to the audience, and she used examples to which the audience could relate. At the end of the day, Amy and her less remarkable partner walked away from the competition with the first-place trophy; and my teammate and I had to be satisfied with third place.

After that experience, I began to change my style of speaking. I smiled more often. I concentrated on making my gestures more natural. I spoke more slowly. I left the speaker's podium more frequently, and I stopped talking 'at' people. Instead, I concentrated on speaking 'with' people. I began to see my audience, no matter the size, as a collection of individuals with a need to be recognized. In short, I tried to engage in *immediacy* behaviours and to establish a greater sense of personal contact and closeness with my audience.

Some mannerisms in delivery achieve the opposite results from immediacy, and they detract from perceptions of sociability. A few years ago, I taught a student (we will call her 'Anne') with a nearly flawless delivery. She was an experienced debater—fluent and confident. She had good volume and clear enunciation. In short, even to an experienced judge of speechmaking, she seemed like a role model. But something was wrong. I searched at length to identify the reason that the audience did not respond warmly or enthusiastically to her speeches. On the final day of class, I asked for some help with diagnosing the problem. One student pointed without hesitation to the nature of the problem. He said that Anne had a tendency to tilt her head slightly backward as she spoke, giving the impression that she was talking down to the group. To audience members, this non-verbal element conveyed the feeling of a patronizing and condescending attitude towards the audience. Anne's verbal style was closer to that of a debater, thus reinforcing the non-verbal impression of someone who is performing in a contrived situation rather than connecting with her audience.

A tendency to hold the head too high can lead to a second problem with delivery. The speaker may appear to have half-closed eyes. The unnatural tilt to the head creates a situation whereby the speaker must look down at the audience.

In concluding this section, it is important to observe that, even though few contemporary public-speaking occasions require that we wear a tuxedo or evening gown, exceptions do happen. A friendly and smiling demeanour may not be appropriate in all circumstances. The family of a deceased member may want pomp and ceremony in the memorial service, and some cultures require a high level of decorum and formality in the celebration of marriage. When these formal rites of passage occur, we must customize our delivery to fit the expectations of the audience and the occasion.

Note especially that 'informal' and 'natural' do not mean 'unrehearsed'. 'Naturalness' does not come easily or spontaneously to most people. The tension felt by many speakers translates into the most unnatural gestures, awkward body postures, and lack of vocal control. Most speakers have to work hard to acquire the ability to present in a spontaneous and conversational way. They move along a continuum in developing this kind of skill. The continuum involves, first, eliminating distracting habits; second, acquiring new skills; and third, practising the new skills so that they appear unrehearsed and natural. The most 'natural' form of delivery appears extemporaneous, as discussed in Chapter 4 on preparing and delivering a speech of introduction.

Finally, the term *conversational* does not imply that speakers should abandon the psychological and physical space that separates speakers from their audiences. As in the classroom situation, the audience should always know who has the floor. A fine (albeit invisible) line always separates a speaker from the audience. If the speaker crosses that line, the audience becomes uncomfortable and the speaker loses her privileged platform. To identify the proxemics of space accorded to any speaker, an instructor need only ask the speaker to roam the room and address the class from different locations. Members of the audience will be able to identify, very easily, when the speakers have crossed the invisible line.

Creating a Sense of Immediacy through Hair and Dress

An interesting example of manipulating speaker immediacy through dress and hair relates to the case of Marcia Clark, lead prosecutor in the O.J. Simpson trial. Clarke underwent a major transformation in image after she tested unfavourably with mock jurors in the period leading to the trial. One mock juror claimed, for example, that Clarke came across as a tough female lawyer. Media consultants feared that her cold and hard veneer could alienate the jurors. They advised that she should alter her image in verbal and non-verbal ways. She should chat with the press about such 'female' topics as shopping and children. She should wear lighter-coloured clothing, softer fabrics, and additional jewellery to soften her appearance. They advised her to change her hairstyle to achieve a more feminine effect.[29]

'Dress for Success' books counsel that women should wear dark colours such as black and navy to create a more professional appearance and to convey a sense of power and authority.[30] In the instance of Marcia Clarke, however, the consultants wanted to de-emphasize the power and authority dimensions and close the psychological distance separating speaker and audience.

The rules for men are not so different from those for women. On one occasion, the president of a teachers' union told a professor to wear slacks, a dress shirt, and sweater to an appeals hearing, instead of a suit. The lawyer told him that his peers would respond more warmly if his dress were not so stiff and formal. Dress can convey warmth and humanity or formality and coldness. Whether the reason for a positive decision was the quality of his argumentation or his sweater, the professor won his appeal. Politicians often use the same technique to convey the impression of having the 'common touch'.

As with all other aspects of communication, culture influences audience perceptions of both dress and hair. Some audiences might perceive a shaved head or long hair as anti-social, and they might be reluctant to approach the person. Others, however, might see the same individuals as highly approachable. In general, source credibility studies tell us that appearance has an impact on audience responses. As superficial as it may seem, the level of a person's attractiveness influences audience receptivity to messages.

Speakers need to observe one other important rule of a pragmatic nature. You should never leave your hair so that it can fall into your face. One of the most common tendencies of novice female speakers is to push back or flip their hair while they speak. Hair should be pulled away from the face and secured with a hair clip, scrunchie, hair comb, elastic band, or headband. In the same way, all speakers (men and women) should avoid clothing that draws the attention of the audience away from the message. Excessive or dangling jewellery, busy scarves, tops that expose too much skin, tight pants, and wild mixes of colour in clothing can create more interest in the speaker than the speech.

Creating a Sense of Immediacy through Physical Proximity

Kenneth E. Bickel, a preacher with Grace Theological Seminary in the US, recounted an experiment conducted by a practising minister.[31] Bickel (who was also a doctoral student) hired a professor of communication from a local college to attend 10 Sunday morning sermons and observe the audience from behind a one-way glass. In the experiment, the minister varied certain elements of his delivery. He stood away from the pulpit for the introduction of each sermon. Then as he made the transition into the main body of the sermon, he moved behind the pulpit to speak. The 100 per cent listener attentiveness that he enjoyed during the introduction quickly dropped to about 30 per cent attentiveness. When he moved to the second major section of his speech, however, he stepped away from the pulpit once again to stand closer to his audience. The observing professor noted that he recaptured a significant amount of audience attention with this change of position. The observer also noted that, when the minister moved to the right side of the sanctuary, larger numbers of that side of the congregation paid better attention; and when he moved to the left side, the situation reversed itself. After repeating the experiment 10 times, the minister became convinced that remaining behind a pulpit represented a significant impediment to listener attention.

A number of studies of the physical environment have demonstrated the impact of putting any sort of physical barrier between speaker and listener. One study of patient–doctor communication demonstrated, for example, that patients felt almost five times more at ease after the researchers removed the desks that separated them from their doctors.[32]

Over many years of teaching, I have noted that audiences respond more warmly in rooms where they feel physically close to other audience members, as well as physically close to the speaker. For events of limited duration, they are usually happier in a small inadequate classroom than in a large room where they feel lost in space. This principle has its limitations, however. Lengthy stays in crowded (particularly overheated) environments can generate negative effects. Hitler applied this principle in an extreme and unethical way, crowding people together in small places to get a unified reaction. Obviously, taking the idea to its extreme is unethical. However, when the intent is to foster a good classroom dynamic and the duration of the speech event is limited, the principle seems appropriate.

Status

Listeners attach greater credibility to speakers with higher status.[33] As discussed below, speakers convey status through dress and vocal cues (including accents and dialects). A related concept is power, which speakers acquire through stance, body language, dress, and a strong, clear delivery.

Dress

In the view of many, a speaker's dress conveys professionalism (or lack of professionalism), judgement (or lack of judgement), and respect (or lack of respect) for the audience. Audiences judge the *status* of speakers by a number of factors, including dress.[34]

An often cited study demonstrated that 'attractive' female speakers (as judged by subjects) experience more success than 'unattractive' female speakers at changing the attitudes of male students.[35] The study manipulated dress as a major means of transforming the appearance of the speaker. Other studies have found a relationship between clothing and judgements of status,[36] and the use of terms such as 'blue-collar' and 'white-collar' workers confirms the perceived relationship between dress and status.[37]

Canadian actress Kathleen Robertson (Theo in *Scary Movie 2*) described her experience: 'One time I wore what I thought was this very cool outfit—a muumuu-type dress with pants underneath and super high sandals. *The National Enquirer* ran a photo of me with a caption saying, "Would you be caught dead in this outfit?" I was thrilled!'

Not everyone shares Kathleen's zest for bad publicity, however, and most speakers seek to build their credibility through positive perceptions of their dress. Norms in dress vary over time; but generally speaking, audiences expect public speakers to be dressed somewhat more formally than they are dressed. Some, such as John T. Molloy (*Dress for Success*), counsel that speakers should always dress in relatively formal attire. An October 2002 *Wall Street Journal* article reported that 88 per cent of US companies adhere to a business casual dress code. These results came from a survey by Rowenta, an iron manufacturing company.[38] The rules, however, are probably less fixed than in the past.

It is my personal belief (based solely on observation) that the best general advice may be to dress *one level above* how you anticipate your audience will dress. In other words, if you think that the audience will wear jeans and casual dress (e.g., on a retreat), you should wear the equivalent of slacks with a sports shirt if you are a man or the equivalent of a skirt or pants with blouse if you are a woman. If you think that male members of your audience will wear slacks with dress shirts and that females will wear the equivalent of dresses or pants with tailored blouses, you might consider wearing a suit and tie or dress slacks with a sports jacket if you are a man. In that situation, women might choose a classical style of dress, suit, or pants suit.

As mentioned above, however, the rules are no longer rigid for how one should dress. A group of youth volunteers, high school dropouts, or street youth may relate more easily to someone in casual dress, as they are less likely to see the speaker as a member of the establishment. Expectancy violation theories also suggest that we are sometimes more successful when we violate expectations. A group of high school students may be pleasantly surprised when a young person, scheduled to speak on high-risk behaviour, shows up in jeans and running shoes.

The research of Virginia P. Richmond, James C. McCroskey, and Steven K. Payne suggests a justification for abandoning fixed norms in dress and accessories:

> Dress and the artifacts one employs to adorn their dress can communicate immediacy or non-immediacy. Informal, but not sloppy, dress usually communicates that one is approachable. Often, people are intimidated by very formal dress. Formal dress is one way of denoting higher status, and heightened status decreases immediacy. In some situations, people wanted to be perceived as having higher status and they want decreased immediacy.[39]

Sometimes audiences have set expectations for how speakers should dress—expectations that diminish the significance of immediacy concerns. On occasion, audiences may perceive 'dressing down' as an insult, a transparent attempt to identify for reasons of self-gain. One Canadian politician learned this fact when he arrived in jeans and lumberjack shirt for a meeting with blue-collar workers. The audience thought that the politician did not show sufficient respect for the group by dressing in such informal clothing.

Accents and Dialects

Audiences also judge the status of speakers on the basis of vocal cues, including accents and dialects. The term *accent* refers to the phonetic sounds of language. The term *dialect*, on the other hand, implies the patterns of speech in a particular region or part of a country—syntax, idiom, and accents. The classic story of Eliza Doolittle in *My Fair Lady* (a musical adaptation of *Pygmalion* by George Bernard Shaw) illustrates how dialect can define status. In response to a challenge, the arrogant and aristocratic Professor Henry Higgins undertakes the daunting task of turning Eliza into a 'lady'. In order to present her as a duchess at a high society ball, he must rid her of a lower-class cockney accent. A more recent version of the Eliza Doolittle story is *The Princess Diaries*. In this film, an American teenager learns that she is next in line to inherit the throne of Genovia, a small Monaco-like country in Europe. Before assuming her new role, however, Mia Thermopolis must learn how to speak and behave like a princess. She accomplishes this task with the assistance of her grandmother, Queen Clarisse Renaldi. Like Eliza, however, Mia makes many mistakes as she undertakes the learning process.

The basic premise of *The Princess Diaries* is not totally unrealistic in the sense that dialects continue to carry meanings associated with status, even in modern contexts. French Canadians, visiting France, often complain that native Parisians refuse to speak to them in French, addressing them instead in English. Not surprisingly, they interpret this refusal as a statement of status. Yet, within Canada, the same kinds of status distinctions manifest themselves. Some Quebecers, for example, regard their accents to be superior to those of northern Ontario or New Brunswick, and some francophones in Ottawa regard their accents as superior to those of their neighbours across the river in Gatineau. In the same way, some French-speaking Canadians consider their accents to be superior to those of the Acadians in southern Louisiana. In short, people still read status into vocal cues; and some studies have found that listeners make status judgements on the basis of single words, without even taking grammatical context or fluency into account.

As a speaker, what can you do about accents and dialects? The answer is 'very little on a short-term basis'. Unless you are truly adept at dialects, like some stand-up comics and stage actors, you may not be able to adopt the dialect of your audience. But you can use good grammar, practise pronouncing difficult words in advance of the speech occasion, and enunciate clearly. A common fault of beginning speakers is the dropping of sounds at the ends of sentences and mumbling. Yet effectiveness of delivery probably hinges more on clarity of speech than on accent or dialect. Also, audiences are often intrigued by accents and dialects different from their own.

Movements, Posture, and Stance

We associate not only composure, but also power, with body stance and movement.[40] Stiffness in delivery conveys lack of confidence and lack of power. Expansive movements, erect posture, feet placed slightly apart, and a relaxed and sociable demeanour carry inferences of power.[41] So if speakers want to be perceived as confident and powerful, their stance and mannerisms must convey this impression.

Many studies have demonstrated the importance of posture and stance in first impressions. Psychologists Loretta Malandro and Larry Barker videotaped 60 pedestrians on New York streets. Later they asked prison inmates, convicted on charges of assault, to assign 'muggability ratings' to the pedestrians. The inmates rated the assault potential of the pedestrians on a scale of one to ten. Ratings at the lower end of the scale meant that the inmate thought the pedestrian would offer little or no resistance. Ratings at the upper end of the scale meant that the inmate thought the pedestrian would offer significant resistance, an assessment that would discourage an assault. The findings of the study indicated that people transmit powerful signals through their body movements, posture, and stance. In this case, the researchers discovered that several body movements, in particular, characterized easy victims:

> Their strides were either very long or very short; they moved awkwardly, raising their left legs with their left arms (instead of alternating them); on each step they tended to lift their whole foot up and then place it down (less muggable sorts took steps in which their feet rocked from heel to toe). Overall, the people rated most muggable walked as if they were in conflict with themselves; they seemed to make each move in the most difficult way possible.[42]

Other studies have found that rapists use postural cues to identify potential victims.[43]

Although audiences will not be judging the 'muggability' potential of speakers, they will be looking for indicators of confidence, status, and expertise. Non-verbal factors play a critical role in these judgements.

Physical Environment

The environment can also affect audience perceptions of speaker status. A plush and comfortable environment can lend an air of credibility to a speaker, enhancing the person's credibility. The number of people who attend the event, as well as the number who remain to the end of the speech, can also enhance or lower credibility.

Competence

The perceived competence or expertise of a speaker is another aspect of source credibility,[44] and studies allege an association between communicators who are competent and those who are assertive, responsive, and versatile.[45] As noted earlier, studies also demonstrate a relationship between perceptions of competence and fluency.[46]

Assertiveness, Responsiveness, and Versatility

Assertiveness displays itself in the posture and voice of speakers. The voices of assertive speakers are strong and animated. Strength in volume conveys the impression of confidence and power. To most Canadians, the lowering of the voice at the end of sentences connotes assertiveness, whereas rising inflection suggests uncertainty (associated with the asking of questions), lack of confidence, and insecurity. But different cultures use language in different ways. Pakistanis raise their inflection for statements and lower their inflection for questions.[47] Canadians who know little about the Pakistani language might interpret the upward inflection as an indicator of hesitancy, a request for validation. And as the example of Ethel Blondin (discussed earlier in the chapter) suggests, we are not always right in our interpretation of the meaning of inflection patterns.

The responsive speaker looks for cues that the audience may be bored, tired, or alienated by the speech. He also looks for non-verbal signs that the audience understands the content of the speech and accepts his message. When speakers sound bored or disinterested or speak in a monotone voice, they project the impression of non-responsiveness. If the attention of the audience appears to be flagging, the versatile speaker will use an attention strategy, catch the eye of disinterested individuals, or strive for a more animated delivery to recapture and refocus attention on the speech. In question-and-answer sessions, the responsive and assertive speaker will answer the questions of the audience in a direct, confident, and energetic fashion.

Expertise

Competent speakers know their material, and they are able to gain and maintain direct eye contact with their audiences. Their expert knowledge enables them to avoid excessive reliance on note cards and manuscripts. Less competent speakers, however, tend to rely too heavily on their written speeches, keep a fixed gaze on the instructor throughout the entire speech, or maintain eye contact with only one side of the audience. Sometimes speakers orient not only their eyes, but also their entire bodies, to one side of the audience. They virtually ignore the other members of the audience. Numerous reasons explain this tendency to prefer one side of a classroom or auditorium. Sometimes the people sitting on one side of the audience are more responsive to the speaker. They may be smiling, nodding, and offering encouragement. Friends may be sitting on the preferred side of the classroom. At other times, more of the seats may be filled on one side than the other. The reasons for choosing to present to one side of the room are usually personal in nature. But whatever the reasons, speakers should always try to maintain eye contact with all parts of the audience—first one section, then another. Speakers should not, however, scan the audience like a rotating fan. In auditorium settings, speakers will not be able to catch the eye of every individual, but if they look in the general direction of different segments of the audience, members will perceive that they have been targeted for attention.

The use of high-quality visual aids can also have an impact on the perceived expertise and authority of a speaker.[48]

Objectivity

A final dimension of credibility that merits discussion is objectivity.[49] While the speaker will establish objectivity predominantly through the spoken text of his speech, he has some opportunities to communicate objectivity through delivery as well. The perceived objectivity of the person performing the introduction, for example, can influence perceptions of the speaker. If a member of the Green Party introduces a speaker, the audience will conclude that the speaker is biased in favour of certain principles.

Audiences also assign attitudes to speakers based on their dress or body ornaments. Rightly or wrongly, the audience may assign significance to the number of earrings in nose, mouth, and ears or—at the other extreme—to highly conservative dress or lack of makeup. They may believe that they know the attitudes and values of the speakers before they utter a single word. How we express ourselves, volume, and tone of voice can also communicate objectivity (or lack of objectivity). As noted earlier, audiences read higher levels of conviction into emotional modes of delivery. On the negative side, when speakers become red-faced, scream at their audiences, and use vituperative language, they run the risk of being rejected by those they seek to influence.

Meeting Technical Challenges

Speakers face a special kind of challenge when cameras televise their speeches. They face the need to accommodate both the audience that is physically present in the speaking environment and the physically remote television audience. Gestures and movements that appear natural in one environment may look contrived and unnatural in the other. And an audience that feels ignored will resent having made an investment in attending the speech event.

On one occasion, I can remember feeling alienated from a speaker who chose to focus on the television cameras at the expense of his audience. I had gone to hear a speech by First Nations Chief Phil Fontaine at Carleton University in Ottawa.[50] I had looked forward to hearing his address and to meeting him, as I have felt a strong empathy with the Native cause. But after reaching the speaker's rostrum, Fontaine turned the podium to face the television cameras, which were positioned away from the majority of his immediate audience. Throughout the speech, Fontaine spoke to the cameras, rarely looking in the direction of his audience. In a similar fashion, prior to his speech, he had distanced himself physically from his audience. While audience members can understand, on a logical level, why speakers sometimes choose the thousands—or even millions—of television viewers over the scores who may be present in the room, they may nonetheless feel resentful that they have taken the time to dress, prepare for the occasion, and make their way through traffic to the speaking location. They wonder why they did not just stay at home instead of becoming wallpaper for the speaker.

Speakers often face the challenge of deciding which audience is more important—the immediate or remote audience. Advanced microphone technologies can help to bridge the two situations, allowing the speaker to reach her immediate audience without having to raise the voice. Gesture and movement are more difficult to reconcile.

Setting Realistic Goals

Many novice speakers believe that successful speaking depends on a near-flawless presentation. But audiences do not expect speakers to be perfect; and they can identify more readily with people who are human, who make mistakes on occasion.[51] When I taught the introductory communication course at the University of Ottawa, I typically asked my students to name the politicians whose speaking styles they liked and disliked. Invariably, during the years in which Brian Mulroney was Prime Minister of Canada, they named Mulroney as a speaker whose style bothered them. They were quick to admit that he was an accomplished speaker, smooth and resonant in delivery. They thought that he dressed well and that he was physically attractive. However, they also noted that they found his style too polished, too flawless, too immaculate to be credible. They found his delivery to be too confident. Studies confirm that we do not assign credibility to a speaker who stumbles and stammers through a speech; but we will tolerate the occasional hesitancy or blip in composure, so long as the speaker appears competent overall.

Visualizing the ideal presentation (see Chapter 2) is one way to improve delivery, and this chapter suggests additional strategies. But realistically, for most of us, the critical variable in improving our delivery is time. Practice translates into comfort at the podium and into improved delivery. We do not become better dancers or skaters or hockey players by sitting in the audience. We have to engage both our bodies and our minds in many processes in order to acquire the skills. The same is true of speaking.

The more often we speak, the better we get. Our gestures become more natural as we gain practice. We stop fidgeting and tugging at our hair and clothes. We cease to sway and prop ourselves against the nearest physical object. We do not race through our speeches, run out of breath, pace like restless lions, or glue our gaze to our note cards. Certainly, we can expect some notable changes in the speechmaking that occurs over the course of a semester, but we must be realistic in what we ask of ourselves and others. We should identify our weaknesses and set small goals to be achieved in each speech. We should realize that some members of the group will have had much more practice at speechmaking than others, and we should not judge our progress against those standards. Let the skills of others inspire but not de-motivate us.

Also, do not lose heart if you have a problem that challenges your ability to be the next Anthony Robbins, Deepak Chopra, or Peggy Fleming (top-billed motivational speakers). Bret Eastburn has no arms or legs; yet he is also a motivational speaker in great demand. Former Prime Minister Jean Chrétien suffered a stroke when he was a young man, which affected his ability to speak from one side of his mouth. Yet he achieved the highest position in Canadian government, one that requires daily speech-

---

Box 6.5 Improve Your Credibility through Delivery!

- Practise your speech in front of a mirror or with a friend.
- Dress appropriately.
- Position yourself so that everyone can see you.
- Wait until you have everyone's attention to begin.
- Use note cards for most speeches; avoid full-sized sheets of paper.
- Be energetic and enthusiastic when speaking.
- Maintain eye contact with your audience.
- If time permits, engage your audience in some activity.
- Be natural and conversational.
- Avoid a choppy delivery.
- Watch your posture; don't lean on the podium or slouch.
- Don't be afraid to leave the podium but don't wander purposelessly.

- Smile when appropriate.
- Avoid a condescending or patronizing attitude and posture.
- If you make a mistake, collect your thoughts.
- Occasionally, you can acknowledge a mistake with humour.
- Be purposeful in your movements.
- Do not fidget with your hands or shift from foot to foot.
- Pause if you are tempted to use fillers such as *uh*, *um*, *like*, etc.
- Use silence to your benefit—for emphasis or effect.
- Avoid strong emotional displays such as crying.
- Vary your rate, volume, pitch, and inflection.
- Avoid rushing your speech.
- Use high quality, professional-looking visual aids.
- Observe time limits.

making. Some highly accomplished speakers are blind, while others deal with the challenges posed by dyslexia, stuttering problems, or lisps. Winston Churchill overcame a problem with stuttering.

Even people who are 'vocally challenged' can succeed if they have sufficient energy, initiative, and dynamism of personality to compensate for their deficiencies. Abraham Lincoln had a rasping, high-pitched voice that became shrill and squeaky when he was excited;[52] yet his Gettysburg Address is still recognized as an oratorical masterpiece. Our ability to succeed as speakers or performers is bound only by the limits that we set for ourselves.

Putting the Significance of Delivery into Perspective

Despite the perceived significance of delivery, audience concerns about the quality of a speaker's delivery rarely take first place in a situation where vital issues are at stake. In the 2004 Canadian election, for example, television commentators and audience members who offered feedback rarely talked about delivery. Instead, they focused on the campaign issues such as health care, subsidized child care, national unity, and fiscal policies.

Speech classes and political commentators may well dissect the debates at some later point and weigh the influence of delivery on audience perceptions. In the case of the 2004 debates, some viewers noted retrospectively that Liberal Paul Martin had looked at the cameras far too often, while Conservative Stephen Harper had looked at his opponents. They also noted that NDP leader Jack Layton showed other weaknesses, such as fidgeting. In the more public debate, however, Canadians focused on issues rather than delivery—whether a vote for the Bloc would translate into separation for Quebec, whether support for the Conservative Party would result in privatized health care, and whether the Liberals could overcome the sponsorship scandal that had threatened the viability of their leadership. Perhaps the situation would have been different if the issues had been less critical to the audience, the election less close, or the delivery of leaders more notably flawed.

The same principle applies to crisis communication situations, where audiences are much more interested in being updated on the crisis than in judging the delivery of the speaker. So yes, delivery is important, but no one should underestimate the ability of a weak speaker to persuade on matters of vital importance to the audience. And from an ethical point of view, that ordering of criteria seems most appropriate.

Finally, no one type of delivery fits everyone, just as no one style in clothing suits everyone. We may admire the slender, tall model or the pre-pubescent teenager who wears the latest Moschino, Calvin Klein, or Betsy Johnson fashions; but we cannot necessarily expect the styles to fit our frames or personalities. The older woman, the teenage boy, and the plus-size woman will choose according to their body builds and comfort level. The same is true of speakers, who have different kinds of voices, personalities, and experiences, and who speak to different kinds of audiences. Martin Luther King Jr was one of the most accomplished speakers of the twentieth century, but his style came from another era (the 1960s), context (civil unrest), country and region (the southern United States), and cultural tradition (Southern Baptist sermon). The most important point to remember is that audiences are most accepting of speakers who

---

Box 6.6 A Question of Ethics

Larry arrived early for his speaking engagement. He positioned the podium so that he could move close to the audience at strategic points in the speech. He had read that speakers can be more persuasive if they invade the personal space of listeners, encouraging an emotional response. For the same reason, he placed the chairs close to each other and raised the temperature to a slightly uncomfortable level.

The purpose of the speech was to encourage the audience of corporate executives and local business owners to support local sports groups. To enhance his credibility with the audience, Larry had brought some slides of his family attending sports events. One photo showed him shaking hands with the coach of the team. Another slide showed him interacting with the players and crowd at a baseball game. He also showed photos of himself at an awards ceremony where he had been honoured for his financial contribution to a local baseball team. Realizing that this particular audience would find his regional accent unattractive, Larry planned to speak with an accent that would be more acceptable to his audience. After reading a book on how to dress for success, he had purchased an expensive dark navy suit and gold tie. He chose colours and styles known to communicate power and influence.

Just before people began entering the auditorium, Larry dimmed the lights and turned up the sound system, which was playing soft music, hoping to create a warm personal atmosphere for the speech. He hoped that these added effects would encourage his audience to support local sports teams. He had also planned the content of his speech to focus on the teams with the best records—the ones that had won the most games in the last season.

How do you feel about Larry's preparations for his speech? Where do you draw the line between ethical and unethical approaches to delivery? Between adapting to your audience and seeking to manipulate them? Should the motivations of a speaker influence your reactions to strategies of the above variety? What if Larry were trying to persuade his audience to give money to a children's hospital? Would your evaluation be different than if he is trying to persuade them to purchase a life insurance policy or to become involved in a get-rich-quick real estate scheme?

---

radiate sincerity and who reveal some elements of their own personality when they deliver a speech.

Conclusion

Other chapters provide an opportunity to prepare speeches that require careful research and extemporaneous, memorized, or manuscript delivery. The impromptu speech, as described in this chapter, provides an opportunity to practise delivery strategies aimed at building credibility. In addition, this chapter has looked at technical challenges in public speaking, the importance of setting realistic goals, and the relative importance of delivery when considered in conjunction with other factors.

Questions for Discussion

1. Describe some situations that require impromptu speaking. What are some of the ways in which speakers prepare for these kinds of impromptu speaking situations?
2. Describe some elements of delivery that you would like to improve. What are the filler words upon which you most often rely?

3. How do you react when speakers pause to take a breath, slow their pace to empha-size a point, or look down to identify the next thought? Are you comfortable with the silence? Are you equally comfortable taking pauses when you speak?

4. Are you comfortable with emotional displays in speaking? Can you think of any speakers who are excessively emotional in their speaking styles, to the point that you are turned off?

5. What do you find most annoying in the delivery of poor speakers? If you were to offer advice to someone on speech delivery, what would you stress?

6. Some of you come from different cultural backgrounds. Compare and contrast acceptable delivery (movement, gestures, eye contact, etc.) in that culture with pre-ferred modes of delivery in mainstream Canadian society or in other cultures.

7. In terms of delivery, what causes us to trust or not to trust a speaker?

8. What are some of the ways in which speakers can create a sense of immediacy or psychological closeness with audiences (restrict your considerations to delivery)?

9. Think of some high-status speakers. How did they dress? Do you believe that one standard exists for appropriate dress in today's environment?

10. Do you think that accents and dialects are always perceived negatively? Give exam-ples to support your point of view.

Appendix: Selected Videos on Public Speaking, Available in Canadian Libraries

How to Make an Effective Presentation, produced by Arthur Heller; co-produced with Alberta Advanced Education Community Program Branch and Access Network (Calgary: Access Network, 1990). Step-by-step guide to preparation and delivery of a speech.

How to Speak, produced and directed by Jamil Simon in collaboration with the Derek Bok Center (Cambridge, Mass.: Derek Bok Center for Teaching and Learning, Harvard University, 1997). Advice by Patrick Winston of the Massachusetts Institute of Technol-ogy on how to present an effective speech.

Persuasive Speaking, produced by Esquire Success (1985). Features clips of speeches by Ronald Reagan, Martin Luther King Jr, John F. Kennedy, and others. Also includes advice from speaking coaches in the world of theatre, business, and politics.

Speaking Effectively: To One or One Thousand, produced by CRM Productions and distributed by Owen Stewart Performances (1992). Gives instructions for organizing and deliver-ing speeches.

Ten Vital Rules for Giving Incredible Speeches and Why They're Irrelevant, distributed by Interna-tional Telefilm (1990).

Time to Stand and Deliver, with Tina Dupree (Princeton, NJ: Films for the Humanities and Social Sciences, 2000–1). Techniques for building confidence as public speaker.

CHAPTER SEVEN

Visual Aids and Software Presentations*

Learning Objectives

- To understand the purposes of using visual aids to complement a speech.
- To become acquainted with the principles governing the use of visual aids.
- To learn about the different kinds of visual supports.
- To find out about the visual presentation of statistical data.
- To learn about computer-generated presentations.

I recall a story from the early 1960s, a time when the arms race was in full swing. People worried that someone in Russia or the United States could inadvertently push a button that would end in a nuclear holocaust. Against that backdrop, then Premier Nikita Khrushchev and President John F. Kennedy decided to establish a hotline to allow instant communication between the two heads of state. A problem arose, however, because the two leaders could not agree on the nature of the hotline. Kennedy wanted a telegraph system, whereas Khrushchev preferred the telephone. These preferences reflected cultural differences in the two societies, with the US valuing the visual and Russia the oral tradition. Scholars in intercultural communication have long stressed the importance of recognizing such cultural preferences. Kennedy would only believe what he could see in writing, and Khrushchev wanted an oral commitment.

In the years since those events, television and the Internet have created even stronger preferences for the visual in technologically advanced societies.[1] People like and expect visual content in presentations of all varieties. Thus, this chapter examines purposes of visual supports, general principles governing the use of visual aids, different kinds of visual supports, and PowerPoint and other software presentations. A sample PowerPoint appears at the end of this chapter.

Purposes of Visual Supports

Visual aids accomplish several major purposes. First, they meet the needs of visual learners (described in Chapter 13). People with visual intelligence learn best from

---

*Please note: The content of this chapter supports assignments for Chapters 4, 8, 10, 13, and 14.

videos, films, photographs, and other materials that appeal to this sensory mode.[2] Because visuals bypass language filters, they are especially appropriate in presentations to multicultural groups. In addition, visual aids give nervous speakers something to do with their hands and draw the attention of the audience away from the speaker. Used properly, they offer important and interesting information but allow the speaker a chance to feel less conspicuous. Visual aids help listeners to understand statistics and other complex material. Finally, we are living in a time when people expect sophisticated presentations. Television has created a generation of people who want to be entertained as well as taught, and computer technologies have fostered expectations of interactive and dynamic content, filled with images. We judge the professionalism of speakers by their visual aids.

General Principles

The following discussion summarizes major considerations in preparing and using visual aids. Visual aids should be uncluttered, simple, and colourful. Lettering and fonts should be bold in effect, and images should be large enough for all audience members to see them clearly. Speakers should display visuals long enough for audiences to absorb the material. One of the most common mistakes of novice speakers is to change the slide or transparency before the audience has had a chance to comprehend the content. Do not rush a presentation. Use a pointer and stay open to the audience when you use visual aids. (*Never* direct a laser pointer towards the audience.)

If someone speaks before you, remove any leftovers from the previous presentation before beginning your presentation. Erase the chalkboard and eliminate distracting features in the speaking environment. Your visuals should not war with photographs or charts still hanging on the walls from earlier speeches. You also need to organize your own materials so that you do not create clutter. When giving a demonstration speech, do not leave paper bags lying on the floor within view of the audience or unnecessary papers and other items on tables. Leave items covered or hidden from sight until you are ready to use them. Have them sufficiently accessible, however, that you are not bent over, digging in bags, to locate them. When you have finished with the visual aid (whether placed on the table or projected on a screen), remove the visual or hide the image from the sight of audience members. You can, for example, use the shutter on remotes that operate data projectors, turn off the overhead projector, or use a paper to hide the upcoming points on a transparency. If you do not take such measures, the audience will continue to focus on the visual rather than on your speech.

Box 7.1 A Question of Ethics

Scanners and computer software programs allow us to edit the words of other people, doctor the images that we present in PowerPoint presentations, and alter photographs to suit our ends. It is possible to put the head of one person on another or omit parts of headlines, changing the meaning of the caption. We can bold, highlight, or lighten selected passages to give them more or less emphasis. Can you think of any examples where communicators have abused the potential of the new technologies?

Daryl Huff wrote a much-publicized book in 1954 titled *How to Lie with Statistics*. Many presenters have followed his advice since that date. At the 2004 California Recreation Conference, for example, Mary Jo Flynn and Katharine James made a presentation titled 'Statistics Can Lie: How to Create Charts that Help to Show your Program in a Positive Light.'* They advocated the use of bold dark colours in pie charts. More compelling than pale pastels, dark colours also appear larger. Flynn and James suggested making selective choices on what to include and exclude in bar graphs. For example, a presenter may depict an increase in soccer participation but omit the declining interest in basketball. Placing the highest values in charts on the right side of the frame creates the impression that they are greater since the eye reads from left to right.

How do you feel about this kind of advice? The presenters were just trying to help cities to improve their participation rates in recreational activities. Their advocacy efforts supported the public interest. Would you feel differently if someone used these same strategies to persuade you to buy new exercise equipment from their company? Does the end ever justify the means? How do speaker motives figure into the ethics equation?

*See Statistics Can Lie Handout, at: <www.cprs.org/confhandouts2004/Res.pdf>.

If you must lower the lighting for any reason, do not leave the audience in the dark for long. Ask someone else to help you with equipment—to turn lights on or off and to operate audio players, VCRs, or media consoles. Be sure that you have the necessary extension cords for overhead or data projectors, laptop computers, and other equipment. Always check your equipment in advance of speaking and, if possible, practise with the person who will be assisting with equipment. Providing the person with a script of your speech can be helpful. If you are operating the equipment yourself, the same rules apply. Practise in advance with co-ordinating slides, overhead transparencies, and video and audio clips. Book all equipment, which is not present in the speaking environment, well in advance. At educational institutions, you may need to secure signatures and provide identification to check out equipment.

Box 7.2 Dead or Alive?

I was giving a demonstration speech on how to make sushi. I'd read that Hawaiians make sushi by ripping the shell off a live shrimp, putting a bit of lemon juice on it, then quickly making and serving the sushi. As I described the process, I held the shell of a large dead prawn in my hand. When I put it down, the prawn rolled a bit. At that point, a woman jumped up and started towards the front with some animal rights comments. Then reconsidering, she turned back and wandered to the back of the room, mumbling to herself. She figured the prawn was alive, but most people saw it for what it was—a playful prop. Still, it's hard to tell when such dramatic bits distract too much from the overall effect.

Vic Williams

Acknowledge the sources on which you have relied in developing your presentation. The credits may appear in a corner of visuals such as photographs or charts. Most important, take your audience and setting into account when making final choices on visual aids. Finally, exercise judgement in your choices of visual aids, especially live ones. Pit bulls are unquestionably inappropriate in a classroom setting. Pigeons, parrots, and cockatoos are distracting. Pets have rarely learned the rules of classroom behaviour, and demonstrations that rely on animals are in the high-risk category.

Different Kinds of Visual Supports

Speakers have a choice of a number of different visual supports, including three-dimensional objects and models; chalkboards, white boards, and flannel boards; flip charts; handouts; posters; overhead and data projectors; slides; statistical charts and graphs; and audio and videotapes. When delivering a motivational talk, a speech of introduction or welcome—or even informative and persuasive speeches—these traditional visual supports are often quite effective. Although classroom instructors, business executives, and trainers make heavy use of PowerPoint and other software presentations, students must be careful in using computer software with five- to 10-minute speaking assignments.

Photo Gill Ferguson

Visuals should always complement, not replace, the spoken word. With PowerPoint presentations, speakers have a tendency to duplicate the words of the speaker on the screen rather than use the PowerPoint presentation as a visual support. With the traditional visual supports, this scenario is less likely. For that reason, I often request that students reserve the use of PowerPoint for business and educational presentations. That is not to say, however, that speakers should not employ computers to show other visual materials.

Three-Dimensional Objects and Models

Be sure that a three-dimensional object is sufficiently large to be visible to all audience members. If an object is too small, too large, awkward, or inappropriate to bring to class, you can construct a model—or you can bring a photograph of the object to class. Locomotives will not fit in the classroom, and the Royal Ontario Museum is not likely to offer a Haida mask on loan. But you can construct models or locate photographs of such items. If you choose the alternative of the photograph, you can make an enlargement at a print shop and mount it on a poster board. You can copy the photograph to a transparency to display on an overhead projector, scan the photograph into the computer for display, or make a slide of the photograph to show on a projector. Check the equipment available to you before deciding on one of these options.

Never circulate objects or photographs among the audience during the course of your speech. When you are ready to talk about the object, position it between yourself and the audience. Sometimes speakers place multiple objects at various locations in the room, sufficiently close for the audience to see the objects without straining. In a demonstration speech, for example, the speaker can ask five or six members from a class of 20 students to work along with her in undertaking a task. If the participating class members are seated in different parts of the room, everyone will feel a greater part of the process than if the speaker demonstrates the task from the front of the classroom.

One student used this approach in demonstrating how to make decorative candles. She gave pieces of wax to about a third of the class. The others were able to observe and follow the process. In another instance, a speaker showed how to make favours for a wedding. She distributed supplies to everyone in the class. Class members worked with her from their desks. Sometimes, speakers walk around the room to display an object. At other times, they wait until the conclusion of the speech to display the object at close range or to pass it around the room. As mentioned above, speakers should never circulate visuals while delivering a speech.

If you take an object apart during a demonstration speech, be sure that you can put it back together again. Also, if you plan to construct an object in class, you should bring a finished product with you. The finished product (e.g., floral arrangement or transformer) enables you to retain a measure of credibility even if something goes wrong, and you do not need to worry if you do not have time to complete the process of construction.

Sometimes your models are life-size. On one occasion, a student brought a dummy to class to demonstrate resuscitation of cardiac patients. Your models can also be live. That is, sometimes students use other individuals in their demonstrations. If you use another person, you should give careful instructions to the individual prior to delivering the speech. The assistant should maintain a serious demeanour before the group. You can ask the person to carry out some action in slow motion (e.g., a self-defence or dance move) while you talk about the action. Assisting individuals should sit down when you no longer require their involvement. You should practise with the person prior to delivering the speech, so that the individual knows exactly what to do. Both the speaker and the person who is the visual prop should be visible to the audience. If someone assists with a demonstration, practice with that person in advance of the speaking event.

Chalkboards, Whiteboards, and Flannel Boards

To the extent possible, speakers should avoid the use of chalkboards. The writing is typically too light to be seen clearly; the board is often dirty; and few people have a clear legible writing style when they are rushing to put information on the board. Moreover, the speaker must turn away from the audience to write on the board. Whiteboards are easier to see, cleaner, and often mobile. Nonetheless, some of the same problems exist. Other kinds of visual supports—ones that can be prepared in advance—are usually superior. On occasion, however, speakers may want to record comments by audience members, or they may want to conclude a speech by writing a Web or e-mail address, telephone number, or postal address on the board. In those instances, the whiteboard works better than the chalkboard. If you do use a chalkboard or whiteboard, you should try to talk as you write and limit the amount of material placed on the board.

Another visual aid is the flannel board, often used by elementary school teachers. The flannel board offers possibilities to speakers who want to add or subtract material as they go along. One student employed the flannel board, for example, in giving a speech on dining etiquette. As she spoke, she placed felt representations of the tableware on the flannel board. The display was colourful, easy to see, and appropriate to the topic of the speech. On other occasions, a person could use a flannel board with felt cut-outs to explain moves in a football or hockey game or stages in constructing a model. Alternatively, the speaker could use this aid to show the locations of people at the time that some event occurred. In a speech on the subway bombings in London, for example, the speaker could show the movement of the perpetrators of violence from one part of the subway system to another.

As with other visual aids, speakers must be careful not to turn their backs to the audience in using the flannel board, and they must not fall silent as they position pieces on the board. An alternative to felt pieces and flannel boards could be magnetic pieces on a metallic board.

Flip Charts

Flip charts, or oversized writing pads, work well in locations that lack electricity or screens. Sometimes groups have retreats in isolated settings, or business people travel to remote locations for their annual meetings. The easels that hold flip charts are inexpensive and easy to construct on location.

If you plan to use a flip chart, check the paper supply prior to delivering the speech. In writing on the pad, use the upper third of the page and never include more than five lines on a sheet. Some flip charts have light blue grid lines that help to align writing. No line should include more than five or six words. Abbreviate long words and use acronyms whenever possible. Use dark-coloured markers; yellows and oranges do not work well. You can alternate colours as you make lists, but you should avoid using more than three colours on a page. Repeat and summarize the ideas as you record them.

If you prepare the materials in advance, you can put your speaking notes on the back of the pages. If you position the flip chart to the side and slightly in front of your speaking position, you can refer to the notes without anyone realizing that you are relying on them. When working in a spontaneous situation (e.g., recording reactions from audience members), you can tape the pages (torn from the chart) to walls for easy viewing. At the conclusion of the exercise, you can give audience members stickers to use in prioritizing the most important points.

Handouts

As noted earlier, speakers should avoid distributing visuals during a speech. If you want to use a handout, place copies (face down) on the desks or seats of audience members prior to speaking. Ask the group not to turn over the handout until you reach the point that you want to use it. Otherwise, they will read the handout while you are speaking. Alternatively, you can distribute the handout at the conclusion of the speech. You may want to colour-code handouts with multiple sections to facilitate reference to the handout. You can also include information that audiences can use to follow up on your ideas. When students give food demonstration speeches, for example, they often distribute copies of their recipes at the end of the speeches. When students give persuasive speeches, they distribute sheets with phone numbers, Web sites, and mailing addresses for information sources and advocacy groups.

Posters

Because few people are highly skilled at creating poster displays, poster presentations are rarely professional in appearance. Even when people have abilities in art, they may not know how to generate exhibition materials. Nonetheless, posters may be the only way to display certain kinds of information, especially if the setting does not include equipment. If you plan to prepare a poster, aim for a display with prominent lettering and graphics that are easy to see from the back of the room. Ask friends to tell you if they can see the lettering, graphics, or photographs from the distance that will separate speaker and the rear of the audience. Most of the time, the audience cannot see the materials on posters. Check the speaking location to ensure that you have a way to hang the poster; if not, bring tape to secure the poster to some surface. Easels for flip charts can also hold posters, but you need a clip to attach the poster to the flip chart.

Overhead and Data Projectors

In low-technology environments, transparencies offer a way to display major talking points and visual material—graphs, charts, and images. You have several alternatives for producing transparencies. (1) You can photocopy material onto a transparency, which you magnify through projection. (Photocopy machines require specific kinds of transparencies; so be sure that you purchase the right variety.) (2) You can scan an image from a book or other source into your computer and then print a copy on a transparency. (3) You can locate an image on the Internet or in your computer files, which you then print on a transparency. (4) You can download an image, make a hard copy, and then use a photocopier to transfer the image to a transparency. Do not copy charts or tables from books. They will rarely be sufficiently large or clear to use on a transparency. Redo the chart on the computer. Number your transparencies and store

Photo Gill Ferguson

them in plastic covers for protection. Business supply stores sell clear plastic sheaths with holes that allow transparencies to be stored in notebooks. Remove the transparencies from their jackets to display them. The plastic sheaths lower the visibility of the transparencies.

Prior to beginning your presentation, check the overhead projector to be sure that the light bulb works. (They give out on a regular basis, but most projectors have a storage place for spare bulbs.) Ensure that the images and print on the transparency can be easily seen when projected. As with other visuals, do not include more than five or six lines on a page or more than six words on a line. Use 30- to 36-point type font for headings, 24-point for subheadings, and 18-point for text. No more than one major idea should appear on a page. Eliminate extra words, including adjectives such as *the* and *an*. For aesthetic purposes, allow the same space at the bottom and top of the transparency. When making your presentation, you may want to cover part of the page in order to reveal points one by one. You can use an opaque sheet to cover points not yet addressed. Avoid looking down unless you are writing. If you do use a blank transparency to record impressions from the group, stay open to the audience when you are writing and speaking.

In high-technology environments, data projectors are the norm. To correct 'keystoning' on data projectors—a wedge-shaped image on the screen, wider at the top than at the bottom—focus the projector prior to beginning your presentation.

During the talk, maintain eye contact with your audience. Position yourself so that you can glance, from time to time, at the projected image—without turning your back to the audience. You may need to dim the lighting to ensure the visibility of projected images. You may also need to speak louder to overcome the noise from an overhead or data projector. When you are not discussing an image, turn off the overhead projector and raise the lighting level in the room. With data projectors, you can use the shutter function on the remote control to hide the image.

Slides

Slide projectors are useful when you do not have access to media consoles, laptop computers, or other sophisticated technologies. Before the advent of digital cameras and software programs, presenters often used slide projectors in speeches about geography, art, and history. When using this technology aid, you need to test the slides before the presentation to be sure that they are not upside down. You also need to know the speech extremely well, because the low lighting levels required in slide shows make it difficult to read note cards. You should practise the timing of your speech in advance so that you know how long to spend on each slide. Most slide projectors have remotes, which permit ongoing eye contact with the audience.

Audio and Videotapes

You should edit audio and video materials to facilitate ease of use. Edited clips prevent loss of time and unnecessary searching for places on a tape. Clips should be brief, often no more than 15 or 20 seconds in length. The length of the speech determines the number of clips and the amount of time that can be given to each clip. Short clips allow the speaker to illustrate specific points or behaviours, such as a negotiation between two people, a gymnastics move, or the dress adopted by trial lawyers. You can use audio recordings in a speech about the characteristics of rap music, bird calls, or noise pollution. Speakers should always check audio or video equipment prior to the speech.

Audio and video clips should supplement and clarify rather than merely repeat points in the speech. If you use music, do not play it too loud. Tell the audience the length of the recording and explain the rationale for using the clip prior to playing it. If you think that the video contains any objectionable material (e.g., old films often contain conversations with sexist and politically incorrect language), mention your reservations and explain why you chose to use the clip anyway. Remain attentive during the playing of the tape. Do not try to talk over a tape with audio content.

Presenting Statistics in Visual Formats

Visual formats make statistical data more comprehensible. This discussion introduces the reader to the most common ways of presenting statistics: simple breakdown tables, pie charts, complex breakdown tables, line graphs, bar graphs, and multiple line graphs.

Simple breakdown tables (Figure 7.1) and *pie charts* (Figure 7.2) show frequency distributions, such as how many people engage in the different forms of gambling (slot machines, horse betting, football pools, and lotteries) or how governments allocate the profits from gambling (e.g., percentages of the profits designated for sports, culture, research, charities, and other). The information in simple breakdown tables and pie charts appears in the form of numbers or percentages.

Complex breakdown tables, on the other hand, break down the information according to factors such as gender, age, region, and income bracket. A complex breakdown table might look at how many men and how many women engage in the different forms of gambling or the income levels of people who engage in the different forms of gambling. Figure 7.3 compares the activities preferred by female and male problem gamblers in Alberta in 1993.

Figure 7.1 Simple Breakdown Table

Source: Statistics Canada, figures for 2001. Cited on 'CBC News Indepth: Gambling', at: <www.cbc.ca/news/background/gambling/lotteries.html>. Accessed 7 July 2005.

Average Household Spending on Government Lotteries	
Newfoundland and Labrador	$249
Prince Edward Island	$231
Nova Scotia	$223
New Brunswick	$226
Quebec	$267
Ontario	$266
Manitoba	$258
Saskatchewan	$211
Alberta	$228
British Columbia	$257

Allocation of Lottery Profits in Ontario

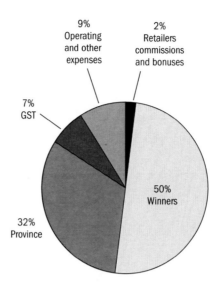

Figure 7.2 Pie Chart

Source: Statistics Canada, figures for 2001. Cited on 'CBC News Indepth: Gambling', at: <www.cbc.ca/news/background/gambling/lotteries.html>. Accessed 7 July 2005.

Sometimes, the speaker wants to show changes over time—that is, trends. Both *bar* and *line graphs* are useful formats for presenting trends. *Bar graphs* are more appropriate when you want to show changes over a short period of time or to focus on discrete points in time. Line graphs, on the other hand, are useful when you want to show the progress of changes over an extended period of time. With line graphs, you are more interested in the overall profile of the trend—the rise and fall of the line over time. Figure 7.4 depicts trends over time in net revenues from government-run gambling. With bar graphs, you focus on a few specific points in time. Figure 7.5 compares trends over

Figure 7.3 Complex Breakdown Table

Source: Adapted from 'Gambling in Canada', National Council of Welfare, at: <www.ncwcnbes.net/htmdocument/reportgambling/Gambling_e.htm#_Toc522256759>. Accessed 7 July 2005.

Problem Gambling in Alberta, 1993		
Percentage Who Ever Bet on Activity	*Current Female Problem Gamblers (%)*	*Current Male Problem Gamblers (%)*
Instant or scratch tickets	92	88
Lotto-type games	78	86
Bingo	76	24
Raffles and fundraising tickets	70	74
Video lottery terminals	41	46
Card games with family or friends	41	64
Break-open, pull-tab, Nevada tickets	41	40
Local casinos	37	46

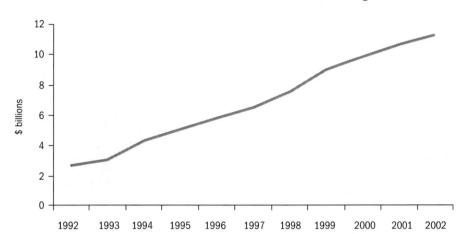

Net Revenues from Government-Run Gambling

Figure 7.4 Line Graph

Source: Adapted from Statistics Canada, 'Perspectives on Labour and Income: Fact Sheet on Gambling', at: <www. statcan.ca/english/studies/ 75-001/ 00403/fs-fi_200304_ 01_ a.pdf>, p. 2. Accessed 7 July 2005.

time in the following gambling activities: lotteries, sports lotteries, casinos, and horse betting.

You can use multiple line graphs to compare trends between or among two or more sets of data. Figure 7.6, for example, compares net revenues from different types of government-run gambling.

Another type of graphic representation is the pictograph. Pictographs use images of objects to show numbers and percentages in bar graphs. The software program Excel has a number of interesting examples of pictographs. One pictograph shows the levels of antioxidant activity in different fruits and vegetables. The bar graphs appear in the colours of the fruits and vegetables that they depict (blue for blueberries, green for spinach, red for strawberries, etc.). A bar graph that shows the popularity of chili pepper consumption uses four chili peppers to represent 40 per cent and seven chili pep-

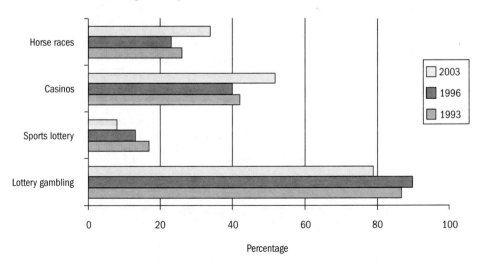

Gambling Activity in British Columbia: Trends over Time

Figure 7.5 Bar Graph

Source: Based on British Columbia Problem Gambling Prevalence Study, Final Report, British Columbia Ministry of Public Safety and Solicitor General, 12 Mar. 2003. At: <www.bcresponsiblegambling.ca/ responsible/bcprobgambstudy.pdf>. Accessed 7 July 2005.

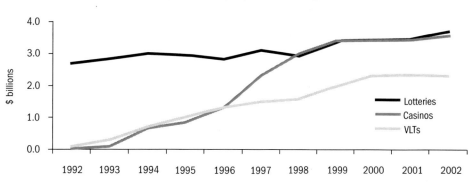

**Net Revenues from Different Types
of Government-Run Gambling**

Figure 7.6 Multiple Line Graph

Source: Adapted from Statistics Canada, 'Perspectives on Labour and Income: Fact Sheet on Gambling', at: <www.statcan.ca/english/studies/75-001/00403/fs-fi_200304_01_a.pdf>, p. 2. Accessed 7 July 2005.

pers to represent 70 per cent. In the third example, dollar bills substitute for the bar graphs. The dollar bills represent the rates charged by different companies for 15-minute weekday calls from New York to Los Angeles.[3]

When presenting statistics in a speech, remember that the audience must be able to grasp and understand the material within the time frame of your discussion. In a short non-technical speech, complex breakdown tables present too much information. In a speech delivered to a group of experts or business people, on the other hand, the situation may be different. You should use strong colours for your line, bar, and pie graphs—sufficiently dark to be seen easily. Present the lines and bars in different colours for maximum clarity and effectiveness. Avoid too many lines, too much clutter, and too many different colours. Include only the most necessary data and clearly label axes and data lines on a graph. Make the bars wider than the spaces that divide them.

PowerPoint and Other Computer-Generated Presentations

In the corporate world, the standard for computer-assisted presentations is high. Communication staff members, trained in graphics and design, create most of these presentations for higher-level managers and executives. They put together 'decks' that are highly professional in appearance, and organizational members come to expect quality in the presentations. An ill-prepared or technologically unsophisticated presentation can create major credibility problems for the speaker. And sometimes, of course, technological difficulties can pose what seem to be insurmountable problems. As Box 7.4 indicates, it is always important to be well-prepared.

The same credibility challenges exist when consultants or other outsiders come into the organization to present their ideas. They have to meet the standards of the organization. Project proposals, sales talks, and debriefings are typical instances where presenters must demonstrate their ability to deliver finely honed and technologically sophisticated presentations. These presentations most often employ PowerPoint, Corel, AppleWorks, or other software programs.

Different software programs work in different ways, and 'help' files come with the software. To elaborate on the details of one out of many software choices would be

---

Box 7.3 Dealing with Disaster: Be Prepared

I recently had the opportunity to make a presentation at a national academic conference. I diligently prepared my PowerPoint presentation and practised my comments for each slide. The time arrived, and I began my presentation before a room filled with 40–50 of my peers, college faculty from around North America.

Before I finished with the third slide (of 24), the power to the building went out, plunging everyone into near-darkness. After waiting several minutes to see if the power would return (it didn't), I decided to continue with my presentation . . . without the PowerPoint. My laptop computer was on battery power, but I couldn't project the slides onto the screen without power to the projector. I thought about turning my computer around so the audience could see the screen, but I realized it would be too small to be seen by anyone but those who were sitting right in front of it. I panicked!

But I knew that, despite the power outage, we had a schedule to keep; so I abandoned the laptop, left the safety of the lectern to stand closer to the audience, and delivered my presentation the 'old-fashioned way', without technology . . . and in the near-dark.

Luckily, I had prepared *very* well for the presentation and had provided participants with a folder of handouts, including a handout of my original PowerPoint presentation. I have since discovered that session evaluations showed that my presentation was one of the best received of the entire conference (even those delivered in rooms with lighting!). It pays to be prepared for the unexpected.

Desirée Devereaux

---

inappropriate. Also the programs are updated on a regular basis. Nonetheless, certain principles apply in using all of the programs; and studies have found that user guides can be as good as hands-on training in learning how to use the presentation software.[4]

The following discussion includes suggestions related to mixed media presentations, aesthetic considerations, considerations related to continuity, use of contrast and colours, typeface and font size, grammar and structure, formatting, and presentation techniques.

Mixed Media Presentations

PowerPoint, Corel, AppleWorks, and other software programs allow speakers to create integrated presentations, involving a mix of text, visual images, and audio content. The programs enable the users to generate charts, graphs, and tables with the click of the mouse. With a few key strokes, they can download images or video clips from the Internet, a digital camera, or camcorder. They can scan materials from books into the computer for download, and they can use programs such as PhotoShop to enhance the quality of the images.

These audio and visual aids add colour and energy to presentations. In a speech on feng shui (the ancient Chinese art of achieving balance in one's environment), for example, a speaker can display graphs that show the growing popularity of this approach to home construction and design. Video clips can demonstrate options in room layouts and ways of arranging furniture and plants. Audio clips can include testimonials from individuals who have had positive experiences with feng shui. In a similar way, a PowerPoint presentation on cross-cultural communication could include text on business etiquette, video clips showing non-verbal transgressions, and audio clips involving conversations between inept communicators.

Aesthetic Considerations

To achieve an aesthetically pleasing presentation, speakers should adhere to a visual theme. On my Web site, I use a Ferguson plaid to represent my company. My Power-Point presentations apply the same theme. You can also establish a common look within the presentation by repeating colours, fonts, shapes, and lines of similar width.

Computer-generated presentations allow for many special effects. While variety is interesting, some novice users overdo the effects. You do not want too many flying images, clanging shutters, or loud zips to distract the listeners. Aim for professionalism rather than entertainment. Use clip art and photographs to add interest to the presentation. Do not be tempted, however, to clutter the slide with an excessive number of visuals. When I first learned to use PowerPoint, I used two or three pieces of clip art on every slide. In retrospect, it was far too much.

Considerations Related to Continuity

To achieve continuity in the presentation, you can continue the wallpaper, which appears as background on the introductory slide, as a sidebar on all subsequent slides. You can also repeat an icon or visual image on slides that talk about the same concept. In a presentation on interview strategies, for example, several slides may discuss techniques for identifying likely employers. The next set of slides may talk about strategies for getting an interview. The third set of slides may talk about dress codes. And the final set of slides may address interview strategies. A new visual image will introduce each new idea cluster: a computer monitor to represent research, telephone for discussion of securing the interview, item of clothing for dress codes, and two people interacting for interview strategies. The audience can only see one slide at a time; consequently, it is easy to lose a sense of organization when attending a lengthy PowerPoint presentation.

Use of Contrast and Colours

Presentations require contrast—either a light font on a dark background or a dark font on a light background. White typeface works well against deep purple or dark blue backgrounds, and dark blue typeface looks nice against a yellow background. In one PowerPoint presentation, I use gold headings and white text against a green backdrop. A swath of purple on each page adds a splash of extra colour without overwhelming the reader. For simplicity and clarity, you can use white against black or black against white, although audiences typically prefer colour. People respond emotionally to colours, and some studies show that they learn better from presentations that employ colour.[5] Avoid backgrounds with patterns or detail that could distract. You should not use more than three or four colours in a presentation.

Typeface and Font Size

Users of computer-generated software presentation packages have a choice of *serif* or *sans serif* typefaces. Serif typefaces have short lines or curls at the tips of letters. Examples include Times, Garamond, and Palatino Linotype. Sans serif typefaces have letters with straight lines. With electronic projection, sans serif typefaces are more readable than serif typefaces. The most common varieties are Arial, Verdana, and Tahoma. They will work with every kind of printer and operating system. Some designers, who say that variety is desirable, suggest using sans serif typeface for headings and serif typeface for text.

Whatever the eventual choice on font size, presenters should avoid highly ornate fonts such as Brush Script MT and Gigi, which are difficult to read; fonts such as Broadway and Audience, which are too wide and dark for presentations; and Agency FB, which is a bit anorexic and compressed. Speakers should also avoid too much variety in typefaces (no more than two or three) and font sizes. Most experts agree that you should use a mix of upper- and lower-case letters. Upper case by itself is hard to read.

Most experts say that the font size should never go below 14 points. The following recommendation appears often in discussions related to formatting of computer presentations: 36 points for major headings, 24 points for subheadings, and 18 points for text. The appropriate size of font depends, in large measure, on the typeface, the distance between speaker and audience, and whether or not boldface is used. Some typefaces are larger or more readable than others, even when they indicate a smaller font size. The space consumed by words written in different typefaces can vary dramatically.

Grammar and Structure

Each slide should support a single idea, such as the spread of HIV among different demographic groups, actions to take in the event of fire, or rules for conducting business in Latin America.

Too often, PowerPoint presentations lose their integrity by sloppy use of grammar. Presenters mix phrases and sentences on the same slide, or they have a hodge-podge of structures that are not syntactically parallel. The following list illustrates both of these problems:

- Running a business without a goal
- Wants profits more than clients
- Lost a large percentage of the business
- In trouble with shareholders and customers
- He's ready to give up.

In the above example, the speaker combines a gerund phrase (*running a business*) with phrases beginning with a present tense verb (*wants profits more than clients*) and a past tense verb (*lost all perspective*). Then she uses a prepositional phrase (*in trouble with shareholders and customers*) and ends with a sentence (*He's ready to give up.*). Even though one central thought is probably present on this slide, the presentation of the ideas creates confusion. When the grammatical structures keep shifting, you have to work harder to figure out what the person is saying.

Aim for parallel sentence structures. You might, for example, begin each bullet with an infinitive, as in the following case:

- To promote the rights of children

- To encourage new child abuse legislation
- To enforce existing laws to protect children.

A second example of parallel structure would be verbal phrases used as nouns:

- Answering the telephone
- Responding to walk-in clients
- Doing the paperwork.

Alternatively, you could use a series of phrases:

- European reactions to war in Iraq
- Domestic reactions to war in Iraq
- Latin American reactions to war in Iraq.

A final example would be the following:

- Spread of HIV in African and Caribbean countries
- Spread of HIV among heterosexuals
- Growing number of women with HIV.

To the extent possible, use phrases rather than sentences. Avoid unnecessary words such as *the*, *a*, or *an*. If you use sentences, they should be short, as in the following example:

Desirable Behaviours in the Event of Fire
- Identify the nearest exit.
- Avoid elevators.
- Do not panic.
- Walk; do not run.
- Avoid pushing and shoving others.

Formatting

Do not try to crowd too much on any slide. Allow sufficient 'white space'—space that does not contain text or visuals. Begin the text at approximately the same place on each slide. Allow the same amount of room on the top and bottom of the slide. Software programs such as PowerPoint assist with this process, because they do not allow you to go below a certain point on the slide.

Use bullets to designate the different points. Note that you always capitalize the first word in a bullet. Place a period at the end of sentences. As with flip charts, you should limit the material to five or six lines on a slide and should not exceed 40 characters on a line.

Presentation Techniques

Most software programs allow you to introduce one point at a time, which works well with certain kinds of content. With cartoons, for example, you can introduce one frame at a time. You can progressively add content to bar, line, or pie graphs in the same fashion.

When delivering from PowerPoint, stand to the side of the screen so that you do not block the view of your audience. Refer as necessary to the screen but do not depend too much on it. Do not peer down at your laptop computer screen. Keep yourself open to your audience and use a remote to change the slides. Some remotes have a shutter device that allows you to hide the image while you are talking about some other point. When you are ready to continue, you can renew the image on the screen by pressing the button a second time. If you require additional note cards for quotations or amplification of points on the screen, limit the number of cards and learn the material prior to presenting. Box 7.5 presents a review of tips for PowerPoint presentations.

In a formal business presentation, delivered to an executive audience, the speaker typically previews the major points to be covered but avoids displaying a detailed outline of the presentation. In a classroom lecture, on the other hand, students expect and need the notes for purposes of studying for examinations. So instructors present a detailed outline of what they will cover during the lecture. Even in that situation, however, speakers are wise to distribute the materials *after* the lecture or presentation. When audience members have a complete set of notes, they do not bother to listen so closely. Some leave the classroom mentally; others walk out the door. The remaining listeners may read the notes rather than listen to the more detailed explanations, reducing their attention to important supplementary material.

In that situation, the two media (aural and visual) compete against, rather than complement, each other. A rule of television production is that a picture should never repeat the script. The two should always work in concert with each other. That same principle applies to the use of visuals in speaking contexts. Visual aids (also audio) should complement and highlight, rather than repeat, the content of a spoken presentation.

Box 7.4 Tips for Using PowerPoint

- Use mixed media (audio and clip art) to add interest.
- Achieve a common look by repeating colours, fonts, shapes, and lines.
- Acquire continuity by repeating icons on slides that pertain to the same idea cluster.
- Limit the number of icons on any slide.
- Use contrasting colours.
- Avoid backgrounds with patterns or excessive detail.
- Avoid distracting noises—clanging and banging of shutters.
- Use sans serif typefaces; avoid highly ornate fonts.
- Keep font size between 18 and 36 points.
- Each slide should support a single idea.
- Limit the material to 5 or 6 lines on a slide.
- Do not exceed 40 characters on a line.
- Don't mix sentences and phrases on the same slide.
- Use parallel grammatical structures.
- Allow sufficient white space on slides.
- Use bullets to designate different points.
- When presenting, stand to the side of the screen; stay open to audience.
- Refer to the screen but maintain eye contact with your audience.
- Use a remote to change the slides.
- Use the shutter device to hide an image and talk about the ideas.

Bring backup copies of your presentation—on CD and hard drive—to your speaking event. Some speakers bring an extra copy of their presentations on transparencies; however, updating the transparencies on a regular basis can be costly.

A final suggestion is to take principles of audience adaptation into account in your presentation. Involve the audience to the extent possible. You can, for example, include photographs of group members among your slides. You can invite comments from the audience or questions at appropriate points during or after the presentation.

Questions for Discussion

1. How important are visual supports to you as an audience member? Do they enhance your learning?
2. Have you ever had a bad experience using a visual aid in an oral presentation? Discuss your experiences.
3. What do you like about PowerPoint and other computer-assisted presentations? What do you dislike about these presentations? Describe one that you found to be very effective. How was it different from one that you found to be ineffective?
4. Discuss some ethical considerations related to the use of visual supports. Refer to Box 7.1 that accompanies the chapter.

Appendix: PowerPoint Presentation

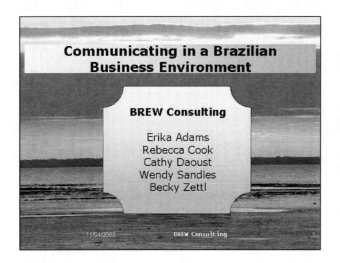

Communicating in a Brazilian Business Environment

BREW Consulting

Erika Adams
Rebecca Cook
Cathy Daoust
Wendy Sandles
Becky Zettl

11/04/2003   BREW Consulting   1

Agenda

10:00 – 10:10	Welcome, introduction, & overview
10:10 – 10:25	Warm-up: Brazilian Trivia
10:25 – 10:35	Brazilian society and people
10:35 – 10:45	Your experience
10:45 – 11:00	Corporate culture
11:00 – 11:15	Storytelling
11:15 – 11:25	Business and corporate practices
11:25 – 11:35	Saúde pausa (health break)
11:35 – 11:55	Negotiation and role of expediters
11:55 – 12:05	Nonverbal interactions
12:05 – 12:20	Role playing
12:20 – 12:30	Fish bowl
12:30 – 12:40	Successful entertaining
12:40 – 12:50	Quiz and recap

11/04/2003   BREW Consulting   2

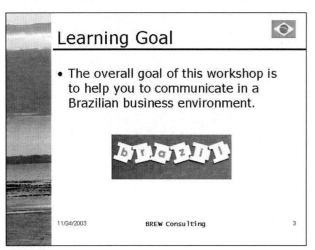

Learning Goal

- The overall goal of this workshop is to help you to communicate in a Brazilian business environment.

11/04/2003   BREW Consulting   3

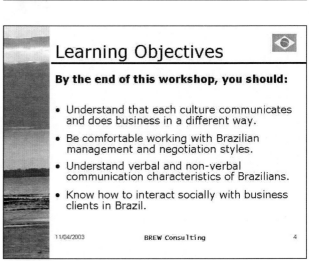

Learning Objectives

By the end of this workshop, you should:

- Understand that each culture communicates and does business in a different way.
- Be comfortable working with Brazilian management and negotiation styles.
- Understand verbal and non-verbal communication characteristics of Brazilians.
- Know how to interact socially with business clients in Brazil.

11/04/2003   BREW Consulting   4

Let's PLAY

11/04/2003   BREW Consulting   5

brazilian TRIVIA

11/04/2003   BREW Consulting   6

Brazilian Society

- Portuguese - national language

- Dominant religion - Roman Catholic

- Personal values – family, education, & achieving socioeconomic status

11/04/2003   BREW Consulting   7

Brazilian People

- Friendly, free-spirited, and warm

- Passionate and opinionated

- Expressive and creative

- Risk-oriented

- Gregarious

11/04/2003   BREW Consulting   8

Your Experience

Have you had an interesting cultural experience in another country?

Tell us about it.

11/04/2003   BREW Consulting   9

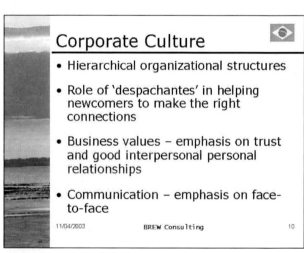

Corporate Culture

- Hierarchical organizational structures

- Role of 'despachantes' in helping newcomers to make the right connections

- Business values – emphasis on trust and good interpersonal personal relationships

- Communication – emphasis on face-to-face

11/04/2003   BREW Consulting   10

Storytelling

Sailing through the Brazilian business style

11/04/2003   BREW Consulting   11

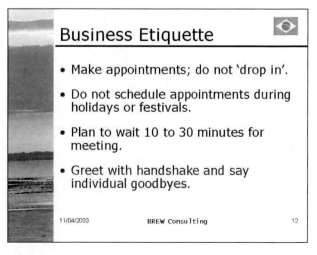

Business Etiquette

- Make appointments; do not 'drop in'.

- Do not schedule appointments during holidays or festivals.

- Plan to wait 10 to 30 minutes for meeting.

- Greet with handshake and say individual goodbyes.

11/04/2003   BREW Consulting   12

Corporate Gift Giving

- Present gifts at social, not business, occasions.

- Options include good quality whiskey, wine, coffee table books, and name-brand pens.

- Gifts for children of business associates are also appropriate.

11/04/2003   BREW Consulting   13

Saude Pausa

Enjoy your brigadeiros!!

- Sweets made with condensed milk and chocolate

- Named after Brigadeiro Eduardo Gomes, an Air Force commander from the 1940s

11/04/2003   BREW Consulting   14

Negotiation Styles

North Americans adopt a direct approach to negotiations.

What is the most common negotiation style in Brazil?

11/04/2003   BREW Consulting   15

Negotiations

- North Americans are more direct; Brazilians are more wordy.

- Brazilians use personal touch to break down barriers.

- Trust comes before negotiations.

11/04/2003   BREW Consulting   16

The Nitty-Gritty

- 'Hype' & casual conversation at onset
- Hard negotiation style
- Emergence of facts over time
- Written agreements at conclusion
- Assistance with contract issues by local accountants and lawyers

11/04/2003   BREW Consulting   17

The Role of Expediters

- Practice of bribery encouraged by bureaucratic inertia
- 'Expediters' hired by multinationals to 'grease the wheels'
- Bribery or 'jeitinho' seen as acceptable

11/04/2003   BREW Consulting   18

Nonverbal Interactions

Body Language

- Physical contact—part of everyday communication
- Touching—sign of friendship and concern
- Eye contact—more intense than in Canada

11/04/2003   BREW Consulting   19

Nonverbal Interactions

Dress
- <u>For men</u>:
  Conservative dark suits, shirts, and ties
- <u>For women</u>:
  Feminine, more 'sexy' than North America
- <u>For both</u>:
  Overall stylish appearance
  Stylish, polished, and well-kept shoes

11/04/2003   BREW Consulting   20

Role Playing

Your experience and mine

11/04/2003   BREW Consulting   21

Verbal Interactions

Brazilians:
- Speak more loudly than Canadians.
- Accept interruptions.
- Are comfortable with verbal confrontation.
- Respond quickly.
- Provide many details when offering info.
- Treat others with courtesy.

11/04/2003   BREW Consulting   22

Verbal Interactions

Courtesies include:

- Summarizing discussion for those who cannot keep up.

- Waiting for less fluent speakers to add their comments.

11/04/2003   BREW Consulting   23

Fish Bowl

'Muddy Waters'

11/04/2003   BREW Consulting   24

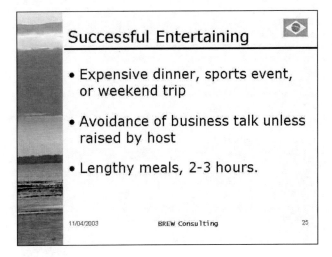

Successful Entertaining

- Expensive dinner, sports event, or weekend trip

- Avoidance of business talk unless raised by host

- Lengthy meals, 2-3 hours.

11/04/2003   BREW Consulting   25

Dining at a Brazilian Home

- Appreciate the invitation—an honor.

- Send flowers before or after visiting.

- Use good dining etiquette.

- Bring a gift.

11/04/2003   BREW Consulting   26

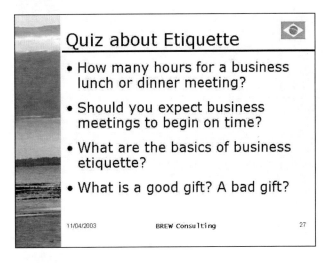

Quiz about Etiquette

- How many hours for a business lunch or dinner meeting?

- Should you expect business meetings to begin on time?

- What are the basics of business etiquette?

- What is a good gift? A bad gift?

11/04/2003   BREW Consulting   27

Recap

This seminar provided the knowledge to better understand and interact with Brazilians in a business environment.

Images: Gill Ferguson, Bruno & Maristela Lepage, Joe Ferguson

11/04/2003   BREW Consulting   28

Reprinted by permission of the authors.

CHAPTER EIGHT

Researching and Supporting Your Ideas

The Informative Speech

Preparing the Informative Speech

The goal of this speech (5-6 minutes in length) is to inform the audience how to do or to make something—in other words, to demonstrate an activity or process—or to prepare an informative speech of a non-demonstrative nature. To assist in achieving your goals, you will use visual aids or props, either animate or inanimate. An outline (prepared in standard format) and at least three bibliographic sources are required. The emphasis in evalu- ating this assignment will be on the quality of your research, the extent to which you have used credible supports for your ideas, and the effectiveness of your visual aids (see Chapter 7). You should continue to apply principles acquired in earlier chap- ters, including the basic components of speechmaking, audi- ence adaptation, and extemporaneous delivery.

Learning Objectives
- To learn about different kinds of informative speeches.
- To learn how to prepare an informative speech.

The purpose of all informative speaking is to impart memorable information that expands and reinforces the knowledge base of the listener. The informative speech may describe a process or procedure; explain an idea or concept; or talk about a person, place, or event.

Topics to be reviewed in this chapter include taking audience adaptation into account in choosing your topic, writing purpose statements and thesis statements, organ- izing your speech, writing preview statements, writing introductions and conclusions, and delivering extemporaneously. The following new concepts will allow you to

Photo Gill Ferguson

continue expanding your knowledge base: researching your topic, supporting your ideas, and using visual aids. The major headings of this chapter draw the reader to consider types of informative speaking, steps to be followed in preparing an informative speech, and a review of basic structural elements in speeches to inform.

Different Types of Informative Speeches

A speech of demonstration describes a *process or procedure*. That is, it gives instruction on how to do or make something, such as how to prepare maple syrup muffins, build a home radio receiver, or use martial art techniques to protect oneself in the event of an assault. Other examples of demonstrative topics include how to see Australia on a budget, recognize signs of drug abuse in family members, or build a positive relationship with a partner. In other words, speeches of demonstration give instruction on how to do or make something. These instructional talks identify a series of steps that lead to a desired result. In the above examples, the desired results could be the following: muffins, a radio receiver, a response set, an inexpensive trip to Australia, the ability to identify drug abuse in family members, and a positive relationship with one's partner.

Informative speeches can explain abstract *ideas or concepts*, such as time warp or conspiracy theories, climate change, or monetary policies. Instructors in college and university classrooms lecture on such theoretical constructs, as do many featured speakers asked to share their expertise. Alternatively, an informative speech can discuss less theoretical ideas such as the history of modern comic strip characters, backup safety features in aircraft, activities of the Canadian Space Agency, the legacy of rap music, or the threat posed by bacterial infections in hospitals. Even when people lecture on abstract and theoretical concepts, however, they should use concrete language and examples.

Informative speeches can also introduce the audience to *people, places, and events*—historical or contemporary. A speaker could talk, for example, about a historical figure such as Louis Riel or a historical event such as the Northwest Rebellion of 1885. Alternatively, informative speeches can look at contemporary figures such as René Lévesque or events such as the patriation of Canada's Constitution or the creation of Nunavut. Some topics, such as the ongoing debate in Quebec over separation, have deep roots in history. You may want to bring historical perspectives to bear on a discussion of these people and events. Informative speeches can also discuss places such as the rain forests of Brazil, the disappearance of old-growth forests in Canada, the incredible diversity of life on the floor of the ocean, or the barren beauty of Canada's Far North.

The following discussion is organized around the sequence of steps to be taken in preparing an informative speech: (1) choosing your topic; (2) framing a purpose statement; (3) writing a thesis statement; (4) researching your speech; (5) identifying points of possible confusion; (6) choosing an organizational pattern; (7) developing an outline; (8) writing a preview statement; (9) writing an introduction; (10) developing your outline with supporting materials; (11) linking the parts of your speech; (12) adding interest with visual aids; and (13) concluding your speech.

Step 1: Choosing Your Topic

When planning your informative speech, you should think back to what you learned in your readings on audience adaptation. In choosing a topic, for example, you should consider audience interests and levels of knowledge on the topic.

Examples of process-oriented topics that have worked well to stimulate the interest of student audiences include how to choose an imaginative gift for your partner, make decorative candles or dried floral arrangements, prepare a table centrepiece for parties, interpret dreams, read someone's palm, or travel lightly in foreign countries. One of my students brought a backpack to class, filled with clothes and travel items. As she removed the items from the backpack, one by one, she talked about the purpose of each item and the ways in which she had economized on space by choosing that particular item.

If the topics are humorous in nature, students may wear special clothing that establishes a mood. One student gave a speech on how to listen to seventies music. He came to class in retro clothes—bell-bottom pants, wide tie, and loud shirt that he had purchased at a second-hand clothing store. He set up an old phonograph player, along with records from the 1970s, in the front of the classroom. His demonstration speech involved detailing the steps required to listen effectively to music from the 1970s.

Students often adapt to the season by selecting topics with holiday themes. When students present demonstration speeches in February, the themes sometimes relate to Valentine's Day. They may talk about how to prepare homemade Valentine candies or cookies for their friends or how to plan for the perfect Valentine evening. One student, dressed as Cupid, spoke about ideas for how to meet and interact with members of the opposite sex. Another spoke on how to identify potential problem dates.

Other popular topics relate to the seasons. With winter close at hand, students will choose demonstration topics that relate to winter sports—skiing, snowboarding, hockey, or figure skating. In the fall, students select topics such as how to prepare for an outdoor camping trip, decorate apartments for Halloween parties, or make apple cider. In the spring, students give speeches on how to establish an herb garden, take creative approaches to looking for summer employment, or guard against pickpockets when travelling abroad. Students enrolled in summer classes prepare demonstration speeches on topics such as hiking, rock climbing, boating, or activities that can be enjoyed on rainy days at the cottage.

Some of the most popular speeches cater to the limited budgets of students: how to plan a low-budget trip to the Caribbean for winter break, prepare an inexpensive but attractive meal for two, shop for bargains at clothing stores, or decorate one's apartment on a shoestring budget.

For students who choose to inform audiences about ideas, people, places, and events, the choices are endless. They might educate their listeners on alternative sources of fuel, human rights abuses in Sudan, the dangers of e-coli bacteria, the proliferation of radio talk shows, peacemakers in the twenty-first century, or the history and origins of earthquakes. The criteria for topic selection are the same as with more process-oriented speeches. Speakers must choose topics with audience interests in mind, and they must gear the development of the speeches to the knowledge levels of listeners.

To test the topic, you should ask, 'What will the audience learn from the speech?' After choosing a topic, you must determine levels of knowledge in audience members. How much does the audience know about the topic? If you assume too little knowledge, you risk boring your audience with information that they already know. But if you judge their level of knowledge to be too high, you may lose them. Will you need to define some terms? Will the audience understand specialized language or jargon specific to this topic area? You should also ask, 'What are the benefits of listening to the speech?' This reason to listen should be articulated when you write the introduction to the speech.

In developing the speech, you should also take audience demographics and psychographics (beliefs, attitudes, and values) into account. If your audience is young and female, use examples that would appeal to a young, female audience. If you are delivering the speech in Thunder Bay, choose examples to which audiences in northern Ontario can relate. Refer to local people and events.

Please refer to Chapter 5 on audience analysis and adaptation for a review of these concepts. Chapter 13 will explore the demands of informative speaking in a classroom context, including the challenges of making a small-group presentation.

Step 2: Framing Your Purpose Statement

After choosing a topic area, you have to decide on a purpose for your speech. The following examples constitute *purpose statements* for selected topics:

- To educate the audience on how to recognize signs of drug abuse in family members.
- To instruct the audience on how to build a home radio receiver.
- To introduce the audience to the benefits of moderate exercise.
- To describe the origins of some modern comic strip characters.
- To explain the process for preparing maple syrup muffins.
- To educate the audience on the threat posed by bacterial infections in hospitals.
- To explain why the Sahara Desert is disappearing.

Notice that the purpose statements are specific, making the desired outcomes obvious. At the conclusion of a successful informative speech, the audience will know more about some process, person, idea, place, or event. Informative speeches increase the knowledge of listeners; they result in cognitive learning. Sometimes you will want to revise your purpose statement after conducting in-depth research on the topic. However, you should have some purpose in mind when you begin your research, even if that purpose later shrinks, expands, or changes in focus.

Step 3: Writing Your Thesis Statement

As we discussed in Chapter 4, *thesis statements* encapsulate the major idea of a speech. Every other point in the speech should relate back to—and support—the thesis statement. Thesis statements can be quite detailed or more general in thrust, as in the following instances:

- Signs of drug abuse can be physical, emotional, or social in nature.
- Building a home radio receiver is fun and easy.
- Tai Chi is a low-impact exercise with high benefits.
- Modern comic strip characters owe their origins to such superheroes as Superman, Captain Marvel, and Wonder Woman.
- Maple syrup muffins are popular, healthy, and easy to prepare.
- Antibiotic-resistant bacteria are thriving and multiplying in Canadian hospitals.
- Recent scientific studies have indicated that the Sahara Desert may be retreating.

Step 4: Researching Your Speech

Once you have decided on the topic and tentative purpose and thesis statements for your informative speech, you must research the topic. You have a number of sources to which you can go—your own knowledge and background, interviews with others who have had first-hand experiences with the subject matter, and secondary sources available in the library and on the Internet. After researching the topic, you may decide to modify your purpose and thesis statements.

Personal Experience

One source of information is your own background. Your experience can make you an expert. In the example below, the student sought to bolster her credibility by pointing to her personal experience with the topic:

> I have consulted numerous government reports, newspaper articles, and Web sites dedicated to aiding those who live with debilitating disorders and disease. Many of these sources recommend the use of marijuana to alleviate the effects of these disorders and diseases. However, none of my library research gave me the insights I gained by watching my grandmother battle throat cancer. I saw first-hand the positive effects of medicinal marijuana. The cancer left my grandmother unable to eat, forcing the doctors to put a feeding tube into her stomach so that she could get the nutrients she needed to survive. Eventually the doctor offered medicinal marijuana to increase her appetite and help with the side effects of the chemotherapy. After my grandmother began to use the marijuana, the difference was remarkable. She was able to eat small amounts of food, and the side effects of the chemo became manageable. She found some relief and comfort for her final weeks.[1]

When you combine your own knowledge with information acquired from other sources, you gain credibility with your audience. Do not make the mistake, however, of relying totally on your own experience. You will increase your credibility if you appear knowledgeable *and* objective, able to bring multiple points of view to bear on the topic.

First-hand Experiences of Others

To adapt your topic to your local audience, you will need to include some local sources. Some of the best sources are experts in your city, whose views are available to you through interviews. Assume, for a moment, that you would like to speak on the topic of crisis help lines. The best places to begin your search for information are local help centres that assist victims of violence and people suffering from depression or contemplating suicide. You can find these centres listed in the Yellow Pages of phone books, as well as on the Internet. Not only can these organizations provide first-hand information to you, but they can also direct you to other sources of information.

Similarly, if you want to speak on the rising cost of university tuition, you might go to someone in your university administration or to a provincial political figure. For anecdotal evidence, you can talk with other university students. Good sources of information on conflict resolution are mediation centres. You can supplement these first-hand sources with newspaper and magazine articles, Internet sources, and recent books on the topic.

A few tips on interviewing will help you to obtain the information that you require. Identify the right people to interview. Plan sufficiently in advance to obtain appointments with these individuals, and if possible, go directly to their offices to make the appointment. Some people are extremely busy, and they will not be able to grant last-minute interviews. Do not rule out people you know. They are often the most accessible and interested in helping you.

Employees of non-profit organizations are usually most willing to grant interviews. They serve the public interest and depend on the goodwill of the community to sustain their organizations. Politicians are generally responsive to members of their constituency; and if they cannot meet personally with you, a staff member will usually try to assist you. Like members of non-profit organizations and politicians, government employees serve the public interest. Their job is to respond to your needs. Consequently, someone usually will agree to speak with you in an interview situation. Of course, the higher you go in an organization, the less likely you are to be able to meet with the executives, because their schedules are often decided well in advance.

Business executives and employees may be more difficult to access than public managers and employees, especially on short notice. Their first obligations are to shareholders and clients. Nonetheless, most forward-looking organizations assume a responsive posture and give support to local initiatives. So your chances of gaining co-operation from these companies are greater than your chances with less civic-minded firms. Your chances of getting an interview (with public- or private-sector employees and leaders) are greatest if you are seeking information on an uncontroversial topic.

Conduct as much library or Internet research as possible before the interview and prepare your questions in advance of the meeting. Open-ended questions such as 'What are the most important aims of this program?' are better than questions that call for 'yes' or 'no' answers. Questions to which you can find answers on the Web or in the library should not appear in an interview. Also avoid expressing your personal opinion on the topic. Remember that the purpose of the interview is to access the knowledge and insights of the other person. When you voice your own opinions, you consume valuable interview time; and you risk alienating the interviewee who does not share your point of view. Avoid leading questions such as 'You do believe that we should have a department of homeland security, don't you?' or hostile questions such as 'Don't you think that your organization has gone a bit overboard with its cuts to arts programs?' If you decide to ask more controversial questions, save them for the latter part of the interview, after you have covered less controversial areas. You do not want your interview to end before you have obtained a significant part of the required information.

To the extent possible, you should frame controversial questions in a neutral way. Assuming that you are interviewing the local police chief about several recent deaths from police use of Taser guns, you might introduce your questions in this way: 'The media has reported 50 deaths in the United States and Canada from Taser guns. Journalists report that stun guns appear to have the most deadly effects on individuals who are in a weakened physical state or under the influence of drugs. How accurate is this statement, in your opinion?' A follow-up question on the topic of Taser guns could ask about the reasons for using the guns: 'I understand that the police have adopted the use of Tasers to protect both the individual and the police officers involved in difficult arrests. Could you describe a typical situation in which you might decide to use a Taser rather than some other method of subduing the person.' You could also ask, 'What were the alternatives to the stun guns in these particular cases?' Even though the subject is highly sensitive (as well as controversial), the calm, reasoned approach and the neutrality of the phrasing create the possibility that the police chief will respond to the question.

Had you worded the question in the following way, the interviewee would probably have bolted: 'I've read about two deaths in the last two weeks from the police shooting victims with Taser guns. Two deaths in two weeks. That's pretty scary. Don't you think that you should reconsider your position on this issue?' The interviewer has committed several offences. She has used loaded language (*police shooting victims*, *scary*). She has also expressed a personal opinion: 'That's pretty scary.' Finally, she has asked a leading question: 'Don't you think that you should reconsider your position on this issue?' The question also calls for a 'yes' or 'no' response, not allowing for grey areas. These kinds of statements will probably result in a defensive response and a premature end to the interview.

Your questions have been prepared. Now you need to plan to arrive at the interview on time, dressed appropriately. Your dress should indicate seriousness of purpose and professionalism. After introducing yourself to the person, remind him of the purpose of the interview. Then set up any equipment—computer, tape recorder, or notebook. With the permission of the interviewee, you can record the interview. However, many people are not comfortable being recorded. So if the person says 'no', do not argue. If two people attend the interview, one can take notes while the other asks the questions.

Flexibility should be your guide when you are interviewing. Be prepared for the person to go off track from time to time or to answer some questions before you have asked them. The order in which the person answers the questions is less important than the fact that he answers them. Do not try to hold the interview to its original course if you are getting interesting information. The person may raise some points that you have not considered. At the same time, you should be aware of the time so that, if some important questions remain unanswered as the interview nears an end, you do not lose the opportunity to ask the questions. Gently steer the interview back on course at an appropriate moment. Ask for clarification when you do not understand a point or ask probing questions if you need more information on a topic.

If you interview a high-level executive, expect the person to take control of the interview. Studies demonstrate that executives like to take the lead and set the direction of interviews. If that happens, do not interrupt. Listen to see how many of your questions are answered during the course of the interview. If the time allotted to the interview nears an end, thank the person for her contribution and say that you have several additional questions that you would like to ask before concluding. Do not exceed the time limit set for the interview unless the person is clearly willing to give more time. Review and transcribe your notes as soon as possible after the interview, before you forget the details.

Libraries (On-site Facilities and On-line Facilities)

Libraries are the repository of the most solid and reliable information. You can obtain access to most secondary sources through your university and local libraries. *Secondary sources* include books, journals, magazines, newspapers, yearbooks, and other published materials in which authors communicate to you through their publications, not in person. You can visit your library in person or on the Web. If you go to the physical facility, you can obtain the help of your reference librarian. Every library has fact sheets on its services, and most offer orientation tours to new students. Unanswered questions can be addressed directly to the librarian on duty.

Until the early 1990s, libraries referenced most of their holdings on cards in filing cabinets. The cards were in alphabetical order according to author, title, key words, and subject headings. Locating a particular source sometimes required skimming through hundreds of individual cards. Few libraries maintain the old-style card catalogues. Although some libraries have retained their old card files, they do not update them. So you will find only the older holdings in the wooden cabinets.

Like the old-style catalogues, the new computerized catalogue lists books, videos, and other library holdings by author, title, key words, and subject. If you are in the library, you can use a computer to access this database and to look up call numbers for books and other library materials. You do not have to be physically present in the library, however, to use the catalogue. You can access the information from a variety of locations—home, office, hotel room, or even another country. So long as you hold a valid permit to use library facilities, you can access the database and its resources.

If you do not know the author or title, the on-line search function in the computerized catalogue allows you to locate materials by inputting key words or subjects. An increasing number of libraries allow you to reserve books on-line. If books, videos, or other materials are checked out of the library, you can put them on hold; and the library will notify you upon their return. If your library does not hold a book, journal article, or video, you can often order the book through interlibrary loan services, a special library unit that helps patrons to secure books from other libraries. To retrieve a book from the shelves, reserve the book, or order the book through interlibrary loan, you need to know the author, title, and call number.

Most libraries have special rooms where they keep current magazines, newspapers, and other periodicals. A few years back, libraries bound and shelved the older periodicals. As binding became too expensive, libraries began to put the older magazines and journals on microfilm or microfiche. Some library floors are still dedicated to these microfilm and microfiche collections, as well as government publications. However, increasingly, libraries have moved to on-line subscriptions, where users access the periodicals via the Internet. Like libraries, government departments also are moving to Web publication, with older materials available in on-line archives.

Why should you go to your university or other library Web site as a point of access for information? Libraries pay institutional fees that allow users to access the information without paying for it. They also reference materials that have been reviewed and approved as legitimate sources of information. If you use search engines such as Alta Vista, HotBot, Lycos, and Yahoo, on the other hand, you will encounter a much more fluid environment. These search engines do not differentiate between Web sites with accurate or inaccurate information. Some Web masters have their own political or social agendas; and they seek to proselytize, not to present unbiased information to Web visitors. Other Web sources are inaccurate or out of date, or they do not list their sources of information. For that reason, the following discussion introduces you to databases that are usually available through university and other library Web sites. Legitimate users can access these sites free of charge.

A number of indexes are available on-line to help you to locate popular magazines, academic and trade journals, and newspapers. The oldest and most consulted index, *The Readers' Guide to Periodical Literature*, can be found in the reference room of some libraries. However, a new *Reader's Guide Full Text, Mega Edition* and *Select Edition* are now available on-line. These new databases contain the full text of magazine articles back to 1994 and abstracts back to 1983. They also reference popular newspapers such as *The New York Times*. Subjects include science, business, arts, entertainment, health, sports and fitness, current events, and many more. *The Reader's Guide Retrospective: 1890–1982* indexes articles that appeared in 375 leading magazines during more than a century.

LexisNexis Academic contains mostly full-text entries from major newspapers, magazines, journals, newsletters, trade magazines, and abstracts. The specialty of this database is law. Other commercial databases, available in many electronic library collections, include ProQuest, EBSCOhost, PsycINFO, MEDLINE, and Info Trac College Edition. ProQuest and Dialog Information Retrieval Service offer electronic collections of millions of books, conference papers, and articles originally published in magazines, newspapers, and scholarly journals. You can search these collections for articles on subjects that interest you or that will help with your research or school work. The Educational Resource Information Center (ERIC) database includes citations for journal articles, conference papers, and original research on all aspects of education.

Other sources specialize in news. NewsLink, for example, connects the reader, to newspapers, broadcasters, and magazines. News and Newspapers Online also contains worldwide linkages to news sources. The Newspaper Association of America references many Canadian newspapers, US dailies, local newspapers, weeklies, business papers, and alternative press papers. Ethnic News Watch is a full-text collection of the newspapers, magazines, and journals of the ethnic, minority, and Native press.

A number of encyclopedias, dictionaries, yearbooks, and other resources—traditionally found in the reference areas of libraries—are now available on-line (see Box 8.1). An increasing number of publishers are also putting their journals and excerpts from books on-line. Many professional associations, which lack complete collections of

Box 8.1 On-line Resources

- *AccessScience*—encyclopedia of science and technology.
- *Canadian Who's Who*—biographical sketches of leading and influential Canadians.
- *Dictionary of Canadian Biography Online*—biographies of significant figures from Canada's past, as well as some lesser-known figures not covered elsewhere.
- *Ancient History & Culture*—coverage of Africa, Egypt, Greece, Rome, Mesoamerica, and Mesopotamia, spanning the period from 3 to 5 million years ago through 1522 CE.
- Bartleby.com Great Books Online—full text of a number of standard reference books, fiction, non-fiction, and poetry.
- *Bartlett's Familiar Quotations*—1901 edition of this popular book of quotations.
- *Contemporary Authors*—biographies of more than 100,000 writers.
- *Dictionary of Literary Biography*—information on literary figures from all time periods in genres such as fiction, non-fiction, poetry, drama, history, and journalism.
- *Encyclopedia Britannica*—the complete encyclopedia, as well as *Merriam-Webster's Collegiate Dictionary* and the *Britannica Book of the Year*.
- *Encyclopedia Canadiana*—bilingual version, authoritative resource on Canadian subjects, with maps, games, quizzes, videos, and references to Internet sites.
- *Canadian Almanac*—Canadian statistics along with general information, astronomical charts, and references to Canadian honours and awards.
- *Grolier* Online—*Grolier Multimedia Encyclopedia*, *The New Book of Knowledge*, *New Book of Popular Science, Lands and Peoples*, and others.
- *Information Please Almanac*—full text of the *Information Please Almanac*, as well as an on-line dictionary and an on-line encyclopedia.
- Literature Resource Center—information on literary figures from all time periods.
- *Oxford Classical Dictionary*, 3rd edition; *Oxford English Dictionary (OED)*, 2nd edition.
- *Webster's Third New International Dictionary*, unabridged.
- *World Book* Online Reference Center—encyclopedia articles, Web links, periodical articles, videos, maps, and more.
- *World Fact Book*—maps, current issues, history, geography, people, government.

their early journals, are asking members to share the missing issues with the associations so that they can put them on the Web.

While the above discussion has emphasized computerized databases as sources of information, you should not overlook the physical library facility. Sometimes the best way to begin a project is to peruse the bookshelves after identifying a few call numbers in the computerized catalogue. Skim books in that general section of the library for bibliographies and ideas that can help you to begin your research project. Many older documents will never be available on-line even though some are important resources.

Internet Search Engines

Popular Internet search engines include Google, Alta Vista, HotBot, Go.com, Lycos, Metacrawler, Webcrawler, Magellan, Infoseek, Excite NetSearch, Ask Jeeves, and Yahoo. Google has now inaugurated a new search engine for scientists and academic researchers: <http://scholar.google.com/>. The new service references scientific citations and peer-reviewed papers, abstracts, books, and technical reports. It also suggests ways to locate materials at libraries that are not on-line. Another new service is Google Print <http://print.google.com/googleprint/about.html>, which locates books with text that matches your search terms. Links will take the reader to the referenced text and to publishers and libraries that hold the book. Publishers and libraries are making an increasing number of their books available in digitized form. The Amazing Picture Machine locates images that can provide visual support for speeches.

Although libraries (on-site and on-line) are the most reliable information sites, Web researchers are going increasingly on the larger Internet for information. According to the *Computer Industry Almanac*, 20.45 million people in Canada (from a population of 32.2 million) had access to the Internet in 2004. Worldwide, 945 million people had access to the Internet. But the numbers are a moving target; by 2007, industry experts project that the numbers will reach 1.46 billion.[2] The Nielsen/Net Ratings listed 8.8 million active users in Canada in June 2004.[3] Active users are those who surf the Internet on a monthly basis.

Certainly, cautions are in order when you rely on the Internet for information. As noted above, many sources are biased, inaccurate, and/or outdated. So ask yourself the following kinds of questions before you decide to use information from a Web site accessed with a search engine: Does the source appear to be an expert in the field? Is the person affiliated with an advocacy organization (e.g., gun control, animal rights, abortion, tobacco, or other)? Is the source missing altogether? Usually the credentials of the author will appear on the Web site. If the author is not listed, does the information appear on a Web site hosted by a credible organization (e.g., reputable market research firm or broadcasting corporation)? Does the author cite statistics, objective facts, and evidence to back up her point of view? Does she include a bibliography of sources? The literacy of the writing may indicate the accuracy of the material. Careful researchers avoid grammatical and typographical errors. Their material is edited and, in the case of academics, is subjected to peer review. Sloppy writing is a good indicator of sloppy research. Look for the last revision date for the material included on the Web site. If no dates appear with the material, you should check its validity by going to other sites for confirmation. If you are using Netscape, you can check the date by going to the *file* menu, selecting *document* information, and selecting *last modified*.

Many university Web sites include links to credible sources of information; and a growing number of professors include course syllabi, along with bibliographies and lecture materials, on their Web sites. They also link their sites to other relevant Web sites. A more limited number of professors have begun to put their published articles or abstracts of their work on personal Web sites. Many universities now include guidelines for writing academic papers, referencing sources, and creating bibliographies. The University of Wisconsin-Madison Web site, for example, includes a summary of the American Psychological Association (APA) format, used by many communication programs: <http://www.wisc.edu/writetest/Handbook/DocAPAReferences.html>. The Humanities Department and the Arthur C. Banks Library at the Capital Community College, Hartford, Connecticut, have generated a comprehensive guide to the Modern Languages Association (MLA) format. Their guide is available at: <http://webster.commnet.edu/mla/index.shtml>. These are just two of many university Web sites that include summaries that conform to popular style guides. Most English programs use the MLA format.

On a day-to-day basis, people use the Internet to research a host of topics from health to current issues to recreational sites, hotels, and airfares. Most news organizations, as well as many magazines, host Web sites with current news and feature items. If you are looking for an interesting parable or colourful story, the general search engines can lead you to many personal Web sites that include quotations and stories. Unfortunately, these sources do not always identify the authors of the quotations or stories, and sometimes the wording is inaccurate. In other situations, you may need to identify the meaning of a word, find the name of the person who won a sports event, research tourist attractions, or locate a recipe. The general search engines offer multiple sources of information on these kinds of topics. However, you should use the criteria discussed above to determine the validity and worth of the information that you intend to use in speeches.

As mentioned earlier in this chapter, you can find the same documents with Internet searches as those that appear in your computerized library catalogues (e.g., references to commercial databases such as ProQuest). However, you will need to pay for much of this information if you do not go through the library where you hold a membership. The fees can be very high. So if you happen to run across an interesting resource when you use the Internet search engines, check your library holdings before you pay for the material.

Box 8.2 A Question of Ethics

Candace was researching the topic of toxic emissions for an informative speech. She was especially interested in this topic because she suspected that the local chemical plant might be releasing unsafe levels of chemicals into the air. A number of people had complained that they could smell the chemicals in the air late at night. They believed that the plant might be waiting until people were asleep to release the toxins into the air. Others said that they had seen heavy smoke coming from the plant stacks at the same time that the air had a smell of noxious gases.

Candace also knew about three employees who had died from a rare form of cancer after working at the plant. The three were only in their mid-thirties; and two were non-smokers, without a history of physical problems. For those reasons, Candace felt strongly about the importance of investigating the topic.

She had already conducted an extensive search of the literature. She had read a large number of newspaper and magazine articles and explored the subject on the Internet. But she wanted some first-hand information from people who worked at the plant. More specifically, she wanted an interview with senior management. She believed that the interview would allow her to ask questions to which she did not have answers, and the interview would give added credibility to her speech.

Candace did not think, however, that a plant manager would grant an interview if he knew the subject of her speech. So she decided to tell the manager that she wanted an interview on a different topic. She said that she wanted to learn more about charitable activities undertaken by the company, such as the sponsoring of a local golf tournament and a run for charity. With this introduction to her research purposes, the public relations person at the plant agreed to arrange an interview for Candace.

Candace did not believe that she was doing anything wrong. She felt that the company's responsibility to the community outweighed any ethical concerns in the situation. Also, she wanted to become an investigative journalist, and she had read about how journalists sometimes misrepresented their purposes in order to secure an interview. Then once on the premises, they revealed their real purpose. Do you think that Candace was right? How do you feel about the ethics of her research methods?

Step 5: Identifying Points of Possible Confusion

Speakers should anticipate the parts of informative speeches that are likely to create confusion or resistance in the mind of the listener. The speaker should ask: What could be confusing to the audience? Has their past experience led them to believe something different from the information that I will present to them? Does my information run against common conceptions of reality? Will they accept my explanation if I do not explicitly recognize their preconceived notions on the topic? Your research should assist you in identifying points of possible confusion. Responding to these questions requires a strategic approach to informative speaking.[4]

Sometimes an audience will be convinced that their interpretation or understanding of an event or concept is the correct one. Imagine that you were informing an audience on the topic of immunizations. Some common misconceptions could influence audience acceptance of your speech. The audience might believe, for example, that the diseases for which we vaccinate children no longer exist in Canada. They may believe that vaccines cause autism in children or that they can overload the immune system, pushing people over the brink. Some people believe that the DTP vaccine triggers infant death syndrome (SIDS) or that the risk from vaccines is greater than the risk from some diseases such as chicken pox (for which we immunize people). If people genuinely believe that immunizations are dangerous, they may tune out the information that you provide on the topic.

People have confused or inadequate understanding of many topics. In fact, when you input the term *misconceptions* into the Google search engine, you obtain over three million references. It would appear that people hold misconceptions about Buddhism, climate change, tornadoes, contraception, hearing, Day of the Dead celebrations in Mexico, quackery, night people, Islam, Florida prisons, depression, Africa, and a range of other subjects too vast to mention. So the person who intends to deliver an informative speech must take areas of confusion into account.

At other times, we speak on topics where the subject matter is counter-intuitive.[5] Many people believe, for example, that chairs are constituted of solid matter; but physicists tell us that they are mostly empty space. Physicists tell us that, if we could eliminate emptiness from the entire planet, the earth 'would weigh as much as it weighs now, but it would only be as big as an orange.' As Wayne State professor Moti Nissani concluded, 'This tells us that common sense and intuition are not infallible guides to reality.'[6]

Other hurdles in preparing an informative speech may relate to the difficulty of the material. In explaining a highly complex concept such as string theory, the speaker must arrive at a strategy to make the material more understandable to the audience. Even physicists have difficulty understanding this theory, which talks about the timeless nature of the universe and parallel existences. A speech on the topic of string theory would need to use many examples and analogies, such as a comparison with the resonating strings of a guitar, to explain the theory.

Step 6: Choosing an Organizational Pattern

When choosing an organizational pattern, speakers must consider what they learned from audience research about levels of understanding of the topic. Speeches to inform typically rely on *chronological*, *spatial*, and *topical* patterns of organization; but they may also use *comparative*, *narrative*, *myth response*, or *transformative* patterns of organization. Where audiences hold misconceptions or have limited understanding of a complex topic, the speaker may need to take a more strategic approach to choosing the organizational pattern.[7]

For purposes of contrast, I have used the same topic, child pornography, to illustrate these five patterns of organization—the ones that you would be most likely to employ in an informative speech.

Chronological patterns of organization are time-based. That is, a time sequence governs the development of the speech: first to last, last to first, past to present, present to past, past to future, future to past. A speech about painting an apartment could rely, for example, on a time-sequenced pattern of organization: first to last. The major ideas could be deciding on a colour scheme (first step), choosing paints that fit your budget (second step), preparing the apartment (third step), and using special techniques in painting (fourth step). In Box 8.3, a speaker uses a chronological ordering to trace the development of legislation governing child pornography. Note that the outline employs phrases, rather than full sentences.

The *spatial* pattern organizes content according to the relationship of the parts in space. Often we are talking about some kind of geographical ordering. In the case of a speech on child pornography, for example, you could talk about initiatives in different countries, such as the United Kingdom, Sweden, Canada, and the United States. Spatial order implies location, such as different parts of a shopping mall (first level, second level, top level), different regions in a country (eastern, central, western, northern), different

---

Box 8.3 Chronological Pattern of Organization

Legislating Child Pornography

I. Passing of Protection of Children against Sexual Exploitation Act in 1978
    A. Outlawed the use of children in the production of obscene materials
    B. Enhanced the penalties for transmission or receipt of obscene materials containing depictions of children
    C. Rejected any measures that would have exceeded the scope of existing obscenity laws

II. Passing of Child Protection Act in 1984
    A. Changed the meaning of sexual conduct to include certain non-obscene pictures of children
    B. Raised the age of 'children' for purposes of the law from 16 to 18, thereby extending the scope of 'child pornography'

C. Increased the maximum fines tenfold
D. Removed the requirement that the transmission or receipt of child pornography have a profit motive

III. Amendment of Child Protection Act in 1986 to include advertising offences
    A. Banning of advertising for any type of exchange of child pornography
    B. Banning of advertising that solicits participation in any sexually explicit conduct for the purpose of creating child pornography
    C. Passing of Child Protection Restoration and Penalties Enhancement Act in 1990 (amended in 1996)

parts of a city (Manhattan, Queens, Westchester, Brooklyn, and the Bronx in New York), or different parts of a page (top of the page, centre of the page, bottom of the page). Box 8.4 demonstrates the use of spatial order in addressing the topic of international initiatives to control child pornography. Like the first example, this outline uses phrases, instead of full sentences.

A *topical* scheme of organization groups ideas according to subject matter. The organization follows some logical ordering of the ideas. A speech on identity theft could include the following ordering of ideas: increases in numbers of people who are targeted, nature of the problem, a profile of people who are most vulnerable, and ideas for protecting your identity. In this example, related ideas cluster under different subject headings. The speaker orders the ideas according to what makes sense—the major points that she wants to cover. In the case of child pornography, speakers using a topical form of organization can examine the ways by which traffickers find their way around the laws, the pros and cons of different approaches to solving the problem, the provisions in the UN Convention on Rights of the Child, the different manifestations of child pornography, or the effects of pornography on children. Box 8.5 illustrates a topical organizational pattern in a speech about the effects of pornography on children. Note that this outline uses full sentences.

A *comparative* scheme of organization places two ideas, concepts, or events side by side—using one to illuminate the other. To demonstrate how the Canadian justice system reflects cultural values, you could compare our correctional system with the one in Thailand. By examining the workings of the prison system in Thailand, we could better understand the uniqueness of our own system. In another situation, a speaker could

---

Box 8.4 Spatial Pattern of Organization

International Initiatives to Address the Problem of Child Pornography

I. Recent initiatives in the United Kingdom
   A. End Child Exploitation Campaign
   B. Establishment of hotlines and the INHOPE forum
   C. Participation in Childnet International

II. Recent initiatives in Sweden
   A. Hosting of the Stockholm Congress on Commercial Child Exploitation
   A. Participation in the UN Convention on Rights of the Child
   A. Joint funding of the UNESCO International Clearinghouse on Children and Media Violence on the Screen
   A. Establishment of the Swedish Save the Children hotline

III. Recent initiatives in the United States
   A. Efforts to produce the Communications Decency Act
   B. Passing of Child Protection Restoration and Penalties Enhancement Act
   C. Establishment of the Cybertipline by the Center for Missing and Exploited Children

IV. Recent initiatives in Canada
   A. Passing of Bill C-15A to modernize the Criminal Code and allow for prosecution of child pornography on the Internet
   B. Signing of the UN Convention on Rights of the Child
   C. Funding of Cybertip.ca
   D. Creation of Beyond Borders, a non-government organization

---

Box 8.5 Topical Pattern of Organization

Effects of Pornography on Children

I.   The availability of pornography increases the chances that molesters will commit acts of sexual violence against children.
   A.   Child molesters use child pornography to stimulate themselves prior to committing rape and other sexual acts against children.
   B.   Child molesters use photographs to encourage children to believe that the activities are acceptable and to gain compliance.

II. The availability of pornography increases the likelihood that children will have more sexually transmitted diseases (STDs) and unplanned pregnancies.
   A.   Pornography divorces sex from responsibility and increases the chances children will engage in sexual activity at a young age.
   B.   By increasing the chances of sexual activity, pornography also increases the likelihood that children will get STDs.

III. Exposure to pornography may lead children to act out sexually with younger children in their families and communities.
   A.   Children imitate what they see, hear, and read in the media.
   B.   Curiosity could lead children to experiment with younger, more vulnerable children.

IV. Exposure to pornography may interfere with a child's psychological development.
   A.   Children are not psychologically ready to deal with sexual relationships.
   B.   Children may develop feelings of shame and guilt that inhibit their development into healthy adults.
   C.   Children may develop the inability to experience sexual feelings independent of viewing pornography.

V.   Exposure to pornography shapes anti-social attitudes and values.
   A.   Pornography results in attitudes that dehumanize women and children.
   B.   After a time, men begin to see violent sexual acts as normal.

---

compare views of women as expressed in the Old Testament and the New Testament. Sometimes the comparison becomes an extended analogy. In the case of child pornography, for example, a speaker might compare the challenges of dealing with child pornography to the challenges of dealing with the heroin trade (see Box 8.6).

Box 8.6 Comparative Pattern of Organization

Challenges of Dealing with Child Pornography Not Unlike Challenges of Dealing with Heroin

I.   Challenges in dealing with heroin
   A.   Addictive
   B.   Profitable
   C.   Easily accessible
   D.   Difficult to control
   E.   Expensive in costs to society

II. Challenges in dealing with child pornography
   A.   Addictive
   B.   Profitable
   C.   Easily accessible
   D.   Difficult to control
   E.   Expensive in costs to society

III. Learning from our mistakes
   A.   Lessons to be drawn from how we have dealt with heroin users in legal contexts—how we have tried to legislate away the problem
   B.   Lessons to be drawn from how we have dealt with heroin users in family contexts—how we have tried to ignore the problem

---

Box 8.6 continued

C.   Lessons to be drawn from how we have dealt with heroin users in school contexts—how we have tried to understand the problem

D.   Lessons to be drawn from how we have dealt with heroin users in psychological contexts—how we have tried to transform the problem

IV.   Provisions of the new legislation—educating the public
A.   Where we've been
B.   Where we are now
C.   Where we are going

A *narrative* pattern of organization simply introduces and defines a term or concept such as *tolerance* and then supports the definition with a number of examples, stories, and analogies (see Box 8.7). Some of the supporting materials will be 'non-examples'.[8] According to the study of semiotics, we often define concepts and terms by *what they are not*. Bravery is not being afraid. Quiet is the absence of noise. Complacency is not caring. We can learn much about the definitions of many words or the meaning of concepts by looking at what they are *not*. By looking at examples of non-tolerance, for instance, we can better understand tolerance.

Similar to the claims pattern (applied in persuasive speeches), a *myth response* scheme of organization involves identifying and negating the misconceptions on some topic. A speech on child pornography, for example, could counter the six myths described in Box 8.8. This organizational pattern would entail identifying the myths one at a time, followed by a clarification and explanation of the real situation.

Finally, the *transformative pattern*, advocated by Katherine Rowan, applies to situations where the new information violates our intuitive understanding of science or

---

Box 8.7 Narrative Pattern of Organization

Child Pornography—Stories about Victims

I.   Introduction of myth that child pornography is a 'victimless' crime

II.   Meeting some victims through stories about their experiences
A.   Story of Nancy, who became pregnant at 13 after being molested by an uncle, who admitted to trafficking in child pornography
B.   Story of Timothy, still haunted by dreams of his molestation by a minister, whose computer contained images of children in sexual positions
C.   Story of Jennifer, raped and murdered by a pedophile, who possessed a large store of illicit magazines
D.   Story of Mark, unable to have a healthy relationship with a woman after years of abuse by a neighbour (a child pornography user)
E.   Story of Kevin, a teenager who abused his younger sister after viewing pornography on a long-term basis
F.   Story of Elizabeth, who turned to drugs on the street after long-term abuse by her father, who admitted to being addicted to child pornography

III.   Arriving at a new definition of 'victim'

Box 8.8 Myth Response Pattern of Organization

Six Myths about Child Pornography and Obscenity Laws

I.   It is impossible to define obscenity.
   A.   In a 1973 judgement (*Miller v. California*), the US courts defined obscenity.
   B.   That definition says that the work must lack artistic or literary merit; violate community standards for normal, healthy sexual interest; and contain sexual content of an offensive nature.

II.   Anti-pornography legislation violates rights to free speech.
   A.   The US Supreme Court has consistently held that some forms of speech, including child pornography, are not protected.
   B.   Criminal elements control the child pornography trade.

II.   Pornography is a victimless crime.
   A.   Studies have shown that many rapists feed on pornography.
   B.   Pedophiles use pornography to encourage their victims to engage in sexual activities of an illicit nature.
   C.   Some children molest other children after being exposed to pornography.

IV.   The prevalence of pornography suggests that many people support it.
   A.   National polls show that most people oppose child pornography.
   B.   You cannot judge community standards by the people who frequent pornography sites or visit adult book stores.

V.   No one has the right to impose his or her morality on another person.
   A.   No one has the right to engage in illegal activities.
   B.   The activities of child pornography traffickers and users threaten others in society.

VI.   Opponents of pornography are sexually repressed and reactionary.
   A.   Dislike of child pornography has nothing to do with sexual interest in adult relationships.
   B.   The pornography business subverts healthy loving relationships into illegal products that degrade the victims.

Source: Adapted from 'Myths about Child Pornography and Obscenity Laws', Morality in Media. At: <www.moralityinmedia.org/index.htm?obscenityEnforcement/cliches2.htm>. Accessed 19 Aug. 2005.

---

other systems of knowledge. The speaker, in that case, should adhere to the following sequence: (1) identify common belief structures on the topic; (2) recognize the seeming plausibility of these beliefs; (3) discuss their shortcomings; and (4) introduce the new information, using examples that are within the experience of the audience and that demonstrate the plausibility of the information.[9] See Box 8.9 for an application of the transformative pattern to our child pornography example.

Box 8.9 Transformative Pattern of Organization

Countering the Perception that Child Pornography Abounds on the World Wide Web

I.   Most people believe that child pornography abounds on the World Wide Web.

II.   Because we see so many links to adult pornography sites, this belief seems highly plausible.

III.   The problem with holding this belief is that we look in the wrong places to find the real offenders.

Box 8.9 continued

A. The real offenders are using e-mail more than the Web to share images.

B. Criminal organizations are using other means to distribute their products.

C. Parents are monitoring the wrong activities, thus putting their children at risk.

IV. In truth, child porn is almost non-existent on the World Wide Web.

A. Most photos of children on the Web are not sexually explicit; the children are riding bikes, swimming, or engaging in some other innocent activity.

B. Family albums, placed innocently on the Web, contain many of the nude photos of children that exist on the Web.

C. Some photos, intended to entrap child pornography offenders, come from police; but those are not sexually explicit.

D. Other photos come from girls and young women with exhibitionist tendencies, who place photos of themselves on the Web; so they are both victims and offenders.

Source: Points I, II, and IV above are based on the research of Judith Levine, *Harmful to Minors: The Perils of Protecting Children from Sex* (Minneapolis: University of Minnesota Press, 2002).

Step 7: Developing an Outline

Recall, from Chapter 4, the standard levels of organization for an outline: first-level headings (I, II, III, etc.), second-level headings (A, B, C, D, etc.), third-level headings (1, 2, 3, etc.), fourth-level headings (a, b, c, d, etc.), and fifth-level headings such as (1), (2), and (3).

I.
    A.
    B.
        1.
        2.
        3.
            a.
            b.
                (1)
                (2)
            c.
            d.
        4.
    C.
II.
    A.
    B.
    C.

As mentioned in Chapter 4, speakers should limit the number of major and supporting points in speeches. A 5–6 minute speech does not usually allow time to develop more than three major points or more than three levels of supporting detail under those points. You should place your most important points either first or last. Research suggests that audiences have the best recall of material that appears at the beginning of speeches (termed *primacy effect*) and end of speeches (termed *recency effect*).[10]

As previously discussed, five rules govern the generation of an outline. First, you should use *either* complete sentences or phrases in developing your outline. Do not mix the two formats. Second, every major point requires at least two supporting details. If you have only one supporting point, the single point should become part of the heading that it supports. So if you have only 'A', you should combine 'A' with the Roman numeral that it supports. If you have only '1', you should combine '1' with the letter that it supports (A, B, C, etc.). If you have only 'a', you should combine 'a' with the number that it supports (1, 2, 3, etc.). The third rule in outlining is to use parallel construction. The ideas that appear at each level or under the same heading should reflect the same organizing principle. The fourth rule requires *indenting* each new point and *capitalizing the first word* in the statement or phrase. The fifth and final rule obligates you to include only one major idea in each point. If you have any questions on these points, review the detailed examples and sample outlines in Chapter 4.

Step 8: Writing a Preview Statement

Preview or statements of structural progression tell the audience where you are going in the speech. In 5–6 minute speeches, such statements are often no more than one sentence in length. These orienting statements point to the organizational pattern of the speech. Examples follow:

- In the following speech, I will acquaint you with the historical uses of maple syrup in desserts, the basic ingredients in muffins, and the steps that you can follow in preparing this delicious snack.
- I would like to share some recent statistics on the retreat of the Sahara Desert, to talk about the reasons for the rejuvenation of these desert lands, and to consider the implications of these environmental shifts for the people of Africa.
- I would like to discuss with you the threat posed by bacterial infections in Canadian hospitals, the major strands of bacteria that constitute the threat, and the kinds of efforts that hospitals are making to deal with the infectious bacteria.
- This speech will focus on the history of comic books, the most memorable superheroes, and the modern incarnations of these heroes.
- My speech will be organized around the following areas: why people use drugs, the most popular choices, and the signs of drug abuse.
- In discussing the ways to make your Australian trip affordable, I will look at choices related to meals, accommodation, transportation, and recreation.

Step 9: Writing Your Introduction

The next step in the preparation process includes writing your introduction. Most people feel creative at the beginning of the speechwriting process; so it is a good time to write your introduction. If you know what you hope to accomplish in the speech, you can also write your conclusion before you add flesh to your outline. In fact, some people write their conclusions before they write their introductions. For organizational purposes, however, I will discuss the writing of conclusions later in this chapter.

When you meet someone, that person forms an immediate impression of you, which influences later perceptions. The speech event is no different. Audiences form first impressions of speakers when they arrive at the podium. These first perceptions of your personality, competency, and level of preparation for the event either help or hinder you in achieving your speech purposes. In the same way, conclusions offer the last important impression and leave the audience with a memorable thought.

When writing an introduction, you should review the material on writing statements of structural progression. Sometimes you will include an explicit purpose statement in your introduction. At other times, the thesis statement (along with statement of structural progression) suffices.

In addition to providing a statement of purpose, thesis, and structural progression, the introduction to an informative speech should accomplish three goals: (1) capture the attention of your audience, (2) give the audience a reason to listen by explaining the benefits that will come from listening to the speech, and (3) establish your credibility to speak on the topic. Why should they listen to *you*? What qualifies you to speak on the topic?

Gaining Audience Attention

Attention-getting strategies used in informative speeches include immediacy strategies; references to the novel; suspense and shock techniques; description; quotations and expressions; activity, drama, and conflict; and humour. Some speakers use gimmicks to gain attention, but these strategies carry heavy risks. The following discussion will review these attention-getting techniques, which the speaker can use in the introduction, body, and conclusion of the informative speech.

Immediacy Strategies

As discussed in an earlier chapter, immediacy techniques help to close the psychological distance between speaker and audience. The speaker may make a reference to someone in the audience, extend a personal greeting or compliment, mention the occasion or surroundings, share personal details, ask a question, use conversational language, or translate a general statistic into one that applies to this specific audience. References to the vital interests of the audience and the familiar also add a sense of immediacy to the occasion. Whereas this chapter focuses on how speakers use language to bridge the divide between themselves and their audiences, Chapter 5 discussed immediacy techniques from the perspective of delivery.

When rock musician and songwriter David Bowie delivered the commencement address at the Berklee College of Music on 8 May 1999, he began his speech by making *reference to a recent event* and *complimenting his audience*:

> Thank you. Thanks very much. Rockers . . . Jazzers . . . Samplers . . . That was a fantastic concert last night. I think both Wayne and myself were just so moved to hear our compositions coming back at us through your ears and abilities. It was dynamite. You don't know how much we appreciate it.[11]

In the second example, a student speaker *congratulates her classmates* on their accomplishments and encourages them to continue to pursue their dreams. She also recalls moments that she has shared with the group.

Leanne, I want to see your face on Global TV. Mario, I would like to see people with your passion for politics. Ruth, your voice—it's so pleasant that you could be the next guru in relaxation techniques. Whatever we all decide to do, let us not forget that we have the potential. Let us not forget the fears that we overcame in this class. And most importantly, let us not forget how good it feels when our voices are heard and we have an impact. Someone once said that everyone in their lifetime will have at least 15 minutes of fame. For me, that 15 minutes started in this class, and for this, I would like to thank you all.[12]

The third example represents an effort to *recognize the person who has introduced the speaker*, to *share a few personal details*, and to *acknowledge the demographics* of the audience:

Thank you for the kind introduction, William. I truly enjoyed reading your book *Boom or Bust*. Whenever William and I get together, we seem to find ourselves comparing notes on our lives as baby boomers. You know, we are the ones born between 1947 and 1966. We often wonder when our children will leave home— for good. And wonder if we could be fired—again. Not a concern. After our third layoff, we know that we can survive inflation, deflation, recession, and depression. We've lived through all of them. And we are still here to talk with you about our hopes for Canada's future—your future. After all, most of you are under 30. So you don't need happy pills to make you optimistic. The future is yours.[13]

In the next example, the speaker uses *questions* to involve the audience. Some questions require the audience to respond by raising their hands or offering verbal feedback. Other questions only require the listeners to ponder the question. Here the speaker employs rhetorical questions that do not demand a visible or vocal response:

Do you become bored easily? Find yourself moving from task to task without completing anything? Are you chronically late and disorganized? Forgetful and unable to stay focused on tasks? Do you become distracted easily? Do you pro- crastinate? If you have answered 'yes' to these questions, you may be an adult with undiagnosed Attention Deficit Disorder (ADD).

As mentioned in an earlier chapter, speakers tend to rely too often on questions to capture the attention of their audiences. Asking several questions of the audience is rarely sufficient to capture their interest. For maximum effectiveness, the questions should be combined with vivid and concrete description or other attention strategies.

References to the *vital*—facts and statistics that relate to our health and well- being—also bring a sense of immediacy to a speech. In the following example, the speaker seeks to inform her audience on the problem of poverty:

Poverty is the most pressing domestic problem of the twenty-first century. Some- one once said that, if poverty were a state, it would be the second-largest in the US, with 'more people than the combined populations of Connecticut, Kentucky, Maryland, Michigan, New Jersey, and Nevada!'[14] Unfortunately, poverty is not just an American problem. And its effects are not limited to the poor. Poverty affects all

of us in terms of increased health-care costs, higher crime rates, and longer com-
muting times for those who flee the cities. There are also costs in credibility as we
slip lower on the list of desirable countries in which to live.

Conversational language can also convey the feeling that the speaker is relating to the
audience on a personal level. The following excerpt from a speech by science fiction
writer Ray Bradbury illustrates this point:

> I went to New York with all of my short stories. I went on the Greyhound bus—four
> days and four nights to New York City. No air conditioning. No toilets. We've had
> many improvements in the last few years. But traveling to New York on the Grey-
> hound bus and then arriving at the YWCA, where I stayed for $5 a week. With a stack
> of manuscripts in my lap, hoping to conquer the editorial field, I met with all these
> editors. They rejected me. On my last night in New York—defeated by my encoun-
> ters—I had dinner with the editor of Doubleday, who said to me, 'What about all
> those Martian stories you've been writing? If you tied them together and made a tap-
> estry of them, wouldn't they make a book called *The Martian Chronicles?*'[15]

References to the *familiar* can also help the audience to feel connected to the
speech. The following example illustrates how you can use the familiar to draw listeners into the speech before introducing novel information:

> We've all heard about DNA—how scientists use DNA to learn more about diseases,
> how criminologists use DNA to free innocent prisoners from jails, and how fami-
> lies use DNA to confirm parentage. But few of us would suspect that our knowl-
> edge of DNA may soon be used to fight spammers. Using knowledge acquired in
> DNA research, scientists at TJ Watson Research Center have developed a new and
> highly effective anti-spam filter. Using pattern recognition, this filter enables com-
> puters to identify patterns or character sequences in spam mail that are not present
> in legitimate mail. The new tool is 96.5 per cent effective.

References to the Novel

Although the familiar can capture audience attention, the novel holds the attention. The
most interesting speeches include *novel* information. One student gave a speech about
ways to save money in planning and booking cruises. She was able to offer many innovative suggestions based on her own extensive travel experience—about the best rooms
for the money, ways to work your way around the world on cruises, and how to save
money in booking cruises. She said, for example, that builders rarely meet their deadlines in building new cruise ships. So, if you request a ship that is still under construction, you have a relatively good chance of getting a free trip. When the ships are not
ready to sail on time, companies offer free voyages or significant reductions to passen-
gers who have been inconvenienced by the time delays.

The following illustrates the interest value that novel examples can add to a speech:

> Residents of Fredericton, New Brunswick—a province long plagued by debates
> over language—experienced a new twist to the debate in July 2004. The unilin-
> gualism of Pavot, a Labrador retriever, became the focus of a heated debate. Yvan

Tessier of Montreal was enrolled in an English immersion course at the University of New Brunswick. This program required that Tessier speak English for 24 hours each day, but guide dog Pavot understood only French commands. So the administrators refused to admit Tessier to the program. Not until hundreds of calls and emails reached Canada from countries around the world did they budge. As one source noted, 'The made-in-Canada brouhaha inspired headlines as far away as England and India. Some news reports observed that Canada's sensitive language issue had found its way into the canine world.' About 70 per cent of the correspondents disagreed with the stance taken by the university. As law professor McIntyre at the University of Ottawa observed, 'That sounds pretty *dog*matic to me.'[16]

Suspense and Shock Techniques

The next example illustrates the use of suspense to gain and hold audience attention:

Audrey. Hugo. Eloise. Floyd. Hazel. Carla. Andrew. Do any of these names sound familiar? They should, because they are the names of mass murderers. Their nationalities are English, French, and Spanish. Cumulatively, they have killed thousands of people. It may surprise you to learn that the females in this list have killed more innocent people than the males. I met Audrey in 1957, when I was a child; and I will never forget her. Who are these dangerous offenders? They are seven of the most notorious hurricanes to originate in the Atlantic Ocean—infamous for the damage they have wreaked and the numbers of lives they have claimed. When an outstanding athlete retires from sports, his team often withdraws his jersey or number, out of respect for the person. In the world of hurricanes, the names of the worst storms are retired from the lottery of names available to meteorological organizations. Audrey, Hugo, Inez, Floyd, Hazel, Carla, and Andrew wreaked so much damage that the most affected countries requested the withdrawal of their names, along with 41 others. The World Meteorological Organization can no longer use these 48 names. The latest offenders, of course, are Katrina and Rita.

The above passage could be used to introduce an informative speech on hurricanes.

Activity, Drama, and Conflict

As illustrated by the next example, activity, drama, and conflict can also pull audiences into speeches.

What is it like to live in a ghetto environment? On a recent bus trip from Chicago to Toronto, I got at least a partial answer to that question. Over the course of the 24-hour ride, a 19-year-old woman named Dolores Rodriguez told me about her life—a story that introduced me to the realities of being poor in one of the nation's largest cities. She explained that she was travelling to Syracuse in hopes of getting work in that city. Her husband Alonso remained at home with their two children. In south side Chicago, Dolores lived in a neighbourhood where the average income was under $20,000 a year. Worse, the neighbourhood was controlled by two warring gangs, the Latin Kings and the Vice Lords. Because Dolores and

Alonso had refused to join either of the gangs, they were under constant threat by both. Whenever they left their apartment, they exited by the back door to avoid contact with gang members who hung around the front of their building. When they travelled in a car, her husband wore a large sombrero to hide his age. Dolores never took her little girl to the park near her apartment, and she feared every step of her two-block walk to the grocery store. She spent most of her days at home watching TV, unable to go out of the apartment. She told me that she was looking forward to the building of a new Wal-Mart in Englewood, because the store would have a number of security guards. The fact is that the situation of Dolores and Alonso is not unusual. Between January and May 2004, the Chicago Police Department recorded almost 15,000 incidences of violent crime in their city. Multiply Chicago by all of the other urban environments in North America, and you will obtain some sense of the scope of the problem. Also realize that these are the *reported* crimes. Large numbers of crimes go unreported, especially where victims fear retribution from their attackers.

Description

Speakers use descriptive language to gain and hold audience attention. The following description by Andrea Ball exemplifies the use of strong sensory-drenched language, which appeals to multiple senses—sight, touch, hearing, and smell.

Each country I've visited has left a lasting, sensual impression on me. In Hong Kong, it was standing on a hill overlooking a lush valley below and listening to the sounds of the wind rustling the bamboo scaffolding of a nearby building. In Bermuda, it was the feeling of being completely surrounded by turquoise water

Photo Gill Ferguson

while sitting on the edge of the battlements of an old British fort. And in England, it was Stonehenge, my favourite place. When we pulled into the parking lot of the tourist centre, a storm was brewing, reminiscent of Macbeth. And by the time we got to the henge itself, the storm felt like a full-fledged hurricane. But for me, the weather only served to make the experience that much more memorable. I slowly walked around the henge, obeying the role boundary and examining the stones, in awe of their size and power. By the time I was halfway around, everyone else in our group had gone inside; but I remained, in the thrall of nature, with the wind buffeting me and the rain washing over me. The dampness filled my nostrils. I was alone, surrounded only by nature, history, and magic. And then, out of the sheets of rain, figures appeared across the stone circle from me. In their dark clothes, huddled together in groups, they looked like druids performing some ancient ritual. I stood breathless as these figures, which appeared to have jumped out of history and fantasy, walked towards me.[17]

The speaker also builds a feeling of suspense as she proceeds with the description.

Quotations and Expressions

Speakers often rely on *quotations or sayings* such as the following to capture the attention of audiences and inspire listeners:

Life should not be a journey to the grave with the intention of arriving safely in a pretty and well-preserved body, but rather to skid in broadside, thoroughly used up, totally worn out and loudly proclaiming, 'Wow . . . What a Ride!'[18]

Motivational speakers rely heavily on this kind of material. Before the proliferation of content on the Internet, they drew their material from sources such *Bartlett's Familiar Quotations* and *Chicken Soup for the Soul*. In the current environment, almost every quotation appears on the Internet. Identifying the sources is more problematic, as they are often cited as anonymous or attributed to multiple sources.

Speakers should avoid worn clichés and overused expressions such as 'murdered in cold blood', 'clear as a bell', 'take the bull by the horns', 'sadder but wiser', and 'better late than never'. To demonstrate the lack of content in clichés, professors sometimes give an assignment that involves using as many clichés as possible.

Humour

Speakers also use humour to capture attention. The most appealing humour is often gentle—the phrase that provokes an unplanned smile rather than the joke that causes a forced laughter. Former President Ronald Reagan was known for his witticisms. While waiting for surgery after a March 1981 assassination attempt, he looked at his doctors and said, 'I hope you're all Republicans.' In the speech referenced earlier, science fiction writer Ray Bradbury brought smiles to his audience when he said:

When I got married, all of my wife's friends said, 'Don't marry him. He's going nowhere.' But I said to her, 'I'm going to the moon, and I'm going to Mars. Do you want to come along?' And she said, 'Yes.' She said yes. She took a vow of poverty, and married me.[19]

Humour that builds on the experiences of people is often better received than the stock joke. Chapter 12 talks more about sources of humour in speeches.

Giving the Audience a Reason to Listen

Introductions to speeches should include a reason to listen to the speech. In other words, the knowledge gained from a speech should be translatable into tangible benefits for the audience. A speaker may promise that the audience will save money if they follow advice given in the speech. Alternatively, speakers may promise rewards such as a sense of satisfaction, a higher grade in school, an adventurous experience, or better relationships. For maximum impact, at least some of the benefits should be ones that listeners can realize in the short term—the immediate future. The speaker may say, for example: 'If you listen to this speech, you will know how to get the best bargains on airfares when you take your next spring vacation.' 'If you pay close attention, you will make a better grade on your next examination.' 'Listening to this speech will translate into money in your next big job interview.' Or you may say, 'If you want a better behaved dog or cat, you might want to pay attention for the next five minutes.' The benefit of listening could be more sleep, a better relationship, or fewer annoyed neighbours.

Building Your Credibility

The third function of introductory comments is to establish personal credibility—to explain why you are competent or qualified to speak on the topic. Do you have a personal stake in the issue? Have you worked in the business about which you are speaking? Do you know someone who has experienced the situation that you are describing or derived the benefit that you attribute to the product? The concept of source credibility is explored in much greater depth in other chapters. However, for the purposes of this assignment, you need to build credibility on three dimensions in particular: *competency*, *trust*, and *composure*. The following example illustrates how a speaker can establish his *competency* to speak on the topic by making reference to his previous experiences:

> During my 10 years in the Canadian Air Force, I had the opportunity to work with the Snowbirds, the Air Force's world-class precision-flying team. Today I want to tell you something about what those experiences taught me.

In the next example, the speaker builds credibility on the *trust* dimension by talking about experiences shared in common with the audience:

> I face the same challenges as you in trying to make my student bursaries and summer jobs pay for my education. Like you, I paid $300 more this semester than I paid last year in tuition fees. My rent increased by 5 per cent. And I had to cancel my plans to go to Cuba on spring vacation after buying eight textbooks for five courses. Some months I eat a lot of Kraft dinners, and I am very familiar with the merchandise at the retro stores. Yes, going to university can be a poverty-inspiring experience. But in this speech, I want to tell you about everything that you will gain from your sacrifices—the long-term financial and psychological rewards of a college or university education.

If you have no first-hand knowledge of the subject, your audience needs to know that you have acquired competency through second-hand knowledge. In the following example, the speaker uses this strategy to gain credibility:

> Since beginning research into this speech topic, I have spoken to a dozen students who have participated in our university's Co-op program. I have reviewed the statistics on job placements with our Co-op office. And I have spoken with several professors who have worked with the Co-op program. This research has given me some very good insights into how the program functions, its benefits, and its short-comings. I would like to share highlights of that information with you in the next five minutes. After hearing this speech, you should be more qualified to make an informed decision on whether to apply to our university's Co-op program.

Note that the speaker also points, in the concluding sentence, to the benefits of listening to the speech.

A final example relates to *composure*. In Chapter 6 we considered composure at length, a credibility factor that some regard as a subset of *competency*. *Composure* refers to the fluency of a speaker and the ability to appear calm and in control.[20] Speakers build credibility on this dimension predominantly through a capable and polished delivery style. However, a few points can be mentioned in regard to the message. Source credibility studies tell us, for example, that we may prefer a speaker who makes an occasional mistake. So if you experience some moment that threatens your composure, a creative recovery can build your credibility on the composure dimension. Christine Vallières recounted how she turned an embarrassing moment to her advantage by joking about the situation:

> As I was speaking, the buttons of my blouse began to set themselves free, opening my chest for all to see. As my situation worsened, people started to notice. I could hear some audience members begin to 'snicker' and giggle. What could I do? I made a joke and said: 'Umm . . . is it getting colder in here? Or is it just me?' People laughed, after which I was able to button my blouse and refocus the audience's attention—on my message rather than my breasts! Lessons learned: No problem is without a solution. Think on your feet. Learning to laugh about yourself is important, and doing it in a positive way keeps your credibility as a speaker. People may remember your embarrassing moment, but they will also remember how skilfully you got out of the situation.[21]

A speaker should never apologize. An apology seriously undermines perception of a speaker's competency and draws attention to possible shortcomings—weaknesses that the audience might not otherwise notice. Speakers should never make statements such as 'I am not an expert on the topic' or 'I am not an accomplished public speaker' or 'I hope you will bear with me. Speaking is not my forté.' They should avoid statements that suggest lack of preparation or time invested in the speech such as, 'I haven't had much opportunity to do reading on this topic.' In the same way, a speaker should never make reference to being nervous or intimidated by the occasion. While speakers often feel as if every nervous gesture is highlighted in bold, the audience may be so interested in the ideas that they pay little attention to nervous gestures or shaky knees.

Step 10: Developing Your Outline with Supporting Materials

Supporting materials clarify, explain, and add flesh to your skeleton outline. They offer proof of the validity of your claims. Authors categorize supporting materials in many different ways. Some use such broad categories as *examples*, *statistics*, and *testimony*. Others become more specific, including *analogies*, *quotations*, *stories*, *explanations*, and various kinds of *instances* (e.g., personal or business). As in so many other areas of communication, the terminology varies from author to author; however, the ideas are constant. For organizational purposes, the following discussion uses these categories: *historical and other facts*; *description*; *analogies*; *proverbs and quotations*; *stories and legends*; *fables and parables*; *poems, ditties, and songs*; *statistics*; *examples*; *explanation and amplification*; and *expert testimony*.

Historical and Other Facts

Facts add interest to a speech. Speakers can provide details about the history behind Bastille Day, catastrophic losses of life at the Battle of Dieppe, or traditions associated with Hanukkah, Ramadan, or the Chinese Lunar New Year. If you talk about karate, you should include details about the Japanese culture that produced karate—who, why, and when. If you talk about mountain climbing, you can introduce the topic by mentioning some of the most famous Canadian climbers. You can tell one or more stories about crises confronted or journeys that ended unexpectedly. If you give a demonstration speech on how to prepare Greek appetizers, you can talk about the Greek culture, their love of good food and good times, and the origins of the individual dishes. Detailing the steps to be followed in preparing the appetizers is not sufficient. When appropriately referenced, the stories of a culture can be interesting additions to speeches. The following example, which talks about the history of the croissant, illustrates this point:

> Food historians debate the origins of this buttery, crescent-shaped puff pastry, but several date it back to the late 1600s when Vienna came under attack by the Turks. According to the legend, the Turks tunnelled under the walled city in the dead of night for a surprise attack. Bakers, who worked in underground kitchens, heard noises and sounded the alarm, thereby thwarting the enemy forces. To commemorate the victory, the bakers made a small roll in the shape of a crescent moon, a symbol on the Turkish flag, to signify that the Austrians had eaten the Turks for lunch.[22]

In speeches of demonstration, speakers should avoid presenting a series of 'what to do next' steps. An interesting speech will do more than outline the steps to be covered in some process or activity.

Description

Just as speakers can use evocative language to capture audience attention, they can use vivid description to support points in their speeches. The following description employs concrete language replete with details and appealing to multiple senses:

For many, Christmas is a season of memories. We remember the sights, the smells, and the sounds of Christmas past. Strings of coloured lights and holly on the mantle. The smell of pumpkin and mincemeat pies set out to cool. The crackling sound of logs about to burst with warmth. And the arrival of people we love, wrapped in wool parkas and scarves, cheeks and hands still cold to the touch as they close the door against the howling snow and wind. These memories, drawn from our childhood, serve as backdrops for later Christmases. But some years we cannot recapture the perfect Christmases of our youth. Something or someone is missing. Maybe we don't have the money for an airplane ticket. Perhaps we have too many assignments to complete over the holidays. Or by chance we may have no special place to go. On those occasions, we may be prone to give in to feelings of loneliness and depression. Untreated, those feelings can lead to unhappy consequences. Statistics tell us that more people commit suicide over the Christmas holidays than at any other time of the year.

Analogies

An analogy is a comparison of two basically dissimilar concepts or objects that share some common characteristics. The comparison of the two concepts or objects allows us to use the familiar concept to learn more about the less familiar concept. In the following example, the inverted triangle helps us to better understand the way in which the army functions:

> The famous World War II British General Sir William Slim once compared an army to an inverted triangle with the huge mass of the army, the supply corps, the general staff, the medical staff and so on, forming the base of the triangle—and existing but for a single purpose: to support the point of the triangle, the individual soldier on the front line protecting the interests of his or her country.[23]

The speaker then proceeds to apply this analogy to the legal and judicial systems that protect individual police officers:

> I think Slim's analogy of the inverted triangle is a good image to keep in mind when thinking about Canada's police officers. In this country, our complex judicial and law-making systems ultimately rest on the shoulders of the individual police officer out there walking the beat or patrolling the streets in a police car. And when we—the federal government, the provincial government or other administrative bodies—develop new laws or regulations, we must ask ourselves, 'How is this going to affect police officers on the street? Will it make their jobs easier or more difficult?'[24]

Proverbs and Quotations

When used to support points in speeches, proverbs and quotations should be relevant to the topic of the speech. A proverb such as the following can apply to many different topics: 'A society grows great when old men plant trees whose shade they know they shall never sit in.' A check of the Internet for references to this Greek quotation reveals applications in the following topic categories: wilderness living, nature, society, service, liberty and patriotism, importance of children, woodworking, landscaping, and change management, among others. Speakers can also find many different applications for a single quotation.

When citing the words of someone else, you should always mention the person's title, position, or other identifying information: 'Canadian author Lucy Maude Montgomery'; 'Aleksandr Solzhenitsyn, winner of the 1970 Nobel Laureate in literature'; or 'radio personality Sheila Rogers'. If the reference is clear, the descriptor can be short: 'Walter Gretzky, the father of hockey legend Wayne Gretzky, once commented, "You miss 100 per cent of the shots you don't take."' If the individual is little known or the contribution requires explanation, however, more details about the person may be appropriate or necessary.

Stories and Legends

Effective speakers often are good storytellers, and some of the most interesting stories are true ones. The following story, told by social anthropologist Bronislaw Malinowski, illustrates this point:

> I once talked to an old cannibal who, hearing of the Great War raging in Europe, was most curious to know how we Europeans managed to eat such huge quantities of human flesh. When I told him the Europeans did not eat their slain foes, he looked at me with shocked horror and asked what sort of barbarians we were, to kill without any real object.[25]

This story could serve as an introduction to speeches about Western habits of consumption, the environment, the warlike tendencies of 'civilized' societies, or a number of other topics.

If you were talking about the worst fires in history, you could begin your speech with the following story about the alleged origins of the Great Chicago Fire of 1871. Although the truth of the story is suspect, people around the world recount the tale:

> According to popular legend, a cow is responsible for the Great Chicago Fire. The cow's mistress, Catherine O'Leary, operated a neighbourhood milk business out of her barn. One evening, she accidentally left a kerosene lantern in the barn. When one of her cows kicked over the lantern, the hay on the floor caught fire. The results are history. On October 8, 1871, Chicago became a city in flames.

A third example comes from Gold River, British Columbia, where federal fisheries officials abandoned a two-year effort to capture and relocate a killer whale named Luna.[26] A speaker could use this example in a speech on beliefs about the afterlife, Native culture, or whales, among other topics:

> After two years of failed efforts by the Department of Fisheries, a four-year-old killer whale named Luna has won the right to remain, at least for the time being, off the coast of northern Vancouver Island. The 1,400-kilogram whale left her pod

almost two years ago to journey 400 kilometres to the coastal waters off Gold River, British Columbia, an area inhabited by a small community of Native Canadians. Fisheries officials have been worried about the increasingly friendly behaviour of Luna, who bumps against boats and stays close to land. But the local Native residents have intervened to thwart efforts to capture and relocate Luna. Whenever the fishery officials set a capture pen, the Natives (led by their chief) lure Luna away from captivity. The Mowachaht-Muchalaht tribe believes that the spirit of their late chief, Ambrose Maquinna, inhabits the body of Luna. A few days before his death, Maquinna promised that he would return, in the form of a whale, after he died. Within days of his death, Luna appeared in the Gold River area.

Again, I would add a caution about time allocation. You do not want stories or anecdotes to be so extended that they consume half of your speaking time. Even in longer speeches, a story or anecdote should be no more than a paragraph in length (maximum of a half-page, double-spaced, in 12-point Times Roman font).

Modern speech theory suggests the effectiveness of self-disclosure—that is, sharing stories about our own experiences. A number of studies have found that students react positively to teachers who use humour, self-disclosure, and narrative (stories) to clarify course content.[27] Nevertheless, you should not reveal details in personal stories that you will regret having divulged after the speech has ended.

Fables and Parables

Fables are short moral stories, usually populated by animal characters.[28] The most famous collection is Aesop's *Fables*. Parables are stories with a moral, philosophical, or religious point, such as the parables told by Jesus (e.g., of the prodigal son), recounted in the Bible. They differ from fables in that they do not typically have animal characters.[29] Many fables and parables circulate, via e-mail, among users of the Internet.

Some fables and parables provide interesting ways to begin speeches, although you need to be careful not to rely on material that has circulated too widely. If you have received a story more than once on the Internet, you should probably avoid using it in a speech. The following parable (paraphrased from an unknown source) has doubtless been used in many motivational speeches and sermons:

> An elderly carpenter told his employer of his plans to retire. Sorry to learn that he was losing such a reliable worker, the contractor asked the carpenter, as a personal favour, to build one last house. The carpenter agreed, but he was tired and unmotivated to do his usual good work. So he economized on materials and labour; he took the easiest and cheapest path to finishing the house. At the end of the project, the employer came as usual to inspect the carpenter's work. But this time, before leaving, he paused at the door. Handing a key to the carpenter, he said, 'This key, this house is yours. It is my gift to you, dear friend and loyal worker.' In deep regret and embarrassment, the carpenter hung his head, unable to look at his long-time employer. Like so many of us, the carpenter learned—too late—the impact of his choices.

Following the telling of the parable, the speaker draws a moral from the story. She might relate the building of the house to how we construct our relationships or live our lives—how we sometimes fail to do our best, not realizing that we are ultimately the real losers.

Poems, Limericks, and Songs

Speakers often use stanzas from poems, lyrics from popular songs, or limericks to support their points. If a speaker were talking about misconceptions of Canada, for example, he could begin with the words from a famous Molson Canadian beer commercial (see Box 8.10).

Limericks are humorous and often nonsensical verses, five lines in length. Short

---

Box 8.10 Joe Canadian Rant

Hey, I'm not a lumberjack or a fur trader.

And I don't live in an igloo or eat blubber or own a dogsled.

And I don't know Jimmy, Sally, or Suzy from Canada,

Although I am certain that they are really nice.

I have a Prime Minister, not a President.

I speak English and French, not American.

And I pronounce it *abOUt* not *a bOOt*.

I can proudly sew my country's flag on my backpack.

I believe in peacekeeping, not policing;

Diversity, not assimilation;

And that a beaver is a truly proud and noble animal.

A toque is hat; a chesterfield is a couch;

And it is pronounced *zed*, not *zee*. *Zed*!

Canada is the second largest land mass.

The first nation of hockey.

And the best part of North America!

My name is Joe, and I AM CANADIAN,

Thank you.

© 2000 Molson Canada.

---

poems or excerpts from poems or songs work better than long ones, because contemporary audiences become bored with long recitations. As with stories and parables, poems, song lyrics, and limericks must be relevant to the content of the speech.

Statistics

The following discussion examines the function of statistics and rules to observe in citing statistics. In the previous chapter, we looked at ways to present statistics in visual formats.

Statistics serve two important functions. First, they allow the speaker to generalize to larger numbers of cases—to express the magnitude of a problem or situation, as in the following example:

> The Center for Incarcerated Mothers Project estimates that at least 600 Ontario children have mothers who are incarcerated. On any given day, over 2 million minor children in the United States have parents in jail.

Second, statistics facilitate comparisons. In the following example, the speaker compares the salary of Michael Eisner, CEO of Disney, to the salaries of Bangladesh workers who sew Disney clothing:

> According to some sources, Michael Eisner, the CEO of Disney, pays himself $133 million a year. That works out to about $63,000 per hour. By way of contrast, the Bangladesh workers who sew Disney clothing earn 12 cents an hour. That means it would take those workers nearly 210 years to earn what Mr Eisner earns in an hour.[30]

In citing statistics, you should observe certain rules. *Audiences should be able to understand the statistics*. Not everyone is an expert in statistical terminology; so speakers should gear their discussion of statistics to the level of the audience. The following statistics, for example, would be confusing and incomprehensible to anyone but specialists—engineers, mathematicians, statisticians:

> The chi-square goodness-of-fit test can be applied to discrete distributions such as the binomial and the Poisson. The Kolmogorov-Smirnov and Anderson-Darling tests are restricted to continuous distributions.[31]

Speakers should translate the statistics into terms that are meaningful to the audience. For many years, speakers at orientation exercises for freshman students made the following kind of statement to their young audience: 'Look at the person on your right. Now look at the person on your left. One of you won't be here next semester. The failure rate for first-year college students is one out of three.' College administrators used this strategy to shock the students into realizing that they had to work hard to stay in school.

This strategy reduces statistics into units that are more meaningful. In the 1993 federal elections, former Prime Minister Kim Campbell translated the country's $600 billion debt into a statistic that made more sense to the voters. By dividing the $600 billion by the number of people in Canada, she was able to say that every Canadian owed $22,000 towards the national debt. She dubbed it our 'national VISA bill.' While no one could visualize the significance of $600 billion, most people could identify with the figure of $22,000. Again, in early May 2005, Matthew Breakey wrote in a letter to the editor of *Maclean's* magazine, 'Taxpayers lost an average of three cents ($100 million divided by 33 million people in Canada) due to the sponsorship scandal, while corporate fraud has wiped out billions of dollars worth of savings and investments.'[32]

In the next example, the speaker translates an abstract statistic into concrete terms that are meaningful to the audience:

> Thirty-three million is an important number. Do you have any idea what it repre-
> sents? Since it's hard to imagine such a large number of anything, let me give you
> some examples. Thirty-three million is half the population of Iran. It is the number
> of people who watched the funeral of Princess Diana, the last episode of *Joe Mil-*
> *lionaire*, and the average number of people who watched the winter 2004 season of
> *American Idol*. Thirty-three million is 70 per cent of the 47 million Americans who
> would like to quit smoking. And last but not least, 33 million is the number of peo-
> ple in the world with HIV. In short, there are 33 million reasons to find an answer
> to the Black Plague of this century.

In pointing to the cost of the Vietnam War, the late civil rights activist William Kunstler
used this same strategy:

> The cost of one modern heavy bomber is this: a brick school in more than 30
> cities; it is two electric power plants, each serving a town of 60,000 population; two
> fine, fully equipped hospitals; it is some 50 miles of concrete highway. We pay for a
> single fighter plane with half a million bushels of wheat. We pay for a single
> destroyer with new homes that could have housed more than 8,000 people.[33]

Practise this strategy by taking any figure and asking yourself what the statistic could
represent in concrete terms. Research the figure on the Internet to see what pops up.

Speakers should round off numbers to make them easier to deliver and for the audience to
comprehend and remember. Rather than saying 3,422 people, you should say 3,400 people.
Rather than saying 15,203 kilograms of steel, say more than 15,000 kilograms of steel.
Always include the source of the statistic; and if you think that the audience will be
unfamiliar with the source, give the qualification. Say, for example, 'According to a five-
year analysis of the National Crime and Victimization Survey, sponsored by the US
Department of Justice, partners and other intimate acquaintances commit an annual
average of more than 600,000 rapes, robberies, and assaults.' If you stop at this point,
however, the audience will not really know whether 600,000 rapes, robberies, and
assaults is a significant number. So you might add: 'In the United States this figure represents 13 per cent of all violent non-fatal crime.'

To add credibility to your speech, include the size of the population from which a statistic is
taken: 'From a population of 40,000 in our city . . . .'

Use statistics sparingly and (when feasible) present them in graphical form (see Chapter 7).
Many speakers tend to overuse statistics, but reciting a long list of statistics bores an
audience.

Examples

Examples can be brief or extended, real or hypothetical, and personal or reflective of the
experience of others. The following excerpt from a commencement address by musician Billy Joel illustrates the use of a number of one-line examples, as well as an
extended personal example:

> And still we hear the same question: So when are you going to get a real job? How
> many times have you been asked this question or some incarnation thereof?

Beethoven heard it. John Lennon heard it. Milli Vanilli heard it. Bob Marley heard it. Janis Joplin heard it. Tchaikovsky heard it. Charlie Parker heard it, Verdi, Debussy. When I was 19, I made my first good week's pay as a club musician. It was enough money for me to quit my job at the factory and still pay the rent and buy some food. I freaked. I ran home and tore off my clothes and jumped around my tiny apartment shouting 'I'm a musician, I'm a musician!' It was one of the greatest days of my life.[34]

In many cases, reference to a series of brief examples is effective. A catalogue of brief examples generalizes a situation, much as statistics do. They make the listener realize that the example is typical—not unique. The extended example, on the other hand, enables the listener to identify emotionally and cognitively with the material in a way not possible with the brief example. The following detailed example illustrates this point:

My work with a very large corporation brought me into intimate contact with the life of a sweatshop worker. In one of our shipments, I found two pairs of scissors. The handles of each were wound with at least three inches of thread. I could tell that the worker had collected the thread for some time, because little scraps of thread were tied together. As well, because the thread was wound so thickly, I knew that the worker needed that material to protect her knuckles from the metal handle. This experience reminded me that, although these sweatshops exist across the ocean, they are still very close to home.[35]

The next example appeared in a speech about risk-taking:

Well into her seventies, my aunt continued to do minor repairs to her roof, to the consternation of the whole community. She eventually took to hiding in the valleys of the roof whenever anyone came near. When the postman caught her on the roof one day and demanded that she come down, she refused, becoming extremely angry. At her age, she declared, she had earned the right to take risks.

The above examples are drawn from real life. Other examples can be hypothetical. That is, the speaker creates a fictitious example to illustrate a point. To be valid, the hypothetical example should reflect a situation that has happened or could happen in the future. Hypothetical examples such as the following can be brief or extended:

Imagine the following scenario. You have just arrived at university. Your bags are still unpacked. The doorbell rings, and you quickly move to the door to greet your new roommate. You met Kim over the Internet. You were very excited to learn that she was beginning classes at the same university. You seemed to have a lot in common. So you made immediate plans to share an apartment. But when you open the door, you find that *she* is a *he*, and *he* is a six-foot-tall, middle-aged man! He smiles and extends his hand while you reach out to steady yourself. Another Internet adventure gone awry!

When examples are hypothetical, the speaker should give notice by using terms such as *imagine, picture this situation,* or a *future scenario could be* . . . . A number of years ago, the NDP in Ontario released a commercial with several hypothetical examples. The campaign commercial suggested that the drinking water in Ontario was unfit and that a government official had abused his expense account. They did not say, however, that the examples were fictitious. As a consequence, some argued that the advertisements had crossed the ethical boundary. Sometimes audiences become irate when they realize that a speaker has duped them. In 1992, students in a law class at the Australian National University made a formal complaint about their professor's use of hypothetical examples concerning sexual assault.[36]

In all cases (hypothetical or real), you should ensure the *relevance* of the examples. The connection should be explicit, not implied. In a speech on the rights of adopted children, for example, you could state:

> We talked about the case of Joan and Margaret, two young women who lived on opposite sides of the country—one in Newfoundland and the other in British Columbia. They never imagined that they had a sister until, one day, they discovered that they shared something very important: DNA. Their example reflects the experience of many people who face life-threatening illnesses. They learn carefully guarded secrets hidden by foster parents. They learn carefully hidden facts about their genetic and personal past. But Joan and Margaret should not have had to wait until they faced a serious health crisis to learn that they had surviving biological family. The laws have changed to allow greater access to personal family history, but children without knowledge of their past cannot take advantage of these new rights.

Be sure that the example is typical of the larger picture. Using atypical examples breaches ethical norms. To emphasize the representative nature of the example, you can tie the example to a statistic: 'You may think that the case of Joan and Margaret is an unusual one, a rare occurrence. In fact, statistics reveal that at least one-third of adoptive parents try to hide their children's past—sometimes for the sake of the children, at other times because they fear being replaced at some point in the future.' The most effective speeches rely on more than one form of supporting evidence.

As with statistics, you should be sure that the audience can understand and identify with your examples. The language should not be above the level of the group. If you are talking to an audience of nurses, your examples should be ones that are within their range of experiences. If a speaker is talking with a young audience about investing for their future, he should use an example with which they can identify—for instance, saving for a university or college education rather than saving for retirement.

Explanation and Amplification

Explanations respond to questions such as 'Why?' and 'How?' The term *amplification* refers to the details added to any speech.

Explanations form the backbone for many speeches because they talk about *causes* and *reasons*. The causes of mould infestations in houses or the reasons for giving to charities, for example, may be the major ideas you develop in a speech. You need to be careful, however, that explanations are not too long and tedious or too general. Explanations are most effective when combined with concrete examples. An explanation that responds to the question *how* follows:

How do you locate an apartment in a city as large as Toronto? The process can be scary and intimidating. If you follow my instructions, however, you will greatly increase your chances of finding a suitable place without succumbing to undue emotional stress. First, you need to place ads in community newspapers. Locals read these small neighbourhood newspapers. Second, you need to post advertisements in desirable apartment buildings and in local supermarkets and variety stores. Third, you should contact churches and community groups who keep lists of homeowners willing to rent rooms or apartments. Fourth, you should ask your employer for help. Universities are another source of information, since turnover is high in the university community. Finally, you can solicit the services of an apartment finder service.

If you wanted to add an example to this explanation, you could continue in the following way: 'To better understand how the process works, let us look at the hypothetical case of Elizabeth. When Elizabeth arrived in Toronto . . . .'

Demonstration speeches, in particular, respond to the question 'How?' Demonstration speeches explain how to juggle, create floral arrangements, spend money wisely, windsurf, or use PowerPoint. They explain how hot air balloons function, how builders create energy-efficient houses, and how culture jamming works.

The next explanatory passage responds to the question 'Why?' The explanation concerns the causes of forest fires:

Forest fires occur for a variety of reasons. Studies suggest that between 67 per cent and 99 per cent of all fires are set by people. Campers leave fires unattended. Smokers throw cigarettes into the brush, or children play with matches in dry areas. Earth-moving equipment, chainsaws, and torches also ignite forest fires. Arsonists set more than 50 per cent of all fires. In a smaller number of cases, nature is the perpetrator. Lightning strikes a tree or ignites a bush, or more astoundingly, thunder causes a fire. On 30 July 2004, the China Net reported that thunderstorms ignited two forest fires. The percentages on causes of forest fires vary because some regions are more susceptible than others to wildfires.

Expert Testimony

We use testimony from experts to add credibility to our arguments. We cite the views of others with experience and knowledge in a particular area. If we speak on government policies, we quote bureaucrats or politicians. If we speak on a medical topic, we cite doctors and other members of the medical community. When speaking on a legal topic, we look to the views of lawyers. Sometimes we cite people who have become experts by virtue of their interest in—or experience with—the subject matter. Erin Brockovich became an expert on water quality when she investigated practices of the Pacific Gas and Electric Company. Princess Diana became an expert on landmines and HIV research through her advocacy efforts.

We can quote experts in our speeches, or we can paraphrase their views. Whichever approach we take, we must give the full name of the expert, as well as the qualifications of the person to speak on the topic. Often we also give the source of the information— where the quote or idea appeared. If we were giving a speech that encouraged the audience to give donate money to the humanitarian efforts in Sudan, for example, we might begin with a quote by Hilary Weston:

> The Honourable Hilary M. Weston, Lieutenant-Governor of Ontario, delivered her farewell address to the Canada Club on December 10, 2001. As you know, the Lieutenant-Governor has many opportunities to connect with Canadians at all levels of society. Her position is non-partisan and largely ceremonial. But it is also a position that allows her to speak to many marginalized groups. In many regards, she has become a voice for these groups. And in her final address, she urged Canadians to extend their compassion to people who are suffering in other parts of the world. She said, 'If some of the planet is suffering massive poverty, none of us can feel smug in our prosperity. If some of the planet is at war, none of us can expect to remain forever at peace.'

Notice that several different things happen in this use of expert testimony. The speaker gives the name of the expert (Hilary Weston), her position (Lieutenant-Governor of Ontario), and the source of the quotation (speech delivered at the Canada Club on December 10, 2001). The speaker also explains why the Lieutenant-Governor is qualified to speak on this particular topic.

In the second example, the speaker refers to a spokesperson for the National Parole Board. She seeks to inform the audience on problems associated with halfway houses:

> A recent Corrections Canada study showed that one-third of parolees placed in halfway houses escape. And a large number commit violent crimes while they are out of the reach of the justice system. In an October 2004 interview, published in the *Globe and Mail*, department spokesperson Suzanne Brisebois said that we should not be too surprised by these figures. The National Parole Board grants early releases to all prisoners who are deemed to be safe. So if someone is in a halfway house, it means that the Board did not think they were ready for early release. She noted: 'Obviously, they're not the most motivated offenders. They're kind of a unique category of offender.'

Again, the speaker gives the name of the expert (Suzanne Brisebois), her qualification (Corrections Canada spokesperson), and the source of the comment (October 2004 *Globe and Mail* article).

Step 11: Linking the Parts of the Speech

As discussed in Chapter 4, transitions, signposts, and internal summaries help audiences to see the relationship among different parts of the speech. The next step in writing the speech is to ensure that you have used effective linking devices and created effective summaries to guide your listeners through the speech.

Transitions

Transitions help the listener to follow a speech, from one point to the next. They connect thoughts, establishing the relationship between different parts of the speech. Sometimes they are single words or short phrases: *in addition to, also, moreover, however, next*. At other times, they are full sentences: 'The next topic I want to discuss is the feeding habits of exotic pets'; or 'Now that we have considered exotic pets, I would like to talk about domestic pets.' Sometimes transitions serve a secondary function of emphasizing points: 'Among the exotic animals that we have discussed, the most dangerous pet is the lion.' This transition can lead the speaker from a general discussion of exotic pets to a consideration of the most dangerous. A second example of a transition that places emphasis is the following: 'More than anything else, you need to understand that exotic pets require a great deal of work.'

Signposts

Signposts are like bookmarks: they position the listener in the speech. Often they are just numbers: 'The *first* exotic pet that I would recommend is . . . . The second exotic pet that I would recommend to apartment dwellers is . . . .' Finally, as the speaker reaches the last part of the discussion of causes, he says, 'My third and final recommendation for exotic pets is . . . .'

An alternative way of signposting is to ask questions as you enter each new area of discussion. For example, a speaker may introduce the first section of the speech by asking, 'What happened in the past?' Once she reaches the next part of her speech, she asks, 'What is the current situation?' She approaches the final section of the speech by asking, 'What can we expect in the future?'

Internal Summaries

Internal summaries also help to ensure the continuity of a speech. Especially important to longer speeches, internal summaries remind the audience of the progress of the speech. The following example illustrates this point:

> *In short*, adopting an animal should imply a lifelong commitment. *As I have explained, however*, not everyone understands the importance of that commitment. People continue to abandon their cats near farmhouses, leave their dogs behind when they move to a new apartment, flush lizards down the toilet, and return birds and fish to pet stores. So how can we create a more enlightened and committed public?

Notice that the internal summary, in this instance, is relatively brief. In extremely short speeches, the summaries may be briefer or even omitted.

Step 12: Adding Interest with Visual Aids

After writing your speech, you should consider the possibility of creating visual supports. Visual aids add interest and colour to presentations. In preparation for a speech on the topic of drunk driving, for example, one student went to the local police station. She borrowed a pair of goggles used in instructional talks on drinking and driving. The goggles allow the user to experience the changes in vision that occur when we consume alcohol. At the conclusion of her speech, the student passed the goggles around the classroom, allowing the class to observe the differences for themselves. People were surprised to see that, after even one drink, a difference occurred in the quality of their vision. After two drinks, the difference was marked. The visual aid was highly effective in making the point that driving and drinking do not mix.

In another instance, a young man brought a mask to the front of the class for his speech of introduction. He said that, for many years, he had hidden behind a mask such as this one, not revealing his true self to people. The mask, he said, had helped him to hide a secret from the world. But it had also kept him from developing open and honest relationships with people. He said that he did not want to hide any more behind masks, and he revealed the secret that he had kept for many years—that he was gay. When the young man held the white mask to his face in the beginning of the speech, it conveyed a sense of the surreal, much like the mask worn by the stage character in *Phantom of the Opera*. The visual aid captured the attention of the audience and helped the speaker to make the point that he was not a real person when he was wearing the mask. Like the revellers who participate in a carnival, he was hiding his true identity.

Demonstration speeches, in particular, rely heavily on visual support materials such as models (live and constructed), charts, photos, and other varieties. See Chapter 7 for a discussion of visual supports and PowerPoint.

Step 13: Concluding the Speech

Conclusions should leave the audience with a memorable thought and provide closure. A brief summary of major points from the speech can serve the function of providing closure. In a five- to six-minute informative speech on why people are turning to cremation as an alternative to traditional burial, for example, your concluding summary could be the following:

> In this speech, we have looked at four reasons behind the shift to cremation as a preferred alternative to embalming: the shortage of available land in highly populated areas, environmental issues raised by designating huge tracts of land for use as cemeteries, the high costs of traditional burial, and finally, shifts in cultural beliefs regarding methods of body disposal.

A second way to provide closure is to refer back to some example or point made in the introduction—a hypothetical or real story, a shocking statistic, or an example. In the following case, the speaker began with a story about her grandmother:

> When I was 17, I went to see my grandmother for the last time. Although she would not pass on for another three years, I found visiting so frustrating. It didn't seem worth the effort for someone I had never known. You see, my grandmother suffered from early Alzheimer disease. I never knew the real person; and towards the end, she rarely put the right name with the right family member. In fact, she thought that she lived in a different decade. Though I can never get to know what my grandmother was like before Alzheimer stole her identity, I can help to support awareness of the disease.[37]

In closing, the speaker returned to the initial idea with this brief statement:

I never got to know my real grandmother, only her disease. Our time with her was brief. There is a myth that only the old are affected by Alzheimer disease; but in my family, we know that is not the reality. The painful reality is that all of us are at risk. We all suffer when a loved one succumbs to Alzheimer's, and we all must work to give researchers the money and tools they need to find a cure.

In concluding his speech to the graduates of the Columbia University College of Physicians and Surgeons, actor Alan Alda returned to the initial and major idea of the speech: 'But there is one thing you can learn about the body that only a non-doctor would tell you—and I hope you'll always remember this: The head bone is connected to the heart bone—and don't let them come apart.'[38]

In terms of support materials, conclusions typically employ quotations, proverbs, or a few lines from a poem. A number of the attention strategies used in introductions are inappropriate in conclusions. For a five- to six-minute speech, a conclusion that is one-third of a page in length should be sufficient.

Conclusion

This chapter has discussed two major components of successful speech-making—researching your topic and supporting your ideas. The chapter has also reviewed the following concepts: taking audience adaptation into account in choosing your topic, writing purpose statements and thesis statements, organizing your speech and writing preview statements, writing introductions and conclusions, and using visual supports.

Questions for Discussion

1. Brainstorm topics for informative speaking that could reflect seasons of the year, holidays, or other special occasions.
2. Identify topics that you would consider to be inappropriate for presentation to the group. Why would you find these topics inappropriate?
3. What are some of the risks and benefits of using Web sources?
4. How could you make use of e-mail in preparing for an informative speaking assignment?

Appendix: Sample Student Informative Speeches

Speech #1: Informative Speech

by Magdalen Dabrowski

Have you ever blown all of your money in one giant shopping spree, only to return later and find that everything you bought had been slashed in price? Have you ever winced when one of your friends talked about a great deal on some item that you had just purchased at full price?

You may attribute your friends' spectacular deals to being in the right place at the right time. However, these people may be what *Seventeen* magazine calls 'super shoppers'—people who have learned the strategic art of sleuthing deals. And today, you are in luck, because I have just learned that my long-term obsession for shopping has a name! So hold on, you're in for a treat, because I am going to let you venture into my closet. I am going to explain how to get great service, save a buck (or much more), and know when the next sale is around the corner. In case you are one of those people who dread even the thought of buying something new, pay attention. These tips are for you.

First, you need to ensure that you will receive the kind of service that you deserve. Achieving this goal means that you must dress up a bit more than you might normally plan to do. Ever notice a pattern to the people who get the best service? That's right, the ones with the shirts that match the pants that match the belts that match the shoes. These people convey the message that they are serious shoppers, and salespeople respond to these non-verbal cues. So if you pull on sneakers and your beer-stained T-shirt from last night's bar hop, you may find that you are closely watched, but for the wrong reasons.

Second, you should select an outfit that represents your taste in clothes. Don't pull out the Christmas sweater that grandma gave to you unless it reflects the style that you like in clothes. And always ask questions. Most shoppers only have a vague idea of what they want; so when the salesperson asks, 'Can I help you?' they are almost certain to say 'no.' At minimum, you should indicate that you would like to take a look first. Or if you know what you want, ask the clerk to help you. They know the store better than you, and they can save time and point to specials.

Assume that you have passed the first two tests for getting great service. You look like a shopper, and the sales clerk is ready to help you. Now you want to move on to your next objective—getting the best buys. To accomplish that goal, you should begin your search at the back of the store, not the front. Stores tend to place their newest merchandise near the front of the store and their sales racks at the back. The newest inventory is generally full price. As super shoppers, you do not want to pay full price for anything.

There is an exception to this rule. Some classic pieces rarely go on sale. Items such as white-collar shirts, brand-name jeans, and black pants tend to be the last to be discounted, because everyone needs these pieces of clothing. Sometimes I buy jeans even when they are regular price.

Another rule in looking for the best buys is to note the items that appear to be in excess. When you see 25 of the same shirt, you should wait to buy that item. It is probably destined for the sales rack in the coming days. Since the store may have additional items in the stock room, you might want to ask if they have a large stock that is not yet on display.

I have also managed to save money by getting discount cards at the stores where I shop the most often. I own a Suzy Shier prestige card that allows me to save 10 per cent, even on sales items. By using my card, I bought this skirt (the one that I am wearing) for $5.00 last summer.

Finally, in terms of getting the best buys, you need to be a regular at the mall. I find that prices change every two weeks. You also have to pay attention to the times of year. Prices will be highest at the beginning of every sales season. Avoid shopping during these periods. You won't lose anything because the new spring line never follows the weather outside. Why not wait to buy those summer shirts until the weather actually allows you to wear them? By then they will be on sale.

How do you know when the next sale is around the corner? Watch for sales patterns and learn when to expect them. There are always sales at the end of seasons and before holidays. I rarely buy things that are brand name. I almost never buy things that are regular price, and lately I have been using the Internet to find better bargains.

With that said, I would like to bring your attention to a few examples of my best bargains. Look at what I am wearing right now. Would you believe that my entire outfit cost less than $20? If you have the patience to dig, you can find remarkable buys at your local chain store outlets. My shirt was $12 before I used my prestige card at Suzy Shier. I bought another $5 skirt on December 23rd, which I wore on New Year's Eve [display skirt]. I got the boots for $30 at half off [point to boots]. I snagged this sweater off the sales rack for $20 [display sweater]. Paying regular price, I bought its clone in black last year for $45.

So if you feel as if your dollar isn't going very far, take my advice and follow these simple steps. After listening to my speech, you should have a better idea of how to get great service, save money, and shop at the right times of the year. Hopefully, you will all become super shoppers with full closets of inexpensive clothing like myself. See you at the malls!

References

Rigaud, Debbie. 'Are you a Super Shopper?' At: <www.seventeen.com/quizzes/qu.fa.ssh.question1.epl>. Accessed 7 Feb. 2004.

Shaver, Sharon. 'Money-Saving Tips to Bargain Hunt your Way to Top Style'. At: <www.focusonstyle.com/shoppingsecrets.htm>. Accessed 7 Feb. 2003.

Speech #2: Demonstration Speech

by Leslie Revere

After living at home for the summer, I was happy to be back in my own apartment, accountable only to myself. You know that feeling. But after a few weeks, I began to miss my mom's cooking. Don't get me wrong. I actually like to cook, but I missed the foods that were uniquely Mom— mashed potatoes, homemade macaroni and cheese, and pie! So what did I do? I got out the recipe book that I hadn't touched since my mom gave it to me in my first year of university. And I looked for a recipe that would satisfy my taste buds.

My roommate's family owns a fruit farm, and she had brought a whole bunch of apples with her when she moved in. So it seemed that the best idea was to bake an apple pie. Now as students, you can understand that I had a dilemma at this point. Not only was I inexperienced at making pies, but also I didn't have a kitchen equipped with any special baking utensils. I was pretty much broke, unable to go out and buy the missing items. So I decided to improvise.

When it was all over, I decided that baking a pie is a skill that everyone should learn. In the next few minutes, I will explain why you should learn this skill, and I will go through the entire process with you, giving some tips on how to improvise when your kitchen is as ill-equipped as mine.

All right, so I bet you are all wondering why you should know how to bake an apple pie. There are three important reasons. First of all, how impressed people will be when you can whip up a pie on demand! If you live at home with your parents, think about how happy your mom will be when she comes home from work to smell a wonderful aroma coming from your oven. Plus, if you are short on money for books, baking your dad a pie will put him in a good mood, making it easier to ask him for a loan. If you have already moved away from home, you can impress your family with your growth and maturity when they come to visit. Or you can just describe the pie that you just made in your next telephone conversation.

But what about the reaction of your friends? Baking a pie can put people in your debt. Negotiate a trade with your roommates where, if you bake a pie, they will do the dishes for three or four days. In my opinion, this is a pretty fair trade-off, because there is nothing that I hate so much as washing dishes. Lastly, when you finish your first pie, you will feel a sense of accomplishment. A beautiful latticed pie is like a piece of art. You admire it and then you get to eat it!

Now let's talk about the supplies that you will need to make the recipe. For the crust, you will need flour, shortening, baking powder, and milk. If you are anything like me, you might not have measuring cups, which can pose a problem when adding the ingredients. If you are lacking in this department, you will just have to eyeball the ingredients and improvise. You can take a mug (like this one), for example, and fill it almost to the top. This mug is pretty close to one cup in size.

Now that you have a way of measuring your ingredients, you will need to locate a bowl. During my first semester in university, we did not have a single bowl that was larger than cereal size. But after looking everywhere, I found a large ice cream bucket, which became my mixing bowl. Use whatever you have in your kitchen.

To make your crust, you will need to combine your dry ingredients—5½ cups of flour and 1 teaspoon of baking powder—with one pound of shortening. If you don't have a pastry blender, use two knives to cut the shortening into tiny bits. Finally, add approximately one cup of milk, just enough to moisten the flour. Mix everything thoroughly together. No utensil works so well as clean hands.

Now that you have made the pastry, you will need to shape the pie. Spread some flour on a clean countertop. Place a ball of dough in the middle of the flour. You will need to find some way to roll the pastry into a pie crust. If you don't have a rolling pin, use a cylinder shaped glass or soft drink bottle. Roll the dough into a circular shape so that you can lay it in your pie pan. Allow some excess to hang over the edges. Then put the pastry aside for the moment.

Arguably, the best part of your pie will be the apples, and I am going to go over a few easy steps for a killer filling. You will need to peel and cut up three and a quarter cups of apples—the equivalent of about seven or eight medium-sized apples. I use a potato peeler to remove the skin, but a small paring knife works equally well. Put the apples aside. Mix together two-thirds of a cup of brown sugar, 2 tablespoons of flour, and if you have some spices, ½ teaspoon of cinnamon and ¼ teaspoon of nutmeg. Sprinkle the flour and spices over the apples, coating each one. Put the apples into the pie shell.

The final step is to roll the top pie crust and finish off the pie. Basically, do the same that you did for the bottom crust, rolling it into a circular shape with your glass or rolling pin. Fold the crust in half, lift it carefully, and place it on top of the apples, unfolding as you go. You will need to poke holes in the top with a knife or cut shapes so that the steam can escape while the pie is cooking. Finally, roll up the sides of the crust to give the pie an edge. Voila, you're done!

Put the pie in a 375-degree heated oven and forget about it for 45 minutes while you are studying. Enjoy the smell of cinnamon wafting from the oven as you watch your favourite rerun of *Seinfeld* or *Friends*. Congratulations, you have just made your first pie!

Despite all of the stereotypes, it is not only moms who know how to bake. Anyone can learn how to make an apple pie, and if you lack utensils or ingredients, you can be creative and improvise. I did it, and I know each of you can as well. So the next time that you are feeling lonesome for a taste of home, or you need to impress your partner or family member, bake a pie. Forget about your problems and just enjoy the moment.

Speech #3: Demonstration Speech

by Joanna Mennie

Today is a very spooky day, sandwiched between two of the spookiest days of the whole year. Yesterday was Halloween (or All Hallows Eve), and tomorrow is All Souls' Day. What better day to sharpen skills that will allow us to answer impossible questions, uncover hidden truths, and transcend barriers of mortality. That's right, folks, welcome to a five-minute seminar on contacting the dead. For the next few minutes, I am going to demonstrate some tricks of the trade in 'mediumship' and divination; and hopefully, we'll all come out alive.

First, when deciding how to approach making contact with the deceased, you have to consider your objective. Do you simply want to know whether or not Dr Ferguson will give an 'A' on your next speech? Or do you want to get some pointers from famous speakers of the past that will blow Dr Ferguson away?

For a simple 'yes' or 'no' answer, you may not need to bother the deceased at all. You can cast dice, with even numbers meaning 'yes' and odd numbers meaning 'no'. Or you can cut a regular deck of cards, designating red cards for 'yes' and black cards for 'no'. For example, 'Will I get an A+ on this speech?'

One of my personal favourites for simple answers is pendulum dowsing, which relies on the interaction between the body and hidden forces in the environment. This technique requires attaching some form of weight to a cord. You can use a necklace with a heavy stone or locket, a ring strung through a chain, or even a thimble tied to a string. After asking the pendulum to give you a sign for 'yes', you watch which way it moves—either back and forth or in a circle. Alternatively, you can ask for the sign for 'no'. That's all it takes. And if you feel that you may be subconsciously tempted to influence certain answers, might I suggest closing your eyes while you ask your questions.

Now, if you're after a more thorough interaction with great aunt Bertha, you'll have to use more sophisticated means. Since I doubt that most of you know a live medium, able and willing to be filled with dead spirits at a séance, I recommend a form of talking board. Ouija boards are a classic example, although you can achieve the same effect with paper letters and a drinking glass. The idea is that spirits use human energy to move the pointer, spelling out words and sentences. I've found this method to be terrifyingly effective, and I'd like to offer a few words of caution. Approach talking boards as you approach Internet chat rooms; you never know to whom you are talking and whether they're going to be friendly. If you're encountering a less than personable spirit, stop immediately. Or if you're determined to proceed, rub a piece of silk across the board to neutralize the negative energy.

Beyond the wonder of Ouija, I find automatic writing to be particularly intriguing. Although this method requires a great deal of patience and practice (and I've never had much luck with it), I wanted to try it out for you today. Basically all you do is hold a pen to a piece of paper and let your mind drift. Supposedly, with your conscious mind suspended, spirits will be able to use your arm to write messages. You should try to forget that you're holding a pen at all; and when the pen starts to move, don't look down. Let's see, grocery list: eggs, milk, butter, beer . . . WHOA! Okay, I did that on purpose, but apparently this technique really can work. Handwriting analysts even testify that the writing styles of some people change entirely when they engage in automatic writing.

Now, if you're really committed to that conversation with Elvis and none of these methods have worked, you can always try table levitation. This complicated technique involves a number of people sitting at a round table with their fingers gently resting under the tabletop, like so. In response to simple questions, the table is supposed to tilt, lift, or thump. If things really get hopping, the table can thump out whole sentences through some sort of complex table language. Again, I would leave this method as a last resort.

Well, friends, this nearly concludes our adventures in the paranormal. But I'd like to offer a few general pointers that I've found helpful. When dealing with spirits, remember that there's no reason to become freaked out. After all, they're people too—they just happen to be dead. This means that they may be privy to some information we are not, and conversing with them in a respectful and responsible manner could prove beneficial. Secondly, avoid using spirits or the paranormal for personal material gain. For example, don't ask your dead grandfather for the winning lotto numbers. That's bad karma and a bad idea. You don't know how messing with the spirit world could come back to haunt you. And finally, it's all about attitude. When approached with an open yet rational mind, anything from drops of candle wax to patterns in egg yolks might just provide you with answers from beyond the grave.

CHAPTER NINE

Ethos, Pathos, and Logos in Persuasive Discourse

A Debate Involving Minority Voices

This classroom exercise involves a debate over a current issue of relevance to one or more minority groups. (See Box 9.1 for ideas on debate topics.) The debate question can be framed as a resolution, as follows:

· Resolved that the justice system should provide alternative methods of punishment such as restorative justice.
· Resolved that corporations should bear a greater part of the taxation burden.
· Resolved that the health-care system should be privatized.
· Resolved that higher education should be free to every qualified student.

For this exercise, the class will divide into two groups. Half of the class will defend the minority perspective on the issue. The other half will argue the opposite perspective. Speakers will not follow a set order. Rather, the speakers may go to the podium on a spontaneous basis to respond to points raised by the other side or to present new arguments. A speaker for the affirmative side (in support the resolution) will begin the debate, followed by a speaker for the negative (opposed to the resolution). Speakers for the affirmative and negative will alternate so that both sides have equal time. The instructor may want to appoint a timekeeper to ensure equity.

All speakers will seek to build their credibility by bringing personal perspectives to bear on the topic—pointing to past experiences, expertise, or knowledge acquired on the topic. (These qualifications may be fictitious.) Speakers will also employ logic and reasoning, as well as emotional appeals, to argue their cases.

After concluding the debate, the class will analyze the credibility strategies employed by various speakers, as well as examine the quality of the argumentation. The evaluation of this assignment (if any) will entail an assessment of the understanding and effective use of credibility, emotional, and logical appeals in persuasive communication.

Learning Objectives
- To learn how to identify and use source credibility appeals (*ethos*).
- To learn how to identify and use emotional appeals (*pathos*).
- To learn how to identify and use logical appeals (*logos*).

Box 9.1 Policy Issues

The following list of policy issues, relevant to minority populations or disadvantaged Canadians, should give you ideas for possible topics for the debate:

- Seal hunting
- Poverty in single-parent families
- Privatized health care
- Rights of victims
- Native fishing rights
- Homelessness
- Panhandling
- Refugee laws and illegal immigrants
- Unemployment
- Accessibility issues for people with disabilities
- Language rights

- Rising cost of education
- Equal opportunity in the workplace
- Glass ceiling for women
- Migrant labour
- Fraud perpetrated against seniors
- Transportation costs
- Invisible disabilities
- Violence in low-income communities
- Racial profiling
- Substance abuse on reservations
- Rejection of immigrants on basis of health issues
- Same-sex marriage
- Denial of insurance on basis of DNA testing
- Mandatory retirement
- Social benefits for people without income

Successful persuasive speaking draws on the Aristotelian concepts of *ethos*, *pathos*, and *logos*. This chapter will discuss how speakers build their *ethos* or source credibility, employ emotional appeals (*pathos*), and develop their logic and reasoning (*logos*) in argumentative discourse.

Ethos as a Persuasive Strategy

From the Socratic period to the present day, rhetoricians have studied the concept of *ethos*—the credibility that audiences attach to speakers. Aristotle looked at how speakers establish their credibility (or *ethos*) through the speech itself.[1] Other classical scholars such as Cicero and Quintilian extended their discussions of credibility to include factors extraneous to the speech. Cicero expected audiences to take into account the actions of a person's life when they judge a message.[2] For Cicero, a good orator was not simply a man of skill, but also a man of personal integrity.[3] Quintilian placed still more stress on the idea of a good man speaking well.[4]

The following components recur most often in early definitions of *ethos*: (1) the intelligence, knowledge, and tangible attainments of the speaker; (2) appearance; (3) character and reputation; (4) personality; (5) perceived sincerity; and (6) the manner in which the speech itself (arrangement, style, memory, invention, and delivery) contributes to the other factors. The prestige influence of the speech of introduction also appears in some definitions.

Beginning in 1949, scholars such as Frank S. Haiman subjected the classical concepts of source credibility to empirical tests in laboratory settings. By the 1950s, Harvard psychologists Carl I. Hovland, Irving L. Janis, and Harold H. Kelley had begun to publish their findings on the factors that constitute source credibility.[5] After completing doctoral research on this topic in 1961,[6] Kenneth E. Anderson joined with

Photo Gill Ferguson

Theodore Clevenger Jr to publish a summary of current research on the topic.[7] In 1966, James C. McCroskey[8] published the results of his efforts to uncover the dimensions of source credibility; David K. Berlo, James B. Lemert, and Robert J. Mertz followed suit in 1970.[9] McCroskey, whose efforts continued over a number of years, became one of the leading authorities in this area.

A number of these and other experimental studies have found that audience perceptions of a speaker influence responses to the message. These studies have identified the following concepts as important considerations in audience reception of messages: the perceived *trustworthiness*, *competence*, *dynamism*, *status*, *composure*, *sociability*, and *objectivity* of the speaker.

True, the terms used in talking about source credibility vary from study to study, and the factors cluster in different ways in different studies. Some researchers refer to the *trustworthiness* dimension of source credibility, whereas others use terms such *safety* or *character* to refer to the same idea. Some use the term *competency*, while others talk about the *qualification* or *expertise* dimension. *Likeability* is another term used to refer to *sociability*, and the term *dynamism* often substitutes for *extroversion*. Some researchers have identified only two dimensions to source credibility: *trustworthiness* and *competency*.[10] Others have identified *competence*, *trustworthiness*, and *dynamism*.[11] Still others have located four dimensions: *trustworthiness*, *competency*, *dynamism*, and *objectivity*.[12] Some studies include *charisma* as a source credibility factor.[13] Others regard *composure* and *status* as components of *competency*, rather than independent variables.[14] So the terms and the organization of the concepts vary, but the basic ideas surface in many studies. For instance, even when *composure* does not appear as a separate factor, discussions about composure appear under other headings.

Chapter 5 described how speakers can influence their credibility through delivery. This chapter focuses on building credibility through speech content.

Variables Related to Credibility

Trustworthiness

Most scholars agree that the most important dimension to source credibility is *trustworthiness*. If the audience does not trust you, you will not achieve your goals as a speaker. Speakers establish *trustworthiness* when they appear to say what they believe. Canadian audiences do not accept 'wishy-washiness' or 'flip-flops' in speakers. One of the most common accusations levelled against the Liberal Party is their flip-flop on the Goods and Services Tax (GST). When the Conservatives brought the GST to the Liberal-dominated Senate in 1991, the Liberals refused to pass it. And when the Conservatives added senators to ensure the passage of the bill, the Liberals filibustered against the GST. They claimed that, once in power, they would dismantle the tax. Of course, the Liberals have been in power since 1993, and the GST remains. As a consequence, Liberal Party leaders still confront questions from a skeptical public that does not trust the government to fulfill its promises.

Audiences tend to trust speakers who violate expectations by taking a stance that puts them at personal risk. Beuenia Brown, a delegate to the 2004 US Democratic convention, noted: 'When a person is outspoken, I think of them as honest. I don't see them as having to connive. They're speaking from the heart.'[15] Many Canadians respected John Crosby, a member of Parliament from Newfoundland who served as a cabinet minister in the Clark and Mulroney governments, not because they always agreed with his politics but because they believed that *he* believed what he said. During that period of time, I sometimes questioned my first-year students about their reaction to various political figures. Almost invariably, a number mentioned Crosby as their favourite politician. (In his later years in Parliament, however, Crosby sometimes took the bluntness to offensive extremes when he jousted verbally with the Liberal 'Rat Pack'.)

Photo Gill Ferguson

In the same way, audiences distrust those who change their point of view to match the situation. US Senator John Kerry faced no end of ridicule for making the statement, 'I actually did vote for the $87 billion before I voted against it', in reference to a vote on funding the Iraq war.

Audiences also trust speakers who are 'one of us'—who share our background, our experiences, and our likely fate. For that reason, speakers often point to similarities with their audiences. Behavioural scientists refer to this phenomenon as *homophily*.[16] When British Prime Minister Tony Blair spoke to the Irish Parliament on 26 November 1998, he sought to establish this sense of oneness with his audience:

Box 9.2 Tips from a Professional: Sincerity Matters
by Brian Creamer

George Orwell, author of *1984*, said that the great enemy of communication is lack of sincerity. Comedian Groucho Marx agreed when he observed, 'Sincerity is everything.' But Marx added, jokingly, 'If you can fake that, you've got it made.' In the realm of public speaking, sincerity is everything—but you cannot fake it. It is the key to communicating with an audience—a necessary condition of connecting with listeners.

Sincerity: A Definition

What does it mean to say someone is 'sincere'? The dictionary gives various definitions: free from pretense or deceit; earnest, genuine, honest, frank. I like this one: the same in reality as in appearance. Think about a speaker whose words touched or moved you at some time. I am willing to bet that you experienced him or her as sincere. I remember one speaker who often appeared on public television at fundraising time. Leo Buscaglia would tell the most amazing stories about his big, wacky Italian family. He talked about life, love, and learning. He was passionate. He was real. And he cared. Audiences adored him—sometimes staying hours after a lecture for one of his famous hugs.

Now think of a speaker who turned you off—a politician, marketer, motivational speaker, or a particular television evangelist. What bothered you about the speaker? Again, I am willing to bet that it related to your perception of that speaker's sincerity. Audiences know a phony when they see one. I recall attending a speech contest a few years back. The speaker gave, in technical terms, a flawless performance. The eye contact was there. The organization and gestures. The vocal variety. But he was not communicating 'in the moment'. Rather, he was play-acting for our benefit, reciting a text from his head. In fact, he didn't seem to know—or care—that an audience was present. His speech felt fake. Not surprisingly, he didn't win. The reality is that we can have all the 'technicals' right. But if we are not believable, we are finished.

How can we 'speak with sincerity'? In keeping with the definition above, one of the most basic ways is simply to be ourselves—to appear to be who we really are. Being the same in appearance as in reality implies being true to our values and beliefs and not putting on airs, play-acting, or throwing in big words in an attempt to impress others. We also communicate sincerity when we speak on subjects about which we genuinely care. After all, if we don't care about our subject, why should our listeners? As I heard one speaker put it, 'I'll believe how much you know when I see how much you care.'

One of the best ways to communicate sincerity is to speak from personal experience. We show that we have a stake in the issue, that our interest is not purely academic. Indeed, who is better placed to speak about something we have lived than we are? At times, this means daring to appear vulnerable before an audience, even looking emotional or sentimental. Risking vulnerability by sharing our personal stories is often the price we must pay to connect emotionally with an audience. Our listeners need to be able to see themselves in us. The clearer and more intimate the picture we paint, the more they can identify with our plight.

Of course, it is not easy to share a moving story or difficult experience. This lesson was brought home to me very poignantly a few years ago. A brother was diagnosed with terminal cancer. The experience of being with someone through the dying process was difficult and new to me. Nonetheless, I decided to share my story in a speech. I spoke about how he and I had struggled with our emotions to connect with one another in the hospital one day—a process that was not easy for either of us. After writing the first draft of the speech, however, I had reservations. I feared my account might be a bit too personal or overly sentimental. And as I often do, I shared my misgivings with a trusted friend. Her advice was simple, 'Leave it in.' So when the time came to deliver the speech a few days later, I trusted her advice and ignored my misgivings. After I had spoken, a woman in the audience came to me to say that she had been very moved by my speech. She said that she was particularly touched by the story of my brother's and my struggling to connect with one another that day in the hospital. Her reaction reinforced in my mind a powerful lesson: we must be willing to share and risk ourselves as speakers. We must be willing to put ourselves on the line if we wish to connect with an audience. When we do, our listeners sense and see that we are genuine.

Communicating sincerity also means focusing on the audience. How can they grow or benefit from our knowledge or experience? Public speaking is not about the speaker. It is about the audience. If our talk is all about us, we will almost certainly fail. By asking for examples or input from the audience and making time for questions, we show that we care and that our presentation is real—not canned.

Finally, to speak sincerely is to say what we mean and mean what we say. This implies, first and foremost, taking responsibility for our language. How many times have you heard prominent public figures avoid responsibility for taking action by speaking in the passive voice?

Notice the difference between these two statements: 'It is important that action be taken' and 'I will act.' Speaking in the passive voice undermines our sincerity because it conveys an impression of distance. We say something must be done without saying who will do it. The active voice leaves no doubt as to where the responsibility for action lies. We respect people who are clear about where they stand on an issue. We experience them as sincere, even if we do not personally agree with their point of view.

Some speakers avoid responsibility for their words by using roundabout or vague phraseology. Notice the difference between one company's pledge to reduce environmental pollutants and another's promise to work towards reducing such pollutants. Other examples of vague terminology are 'in due course' and 'at the proper juncture'. Listeners are familiar with such gobbledygook, and they sense that speakers who use such language are not levelling with them. Speaking with sincerity means eliminating the 'wiggle room' that leaves doubt about our motives and our intent.

Conclusion

Sincerity does matter—probably more today then ever. In an age of information overload, audiences have little time for speakers who are less than genuine. Technical competence is not enough. Audiences relate to real human beings who show that they care—about their subject and their audience. Speakers must mean what they say and say what they mean.

An experienced speaker and speech coach, Brian Creamer is the author of Successfully Speaking: Seven Keys to Unlock Your Speaking Potential. He can be reached through his Web site: <www.successfullyspeaking.ca>.

Ireland, as you may know, is in my blood. My mother was born in the flat above her grandmother's hardware shop on the main street of Ballyshannon in Donegal. She lived there as a child, started school there and only moved when her father died; her mother remarried and they crossed the water to Glasgow. We spent virtually every childhood summer holiday up to when the troubles really took hold in Ireland, usually at Rossnowlagh, the Sands House Hotel, I think it was. And we would travel in the beautiful countryside of Donegal. It was there in the seas off the Irish coast that I learned to swim, there that my father took me to my first pub, a remote little house in the country, for a Guinness, a taste I've never forgotten and which it is always a pleasure to repeat.[17]

In a farewell address, Hilary Weston (former Lieutenant-Governor of Ontario) spoke of how Canada is one with the rest of the world:

> The globalization of commerce and communications has made us all partners in each other's well being. If some of the planet is suffering massive poverty, none of us can feel smug in our prosperity. If some of the planet is at war, none of us can expect to remain forever at peace.[18]

To establish credibility on the trustworthiness dimension, speakers should acknowledge divergent points of view, use respectful terms when referring to opponents, remind audiences of shared experiences and common values, speak in concrete terms to avoid an impression of wishy-washiness, be willing to take a stand on controversial issues, and demonstrate consistency in belief structures over time. Some studies in classroom settings have found that instructors lose credibility with students when they engage in sarcastic put-downs or make verbally abusive comments.[19]

Competence

The second most frequently acknowledged factor in source credibility is *competency* or expertise.[20] Experimental studies support the connection between expertise and ability to persuade. Two classical studies found, for example, that subject attitudes changed more dramatically when the information source was revealed to have expertise related to the topic under discussion, as opposed to someone without expertise on the topic.[21]

We assign credibility to speakers who are recognized for their knowledge in an area. Prime Minister Paul Martin is well-known, for example, for his significant experience as finance minister. Most Canadians are confident that Martin is well-equipped to deal with the country's financial issues. So when he speaks on budgetary issues, he has a high level of credibility. On other topics, he has less credibility. When Martin meets with western Canadians, for example, he has to work hard to establish his expertise on issues related to lumber, oil, and the environment. The sponsorship scandal also diminished his credibility in areas related to ethics, as he was forced to bear responsibility for the alleged mistakes of his predecessor, Jean Chrétien.

Afraid of being associated with the previous government in the 2004 election, Martin refused to publicize his successful record as finance minister. He could not easily promote his years in cabinet or *expertise* without raising questions of *trustworthiness.* Since his opponents did not let the issue of trustworthiness escape the attention of the public, Martin may have lost more than he gained by avoiding discussion of his record as the finance minister who tamed the budget deficit and brought budget surpluses to the Canadian government. Ironically, Martin faced the same dilemma that Chrétien had confronted. Despite his extensive experience in cabinet, Chrétien chose to distance himself from the legacy of the Trudeau years. In so doing, however, he also forfeited the credibility he had acquired as an experienced and distinguished member of cabinet.

Box 9.3 A Question of Ethics

Darrell presented a speech on the topic of political fraud and corruption. He spoke, in particular, about a recent scandal involving a number of high-profile public officials. He decided to name the guilty officials, all of whom belonged to the same political party. Darrell realized that not all members of this party were dishonest, and he knew that his speech would offend audience members who supported the political party accused of wrongdoing. In addition, his instructor had told the class to avoid topics such as politics and religion. Still, Darrell believed that public officials have a special responsibility to behave in an ethical way. He also believed that public servants have an obligation to answer to their publics. Darrell did not agree with his professor that students should avoid topics such as politics, but he believed that religion was a different matter. Do you agree? How do you feel about discussing political topics in a classroom speaking environment? Religious topics? Should speakers be allowed to attack the credibility of public figures? In all circumstances? In certain prescribed circumstances? Is name-calling ever justified in a speech?

Another factor played into this situation, as well. Darrell did not tell the audience that his cousin was running for political office, against the candidate he was accusing of wrongdoing. Darrell did not think this information was relevant, since he believed the candidate was guilty and he would not have supported him under any circumstances. Yet, he did want his cousin to win the election, and he hoped his speech would make a small contribution to that end.

In the question session that followed the speech, one student accused Darrell of having a hidden agenda. Should Darrell have been more forthcoming about the purposes of his speech? Is it unethical to conceal purposes in a speech? Many politicians are really campaigning for office when they accept 'goodwill' speaking occasions. Should they tell the audience why they accepted the speaking engagement?

In October 2001, Margaret Newall delivered a convocation address to graduating students at the University of Manitoba. At the time, Newall chaired the Prairieaction Foundation of Calgary, Alberta, a charitable organization that funds research aimed at preventing and combatting abuse and violence. Since an introductory speech had acquainted the audience with her credentials, Newall was able to focus on the personal dimensions of her acquaintance with domestic violence:

> My own awareness of family violence began to emerge over twenty-five years ago, in a Grade 3 classroom in the suburbs. I had taught a lesson, and was walking up and down each aisle making sure that the children understood the assignment that I had given to them. It was a bright sunny day. My shadow fell across one child, who cringed and threw up his arm to protect his head. 'Andy,' I told him, 'I would never hit you. You can count on me.' To myself, though, I thought, 'Someone must hit him on a regular basis, that his defensive reflexes are so well developed.' Over the years my awareness grew.[22]

If you have no first-hand knowledge of the subject, your audience needs to know that you have acquired competency through second-hand knowledge. In the following example, the speaker uses this strategy to gain credibility:

> You may wonder how an 18-year-old can identify with the plight of an older worker. First, I can identify because I have a father who was laid off from his work

at General Motors at the age of 44. He never got another job that paid as well or offered the same benefits. Our entire family experienced the consequences of my father's layoff. Second, I have done extensive research to learn more about a problem that has created untold distress for hundreds of thousands of Canadians. Statistics, case studies, and personal instances all paint the same bleak picture. In the context of modern technological society, many older workers face discrimination and unfair competition to maintain their jobs.

The final example comes from a speech by television and screen actor Alan Alda, delivered in May 1979 to the graduating class of the Columbia University College of Physicians and Surgeons.[23] At the time, Alda had achieved fame for his role as a field doctor in *M★A★S★H*, a long-running television show about the Korean War. He enjoyed celebrity status. The selection of an actor as a commencement speaker was, however, 'a departure from the tradition of inviting prominent physicians as commencement speakers'.[24] Thus, Alda faced the challenge of building credibility with audience members who knew far more than he did about the technical and scientific aspects of doctoring. The following excerpt illustrates how he accomplished this end:

> Ever since it was announced that a non-doctor, in fact an actor, had been invited to give the commencement address at one of the most prestigious medical schools in the country, people have been wondering—why get someone who only pretends to be a doctor when you could get a real one? Some people suggested that this school had done everything it could to show you how to *be* doctors and in a moment of desperation had brought in someone who could show you how to act like one. It's certainly true that I'm not a doctor. I have a long list of non-qualifications. In the first place, I'm not a great fan of blood. I don't mind people having it. I just don't enjoy seeing them wear it. I have yet to see a real operation because the mere smell of a hospital reminds me of a previous appointment. And my knowledge of anatomy resides in the clear understanding that the hip bone is connected to the leg bone. I am not a doctor. But you have asked me, and all in all, I think you made a wonderful choice. I say that because I probably first came to the attention of this graduating class through a character on television that I've played and helped write for the past seven years—a surgeon called Hawkeye Pierce. He's a remarkable person, this Hawkeye, and if you have chosen somehow to associate his character with your own graduation from medical school, then I find that very heartening. Because I think that it means that you are reaching out toward a very human kind of doctoring—and a very real kind of doctor.[25]

Rather than compete with the knowledge of the audience, Alda talks about the personal qualities of the character that he played for so many years, Dr Hawkeye Pierce. Since Pierce was allegedly modelled after Dr Keith Reemtsma, a professor and chairman of surgery at Columbia from 1971 to 1994,[26] this approach was especially appropriate.

To establish credibility on the competency dimension, speakers can refer to earlier experiences, knowledge of the topic, or positions held in the past. Speakers can also transmit a sense of authority and competency by using a variety of support materials—statistics, examples, and expert testimony. References to personal acquaintance with experts or earlier encounters with similar audiences support the impression that the speaker is not a novice to the subject at hand. The use of examples from these earlier experiences can greatly increase the credibility of the speaker, as well as humanize the topic. When speaking to an audience of experts, speakers gain credibility by using the terminology of the field.

Guest speakers gain additional credibility on the competency dimension when the introductions to their speeches are complimentary. Introductory speeches typically include references to the background and accomplishments of the guest speaker. (The speaker often provides this summary, thus making an active contribution to the building of his own *ethos*.)

Speakers lose credibility on the expertise dimension when they do not know their topic or speech, make statements that cannot be supported with evidence, and make poor choices with language and grammar.

Box 9.4 Improve Your Credibility through Speech Content

- Ask a well-respected person with status to introduce you.
- Refer to members of the audience.
- Mention your experience with—or expertise on—the topic.
- Demonstrate objectivity by giving both sides of the issue.
- Use solid evidence and reasoning to support your position.
- Mention your commitment to shared audience values such as family.
- Use examples that show that you are 'one of us.'

- Use strong, colourful language; avoid weak, non-assertive language.
- Be consistent; do not shift from one position to another.
- Do not be afraid to put your views on the line; audiences respect people who are willing to stand up for their views.
- Give examples that show your commitment to change and progress.
- Do not demean anyone; demonstrate respect for your audience and those who oppose your position.
- Do not apologize for mistakes.
- Do not thank the audience for attending the speech.

Status

A related concept, which many include under the category of competence, is *status*. If we perceive the speaker to have an elevated place in society and to be respected, we are more likely to see the person as credible and to pay attention to what he has to say. We typically derive our impressions of status from the reputation, appearance, and occupation of the speaker. Chapter 6 described how speakers use dress to establish status. This chapter discusses how they use references to reputation and occupation to construct status.

A number of years ago, the US Public Health Service published a study that suggested a causal relationship between smoking and lung cancer. The release of the study had little influence on the attitudes of the public until 1964, when the Surgeon General called a press conference to publicize the findings of the study. Subsequently, many Americans claimed that they had stopped smoking. Communication researchers concluded that the status of the source had a significant impact on the receptivity of the audience to the second release of the information.[27] As studies have proved, scientists have enormous credibility with audiences. In a classic experiment by Stanley Milgram, the most compliant subjects in the experiment administered what they believed to be dangerous (even lethal) electric shocks to others.[28] They did so on the orders of a man in a white laboratory coat, whom they believed to be a scientist.

Seasoned speakers recognize the role that perceived status can play in their ability to gain credibility with their audiences. To enhance her credibility when speaking at an Ottawa awards ceremony, Adrienne Clarkson, then Governor-General of Canada, mentioned previous invitations to make awards for bravery:

> Giving decorations like these is one of the most inspiring functions for me as Governor General. A week ago, I was in Winnipeg to give to the 2nd Battalion of the Princess Patricia's Canadian Light Infantry the Commander-in-Chief's Commendation for their actions in the Medak Pocket in Croatia nine years ago.

Speeches of introduction often talk about awards or recognition received by speakers. Speakers build their own credibility when they talk about affiliations with people or organizations with status. The endorsement of high-status individuals also adds to credibility, while the endorsement of low-status individuals detracts from credibility.

Hesitations such as '*Well, uh,* I suppose' and 'I wish that you—*er*—would be more considerate' strip language of its power and speakers of their status and composure. Speakers also dilute language when they use *hedges* such as '*I think* that I would like to spend tomorrow at the beach' or '*I guess* that you can use the car.' More powerful language would be 'I would like to spend tomorrow at the beach' or 'You can use the car.'[29]

Disclaimers give wiggle room to speakers. The person makes an excuse before making the assertion. 'I really shouldn't admit that I wrote the essay, but . . .' or 'I know that I shouldn't have gone to the show after hearing the bad reviews, but . . .'[30] *Qualifiers* such as *maybe, perhaps,* and *possibly* achieve the same purpose, removing the edge in the event that the listener disagrees. Excessive politeness also strips the speaker of power.[31]

Tag questions are powerless because they demonstrate uncertainty on the part of the speaker. The speaker makes an assertion and then questions her own statement: 'That movie is wonderful, *don't you think*?' 'Sally should have won that award, *shouldn't she*?' 'You do want to go, don't you?' To be more assertive, the speaker could have said 'That movie is wonderful' or 'Sally should have won that award.' Tag questions add a negative to the end of sentences: 'isn't it?'; 'don't you think?'; 'shouldn't she?'; 'wasn't it?'; 'didn't it?'[32]

Intensifiers achieve the opposite of what the term implies. Rather than strengthening a thought, they weaken it. Examples of intensifiers are 'I am *so* anxious to go,' 'I *really* want to see her,' and 'I am *so* angry that he broke his promise.'

In informal communication, people may deliberately strip language of some of its power out of respect for norms of social interaction. They may use *polite forms* such as 'Forgive me, sir, but would you be willing to change seats so that I can be close to my grandchild?' The tone is beseeching, and the language is powerless. Phrases such as 'forgive me, sir' and 'would you be willing' convey the impression that the speaker has little power or status in the situation.

When you deliver a speech, you should use powerful language—language that is strong and assertive rather than weak and unassertive. In his book *Influence: Science and Practice,* Robert B. Cialdini tells us that people are influenced by those whom they perceive to have power.[33] *Non-verbally,* speakers convey an impression of power through the clothes they wear and through vocal characteristics, stance, posture, and gestures.

Verbally, speakers communicate power through strong and assertive language. It should be noted, however, that behaviours viewed as assertive in men are sometimes seen as aggressive in women.

Dynamism

Canadian audiences also assign credibility to speakers who are *dynamic*—bold, energetic, and assertive. In his next-to-last campaign for Prime Minister (and his only defeat), the late Pierre Trudeau appeared tired and worn. Journalists said that he could no longer excite Canadian audiences.[34] When Jean Chrétien (one of Trudeau's closest associates) ran for the leadership of Canada, he faced the dilemma of having been associated with the Trudeau years. Some called Chrétien 'yesterday's man'. In this situation, Chrétien confronted the challenge of positioning himself as a member of the contemporary Canadian scene. He accomplished this end by planning (or taking advantage of) photo opportunities on university campuses, participating in athletic activities, and surrounding himself with advisers of different ages.

In terms of message strategies, a speaker can build credibility on the dynamism dimension by using forceful, active language. To establish oneself as a member of today's generation, a politician can speak about change and progress, new ideas, and current legislation and policies. US Senator Barack Obama's speech to the 2004 Democratic convention, in which he issued a call for action and change, illustrates the use of strong, powerful, and dynamic language:

> Democrats, Republicans, Independents—I say to you tonight: we have more work to do. More to do for the workers I met in Galesburg, Illinois, who are losing their union jobs at the Maytag plant that's moving to Mexico, and now are having to compete with their own children for jobs that pay seven bucks an hour. More to do for the father I met who was losing his job and choking back tears, wondering how he would pay $4,500 a month for the drugs his son needs without the health benefits he was counting on. More to do for the woman in East St. Louis, and thousands more like her, who has the grades, has the drive, has the will, but doesn't have the money to go to college.[35]

At other times during this keynote address, Obama talked about having 'energy' and 'urgency' and pursuing and defeating enemies.

Sociability

Audiences like speakers who are *sociable*. When politicians fail to show signs of sociability, as happened in Kim Campbell's 1993 campaign to be elected Prime Minister of Canada, they become the objects of severe criticism. Campbell invoked the ire of hundreds of thousands of Canadians when she remarked that she could not relate to anyone who sat around in an undershirt, drinking beer and watching a hockey game on TV. Since many Canadians more or less fit that description, Campbell hit a sensitive note that stamped her as unsociable and elitist. Her losing campaign was the price paid for this and other errors of judgement. Like the trustworthiness dimension, the sociability or likeability dimension has links to the concept of identification. We like people we perceive to be similar to us. If Kim Campbell does not like hockey, beer, and watching TV in an undershirt, then she is dissimilar to a large number of Canadians.

Speakers use strategies of *immediacy*, discussed in earlier chapters, to build rapport with audiences and enhance their perceived sociability. The term *immediacy* refers to the extent to which we feel physically or psychologically close to another person.[36] To build this sense of closeness, the speaker may refer to someone in the audience, extend a personal greeting or compliment, mention the occasion or surroundings, or ask a question of the audience. Showing respect for the audience and pointing to similarities in background can also enhance credibility on the likeability dimension.

Classroom studies have found that students like instructors who are friendly and know their names, use a number of examples to explain concepts, recount interesting stories, use a conversational tone and rate of speech, have an expressive voice and dramatic manner, use humour that is spontaneous and relevant to the course content, encourage students to talk, address the issues raised by students, and show openness and a willingness to disclose personal information.[37] Most scholars believe that we can apply these findings to speaking in general. As discussed in Chapter 5, we can certainly see that audiences like media personalities such as Oprah Winfrey, who share many personal stories and self-disclose to the audience. Winfrey comes across as highly immediate.

We also identify with people who share some of our weaknesses and vulnerabilities. In a speech delivered to the APEX symposium in June 2002, Alex Himelfarb (Clerk of the Privy Council, Secretary to the Cabinet, and head of the Public Service of Canada) spoke with great humility about his accomplishments:

> You know, I think every day what a privilege it is to be a public servant. I feel that more today than I did when I first arrived 20 years ago. I'm sometimes in a room with decision-makers and I keep wondering, 'Will they notice me or will they ask me to leave? How did I get here?'[38]

In the same way, one has a sense of meeting the real person in this next excerpt from a speech by science fiction writer Ray Bradbury. Bradbury demonstrates a humility and humanity that appeals to most listeners:

> I had a thing happen to me when I was 9 years old, which is a great lesson. That was in 1929—the start of the Great Depression. And a single comic strip in the newspaper sent me into the future. The first comic strip of Buck Rogers. In October 1929 I looked at that one comic strip, with its view of the future, and I thought, 'That's where I belong.' I started to collect Buck Rogers comic strips. And everybody in the fifth grade made fun of me. I continued to collect them for about a month, and then I listened to the critics. And I tore up my comic strips. That's the worst thing I ever did. Two or three days later, I broke down. I was crying, and I said to myself, 'Why am I crying? Whose funeral am I going to? Who died?' And the answer was, 'Me.' I'd torn up the future. And then I sat down with myself, and I was crying, and I said, 'What can I do to correct this? And I said, 'Well, hell, go back and collect Buck Rogers comic strips!' . . . And that's what I did. I started collecting Buck Rogers again.

Objectivity

A final dimension of credibility that merits discussion is *objectivity*.[39] When you cite statistics, expert testimony, specific instances, and illustrations, you avoid the appearance of relying strictly on personal opinion. You appear unbiased and objective.

Shifts in Credibility during Speech

The credibility of a speaker can vary from the beginning to the end of a speech. So researchers talk about *initial*, *derived*, and *terminal* credibility.[40] *Initial* credibility refers to audience perceptions of the speaker at the moment that she starts to speak. *Derived* credibility refers to how the speaker gains credibility during the process of delivering the speech. *Terminal* credibility concerns audience perceptions of the speaker at the end of the speech.

Audience reaction to a controversial speech by former Congressman and Louisiana Governor Edwin Edwards illustrates how speakers can dramatically alter initial audience perceptions. In 1969, at a time of great controversy over the busing of children to other school districts, Congressman Edwards spoke to members of the Louisiana Education Association on this contentious issue. His stance was moderate—favoured by neither blacks nor whites. J.K. Haynes, a spokesman for African-American educators, introduced Edwards as 'a former friend' of the black community. Jim Baronet, a television news broadcaster, described the dilemma confronted by Edwards in the following way:

> It was a hairy type of situation. He [Edwards] knew that there was nothing he could say that would please them [the audience], without cutting his own throat. Yet he impressed the group—gave a particularly good speech. He was very blunt. He said in essence that everyone was going to have to be fairer. . . . Not in the particular way that most politicians usually have about them, trying to slice up the pie so that everyone can have a piece. He somehow managed to say things bluntly, almost brutally, and I suppose in mere relief, they appreciated it to the point that they gave him a standing ovation for about six or seven minutes.[41]

This example demonstrates how a speaker can move from low initial credibility to high terminal credibility. Edwards achieved this shift in audience perceptions because he delivered a credible message. Initially, the audience distrusted him; and the introduction by Haynes only worsened the situation. But audience perceptions changed when they began to see the speaker as sincere, willing to risk his popularity for his personal convictions. The fact that Edwards was prepared to state his point of view, no matter the consequences, created trust in the audience. One audience member made the following observation, 'Well, he may be stupid, but at least he's honest.'[42] A television newsman commented on audience attitudes towards the speech content, 'I can't say that the audience necessarily agreed with him, but they gave him a standing ovation at the end.'[43]

As noted already, many factors can influence audience views of a speaker's credibility. The audience may have prior knowledge of the speaker, which determines their initial perceptions. The actions or behaviour of the speaker in the moments leading to the speech can mitigate these initial perceptions. Introductory comments can also influence the initial credibility of the speaker. The quality and relevance of the speech, as well as the speaker's delivery, can lead to higher levels of derived credibility. The terminal credibility of the speaker results from the interaction of initial perceptions with the immediate experience.

Pathos as a Persuasive Strategy

Speakers must appeal not only to the rational thought processes of their audiences, but also to their emotions. Aristotle applied the term *pathos* to the use of emotional appeals in speaking. Like later rhetorical scholars, Aristotle considered emotional appeals to be not only ethical, but necessary to the achievement of speaker goals. Speakers seek to invoke feelings in listeners such as compassion, anger, fear, pride, empathy, guilt, humility, and respect.

When we react emotionally to an event or person, we experience physiological changes. Minute alterations in blood chemistry affect our breathing, digestive processes, heartbeat, and muscle control. We may tremble or cry in an emotional moment. Emotional arousal is a very individual phenomenon, however. What causes an emotional response in one person may create no reaction in another. Mohawks, for example, are known for their abilities as high-steel workers. They are able to walk across small beams, hundreds of feet above the ground, without experiencing the sort of transformed physical state or fear that most of us would find debilitating. The same person, however, might sweat uncontrollably if confronted with the need to address an audience of 20 students.[44]

Many people, particularly in Western societies, consider overt emotional responses to be a sign of weakness. They seek to control their emotions in public. Although scholars recognize the importance of touching people emotionally with our words, speakers and audiences often think of such emotional arousal as an unnatural and undesirable state of being. In reality, feeling is a prerequisite to understanding and acting. Moderate emotional appeals help to hold the attention of an audience, focus on their needs, motivate them to think seriously about a topic, improve understanding, and encourage intelligent behaviour. If we have no feelings, we will not act—intelligently or unintelligently.[45]

At the same time, our emotions should not overwhelm our ability to think rationally about a topic. Unethical speakers seek to arouse emotions to an extreme that inhibits intelligent decision-making. Ethical speakers try to achieve a balance by using sufficiently strong appeals to facilitate intelligent responses but not so intense that listeners react without thinking. We tend to react emotionally when we perceive that a speaker is meeting our needs in some way, and surely that should be the aim of every speaker.

The most arresting examples of emotionally compelling rhetoric occur in periods of war, conflict, and great tragedy—World War I, World War II, the Cold War, Vietnam, the Gulf War, and most recently, the war in Iraq. Many of our most powerful literary pieces have come from the pain of individuals and societies at war with others or themselves.

In the film *The Third Man* (scripted by Graham Greene in 1949 and later made into a radio series and television production), character Harry Lime (played by Orson Welles) delivered these famous words: 'In Italy, for thirty years under the Borgias, they had warfare, terror, murder, bloodshed—they produced Michelangelo, Leonardo da Vinci and the Renaissance. In Switzerland, they had brotherly love, five hundred years of democracy and peace, and what did that produce? The cuckoo clock.'[46] This tongue-in-cheek comment holds some truth for rhetoric also.

The rhetoric related to the terrorist attacks on the US of 11 September 2001 and the 'war against terrorism' also reflects this need to connect with emotionally laden values such as love of country and the most deep-seated need for security. On 11 September 2004, President George W. Bush commemorated the victims of 9/11 in his weekly radio address from the Oval Office. This speech demonstrates the use of emotional language to stir the feelings of the audience:

> Three years ago, the struggle of good against evil was compressed into a single morning. In the space of only 102 minutes, our country lost more citizens than were lost in the attack on Pearl Harbor. Time has passed, but the memories do not fade. We remember the images of fire, and the final calls of love, and the courage of rescuers who saw death and did not flee.[47]

Remarks of this nature are compelling because they speak to vital issues and reflect shared values. Health-related issues such as HIV/AIDS, deaths resulting from drunk driving, and breast cancer also produce rhetoric with strong emotional appeals. In the following excerpt from a speech on the rising costs of snowmobile insurance, the speaker appealed to audience needs for safety and security:

> If nothing is done to lower the cost of insuring safe trails, the results are certain. Your neighbour, who works for the local snowmobile dealership, will be out of work. Your aunt's coffee shop will see a massive decline in sales during the winter months. And worst of all, robbed of a safe trail system, a friend or family member will be hurt or killed while snowmobiling in unfamiliar territory.[48]

Speakers use vivid and concrete language, balanced and parallel sentence structures, antithesis, repetition, alliteration, first and second voice, rhythmic triads and quads, comparison and contrast, metaphors, similes, personification, analogies, and rhetorical questions to evoke powerful emotions in their audiences. Chapter 10 will discuss these strategies.

A final area of consideration concerns the use of fear appeals in persuasive speaking. In general, scholars do not agree on how best to employ fear appeals. The majority argue that mild or moderate fear appeals work better than strong appeals.[49] They say that people tend to react defensively and tune out overly gruesome statistics and images. A few studies suggest, however, that when persuaders succeed at creating high levels of fear in audiences, the persuasive effect is greater than would otherwise be the case.[50] Teenagers, on the other hand, tend to react more to threats of rejection or social embarrassment than to threats of bodily injury. Most agree that speakers should provide audiences with explicit instructions on actions that will enable them to cope with the problem and reduce their fears. In a speech on prevalence of thyroid cancer in young people, for example, the speaker could assure the audience that the cancer can be safely and easily removed. In a speech on the risks of smoking, the speaker could advise the audience on specific places to go to seek help.[51]

Logos as a Persuasive Strategy

The term *logos* refers to argumentation and reasoning—the use of logical appeals in persuasion. The following discussion describes the processes of reasoning from examples, reasoning from generalizations, causal reasoning, and reasoning from sign. Chapter 11 considers common flaws in these reasoning processes.

Reasoning from Examples

Inductive reasoning involves reasoning from example. The speaker reaches a general conclusion on the basis of a number of specific instances. President Franklin D. Roosevelt's declaration of war on 8 December 1941 illustrates the process of inductive reasoning:

> The attack yesterday on the Hawaiian islands has caused severe damage to American naval and military forces. Very many American lives have been lost. In addition, American ships have been reported torpedoed on the high seas between San Francisco and Honolulu. Yesterday, the Japanese government also launched an attack against Malaya. Last night, Japanese forces attacked Hong Kong. Last night, Japanese forces attacked Guam. Last night, Japanese forces attacked the Philippine Islands. Last night, the Japanese attacked Wake Island. This morning, the Japanese attacked Midway Island. Japan has, therefore, undertaken a surprise offensive extending throughout the Pacific area.[52]

In a fireside chat, broadcast on radio on the following evening, Roosevelt again reasoned from examples to support his claim that the actions of Hirohito in Asia, Hitler in Germany, and Mussolini in Italy had become more than parallels; they offered proof of active collaboration among fascist forces in the three countries:

> In 1931, ten years ago, Japan invaded Manchukuo—without warning. In 1935, Italy invaded Ethiopia—without warning. In 1938, Hitler occupied Austria—without warning. In 1939, Hitler invaded Czechoslovakia—without warning. Later in 1939, Hitler invaded Poland—without warning. In 1940, Hitler invaded Norway, Denmark, the Netherlands, Belgium, and Luxembourg—without warning. In 1940, Italy attacked France and later Greece—without warning. And this year, in 1941, the Axis powers attacked Yugoslavia and Greece and they dominated the Balkans—without warning. In 1941, also, Hitler invaded Russia—without warning. And now Japan has attacked Malaya and Thailand—and the United States—without warning. It is all of one pattern.[53]

Reasoning from Generalization

In the case of deductive reasoning, the speaker reasons from the general to the specific. A classic example follows: 'All people are created equal. I am a person. Therefore, I was created equal.' Hillary Rodham Clinton (now US Senator, formerly First Lady) demonstrated a loose form of reasoning from generalization in a speech delivered at the Fourth World Conference on Women. The implicit reasoning went as follows: 'We should protect victims of human rights violations. The most frequent victims are women. Therefore, we should protect women from human rights violations.' She used the following examples to back up her claim that the most frequent victims are women:

> It is a violation of *human* rights when babies are denied food, or drowned, or suffocated, or their spines broken, simply because they are born girls. It is a violation of human rights when women and girls are sold into the slavery of prostitution. It is a

violation of human rights when women are doused with gasoline, set on fire and burned to death because their marriage dowries are deemed too small. It is a violation of human rights when individual women are raped in their own communities and when thousands of women are subjected to rape as a tactic or prize of war. It is a violation of human rights when a leading cause of death worldwide among women ages 14 to 44 is the violence they are subjected to in their own homes. It is a violation of human rights when women are denied the right to plan their own families, and that includes being forced to have abortions or being sterilized against their will.[54]

Causal Reasoning

With cause-effect reasoning, speakers observe effects and look for the causes. If we have an increase in violent crime (effect), we may seek to identify the causes of the increase. If we see that more people are unemployed (effect), we may look for the causes of the unemployment. If we find that more people are dying from heart disease (effect), we may seek to uncover links with dietary habits. We ask: 'What is the cause of this problem?' 'What has generated this effect?'

Using the first example, let us consider the case of two speakers. Perhaps the first speaker sees that violent crime is on the increase. Researching the topic, she believes that she has discovered a link between violent crime and firearms. She may learn, for example, that guns are the cause of most homicides, the weapon of choice in domestic violence, and the most frequent cause of accidental deaths among children. She develops her speech, using statistics, examples, and other evidence to support her claim that the availability of firearms is responsible for increases in violent crime.

Another speaker may disagree with this perspective. He may take a different route with his research. He may believe that he has found a more compelling association between poverty and violent crime. He may believe that poverty is at the root of the problem and that firearms only provide a means to express anger and frustration with

---

Box 9.5 Tips for Using Evidence

· Does the evidence come from a credible and unbiased source?
· Is the evidence up to date?
· Is the evidence representative of other findings on the topic?
· Does the evidence support the points that you are making?
· Have you given sufficient evidence to support your ideas?

---

the system. He may believe that the large numbers of accidental deaths among children are due, not to the presence of firearms in the home, but to the lack of parental supervision and the absence of old-fashioned family values. Like the first speaker, he will use statistics, examples, and other support materials to substantiate his position.

Acceptance of the causal reasoning of either speaker will depend on the quality of the supporting evidence, the credibility of the speaker, and the extent to which the audience is disposed to consider the arguments of the speaker.

Reasoning from Sign

Reasoning from sign is similar to causal reasoning. With causal reasoning, you see an effect and you try to figure out the cause. With reasoning from sign, you see a visible indicator—or physical manifestation—of a condition. You try to figure out what the sign means. Does someone with a cough, high fever, and headache have the flu? Possibly. You may see bruises, fractures, and bumps in a child. Has the child been abused? Maybe. You see someone with a modest home, economy-priced car, and frugal spending habits. Does the person fall into a middle income bracket? Perhaps. The person with the above symptoms may or may not have the flu. He may have pneumonia or other serious lung condition. The child with bumps, bruises, and fractures may be abused or may be accident-prone. The person with the modest home, economy-priced car, and frugal spending habits may be limited in access to funds, miserly, extremely generous in giving to charitable causes, or spending all of her money on a family member with problems.

Reasoning from Parallel Cases

When you reason from a parallel case, you look at one situation and extrapolate its characteristics to a second situation. You may, for example, have had an easy time finding an apartment in Montreal. Moving to Vancouver, you assume that you will have an equally easy time—that the characteristics of the two situations are approximately the same. You use one case as a model for another case. In argumentation, you attempt to convince the audience that the two cases share enough similarities that the model is transferable between cases. Leaders of Western democratic countries argue, for example, that the practices of their countries can be replicated in developing societies. Many of the emerging Eastern European societies are attempting to adopt Western economic models. In past years, Canadians looked to the Japanese for management models.

The difficulty, of course, with reasoning from parallel cases derives from the fact the characteristics of two situations may be dissimilar. Some African and Latin American countries may not have sufficiently developed infrastructures to support Western economic policies. In unstable countries, a more authoritarian manner of governance may be the only way to prevent a never-ending sequence of military coups. Former East bloc countries may be culturally different from the Western societies they seek to emulate, especially after so many years of Soviet rule. And Canadian managers may operate in different circumstances from Japanese managers. Western values favour the individual, and Japanese values favour the collective. Canadian managers like to maintain control of their own decisions, and the Japanese rely on a consensus-based model.

In persuasive speaking, speakers often argue that one policy is transferable to a second situation. They may seek to convince the audience that an innovative practice in one educational system will work in other educational systems. They may argue that the United States, Mexico, and Canada should adopt a common monetary system, similar to that used in the European Economic Community. Or they may seek to persuade their listeners that environmental legislation in one province will work equally well in a different province. Chapter 10 will look at common fallacies in reasoning from parallel cases.

Conclusion

This chapter has examined how speakers use *ethos*, *pathos*, and *logos* to develop their speeches. A later chapter will consider issues of accountability related to unethical practices—fallacies in argumentation and reasoning and appeals designed to bypass rational thought processes.

Questions for Discussion

1. In analyzing your own source credibility, what would you consider to be your strengths and weaknesses as a speaker? Does your credibility vary from topic to topic? Give examples to illustrate this point.
2. Do male and female speakers face different challenges when building their credibility? Are the expectations the same for men and women?
3. How can a speaker with initial low credibility improve her credibility?
4. Why does war produce some of our greatest speeches and novels? Would the kind of rhetoric produced during war be deemed as overly emotional in peacetime?
5. List examples of jargon from various professions (e.g., law, medicine, various academic disciplines, government). Does such language ever serve a useful purpose? When would its use be appropriate or inappropriate?

CHAPTER TEN

Speeches to Convince, Stimulate, or Actuate

Preparing a Persuasive Speech

This assignment requires the preparation of a speech to convince, stimulate, or actuate. After conducting audience research, the speaker will decide on the specific purpose. A six–eight minute speech should follow one of the organizational patterns described in this chapter. A question–and–answer session should follow the speeches. This assignment stresses conforming to persuasive patterns of organization, supporting your ideas with sound evidence and reasoning, achieving eloquence of language, and delivering a speech with memorized passages. The most famous speeches in historical terms are those that employ such linguistic devices as repetition, metaphors, and analogies. The wording of the speeches has been carefully honed. The language is precise, requiring the speaker to rely on memorized passages.

Learning Objectives

To learn how to prepare and present a persuasive speech, including finding out how to:

- Select a topic.
- Write a tentative position statement, and make adjustments to this later if necessary.
- Define a general purpose.
- Research and identify levels of audience knowledge and attitudes.
- Decide on a specific purpose or desired outcome.
- Choose an organizational pattern.
- Write an introduction.
- Develop supporting materials.
- Research and adapt materials to your audience.

- Write transitions and internal summaries.
- Use evocative language to express your ideas.
- Write your conclusion.
- Speak from memory or note cards.
- Respond to questions from your audience.

The persuader may have three potential purposes: to *convince* (change existing attitudes or effect a shift in position), to *stimulate* (reinforce existing attitudes or stances), or to *actuate* (move an audience to act on their beliefs or to eliminate an unwanted behaviour). In this chapter, we will discuss how to prepare a persuasive speech that seeks to convince, stimulate, or actuate. That process involves (1) selecting a topic, (2) writing a tentative position statement, (3) defining a general purpose, (4) researching and identifying levels of audience knowledge and attitudes towards your position, (5) deciding on a desired outcome, (6) choosing an organizational pattern, (7) writing an introduction, (8) developing supporting materials, (9) researching and adapting to your audience, (10) writing transitions and internal summaries, (11) choosing evocative language, (12) writing your conclusion, (13) memorizing and delivering your speech, and (14) responding to questions at the conclusion of your speech.

Step 1: Selecting Your Topic

Your initial task is to select a topic that is meaningful to you *and* relevant to your audience. To achieve this goal, you may want to think about causes that matter to you, policies and laws that you would like to change; or policies and laws that may be at risk.

Photo Gill Ferguson

Persuasive discourse aims to *change* or *reinforce* existing attitudes and practices. Typically, if everything is going well and everyone agrees with us, we do not see the need to engage in persuasive discourse. Finally, you should also take ethical considerations into account.

Think about Causes That Matter to You

In selecting a topic, think about causes that matter to you. All of us have some causes in which we believe. A *cause* is a goal, principle, or practice to which we are strongly committed. These commitments reflect our values and our concept of an ideal society. What would such a world resemble? Obviously, a utopia constructed by one person would look quite different from a utopia constructed by another. In the same way, our causes would be different.

If we think in terms of political and social activism, we can arrive at causes that matter to other people. Tree huggers would say that their cause is environmental sustainability. People for Ethical Treatment of Animals (PETA) argue for animal rights. The advocacy group Victims of Violence stands for the rights of victims of violent crime. Some argue against Canadian participation in rebuilding Iraq. Other social and political activists have causes that relate to the rights of women, men, grandparents, children, gays and lesbians, and various minority groups. Environmental groups have a wide-ranging list of causes to which they subscribe. Most causes find their voice in advocacy groups. For ideas on causes about which to speak, look for advocacy groups on the Internet or in the media.

Our values are strongly reflected in the causes to which we commit our time and resources. Consider the following list of values identified by Milton Rokeach, which he says are common to most cultures in the world: achievement, activity, competence, compassion, generosity, obedience, freedom, imagination, independence, intelligence, logic and intuition, a comfortable life, honesty, world at peace, world of beauty, responsibility, sociality, and family orientation. A number of other researchers have added individualism, patriotism, progressiveness, optimism, and efficiency to the list.

Many of these values (equality, independence, a world at peace, and others) are at the heart of the causes discussed above. So when you argue about causes, you are really arguing about values. If you are arguing for a cause or value, you might seek to convince listeners that vegetarianism will save our environment, the arts should receive greater funding, or residents of urban centres should use public transportation in preference to automobiles. In these three instances, you are urging people to change opinions or practices that violate values related to responsibility and aesthetic concerns.

Think about Policies and Laws You Would Like To Change

Policies and laws emerge from decisions made by governments (federal, state, municipal), schools, businesses, sports and recreational organizations, fraternities and sororities, churches, the courts, and other organized groups. Whereas policies emerge from administrative decisions, laws result from legal decisions. Policies are often formalized and usually recorded in print; that is, they appear in a document (legislative acts, charters and operating rules of organizations). At other times, they are unwritten, but everyone knows that the rule or regulation exists. Laws are always formalized, emerging from the legal structures of governments. Laws are subject to interpretation by courts in democratic societies.

Since people do not confront the need to persuade on policies and laws that everyone supports, the speaker will want to identify policies and laws that have given birth to *issues*. Issues result from policy decisions and laws that are not widely accepted. We have many different kinds of issues: political, social, economic, technological, health, environmental, educational, and other. Activists attach themselves to these issues. They may call for stiffer penalties for white-collar crime or better legal representation for offenders. They may demand the abolition of hazing practices in the military, bonfires on university campuses, or drinking competitions in fraternities. In the workplace, they may argue for policies that facilitate greater employee participation. In a sports organization such as the Professional Golfers Association (PGA), they may speak in favour of allowing golf competitors who are disabled to use motorized golf carts or argue to change participation requirements.

To qualify as an issue, the policy question or law must conform to three criteria. *First, the policy or law must have elements that are debatable.* That is, there must be at least two conflicting points of view on some aspect of the subject, with some people in agreement and others in disagreement. A cosmetic firm, for example, may have a policy of using animals in its research; some will support and some oppose the policy. The federal government may be considering new security screening measures or 'no-fly' lists at airports. Some will believe these measures are necessary to protect people, while others will oppose any policy that threatens the privacy of individuals. Border agents may use racial and ethnic profiling to identify people for strip searches; some may agree and others disagree that such measures are necessary or appropriate.

Second, by definition, issues relate to policy questions that are unresolved in people's minds. Once the public accepts policies and laws, they move out of the issue category. However, some issues (e.g., abortion and capital punishment) will probably never go away. The same is true of the debate over gun control. No matter what kind of legislation is passed, this debate will continue for a long time. The act of passing legislation or adopting a policy or practice will not assure the acceptance of the law or policy. So long as people do not accept a particular policy decision, the question remains active.

Third, values reside in policy questions, just as they are at the centre of causes in general. The debate over abortion pits the sanctity of human life against the right to self-determination. Policy debates related to military spending position the value of state security against the value of a world at peace. Of course, those who persuade often adopt strategies that link their causes to multiple values. When pro-choice advocates wear T-shirts that depict a coat hanger, they invoke a value more potent than the right to *self-determination*. Like the anti-abortionists, they argue on the basis of the *sanctity of human life* (in this case, the woman's life). When military and political leaders argue their case for increased defence funding, they say that their troops will be at risk if the government does not allocate the necessary funds (the *sanctity of human life*). They also say that they are fighting to secure a *world at peace*. And they invoke the values of *compassion* and *humanitarianism* when they say that they will secure the rights of others against authoritarian and despotic regimes. Frequently, advocates for increased military funding call on the value of *patriotism*. Box 10.1 lists additional examples of topics that give birth to issues.

Imagine that someone said to you, 'You have the power to change any policies or laws with which you disagree. Which ones would you change?' In response to this question, I would say, 'I do not believe that the legal system offers adequate resources to

Box 10.1 Persuasion Topics: Issues

Legalized gambling	Cost of wars (human, financial)
Privatized health care	Costs of insurance (car, house, etc.)
Proliferation of street gangs	Violence on the Internet
Motorcycle gangs	By-products of video games
Cosmetic surgery	Male and female roles in society
Panhandling	Costs of legal suits
Violence in schools	Insurance fraud
Addiction to video games	Identity theft
Climate change/global warming	Internet scams
Establishment of government spy agencies	White-collar crime
Surveillance practices by government	Garbage disposal sites
Child trafficking	Disposal of hazardous wastes
Poverty	The costs of plastic society
Custody laws	Increases in allergies
Risks of inoculations	Costs of aging society
'Super bugs' (antibiotic resistant bacteria)	Equity in health care for the elderly
Biological terrorism	Immigration quotas
Clean water	Costs of conformity/loss of individuality
Fishing/hunting rights for Aboriginals	Congested highways
The role of the courts in deciding laws	Pollution in cities
Subsidized child care	Risks associated with travel abroad
Eating disorders (anorexia, bulimia, obesity)	Risks associated with domestic travel
Consumption as a way of life	Cost of education
Medical errors	Full-time student, full-time employee
Protection of animals	Risks associated with amusement parks
Endangered species	Costs of partying in universities
Exotic pets	Children who kill their parents
Sexually transmitted diseases (STDs)	Date rape
Overpopulation	Internet predators
Criminalization of drugs	Airline safety
Cost of being a drug 'mule'	Racial profiling
Medical uses of marijuana	Employment practices
Burial practices	Sexual harassment
Spousal violence	Branding of society/designer society
Gun control	Polygamy
Suicide rates among undercover police	Suicide in teenage populations

victims. I do not believe that governments should allow tobacco companies to operate. I do not believe that gambling should be legalized. I believe that governments should place stronger restrictions on violent or pornographic content on the Internet. I do not believe that charity organizations should sell the names of donors for profit.' If I were a political or social activist, several of the above would be my causes; and I would argue to change or strengthen the laws that allow these policies and practices to continue.

Of course, not everyone would agree with me. Many people would say, 'No, I like gambling. I don't agree that we should ban it.' 'No, tobacco companies have the same right to seek profits and markets as chemical companies and pharmaceutical companies.' 'No, we should not regulate content on the Internet.' So issues would arise from my choices. Values would be at the foundation of both perspectives. And obviously, if we are debating the question, the matter is unresolved.

Think about Policies or Laws That May Be at Risk

Alternatively, you might want to talk about policies, laws, or practices that are at risk of being discontinued or eliminated. A university, for example, may be rethinking the matter of subsidized child care for students. A public recreation facility may be considering instituting or increasing user fees. A government may be contemplating changes to family law. Opposition to a change in any one of these policies could be the subject of a persuasive speech in which you argue to support the status quo. The speech purpose is to convince an informed audience to agree with you or to move the audience to action. If a persuader perceives that audience members agree strongly with his point of view, he may ask the audience to act on their beliefs by writing letters to lawmakers, petitioning justice departments, or taking other actions.

Photo Gill Ferguson

Sometimes people accept the basic concept of a policy or law but disagree on the definition of terms. They may support benefits for families, for instance, but disagree on the definition of *family*. The same kinds of arguments arise with regard to the definition of *marriage* and *spouse*. In a September 2004 audience with the Canadian ambassador to Italy, the late Pope John Paul II argued that the term *spouse* should not include a same-sex partner and that the term *marriage* should refer only to the union of a man and woman.

In other situations, people may agree with the *intent* of legislation or policies but disagree with how governments or other organizations interpret, implement, or enforce the policies. They may agree, for example, that refugees should be allowed to enter the country but disagree on implementation of the legislation, believing customs officials to be too lenient or too strict in their interpretation of the law. Alternatively, they may disagree with criteria set in place to determine who qualifies for refugee status.

Think about Controversial Claims You Would Defend or Dispute

Many people and groups make claims that cannot be definitively proved. Because the claims have not been proved, they are subject to controversy. Scientists speculate, for example, that the virus associated with AIDS originated in the rain forests. A number of communication scholars claim an association between violence on television and criminal behaviour. Members of groups interested in UFOs claim that aliens visit our planet on a regular basis. You may choose to speak in defence of—or against—one of these controversial claims.

Take Ethical Considerations into Account

On some occasions, you may want to reconsider your choice of topics for ethical reasons. Imagine that you have decided to deliver a speech supporting a French law, passed in 2004, that bans the presence of religious symbols in schools. Banned symbols include Christian crucifixes, Jewish skull caps, and, most contentiously, Muslim headscarves. At the time that you plan to deliver your speech, extremists are holding two French hostages and demanding that France rescind its law. The situation is tense and emotional, and the lives of two men are at stake. You learn that some students have expressed anger towards your position statement. Views appear to be polarized along religious lines. Some do not believe that you should use classroom time to promote a point of view that trespasses on their religious convictions. In a case such as this one, you should consider selecting another topic. Where levels of hostility are too strong and latitudes of rejection are too large, you must ask yourself whether you can accomplish any purpose in the speech.

Step 2: Framing a Tentative Position Statement

Next you should frame a tentative position statement—your position on the question you have chosen. You could say, for example:

- I believe that gambling should be abolished.
- I believe that people should do more to protect the rain forests.
- I believe that working parents should have access to subsidized child care.
- I believe that increases in university tuition force many students to work unrealistically long hours to pay for their education.
- I believe that the staggering debt accumulated by students in their university years is unfair.
- I believe that present child custody laws put many children at risk.
- I believe that vegetarianism offers many benefits to people.
- I believe that some diet regimes put one's health at risk.
- I believe that governments should offer subsidies to organic farmers.

Some of the above position statements concern policies and laws; others concern values and personal choices. The statements about vegetarianism and diets, for example, relate to personal choices and values rather than existing policies. Note that all examples, however, have controversial elements; and even the policy statements are value-based. Moreover, some value statements could lead to policies if enough people begin to hold the belief or value. Beliefs, values, and policies interact.

Step 3: Translating Your Position Statement into a Thesis Statement

- After framing a position statement, you must convert that statement of personal belief into a thesis statement for your speech, such as:
- Video games contribute to violence in society.
- The new gun control legislation will save lives.
- Large-scale consumption of beef is destroying our environment.
- Governments should offer larger subsidies to dairy farmers.
- Legislatures, not courts, should decide matters such as same-sex marriage.
- Universities and colleges should lower their tuition fees.
- Gambling destroys families.
- Fashion television provides unrealistic role models for young women.

Step 4: Researching Your Audience

After framing a thesis statement, you should research audience views on the topic. As discussed in Chapter 5, you want to learn more about audience demographics (e.g., level of education, occupation and income, age, gender, race, ethnicity, and prior experience with the topic), psychographics (beliefs, attitudes, and values), personality (e.g., open- vs close-minded, high or low esteem), and situation (e.g., environmental constraints). This information will allow you to generate a profile of your audience so you can better meet their needs and achieve your purposes.

You can keep a weekly journal in which you make notes about the interests, abilities, and experiences of your classmates. A well-kept journal can give valuable clues to audience attitudes on topics. A second way to learn about audience attitudes is to elicit responses to a questionnaire, which requests feedback on your topic. This questionnaire will enable you to identify audience attitudes on your specific topic.

Persuasive speakers face audiences with four potential attitudes on any topic: supportive, undecided, hostile, or apathetic (not really caring one way or the other). Audiences are also at different places on the persuasion continuum. Some are ready to be persuaded. Others have not received the necessary preparation to understand the speech. They may lack information or awareness of the significance of the topic. They may not be able to see how the topic applies to their lives. Some have large latitudes of acceptance; others have large latitudes of rejection. (See Chapter 5 for a review of these concepts.)

Step 5: Defining Your General Purpose

After articulating a position statement and researching audience views on the topic, the speaker defines a general purpose to be achieved in the speech. Informative speaking aims to increase the *knowledge or awareness* of audiences. Persuasive speaking, on the other hand, aims to influence *beliefs*, *attitudes*, and *actions* of audiences. Despite the popularity of a long-standing distinction between informative and persuasive purposes, studies have demonstrated that changes in awareness, attitudes, and actions occur on a continuum. That is, higher levels of awareness are necessary before changes in attitudes or actions can take place. The following kind of continuum exists:

Speech → Change in awareness → Change in attitude → Change in behaviour

What does this finding mean for the persuader? First, the existence of a continuum means that the persuasive speaker will often need to include a strong informative element in the speech. This informative element typically appears in the problem or need and solution steps. The less informed the audience and the more complex and controversial the issue, the more information may be required to bring about changes in beliefs or attitudes. Attempting to effect changes in audiences with low knowledge levels is unrealistic.

Second, the necessity to move audiences along a continuum means that the speaker will need to be flexible on purposes. Speakers who confront a well-informed audience will have a choice of speech purposes. The persuasive choices will be to reinforce existing attitudes, to convince the audience to change attitudes, or to move the listeners to action. If the audience holds *positive attitudes* towards the position of the speaker, the persuader can choose to reinforce those attitudes or encourage the audience to act on their beliefs. If the audience is *relatively neutral* or *non-committed*, the persuader may aim to shift their anchor positions in the direction of acceptance. If the audience is *hostile* to the position advocated, the speaker may want to convince the audience to change their opinions. Realistically, however, the speaker should expect little change with hostile listeners. At best, the speaker can hope to move the person marginally into the non-commitment zone. Until attitudes move into the zone of acceptance, the speaker will be unable to affect shifts in behaviour. Aiming for behaviour change in this situation is unrealistic.

Step 6: Framing a Desired Outcome

To frame a desired outcome, change the wording of your position statement to reflect what you would like your audience to believe or to do at the conclusion of your speech.

- I want my audience to understand why charity organizations should not spend their money on publicity targeted at existing donors.
- I want the audience to agree that governments should ban gambling.
- I want my audience to send letters to their members of Parliament, demanding better protection of children against Internet predators.
- I want the audience to demand that the disposal of toxic wastes be discontinued in populated areas of the province.

These outcome statements will embody the general speech purposes, aimed at informing, convincing, or moving audiences to action. They will, however, become more specific in nature, reflecting the content of the speech.

A number of influences mediate the ability of persuaders to achieve their desired outcomes. As discussed earlier, listeners fall at different places on the persuasion continuum. They also have different latitudes of acceptance, hold different beliefs and values, and have personality characteristics that influence their willingness to learn, change their attitudes, and adopt new behaviours. As mentioned in Chapter 5, you are unlikely to convince pig farmers to become vegetarian. Their latitude of rejection is too large. You may aim, however, for some more realistic outcome, such as a commitment to treating their animals well.

A need for flexibility in framing desired outcomes derives from an understanding of audience composition and psychology. The statement of desired outcomes should reflect the results of audience research—an identification of how much the audience knows about a topic, their opinions on the topic, the values that could influence the persuasion process, and personality characteristics of the audience.

Step 7: Matching Audiences with Organizational Patterns

In the following discussion, we will look at the most common organizational patterns for persuasive speaking, as well as considerations in ordering arguments.

Choices of Organizational Pattern

Here we will consider the problem and/or solution, reflective thinking, causal, comparative advantages, criteria-satisfaction, claims, and motivated sequence patterns.

Problem and Solution Patterns

A *problem* speech limits itself to the description of a condition requiring change—in other words, a perceived need. A *solution* speech offers answers to perceived need(s). A *problem solution* speech, on the other hand, both explores the problem and proposes a viable solution to the problem.

Consider how to develop a problem solution speech on obesity. Discussion of the problem could potentially include the background and nature of obesity, its causes, and its effects. The solution step could include an explanation, a description of how the solution will alleviate or eliminate the problem, references to the practicality of the solution, and the benefits of adopting the solution. Some speeches substitute an action step for a benefits step. Box 10.2 outlines a problem-solution speech, which includes benefits but not an action step.

The problem-solution pattern can be used with an audience of any disposition. The

---

Box 10.2 Problem-Solution Pattern of Organization

I.   *Introduction.* According to the Canadian Institute for Health Information, almost one out of two Canadians is overweight. One out of seven is obese. The statistics apply to men and women of all ages, all ethnic and racial types, all educational levels, smokers and non-smokers.

II. *Nature of the problem.* Obesity causes serious health risks to individuals.
  A.   People who are obese have a high risk of cardiovascular disease.
  B.   Obese people are at higher risk of diabetes.

  C.   Obese people have more back, hip, and foot problems as a result of the strain that obesity places on the body; they also have more varicose veins.
  D.   Obese people have a greater chance of getting colon or breast cancer.

III. *Causes of the problem.* The causes of obesity are numerous.
  A.   People are overeating.
  B.   People are eating too much fast food.
  C.   People are not exercising.

Box 10.2 continued

IV. *Effects*. Obesity has serious implications for individuals, our health-care system, and our social fabric.
   A. People are dying.
   B. The health-care system is faltering under the burden imposed by people in poor health as a result of obesity.
   C. The military does not have an adequate pool of people from which to draw its recruits.
   D. Airlines are concerned about tragedies resulting from excessive weight in planes, and transportation providers in general have to provide special accommodations for the growing number of overweight clients.
   E. Young people who are obese sometimes suffer poor self-image.

V. *Solution*. Since the problem is complex, any solution must be multi-faceted.
   A. Governments need to regulate the fast-food industry.
   B. Schools need to include mandatory exercise programs in their curricula.
   C. Schools should remove candy and soft-drink machines from their premises.
   D. Schools should not allow advertisements for fast foods in bathrooms, halls, or cafeterias.
   E. Restaurants should serve smaller portions and eliminate 'all-you-can-eat' buffets.
   F. Health services and clinics need to make educational materials on healthy lifestyles readily available to the public.
   G. Advertisers should not place fast-food commercials in proximity to children's TV programs.

VI. *Benefits*. The benefits of solving the problem are obvious.
   A. People will live longer, healthier lives.
   B. The costs of health care and other social services will decrease.
   C. The cost of restaurant meals will decrease if owners serve smaller portions.
   D. Our military system will have a larger pool of fit applicants.
   E. Young people will have a better self-image.

VII. *Practicality of the solution*. The solution makes sense because no one group in society will bear all of the costs or responsibility for alleviating the problem.

---

quality of the supporting evidence will doubtless determine the effectiveness of this pattern with *undecided* audiences. When facing *disinterested* audiences, a speaker may want to include a discussion of the benefits in order to rouse the audience from its state of apathy.

Reflective Thinking Pattern

Philosopher John Dewey developed a variation on the problem-solution pattern of organization: the *reflective thinking* pattern.[1] This organizational pattern follows a five-step sequence: defining the problem, analyzing the problem, establishing criteria for a solution, identifying possible solutions, and selecting the best solution based on the criteria. Using the earlier example of obesity, the outline could look like that shown in Box 10.3.

Like the problem-solution model, the reflective-thinking model applies to most audiences. While no one can guarantee a positive response from a hostile audience, this organizational scheme may be more effective than others in reaching well-educated listeners who disagree. The logic and objectivity of the organizational scheme probably holds appeal for educated audiences. If the speaker also provides sound supporting evi-

Box 10.3　Reflective Thinking Pattern of Organization

I.　*Introduction*. According to the Canadian Institute for Health Information, almost one out of two Canadians is overweight. One out of seven is obese. The statistics apply to men and women of all ages, all ethnic and racial types, all educational levels, smokers and non-smokers.

II.　*Definition of the problem*. Obesity, a condition that results from an excess number of fat cells in the body, causes serious health risks to individuals.

   A.　People who are obese have a high risk of cardiovascular disease.

   B.　Obese people are at higher risk of diabetes.

   C.　Obese people have more back, hip, and foot problems as a result of the strain that obesity places on the body; they also have more varicose veins.

   D.　Obese people have a greater chance of getting colon or breast cancer.

III.　*Nature of the problem*. The problem results from the actions of individuals, advertisers, institutions, and the food industry.

   A.　The lifestyles of individuals contribute to the problem.

      1.　Overeating adds billions of fat cells to the body.

      2.　A diet of fast food also contributes to the fat cell count.

      3.　People are not exercising, which is one way to keep the fat cell count in check.

   B.　The advertising industry contributes to the problem.

      1.　Advertisers often promote unhealthy food choices.

      2.　Advertisers place their commercials at times in the evening when people should not be eating carbohydrates and sweets.

      3.　Advertisers put promotional materials in schools.

   C.　Institutions contribute to the problem.

      1.　Schools allow the placement of soft-drink, candy, and other vending machines on their premises.

      2.　Governments have done little to regulate the advertising or fast-food industries.

   D.　The fast-food industry and restaurants contribute to the problem.

      1.　Hamburger, pizza, and other fast-food chains offer too much volume and too few healthy choices.

      2.　Some restaurants economize by offering fries with every meal.

IV.　*Criteria for solution*. Any solution must meet the following criteria:

   A.　The solutions must not put the person's health at risk.

   B.　The solutions must be sustainable over time.

   C.　The solutions must be practical in terms of cost.

   D.　The solutions must be realistic in terms of implementation.

V.　*Possible solutions*. Below are possible solutions; some are better than others.

   A.　Individuals with long-term and serious problems of obesity may want to seek medical help with reducing the number of fat cells.

      1.　Medications are available.

      2.　Surgery is an option for some people.

   B.　Advertisers should adopt self-regulatory policies.

      1.　Agencies should advise their clients to place ads for high carbohydrate foods in daytime and early evening hours.

      2.　Advertisers should adopt ethical guidelines related to fast-food sales.

   C.　Parent groups should insist that schools prohibit advertisements and vending machines, promote healthy food in cafeterias, and build mandatory exercise programs into their curriculum.

      1.　Advocates for healthy eating should insist that local candidates build this issue into their platforms.

      2.　Advocates should seek to gain representation on school boards.

Box 10.3 continued

D. Governments should regulate the advertising and fast-food industries.
   1. Agriculture Canada and Health Canada should get involved.
   2. Provinces and territories should adopt new policies.
   3. Governments should sponsor campaigns for healthy eating and exercise.
E. Consumer groups should promote and monitor the fast-food and restaurant industries.
   1. Consumer groups should approach local restaurants and fast-food outlets to request help with solving the problem.
   2. Consumer groups should establish checklists and monitor the situation.
   3. Local consumer groups should publicize the results of their efforts and make recommendations to youth on where to eat.
   4. Consumer groups should urge advertisers to educate their clients on the negative impact of some choices.

VI. The following solution will meet the criteria of being safe, sustainable over time, practical, and realistic.
   A. Consultation with doctors will help individuals to choose appropriate medical and exercise options.
   B. Parent groups should become more active in promoting healthy foods in cafeterias, insisting on the removal of vending machines and urging school boards to include mandatory exercise programs.
   C. Governments should sponsor campaigns for healthy eating, just as they sponsor anti-tobacco campaigns.
   D. Local consumer groups should monitor progress on the part of local restaurants, schools, and advertisers; and on that basis they should make recommendations to city councils and others with regulatory powers.

dence, she may have some opportunity to effect change of a limited nature, even with those who are fundamentally opposed to her position.

Causal Pattern

Speeches that employ *causal* patterns of organization are concerned with linking causes and effects. Thus, like the problem-solution and reflective-thinking models, this organizational pattern addresses problems. The causal pattern does not, however, concern itself with solutions, only with addressing the relationship between the causes of problems and their resulting effects on people, institutions, and systems. Perhaps the speaker sees an *effect* or manifestation of a problem in society: violence, increasing suicide rates among teenagers, growing numbers of homeless people on the streets of Toronto, or an increasingly obese population. Then she asks the question 'Why?' *Why* do we have violence in society? *What explains* the increases in suicide rates among young people? *Why* do we have so many homeless people on the streets of Toronto? *Why* are so many people obese?

Scientists have recently announced the discovery of a relationship between date of birth and longevity. More specifically, they have found that people born in May, June, or July tend to die, on an average, nine months earlier than those born in other months of the year. (The statistics vary in Australia, which has a different seasonal pattern.) The researchers have been engaged in an effort to discover the causes, or reasons, for this phenomenon.[2] Like the earlier topics, this subject would call for an *effect-cause* pattern of organization.

Alternatively, a speech on the topic of homelessness could begin by talking about the *causes* of homelessness: lack of subsidized housing, legislation that limits the stay of mental patients in institutions, and the overcrowded conditions in psychiatric facilities. These overcrowded conditions push people onto the streets before they are able to take care of themselves. Afterwards the speaker could talk about the *effects* of underfunding, such as growing numbers of people on the streets of large urban centres, deaths from harsh cold winters, and rootless families. A speech on obesity, which employed a causal pattern, could concentrate on parts III and IV of the above outline. The speaker could seek to establish a relationship between the causes and effects of obesity (see Box 10.3).

Persuasive speakers employ causal patterns with audiences who question the basic premises of a position—people who do not accept the causal relationships in an issue. Some people, for example, attribute homelessness to lack of motivation on the part of homeless people. They may not understand the large numbers of homeless people with mental problems. They may not know that, in past years, some families of non-commissioned military personnel have had to join the food lines at shelters as a result of low pay. They may not understand the relationship between unemployment and homelessness. Discourse that employs causal patterns is well-suited to less informed, skeptical, and hostile audiences, who need to understand and be convinced of the source of problems before they will take action.

Comparative Advantages

Whereas the causal pattern focuses on the problem, the *comparative advantages* pattern focuses on the solution. This model is appropriate in situations where most audience members would agree that a problem exists. They would not, however, necessarily agree on the best solution. For this reason, speeches that employ the comparative advantages pattern of organization concentrate on solutions and make only passing reference to the problem. With this model, the speaker looks at the advantages of one solution over the others, as in Box 10.4.

Box 10.4 Comparative Advantages Pattern of Organization

I.   *Introduction includes a brief description of the problem.* According to the Canadian Institute for Health Information, almost one out of two Canadians is overweight. One out of seven is obese. The statistics apply to men and women of all ages, all ethnic and racial types, all educational levels, smokers and non-smokers.

II. *Medical solutions are not the answer to obesity.*
   A.   Medical solutions are costly.
   B.   Medical solutions pose health risks in some individuals.
   C.   Medical solutions focus on the symptoms rather than the underlying causes.

III. *Lifestyle changes are a better answer to the problem of obesity.*
   A.   The results are long-term.
   B.   Lifestyle changes carry no risks, only benefits.
   C.   Lifestyle changes get at the root of the problem, which may be psychological as much as physical.

Criteria-Satisfaction

Like the comparative advantages model, the criteria-satisfaction pattern of organization focuses on solutions and makes only passing reference to problems. With this model, the speaker examines a solution against a set of criteria. You will recall that the reflective-thinking model also includes a criteria satisfaction component. The comparative advantages and criteria-satisfaction models are appropriate patterns to use with well-informed audiences who understand the problem but disagree on solutions. While listeners may not need to be convinced that a problem exists, they may hold various views on solutions (see Box 10.5).

Box 10.5 Criteria-Satisfaction Pattern of Organization

I. *Brief introduction to problem.* According to the Canadian Institute for Health Information, almost one out of two Canadians is overweight. One out of seven is obese. The statistics apply to men and women of all ages, all ethnic and racial types, all educational levels, smokers and non-smokers.

II. *Criteria for solution to solve problem of obesity.*
   A. The solutions must not put the person's health at risk.
   B. The solutions must be sustainable over time.
   C. The solutions must be practical in terms of cost.
   D. The solutions must be realistic in terms of implementation.

III. *Evaluation of solution against criteria (proposal of lifestyle changes as optimum solution to problem of obesity).*
   A. Lifestyle changes do not put the person's health at risk.
   B. By definition, lifestyle changes involve the long term.
   C. Individuals can tailor their diets and exercise regimes to their budgets.
   D. Individuals control what happens; they do not have to depend on others to change laws or policies.

Claims Pattern

Alternatively, the speaker may choose to argue a series of *claims*, which he supports with reasoning and evidence. The organizational format would be as follows: attention, claims, and supporting material (logical, credibility, and emotional appeals). Alternatively, the speaker may counter the claims of another party. In the last scenario, the speaker follows the articulation of claims with counter claims and supporting material (see Box 10.6).

Motivated Sequence

The *motivated sequence*, developed in the 1930s by Alan H. Monroe, goes beyond the problem solution speech in its inclusion of visualization and action steps.[3] The motivated sequence pattern includes *attention, need, satisfaction, visualization,* and *action* steps.

The *attention* step captures the interest of the audience. The *need* step defines the problem, discussing weaknesses or risks in the present situation. The *satisfaction* step proposes a solution and describes how the solution will meet the need. To this point, the speech is like the problem-solution speech, which includes introduction, problem, and solution phases. The next two steps, however, extend the problem-solution model.

Box 10.6 Claims Pattern of Organization

I.   Get the attention of the audience.
  A.   Mention the opening of the first school for obese high school students.
  B.   Ask for a definition of obesity.
  C.   Introduce overall claim that the problem of obesity is overstated.

II.   Claim #1: Statistics related to deaths from obesity are overstated.
  A.   The *New England Journal of Medicine* (January 1998) says that data supporting a link between weight and mortality is weak.
  B.   So many factors interact in the case of premature deaths that it is impossible to contribute the deaths to any one cause.
  C.   A study reported in the *Gerontologist* says that the risks of dying from obesity have been exaggerated 15-fold.
  D.   The Center for Disease Control says that the problem has been overstated.

III.   Claim #2: Some measures of obesity are flawed.
  A.   The body mass index (BMI) is flawed, because it fails to distinguish between weight from body fat and weight from muscle.
  B.   Using body mass index, many fit athletes and weight lifters would fall into overweight categories.

IV.   Claim #3: Obesity does not cost Americans $117 billion each year.
  A.   Only one source supports this figure: the *Obesity Research Journal*.
  B.   Reliance on the wrong body mass index number added ten million Americans to the calculation, who should not have been included.
  C.   The data are inconclusive.

V.   Claim #4: Older Americans are no more likely than young Americans to die from obesity.
  A.   A study by the *Gerontologist* found that obese seniors are less likely to die than non-obese seniors.
  B.   Since older Americans often die from a combination of factors, one cannot attribute their deaths to any one cause.

VI.   Conclude with the observation that obesity is not as serious a problem as the pharmaceutical industry, lawyers, and animal rights groups would have us believe.

Source: The above information came from Web sites such as the Heartland Institute <www.heartland.org/Article.cfm?artId=15400> and the Center for Consumer Freedom, <www.consumerfreedom.com/news_detail.cfm/headline/2863>. David Martosko is the author of the first article, which appeared in *Health Care News*, 1 Aug. 2004. The article is based on Martosko's testimony to the Food and Drug Administration on 23 Oct. 2003.

The *visualization* step asks the audience to imagine a future with or without the preferred solution. The speaker uses vivid (but not unrealistic) language to describe this possible future. Some speeches include positive and negative visualization steps—painting a future with the preferred solution and a second future without the preferred solution. Others employ one or the other. The following example illustrates a negative visualization:

But what will happen if we do nothing, if the situation persists? Imagine the following scenario, an alternative future. You walk down the streets of your town. Two out of three pedestrians are seriously overweight, and the bicycle paths are almost deserted. You see fewer people over 60 on the streets. A friend notes that many of his older acquaintances have died from heart attacks, strokes, and diabetes—

conditions aggravated by their weight problems. You try to get an appointment with a doctor, but you learn that no one can see you for nine months. There are fewer sports teams, fewer athletes to represent the country in Olympic competitions, and fewer people who are fit for military service.

In the *action* step, the speaker summarizes the main points of the speech and appeals to the audience to take action. She offers specific, concrete suggestions. Sometimes the speaker also states personal intent to take action and challenges the audience to do the same. The speaker may say, for example: 'In the last five minutes, I have discussed the serious nature of the shortage of blood in our community. When I leave this class, I intend to go to the on-campus blood clinic to give my blood. If any of you are willing to join me, I will be pleased to offer you a ride.'

Theories related to social learning suggest that messages should specify the exact nature of the behaviours expected from audiences, especially in fear-arousing situations.[4] They also say that audiences are most likely to act if communicators make suggestions that they can follow in the near future. In other words, the speaker should suggest actions that listeners can perform in the days and weeks immediately following the speech. Persuaders should also encourage people to find a visible means to show their commitment to these behaviours—wearing a button or making a speech to support the new behaviour. If a persuader fails to specify actions, the audience will usually do nothing.

Box 10.7 illustrates the development of a speech using the motivated sequence. Note that, in practice, the attention step for all speeches (problem-solution, reflective thinking, causal, motivated sequence, and others) is only one part of a larger introduction, which includes statements of position, purpose, reason to listen, credibility, and orientation or structural progression.

Box 10.7 Motivated Sequence Pattern of Organization

I. *Attention.* According to the Canadian Institute for Health Information, almost one out of two Canadians is overweight. One out of seven is obese. The statistics apply to men and women of all ages, all ethnic and racial types, all educational levels, smokers and non-smokers.

II. *Need.* Obesity is creating serious health problems for Canadians.
   A. People who are obese have a high risk of cardiovascular disease.
   B. People who are obese are at higher risk of diabetes.
   C. Obese people have more back, hip, and foot problems as a result of the strain that obesity places on the body; they also have more varicose veins.
   D. People who are obese have a greater chance of getting colon or breast cancer.

III. *Satisfaction.* Solutions require partnerships among all levels of government, schools, parents, the restaurant industry, advertising firms, and individuals.
   A. Governments need to regulate the fast-food industry.
   B. Schools must include mandatory exercise programs in their curriculum.
   C. Schools should remove candy and soft-drink machines from their premises.

Box 10.7 continued

D. Schools should not allow advertisements for fast foods in bathrooms, halls, or cafeterias.

E. Restaurants should serve smaller portions and eliminate 'all-you-can-eat' buffets.

F. Health services and clinics need to make educational materials on healthy lifestyles readily available to the public.

G. Advertisers should not schedule fast-food commercials in association with TV programming for children.

IV. *Visualization (positive).* Imagine a future in which we return to the past. Visualize the return of a time when . . .

A. Young and old alike lead active lives.

B. Seniors are able to remain in their own homes for most of their lives, since they are healthy and fit.

C. School cafeterias offer a healthy array of foods instead of providing vending machines.

D. School hallways showcase the artwork of students and teachers instead of the advertisements of jean companies.

E. Families and communities get together on the weekends for picnics, swimming, and outdoor activities that require active engagement.

F. Our military has a large pool of fit applicants and recruits.

G. Our health-care system is able to channel funds to treat those most in need.

V. *Visualization (negative).* But what will happen if we do nothing, if the situation persists? Imagine an alternative future without my solution.

A. Four out of five Canadians are seriously overweight.

B. The waiting list for hip replacements is five years.

C. You see fewer people over 60 on the streets because many have died from heart attacks, strokes, and diabetes—conditions aggravated by their weight.

D. Getting an appointment with a doctor requires months of waiting because the health-care system is seriously overtaxed.

E. There are fewer sports teams, fewer athletes to represent our country in Olympic competitions, and fewer people who are fit for military service.

VI. *Action.* The solutions rest with you.

A. Do not give business to restaurants that offer only unhealthy options.

B. Tell the managers of restaurants how you feel about their menus when asked to fill out comment cards.

C. Demand that school boards enact new policies; attend local meetings and make your views known.

D. Protest the presence of vending machines and advertisements in schools.

E. Run for office on school boards and press for changes once in office.

F. Ask your local health clinics to distribute materials on the problem; get doctors involved.

G. Petition governments for more research funds to identify the causes of obesity.

H. Ask community centres to sponsor more recreational events for families.

The motivated sequence works well with topics where the audience is not polarized and does not hold passionate feelings on the subject. The existence of an action step implies that the speaker can realistically hope for action on the issue. The position of the speaker, in other words, probably falls within the latitude of acceptance of the audience if he selects this organizational scheme. Perhaps the speaker is asking for more people to sign organ donation cards, vote in elections, or participate in a walkathon for charity. If the speaker can realistically expect both compliance and action to result from the speech, the motivated sequence may be the right organizational choice. The inclusion of need and solution steps, on the other hand, implies that the audience may need to know more about the topic.

Considerations in Ordering Arguments

Within the chosen organizational framework (problem and/or solution, reflective thinking, causal, criteria-satisfaction, comparative advantages, motivated sequence, or claim), you may need to make decisions on how to order your arguments.

One-Sided versus Two-Sided Argumentation

On the whole, research has found that two-sided arguments are more effective than one-sided arguments in gaining audience compliance.[5] That is, the most persuasive messages present both points of view but refute the opposing arguments. If you seem flexible and balanced, audiences are more likely to listen to your arguments. One dimension of source credibility is objectivity. Audiences are more likely to accept statements from speakers who appear to be objective. You can also improve your credibility in areas such as expertise and trustworthiness when you show a broad understanding of the topic.

Well-educated and well-informed audiences, as well as those who disagree with your position, are particularly responsive to messages that acknowledge both points of view before stating a biased perspective.[6] One-sided argumentation has been found to be effective with less-educated audiences, but only if they are not hostile to your message. When offering both perspectives, which side should you present first? Studies suggest that you should present your side first when audiences do not know much about the topic or disagree with you. After that, you present and refute the opposing arguments.[7]

You may also want to use two-sided argumentation if you know that the audience will hear the other side of the case at some future date. In essence, you 'inoculate' your audience by preparing them for the opposing argument.[8] Although you may present both sides of the argument, you will usually place more emphasis on your position.[9] Some legal analysts claim that the prosecuting attorneys in the Scott Peterson murder trial followed a very unusual strategy. They presented not only their own case, but also the defence case. After presenting the defence arguments, they answered them. In essence, they inoculated the jury against the arguments, preparing them with counter arguments. In the same way, political candidates often warn voters of strategies their opponents might use to damage their credibility.[10]

Reviewing the organizational patterns, we can see that the reflective thinking, motivated sequence, causal, and comparative advantages models allow the possibility for two-sided argumentation. The reflective thinking and motivated sequence patterns, in particular, allow the speaker to present alternative solutions before proposing an optimum solution. The causal pattern allows the speaker to explore various possible causes or effects before reaching conclusions. The comparative advantages model enables the speaker to argue the advantages of one solution over another one.

Ordering of Arguments According to Strength

Debates have occurred over where to place the best or strongest arguments in a persuasive speech. *Primacy* research supports the practice of placing the strongest arguments at the beginning of speeches. This research suggests that arguments appearing early in argumentation have a greater influence on audience attitudes than those appearing later. *Recency* research, however, concludes that audiences are most likely to recall arguments appearing at the end of speeches.[11] Still others say that it does not matter—that the findings are inconclusive.[12]

Finally, some communication scholars say that the response to questions of order depends on the *initial attitudes* of the audience (their orientation towards the topic) and the *importance of the topic* to the audience (level of concern that they feel). Some studies suggest, for example, that the strongest arguments should appear first when audiences care about the topic.[13] Others point to the opposite—that the strongest arguments should appear first when audiences do not care[14] or have not made their minds about what to believe or think.[15] Still other studies conclude that the strongest arguments should appear early in the discourse in order to reach the maximum number of listeners. The assumption is that some people always leave early.

Whatever the disagreements on *primacy* and *recency* effects, most studies concur that arguments appearing in the middle of a discussion have less impact. And the weight of most experts appears to come down more heavily on the side of sooner rather than later for the strongest arguments. Thus, in a one-sided presentation, you would do best to proceed from strongest to weakest argument. If you are making a two-sided presentation, designed to inoculate the audience or to meet the needs of better-educated, better-informed, or hostile audiences, you would also begin with your strongest arguments. The arguments of the opposition (the ones to which you do not adhere) would appear later in the discussion.

In conclusion, most of the time, you will want to present both sides of the argument. You will present your perspective first, and you will begin with your strongest arguments. Then you will present and refute the arguments of the opposing point of view.

Step 8: Writing Your Introduction

After deciding on an organizational pattern, you should write the introduction to your speech. The following five elements can appear in the introduction: attention strategy, purpose, position, reason to listen, and basis of credibility. Sometimes an explicit statement of purpose may not be necessary. You should, however, always have the purpose firmly in mind as you write the speech. The other components are mandatory.

Remembering Attention Strategies

Whatever organizational scheme you adopt, attention strategies constitute the first step in preparing your introduction. The strategies most often used in persuasive speeches are immediacy strategies; personalization; references to the novel; suspense and shock techniques; activity, drama, conflict; and quotations. The following discussion will briefly review attention-getting techniques discussed in previous chapters, as well as add a discussion of personalization strategies, often employed in persuasive discourse.

Immediacy Strategies

The persuasive speech is often more dramatic and less conversational than informative speeches. A less chatty tone characterizes the introductions and conclusions of persuasive speeches, in particular; and immediacy strategies are more focused on establishing the vital nature of the subject matter. The persuasive speaker often hopes to shock the audience into recognizing a problem or acting on a solution. References to the *vital* interests of the audience—their health and well-being—characterize most persuasive speeches.[16] The following example illustrates this immediacy strategy:

> You may be feeling pretty safe here in Halifax, but the fact is that kidnappings for profit occur in a surprisingly large number of countries frequented by Canadian tourists. Members of the Chinese community say they are common in their home countries. They are also on the rise in Mexico, a favourite destination for many college and university students on spring break. The high-profile case of Natalee Holloway, missing in Aruba, reminds us that even the most tranquil tropical locations can be risky. And this next fact may surprise you. On a list of 10 countries that share this problem, the United States ranks in seventh place, ahead of Venezuela, India, and Ecuador! So take care on your next trip, whether windsurfing in Cancun, hiking in the Rocky Mountains, or sunning on the beaches of Miami.

Chapter 5 talked about the hierarchy of human needs described by Abraham Maslow, who said that our most basic needs (physiological and safety/security needs) must be satisfied before an individual can think about meeting higher-level needs (love/belonging, esteem, and self-actualization). When speakers appeal to the vital interests of audiences, they seek to establish linkages between their issues and audience needs for safety and security.

Speakers may also ask *questions* of audiences. In the following example, the question is rhetorical, not demanding a visible or vocal response of the listeners:

> Have you ever noticed the skid marks on the highway that runs through Jacques Cartier Park? They usually come in close proximity to signs that warn about moose and deer crossings. Or maybe you haven't noticed the signs either? I never used to notice. The warning signs were invisible to me until one night when our headlights showed a nine foot moose standing directly in the path of our fast-moving vehicle. Space and time collapsed, and we were upon the moose before we knew what had happened. At the last minute, we swerved in time to avoid catastrophe—hitting the rear, rather than the side, of the moose. And the next day, when we returned to the scene, we noticed the now familiar remains of tire marks etched into the highway—our tire marks. We also noticed the large warning sign.

As noted in previous chapters, for maximum effectiveness, speakers should usually combine questions with some other attention strategy. In this case, the speaker builds action and drama into the story.

Personalization

Another often employed technique in persuasive speaking is *personalization*. When we personalize accounts, we describe the experiences of people (real or hypothetical) in an effort to humanize the dry facts and statistics. Programs that seek sponsors for children in developing countries make effective use of this technique. In public service announcements or paid commercials, they show pictures of individual children in deprived conditions. They ask people to sponsor one child, whose plight can become real for the donor. They send photographs and letters from the sponsored child to the donors to create a small personal connection.

Animal rights groups use the same approach when they do mass mailings containing images of abused animals. People often feel impotent to do anything about the larger crisis, but if they see one person or animal in peril, they feel empowered to help. The 'angel tree,' seen frequently in shopping malls over the Christmas season, operates on the same principle. People take a name from the angel tree and provide Christmas for that child. The media use the same strategy to evoke concern when they publish the picture of a lone individual or family who have suffered the effects of war.

Pro-lifers often rely on strategies of personalization in their campaigns. On one occasion, for example, they appeared on the steps of a hospital, where they presented administrators with small coffins for the burial of fetuses. In another instance, they thrust baby gifts at Chantal Daigle, a Montreal woman involved in a legal fight for the right to an abortion. (Her boyfriend had asked the court to revoke that right.) The following excerpt from an anti-abortion speech by Sonia Genovesi illustrates how one student used personalization to persuade her audience:

> Many of you would shrink at the idea of murder, killing a person. But when does one become a person? Is it at conception? Two weeks? Three months? Six months? At birth? *There are things I never saw, and these are the things I miss: her first smile, her first words.* Some would argue that personhood emerges at conception—the time, in their view, when the soul meets the body for the very first time. Others consider that personhood has occurred when a clearly distinctive DNA code appears in the mother's womb, a few hours after conception. Does life begin when the heart starts beating at 18 days or at three months when the fetus starts to resemble a baby? Or is it simply at the materialization of thought or measured brainwave patterns? *These are the things I never saw, and these are the things I miss: seeing her ride a bike for the first time, consoling her when she scraped her knee.* In the first three months after conception, we can observe the baby sucking his thumb, swimming around in the amniotic fluid, even grasping at the umbilical cord. At two months after conception, if you tickle the baby's upper lip with a hair, it can move its entire body to avoid the stimulation. Is it possible to assume the baby can experience sensation? *These are things I never saw and these are the things I miss: her first day of school, helping her with her homework.*[17]

Instead of using the most common shock techniques, Genovesi talks about the simple pleasures of being a mother—pleasures that will be missed if the woman gives up the opportunity to experience motherhood. She attempts to evoke an emotional response from the audience by relying on the strategy of personalization. In the later development of the speech, she spoke of how she would miss making Halloween costumes and trick or treating with her child, attending piano recitals and ballet rehearsals, and watching her daughter blossom into a young woman and fall in love.

In another highly emotional speech, a student brought a stuffed animal to the front of the classroom. The topic of her speech was suicide among young people, and the stuffed animal represented the last treasured gift from her best friend, who had committed suicide in high school.

References to the Novel

The most effective persuasive speeches include *novel* information. The following example reflects the use of novel information to gain audience attention:

> Did you know that kidnapping for profit is one of the leading domestic industries in Colombia? It generates millions in revenues. The major group that carries out the kidnappings is the Revolutionary Armed Forces, or FARC for short. Last year FARC kidnapped over 3,700 wealthy landowners, prominent government officials, *and* foreign tourists. In a typical scenario, victims are seized from airports or hotel rooms and held in hiding while the kidnappers extort a ransom payment from relatives. Kidnapping has become so much a business that there are set ransom fees. You might be interested to know, for example, that our instructor's value as a kidnap victim is approximately $8,000, the standard ransom for university professors.

Suspense and Shock Techniques

The next example illustrates the use of suspense to gain and hold audience attention:

> A killer is now in our community. When last seen, the strangler was moving along Highway 105, headed towards Chelsea. The risk to the community is high, because no one has any idea how to control this murderous *dog-strangling vine*. Does this sound like the old movies about giant man-eating tomatoes or lizards? Unfortunately, the threat is much more real. Dog-strangling vines *do* exist, and they *are* a real threat to our national parks and gardens, if not to dogs.

Activity, Drama, and Conflict

Persuasive speeches often include strong elements of drama and conflict that build to a climax. In the following instance, the speaker describes such an event:

> The police arrived at 2:00 a.m. They tried to get the man to open the door, but he did not respond. Others had gathered in the hall, drawn by the commotion. The scene was chaotic. When the police finally broke down the door, the man rushed at them, holding a knife in one hand and a baseball bat in the other. One of the police officers tried to subdue the man with pepper spray, but his efforts were unsuccessful. The man was high on cocaine. With no other clear alternative, the officer responded by shooting the man with a Taser gun. Stunned, the man fell to the ground. When the police checked his pulse, they realized that he had stopped breathing. They called an ambulance to come to the rooming house, but it was too late. The man was dead, and the media took the story and ran with it. Fifty men, they reported, have died in the Canada and the United States in the last year from the use of stun guns by police.

Quotations

Quotations, proverbs, and poems are also used to gain audience attention in persuasive speeches. The following quotation introduces a speech on poverty:

> As a report by the Royal Commission on Women noted, 'Poverty is to be without sufficient money, but it is also to have little hope for better things. It is a feeling that one is powerless in a society that respects power.'[18]

When citing the words of someone else, you should always mention the person's title, position, or other identifying information: 'Canadian astronaut Julie Payette', 'the well-known Canadian author Carol Shields', or 'Assembly of First Nations National Chief Phil Fontaine'. If the reference is clear, the descriptor can be short.

Reviewing Other Elements in the Introduction

After getting the attention of your audience, you should state your purpose and position, give people a reason to listen, establish your credibility to speak on the topic, and/or give a preview statement. The ordering of these elements is flexible. Since we have already discussed these points in a previous chapter, I will offer a review in the form of an example. Look at the following excerpts from a persuasive speech, intended to get the audience to contribute to the work of a local heart institute:[19]

Attention strategy (personal story):

In March of 1986, my grandfather had a heart attack. I was not quite two years old. The hospital in my home town of Winchester transferred him to the Ottawa Heart Institute, where he could receive more specialized care. Here the doctors determined that his only hope for a healthy life was a valve replacement. As a result of this successful procedure, my grandpa was in my life for another 12 years. I was able to get to know him and still have memories of him.

Credibility to speak on the topic:

Heart problems run in my family, and so the Ottawa Heart Institute has played an important role in the health of some of my closest relatives. For this reason and others, this topic is important to me; and I have done extensive research to provide you with credible and reliable information.

Reason to listen (why should you care):

Many of you—I suspect all of you—also have a friend or relative who has experienced heart problems. Listening to my speech will give you important information on how to help this person by contributing to the activities of the University of Ottawa Heart Institute.

Purpose and position statements:

At the conclusion of my speech, I hope you will take some of the actions identified in my talk. I believe we can reduce the deaths and disabilities from heart disease if we put our minds, pocketbooks, and bodies into the effort.

Preview statement:

In the next few minutes, I will give you some facts about heart disease, discuss the research efforts of the Heart Institute, and tell you what you can do to help the Institute in its fight against cardiovascular disease.

Step 9: Supporting Your Ideas

Chapter 7 discussed the importance of conducting primary and secondary research on your speech topics. The chapter also described the range of support materials available to a communicator. Those supports include *historical and other facts, description, analogies, proverbs* and *quotations*, *stories* and *legends*, *fables* and *parables*, *poems* and *songs*, *statistics*, *examples*, *explanation and amplification*, and *expert testimony*. Like informative speakers, persuasive speakers often translate their statistics into *visual supports*.

Speakers can use any of the above materials to develop their speeches. Studies have found, however, that some supporting materials are better than others in effecting attitude change. Examples, illustrations, and case histories, for example, have a greater impact on attitudes than statistical or other data summaries.[20] In addition, attitudes formed on the basis of examples and case histories are more stable over time than attitudes stimulated by data summaries.[21]

Most difficult to refute is argument by example. A personal instance or story can have a greater impact than the most exhaustive statistics. In some countries, such as Kenya, personal testimonials are regarded as the best and most reliable form of evidence.[22]

Even though current wisdom suggests that speakers should rely more heavily on narration, self-disclosure, and visual supports,[23] many speakers still rely too heavily on statistics. They fail to use some of the most acclaimed speeches in history as a model for their persuasive discourse. Speeches by noted politicians, Nobel Prize winners, and others often make limited use of statistics. Reference to any 'top speech' site confirms this statement.

Because persuasive speaking is serious business, however, you will use less humour in persuasive discourse than you might use in an informative or special occasion speech. The necessity to prove your case means that you should use a *variety* of support materials, and expert sources should be highly credible and unbiased. Your materials should be *current*, *representative* of other findings on the subject, *relevant* to the points in question, and *sufficient* in numbers. You should be specific in citing your sources. And despite the above discussion of the effectiveness of using anecdotal information, statistics and other forms of evidence do enable the speaker to generalize a particular idea or event to the larger population. Observation of the rules associated with statistics will help you to make your statistics meaningful. For a review of support materials, refer to Chapter 8 on informative speaking.

In addition to logical supporting materials, you should use emotional appeals in a strategic fashion. That means thinking about the needs, beliefs, values, and attitudes of your audience as you write your speech. When you seek to persuade, you must establish your credibility early in the speech. Why are you qualified to speak on this topic? And why should we believe what you have to say?

Step 10: Choosing Evocative Language

Speakers use literary techniques such as vivid and concrete language, balanced and parallel sentence structures, antithesis, repetition, alliteration, first and second voice, 'the rule of threes and fours,' comparison and contrast, metaphors, similes, personification, analogies, and rhetorical questions to evoke powerful emotions in their audiences.

Concrete and Vivid Language

When speakers use concrete language, they translate abstract concepts into more tangible realities. 'One of my supporters' becomes 'Tom'. Instead of saying 'A bird chirped', we say "'A yellow finch chirped.' A house is ranch or Victorian or log cabin. The following excerpt from a speech by former Prime Minister Kim Campbell illustrates how a speaker translates abstract concepts into concrete examples:

> When you go to Ottawa, you get used to hearing all sorts of words, big words, clinical words, words created for the world of memoranda, not the world most Canadians live in. You've heard those words yourselves. Global competitiveness. Structural adjustment. I don't know what those terms mean to a banker. But I do know what they mean to Canadians. They mean the young person in Kitchener who leaves school without skills, who can't find a job in an industry where skills matter. They mean the young single mother in Fredericton, who must work, but who wants to learn, yet can't afford the time and the money to do that. They mean the middle-aged worker in Montreal, laid off in an industry that is fading, with little hope of retiring, without the skills and training for different work. And they mean the sad, empty fate of too many young people, everywhere, who know about rap, but not reading, much more about Muchmusic than math.[24]

In the early 1970s, lawyer and activist William J. Kunstler presented a powerful anti-war speech to 3,900 audience members (mostly students, including myself), who packed the Indiana University auditorium. Kunstler's credibility was high. He had acquired celebrity status through his defence of Martin Luther King Jr, H. Rap Brown, and Stokely Carmichael. He had also acted as legal counsel to the 'Chicago 7', a group of activists charged with conspiracy, inciting to riot, and other violent protests at the 1968 Democratic National Convention. The trial had been a circus. The judge charged both defendants and defence lawyers with contempt of court. Defendant Bobby Seale was bound and gagged for the courtroom proceedings. The following excerpt from the speech by Kunstler demonstrates the power of concrete images:

> Wherever you go, wherever discussions are heard, people are going to say, 'What about violence on campus? How can you condone the destruction of a building in which a man died, and people are going to forget that every day B-52's go out over South Vietnam; people are going to forget what happened to the demonstrators on Lower Wall Street in New York; people are going to forget who was responsible for the defoliation of millions of acres in Vietnam; people are going to forget about six black men who were shot to death by policemen in Augusta, Georgia, for the capital crime of stealing a television set during a disorder; people are going to forget who killed the students at Kent State and who killed the students at Jackson State; people are going to forget My Lai 4 and the bayoneting of grandmothers and babies; people are going to forget where the real violence exists; people are going to forget that Fred Hampton was murdered in his bed on Sept. 4, 1969 and that no one will ever answer for that crime.[25]

Balanced and Parallel Sentence Structures

Eloquence of spoken language relies on the balancing of sentence structures, so that one part of the sentence 'weighs' the same as the other part. We use this kind of language in more formal and ceremonial speeches.

The following statements demonstrate the principle of balanced sentence structures. 'She was not so much confident, as determined; not so much fearless as committed.' 'The more we learn, the more uncertain we become.' In each case, the second half of the sentence 'weighs' the same as the first half. In the first example, there is also balance within the clauses. See the following example, drawn from a speech by British Prime Minister Tony Blair: 'I reflect on the sheer waste of children taught to hate when I believe passionately children should be taught to think.'[26]

In urging the citizens of Quebec to vote against separation, Prime Minister Jean Chrétien used both parallel sentence construction and repetition:

> Other countries invest in weapons; we invest in the well-being of our citizens. Other countries tolerate poverty and despair; we work hard to ensure a basic level of decency for everyone. Other countries resort to violence to settle differences; we work out our problems through compromise and mutual respect.

Speaking from the floor of the House of Commons, former Prime Minister Joe Clark delivered an eloquent tribute to Pierre Elliott Trudeau. In this speech eulogizing his long-time political opponent, Clark employed the technique of balanced sentence structure: 'While I never thought that I knew him well, it was here that I knew him best.' An earlier tribute by Clark to former Prime Minister John G. Diefenbaker was equally eloquent:

> John Diefenbaker is home—at the end of a life which started in another century, and embraced most of the history of our Canada. . . . As a child, he talked to the buffalo hunters. As a man, he led his country and dominated its Parliament.

Sometimes the balance occurs in adjacent sentences. In a farewell address, Lieutenant-Governor Hilary Weston spoke of the impact of her interactions with the people of Ontario: 'I wasn't just informed by them. I was transformed by them.'[27]

Ordinary conversational language, on the other hand, is typically unbalanced. We do not try to achieve an equal weighting for the different parts of a thought. Examples of unbalanced sentences are the following: 'She didn't show much confidence when she stood up to deliver the speech to a crowd of stone-faced spectators.' 'The boys were frustrated to see that every attempt to pass the ball or to locate a receiver failed.' Although you may not want to aim for the same number of balanced sentences in an informal speaking situation, that kind of structure is easier to deliver. There are ample places for pauses and breaths in balanced sentences with parallel structures.

Antithesis

Antithesis, one kind of balanced sentence structure, involves the use of 'not,' 'not/but', and 'never/but' in offering a contrast between two ideas. In a speech to the Confederation Club of Kitchener, Ontario, former Prime Minister Kim Campbell said: 'I believe there is a role here for Canada. . . . Not to force, but to facilitate. Not to act apart, but to work together with others.' In a speech arguing against Canada's engagement in the Gulf War, Audrey McLaughlin (then leader of the New Democratic Party) said: 'We will not engage in debates that are simply about who is right, but we will pursue that international vision based on a new world order.'[28] In a much-acclaimed speech on AIDS, delivered to the 1992 Republican National Convention, Mary Fisher said, 'I bear a message of challenge, not self-congratulation. I want your attention, not your applause.'[29]

John F. Kennedy's 1961 inaugural address was characterized by its riveting use of antithesis. The most famous line from the speech was 'Ask not what your country can do for you . . . ask what you can do for your country.'[30] Another well-known example from the same speech was 'Let us never negotiate out of fear, but let us never fear to negotiate.'

Repetition

Repetition is another key linguistic strategy. As Patrick Gossage, speechwriter to former Prime Minister Pierre Trudeau, observed, 'Repetition is the bread and butter of a speechwriter's trade.'[31] Christopher Dunkin used repetition when he spoke against Confederation in the Canadian House of Parliament on 27 February 1865:

> Always I have been, and now I am, a unionist in the strictest and largest sense of the term. *I desire* to perpetuate the union between Upper and Lower Canada. *I desire* to see developed, the largest union that can possibly be developed . . . between all the colonies, provinces, and dependencies of the British Crown. *I desire* to maintain that intimate union which ought to subsist, but which unfortunately does not subsist as it ought, between the Imperial Government and all those dependencies. I am a unionist, who especially does not *desire* to see the provinces of Upper and Lower Canada disunited.[32]

University of Calgary professor Leslie Tutty made effective use of repetition in a speech commemorating the eleventh anniversary of the massacre at Montreal's École Polytechnique. She responds to the question 'Why do we remember the 14 young women murdered in Montreal?' in the following way:

> *We remember* because they might have been our daughters, sisters, friends. This was the first incident in Canadian history, perhaps in recent world history, when a group of people were targeted and murdered simply because they were women. This must not happen again. *We remember*, not to punish men for the violence that other men perpetrate against women, but to appreciate the men who do advocate for women's rights—the men who create white ribbon campaigns and join us today in memoriam. . . . *We remember*, because of the seldom-heard voices of other Canadian women who live every day with the threat of violence and even death. . . . And so, *we remember* the 14 young women because it reminds us that countless Canadian women live with violence every day and we need to do something to address this sad fact. *We remember*, so we can channel today's grief into action, to read, do research, advocate and protest any act of violence against others, but for today, especially, violence against women. . . . Finally, *we remember*, because it would be dishonourable to the memory of the 14 young women killed in the Montreal Massacre, to forget.[33]

In another emotionally compelling address, delivered in the British House of Commons on 4 June 1940, Winston Churchill spoke of the commitment of the British to fight to the end in World War II. The passage is well-known for its cadence and rhythm, as well as its eloquent use of repetition:

> We shall not flag or fail. We shall go on to the end, *we shall fight* in France, *we shall fight* on the seas and oceans, *we shall fight* with growing confidence and growing strength in the air, we shall defend our Island, whatever the cost may be, *we shall fight* on the beaches, *we shall fight* on the landing grounds, *we shall fight* in the fields and in the streets, *we shall fight* in the hills; we shall never surrender.[34]

Beginning speakers often employ repetition without infusing sufficient variety into their writing. Some of the above examples illustrate how experienced speakers avoid the repetition of entire sentences. They have different endings to speeches that begin with a repetitive phrase. Or after several repetitions, they change the wording. Most often, they sprinkle repetitive phrases into a longer dialogue, where they build variety into the paragraphs that separate the repetitious chant.

The following example, from a speech by former Prime Minister Kim Campbell, shows how a variation on the repeated phrase can be effective: '*The trend is toward* an industry that adds value. *The trend is towards* the provision of services, rather than the production of goods. *The trend is away from* the idea of harvesting to the harvesting of ideas.'[35] The final example comes from student Andrew Gowing, who spoke on the rising costs of snowmobile insurance in Ontario:

> I regret to inform you that I am the bearer of bad news. *The bad news* is that an organization exists, whose policies threaten the jobs of over 30,000 Canadians. *The bad news* is that these policies threaten to eliminate nearly $1.3 billion from our economy. I'll repeat that: $1.3 billion from the Ontario economy. And the *worst news of all* is that these same policies put the lives and safety of nearly 175,000 snowmobilers at risk.[36]

Sometimes speakers overdo repetition. When strategies become too obvious to an audience, they lose their effectiveness. In a speech delivered at the Liberal leadership convention in June 1984, candidate Jean Chrétien went a bit overboard with his use of repetition. First he used the phrase 'Should we Liberals distance ourselves . . .' six times, ending each repetition with 'Not this Liberal.' Then he proceeded to use the phrase 'I will be satisfied with nothing less' or 'I can be satisfied with nothing less' seven times. Next he repeated the phrase 'We are not choosing' or 'We are choosing' five times. A more limited use of repetition in the speech would have been effective. However, the excessive use of repetition in the speech made the words seem contrived and made Chrétien seem insincere.

Alliteration

Alliteration involves repetition of a letter or sound at the beginning of words, as in 'She slid down the slippery slope at Sedona.' Unlike poets, who sprinkle alliteration throughout their work, speakers often limit the recurrence of alliteration to two words in a phrase. In a particularly gripping anti-war sermon, Harry Fosdick made use of alliteration: 'spoke at sunset', 'best of your breed', 'men like myself', 'blown to bits', 'Somme battlefield to the southern trenches', 'prostitution of the noblest powers', 'self-sacrifice', 'submarines off the shores', 'lies it lives', and 'somehow make the world safe'.[37]

In 1961, newly elected President John F. Kennedy delivered a farewell address to the people of Massachusetts, whom he had served as US Senator. In this speech, titled 'History Shall Be Our Judge', Kennedy used a number of literary devices, including alliteration:

> And so it is that I carry with me from this state to that high and lonely office, to which I now succeed, more than fond memories and fast friendships. The enduring qualities of Massachusetts—the common threads woven by the Pilgrim and the Puritan, the fisherman and the farmer, the Yankee and the immigrant—will not be and could not be forgotten in this nation's executive mansion.[38]

He also used alliteration with great impact in his 1961 inaugural address when he said: 'Let every nation know, whether it wishes us well or ill, that we shall pay any price, bear any burden, meet any hardship, support any friend, oppose any foe, in order to assure the survival and the success of liberty.'[39]

In an address to the 1984 Liberal leadership convention, Jean Chrétien used alliterative phrases such as 'left a legacy', 'what you're going to get', and 'crystal clear'. Other examples of alliteration by Canadian speakers include 'the forests and the fish';[40] 'caring, more compassionate society';[41] 'serious systemic deterrent';[42] and 'to be heard and to be heeded'.[43]

If not overdone, alliteration enhances the aesthetic quality of speeches. The technique adds a rhythmic quality to the speech.

First and Second Voice

The importance of audience adaptation means that speakers typically make limited use of first-person singular voice (*I*) in a speech. Instead they use first-person plural (*we*) and second person (*you*) to involve the audience. On occasion, however, speaking in the first person can have a powerful impact on an audience, especially in a situation where the speaker has high credibility and a strong desire to assert responsibility for his words and actions. Those variables were at work on 20 April 1964, when a young Nelson Mandela spoke from the prisoner's dock in the Pretoria, South Africa, Supreme Court building. The 1990s would see Mandela assume the leadership of South Africa, but not before he had spent 27 years in prison. On this day, in 1964, Mandela faced the possibility of death if convicted of the crimes with which he was charged. You can see his acceptance of responsibility in his opening statement to the courtroom:

> I am the First Accused. I hold a Bachelor's Degree in Arts and practised as an attorney in Johannesburg for a number of years in partnership with Oliver Tambo. I am a convicted prisoner serving five years for leaving the country without a permit and for inciting people to go on strike at the end of May 1961. At the outset, I want to say that the suggestion made by the State in its opening that the struggle in South Africa is under the influence of foreigners or communists is wholly incorrect. I have done whatever I did, both as an individual and as a leader of my

people, because of my experience in South Africa and my own proudly felt African background, and not because of what any outsider may have said.[44]

For dramatic effect, some speak in the first person to give voice to some historical person or group. In the following example, drawn from a speech on the history of wars, I used the first person for dramatic effect: 'I lie in Flanders Field. I am the voice of the soldier slain. Above my grave there stands a small white cross. The sky overhead spreads a canopy of azure over me; and the poppies, rippling in the summer breeze, form a crimson coverlet over my bed. I am one of many soldiers slain on foreign fields of war.'

More commonly, speakers employ the first-person plural (*we*) or the second person (*you*)—inclusiveness strategies that bring the audience into the speaker's frame of reference. Prior to the 1980 referendum to decide if Quebec should leave Canada, Trudeau spoke to a large rally for the 'No' side at the Paul Sauvé Arena in Montreal. Speechwriter Patrick Gossage characterized this speech as one of the best in the history of political rhetoric in Canada. Gossage noted that Trudeau had written and practised his speech for three days before delivery.

> You, the supporters of the NO side, you know the divisions this referendum has caused. You have seen the divisions it has caused with families. You have seen the hatred it has created between neighbours. You know it has widened the generation gap. You know that the deep suspicion and mistrust between supporters of the YES side and those of the NO side will last for a long time to come. . . . Well, we are saying NO to that. No, it will not go on.[45]

Rule of Threes and Fours

Writers and speakers tend to cluster their phrases into groups of three or four (rhythmic triads or quads). In eulogizing Trudeau, Jean Chrétien said that 'Pierre Trudeau was a colleague, a mentor and a friend.'[46] Former Lieutenant-Governor of Ontario Hilary Weston offered her best wishes to her successor in the following way: 'I wish that fortunate person will be as blessed as I have been by all the people I've met, all the places I've been, and all the activities I've seen.'[47] At other times, the 'rule of threes' manifests itself in a series of three sentences. In a speech that recognized acts of bravery by Canadians, Governor-General Adrienne Clarkson asked the following sequence of questions: 'What is normal? What is normal for the person who is rescued? What is normal for somebody who has risked their own life to rescue someone from death?'[48]

Many Aboriginal peoples believe that four is a mystical number that helps to shape thought and speech. In a speech to the Indigenous Leaders Summit of the Americas on 29 March 2001, Matthew Coon Come illustrated the 'rule of fours': 'We always knew that we were not inferior societies, that we are a nation, that we are a people, that we have the right to self determination.'[49] The following famous quotation from a speech by Winston Churchill, delivered to the

Matthew Coon Come, then National Chief of the Assembly of First Nations, at the opening ceremony of the annual assembly, Kahnawake, Quebec, 16 July 2002. (CP PHOTO/Ryan Remiorz)

Canadian Parliament on 30 December 1941, also illustrates the 'rule of fours': 'We have not journeyed across the centuries, across the oceans, across the mountains, across the prairies because we are made of sugar candy.'[50] Joe Clark applied the 'rule of fours' in his eulogy to Trudeau: 'He was an enigmatic man—tough and kind and cold-blooded and sympathetic.'[51] In this final example, drawn from Chrétien's eulogy to Trudeau, the rule of fours involves a sequence of four sentences:

> He came to this House of Commons to build a country in which French-speaking Canadians have their rightful place—from sea to sea. A Canada of two official languages. A Canada that celebrates diversity. A compassionate Canada that affords all of its citizens an equal opportunity to succeed in life; whatever their backgrounds; whether rich or poor. A Canada that is active in the world; engaged in the cause of freedom, peace and justice.

Comparison and Contrast

Comparison reveals similarities between ideas or concepts, whereas contrast shows differences. The following statement examines similarities in two disorders that lead to shoplifting:

> Like kleptomaniacs, people with addictive-compulsive disorders cannot resist the urge to steal. And like kleptomaniacs, they may have absolutely no need for the shoplifted objects. Nonetheless, they feel a sense of relief and pleasure at the time that they commit the act of theft. Neither the kleptomaniac nor the addictive-compulsive thief is a bad person, in the sense of being uncaring or anti-social. Most are good, otherwise law-abiding citizens.

In a speech delivered on 19 October 2001, former Ontario Lieutenant-Governor Hilary Weston draws a contrast between the normal preoccupations of people in the fall season and their preoccupations after 11 September 2001:

> This is normally a time of year when we savour the pleasures of the Ontario Fall—glorious foliage, country fairs, hot cider to remind us that winter is on its way. But this year it's not the same: the subject on everyone's mind is terrorism, as hundreds of Canadian families forlornly wave their loved ones off to war.[52]

In a second speech, delivered to the Canadian Club, Weston contrasts the reactions of men and women to signs of heart disease:

> A few months ago, on a visit to the Women's Health Care Centre at Toronto General Hospital, a top doctor offered me a fascinating, but disturbing, explanation of why more women are dying of heart disease (as opposed to cancer) than men. When a man gets a chest pain, she explained, he assumes he's having a heart attack due to stress or overwork, immediately rushes off to a hospital, and is told to relax, etc. But when a woman gets a chest pain, she'll often dismiss it as a bit of indigestion, a bit of neurosis, nothing serious. She'll take a pill and go on because she can't afford to relax, so her actual condition is not discovered until much later and, by then, it's more acute and often fatal.[53]

In the next and final example, the speaker compares the number of cancer-related deaths to losses from airline crashes and then contrasts the way in which we treat airline companies and tobacco companies.

> If 800 fully loaded jumbo jets crashed each year, killing all 400,000 passengers, would we take action against the company that made the planes? The answer is *yes*. Yet the same numbers of people die each year from lung cancer, and we do nothing to close down the companies or seize their profits. What is the logic behind such contradictory behaviour?

Metaphors

A metaphor is highly compressed comparison. It compares two ideas or concepts by saying that one *is* the other. The classic example is 'Life's but a walking shadow; a poor player' (Shakespeare, *Macbeth*). In a speech on the importance of education, former Prime Minister Kim Campbell said, 'Illiteracy is a prison.'[54] In the same way, Winston Churchill often spoke in metaphorical language, saying in one often-quoted line: 'We are still masters of our fate. We are still captains of our soul.' In a rallying speech that followed the collapse of France in World War II, he asserted:

> Hitler knows that he will have to break us in this Island or lose the war. . . . If we fail, then the whole world, including the United States . . . will sink into the abyss of a new Dark Age made more sinister, and perhaps more protracted by the lights of perverted science. Let us therefore brace ourselves to our duties, and so bear ourselves that if the British empire and the Commonwealth last for a thousand years, men will still say, 'This was their finest hour.'[55]

Many consider the final line of this passage to be one of Churchill's most memorable rhetorical moments. Metaphors in the above passage include 'the abyss of a new Dark Age' and 'the lights of perverted science'. At other times, Churchill speaks of England's passage through a 'dark and deadly valley' [of war].[56]

In his eulogy to Trudeau, Joe Clark spoke of Trudeau as 'a bold page in the story of the nation'.[57] The inaugural address of John F. Kennedy, considered to be one of the best examples of American rhetoric, is rich in metaphorical language. Kennedy asserts, for example, that 'those who foolishly sought power by riding the back of the tiger ended up inside.' He also uses metaphors such as 'beachhead of co-operation' and 'jungle of suspicion' as he pursues the tropical theme.

Finally, in one of the most moving of rhetorical moments, Martin Luther King Jr delivered his last speech on 3 April 1968 to an audience gathered at the Masonic Temple in Memphis, Tennessee. The day after delivering this speech, King died at the hands of an assassin, shot to death on the balcony of his Memphis motel at the age of 39. In this speech, King's journey to the top of the mountain is a metaphor for the realization of his hopes for a just society. The image of the mountaintop also evokes the Biblical account of Moses, who went to the top of Mount Sinai to receive the Ten Commandments from God. Moses led his people out of Egypt to the promised land but never got there himself. As in his other speeches, King, a Southern Baptist minister, delivered this talk in the manner of a sermon, with predictable rising and falling cadences.

Well, I don't know what will happen now. We've got some difficult days ahead. But it doesn't matter to me now. Because I've been to the mountaintop. And I don't mind. Like anybody, I would like to live a long life. Longevity has its place. But I'm not concerned about that now. I just want to do God's will. And He's allowed me to go up to the mountain. And I've looked over. And I've seen the promised land. I may not get there with you. But I want you to know tonight, that we, as a people, will get to the promised land. And I'm happy, tonight. I'm not worried about anything. I'm not fearing any man. Mine eyes have seen the glory of the coming of the Lord.[58]

Similes

A metaphor, as we have seen, states that 'this is that.' Similes, on the other hand, are explicit comparisons that employ *like* or *as*: 'My love is like a red, red rose' (Robert Burns) or 'The evening is . . . like a patient etherized upon a table' (T.S. Eliot). Unlike similes, metaphors do not use terms such as *like* and *as*. An example comes from a caustic comment by Jack Layton, leader of the National Democratic Party. Layton accused Prime Minister Paul Martin of 'eating a Big Mac while [pretending] you're a vegetarian'.[59] He was referring to the government's ambiguous position on backing the US missile defence system. Although *like* and *as* do not appear in the comparison, they are implicit in the statement. Layton says, in essence, that the government is behaving like a vegetarian who eats a Big Mac. In an equally cynical comment, David Kilgour, a Liberal MP from Edmonton, claimed that his party 'is seen as looking on the public trust as a vulture looks on a dying calf.'[60]

Personification

Personification involves attributing human characteristics to an abstract idea or concept. In the following excerpt from the speech cited earlier, Mary Fisher personified the problem of AIDS:

> The AIDS virus is not a political creature. It does not care whether you are Democrat or Republican. It does not ask whether you are black or white, male or female, gay or straight, young or old. Tonight I represent an AIDS community whose members have been reluctantly drafted from every segment of American society.

In the early days of World War II, Winston Churchill delivered a speech to the British House of Commons in which he urged his colleagues to concentrate on their present task and to put aside fault-finding and recriminations: 'Of this I am quite sure, that if we open a quarrel between the past and the present, we shall find that we have lost the future.'[61] This sentence also illustrates parallelism.

Analogy

Analogies locate the similarities in two different ideas or items. The analogy uses a known concept to explain an unknown or less familiar concept. Although analogies are like similes in comparing two different concepts, they are often longer and they involve a reasoning process. That is, an analogy seeks to establish the logic in the relationship between the two dissimilar ideas. In his historic address 'I Have a Dream',

Martin Luther King Jr developed a powerful analogy in which he compared the treatment of African Americans to the predicament of someone given a cheque for insufficient funds.

> In a sense we have come to our nation's capital to cash a check. When the architects of our republic wrote the magnificent words of the Constitution and the Declaration of Independence, they were signing a promissory note that all men, yes black men as well as white men, would be guaranteed the inalienable rights of life, liberty, and the pursuit of happiness. It is obvious today that America has defaulted on this promissory note insofar as their citizens of color are concerned. Instead of honoring this sacred obligation, America has given the Negro people a bad check, which has come back marked 'insufficient funds'. But we refuse to believe that the bank of justice is bankrupt. We refuse to believe that there are insufficient funds in the great vaults of opportunity of this nation. So we have come to cash this check—a check that will give us upon demand the riches of freedom and the security of justice.[62]

Rhetorical Questions

In an address to the nation on 25 October 1995, Prime Minister Chrétien used a series of rhetorical questions in exhorting the people of Quebec to vote against separation from Canada. This example also illustrates the use of repetition:

> Do you really think that you and your family would have a better quality of life and a brighter future in a separate Quebec? Do you really think that the French language and culture in North America would be better protected in a separate Quebec? Do you really think you and your family will enjoy greater security in a separate Quebec? Do you want to turn your back on Canada? Does Canada deserve that? Are you really ready to tell the world—the whole world—that people of different languages, different cultures and different backgrounds cannot live together in harmony? Do you really think that ties of friendship and understanding . . . ties of mutual trust and respect can be broken without harm or rancour? Have you found one reason, one good reason, to destroy Canada? Do you really think that it makes any sense—any sense at all—to break up Canada? These are the questions I ask you to consider. It's a big, very big responsibility.

Biblical References

The most common marker of US presidential rhetoric is the invocation of the deity. Few presidents have ended their speeches without asking for a blessing upon the country. By way of contrast, Canadian politicians in recent years have rarely used Biblical references in their speeches.

When the space shuttle *Challenger* was lost on 28 January 1986, former US President Ronald Reagan delivered the following words of sympathy:

> The crew of the space shuttle *Challenger* honored us by the manner in which they lived their lives. We will never forget them, nor the last time we saw them, this morning, as they prepared for their journey and waved goodbye and 'slipped the surly bonds of earth' to 'touch the face of God.'[63]

When the space shuttle *Columbia* fell from the skies on 1 February 2003, President George W. Bush drew upon religious references to express his grief and condolences to the families of crew members:

> In the skies today we saw destruction and tragedy. Yet farther than we can see there is comfort and hope. In the words of the prophet Isaiah, 'Lift your eyes and look to the heavens. Who created all these? He who brings out the starry hosts one by one and calls them each by name. Because of His great power and mighty strength, not one of them is missing.' The same Creator who names the stars also knows the names of the seven souls we mourn today. The crew of the shuttle *Columbia* did not return safely to Earth; yet we can pray that all are safely home.[64]

Bill Clinton concluded his inaugural address on 20 January 1993 with a number of Biblical references:

> The scripture says, 'And let us not be weary in well-doing, for in due season, we shall reap, if we faint not.' From this joyful mountaintop of celebration, we hear a call to service in the valley. We have heard the trumpets. We have changed the guard. And now, each in our own way, and with God's help—we must answer the call. Thank you, and God bless you all.

While most Americans consider Biblical references in presidential speeches to be the normal practice, the leaders of most other countries (with some notable exceptions) do not include the same number of religious references in their speeches. Such references rarely appear in addresses by contemporary Canadian politicians.

Step 11: Adapting Your Materials to Your Audience

Speakers adapt to their audiences through strategies that recognize audience demographics, psychographics, needs, and personality profiles.

Demographics

Audience demographics such as level of education, occupation and income, age, gender, race, ethnicity, and prior experience with the topic should influence your approach. Without being condescending, you should gear your language to the educational level of your audience. You should include more definitions, explanations, and examples with audiences who are less familiar with the subject. You will need to include more evidence to support your case with hostile audiences. To capture and hold the attention of apathetic audiences, you will need to emphasize the benefits of listening to the speech. You can use jargon with people who share your profession but not with those who do not share a common language.

Age affects our knowledge of—and perspectives on—issues. Many older adults have difficulty understanding the language and value sets of younger people. They may think, for example, that words such as *dating* have the same meaning as when they were young. They may anticipate that living together implies the same commitment as marriage. People within bracketed age groups also share some life experiences. People who lived through the Great Depression of the 1930s, 'Trudeaumania' of the late 1960s, imposition of the War Measures Act in Quebec during the October Crisis in 1970, or the 1998 ice storm in eastern Ontario and southern Quebec have accumulated some shared life experiences (even if their perspectives on these events vary). When presenting to some audiences, speakers can make brief references to such events without having to offer supporting details. They can assume general knowledge of the events and sometimes shared perspectives, as well.

In addition, speakers can assume some shared concerns among people in the same age group. Young adults are often worried about getting an education, finding a partner, locating suitable employment, purchasing an automobile, and finding reasonable housing. Middle-aged adults are more concerned about paying off their mortgages, getting promoted at work, helping their children through university, building their pensions, and finding ways to lower their taxes as they move towards their peak earning years. Older adults tend to be most concerned about issues such as health care, transportation, and housing. An overriding concern is to find ways to maintain their independence for as long as possible.

Women have some issues and interests that are not equally important to men—and vice versa. Women experience the loss of ability to conceive children much earlier than men. They confront diseases, such as ovarian and uterine cancer, not experienced by men. They enjoy sports such as figure skating more than their male counterparts. Women converse more than men about personal relationships. Men tend to focus more on sports, finances, and business. Of course, many exceptions exist, and sexual stereotyping is always risky.

Although some studies indicate that speakers achieve maximum opinion change when they draw explicit conclusions for their audiences, others suggest that more educated and better-informed audiences prefer to draw their own conclusions.[65]

The same kinds of considerations apply to demographic groupings based on income, ethnicity, race, occupation, and region. People from certain racial and cultural groups, for example, may feel more strongly than the general population about issues such as racial profiling and equity legislation. People in particular occupations or income groups will often look at arguments from the perspective of self-interest. How will this proposed change or policy affect me? Will I lose my investment or savings? Will I have a reduced pension when I retire? At other times, audiences may perceive the information to be irrelevant to their circumstances. So speakers need to identify ways to answer objections based on self-interest and to clarify the relevance of the proposals for other audiences.

Psychographics

Often, the speaker has to move the argumentation to the level of values—to appeal to the patriotism, altruism, generosity, competitiveness, or other value orientation of audience members. To the extent possible, the speaker should look for values that she holds in common with the audience—a place where the two can meet and connect.

Needs

As discussed in Chapter 5, audiences look for ways to satisfy their basic physiological, safety, love, esteem, and self-actualization needs. When persuasive speakers can convince an audience that their ability to meet those needs has been compromised or when they can demonstrate that their solutions will overcome the obstacles, audiences will listen.

As discussed earlier, speakers sometimes use fear appeals to persuade audiences. Those fear appeals may involve threats to the safety, security, esteem, or other audience needs. Inciting fear is not enough, however, to accomplish persuasive aims. The speaker must also offer the listeners explicit advice on how to reduce or eliminate the threats. In addition, most experts agree that mild to moderate fear appeals are more effective than strong fear appeals and that teenagers react more to threats to their ego and self-esteem than to safety appeals.[66]

If audiences stand to lose from the proposed stance or solutions (e.g., to receive a lower pension with changes to social security), speakers need to explain how the long-term benefits outweigh the short-term costs. In other words, speakers need to identify a strategy for persuading the audience. But the first step is to recognize audience feelings on the topic. Audience members may feel insecure, threatened, or even angered by the proposed policy. They will reject the arguments of anyone who does not recognize their situation. So the argumentation must include recognition of audience sentiments on the topic.

Personality

Other considerations include factors such as personality. One can speculate, with some degree of certainty, that audiences populated by CEOs, Olympic athletes, and successful entrepreneurs probably do not suffer from low self-esteem. Thus, these audiences are likely to prefer messages that leave the choices open to them, not limiting their options or giving high levels of direction. They are more likely to respond to arguments based on logic and sound evidence than on loose opinions, since they do not depend on outside authorities to the same extent as low-esteem individuals. They do not tend to be conformists who seek the approval of others. They are more likely to respond to optimistic than pessimistic messages. The task of persuading an audience of high-esteem individuals can be a formidable one.[67]

When speaking to a group of low-esteem individuals (e.g., recovering drug addicts or teenagers with weight problems), the persuader may want to adopt a different strategy—more directive messages and greater use of role models drawn from peer populations. Alcoholics Anonymous, run by alcoholics for alcoholics, exemplifies this approach. The speakers at AA meetings are themselves recovering addicts.

Some of the same persuasion strategies that work with high-esteem audiences apply to open-minded audiences. Open-minded audiences tend to be more optimistic than close-minded audiences. They are also less reliant on authorities. They are able to place problems in a larger context than more close-minded individuals, and they try to find a way to accommodate the new information within their existing framework of beliefs. Thus, persuaders can feel more comfortable introducing new and controversial ideas to an audience populated by open-minded individuals. Speakers can be more optimistic in their approach to solutions, and they can rely more on expert opinions and less on authority figures to support their positions.[68]

With more close-minded audiences, on the other hand, persuaders may need to work harder to gain acceptance for controversial or new ideas. They should expect that the audience may be pessimistic in the first place towards proffered solutions, and they may need to rely more strongly on sources trusted by the audience to gain acceptance and compliance.

Box 10.8 A Question of Ethics

William was strongly in favour of gun control. One of his cousins had died in an accidental shooting several years previously. Nonetheless, he decided to argue against gun control in his persuasive speech. His decision resulted from the feedback he had received on his speech topic. A number of his classmates expressed annoyance when they learned that he planned to argue for stricter gun control legislation. Living in a rural area, many students were hunters. They believed that they knew how to use guns in a responsible way and that they had the right to purchase guns for recreational use. Worried that he would offend his classmates if he took such a controversial position, William decided to argue a position he did not believe to be morally right. Evaluate the decision of this speaker to abandon his original position.

Meredith, on the other hand, delivered a persuasive speech on the topic of overpopulation. She decided that the speech would be more interesting if she generated a hypothetical example in which she described the likely consequences of uncontrolled population growth. Her hypothetical example involved a country in western Africa. She also generated statistics to support her example. She did not inform her audience that the example and statistics were fictitious or exaggerated, generated to dramatize

the worst possible effects of overpopulation. She also said that the negative consequences were not just likely, but certain, if people did not act. And she presented two alternatives: support her solution or face disaster.

After Meredith sat down, a young man from Africa questioned her statistics and conclusions. When he learned that the example was hypothetical, created to provoke interest in the topic, he was extremely angry. He said that the speaker had falsified information rather than taken the time to research actual cases and gather valid statistics. Meredith, on the other hand, defended her speech on the grounds that her motives were honourable. She said that many people would die in the future if nothing happened to change the situation. Moreover, she argued that the country chosen for the example was the most likely to experience problems and that the statistics reflected patterns already developing. Was Meredith justified in using a hypothetical example in this way? Was she justified in creating or exaggerating statistics to support her claim? In simplifying a complex situation and encouraging the agreement of the audience by presenting only two alternatives? In pretending to be certain about the outcome of failure to act? Discuss the ethics of Meredith's approach.

General Considerations

Speakers should realize that a single speech will do little to effect major changes in audiences. Often the speech only stimulates the audience to think more seriously about the topic under consideration. Using extensive research as a basis for their decisions, politicians tend to target their communications to those most likely to be persuaded—the undecided. They also seek to reinforce the positive perceptions of audience members who favour their point of view and to energize those who are apathetic. Typically, they pay less attention to those who are hostile to their point of view, recognizing that change is highly unlikely in the 'decided' population.

Persuaders, in general, face the same decisions. To what extent should they target their communications to some audience segments and ignore others? Wanting to reach every audience member is a laudable objective; however, it is rarely realistic. For that reason, most persuasive speakers direct their speeches to those audience members with whom they can have the greatest impact. To identify those audiences and to aim for realistic outcomes, they must conduct research.

Step 12: Linking Your Ideas

As discussed in Chapters 4 and 8, *transitions*, *signposts*, and *internal summaries* help speakers to see the relationship among different parts of the speech. These linking devices and summaries guide the audience through the speech. Listeners cannot go back to confirm the organization of the speech, as they can when they read a book or article. So they must depend on the speaker to give orienting signals as they progress through the speech. Box 10.9 reviews the role of transitions, signposts, and internal summaries within the larger speech structure.

Box 10.9 Transitions, Signposts, and Internal Summaries

Attention: Justice has a face. The children in Inuktituk tell me the face is white. Justice has a home. The children in the Yukon say that they have never seen the home. It must be far away. Justice has a job—to see that all of us are safe from those who err and lose their way. The children of the Northwest say that they do not feel safe. They do feel lost. Justice is a southerner, who wears spiked heels in Toronto, pin-striped suits in Ottawa, and designer clothes in Montreal. Justice does not wear the dress of those who live in Nunavut or hunt caribou on frozen tundra. *Thesis statement:* More culturally appropriate models are required to ensure justice for Native Canadians. *Preview statement:* In this speech, I will identify some of the biases in the Canadian justice system, especially as they relate to Native Canadians. Then I will suggest some creative solutions to these problems, focusing on cultural fit. *Signpost:* First, let us consider biases in the system. (A discussion of biases comprises the first part of the body of the speech.) *Internal summary:* Let us pause for a moment to reiterate what we have just said. First, we have seen that our justice system does not effectively protect every Canadian. Some groups, such as our Native population, 'fall through the cracks.' We have also seen that the design and operation of our penal institutions are culturally biased against Natives. *Transition:* Therefore, we can conclude that many different factors are at play in the situation. *Signpost:* Now let us look at three possible solutions. Then you will be in a position to select the best option. They are as follows . . . (The solution part of the speech comes next.) *Conclusion:* Thus, while we may believe in a system that protects the rights of all citizens, we are not always able to realize that goal. But change is possible. We can work towards ensuring that our prisons are not populated by the poorest in our society. We can change the conditions that nurture crime in our northern communities. We can ensure that every Canadian has equal access to competent legal counsel. We can strive to establish penal systems based on culturally appropriate models, whether that system be healing circles or modern correctional facilities. The key to solving the problems are the two words 'We can'. In a recent interview, Larry King asked Bill Clinton why he had the affair with Monica Lewinsky. Clinton responded, 'For the worst of all possible reasons—because I could.' Conversely, I challenge you today to commit yourself to ensuring justice for the people who live in Rankin Inlet and Frobisher Bay and all of the other northern communities—for the best of all possible reasons—because *you can.*

Step 13: Writing Your Conclusion

As with other speeches, conclusions should provide a brief summary of major points from the speech and leave the audience with a memorable thought. Speeches to convince typically employ quotations, proverbs, or poems in conclusions. Speeches to actuate often include a challenge to the audience, as well as a quotation, proverb, or poem. Sometimes speeches to actuate ask the audience to visualize a future with or without the desired solution. Some attention strategies (e.g., use of humour) are inappropriate in speeches of a serious persuasive nature.

The following example illustrates a conclusion that summarizes the major points in the speech. The conclusion also challenges the audience to make difficult choices.

> I hope I've succeeded in explaining what the government intends to do on the health-care issue and in describing your options as a consumer of health-care services. Do you want a system that will still be with us in 20 years? 30 years? Do you want a system that will offer your children the same or better benefits than you enjoy? There is a way to ensure a quality health-care system for your children, but you must be prepared to make the sacrifices I have outlined to you. Mark Twain said, 'The only way to keep your health is to eat what you don't want, drink what you don't like, and do what you'd rather not.' Well, I would say that the only way to fix our health-care system is to accept that our choices may not always be what we *want* to do, *like* to do, or would *prefer* to do. But they can lead us to a solution with long-term and sustainable results. In this case, three negatives can lead to a positive.

In addition to leaving the audience with a memorable thought, conclusions should provide closure. So they will often include a brief summary such as the one above. Often, speakers refer back to some example used in the introduction to the speech to give a unity to the speech.

The conclusions of speeches to actuate (e.g., the motivated sequence) will suggest specific actions to be taken by the audience. The conclusions of speeches to convince will not include an action component. As noted in the discussion of the motivated sequence, if you include an action step, your requests for action should be specific. For a six- to eight-minute speech, a conclusion that is half of a page in length should be sufficient.

Step 14: Delivering Your Speech

Extemporaneous speaking from note cards is the preferred form of speaking for most occasions. Exceptions occur, however, when speakers compete in oratory contests, deliver addresses at ceremonial events, or aim to capture a place in the annals of history. In those situations, the speakers will create a manuscript speech, carefully worded and refined, which they read or deliver predominantly from memory. Eloquence of language is very important in those circumstances. The speeches we study as examples of great oratory were not improvised. Few orators deliver such speeches in an impromptu or extemporaneous fashion. For the most part, the speakers know, in advance, exactly what they are going to say. Either they or their speechwriters have spent hours on the wording of the speeches.

The difference between an extemporaneous speaking event and a memorized presentation should not be the presence or absence of note cards. Rather, the difference should be the extent to which you strive for spontaneity in wording. With an extemporaneous delivery, you vary your wording from practice to practice so that you will appear to be totally 'in the moment'. With a more memorized delivery, you strive to remember each word as you have written it. You want the audience to savour the words and to appreciate special turns of phrase. In some cases, you will be striving for lyricism and poetic of expression. The rhythm with which you deliver the words may be important.

Some speaking competitions prohibit the use of note cards. These occasions demand that speakers rely totally on recall. Most occasions, however, allow speakers to bring whatever memory devices they choose to the podium. So even if you plan to deliver a memorized speech, you may feel more comfortable bringing a few notes to the stand with you. Should you forget your speech, you can refer to the note cards. Finding your place in the full manuscript would be much more awkward and difficult.

The challenge for most speakers will be to refrain from going to the note cards when it is unnecessary. For that reason, you should restrict your notes to the major points and wording of hard-to-recall passages. Bring the cards with you as a reminder, should you need them; or use the cards for long quotations or stories that may be difficult to remember. Above all, the goal of memorized delivery is to respect the exact wording of the speech. In practising the speech, think about the sequence of ideas. Memorize the sequence and then memorize the wording.

When delivering the speech, focus your attention on your purpose in speaking and on your audience so that you do not sound robotic. If you forget a part of the speech, stop and find your place. If necessary, improvise until you are back on track.

Step 15: Responding to Questions

The question-and-answer session following a speech is an opportunity to demonstrate the breadth and depth of your research. You should listen carefully to the questions, restate them before responding, and then answer clearly and succinctly. You should never dismiss any question as unworthy, and you should try to engage a maximum number of people. If you cannot answer a question, offer to get back to the person with a response. Do not pretend to know something that you do not know. Finally, you should respect the time period assigned for responding to questions from your peers.

As noted in the introduction, persuasive speeches may aim to convince (change existing attitudes or effect a shift in position), stimulate (reinforce existing attitudes or stances), or actuate (move an audience to act on their beliefs or to eliminate an unwanted behaviour). The process of writing such a speech involves selecting a topic and defining a general purpose, writing a tentative position statement, researching and identifying levels of audience knowledge and attitudes towards your position, deciding on a specific speech purpose, choosing an organizational pattern, writing an introduction, developing supporting materials for your outline, adapting to your audience, choosing evocative language, writing transitions and internal summaries, writing your conclusion, memorizing and delivering your speech, and responding to questions at the conclusion of your speech.

Questions for Discussion

1. If you had to choose some cause to which you would leave your inheritance, what would it be? How does this cause represent values of importance to you?
2. Have you ever been held responsible for breaking a law that you thought should be eliminated? How could you use this idea in a speech to persuade? Form a position statement on the issue. How would your audience feel about your position? Are

they likely to be supportive, undecided, hostile, or apathetic? How could you approach your topic in a manner that would allow you to overcome any hostility or apathy?

3. Can any contemporary speakers compete with the rhetorical talents of speakers such as Winston Churchill and Pierre Elliott Trudeau? If so, who? What are the characteristics of that speaker in terms of language usage? Does the person speak in eloquent terms or use more conversational language?

Appendix: Sample Student Persuasion Speeches

Speech #1: Problem Pattern of Organization

by Emily Goucher

James Murray Davidson, beloved husband of Elizabeth and the late Evelyn. Cherished father of Jane, Cathy, Martha, David, Nancy, and Angus. Much loved stepfather of Pat, David, Paul, and Judy. Missed terribly by his daughters and sons-in-law. Beloved and respected grandpa of 13. Memorial donations to the Canadian Cancer Society.

What I just read to you was my grandfather's death announcement. On May 3, 2004, cigarettes killed my grandfather, who died of lung cancer. I am not here today to preach to you about the dangers of smoking. You've all heard that message many times. Rather, I would like to share with you the reality of smoking. I would like to suggest that a decision you make today affects not only you, but also everyone connected to you. Cancer did not just end my grandfather's life. It also took away a husband, a father, and a grandfather.

My grandfather survived the Great Depression. He was shot twice during World War II. And in his career as a civil engineer, supervising some of Canada's most northern highways, he was no stranger to danger. But what ended up killing him was cigarettes. To the smokers in this class, I ask you: Sixty years from now, do you want your grandchild to be standing in front of her peers, uttering the words, 'My grandfather died of lung cancer'?

I understand how difficult it is to quit smoking. I've watched countless family members struggle to quit in the months after my grandfather's death. But you know what, watching a loved one die of lung cancer is not easy either. My grandfather had lived a long and productive life, but it did not ease the pain of watching him struggle in the months preceding his death. Lung cancer has acquired the reputation of being a silent killer. By the time you realize

that it has claimed a space in your life, you have little hope of a cure. When I was home for winter break in late February, my grandpa was making his own wine and snow-blowing his neighbours' driveways. By the time I returned home for Easter break, they had given him weeks to live. The rapidity of his decline was hard to accept and part of the reason that I am so passionately against smoking.

I am not telling you to quit smoking. That is not my place. I am, however, asking you to think hard about your choices and what they will cost you down the road. An article in *Men's Health Magazine* predicts that, on average, smoking removes 15 years from a smoker's expected lifespan—a large chunk of your life for the pleasure of a few puffs a day. Recent statistics also tell us that lung cancer has now replaced breast cancer as the leading cause of cancer-related deaths in women. So why don't we have runs and special charities for lung cancer victims?

The overall rates of death from cancer are twice as high among smokers as non-smokers, with heavy smokers having rates that are four times greater than those of non-smokers. More people die from smoking than from traffic accidents, AIDS, and suicide combined. The government invests millions of dollars in cancer research each year, but we all know that the major cause of cancer is sitting in the coat pockets of Canadians, including some members of this class.

The fact is that 99 per cent of all deaths from lung cancer are smoking-related. Notice the word 'related'. Not everyone who dies from lung cancer is a smoker. Exposure to second-hand smoke holds the same hazards as smoking, but the myth persists that only smokers get lung cancer. So if you have been sitting here, comfortable that this speech does not apply to you, you should take notice.

A depressing picture, yes, but change is possible. In the 1970s, 50 per cent of all people in our age group smoked. Today that number hovers at around 22 per cent. We are making progress, but we have a long way to go. For the smokers in this class, you have two choices. You can quit or you can continue smoking. I realize that the decision is yours. My aim is simply to put a human face on cancer—to expose the problem. My grandfather died of cancer, and I miss him terribly. Cigarettes accomplished what the Great Depression, a world war, a stressful career, and 10 children could not. So the next time you consider your options, remember that 15 years is a long time to lose and cancer is no way to die. We can't change what happened to our grandparents, but we can change what happens to our grandchildren.

References

Balance TV. Tips for Talking to your Kids about Smoking Day. www.balancetv.ca/balancetv/client/en/Wellness/DetailNews.asp?idNews=542

Canadian Centre for Adolescent Research: Smoking Statistics http://ccar.briercrest.ca/stats/smoking.shtml

CP News Wire: Lung Association www.newswire.ca/en/releases/archive/January2004/18/c9976.html

'Smoking Facts and Smoking Statistics on Dangers of Smoking Hazards', *Men's Health Magazine*, on-line edition: www.men-health-magazine-online.com/smoking-facts.html

Prevention Source, British Columbia. Smoke Signals, Teen Smoking in BC 1997 www.preventionsource.bc.ca/factsheets/15.html

Speech #2: Comparative Advantages Pattern of Organization

by Crystal Cuthbert

Archaeological data tell us that the burial of bodies dates back to the Stone Age, or about 3000 BC. This practice occurs in countries around the world, including Asia, North America, and Europe. Our ancestors saw burial as returning to the elements, with everyone sharing the same eventual destiny. Churches filled catacombs with the deceased and layered the dead in cemeteries. The practice of layering bodies on top of each other occurred because, even several hundred years ago, space was limited in some parts of the world.

But even the layering of bodies has not solved the bigger problem—what to do with the remains of a growing world population. Environmentalists argue that we should be making better use of space in our cities and populated areas of the world. Health experts declare that many cemetery spaces are carriers of disease. Some studies have found that bodies from the eighteenth century still contain bacteria from diseases such as the bubonic plague. Celebrities are often entombed in concrete structures to avoid the ravaging of their grave sites. Burials have become extravagant affairs, involving the purchase of expensive plots of land, caskets, and headstones. Many families cannot afford this kind of expense.

In short, most people would agree that traditional forms of burial carry significant risks, but not everyone understands the advantages of alternative methods of disposal. In this speech, I will compare the advantages and disadvantages of five kinds of body disposal, including city graveyards, garden cemeteries, transfer of bodies to other locations for burial, cremation, and woodland burials. By the accounts of many people, the best alternatives are cremation and woodland burials.

What are the advantages and disadvantages of these various methods of burial? Obviously, city graveyards are convenient, easy to access for purposes of funerals, and easy to visit. Many people like to know that loved ones are close at hand. City cemetery plots come with many disadvantages, however. They are often relatively shallow, making it easy for thieves to snatch bodies from their graves and leave bones scattered about the graveyard. Two hundred years ago, numerous rundown cemeteries in Europe were closed after being declared a magnet for disease and delinquency. The closing of some cemeteries, however, only made the problem more serious for those that remain open for burials.

In cities such as London, England, archaeologists are stymied by the inability to conduct archaeological digs in areas where bodies are buried—a significant problem since the ancestors of the Londoners did not pay a great deal of attention to where they placed the bodies of their family members. To relocate the bodies involves huge expenditures of money, generally not seen as worth the investment.

In some communities, residents have moved cemeteries outside city boundaries in order to prevent the spread of disease. Their solution was to create garden cemeteries—sprawling landscaped areas, replete with benches, monuments, and yes, the deceased. We can find such communities in Canada, close to most towns and cities. They are certainly attractive, and like parks, they allow people to stroll in quiet spaces. But these garden cemeteries consume large amounts of space that cannot be used for other purposes. Consider the following statistics. Approximately 224,000 people die each year in Canada. If each person has a traditional interment (2.8 metre by 2.7 metre plot), they will consume about 1,700 square kilometres of space. This calculation does not take into account the space between grave sites.

Moreover, once a tract of land has been declared as a burial site for human remains, no building can be zoned for that area. In more senses than one, this space has become a 'dead' zone, claimed by the dead for the dead, impossible to be employed for the purposes of the living. While in the 1920s, many people took Sunday strolls in these garden cemeteries, they no longer spend their Sundays in this way. In short, the creation of garden cemeteries has not proved to be a good solution. The cemeteries could be put to better use as farmland for crops and the grazing of animals, wildlife preserves, or residential areas.

In cities such as Hong Kong, families have solved the space problem by transporting the bodies of their loved ones to the mainland. But this solution is only a temporary one. With the continuing growth of populations in countries such as China, available spaces for burial will become scarce over time.

What are the alternatives to these city and garden burial sites? The first alternative is cremation. Ashes to ashes, dust to dust. Cremation returns you to the elements immediately. With cremation, you do not decompose slowly over time. A box or coffin containing the body is placed in an oven structure. The crematorium burns the body at 1,000 degrees centigrade, reducing the body and its container to ashes and small bone fragments. The bone fragments are later crushed into a fine powder. The remains, which weigh about four pounds, are placed in an urn, which can be buried in a small plot or placed in niches above ground. Alternatively, family members can spread the ashes in a location desired by the deceased. It is important to check with local officials before proceeding with the spreading of ashes in public domains.

In Canada, about 42 per cent of all deceased are cremated. Despite some minor problems, such as the potential for mixing of ashes with the bodies of other cremated individuals, many people choose this alternative to traditional burials. Some religious groups also choose cremation over alternative methods of burial.

If cremation violates the religious beliefs of a person or group, however, a second alternative exists. Woodland burials involve placement of a body in a biodegradable casket, which is buried in the ground. Caskets can be made of bamboo, wicker, or pine. Instead of a headstone, the family plants a tree above or beside the plot. In time, the box will decompose, as will the body, fertilizing the tree. Although the lands still qualify as cemeteries, they could be designated as wildlife preserves. Once full, they could become woodlands. Instead of having tracts of wasted land, void of vegetation, the cemeteries would be preserves of nature.

Woodland burials make sense not only from an environmental point of view, but also from a financial perspective. Woodland burial caskets are more economical than traditional ones. They cost an average of $1,000 less than other kinds of coffins. Neither cremation nor woodland burials require the purchase of headstones, which can cost upwards of $400. Cemeteries also require constant upkeep, and the families of the interred must pay for these services. Woodlands do not require the same level of maintenance, and cremation requires no services by others if the family retains the urn.

In a world where the land mass is limited and the population is expected to rise to nine billion, we cannot afford to allocate so much space to the deceased. In a world where ancient rain forests are destroyed to support cattle, we cannot afford to waste grazing land on the dead. With space becoming scarcer in cities and cemeteries encroaching upon rural communities, we cannot afford to waste more time before shifting to alternative methods of body disposal.

One reason for the popularity of traditional burials was to ensure that the deceased really were deceased. That argument no longer holds, since most bodies are embalmed prior to burial. We no longer have to bury people with communication devices to ensure that they can alert us if they happen to awaken after being buried. We know when brain activity has ceased. The old excuses for traditional burials no longer work, and we must abandon a past bogged down with foolish superstitions and land-wasting traditions. Add your voice to the growing numbers of those who care about our environment and our present and future needs. Reclaim our land for the living.

References

Beechwood Cemetery (2004). *Beechwood: A Place for Living.* At: <www.beechwoodcemetery.com>. Accessed 24 Nov. 2004.

Hallam, E., and J. Hockey. *Death, Memory and Material Culture.* New York: Oxford University Press, 2001.

Robinson, B.A. *Cremation vs. Burial.* At: <www.religioustolerance.org/crematio.htm>.

Salisbury, M. *From My Death May Life Come Forth: A Feasibility Study of the Woodland Cemetery in Canada.* At: <www.earthartist.com/research/thesis>. Accessed 24 Nov. 2004.

Taylor, A. *Burial Practice in Early England.* London: Tempus Publishing Limited, 2001.

Speech #3: Claims Pattern of Organization

by Carly Fridman

They pass you on the street. They are in your classes. They may be sitting next to you or standing right in front of you. They are people with learning disabilities—people like me. No, I am not slow or stupid. Nor do I have a disease. I am dyslexic, and I am not alone. According to the International Dyslexia Association, between 15 per cent and 20 per cent of Canadians have a language-based learning disability. That statistic means that at least two or more of you can identify personally with what I am saying.

People like me are not less intelligent than other people. In fact, we can be academically gifted and highly motivated achievers. But we are unable to communicate our intelligence because we learn in a different way. That is, a person with a learning disability experiences a large gap between personal strengths and weaknesses. I am very good, for example, at problem-solving and oral expression. But when it comes to reading and writing, as well as spelling and math, I am below average. These weaknesses sometimes make it impossible for me to communicate my strengths.

At times, I have felt hopeless, as if I were climbing a hill covered in ice, fighting to keep my grip. My successes have come from getting help and accommodations from teachers and peers. Accommodations—this word is a vital part of my success, but a misunderstanding of its importance has also made my journey very difficult at times. Today I will educate you on why these accommodations do not give me an upper hand or constitute abuse of the system. I will explain why people with learning disabilities, including myself, need these accommodations in order to accomplish our personal learning goals. And I hope to dispel the myth that accommodations constitute an unfair practice, giving some students an advantage over others.

My university offers a range of vital services to students with disabilities, including note-takers, taped texts, and test-ing accommodations. These services are not accessible to everyone. You cannot just walk in and say, 'I have a learning disability and I need accommodations.' You must have a valid assessment. An assessment is a series of tests that evaluate the learning abilities and outline the needs of the individual. By law, the person with the learning disability must receive the accommodations suggested by that needs assessment.

I can tell you, however, that the matter is rarely that simple. This assessment does not ensure willing compliance. No matter where I go, I find that I must fight and stand up for myself. I must argue to receive the accommodations that help me to succeed. In my case, I require extra time, access to a computer, and carbon paper. At times, I also need certain kinds of technical assistance.

On one occasion, I almost had a panic attack when a professor gave a pop quiz in class. I knew that, despite my understanding of the subject, I would not be able to communicate my knowledge in writing. Yet I had no choice; so I wrote the quiz. When I got the results, I was not surprised to see that I had failed the quiz. I did what I always do. I went to the professor's office to explain my need for special accommodations. Without hesitation, she said, 'Well, I can't do anything about it. If I give special treatment to you, I will have to give special treatment to everyone and that's not fair.'

Let's talk about fair. Do you believe in equal opportunity? Well, accommodations give me equal opportunity. They make life a little fairer for me. When talking about learning disabilities, accommodations, and the concept of fairness, the following example comes to mind. If Danielle were to fall unconscious, would I say, 'I can't give her CPR because if I do, I would have to give CPR to Mike and Adrienne and Ashley'? Does that seem logical to you? It doesn't to me. I know that this example is a bit extreme, but that's how I feel when a professor says, 'I can't do this for you because it's not fair to others.'

Well, it is fair. It is fair to have someone read an exam to you if you can't decipher the questions. It is fair to have someone read your answer out loud when you cannot differentiate what is on the page from what is in your mind. And it is fair and reasonable to expect access to a dictionary that allows you to check for spelling errors. These kinds of supports do not give an unfair advantage to a student with dyslexia. Rather, they put us on the same playing field as the rest of you.

Please, can someone tell me what this says? *Dis ri p the co ns e bt of he j m o n y*? Sabrina? Imagine this gibberish was an exam question. This is how people with dyslexia sometimes see things when they are trying to read. In doing this short exercise, you put yourself in their shoes. How do you feel? I don't have quite this much difficulty reading, but it is still tough. I expend as much energy reading the question as writing the answer. By the time I have finished one question, I'm exhausted. That's why the accommodation of time and a half is so important to me. In order to have the proper time to answer the question, I must have more time to read the question.

The same principle applies to taking notes. I have to concentrate so much on spelling the words that I miss information. For this reason, I often ask classmates for a copy of their notes. But many of my peers are hesitant to share. I always get the same response, 'Why don't you just take notes? It's not fair that I have to take them for you, while you just sit there.' In response I ask, 'Is it fair that I will miss half the lecture trying to figure out how to record a thought? Is it fair that, even if I get most of the lecture, when I go home to review it, it is so misspelled that I cannot read my own hieroglyphics? Is that fair?'

Today, I have given you some clear examples of why accommodations given to students with learning disabilities are crucial for their success. Everyone has the right to learn. Everyone who expends the effort has the right to succeed. Shouldn't everyone have the opportunity to become productive and contributing members of society? I hope that today I have opened your mind and dispelled the ignorant claim that accommodations offered to students with learning disabilities are a type of hand-holding, a freebie. Because nothing I have done has been easy. Achieving an education has been a battle for me, and everyday I confront the enemy.

I hope that the next time someone asks you for a special accommodation, you will remember this speech and consider the possibility that *fair* can have different meanings in different contexts. And if you look around our classroom and say, 'We do not have five members of this class who are dyslexic; the statistics must be wrong', consider the possibility that the other 15 per cent may have grown tired of coping with the mantra 'I can't help you because it would be unfair.'

References

Fletcher, J.M., Coulter, W.A., Reschly, D.J., and Vaughn, S. (2004). Alternative approaches to the definition and identification of learning disabilities: Some questions and answers. *Annals of Dyslexia* 54 (2): 304–31.

International Dyslexia Association. At: <www.interdys. org/>. Accessed 21 Mar. 2005.

Kurnoff, Shirley (1995). *The Human Side of Dyslexia*. London: London Universal Publishing.

Shivers, Maria (2001). *Practical Strategies for Living with Dyslexia*. London: Jessica Kingsley Publishers.

The Dyslexia Institute. At: <www.dyslexia-inst.org.uk/>. Accessed 20 Mar. 2005.

Speech #4: Motivated Sequence Pattern of Organization

by Elizabeth Buryk

Attention

Every two seconds, someone in North America requires a blood transfusion to save his or her life. By the time that I finish this speech, blood donations will have saved 240 lives. By the time we finish this class, 5,400 lives will have been saved by blood donations. By the end of the day, these acts of caring will have saved the equivalent of the population of this university. It takes less than one hour to donate your blood, and one donation can save up to four lives. Blood donations make a difference.

I am, unfortunately, not eligible to give blood because I have iron deficiency anemia. Nonetheless, I think that giving blood is a very important cause about which people should be educated. And I have done extensive research in order to share some of the most important facts on the topic. In this speech, I will talk with you about the importance of donating blood, tell you how to donate, and explain who benefits from donated blood.

Need

At the moment, Canada's blood reserve is in a 10-year decline. Three and a half per cent of Canadians donate blood each year, but to keep our blood supply at an acceptable level, Health Canada needs at least 5 per cent of Canadians to donate. The aging population in Canada will create a situation of even greater need than in the coming years. Blood donations may not affect you personally right now, but statistically speaking, one in 10 people will need a blood transfusion in a lifetime. That means that at least two people in this class will require donated blood to stay alive. But even if the person receiving the blood is a stranger to you, he or she is someone else's mother, child, best friend, or partner.

Eighty per cent of Canadians think that donating blood is a good idea, but only a small percentage of that number actually donate. People use excuses such as, 'I don't want to feel weak afterwards' or 'I don't have enough time.' In reality, the entire process of giving blood takes less than one hour. It is a simple procedure, which responds to a serious problem.

Satisfaction

To qualify as a donor, you must be between the ages of 17 and 71 and weigh at least 110 pounds. It can be dangerous to give blood if you are not in good health. This requirement protects the donor, not the recipient. Nor can you have any piercing or tattoos in the last year. Since tattoos and piercing can transmit HIV, the blood foundations ask you to wait a year to be sure that you are not carrying a virus unknowingly. This requirement protects the recipient.

A nurse will ask a few confidential questions, intended to screen donors to be sure that they are not at risk and that the recipients of the blood will not be at risk. Some sample questions include, 'Are you taking medication? Have you had the flu in the last two days?' Following the interview, the nurse will ask you to take a quick hemoglobin test to measure your iron count. If you qualify, the actual donation process will take less than 10 minutes. In less than one hour, you can save up to four lives with your blood. The donated blood will be taken, tested, and put into a blood bank, to be distributed to hospitals. Britain is presently working with an acceptable level of blood donations. Blood is readily available to all people in need—accident victims, surgery patients, and those with anemia and leukemia.

Visualization

Imagine that we were working at the same level in Canada as Britain. We would have more than enough donated blood in our system. No one would have to postpone surgery because of an inadequate blood supply. Hospitals would always have enough blood on hand. Patients at risk of dying would not have to wait for it to be shipped from central donation banks. A different future could occur, however, if the donation rate continues to decline. Hundreds, even thousands of Canadians, could die needlessly. The baby boomers, our parents' generation, will suffer the most.

Action

We can ensure a different scenario if we donate and encourage others to do the same. This university is holding a blood donation clinic this Wednesday, November 19th, at 550 Cumberland. You can arrive without an appointment, or for more information, you can call 1–888–2 DONATE. As students, you may not have extra funds to give to charities, and you may not have the time to volunteer for food banks or at homeless centres. But you can save lives by donating one hour of your time and giving the most precious gift of all—your blood.

Only a couple of months ago, my best friend's father made a successful recovery from prostate cancer because he was able to receive donated blood following his surgery. He harvested his own blood before surgery, but complications required him to receive more blood than originally anticipated. The hospital used donated blood to save his life. Without that donation, my friend would have lost her father. The next person in need could be your father, your brother, or your best friend. 'Blood—it is in you to give.'

References

Abbott Laboratories. *The Use of Blood*. Chicago: Abbott Laboratories, 1961.

Canadian Blood Services. At: <www.bloodservices.ca>. Accessed 9 Nov. 2003.

Hagen, Piet J. *Blood: Gift or Merchandise: Towards an International Blood Policy*. New York: A.R. Liss, 1982.

Harmening, Denise M., ed. *Modern Blood Banking and Transfusion Practices*. Philadelphia: F.A. Davis, 1999.

'Hospital Waiting Times/List Statistics'. United Kingdom Government. At: <www.doh.gov.uk/waiting times/2002/q2/qm08r_s_821.html>. Accessed 9 Nov. 2003.

'Numbers,' *Time* 162 (2003): 29.

Weiner, Melvin. *Personal and Social Consequences of Blood Donors and Non-Donors*. Ottawa: National Library of Canada, 1980.

Speech #5 Common Variation on Motivated Sequence Pattern of Organization

by Lee-Ann Cass

Attention Step

As some of you may have noticed, I am wearing a green ribbon today. Do you know what the ribbon represents? For those who don't know, the ribbon symbolizes organ donation, the topic of my speech.

I have been a supporter of organ donation for over ten years now. Let me explain why. In the early nineties, my brother was diagnosed with an unknown lung disease. He was 22 years old, the same age as some of you. Before his diagnosis, he was very active. Throughout high school, he was a cadet, going to army training camps every summer. He loved to play hockey and worked out regularly at the gym. While manual labour wasn't his first love, he knew the value of a hard day's work. One of his jobs involved working on a farm, where the doctors think that he contracted the lung disease. While there is no name for his disease, it is common among people who work with animals. The symptoms are similar to cystic fibrosis, where fluid builds up in the lungs.

Doing the simplest tasks, such as climbing the stairs in our home, became unbearable for my brother. My family spent so much time at the hospital that the doctors and nurses knew our family members by name, and my brother rarely had to wait in the ER. He would walk into the emergency room, find a vacant bed, and hook himself to the oxygen machine while we checked him into the hospital. After several years and many surgeries, the doctors decided that he required a lung transplant.

After a year on the waiting list, my brother's condition deteriorated seriously. At that time, I was only 16. I didn't realize that, if he had not received his lung when he did, he would not have survived the following 24 hours.

Need Step

For the next several minutes, I will share with you the benefits of organ and tissue donations. I will lay to rest some of the fears or concerns that you may have regarding organ donation. And finally, I will let you know how you can help to save lives.

As of this minute, more than 3,500 Canadians are waiting for an organ—a heart, lungs, kidney, liver, or pancreas, just to name a few. By this time next year, 150 of those 3,500 people will have died. One hundred fifty families will have lost a mother, father, sister, son, or daughter, because

only 15 out of every one million people in Canada have chosen to become a donor.

I would like to translate this statistic into something more real for you. The following statistics come from the Quebec government Web site:

Number of Quebec Patients Waiting for a Transplant in 1996

Kidney	Kidney/ pancreas	Pan- creas	Liver	Heart	Heart/ lungs	Lungs	Total
471	16	5	32	24	1	28	577

My brother was one of these numbers. In 1996, he was one of 10 people who received a lung donation:

Number of Transplants in Quebec in 1996

Kidney	Kidney/ pan- creas	Pan- creas	Liver	Heart	Heart/ lungs	Lungs	Kidney (live)	Total
184	1	2	95	37	0	10	14	341

And my family thanks God that he was not listed on the next chart, the number of people who died while on this list. The total number of deaths is unknown, since no data are available in some categories:

Number of Quebec Patients Who Died on the Waiting List in 1996

Kidney	Kidney/ pancreas	Pancreas	Liver	Heart	Heart/ lungs	Lungs
N/D	N/D	N/D	14	11	0	7

Unfortunately, many families are not as lucky as my family.

Satisfaction Step

What can be done to change these statistics? The number-one solution is for more people to become organ donors. Some of you may be asking: Exactly what does becoming a donor entail? To answer your question, there are two kinds of donors—living and dead. The most common organ donation by living donors is the kidney. Economically, it makes much more sense for someone to receive a kidney transplant than to be on dialysis for years. The cost of a kidney transplant can be as low as $20,000. The cost per year for someone to stay on dialysis is $50,000—a saving of $30,000 to our health-care system in the first year alone. Not only that, the transplant allows for a person to resume normal activities, while dialysis is only a temporary fix.

The second type of donation can be made when you die. While this topic of conversation may not be pleasant, an uncomfortable conversation at this time can save up to seven lives, if not more, in the future. Some people are hesitant about donating their organs because they don't know the facts. That is why I am here today, to set the record straight. The perfect donor candidates are those with severe head trauma, who have been declared brain dead. These traumas may be the result of a car accident, a gun shot, a lack of oxygen to the brain, or cerebral bleeding.

Everyone can become a donor, regardless of health. In fact, the oldest donor was over 90 years of age. Most religions support the concept of organ donation, including Judaism, Christianity, Buddhism, even Quakers. Most of the other religions leave it up to the individual to decide.

Willing your organs does not mean that doctors will deliberately let you die to increase their organ bank. On the contrary, every attempt will be made to save your life; and the doctors who care for you will have nothing to do with the transplant. Their primary concern will be preserving your life. They will only ask about your status as an organ donor after they have made every effort to save you.

Others may not want to donate for fear the recipients of their organs are smokers or alcoholics. While every concern is valid, one must ask: Is the life of a smoker any less important than the life of a non-smoker? What if it were your mother or your uncle? Most of us have some family members who became addicted before cigarettes were declared deadly? In addition, being on a transplant list requires adherence to strict rules. If you are waiting for a liver, for example, and you have even one drink, you are kicked off the list indefinitely. The same applies to smoking of cigarettes.

Action Step

You are now better prepared to decide whether you want to become an organ donor. If you have decided to give the gift of life, you must take several actions. First, take out your medical card. On the back of the card is a place for a signature. If you sign the card, the doctors will ask your family for permission. If your family declines, your organs will not be taken.

My family has been on the giving, as well as the receiving, end of a donation. My cousin had a burst blood vessel in his brain. While he lived for several months, medical science could not save him. After his death, his mother donated his organs. Not all were healthy enough to use in transplants, but those that were helped to save and improve the lives of recipients. Believe me when I say that families can feel a great deal of comfort knowing that their loved ones, although gone, helped to save the lives of others.

To register to be a donor, go to the following Web sites: www.organ-donation-works.org/, http://secure.cihi.ca/cihiweb/, or www.hc-sc.gc.ca. Individual provinces have additional locations for registration on the Web. Registration ensures that doctors will not need permission from your family. Another alternative to secure your gift of life is to make a living will.

Visualization

A year after my brother received his new lung, I was involved in a serious car accident. I was unable to move for months, confined to the house for a year. Without the generosity of one person and his family, my brother would not have been there to help me recover. Think of it this way. The heart, kidney, or lung that you donate today could help to save the life of the doctor who cures cancer or AIDS or lung disease tomorrow. Imagine a future without these diseases. Imagine a future in which the figures in this second chart outnumber those in the third chart—if the number of organ donations was not 23 people out of every million but 100 or 200 out of every million. Imagine the reduced suffering and the savings to the health-care system that could result from a higher percentage of Canadians sharing their most precious gift of life with someone else. Just imagine . . . and then give.

References

Cline, A. Ethics of organ transplants. Agnosticism/Atheism. At: <http://atheism.about.com/library/weekly/aa052302a.htm>. Accessed 21 Mar. 2004.

Canadian Association of Transplantation. At: <http://transplant.ca/test2.htm>. Accessed 21 Mar. 2004.

Health Canada. Organ and Tissue—Canada's National Information Site. At: <www.hc-sc.gc.ca/english/organandtissue/index.html>. Accessed 21 Mar. 2004.

Knoll, G., Mahoney, J. (2004). How to improve organ donation rates. *Canadian Medical Association Journal* 170: 319.

Langone, A.J., Helderman, J.H. (2003). Disparity between solid-organ supply and demand. *New England Journal of Medicine* 349: 704–6.

Nation Foundation for Transplants: Organ/Tissue Donation. At: <www.transplants.org/OrganTissue Donation.php>. Accessed 21 Mar. 2004.

Quebec-Transplant. At: <www.quebec-transplant.qc.ca/ anglais/public_e.htm>. Accessed 21 Mar. 2004.

Trillium Gift of Life. At: <www.giftoflife.on.ca/flash. cfm>. Accessed 21 Mar. 2004.

CHAPTER ELEVEN

The Language of Propaganda

SUGGESTED ASSIGNMENT

Engaging in a Coffee Shop Discussion on Ethics

This session will involve a 'coffee shop' discussion on ethics, preferably held in an informal setting. Groups will use the ideas and examples in this chapter as a basis for talking about the concepts relating to unethical uses of language, extreme emotional appeals, and fallacious reasoning. The instructor may also want to distribute a current speech to be included in the analysis. Class members can also refer back to the ethics boxes accompanying each chapter. Each group should appoint a recorder to make notes on the content of the discussions and to present their views to the class. Following the small-group discussions, representatives of each group will join a round-table discussion, which will be followed by comments and questions from the remaining class members.

Learning Objectives
- To learn both classical and modern definitions of *propaganda* and *demagoguery*.
- To find out about the toolbox of the propagandist.
- To understand fallacies in reasoning.
- To learn about the problems related to improper use of statistics.
- To discover the application of the critical communication model.

This chapter looks at classical and modern definitions of *propaganda* and *demagoguery*. We will also consider the toolbox of the propagandist—strategies used to manipulate audiences. Finally, the chapter will consider fallacies in reasoning, problems with improper use of statistics, and the application of the critical communication model.

Defining Propaganda

The word *propaganda* has acquired different meanings over time. Until the seventeenth century, *propaganda* simply meant 'the dissemination of ideas and information'. But the

term lost some of its neutrality when the Roman Catholic Church attached the label to a committee of cardinals responsible for opposing Protestantism and disseminating the Church's word in the colonies.[1] By the late nineteenth century, governments around the world had begun to use the term to refer to their efforts to promote political ideologies such as socialism, communism, or democracy. The growth of mass society and new media fuelled this expansion of propagandistic activity. Any remaining hint of neutrality in the term disappeared with the establishment of the German Ministry of Propaganda in the years leading to World War II.[2]

Defining Propaganda in the Context of World War II

Jacques Ellul, a contemporary of Adolf Hitler, defined propaganda in the following way: '[Propaganda is] a set of methods employed by an organized group that wants to bring about the active or passive participation in its actions of a mass of individuals, psychologically unified through psychological manipulation and incorporated in an organization.'[3] In further discussion, Ellul says that groups engaging in propaganda will manipulate the truth in any way necessary to achieve their ends.

Expanding on this idea, Ellul says that propaganda efforts can succeed only when the audience has an internal need for the propaganda. This need manifests itself most strongly when people feel vulnerable. While awaiting trial at Nuremberg, Vice-Führer Hermann Göring (head of the Gestapo in Nazi Germany) explained why people are willing to listen and act on the rhetoric of propagandists in periods of uncertainty and conflict:

> Naturally, the common people don't want war; neither in Russia, nor in England, nor in America, nor for that matter in Germany. That is understood. But, after all, it is the leaders of the country who determine the policy and it is always a simple matter to drag the people along, whether it is a democracy, or a fascist dictatorship, or a parliament, or a communist dictatorship. . . . Voice or no voice, the people can always be brought to the bidding of the leaders. That is easy. All you have to do is tell them they are being attacked, and denounce the pacifists for lack of patriotism and exposing the country to danger. It works the same in any country.[4]

Removing the idea of the audience as innocent victims of propaganda, Ellul sees society as participating in acts of propaganda. The consequences of this manipulation of the emotions can be positive or negative in results. Speakers at funerals also manipulate the emotions of the audience, but expectations and occasion influence our assessments of the rhetoric. As the model presented in the first chapter illustrates, one must also take motive and impact into account in deciding whether the communicator has acted in a responsible and ethical fashion. How a speech is framed (strategies and language) is one of several considerations.

Another term associated with early definitions of propaganda is the term *demagogue*. As practised by Josef Goebbels, Minister of Propaganda for Hitler, the term *propaganda* came to be synonymous with the language of demagoguery. In the WordNet dictionary, a *demagogue* is 'an orator who appeals to the passions and prejudices of his audience'.[5] The 1913 *Webster's Dictionary*, on the other hand, defines *demagogue* as 'one who attempts to control the multitude by specious or deceitful arts' and 'an unprincipled and fractious mob orator or political leader'.[6] Putting these definitions together, the demagogue uses emotional appeals and manipulation of the truth to gain power and to control the masses. The rise of Hitler imbued the term with many additional layers of meaning.

Problems with Defining Propaganda in a Modern Context

Some scholars claim that definitions of *propaganda* are problematic. In a modern context, communication scholars ponder the distinction among the terms *information*, *persuasion*, and *propaganda*. Every democratic government, for example, has a mandate to educate its citizenry on affairs of state. This task involves the distribution of information. At the same time, democratic governments must persuade their constituencies to accept their policies and programs if they are to remain in power. Without consensus, political parties soon lose their mandates to govern; and without a mandate, individual politicians do not remain long in positions of authority.[7] So the information and persuasion functions work together.

In the same way, health communication campaigns seek to inform the public on health risks and best practices; but they also seek to persuade us to follow their suggestions:

> While health communication researchers and practitioners prefer to call their work 'health education interventions' or 'public health campaigns', the truth is that their ultimate goal is to manipulate people into practicing healthy behaviors. For example, doctor-patient researchers study how to make patients feel satisfied with medical encounters (i.e., manipulate patients into feeling a certain way about a medical interaction) or how to make patients comply or adhere to medical advice (i.e., manipulate patients into doing what physicians want them to do).[8]

Persuasion, in this context, is simply an attempt to influence public perceptions, attitudes, and/or behaviours. In common usage, persuasion can imply a friendly effort to prod someone to action or (at the other extreme) to coerce or bribe the person. The latter is an act for which a person can go to prison. So the term itself is neutral, although a persuader may employ ethical or unethical means to achieve personal ends.

According to one definition, propaganda is the 'deliberate and systematic attempt to shape perceptions, manipulate cognitions, and direct behavior to achieve a response that furthers the desired intent of the propagandist.'[9] Thus, like persuasion, propaganda becomes an activity aimed at influencing publics and achieving the purposes of the pro-

---

Box 11.1 A Question of Ethics

A recruiter delivered a speech to a group of high school students, urging the young men and women to make a career in the armed forces. She included almost no facts in her speech. Instead she relied on patriotic appeals, talking about the vastness and greatness of the country, the pride of being Canadian, and the influence of Canada in the world. She spoke in abstract terms and glittering generalities about the importance of serving one's country and being loyal to Canadian values. In other words, she 'waved the flag.' How do you feel about this kind of speech strategy? In times of war, should speakers be able to use patriotic appeals to strengthen the resolve of troops and people at home?

Another student gave an anti-war speech with strong fear appeals. He described what happened to the four Canadian soldiers killed by 'friendly fire' in Afghanistan. He also described the kinds of injuries suffered in war and the torture techniques used with prisoners of war. Prior to giving his speech, the speaker had learned that two members of the class had relatives currently on duty in Afghanistan. Feedback forms also told him that some students thought that the anti-war content was disrespectful to people serving in the military. Others worried that the graphic descriptions of injuries and torture could create high levels of stress and anxiety in class members who might have made a prior commitment to military service. These students argued that their attendance was a class requirement; they were not voluntarily choosing to be subjected to the speech. Therefore, they believed that the speaker was wrong to pursue such a controversial topic.

The speaker chose nonetheless to present the speech, believing that the subject matter was sufficiently important to justify making people feel uncomfortable. He believed that Canada's involvement in the Middle East, even in a peacekeeping capacity, was interventionist and wrong. Whose perspective do you support? Was the speaker right to give the speech, even against such protest? If so, why?

A third speaker accused a politician of involvement in a scandal. She said that the politician had dined with a man accused of fraud. At a later date, the politician had received a thank-you letter from this person. The speaker did not, however, offer any evidence to support the alleged link between the breakfast meeting, the correspondence, and the acts of fraud. But the audience was led to infer that a link existed. Based on your chapter reading, what was the speaker's strategy? Was the strategy ethical?

---

pagandist. This modern definition of propaganda sounds pretty much like definitions of persuasion. With the proliferation of mass media and advertising, many believe that propaganda has become an institutionalized part of modern society. They claim that we are subjected daily to huge doses of propaganda from commercial organizations, governments, and even non-profits.

Whether the terms *propaganda* and *demagogue* are in fashion or out of fashion is not very important in the context of this discussion. What is important is that some speakers (whether you call them *information providers*, *persuaders*, *propagandists*, *ideologues*, or *demagogues*) use unethical means to achieve their ends. Such speakers employ a number of strategies to confuse and unfairly influence the opinions of their audience.

Despite the difficulty that academics experience in defining terms such as *information*, *persuasion*, and *propaganda*, the average person uses the term *propaganda* in a negative context. If you proclaimed to your family, 'I've just taken a job as a propagandist!' they would look with surprise upon your pronouncement. The word has acquired values associated with unethical efforts to manipulate the public, even though the precise definitions of propaganda do not require this negative interpretation.

If modern concepts of propaganda teach us little that allows us to differentiate between ethical and unethical attempts to persuade, perhaps we can learn from the practices of men such as Adolf Hitler and his colleagues. Few would claim that these persuasion efforts fell within the boundaries of ethical communication. Unfortunately, Hitler does not stand alone in his efforts to motivate people to act solely on emotional (as opposed to rational) grounds. Just as the rhetoric of war provides examples of some of the most eloquent discourse, the language of war also offers examples of the most questionable in ethical terms.

The Toolbox of the Propagandist

The following discussion looks at common strategies for compliance, which many would place in the category of propaganda: eliciting signal responses, manipulating the truth, softening the truth, oversimplifying complex issues, relying on generalities and patriotic platitudes, stating the obvious, speaking in the third person, using extreme fear appeals, pretending to be someone that we are not, getting on the bandwagon, engaging in name-calling, and labelling people as guilty by association.

Eliciting Signal Responses

In the effort to shape perceptions and manipulate cognitions, the propagandist relies heavily on emotional appeals. As noted in Chapter 9, emotional appeals are important in persuasive discourse. But we must understand the difference between ethical and unethical uses of emotional appeals. Distinguishing between *signal* and *symbol* responses helps us to understand the difference. Winston Brembeck and William Howell tell us

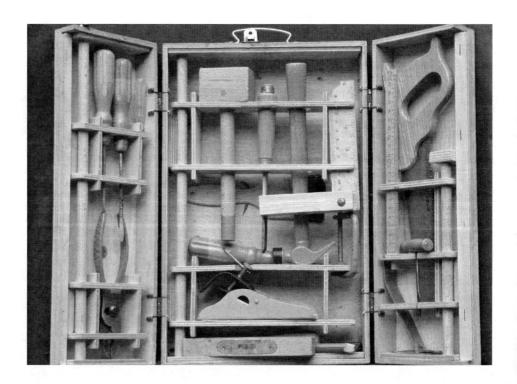

that *signal responses* are 'immediate, unthinking, largely automatic, uncritical responses'. *Symbol responses*, on the other hand, are, at least to some degree, 'deliberate and discriminating'.[10] They cite the work of linguist S.L. Hayakawa, who taught a chimpanzee to drive an automobile. The chimpanzee handled mechanical operations with ease. When he came to a red light, he stopped; and when he approached a green light, he started the car. One significant difference, however, separated the actions of the chimpanzee from those of human drivers. When the light turned green, he accelerated, whether or not the way was obstructed. He did not modify his response to take his environment into account.[11] Instead, his response was 'automatic and uncritical, exemplifying the pattern of the signal response.' When speakers aim for such an uncritical response from listeners, they are engaging in communication behaviour that characterizes the kind of unethical persuasion that we often call *propaganda*. The aim of the propagandist is to bypass our reasoning processes and gain immediate access to the emotions.

Used ethically, emotional appeals stimulate an audience to think seriously and to care about a topic. Sometimes they can even move an apathetic audience to action. Emotional appeals are not, in themselves, unethical. To use an analogy, water is vital to survival; however, if we consume it in excess, we drown. The same is true of emotional appeals. Used in excess, they overpower, rather than stimulate, rational thought processes. Used unethically, they encourage listeners to respond without thinking. In *Mein Kampf*, Hitler advocated the exclusive use of emotional appeals to reach his listeners (Box 11.2).

Box 11.2 Hitler on Appealing to the Emotions

He [the speaker] will always follow the lead of the great mass in such a way that from the living emotion of his hearers the apt word which he needs will be suggested to him and in its turn this will go straight to the hearts of his listeners. . . . Since the masses have only a poor acquaintance with abstract ideas, their reactions will lie more in the domain of the feelings, where the roots of their positive as well as their negative attitudes are implanted. . . . The emotional grounds of their attitudes furnish the reason for their extraordinary stability. . . . And the driving force which brought about the most tremendous revolutions on this earth has never been a body of scientific teaching which has gained power over the masses, but always a devotion which has inspired them, and often a kind of hysteria which has urged them into action. Whoever wishes to win over the masses must know the key that will open the door to their hearts.

Adolf Hitler, *Mein Kampf*, vol. 1, ch. 12 (1925), trans. James Murphy

---

The orators of Hitler's Third Reich used many means to stir the emotions of audiences. They complemented their rhetoric at rallies with flamboyant displays of pageantry, dramatic lighting, and martial music. They used posters, slogans, and symbols such as the swastika and military dress to encourage displays of patriotism to the 'fatherland'.

Hitler also identified enemies of the state for censure, picked out one enemy in particular for vilification, and played on stereotypes.[12] Believing that life is a struggle where the fittest survive, he also advocated vehemence of expression. In short, Hitler and his adherents engaged in a form of persuasion that relied almost completely on emotional appeals, without concern for rationality, truth, or common concepts of morality.[13] All of these rhetorical strategies came to be associated with the language of demagoguery, the most unethical manifestation of propaganda.

Manipulating the Truth

They say that the first casualty of any war is truth. In the aftermath of World War II, analysts looked at the ways in which Hitler had manipulated the truth through means such as 'the big lie', failure to qualify statements, and offering only one side of any argument. Hitler adhered to the view: the bigger the lie, the more likely it is to be believed. During the Gulf War, I was sitting with my husband, watching television. To my dismay, I heard a young Kuwaiti woman explaining that the Iraq military had come into the nursery where she worked, taken infants from incubators, and thrown them on the floor. I expressed my feelings to my husband, who had been a fighter pilot in the Royal Air Force during World War II. He responded with a simple caution, 'It may not be true. In war, people lie.' Two years later, the story was proclaimed to be untrue, manufactured by an organization calling itself 'Citizens for a Free Kuwait'. The young woman was a relative of the Kuwaiti ambassador to the United States. Representatives from Hill & Knowlton, an international public relations firm, had allegedly coached the 15-year-old girl for her appearance before a US congressional committee. An account that appeared in the British press described the incident in this way:

> Take the Kuwaiti babies story. Its origins go back to the first world war when British propaganda accused the Germans of tossing Belgian babies into the air and catching them on their bayonets. Dusted off and updated for the Gulf war, this version had Iraqi soldiers bursting into a modern Kuwaiti hospital, finding the premature babies ward and then tossing the babies out of incubators so that the incubators could be sent back to Iraq. The story, improbable from the start, was first reported by the *Daily Telegraph* in London on September 5, 1990. But the story lacked the human element; it was an unverified report, there were no pictures for television and no interviews with mothers grieving over dead babies. That was soon rectified. An organisation calling itself Citizens for a Free Kuwait (financed by the Kuwaiti government in exile) had signed a $10m contract with the giant American public relations company, Hill & Knowlton, to campaign for American military intervention to oust Iraq from Kuwait. The Human Rights Caucus of the US Congress was meeting in October and Hill & Knowlton arranged for a 15-year-old Kuwaiti girl to tell the babies' story before the congressmen. She did it brilliantly, choking with tears at the right moment, her voice breaking as she struggled to continue. The congressional committee knew her only as 'Nayirah' and the television segment of her testimony showed anger and resolution on the faces of the congressmen listening to her. . . . In the Senate debate on whether to approve military action to force Saddam out of Kuwait, seven senators specifically mentioned the incubator babies atrocity and the final margin in favour of war was just five votes. John R. Macarthur's study of propaganda in the war says that the babies atrocity was a definitive moment in the campaign to prepare the American public for the need to go to war.[14]

Most disturbing in this regard—and why propaganda and lies are especially insidi-ous—is that first impressions are often lasting impressions. If people remember the

Kuwaiti babies incident at all, they may recall it as a barbaric act of Iraqi troops, not as a political lie.

Softening the Truth

Transfer involves using words or images that evoke associations of a positive nature. In the debate over cloning and stem cell research, both sides use this strategy to argue their cause. Supporters of cloning and stem cell research use terms such as *therapeutic cloning*, *somatic cell nuclear transfer*, and *nuclear transplantation* to transfer the positive values of medical research to cloning. The term *ethnic cleansing* became popular during the Serbo-Croatian conflict. Many worried that the positive associations of the word *cleansing* were transferred to acts of genocide.

Euphemisms are words or phrases such as the above that we substitute for more offensive or less comfortable words. We use euphemisms to soften the impact of death, war, and other unpleasant phenomena. Euphemisms for death include *passed away*, *crossed over*, *kicked the bucket*, *cashed in his chips*, and *went to his final reward*. Euphemisms related to firing and layoff practices include *downsizing, rightsizing, streamlining, outsourcing, repositioning, transitioning, re-engineering, restructuring*, and *personnel enhancement*.

In times of war, people often use euphemisms to distort or hide the truth behind words. George Orwell, for example, wrote about the kinds of euphemisms that characterized the rhetoric of World War II.[15] When military forces invaded Grenada, they spoke of the attack as a *pre-dawn vertical insertion*, meaning an early morning invasion. During the Vietnam War, the Military Assistance Command Office used similarly obtuse terms in their press releases. Then the Gulf War generated a whole new set of terms to talk about war (see Box 11.3).

Box 11.3 War Terminology To Soften the Truth

MILITARY TERMINOLOGY IN WORLD WAR II

Pacification (bombing and destruction of villages)

Orderly retreat (running from the enemy)

Elimination of unreliable elements (imprisonment, execution, and exile of political enemies)

Rectification of frontiers (forcing people to abandon homes and possessions)

MILITARY TERMINOLOGY DURING VIETNAM WAR

Accidental delivery of ordinances (we bombed our own troops)

Incendiary jelly (napalm)

Friendly fire (accidentally firing on one's own troops)

Mobile manoeuvring (trying to retreat in the face of enemy confrontation)

Free fire zone (everything is a military target)

Civilian irregular defence unit (mercenaries)

Search and clear (search and destroy)

Rallier or returnee (deserter)

Redeployment (strategic retreat)

Combat emplacement evacuator (shovel)

Protective reaction air strike (bombing that involves aircraft)

Greenbacking (paying mercenaries)

MILITARY TERMINOLOGY DURING THE GULF WAR (1991) AND IRAQ WAR (2003-   )

Delivered ordinances (dropped bombs or missiles)

Dropped their payload (dropped bombs)

Security contractors (mercenaries)

Collateral damage (civilian casualties)

Incontinent ordinance (bomb or missile that misses target and kills civilians)

Box 11.3 continued

Repositioning assets (relocating troops and
   equipment)
Gave an official assist (CF-18s from Canada helped
   the US to stop Iraqi vessels)
Targets of opportunity (the enemy)

Shock and awe (massive bombing with resulting
   firework displays)
Non-operative personnel (dead soldiers)
Servicing the targets (killing the enemy)
Surgical strike (bombing or shelling)

With a twist on Orwell's references to *newspeak*, William Lutz refers to these kinds of examples as *doublespeak*—language that is deceptive, contradictory, and evasive. His examples include terms such as *terminate with extreme prejudice* (to kill) or *negative patient care outcome* (death of patient). These examples illustrate the language of non-responsibility.[16]

Oversimplifying Complex Issues

Polarization involves oversimplifying complex issues and concepts so that only two positions appear possible: 'You are either for me or against me.' The most recent example of this strategy appeared in the rhetoric of George W. Bush when he proclaimed, 'You're either with the terrorists, or you're with us.' This type of statement leaves no middle ground for those who oppose terrorism but also question the decisions of the government. Early studies of propaganda termed this process as 'two-sided orientation'. With two-sided orientation, persuaders describe people as saints or sinners, good or bad, intelligent or stupid. The language of polarization also makes use of *god terms* and *devil terms*, a concept attributed to Richard Weaver.[17] Language used to characterize one's own position is always positive, while language depicting the other party's position is always negative.

In the debate over cloning, for example, *opponents* use devil terms such as 'Nazis', 'a race of supermen', 'exploitation', 'disrespect for life', 'manufacturing process', 'clone-and-kill bill', 'baby-making', 'objects of manipulation', 'made in laboratories', 'spare body parts', 'engineered to custom specifications', 'genetic cocktails', 'Frankensteinian research', and 'the dead unborn'. They refer to their own position with god terms such as 'moral high ground', 'pro-life', 'dignity of human procreation', 'strong ethical verdict', 'compassionate nation', 'highest of ethical standards', and 'respect for human life'. For *those in favour of cloning*, the god terms are 'therapeutic cloning', 'tools of medicine', 'wonders of discovery', 'saving human lives', and 'providing a range of choices'. The devil terms for those in favour of cloning are terms such as 'radical anti-abortion right', 'closed-minded intolerant religious fanatics', and 'muzzling our minds'.

As you can see, the typically loaded language of polarization often involves name-calling. Neutral and objective terms rarely characterize the rhetoric of polarization. Yet, democracy depends on the ability of citizens to voice their concerns and to engage in lively public debate over issues.

Relying on Glittering Generalities and Patriotic Platitudes

Sometimes speakers cross the boundaries of ethical communication in their over-reliance on highly abstract words that sound virtuous but lack concreteness. They are 'feel-good' words, such as *freedom*, *justice*, and *fatherland*. The rhetoric of Adolf Hitler was filled with these kinds of glittering generalities and platitudes. The following passage is drawn from his autobiography, *Mein Kampf*:

> He [the Aryan] is the Prometheus of mankind from whose bright forehead the divine spark of genius has sprung at all times, forever kindling anew that fire of knowledge which illumined the night of silent mysteries and thus caused man to climb the path to mastery over the other beings of this earth. Exclude him—and perhaps after a few thousand years darkness will again descend on the earth, human culture will pass, and the world turn to a desert.[18]

The lack of specificity and concreteness in this kind of rhetoric raises ethical questions. The audience cannot be sure what the speaker means or what he is asking them to accept, sanction, or undertake. Many of the *god terms*, discussed earlier, also fall into the category of 'the glittering generality'.

Using patriotic platitudes, abstract in nature, the speaker makes references to the greatness of the country, its moral strength, and its potential for victory over its enemies. He 'waves the flag' to get his audience to act.

In some situations, however, speakers use ambiguous language to bridge cultural gaps. In the United Nations, for example, speakers often use highly metaphorical language to reach people from many different social, economic, religious, cultural, and political backgrounds. UN representatives rely heavily on the archetypal metaphor, which draws comparisons between light and darkness, the various seasons, heat and cold, and other natural forces. Common in United Nations rhetoric are terms such as the 'icy winds of change', 'seeds of life', 'flowers of peace', 'tides of self-determination', and 'fruits of aggression'.[19]

Stating the Obvious

When a speaker uses tautological language, she states the obvious, as in the following examples: *Life is for the living. Nothing succeeds like success. Victory is enjoyed by those who win. Our future lies in front of us. If we don't succeed, we run the risk of failing.* Like platitudes, tautological language is bereft of meaning.

Speaking in the Third Person

Sometimes speakers remove themselves from responsibility for their actions by referring to themselves in the third person. This strategy has become more common in the last few years. In a July 2004 court appearance in Iraq, Saddam Hussein spoke of himself in the third person. Brigadier General Janis Karpinski did the same in August 2004 when she denied responsibility for abuses at the US military prison at Abu Ghraib in Iraq. She claimed that a conspiracy had prevented her from knowing about prisoner abuse at the jail: 'From what I understand . . . it was people that had full knowledge of what was going on out at Abu Ghraib who knew that they had to keep Janis Karpinski from discovering any of those activities', she added.[20]

For different reasons, former Alliance leader Stockwell Day and hockey player Wayne Gretzky have, on occasion, referred to themselves in the third person. Although one can only speculate about the reasons, the result is that the person assumes the status of a third party or a product. A disconnect occurs between the individual and the act.

Using Extreme Fear Appeals

Extreme fear appeals are not only questionable on ethical grounds, but also prove ineffective most of the time. Those working in health communication have learned that strong fear appeals (involving threat of death and personal injury) often lead to defensive avoidance of the message. Listeners tend to tune out messages that are too gruesome or scary. Cancer patients say that they do not remember anything that the doctor says after she says, 'You have cancer.'[21] In the same way, we often switch the television channel when we see images of the human victims of famine, drought, and war; and we throw away the pamphlet that depicts a badly abused animal. The images are too strong. In the case of health issues, we may rationalize by concluding that the claims are exaggerated; and we dismiss the arguments.

According to some researchers, even moderate fear appeals are limited in their effectiveness. They tend to have the greatest impact in the following three conditions: when speakers are highly credible, when they discuss the problem in very specific terms, and when they offer reasonable courses of action.[22] The audience should be placed in a position to take immediate action to reduce the state of anxiety.[23]

Some studies demonstrate that fear appeals are more effective at achieving short-term than long-term results.[24] Most effects disappear within 24 hours.

Pretending To Be Someone We Are Not

Another persuasive strategy has been dubbed 'plain folks'. In essence, the person says, 'I'm just a simple country boy.' This 'plain folks' or 'common folks' strategy appeals to those who have achieved success by hard work and perseverance. We recognize the strategy when we see Canadian politicians in blue jeans and lumberjack shirts. The following account of Jean Chrétien's behaviour on the eve of the 1997 election recalls the 'plain folks' strategy:

> In early April, Jean Chrétien was in British Columbia for several events that included a lunchtime meeting with Liberal candidates in a McDonald's restaurant in Surrey. After lunch (Big Mac, large fries with no ketchup and cola for the Prime Minister), Chrétien decided to visit the restaurant staff behind the counter. He shook hands with several cooks and servers, then spotted a woman working at the drive-through window. 'Would you mind?' he asked, stepping past her with a smile. The next three customers pulling up to the window were given, along with their orders, a smile, a proffered handshake and the announcement: 'Hi, I'm Jean Chrétien, the Prime Minister.' The predictable result, one Chrétien aide recalls, was 'utter astonishment. One woman looked as though she didn't know whether to giggle or faint.'

Politicians face risks, however, when they use this strategy. The image of Pierre Trudeau paddling a canoe in the Canadian wilderness was within reach of a great many Canadians in most social strata. On the other hand, when Progressive Conservative leader Robert Stanfield's handlers sought to burnish his stodgy image during one campaign against Trudeau by bringing a football on the campaign bus, the subsequent press photos of Stanfield awkwardly stooping to get the ball he dropped had the opposite effect. In the US, George W. Bush telling one folksy story after another in the 2004 presidential campaign presented a reality that was only a partial truth. And that is why some question the use of the 'plain folks' strategy. They believe that a speaker should not rely too strongly on this kind of emotional support, particularly if the person is not really a 'simple country boy'. Nonetheless, many speakers do use this strategy as a means of identifying with their audiences; and some consider the strategy to be legitimate if, in fact, the representation of the person is genuine rather than contrived.

Getting on the Bandwagon

The 'bandwagon argument' seeks to convince the audience that they should accept an idea or join a movement because everyone else is doing it. 'Get on the bandwagon. Join the crowd of supporters.' Speaking on 15 January 1991 in support of Canada's engagement in the Gulf War, Prime Minister Brian Mulroney said:

> It should not be surprising or offensive that the views of free nations often coincide. In fact, in this case the views of all of the leading Western nations—led by governments of very different political stripes—including the United Kingdom, Italy, Australia, France, the United States and Canada are in harmony.... Prime Minister Bob Hawke of Australia, the leader of the Labour Party in his country ... told his Parliament on December 4 that 'if conflict occurs of a kind which is contemplated and authorized by the [UN] resolution, [Australian] ships will be available to participate in action with the allied fleet.' François Mitterand, President of France and leader of his country's Socialist Party, has made clear his country's position when he said that 'France considers a complete withdrawal from Kuwait to be an inviolable principle. ...' In the United Kingdom, Prime Minister Major has been equally clear and consistent on this point. And Neil Kinnock, the Leader of the Opposition in the UK, said last week that the Labour Party 'will not, in the interests of distancing ourselves from the government, distance ourselves from our forces or from the United Nations.' And we know now that both chambers of the US Congress as well have voted to support the US Administration in the implementation of UN Resolution 678—to get Saddam Hussein's forces out of Kuwait.[25]

This kind of argumentation seeks to impress the listeners by pointing to the number of people who agree with your position. Obviously, not every effort to point to support for one's position qualifies as unethical use of language. Where other valid argumentation supports a position, the use of the bandwagon argument can be justified. However, when speakers rely strictly on emotional appeals to support their positions—whether those emotional appeals are bandwagon or other forms of argumentation—their usage moves into the category of the questionable.

Calling Names and Labelling by Association

Name-calling involves a verbal attack on the person with terms considered to be denigrating, such as *hawk*, *wimp*, or *Commie*. The attack sometimes involves the use of sexist or racist language. *Guilt by association*, on the other hand, involves bracketing the person with another person or concept that has a negative association. During election years politicians try to distance themselves from colleagues with reputations they deem unprofitable. During the 2004 and 2006 elections, the opposition parties repeatedly attempted to bracket Paul Martin with the scandal-plagued Chrétien government. They stressed Martin's former role as finance minister, thus reminding voters that he was a central player in the previous government. In a similar fashion, the Conservatives had bracketed Jean Chrétien with the Trudeau years when he ran for Prime Minister in 1993; and the Liberals stressed Kim Campbell's association with the no longer popular Mulroney government. In an attack on US presidential hopeful John Kerry, Vice-President Dick Cheney said that terrorist Osama Bin Laden wanted Americans to elect Kerry as President of the United States.

One of the most common applications of 'guilt by association' involves bracketing the person with elite monetary interests. On a number of occasions, US Democrats have bracketed the Bush family with monetary interests associated with the war in Iraq. In Canada, critics called former Prime Minister John Turner a 'Bay Street politician', suggesting an association with elitism and wealth.

Sometimes the results of guilt by association can be tragic, as in the case of the young Brazilian electrician shot by London police in July 2005. He had been labelled as a terrorist because he emerged from a building in which suspects lived.

Fallacies in Reasoning

Fallacies in reasoning can occur with circular reasoning, the slippery slope argument, reasoning from specific examples, generalizations, sign, causes, parallel cases, and red herrings.

Circular Reasoning

A university department wanted to establish a graduate program. When the chair and committee approached higher-level administrators, they were told they needed more professors to establish a graduate program. But when they asked to hire more professors, they were told that they could not hire more professors because they did not have a graduate program. The departments with graduate programs had priority. It took many years of negotiation for the department to escape this circular pattern of reasoning. Usually, circular reasoning is employed to support the status quo. Circular reasoning produces entrapment so that parties cannot escape without breaking the pattern.

Slippery Slope Reasoning

When people use slippery slope reasoning, they argue that one step will lead to the next. That step, in turn, will create its own set of predictable consequences and so on. The process is a bit like the line of thinking that emerged during the Cold War, when American politicians argued that if one government fell to Communism, another would follow. When that government fell, a third government would follow suit and so on. They argued that the US must prevent the first country from falling into the hands of Communists in order to prevent the worldwide spread of Communism.

That reasoning process became known as the 'domino effect'. In other words, if you push down one domino, it will cause all of the others to fall. One event inevitably leads to a second, the second to a third, and the third to a fourth. Prime Minister Brian Mulroney applied this strategy in a speech delivered to Parliament in 1991, following Iraq's invasion of Kuwait:

> Were Saddam Hussein to succeed in his annexation of Kuwait, he would be in a position to threaten the entire Middle East. . . . After Iran and Kuwait, who would be his next target? Saudi Arabia? Jordan? . . . . Saddam Hussein has threatened to attack Israel.[26]

Audrey McLaughlin, leader of the New Democratic Party, likewise referred to the likelihood of a domino effect in her speech, delivered in response to Mulroney's address. McLaughlin reached different conclusions, however, as to what would happen in the Middle East if Saddam Hussein were removed from power:

> Look at the region, Mr. Speaker. . . . If Iraq is destroyed, Iran may very well rise again as the dominant power in the region. If Iraq is destroyed, Turkey, Syria and Iran may decide to fight to control what is left of Iraq. The Arab governments that decided to support the war will face the fury of their citizens. A holy war is a real possibility.[27]

People who smoke are also prone to engage in slippery slope reasoning. The typical line of logic follows: If I stop smoking, I will gain weight. If I gain weight, I will be more likely to have a heart attack. If I have a heart attack, I may die. Therefore, the best way to protect my health is to continue smoking. Logical? Of course not. Not everyone gains weight, and not all overweight people die of heart attacks. People can choose to exercise more and to pursue a healthy lifestyle. The fallacy in all of these examples is that one consequence does *not* necessarily lead to the next in the complicated world of causes and effects.

Reasoning from Example

The following example illustrates the risks in *reasoning from example*.

> Mary got the flu after visiting an amusement park in Ontario.
> Jennifer got the flu after visiting an amusement park in British Columbia.
> Randy got the flu after visiting an amusement park in New Brunswick.
> Therefore, all children will get the flu if they visit an amusement park.

An insufficient number of examples can lead to the wrong conclusion, a hasty generalization. We often develop fears on the basis of events that appear frequently on the news. We worry that our children will be kidnapped, that we will become victims of violent crime, or that our identities will be stolen. In reality, however, these kinds of events may be featured on the news because they are rare or unusual. If we experience three or more instances of rude drivers in Toronto, we may conclude that all drivers in Toronto are rude. This conclusion is based on an insufficient number of examples.

Another problem arises if you select your examples on the basis of what supports your claim and disregard examples that could call your claim into question. Sometimes these errors in reasoning occur inadvertently because we lack sufficient knowledge. We may erroneously assume similarity in all cases.

Reasoning from Generalization

The next example illustrates a fallacy in *reasoning from generalization*.

> People who live in hurricane-prone areas tend to have more property insurance than people who live outside hurricane-prone areas.
> Janet Crosby lives in St Bride's, Newfoundland, which suffered extensive damage from Hurricane Gert in 1999.
> Therefore, Janet Crosby is likely to have more property insurance than people who live in less hurricane-prone areas.

If the basic premise (people who live in hurricane-prone areas tend to have more property insurance) is inaccurate, then any conclusions drawn from the statement will also be inaccurate. Also, Janet Crosby may have less money after paying for the damages incurred by Hurricane Gert, or insurance companies may not give the same coverage to people who live in an area such as St Bride's.

Some of the most common fallacies in reasoning from generalization occur in the area of culture. We may unfairly ascribe general characteristics of a culture to every member of the culture: 'All Italians are emotional. Antonio is Italian. Therefore, Antonio is emotional.' Or, we may attribute the characteristics of women in general to individual cases. 'Women tend to be more nurturing than men. Lisa is a woman. Therefore, Lisa must be more nurturing than her male counterparts.' In some (or many) instances, the generalization is not true. Women are not always more nurturing than men. In other cases, the person may be an exception to the general rule. Women, in general, may be more nurturing than men; but Lisa may be the exception to the rule.

Sometimes our definition of terms influences our views of the validity of the argumentation. See the following example.

> Countries without a national deficit and debt enjoy a higher quality of life than countries with a national deficit and debt.
> Kuwait has no national deficit or debt.
> Therefore, Kuwait enjoys a higher quality of life than countries with a national debt.

Using this argumentation, Kuwait would have a better quality of life than most countries in the world, including Canada, France, Britain, the Netherlands, Germany, and Sweden. In this context, *quality of life* implies materialistic well-being. However, you may disagree with this conclusion if *quality of life* means something different to you. To accept argumentation, everyone must agree on the meaning of the terms that are employed.

In brief, problems arise when the basic premise is flawed (all women are nurturing or all Italians are emotional). Problems also arise if you do not recognize the possibility for exceptions from the rule (Lisa may not be like all women, and Antonio might not be like all Italians). Finally, problems may occur if the terms are ambiguous, where not everyone interprets them in the same way.

Reasoning from Sign

Reasoning from sign is extremely risky. Consider the following: 'I have a headache. Since headaches can be a sign of encephalitis, I conclude that I have encephalitis.' In fact, headaches may be a sign for many different illnesses, the least common in Canada being encephalitis. So I may or may not have encephalitis. The conclusion is not supportable on the basis of such limited information. I have often heard that first-year medical students 'develop every illness they study'—at least, according to their own first diagnosis! Once they have learned the symptoms of certain serious and rare diseases, they tend to interpret the appearance of similar symptoms in themselves as manifestations of these dread diseases. Yet, more often than not, the symptoms are indicators of much less serious conditions. In other words, the medical students engage in fallacious reasoning from sign.

Grey hair is usually a sign of aging, but some young people have prematurely grey hair. A large stomach in the Western world is usually a sign of plentiful food; however, a large stomach in famine-stricken countries is a sign of malnutrition. In children, bruises, fractures, and bumps may be a sign of parental abuse. They may also be a sign of children who are overactive and negligent in their play or a sign of a blood disorder or other illness. Many Canadians experience extensive breakage of blood vessels under the skin and extraordinary bruising. This situation may be a sign of intravenous drug usage. Alternatively, the bruising may be a sign that the person takes blood thinners for a heart condition or prednisone for arthritis. All of the above examples indicate the dangers of reasoning from signs. Fallacies in reasoning from sign occur when someone fails to recognize that signs may have many different meanings and interpretations.

Causal Reasoning

When seeking to identify the *causes of problems or other conditions*, we must be careful to establish clear and compelling connections between effects and their causes. The most common error is to attribute all of the blame to one cause. In essence, that cause becomes a scapegoat. But that kind of reasoning is too simplistic. Most conditions result from the interaction of many different variables. Cancer, for example, has been linked to many different causes—both environmental (e.g., smoking, dietary habits, and exposure to chemicals in the air and water) and genetic. Insomnia has been linked to stress, lifestyle, consumption of caffeine, and the use of certain medications, as well as many other influences. Dropouts in school result from emotional and financial as well as intellectual factors.

Because so many factors can influence any of these situations, we must be careful not to make the wrong connections or to attribute undue influence to one cause. Hurricane Jeanne devastated much of Haiti. The hurricane caused extreme suffering and misery among the Haitian people. Nonetheless, it would be a fallacy to conclude that Hurricane Jeanne is responsible for famine in Haiti. Long-term civil unrest and poor crop yields had created the conditions for famine before the first flood waters hit Haiti.

News accounts, appearing in early August 2004, warned that Haiti was on the brink of a famine. A German aid agency said that Haitian farmers, without alternative food sources, were being forced to eat reserves of seed that should be planted. Agency representatives warned that famine loomed on the horizon for Haitians.[28] The major cause of famine in Haiti in September 2004 was not the hurricane, even though famine followed close on the heels of the hurricane. Nonetheless, Hurricane Jeanne hastened the onset of famine in a country already facing lack of food. The flooding, high winds, and mudslides pushed an already vulnerable population over the edge. Furthermore, during the same year, Floridians experienced far worse weather—four times—without experiencing famine. So the hurricane-famine connection is too simplistic. The fact is that poverty, unstable governments, and lack of adequate infrastructures in Haiti have made the population vulnerable to even small disturbances in the environment.

We often face the dilemma of having to separate causes and effects. The task is not easy, as we discover if we debate the following question: Does poverty create crime in the inner city, or does crime create poverty by causing merchants to flee inner-city neighbourhoods?

Reasoning from a Parallel Case

You are good at skateboarding, and you have decided to try your skills at snowboarding. You assume that the two situations are analogous—that your skills in skateboarding will transfer to snowboarding. But travelling downhill on a snowboard may be quite different from skateboarding on city sidewalks.

The following two examples illustrate the difficulties in extrapolating from one situation to another—in this case, using the policies and practices of one country to guide the development of policies and practices in another country. Not too long ago, the mayor of New York City went to Mexico City to advise his counterpart on setting up a system that could deal with the kidnappings and institutionalized corruption in the city's justice system. But cultural differences undermined the possibility of transferring the system from one city to the other. The differences in the two cases outnumbered the similarities.

My husband taught for a time at a West African university. He said that, on one occasion, agricultural experts from a Midwestern university arrived in the region with high ambitions of establishing agricultural systems similar to those in the US. One of their first experiments involved asking the natives to cut down the tropical forest and to plant rice in the clearings. Although the Africans looked a bit confused at this advice, they complied with the request of the 'experts'. They cleared the forest and planted the fields with rice. Then the monsoon season arrived, and all of the topsoil from the cleared land washed away—topsoil that had taken centuries to accumulate. The rice went with the topsoil. Too late, the scientists realized their mistake. In fact, the Africans had been growing crops among the trees for centuries. They knew that the trees held the soil in place. The newcomers had assumed that their models would work equally well in Africa. The price of their learning was high for the African community.

Red Herrings

A couple may argue about the amount of overtime that one is working. But the argument soon encompasses a much wider range of issues—choice of friends, spending habits, dress, and family relationships. The couple may even completely abandon the original issue as they enter the territory of other emotional concerns. These issues are 'red herrings', not relevant to the main topic under discussion. In another situation, someone says that motorboats should not be allowed on a lake because they create excessive noise and pollution. Rather than arguing the point about noise and pollution, the opponent argues that boating is one of our most popular recreational activities. The popularity of the sport, however, has nothing to do with the argument raised by the first party. The second party has introduced a 'red herring'. Like a coronary bypass, the red herring diverts discussion into a different and unrelated vein.

Politicians receive media training to learn how to divert questions from one area to another. The reporter asks, 'What do you intend to spend this year on health care?' The politician answers, 'Health care is important, but we can only improve the health of our nation by reducing our deficit. This is where we want to go. I plan to introduce a three-point plan for reducing the national debt. This plan will have some important implications for our long-term economic health.' Suddenly, the topic has switched from expenditures on health care to a plan for reducing the deficit. Alternatively, the politician might say, 'I'm glad that you raised that point. But we really should be talking about the *cost* of health care. It is spiralling out of control in some provinces.' In both cases, the responses have little to do with the question asked by the reporter. They are red herrings, designed to distract the reporter into areas that the politician wants to discuss and to set the media agenda.

Problems with Statistics

Statistics can lie when the speaker does not offer complete information. Governments often tell us, for example, that crime is going down. If you consider all categories of crime (vehicle theft, burglary, robberies, theft identity, forgery, etc.), the statement is true. However, *violent* crime (murder, conspiracy to murder, and serious assault) has increased dramatically in many of the countries where governments talk about lowered crime rates. Sometimes the increases are as high as 15 per cent. One writer expressed the situation in this way:

> We've never had it so good, but we've also never had it so bad. The latest crime statistics paint different pictures of Britain. There were nearly 6 million crimes recorded by police last year, one per cent up on the previous year. For the first time, over a million of those were violent crimes, up 12 per cent, but the British Crime Survey paints a rosier overall picture. So who's right? Is it up or down? First, the gospel according to the British Crime Survey. Since a peak in 1995, crime in England and Wales has fallen by 39 per cent, fuelled mainly by drops in vehicle crime and burglary, that's a fall of 5 per cent in the past year. But in the separate data for recorded crime, the statistics suggest that the most serious type of violent offences have gone up by 15 per cent in the past year. That figure includes attempted murder up 8 per cent, conspiracy to murder up 23 per cent and serious wounding which endangers life—up 8 per cent on last year.[29]

Sometimes speakers cite statistics that are limited in time or scope, not reflecting trends. Perhaps a much larger number of people made charitable donations to non-profit organizations after the Asian tsunami of December 2004. An inaccurate or unethical presenter could say, 'The number of people donating to charities has increased by 20 per cent.' But that increase may be an unusual spike in donations, not sustained over time. The same applies to scope. If you are talking about a 20 per cent increase in a population of 5,000, that figure is more meaningful than if you are talking about a 20 per cent increase in a population of 10 people.

In a speech delivered to an Internet conference in 2000, Mel Cappe (then Clerk of the Privy Council and Secretary to the Cabinet) faulted governments and others for using statistics in a sloppy and unclear fashion. Referring to discussions about the impact of globalization, Cappe said:

> We sometimes resort to the blur of big numbers to make our point. It's $X trillion of this, and Y terabytes of that and, more recently, Zed billion cubic tonnes emitted. The problem is that big numbers can distil out the human element. What we see is a parsed view of the universe; what we lose is the human perspective.[30]

Visual presentations of statistics can also give an erroneous impression. A classic book, *How to Lie with Statistics*, showed how the elongation of a boxed graph, in one direction or the other, can cause the statistics to look more or less impressive (see Figure 11.1).

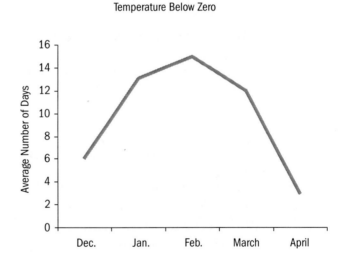

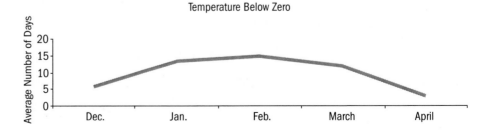

Figure 11.1 Visual Presentations That Distort

The Critical Communication Model as a Basis for Assessing the Ethics of Communication

In assessing any speech event, you must look at *intent* (speaker motives and purposes), *means* (rhetorical strategies and delivery), *environment* (economic, technological, political, social, and cultural factors within which the speech event occurred), *impact*, and *ethical costs of achieving one's purposes*. This chapter has concentrated largely on the message delivered by speakers—that is, *means*. However, other chapters in the book have presented a series of questions and exercises related to ethics. Taken as a whole, these questions address the remaining components of the critical communication model—intent, environment, impact, and ethical costs of achieving one's ends. Some scenarios, posed in the previous chapters of the book, have required you to make choices as a speaker; others have necessitated that you judge the rhetorical efforts of other speakers.

The critical communication model implies the necessity to take many different variables into account. Hitler would clearly fail in most categories—intent, means, impact, and ethical costs. In other cases, however, the assessment of the speaker may be more complex and more controversial. Maurice Duplessis (Premier of Quebec from 1936–9 and 1944–59) was beloved by many, who saw him as the protector of a traditional French Canada. They saw the positive outcomes of his administration—a stronger Quebec within Canada, the creation of enormous public works projects (highways, hospitals, universities, and schools), and the 'electrification' of rural Quebec.

Those who opposed Duplessis, however, viewed him as a demagogue, who maintained his rural conservative Catholic base by allowing the Church to run the province's schools. He held on to power by developing an extensive patronage network, which allowed political cronies and supporters to benefit from plum construction projects. In the Quebec legislature and on the stump, he frequently resorted to name-calling. He called the founder and dean of the social sciences faculty at Laval University 'the little red' and eventually cut off all government funding to the faculty because they were 'socialists or Communists'. He was also responsible for the infamous Padlock Act, which allowed the police to lock any building where Communists or socialists (including union workers) might be meeting. He encouraged brutal treatment of striking workers at Asbestos, Quebec, in 1949.[31]

Conclusion

The moral borderline in the spectrum of persuasion depends, in large measure, on the interpretation of the individual. People frequently push this borderline around on the assumption that 'the end justifies the means.' The risks in accepting this sort of fluidity in defining the limits of ethical persuasion, however, are high. As mentioned in the opening chapter of this book, a speaker must look at the legitimacy of his or her own motivations (speaker intent and purposes), the means used to achieve the ends (strategies, language, and modes of delivery), environment (technological, economic, political, social, cultural), and the impact of success in ethical costs. Ultimately, however, the listener must decide what to accept and to reject.

Questions for Discussion

1. What does the word *propaganda* mean to you? Does the term carry negative connotations? How would your family feel if you told them that you intended to pursue a career in propaganda? How would they feel if you said you were going into advertising or public relations or that you found a summer job as a political strategist? What are the differences among these terms?

2. In what contexts do we typically use euphemisms? In talking about what kind of topics? Do euphemisms serve a purpose? Is that purpose ethical or unethical?

3. Can you think of any modern speaker who uses the 'plain folks' strategy to his advantage?

4. Are you familiar with anyone who speaks of himself in the third person?

5. When thinking about the 'war on terrorism', what are some of the god terms used by politicians? Devil terms? What is the potential impact of using these kinds of labels? Has the rhetoric of the 'war on terrorism' become extreme in the reliance on fear appeals?

6. Do Americans tend to use more patriotic platitudes in their speech-making than Canadians? If so, does this mean that Americans are more patriotic?

7. How do you react to politicians who engage in name-calling? Is this strategy effective with audiences? Is it ethical?

8. Give some examples to illustrate problems with circular and slippery slope reasoning, reasoning from sign, and reasoning from generalization? What is an example of a red herring argument?

CHAPTER TWELVE

Speaking in Social Contexts

The Social Occasion Speech

SUGGESTED ASSIGNMENT

Preparing a Social Occasion Speech

Students should write and deliver one of the following kinds of social occasion speeches: after-dinner, roast, wedding toast, graduation, award, acceptance, tribute, eulogy, or speech of introduction. Speeches should incorporate all of the elements of speech-making discussed in previous chapters. In marking this assignment, the instructor will ask: To what extent does the speech reflect best practices for the genre that it represents (after-dinner, eulogy, or other)? If the speech employs humour, the instructor will assess the quality and appropriateness of the choices.

Learning Objectives
- To learn about the speaking requirements for various kinds of social occasions—after-dinner, roast, wedding toast, graduation, award and acceptance, tribute, eulogy, and introduction to another speaker.
- To learn about strategies, cautions, and delivery techniques for using humour.

A best man presents a toast to the bride and groom. A statesman rises to present a eulogy to a fallen leader. Friends and fellow workers gather to roast a retiring member of their organization. The soccer coach presents an award for most valuable player of the year. An invited speaker delivers a speech following the annual banquet for members of a social club. An actress accepts an award for best performance in a dramatic film. A student delivers a graduation address at spring convocation. Special circumstances call for special kinds of speeches, customized to meet the demands of that occasion. For many people, the social occasion speech is the one that they are most likely to deliver outside of the workplace; and ceremonial speaking is especially important in collectivist cultures.[1] The first part of this chapter describes some of the most common social speaking occasions. The second part discusses strategies and cautions in using humour, as well as delivery techniques.

Types of Social Occasion Speeches

The most common social occasion speeches are the following: after-dinner, roast, wedding toast, graduation, award and acceptance, tribute, eulogy, and introduction.

After-Dinner Speeches

The after-dinner speaker aims to entertain her audience. Most often, she presents this kind of address in a banquet environment. The speech should not exceed 20 minutes in length. While the person speaks, others are often finishing the last of their desserts and coffee.

Although the majority of after-dinner speeches aim to entertain, the speaker may have a secondary purpose of equal importance. She may offer information to her audience. She might, for example, talk about the history of tsunamis, haunted museums, or the economic forecast for the coming year. Most after-dinner speeches include some humorous or whimsical content, even with the most serious of topics.

Roasts

Another social occasion speech is the 'roast', where work colleagues, family members, and friends pay tribute to an individual who is retiring, leaving the organization, or being recognized by colleagues. Roasts have a mistress of ceremonies (MC) or roast master, who introduces the speakers. Pre-selected members of the audience take turns presenting short speeches that poke fun at the person. Usually the speeches target and exaggerate some distinguishing characteristics or eccentricities of the person. So if the person is often late for appointments, one or more speeches might centre on past instances of missed appointments. Each 5–10 minute speech will usually have a theme, based on idiosyncrasies identified by the speaker, family members, colleagues, or friends.

Research may be required (e.g., interviews with friends and family members) to identify the most humorous stories that relate to this eccentricity. Sometimes the speakers will present little gifts that make fun of this dominant characteristic. If the person's distinguishing characteristic is being late for appointments, for example, the speaker might present the person with a calendar or a very ostentatious and ugly watch. The gifts are often inexpensive and humorous in nature.

Roasts employ many of the same humorous strategies as the after-dinner speech. Incongruity and unexpected twists often characterize these speeches. A speaker might say, for example, 'Although late for most events, Bill was always on time for the really important occasions—the office Christmas party, union votes for salary increases, and Friday afternoon dart challenges at Chelsea's Pub. Is that true, Bill?'

At the end of a retirement or resignation roast, at least one person will deliver a more serious address that pays tribute to the past contributions of the person, expresses some regret about the impending departure, and wishes the person well in future experiences. Sometimes, however, roasts celebrate a birthday or an accomplishment, rather than the impending departure of a person.

Wedding Toasts

Wedding toasts offer a mix of serious and humorous moments. As with many other kinds of social occasion speeches, the speaker reflects on past memories and offers a toast to the future happiness of the bride and groom. The typical order of wedding toasts follows: best man, father of the groom, father of the bride, groom, bride, friends and relatives, maid or matron of honour, groom's mother, bride's mother, and miscellaneous others.

Speakers should wait to begin speaking until everyone has received a drink to be used in the toast. Since not everyone will know the speakers, you should introduce yourself and explain your connection to the bride and/or groom. Because a number of people present toasts, each speech should be short, no more than three or four minutes in length. Less is appropriate. Some toasts may be only one line in length, such as 'May your problems be as far away as yesterday and your happiness as close as tomorrow.' Others may include rhyme: 'May the sun eclipse the shadows, may your friends outwit your foes, may your hopes cast out your fears, and may your love outlast the years.' One of my favourite Irish toasts is 'May the road rise to meet you, may the wind be always at your back.' Another simple but eloquent toast says, 'May the strength of three be in your journey.' One of the most popular wedding toasts, of unknown origins, is the following: 'If you cheat, may you cheat death. If you steal, may you steal one another's heart. If you fight, may you fight for one another. And if you drink, may you drink with me.' Other examples include 'To the newlyweds, I say: May "for better or worse be far better than worse"' and 'Today I wed my best friend.'

Longer wedding toasts usually include some light, as well as sentimental, moments. The lighter moments will involve humorous accounts of experiences involving the bride and groom—for example, a time when one partner brought the wrong load of laundry back from the laundromat, confusion over having the same last names, or how the couple *really* met. Other moments will be more inspirational, talking about the love shared by the couple, sacrifices made to be together, or the significance of their having found each other. Like the humorous moments, many of these serious thoughts will appear in the guise of stories (e.g., a story about how the couple met or how one spontaneously took a plane to Paris to spend a weekend with the other person). Each speaker draws on his or her repertoire of past experiences with the bride and groom in planning the wedding toast. The longer wedding speeches will often end with a one-line toast. Whether lengthy or brief, wedding toasts should always steer away from vulgar language and stories that involve other partners. The stories should make the couple smile, not blush with embarrassment.

The style of language and presentation should be conversational, warm and friendly in tone. You are speaking to a room of friends, people united in their desire to wish the couple a healthy and happy marriage.

Graduation Speeches

Keynote speakers or invited commencement speakers have three major goals: to congratulate the graduates on their past accomplishments, to offer some advice, and to wish them well in future undertakings. The speeches should be inspirational in nature. When universities and colleges select commencement speakers, they choose them on the basis of some life accomplishment. The keynote speaker will have excelled in some career area or made a notable contribution to society. Sometimes the person will be a noted political figure, a writer, or a celebrity. Not infrequently, commencement speakers have special ties to the university, college, or town in which the educational institution is situated. The person may be a former graduate or a native of the community, or their daughters or sons may attend the school. The university or college typically awards an honorary degree at the graduation ceremonies to the keynote speaker(s). Because of its bilingual nature, the University of Ottawa features two keynote speakers at each graduation exercise. One speaker delivers in English, the other in French.

Unlike keynote speakers, valedictorians, salutatorians, and class speakers are members of the graduating class. These individuals will have achieved a position of status within their class by virtue of academic achievements. The salutatorian speaker typically has the second highest average in the graduating class; the valedictorian has the highest average. Salutatorian speakers greet the graduating class, and valedictorian speakers bid the class farewell. Both speakers recall the highlights of shared school experiences, note the accomplishments of their classmates, and wish their classmates well in future endeavours.

Salutatory and valedictory addresses are part of long-established rituals with symbolic significance and emotional impact on the participants. The speeches may, nonetheless, contain moments of humour. Conforming to historical traditions, salutatorians at Princeton University deliver the salutatory address in Latin. Only the news media receive an English translation of the address. The graduating students, for their part, receive a copy in Latin, which indicates appropriate places to laugh, applaud, groan, or otherwise react to the speech. To attending members of the audience, it appears that the students have a complete grasp of Latin, whereas in reality, the planners have manipulated the occasion for humorous effect. Unless they are scholars of Latin, the audience members will have no idea of what is said in the salutatory address.[2]

Award and Acceptance Speeches

The presenter of an award must accomplish the following. He must give the name of the award, the reason for its establishment, and any criteria for granting the award. Subsequently, he must identify the winner of the award and talk about how the person meets the criteria for award winners. The presenter may conclude by talking about feelings of pride associated with being selected to give the award. When speaking of the qualities of the winner, the presenter should be specific and concrete, giving examples to illustrate the points. If the audience includes members who competed for the award and lost, the speaker should also acknowledge the quality of the competition. Speeches of presentation rarely exceed four or five minutes in length.

In accepting an award, speakers should express appreciation for the award and acknowledge those who played a contributing role. They should thank both the donor(s) of the award and the presenter. The speeches should be short, to the point, and humble in tone. Being acquainted with the history of the award (its establishment and former winners) will allow the person to comment on what the award means in personal terms. Recipients of awards should avoid saying that they do not deserve the award. Such statements degrade the choices of the committee that selected the award winners. The speaker may say that he will try hard to represent the values of the organization that selected him.

On most occasions, the language of the acceptance speech will be relatively formal and dignified in tone. Any humour should be gentle, evoking smiles rather than guffaws. Sometimes speakers accept awards for others who are absent. The same rules apply to those speakers. Speeches should not exceed several minutes in length.

At times in past years, winners of Academy Awards have chosen to use the award ceremony as a platform for expressing their political views. In 1973, Marlon Brando asked an unknown Native American, Sacheen Littlefeather, to speak on his behalf at the awards ceremony. Forced by show producers to abandon her plans for a 15-minute speech, Littlefeather appeared in full Apache dress to say that Brando would not accept the award for best actor in *The Godfather*. The refusal was in response to the film industry's poor treatment of Native Americans. Some audience members clapped, but many booed.

In 2003, amid hisses and boos, best documentary film winner Michael Moore invited the other documentary nominees on stage to denounce George Bush. Moore proclaimed, 'We are against this war, Mr Bush! Shame on you, Mr Bush, shame on you!' The audience did not appreciate his actions. In such a situation, audiences are often resentful. They feel that the person has taken advantage of a position of privilege, a gift. Speakers who choose to promote their personal agendas must accept the risks associated with these actions.

Tributes

Speeches of tribute celebrate the life of a person, recall an event of significance, or commemorate a cause. In Canada, we celebrate Remembrance Day, Canada Day, St Jean Baptiste Day (in Quebec), old soldiers, and the repatriation of our Constitution with speeches and festivities. We also pay tributes on sadder occasions, such as the anniversary of the massacre of 14 young women at the L'École Polytechnique in Montreal.

Tributes to people are often emotional and personal. The speaker uses language to paint a portrait of the person. Rather than just say that the person was generous, the speaker describes actions performed by the person—the time that the person sent a bag of groceries to the home of someone without money, drove an extra 200 miles to assist someone whose car had broken down on the highway in mid-winter, or took meals on a weekly basis to homebound seniors. The specifics allow us to obtain an understanding of why the person should be admired.

No one format exists for speeches of tribute. The speaker may build a metaphorical comparison, construct a series of stories about the person, or simply detail characteristics with supporting examples. Whatever the organizational pattern, the speaker should pursue a central theme. The nature of the occasion will dictate the length of the speech.

Our most central values lie at the heart of speeches of tribute. We talk about what matters most to us in terms of personal qualities, causes, and events of significance. We identify our heroes and talk about the ideals for which they stand and for which we should strive. Many speeches of tribute explicitly acknowledge the shared nature of the values held by speaker and audience. They are often inspirational in nature, encouraging the audience to stretch their goals and extend their reach.

Eulogies

Eulogies are speeches of tribute to those who have died. Ministers, family members, and close friends deliver eulogies at memorial services and funerals. A Greek derivative, the term *eulogy* means 'good word'. Audiences anticipate that eulogies will pay respect to the person who has died by praising his or her good qualities and contributions while living. More specifically, eulogies recognize the death of the person, establish the relationship of the speaker to that person, talk about the impact of the deceased on the speaker and others, and offer consolation to the family and friends of the deceased. Eulogies do more than talk about the accomplishments of an individual; they also talk about how the person lived his life.

Eulogies usually have a spiritual dimension, where speakers reassure the audience that life continues beyond the moment of death. If the eulogy does not contain such a religious bent, the speaker will reassure the audience that the good deeds of the person will continue to live in the memories of those who knew him.

When offering a eulogy, speakers should take care not to overextend their praises so that the eulogy rings false. Most people have faults; they are not perfect. So eulogies should concentrate on the strengths that will be recognized by audience members— love of family, dedication to hard work, or generosity of spirit. The speaker should bolster the assertions with stories that demonstrate the best qualities of the person. Eulogies should address a limited number of character or personality traits. If you try to talk about too many qualities of the person, you will not have time to develop the ideas with stories and examples. The language of eulogies should be simple but eloquent.

When offering a eulogy, the speaker will often speak of her profound sense of loss, her sadness. Although some speakers inject gentle humour into eulogies, the overall tone is sombre and dignified.

Speeches of Introduction

Chapter 2 discussed the demands of introducing oneself to an audience. The following discussion offers guidance for when you introduce another speaker to the audience. In such a situation, you will greet the audience in a warm fashion, introduce yourself if you are unknown to the audience, introduce the speaker and the topic of the speech, and talk about the qualifications of the speaker to present on this particular topic. In other words, your aim is to create a warm, friendly climate for the speech and to build the credibility of the speaker. You should also establish the importance of the topic for the audience. Why should they care about listening to the speech? What can they get from the occasion? You want to instill a sense of anticipation in the audience, but you do not want to oversell the speaker. Excessive praise can make a speaker feel unable to rise to the occasion.

Speakers usually provide biographical statements to those who will introduce them. The presenter should study the statement prior to introducing the speaker and integrate the comments into her presentation. Even though the practice of providing biographical details is often necessary, the speaker does not want to focus audience attention on the prepared statement. Otherwise, it will appear that the person being introduced is promoting herself. Rather, the details included in the biographical summary should appear to originate with the person offering the introduction. The presenter should emphasize those details that are most relevant to the occasion and topic.

Statements of introduction should not exceed three to four minutes in length. Prior knowledge of the speaker should dictate the length of the introduction. The better known the speaker to the audience, the less needs to be said. You can create a greater sense of drama when you withhold the speaker's name until the final moment.

You should check with the speaker, prior to delivering the introduction, to verify details and check for acceptability of the comments. Also be certain that you can pronounce the speaker's name. Los Angeles Democrat and Assembly Speaker Fabian Nunez mangled the names of two California Supreme Court justices in introducing their 'State of the State' addresses. After mispronouncing the last name of Justice Kathryn Mickle Werdegar, Nunez introduced Justice Ming Chin as 'Ming Ching'.[3] Finally, you should be certain of the appropriate title to be used in the introduction. European and Canadian professors, for example, often use the term 'Professor' in preference to 'Doctor', while American professors tend to use the term 'Doctor'. Women may have a preference for 'Mrs' or 'Ms'. Governors-general use the term 'His/Her Excellency' during their terms in office. In Canada, prime ministers, chief justices, and governors-general acquire the right to the title 'Right Honourable' for life. The term 'Honourable' applies to members of Parliament, upper court judges, and lieutenant-governors.

As with all other kinds of speeches, you must adapt speeches of introduction to the audience and occasion. More formal occasions demand more formal introductions. Comments should be in the spirit of the occasion and never violate standards of good taste.

The Use of Humour

Speakers use a number of strategies to add humour to their speeches. Those strategies include exaggeration or overstatement; understatement; incongruous and sometimes absurd comparisons; pairing personality characteristics with inanimate objects, events, or activities; playing on stereotypes; puns; irony; and oxymorons.

Humorous Strategies

Speakers and comedians use *exaggeration* for humorous effect. 'If you drove any slower, we would need to requisition the foot patrol for a walking permit.' 'Her fur looked so real that I offered to feed it.' 'It was so cold that a flea could have done a slalom run in my ear canal.' Comedian Robin Williams used exaggeration for humorous effect with the following comment: 'The only people flying to Europe will be terrorists, so it will be, "Will you be sitting in armed or unarmed?"'[4]

A second technique involves *understatement*. 'In the event of a nuclear disaster, expect some delays in your mail service.' 'No, I'm not upset. Would you like to share a cup of CLR with me?' Comedienne Joan Rivers once remarked, 'I knew I was an unwanted baby when I saw that my bath toys were a toaster and a radio.'[5] Had the comment been genuine, *unwanted* would have been an understatement of her parents' feelings.

Sometimes speakers use *comparisons* for humorous effect. 'Forgetting your wife's birthday is like sudden death in tennis. The game's over.' 'Fighting for peace is like shouting for quiet.' 'A narcissistic personality is like a mummy—all wrapped up in herself.'

Another technique involves *pairing personality characteristics with inanimate objects, events, or activities*. American Comedy Awards winner Margaret Smith once joked, 'My uncle Sammy was an angry man. He had printed on his tombstone: What are you looking at?'[6] In this case, the speaker achieves humour by combining a common occurrence (people visiting gravesites) with a personality characteristic (anger). If you put together a different personality trait (slowness) with a common activity (swimming), you can see how it works:'Johnny liked to swim with his dog. But it was quite a job for the dog, paddling backwards to keep up with him.'

Humour sometimes depends on audience acquaintance with *stereotypes*. Robin Williams once joked, 'We had gay burglars the other night. They broke in and rearranged the furniture.'[7] Comedian Chris Rock calls on our acquaintance with a number of stereotypes in the following joke:'You know the world is going crazy when the best rapper is a white guy, the best golfer is a black guy, the tallest guy in the NBA is Chinese, the Swiss hold the America's Cup, France is accusing the US of arrogance, [and] Germany doesn't want to go to war.'[8] As I will discuss in the second part of this chapter, those of us who do not qualify as comedians must take great care not to cross ethical boundaries with regard to evoking stereotypes.

Box 12.1 A Question of Ethics

Asked to speak at a roast honouring Willard, a work colleague, Charlie thought at length about what he could use as focal points for the speech. He thought about Willard's habit of triple-checking everything. Willard also mumbled to himself when he was upset with someone, especially his boss. A third habit involved making appreciative comments about an attractive female employee. Charlie decided to use these traits as the basis for his speech. On the night of the roast, Charlie strode confidently to the podium. He began the speech by talking about Willard's admiration of female employees, especially Barbara. Out of the corner of his eye, Charlie saw Barbara stiffen; her husband looked angry. Willard's wife didn't look too happy either. Caught off guard, Charlie fumbled over the next several sentences before reaching the part about his colleague's triple-checking everything. He glanced in the direction of Willard, as the room grew quiet. No one was laughing, and Willard's face now matched the colour of his burgundy tie. Charlie didn't know what to think, and he wanted to be anywhere but in front of this audience. Only

afterwards did someone tell him that Barbara and her husband had been having marital difficulties related to jealousy, and Willard struggled with an obsessive compulsive disorder that involved repeating actions multiple times. Willard's boss laughed when Charlie talked about his employee's tendency to complain about his requests, but Willard did not look happy.

Ellen had a similar problem. She delivered a wedding toast to her best friend, Melanie. In the toast, she talked about Ellen's efforts to hide her relationship from her family and their friends in the months leading to her engagement. Living secretly with her boyfriend, Melanie was afraid to tell her family, whose religion did not sanction intimacy outside of marriage. When Ellen talked about Melanie's efforts to deceive her family, a hush fell over the room. Melanie blushed in shame and her family looked shocked and upset. Ellen thought, 'Oh no, what have I done?'

What can we learn from the mistakes of Charlie and Ellen? Have you ever been witness to—or made—a similar mistake?

Speakers sometimes use *puns* or plays on words for humorous effect. Sometimes puns involve gaining humour from double meanings of words. The next example illustrates this point:'I used to work for a tow company, but it got to be too much of a drag.' At other times, the humour comes from slight changes in the wording, as the following example illustrates: 'Fullerton (California) divorce lawyer Linda Ross has a sign in her office that reads, "Satisfaction guaranteed or your honey back."'[9]

The next and final example demonstrates how plays on words can also involve mispronunciations:

A robbery took place at the home of an elderly immigrant woman. As the robbers ran from the house, her neighbours heard her frantic shouting, 'The *bully's* coming. The *bully's* coming.' Worried that the woman was unable to get a grip on herself, the neighbours rushed to her side. They pointed to the departing truck of thieves, 'See, they're going. We'll call the police.' 'No need, I called already,' the woman replied in an agitated voice. 'The *police* coming. The *police* coming.'

Stories and anecdotes sometimes come with an *unexpected twist*. In a twist on an old joke that typically relates to men, comedian Carol Leifer commented, 'I don't have any kids. Well . . . at least none that I know about.'[10] There is also a certain degree of irony present in this example.

Irony involves drawing a contrast between the expected and unexpected. The following comment by actor Michael J. Fox, diagnosed with Parkinson's disease, illustrates the nature of irony: 'I'm perceived as being really young, and yet I have the clinical condition of an old man.' When applied in the context of humour, irony involves interpreting words in a way that is contrary to their literal meaning. Sometimes irony entails saying the opposite of what we mean: 'My husband loved me so much that he bought me a seat on Pan Am 102—for a trip to the Middle East—on September 11th.'

Sometimes speakers use *oxymorons* for humorous effect. An oxymoron contains a contradiction. A speaker could say, for example, 'She had a genuine fake fur' or 'It was real imitation leather.' Other examples of oxymorons are 'paid volunteer', 'virtual reality', and 'small crisis'.

Cautions in Using Humour

Humour should always bear a strong relationship to the content of a speech. Even with after-dinner speeches, the linkages should be obvious and explicit. You say, 'As Jerry learned when he leapt from the top of the Eiffel Tower, our perspective changes as we get closer to the ground.' Otherwise, the speaker runs the risk of appearing to be a stand-up comedian, moving from one joke to the next.

Speakers must also recognize the ethical limits of using humour—not the same as those that govern comedians. Because comedians operate in the theatre of the absurd, we allow them a wider margin and special privileges. Comedians earn their living by making fun of human frailties and weaknesses. The assaults on character are often strong; and no one is safe, especially politicians and celebrities. Speakers, for the most part, are held to higher standards.

In general, speakers must shy away from ethnic and sexist jokes, as well as character slurs. Research suggests, however, that members of oppressed groups (as defined by gender, race, politics, religion, economics, physical characteristics, or sexual orientation) tend to use more self-deprecatory humour—humour directed at themselves—than do members of other groups.[11] Generally speaking, we can poke humour at groups in which we hold membership, but we cannot use humour at the expense of groups in which we do not hold membership. Lawyers can make jokes about lawyers, and doctors can make jokes about doctors. Lesbians and gays may refer to themselves as *queers*, but they will take offence if others use the term as a source of humour. But there are limits even with humour that we use at our own expense. Some feminists resent the use of stereotypes in jokes about women, even if the remarks come from comediennes. Comedian Bill Cosby argues that the use of derogatory labels is unacceptable, whether coming from black or white performers.[12]

The above examples illustrate a continuum of risk borne by speakers who use self-deprecating humour. In most instances, lawyers and doctors can tell jokes about their own community or profession without unhappy consequences. They have not suffered from their association with the profession that they practise; in fact, they profit and gain credibility from the association. They do not feel vulnerable. Seniors have not suffered *en masse* from outside persecution, but advocacy groups argue the need to combat societal stereotypes of seniors as old and frail. They say that aging occurs on a continuum. So some seniors will be sensitive, but most seniors are able to laugh at themselves. Therefore, when a senior makes a joke about seniors, the person is relatively safe—but maybe not so safe as lawyers or doctors who use self-deprecating humour.

Members of the gay community assume a higher risk in joking about their issues and using terms that are politically incorrect, because many feel vulnerable. In the same way, people of colour risk a great deal when they use politically incorrect terms and self-deprecating humour, because many members (especially the older generation) cannot laugh at stereotypes that carry such painful memories. And at the far end of the continuum, I would argue that it would be difficult to find members of the Jewish or Muslim communities who would joke about their issues in the current context. We can laugh at ourselves in some situations, but not in others. Speakers must evaluate the tolerance of the audience and the larger society for humour that is self-deprecating. Generally, the more vulnerable the audience feels, the lower the tolerance level for even self-deprecating humour.

As will be discussed in Chapter 15 on ghost-writing, differences also exist between males and females in terms of their appreciation and use of humour. Men tend to enjoy jokes with a punch line more than women, whereas both men and women appreciate anecdotal humour.[13] Women often have a hard time telling a stock joke without forgetting or messing up the last line of the joke. They tend to be much more comfortable with experiential humour, which involves telling stories about themselves and their families (extensions of themselves).[14] Men, on the other hand, say that they like to tell jokes.[15] As mentioned earlier, the humour of women is more likely than that of men to be self-deprecatory. It is also more likely to be aimed at power structures and figures.[16]

Delivering Humorous Content

In terms of delivery, humorous speeches call for a more theatrical presentation than other kinds of speeches. Speakers may use larger and more exaggerated arm and hand gestures, broader facial expressions. They move their eyes in ways designed to get a humorous reaction or drop their jaws, as if in astonishment. Like the comedian, they insert pauses after punch lines. The after-dinner speaker, who aims to entertain, may use more extreme inflections of the voice, mimic sounds, or impersonate a person or animal. He may deliver from note cards or, in the case of a more formal event, a manuscript. Often the speaker leaves the podium and employs the entire body in his presentation.

Conclusion

Most of us will present a social occasion speech at some point in our lives, because social occasion speeches celebrate the highs and lows in our lives. Although some, such as eulogies, are more formal and sombre in nature, others, such as retirement roasts, focus on the light and whimsical. But even when the speeches are light in tone and whimsical in spirit, they usually have some inspirational moments.

Questions for Discussion

1. Have you ever delivered one of the kinds of speeches discussed in this chapter? If so, what was your experience?
2. Have you ever attended a social occasion such as a wedding or shower where the speaker offended the persons he was supposed to be honouring? How did the audience react to the derogatory comments? How did the subject(s) of the jokes react? Were they embarrassed? Offended?
3. Can you recall an eloquent speech delivered at a funeral or other sombre occasion? What made the speech memorable and special?
4. As a speaker, are you comfortable using humour? Do you prefer to tell jokes with a punch line or to recount stories with humorous content? As a listener, what kind of humour do you prefer?
5. Is it acceptable to poke fun at groups in which you hold membership? What if the jokes enter the public arena?

Appendix: Sample Social Occasion Speeches

Speech #1: Sample Acceptance Speech

by Arcade Kakunze

It is an honour to accept this basketball trophy for 'most valuable player' on behalf of Stephane Nkakibirerero, who cannot be here tonight. I've known Stephane since he arrived in this country from Burundi, and I would like to share with you guys how much this award means to Stephane.

From grade nine, Stephane and I have been a part of this team, contributing our skills and talent. But, as I'm sure you remember, it wasn't easy. We had to work really hard to improve our basketball skills. Well, there wasn't much that I could do because I was too short. And it didn't really help to have a little belly that slowed me down. But you guys don't know Stephane's story. How did Stephane go from the basketball player who ran with the ball instead of dribbling it to the all-star player that he is today? Well, I know, because I was there every step of the way.

You really have to put yourselves into Stephane's shoes to understand how this great transformation came about. First, picture a tall African high school kid who just came straight from his homeland. Then remember that Burundi is all about soccer, not basketball.

When Stephane first picked up a basketball, he could neither dribble nor shoot the ball. And he always played by his own rules. He ran with the ball every time that it was passed to him. After seeing him play for the first time, I was certain that there was no hope for him in basketball. Soccer, maybe, but not basketball. Stephane was definitely not a good basketball player when he first started five years ago. But no matter how embarrassing his skills, he always loved the game and never stopped trying. In Grade 10, Stephane and I spent almost every day playing basketball after school, so that we could improve for the coming season. Even when it started getting cold, we continued playing in our winter coats and gloves. Now when you hear that two Africans are outside playing in the winter, you automatically know there's a problem. Stephane was allergic to the cold Canadian winters. His thin body had not adjusted to the horrible conditions. But he still managed to practise in the freezing cold because of his love of the game.

Over the years that I've known Stephane, I have come to realize what a great achiever he is. When he first started playing for this school, he sat on the bench most of the games—right next to me. And for three straight years, Stephane and I sat together on the bench, watching instead of being a part of the game. Remember, I had an excuse for being on the bench. I was too short, and my little belly slowed me down! It wasn't my fault; I loved hamburgers and hot dogs back then. I'd never eaten such foods in Burundi.

But Stephane made no excuses for himself. He wanted to play. He was tired of entering the game with only a minute left, giving a break to those who had played most of the game. I said to him: 'Stephane, this coach is never going to give us a chance. It's embarrassing to be on the bench all of the time. Let's just quit and go have a burger.' He looked me in the eyes (like this) and told me, 'Arcade, I won't quit and eventually I will be the best!'

Stephane surely proved me wrong. He did become the best the following basketball season. He averaged over 15 points a game and went from playing two minutes to playing the whole game. He proved himself to everyone who thought that he would never be a good basketball player. And he definitely proved himself to me. Stephane turned a dream into reality through his hard work, determination, and spirit. This is a man we should all respect for his achievements—and not only on the basketball court. But academically and as a person. Once again, let's give a round of applause for this year's most valuable basketball player.

Speech #2: Mock Commencement Address

by Christine Gravelle

In the now famous speech, the class of 1997 was advised to 'Wear Sunscreen.' Tonight, friends and fellow students of the class of 2003, I would like to tell you to 'lose your bra!'

Most of you are probably saying to yourselves right now, 'What is she smoking?' and 'Where can I get some?' I would like to share a little story from my university career to demonstrate what I mean when I say, 'Lose your bra.'

As for many of you, my first year of university was one of adjustment. I arrived at our university, not knowing a soul. I questioned my sanity at going so far from home, into a new and alien environment. In high school, I had been rather quiet and shy. The thought of public speaking or being in the spotlight froze me with fear. I would rather have written a 30-page paper than talk in front of a classroom of my peers.

One night during frosh week, a group from my floor went down to Faculty Hollow to hear the Philosopher Kings. In the middle of one song, the lead singer said to the audience, 'If you give a little, we'll give a little.' I guess this request appealed to Chloe, the bad angel who sits on my right shoulder, because—all of a sudden—my bra was sailing through the air. It landed squarely on stage in the glaring spotlight. I felt free—in more ways than one!

In later years, I have come to view that moment as the symbolic gesture of throwing off my adolescence, overcoming my fears of expressing myself, and growing up a little. Today, instead of asking ourselves where we would like to go to university, we are asking ourselves, 'What do I want to do with the rest of my life?' The answers are scary. We are leaving the comfort and routine of university life to go out

into the 'real world.' Basically, the bra—and I'm not trying to be feminist here—represents all of our fears and inhibitions that we have regarding the unknown and the novel.

So I urge you tonight, when the bra is weighing you down, too tight to be comfortable, lose it. Take all those fears and doubts and throw them away. And when you ask yourself, 'Should I take this job out in British Columbia?' Lose the bra. 'Do I want to move in with my boyfriend or girlfriend?' Lose the bra. 'Do I want to do my Master's?' Lose the bra. Even if things turn out badly, everything (as our parents have often told us)—good or bad—is experience. And everything happens for a reason.

I expect to be throwing my bra many times this year. Not only am I about to receive my diploma, signifying my freedom from 19 years of educational drudgery, my parents are moving halfway across the country. I will be sharing a house with my friends and hoping that they will not turn into my enemies. I have no clue what type of career appeals to me, nor do I have a permanent job, unlike some of my peers who have already established themselves in various organizations.

Back in first year, we had to lose the bra in order to mature. Today we need to lose the bra in order not to fear what the future holds. Over at our sister institution, the valedictorian has just spent a half-hour talking about how much he will cherish his university experience and how his education has prepared him for the workforce. I just spent five minutes telling you to get naked. Guess who lucked out?

Speech #3: Speech of Tribute

by Adam Brown

Last week my Grandma died. This past weekend I returned home to remember her and to say goodbye. Her death was a moment of clarity and reflection for me. It was an opportunity for the reality of mortality to truly sink in and manifest itself within me. Thoughts that had been contemplated over and over again in my head throughout the summer returned and have been revisited. Just over four months ago, my Grandpa passed away. The odd juxtaposition of their deaths is comforting, in a sense, as they blend together in my mind as one event.

It was somehow easier this time around, as I could trust in the closure that Grandpa's death had provided me. I would like to speak a bit about my relationship with Grandpa, as he and I were a little closer than Grandma and I. My journey home was an opportunity to say one final farewell to both, who have joined each other somewhere, if only in my mind.

On Saturday, I had an eight-and-a-half-hour drive home from university. And on that trip, I spent a great deal of time thinking about Grandpa—about his life, his accomplishments, his ethics and morals, his faith, his genuine nature and gentle approach. I thought about crokinole (a favourite pastime), buckets of lawn mulch in the garage (I never knew the reason for the mulch), the woodshed behind their house (a great place to play), rhubarb (Grandma made him pies from a huge rhubarb patch), the rub of his whiskers across my face when I was a child, and his quiet little chuckle. He was always 'pretty fair'. The seasons went in cycles (some years being dry and hot, others being wet and cold). The weather has always been hotter and always been colder.

On that trip, I thought about my grandparents, the things I have thought and never said. I thought about the letter I never wrote. And let me tell you, I often thought about writing it, just never did.

It was after I graduated from high school that Grandpa and I became really close. On my trips home from university, I always tried to reserve an afternoon, with at least an hour and a half, so that I could visit with Grandpa and

Grandma. We talked about a lot of things. Among others were politics, history—Canadian and American history, world history, and family history. His past, my future, and God. It was a rare moment when Grandpa wasn't familiar with a topic, but when he wasn't, he was upfront about it and we moved on.

It is important that I express a little of what Grandpa taught me during our many conversations about God. For a little background, I come from a Quaker family. Quakers are pacifist Christians who believe in the good in everyone and in the ability of everyone to have a personal relationship with God. Our services do not have preachers or pastors. The service is conducted in silence until someone feels touched to say something. It could be a poem, a scripture, or just a thought. Funerals are conducted in the same way.

Grandpa showed me that God is accessible, visible, active, and loving. Most of my faith has found root both in what Grandpa has told me and in who Grandpa is. In life, he was a profoundly good person because of his relationship with God. Whenever he explained to me a virtue from his faith, I saw that virtue in him. Patience. Kindness. Selflessness. Humility. Peace. Generosity. Inclusiveness. Tenderness. Love. Compassion. Commitment. Forgiveness. Understanding. Work ethic. All of these traits that Grandpa wore so easily found their origin in his understanding of God.

As his grandson, who falls short in so many of these categories, I am overwhelmed by the magnitude of this man's spirit. And I recognize how fortunate I am to have been able to spend time with him—learning, sharing, and growing. In my mind, Grandpa is the epitome of Christianity. In my mind, he personifies what Jesus was trying to tell us over two thousand years ago. How wonderful it is for a message to be so fresh—and alive—and accessible to us here today.

There has been a powerful feeling that has been constantly invading me over the past few days. My grandparents are together and young again. I love my grandparents very much and will miss them dearly. And this is the letter that I wish I had sent. These were the words I wish I had said.

Speech #4: Speech of Tribute

by Claude Pike

She stands a symbol of virtue. A symbol of strength. A symbol of resilience. She is a homemaker, a dressmaker, a shoemaker, a baker, and a tailor. She is a disciplinarian, a teacher. She is a psychologist, nurse, wife, and a compassionate friend.

Her mother called her 'Eula', her friends call her 'Galy', others call her 'Mother'. But I call her 'Mama'. I stand here today to pay tribute to a lady who gives her all in expectation of nothing in return. I stand in recognition of my mother.

My mother has 10 children. Her life has been one of self-sacrifice in the rearing of the 10 of us. As a child, I was amazed at the fact that she was always the last to go to bed at night and the first to wake in the morning. She just had to make sure that we were all safe and accounted for in the home. This is Mama the protector.

There were times when we were sick with the cold or the flu. This lady would be up at 2 a.m., preparing a hot poultice and rubbing a back or chest with eucalyptus oil. The warmth of her hands and her gentle touch of love never failed to speed our recovery. This is Mama the nurse.

One of Jamaica's famous dishes is the traditional rice and peas. The main ingredients are kidney beans, rice, and coconut. Anyone who knows anything about rice and peas knows that the best rice and peas are cooked over a slow fire until all the rice grains split. Mama knows this—and almost everything else there is to know about cooking and serving a meal. This was how she earned the name 'Galy', as she is always found around the fireplace, or galie, at weddings, parties, church and community functions. She is

famous—not only among us, but throughout the community—for her cooking. This is Mama the cook.

My mother is a devoted Christian. She believes that God placed her on this earth to be of service to others. For this reason, she has always adopted an elderly person in the community who does not have any relatives. She performs household chores for this person and ensures that they have a warm meal every day. This is Mama the social worker.

My mother is a firm believer in the phrase 'It takes a village to raise a child.' Every child was her child. For this reason, our home was a place where every child was welcomed. And she treated them as she treated us. She was a strict lady, but even the most rebellious child in the community gravitated toward her. This is Mama the caregiver.

As a family, we saw rough times. Money was not always available. But we were always clean and fed, and she ensured that we all went to school, no matter what. She believed that a good education was important if we were to get the most out of life. She was always encouraging not only us, but also our friends, to get good grades and to become involved in extracurricular activities. This was Mama the motivator.

The wise man Solomon said, 'Who can find a virtuous woman? For her price is above rubies. The heart of her husband doth safely trust in her. She seeketh wool, and flax, and worketh willingly with her hands. She riseth also when it was yet night and giveth meat to her household. Her children shall rise and call her blessed. Many women have done well but thou excelest them all.' Mama, you have truly excelled them all.

Speech #5: Speech to Entertain

by Nicholas Kowbel

Today is December 1st, and it is indeed a special occasion. Only 23 more days to shop the malls, in search of that perfect Christmas gift—or let's face it, for some people, any gift at all. As consumers, we head to the malls, sharing Christmas cheer with throngs of other shoppers—shoppers who grow increasingly more desperate as the number of chocolates disappear from their Advent Calendars.

As it happens, I am not just a consumer. Like many of you, I am also a student who earns extra money through

part-time jobs. I earn that money working as a sales clerk at Pharma Plus, and this year will be my third retail Christmas. Because this is the first day of December, our last day of classes, I thought that I would share with you some of my favourite Christmas moments. This is our story, mine and yours, of a retail Christmas.

As we wander the malls, some of our favourite Christmas songs fill the air—'Jingle Bell Rock', 'I Saw Mommy Kissing Santa Claus', and the seemingly endless 'Twelve

Days of Christmas', each day more riveting than the last. I know these songs well, because as of the first of December, they will be the theme song of my life—repeated in sequence, every 20 minutes, for the next 23 days. The monotony of the soundtrack seems as endless as the streams of people lining up at the cashes.

I can still remember my first retail Christmas. It was December 1, 1999, about 9:45 p.m. I was 16 and not nearly so jaded as I am today. The malls were busy that day. Customers were entering the store in hordes, ravaging our displays, leaving their coffees and soft drinks on our shelves, filling their hands with more junk than they would ever need at any other time of year. They came through our cashes with wrapping paper, gadgets, decorations, gift baskets, and chocolates.

We were four cashiers that evening, and I had already seen one fall. An angry woman cried vengeance on poor Nathalie when she discovered that we had run out of Planters peanuts—as if it was Nathalie's fault. Tears welled up in Nathalie's eyes as she fled the ever-expanding lines of shoppers for the solitude of the store bathroom. 'Not me,' I said, 'I shall not fall.'

The tension mounted as customers continued their campaign of pillaging with their credit cards and gift certificates. Another agitated shopper looked in my direction as she remarked loudly to her friend, 'This is ridiculous. They should really open another cash.' I wondered what she expected me to do—build one right there, out of the stack of empty coffee cups lining our stockroom desk. The sweat was beginning to bead down my face as we struggled to move faster and faster. Out of the corner of my eye, I noticed a man step out of line. He had a roll of wrapping paper and a travel-size bottle of Listerine. He glared at me, eyes wide open. His face, which under non-Christmas conditions would have been normal, had turned a bright red. As he drew nearer to the front of the line, I was sure that conflict was eminent. It was obvious that he intended to perform a 'bud'—and without the permission of the gentleman in front of him. In elementary school, we learn that the consequences of budding without permission can be dire. Were my vibes right? Was he about to commit this transgression?

Another customer called out, 'Hey, that's not right!' pointing at the red-faced gentleman. He had been caught. He turned his glance toward me, demanding that I offer his very important person some special consideration. 'I'm sorry, sir, but you'll have to follow the line', I said firmly. Then the Christmas spirit hit me, literally. It struck me in the form of a bottle of Listerine and a tube of wrapping paper, hurled toward my post. I turned to protect my head, but left my back exposed to assault from the travel-size Listerine. I bore many scars that night—and not just from the customer's choice of projectiles.

December 1st is an important day, you see. There are only 23 days left to shop. It is the first day of that wonderful soundtrack. Most importantly, it is a day when the consumer-retailer relationship enters its bitter transformation. I tell you this from the eyes of a retailer. And yet I know that I am not all that patient when I journey to those suburban jungles that we euphemistically call malls. This year, however, my theme song will not be of a partridge in a pear tree, but of John Lennon, as I ask myself, 'And so this is Christmas and what have you done?'

Speech #6: Roast at a Shower for a Bride

by Rosalind Marchut

Dear family and friends. We are gathered today to remember and celebrate the life of Anna. Anna was beautiful, youthful, and energetic. But sadly, Anna's life, as we know it, is no longer. As her best friend, I remember her favourite pastimes. She loved hanging out with her girlfriends and going to the bar on weekends. She loved shopping and cruising around the town with friends in her cute convertible. She liked watching funny romantic films and taking long hot baths in her impeccable bathroom. I remember how excited she was when she first fell in love. I remember how much she loved moving into her own apartment—the time she danced atop the counter at the Lebanese shwarma place. I remember all the hours we spent doing each other's hair and gossiping. I remember our weekly girls' night watching *Friends* and *Will and Grace*. I recall the road trips we would take every summer. But sadly all of this has come to an end, and we must say goodbye to Anna. Anna has left the world of singletons to be joined in holy matrimony, and some would say that a wedding is a funeral where a woman smells her own flowers.

It is always sad when such a thing comes to someone so young. Anna always dreamt of backpacking in Europe and learning to surf in Australia. She thought for sure that she would have the opportunity to become a model. But Anna was unable to escape the vice grip of love. Shackled, she carried these chains with her for years, desperately seeking a means of escape; but after a long struggle, she could not fight any longer.

Sometimes we ask ourselves 'Why has this happened? Why is she being taken from us?' But we must remember that fate works in mysterious ways and that Anna will always be with us in spirit and in memory. Even if she can no longer fly to Vegas with us for Christmas, we will think about her at home with her new husband and mother-in-law.

And many new experiences await Anna. Instead of going out to lunch with the girls, she can accompany her husband to the pub for wings and beer. Instead of enjoying her clean bathroom, Anna can enjoy scrubbing the bathroom clean.

Instead of driving in her convertible, Anna can watch her husband spend countless hours trying to fix it without success. Instead of wearing lingerie to bed, she can wear earplugs. Instead of watching her romantic comedies with Julia Roberts, she can watch action films with Arnold Schwarzenegger. Instead of watching *Friends* and *Will and Grace*, she can search for the humour in Jimmy Kimmel and *The Man Show*. Road trips will be replaced by fishing trips, girls' night by poker night, and her little black book by babysitting numbers.

And so while we may be feeling sorry for ourselves for losing Anna in our everyday lives, we should really be feeling sorry for Anna. Being a carefree single girl is not something you can easily get back. Let us take the time to say goodbye. Goodbye to girls' night out, goodbye to clean bathrooms. Goodbye to lingerie and to road trips. Goodbye to the little black book. Goodbye Anna. For a woman may be incomplete until she is married, but after that, she is finished.

Speech #7: Spoof Acceptance Speech

by Jennifer Pierce

Thank you! Thank you so much! Wow, this is such an honour. I am truly shocked. I never expected to be Employee of the Year at Bob's Burger Barn—such a great place to work and be part of. It is an honour that I truly accept graciously.

You know, I can still remember the first day I walked through the Bob's Burger Barn doors. It was my first shift, and Daddy had got me the job because Momma is actually Bob's fifth cousin by marriage—or is it, seventh just plain cousin? Oh well, never mind, you all know how everyone in this town just seems to be related somehow.

Anyway, I was a nervous wreck that first day on the grill, let me tell you. I was putting bacon on the Barneriffic mushroom melt (which we all know should just have cheese) and Barn BBQ sauce on the Bawk Bawk Barn chicken burger, which of course only requires mayonnaise. Man, what a day! I was so down, really having lost all hope of succeeding in this place. And as the orders piled in front of me, I thought, 'I can never be a grillin' girl. Look at this. I'm messing up right and left.' And that's when my now best friend Bobby Jane got beside me on that grill, told me to pull myself together, stand tall, and turn my frown upside down, because I was a Triple B girl now.

She told me that, as a Bob's Burger Barn employee, I had to strive for perfection and be composed at all times. It was now my duty to make sure that every man, woman, and child's order was a-okay so that they too could have a Barneriffic day and walk out of here with a smile on their faces. I watched her, completely mesmerized by her quickness; learned from her; and soon mastered my grilling skills. To this day, I live by the words she said to me on that first shift. And I never forget my purpose here. I would like to give a very special thank you to Bobby Jane for helping me on that one fateful day and for nominating me for this prestigious award. Without you, I would not be standing here right now.

Next I would like to thank another colleague, one who helped me to push the envelope and exceed the Triple B employee standard, setting a new record. Tommy Rae, I will never forget that cold, blustery night last month when those two buses pulled into our parking lot. They were old folks, headed down to Las Vegas, looking for food to fuel them up before they gambled their pensions away. I can still picture Tommy Rae's face as he yelled, 'Code Red, Code Red, man your stations', as dozens of hungry seniors came bursting through the Barn doors. I turned and told him not to worry: we were ready and trained, and we would do this together. And do it we did. And as most of you know, that night I broke the record for the most perfect orders served in one hour. The previous record was 68, and that night I put out 162 perfect orders in 60 minutes. What a complete rush that was, and Tommy Rae, I could not have done it without you, buddy. You manned that cash like a pro, taking those orders without missing a beat. Thank you so much.

Next month will be my seventh year here at this wonderful place, and I truly feel it is my second home. The Triple B staff have become like a family to me. You are all assets to this company in your own ways—and an inspiration to me

personally. And next week, when I am promoted to Barn Supervisor #2, I will strive to continue the Burger Barn tradition of teamwork, exceeding customer expectations. I will push even harder for perfection with each and every order.

Lastly, I would also like to thank my general manager Jimmy Henkle and Barn Supervisor #1 Bobby Lynn Sauvé for choosing me for this award. This is a dream come true, and I am truly honoured to be accepting it today. But most of all, I am proud to be a part of this great team and proud to say that I am a Bob's Burger Barn employee. Thank you all again, and wow, this has just been the most Barneriffic day ever! Thank you!

Speech #8: Speech to Entertain

by Chris Ratcliffe

As some of you may have noticed, I have had my hair trimmed. Just a little bit off the top.

In one of my classes, we had a discussion about the possible motivations for cutting my hair. There were many suggestions—none of which were right. The real reason is a deep-seated psychological need that manifested itself as early as five years of age. In hopes of shedding some light on my internal motivations, I would like to describe an incident that occurred when I was in kindergarten.

It was arts and crafts time and—as all good children do—we were sitting around our table, eating paste and cutting paper to eat later. At that particular point, I had a thought—perhaps inspired by the paste, perhaps evidence of my struggling creativity. In this moment, I was inspired. The muses of art and beauty struck. I decided that I was going to create the greatest art the world had ever seen. That's right. I decided to cut my own hair.

I knew that this inspiration would not last long; so I decided to cut my hair right there in the classroom. The rebel inside me was screaming for release. I was challenging the norms set down by our elders. My classmates were awestruck by my audacity. My friends tried to stop me, but I would not hear their arguments. I was breaking free. No more bowl cut for this kiddo!

But first I needed to test the scissors to ensure that they would make a clean cut. So I applied them to the bottom of my shirt. The large chunk of fabric that fell away before the awesome power of these shears was a testament to their designer and manufacturer.

Having seen clear evidence that my tool of choice worked, it was time to select the canvas for the expression of my creative juices. I chose a swath of my hair an inch wide directly over my left eye. This would be an ideal location to showcase my talent and my struggle for independence. With the site chosen, I carefully removed the selected follicles, in a manner similar to the clear-cutting of a forest.

When I got home, my parents were not as impressed with my art as my friends had been. In fact, they saw it as some sort of vandalism. They demanded an explanation. I was cornered. I had to think fast. If my parents knew that I was a rebel at heart, I would never again be allowed to roam free. So I devised a tale so ingenious that not even the great detective Sherlock Holmes would be able to figure out what had happened.

My first tactic was denial. 'What do you mean what happened to my hair? Nothing happened.' It would seem that my parents were smarter than I had reckoned. They examined my hairline closely and demanded to know who had cut my hair. The piece missing from my shirt seemed to lend credibility to their theory that something had indeed happened, and they suspected that I had done it myself. I could see it in their eyes. Time for my backup plan. 'Uhh, I didn't cut it off.'

They demanded to know, if it wasn't me, then who was it? I chose the most logical answer I could. 'Ummm . . . I was on the playground at recess and . . . uhhh . . . a kid came up to me with scissors and . . . attacked me, cut my shirt, and cut off my hair.' The words tumbled out of my mouth.

My parents wanted to know more. Who was this crazed hairdresser? What did he look like? The interrogation was brutal, but I kept my cool. 'Uhhh . . . I don't know his name, but I think he is in . . . umh . . . grade six.'

I gave the best description I could conjure. 'He was wearing a jacket that was red and black and grey (the same colours as my own vest). And I think that he had a bowl cut.' I was brilliant, a masterful storyteller. Someday I would be a player in the international game of espionage.

My parents looked concerned and puzzled. My dad tried to break me. He said, 'Now look, Chris, you won't get in trouble if you just tell us the truth.' Yeah, right. I'd heard that one before. I stuck to my story. It became a war of attrition, one that I was determined to win.

The next day, my parents again tried to force me to reveal my secrets. They tried to convince me of the value of being honest. But I had carefully evaluated the situation and developed several scenarios. I was prepared for every possible tactic that they could use to tame my wild nature and regain their hold over me. Soon it would be time for me to strike out on my own, and this situation had become a way for me to break free of my parents' mind control.

On the third day, my dad came to my school and pulled me out of class. We went down the hall to the sixth grade classroom to identify the culprit. My emotions were riding a stand-up looping rollercoaster. I imagine the feeling was somewhat similar to what a death row inmate feels on his way to the execution chamber. This was not an action I had anticipated. I gave the only answer I could. 'Nope, I don't see him.'

Now for those of you who remember the size difference between a kindergarten student and a grade sixer, you can well imagine my terror at facing a whole classroom of giants. I was stunned that my daddy would try something so evil to force my hand.

Later that night, at dinner, my father informed me of the actions to be taken. He told me that, since I was unable to identify the barbarian, the entire grade six class would lose their recess privileges until the guilty party came forward.

'Oh, the humanity of it all!' If my parents were willing to go to such lengths and punish others to force my confession, I was obviously in a battle I could not win. I had underestimated my parents and their desire to crush my spirit. I had fought a hard battle, but I could not allow others to suffer for the actions of a heroic freedom fighter such as myself. Of course, the other consideration was that the grade six class would eventually discover who was behind their loss of privilege. This would no doubt result in some serious bloodletting. And since I was a fat little kid, I was convinced the blood would be mine.

I confessed, but I still managed to strike a blow for posterity. Class pictures were the next week, and the evidence of my fight against conformity was centre stage. And so, for those of you still wondering about my motivations for cutting my hair this time, it should be obvious that it was simply a manifestation of my desire to be a heroic freedom fighter. Or maybe I was just having paste flashbacks?

Speech #9: Speech to Entertain

by Tim Mowrey

Picture this. The morning sun is just edging over the horizon, splashing the dew-covered lawns with the bright yellows and oranges of a new day. Robins and sparrows are perched outside my window, chirping a friendly welcome to the dawn. The air is crisp and fresh. The sounds of my favourite radio station, playing my favourite songs, chime from the alarm clock near my head. And I swing at it with all of my might, hoping to dislodge it from the wall outlet! Cause long-term damage, if I can.

The birds, thank you lord, are long since gone. Their incessant and obscenely cheery chirping goes to someone else's window. You see, I hate mornings. A lot. I know that some of you are probably what we call 'morning people', or what I like to call 'weird'. But I'm certainly not one of you. Nothing can drag me out of bed in the morning. Nothing, that is, except for a grandpa breakfast. Actually it's one of only two things that can get me out of bed in the morning—the other being a house fire. But even that isn't as effective as a grandpa breakfast.

What is a grandpa breakfast, you ask? Well, it's a breakfast made by Grandpa. But not just any grandpa . . . my grandpa. You see, he's been in the breakfast business for a long time, serving tens upon tens of family, and . . . well, mostly family. But he's been making them for as long as I can remember.

A grandpa breakfast is not spectacularly complicated. It's not fancy or frilly. A grandpa breakfast is not a gourmet meal. But a grandpa breakfast is made from the heart. It is served with a smile and a laugh. A grandpa breakfast is simply the best breakfast that I've ever eaten. Picture this. Eggs, over easy. Enough to cover the entire flat iron skillet a few times over. Pancakes, their outsides grilled to a golden brown, their insides light and fluffy. Thick maple sweetened bacon—I've only ever tasted bacon this good at Grandpa's.

Now it's usually at about this time that the scent of breakfast cooking wafts down the hall at Grandma's and Grandpa's place and plays tricks on my brain. It makes me think that I like mornings. It makes me think that I look good enough to wander out into the kitchen without first doing something to my 'bed head'. This is pretty powerful stuff.

Now comes the big moment. . . . Grandpa brings everything over and . . . starts digging in himself. I'm lucky if I can get the pancakes before he does. Not to mention the fact that Grandma has already commandeered the eggs and will only pass the bacon if you hand her the syrup. For a grandpa breakfast, not only do I have to get up early. I've got to be at the top of my game to fend off senior citizens who are surprisingly quick. It takes them 20 minutes to answer the door, but for breakfast, they'd make Donovan Bailey look like slow maple syrup.

Now that I've mentioned Grandma, you may be wondering how she fits into a grandpa breakfast. Well, Grandma happens to be a breakfast architect. I learned from Grandma at an early age that the only way to eat a grandpa breakfast is to stack everything strategically—starting with the pancake on the bottom, then the egg, then the bacon, and then, of course, cover the whole construction with syrup. The beauty of this method is that, when you go for seconds, you can never get just one more thing. If you want to eat another pancake properly, then you've got to get another egg and a slice of bacon. That Grandma . . . she's a genius.

When breakfast is finished and I've put away all of the dishes and cleared the table (Grandma and Grandpa aren't so quick now, are they?), the whole day waits ahead. I'm up, I'm fed, and I'm extremely satisfied. The sun has arched its way westward for what's bound to be a warm, sun-filled day. So what better to do than go back to bed? Picture this. One happy kid.

Speech #10: Greetings by a Town Crier on the Final Day of Class

by Julie Huot

Oyer, oyer, oyer, citizens of the public speaking class!
The distinguished Brian Creamer is our special guest.
He comes with credentials, knowledge, and public
    speaking prowess.
On behalf of our class, I welcome you here today.
It is a special occasion.
Let it be known to all persons here gathered today that
Monday, the 1st day of the 12th month of the year 2003
    marks the end of Public Speaking 101.
On this, our final day, with the designated theme 'special
    occasion speeches', I invite you to listen attentively and
    to gain knowledge and wisdom from those presenting
    before you today.
But firstly, hearken back to that initial class, three months
    ago, when we nervously stood in this same stark,
    uninspiring classroom to give our first introductory
    speeches.
For many, it was the first time to formally present.
No one really knew what the audience would say.
Public speaking was not our forté.

Citizens, one and all, recall your thoughts, impressions, and
    nervous tensions.
Now remember the demonstration speeches.
Citizens shared their experiences and taught us new skills.
We learned about proper etiquette,
    how to spit shine shoes,
    how to make tried and true recipes,
    how to pack a suitcase, just to name a few.
Let it be known that these speechmaking citizens rose to
    the challenge and gained new confidence in the art of
    public speaking.
Demonstrations left all citizens with positive impressions.
Public speaking was becoming commonplace.
Persuasive speeches were our next challenge.
It was clear that we citizens have strong opinions and can
    be persuasive.
Our peers spoke passionately about drunk driving,
    international adoptions, threats to fresh water, and the
    right to hunt, for one and all.
The audience was convinced as the orators expounded.

Persuasive public speakers were now amongst us.

Let it be known that this public speaking class is here to be reckoned with, that we have successfully shed our formative past.

The audience has been impressed, the professor has seen us progress.

That, citizens of Public Speaking 101, brings us to the final chapter.

This is a special occasion, a fete, a party, a bash, a shindig, a fiesta, a festival of public speaking.

Marking this special occasion, I am your town crier.

Criers are a part of our heritage, examples of orators extraordinaire.

As class crier, I announce special occasions.

I speak in a commanding voice.

And I am in charge of marking the opening of this celebration.

Hear ye, hear ye, hear ye.

It is time for celebrations to begin.

Citizens, it is our final class.

We have mastered the art of public speaking.

The world is ours.

We will put these skills to good use, giving us a personal boost.

With presentations for other classes, for jobs today and tomorrow,

these skills will come in handy.

So let us indulge, let the fun begin.

Bring on the food to inspire our celebratory mood.

Good work has been done in friendship and in fun.

Join in and mark this special occasion.

God save the Queen.

CHAPTER THIRTEEN

Speaking in Classroom Contexts

Team Presentation

Making a Team Presentation

Groups of four or five students are responsible for planning and delivering a team presentation, approximately one hour in length. Every group member must participate in the design of the presentation and must have an active speaking role. The group should employ a variety of teaching strategies (e.g., short lectures, small-group discussions, simulation exercises, role-plays, and/or case studies). None of the lecture segments should be longer than five minutes in length. Participation among members should be balanced so that everyone makes a contribution that is capable of being marked. The groups may divide roles to fit the talents and interests of individual group members. The groups should use PowerPoint for lecture components. See Chapter 7 for rules governing PowerPoint presentations.

Learning Objectives
- To understand what is involved in preparing and presenting a successful team presentation, including choosing a theme, establishing teaching and learning objectives, and determining an agenda of learning activities.
- To learn how to manage group dynamics, including drawing the audience into question-and-answer and other interactive activities.
- To find out how to integrate the various components of a team presentation.

Imagine the following scenario. The course instructor has assigned Nancy, Jim, Belinda, and Rodney a group presentation on risk management. The four students meet to discuss their strategy for the one-hour presentation. Nancy volunteers to deliver a lecture on current health and environmental risks such as mad cow disease, bio-terrorism, and the potential for new viral strains of the avian flu. Jim offers to research and present a discussion on current theories related to managing health and environmental risks. Belinda assumes the task of putting together a presentation on how to engage in planning for risk management. Rodney says that he will research and discuss the efforts of several major corporations in the area of risk management. Having allocated tasks successfully, the four leave the meeting with a sense of confidence that they have achieved a credible plan. Sound familiar?

The day arrives for the group presentation. Each member rises and makes a 15-minute PowerPoint presentation to the class. The quality varies from one presentation to the next, depending on the skills of the presenter. At the end of the four lectures, the members sit down, satisfied that they have fulfilled the requirements of the assignment. Certainly, they have achieved the most basic goal of delivering an oral presentation on a selected topic. Chances are that presentations by the other students will look and sound much the same. But a learning theorist might have some questions. What were the teaching and learning objectives for the presentation? Did the group choose the right strategies and use their time wisely? Did the audience learn anything from the group presentation? What do audience members remember? Could the class answer content-based questions at the end of the presentation?

Too often, the response to these questions is 'no', because the presentations do not reflect broadly accepted design, learning, teaching, and oral presentation strategies. Rather, the group has relied on the most common teaching technique, the lecture; and they have equated hearing with learning. The selected process to transmit knowledge has been one-way, offering little opportunity for feedback outside of possible questions and answers at the end of the presentation. This scenario is repeated again and again in

Photo Gill Ferguson

classrooms around the country, in a range of subjects from business to engineering to communication.

As the numbers of students in classrooms increase, instructors find that time often does not permit individual presentations of material; and they call on their students more and more frequently for small-group presentations. Oral presentations by groups create new challenges, different from the requirements for individual presentations or speeches. At the same time, group presentations offer new teaching and learning opportunities for students. The classroom can become an exciting forum for learning when students exercise creativity and strategy in their oral presentations, engaging their audiences through active learning techniques.

This chapter introduces the basic principles of how to design and deliver an effective small-group presentation—one that will depart from the expectations associated with other speaking genres. More specifically, we will examine how to choose a theme for the presentation, establish teaching and learning objectives, decide on an agenda of learning activities, manage the group dynamics, and deliver the presentation. The material in this chapter is geared to students with an interest in educational and professional training careers, as well as group facilitation and organizational development. The principles apply to a broad spectrum of learning environments (including university classrooms), where the students can experiment with more active learning strategies.

Box 13.1 A Question of Ethics

A major concern in academia relates to the right of professors to teach what they please, without being subjected to the normal rules of legal society. That is, traditionally professors have enjoyed *academic freedom*—the right to express their views freely without fear of being disciplined or fired for their beliefs. The aim of this principle has been to protect the rights of professors to disseminate knowledge without worrying about being challenged in courts of law or imprisoned for their teachings. In many countries in the world, academics can teach only the doctrines that are acceptable to political or religious authorities. Democratic countries do not believe in these forms of censorship.

In recent years, however, this principle of academic freedom has been challenged in the courts. Accusers claim that professors are as responsible for their words as anyone else in society. Several recent cases have highlighted the murky and often disputed nature of academic freedom. In the first instance, a high school instructor taught that the Holocaust never took place—that it was a conspiracy created by people of Jewish descent to justify aggressive actions against Palestinians. In a second

instance, a university professor publicized research demonstrating that some racial groups are more intelligent than other racial groups. A prominent researcher made a presentation that accused pharmaceutical firms of hiding results that do not support their products. Representatives of the pharmaceutical firms attended the speech event. Threatened with potential loss of funding from the pharmaceutical companies, the university cancelled the employment contract of the researcher. (The university did not, however, admit that the dismissal of the researcher was related to this speech.) What if a professor were to urge his students to boycott Wal-Mart and give their business to local merchants?

What are the similarities and differences in these examples? Do you believe in the principle of academic freedom? If so, do limits exist? What are they? When publicly funded institutions employ professors, should they be as accountable for their words as politicians are expected to be? Should they be able to promote their own political views in a classroom setting? What are the risks of failure to protect the principle of academic freedom?

Choosing a Theme

First, the group must meet to decide on a theme for the presentation. In a presentation on communication planning, for example, I focus on the relationship among different kinds of planning—strategic, operational, and work planning. I show how everything fits together. This focus governs the organization of the presentation. If you are making a presentation on cultural differences in communication, you might have a theme such as 'different but equal'. Or your theme for a talk about e-mail communication could be 'E-mail Etiquette'. If you have titled your presentation, you have probably selected a theme for the presentation. If ideas are too scattered, your presentation will seem confused and disorganized. So choosing a theme, early in your planning, will prevent a disoriented approach to the subject matter.

Setting Teaching and Learning Objectives

The next step in the process is to establish teaching and learning objectives. These objectives flow directly from the theme of the presentation and define what a group wants to achieve in the presentation. For example, in the scenario cited in the introduction to this chapter, the group members might decide on the follow *teaching* objective or goal: 'To convey the importance of risk management in the current business environment and to identify strategies for dealing with high-risk situations.' Teaching goals are written from the perspective of teachers, or in this case, small-group presenters.

The group should also write *learning* objectives, which they frame from the perspective of the audience.[1] Learning objectives are audience-centred. They tell the listeners what they will acquire from the presentation in the way of information and/or skills. When the listeners leave the room, what will they take with them? In framing learning objectives for their presentation on risk management, Nancy, Jim, Belinda, and Rodney can say that (at the end of the group presentation) the class should be able to:

1. Discuss at least three reasons why risk management has become a current topic of importance to those who work in health and environmental spheres.
2. Identify four current threats to our health and environment.
3. Reflect in writing upon several contemporary theories of risk management.
4. Pinpoint six common elements that appear in the strategies of corporations noted for successful risk management practices.
5. Generate at least two statements that could appear in each section of a risk management plan and explain how these statements reflect current theories and best practices.

Thus, learning objectives should be audience-centred, written in a way that shows what the audience will take away from the group presentation. The objectives should also be specific, unambiguous, measurable, positive, and realistic,[2] although some learning theorists disagree on the desired level of specificity.[3]

The means to evaluate the achievement of a learning objective should be immediately obvious. In other words, in the above example, the presenting group could test for knowledge of risk management theories by giving a quiz to the class or could test for ability to apply the theories and best practices by asking the class to generate a skeletal risk management plan.

Some of the above learning objectives are more specific than others. If you wanted to become more specific with objective two, for instance, you could write 'In a role play, demonstrate knowledge of several contemporary theories of risk management.'

The following examples relate to teaching and learning goals for a presentation on assertiveness training. The teaching goal would be 'to provide skills in assertiveness'. The learning objectives, written from an audience perspective, would be the following. At the end of the session, audience members should be able to:

- Analyze their own communication styles.
- Diagnose situations that call for more assertive behaviours.
- Identify the techniques for communicating assertively.
- Apply assertiveness techniques in interactions with aggressive personalities.

The above learning objectives are audience-centred. They are also clear and specific in wording. They are measurable in the sense that the presenters could test the ability of the audience to analyze their own communication styles, diagnose situations that call for assertive responses, identify assertive communication behaviours, and apply the techniques in a simulated situation. The objectives are positive in wording, and they are realistic and achievable.

Most theorists believe that the framing of learning objectives contributes to the reduction of anxiety,[4] focuses audience attention on relevant concepts,[5] and increases learning.[6] Stating and reiterating these learning objectives in opening and closing the group presentation is important. If you put the teaching and learning objectives on transparencies or PowerPoint, they will be most clear to the audience.

Deciding on an Agenda of Learning Activities

The agenda will involve a mix of different activities. Decisions on the agenda should be based on application of sound learning theories and principles of audience adaptation. They should involve a variety of activities that take different learning styles into account.[7]

Taking Learning Theories into Account

One study has suggested that learners retain 10 per cent of what they read, 20 per cent of what they hear, 30 per cent of what they see, 50 per cent of what they see and hear, 70 per cent of what they say, and 90 per cent of what they say and do.[8] In classroom situations, a retention rate of 10 per cent is common,[9] probably in large part because of heavy reliance on lectures as a dominant method of conveying information. What does this finding imply for the design of group presentations?

First, learning theory suggests that oral presenters should actively engage their audiences in the learning process. This necessity conforms to current trends in society and in educational theories. Stand-alone lectures violate the principles of engagement. Lectures offer a fast, efficient way of transmitting large quantities of information, but the results in terms of learning are often questionable. Some say that, instead of trying to 'cover' the content, instructors should aim to 'uncover' the material by using a number of interactive demonstrations and problem-solving activities that engage the learner.[10]

A second principle relates to organization of materials. Educators have learned that lectures should be broken into no more than 15-minute learning 'chunks'.[11] My own experience has demonstrated that, in a one-hour presentation by students, groups should limit lecture components to five-minute chunks for maximum effectiveness. Lacking the experience of their instructors, student presenters have a harder time holding attention in lectures, especially if they select relatively dry facts for presentation. Other more interactive parts of a small-group presentation can, however, be longer than five minutes.

A third principle that has emerged in learning theory is that individuals vary greatly in how they prefer to acquire information. Some people prefer to learn new material by listening (auditory), by reading or viewing (visual), by touching (tactile), or by doing (kinesthetic).[12] Auditory learners might get the most out of hearing an audiotape of a speech or listening to music while they work. Visual learners might want to examine photographs, see graphical depictions of the material, or watch a film or television show. Those with a preference for the tactile might like to work on the computer, using their hands in some way or taking notes. The kinesthetic learner likes to practise the skill.

In 1983, Howard Gardner, professor of education at Harvard University, developed a comprehensive theory of multiple intelligences that explains and amplifies the above ideas.[13] The number of references when you input 'theory of multiple intelligences' into Google (480,000 in October 2005) suggests the popularity of Gardner's ideas. This theory advocates the existence of nine potential pathways to learning (originally, Gardner proposed seven avenues to learning):

- Linguistic intelligence (ability to understand, use, and appreciate words)
- Logical-mathematical intelligence (ability to think in logical terms, to reason abstractly, and to see numerical patterns)
- Visual-spatial intelligence (ability to think in images and pictures and to discern visual and spatial patterns)
- Bodily-kinesthetic intelligence (ability to exercise control over body movements and to handle objects with agility)
- Musical intelligence (ability to produce and appreciate melody, rhythm, pitch, and timber)
- Interpersonal intelligence (ability to interact easily with others, to understand their socio-emotional needs, and to respond in a way that furthers the relationship)
- Intrapersonal intelligence (ability to connect with one's inner feelings, motivations, and values)
- Naturalist intelligence (ability to appreciate and relate to the world of nature).
- Existentialist intelligence (ability to ponder and enjoy contemplating deep questions about the meaning of life and human existence).

According to Gardner, all human beings possess the totality of the nine intelligences; however, people vary in the extent to which they possess any single intelligence. Therefore, one person may be very good at calculating the distance of stars from earth (logical-mathematical intelligence) but limited in the ability to play soccer (bodily intelligence) or to feel comfortable in a social setting (interpersonal intelligence). Another person might win accolades for musical intelligence but have a difficult time creating images on paper (visual-spatial intelligence). A third person might have the ability to survive in an arctic environment under the harshest of winter conditions (naturalist ability) but be unable to articulate his feelings to himself or others (intrapersonal and linguistic intelligences).

When oral presentations by groups depend strictly on words, some audience members may be unable to relate to—or learn from—the presentation. The bodily-kinesthetic learner may grow restless and anxious to find a way to express herself in a more dynamic way. The visual learner may want to see pictures and photographs that illustrate the ideas being discussed. The interpersonal learner may become bored with one-way communication that disallows the opportunity for interaction. To satisfy this need, she may write notes to the person sitting next to her in the classroom, while the musical learner quietly slips a listening device into one ear. The logical-mathematical learner may drift into his own reverie, wondering if he could create a chart that compared and contrasted the ideas in some more quantitative fashion; and the naturalist learner may pay more attention to the squirrels on the lawn outside the classroom than to the speakers. In such a situation, the linguistic learner may be the only person whose needs are recognized and met.

Learners also vary in whether they like to work alone, in dyads, or in small groups.[14] Some studies have identified differences between introverted and extroverted learners.[15] Introverted learners prefer activities such as questionnaires, handouts, worksheets, gallery exercises (discussed later in this chapter), and computer exercises they can do at home or in some quiet setting. Extroverted learners like activities that bring them into contact with other people. Examples include icebreakers, brainstorming, games and simulations, read-arounds, role-plays, discussions, and psychodramas. Extroverts are not shy about expressing their points of view, and these activities enable a dynamic exchange with other people. Some people prefer to learn from their peers and coworkers, while others like to draw their knowledge from authority figures.

Gender and personality variables also intervene to influence learning preferences. Women in general prefer a wider variety of activities than men, and they have stronger needs for collaborative sharing of ideas. Men in general (especially younger men) prefer a more analytical and active experimenter style of learning. But . . . it's not that simple. More apprehensive women also like the more analytical and active experimenter style of learning—that is, 'watching and doing'; less apprehensive women prefer innovative approaches to learning.[16] Less flexible personalities favour a more direct and formal teaching style (e.g., lectures), and more optimistic personalities appreciate a wide variety of learning activities.[17] In short, people have many different preferences as to how they want to learn, which creates the need for more flexible and eclectic approaches to classroom instruction.

Applying the Learning Theories

In short, group presenters should establish an agenda that recognizes the learning profiles of all members of the class and seeks to engage them in active learning. A 'something-for-everyone' approach means that the presentation must include diverse kinds of activities. The group may want to use music, art, role-plays, multimedia, inner reflection, and other techniques to transmit the material. They may want to ask participants (a better word in this context than 'audience') to represent an idea in graphical terms or use finger paints to create a colourful visual representation of their feelings on a topic.

Examples of activities that appeal to different senses include the following: auditory (lecture, discussion, music, read-arounds, storytelling), visual (handouts, overheads, gallery exercises, maps, timelines), tactile (worksheets, card sorting, artwork), and kinesthetic (movement/sorting, practice role-plays, psychodrama).[18] In adopting a 'something-for-everyone' approach, group presenters call on a variety of techniques to transmit content.[19] They may ask the class, for example, to reflect on a passage from a poem (individual learning), then to discuss the passage with another classmate (learning in dyads), and finally to share their findings with the larger group (learning through group interactions). Using videotaped interviews with experts or quoting authority figures can appeal to the learners who prefer to get their information from experts or people in positions of influence or power.

In a recent classroom presentation on the nine intelligences, a group fabricated a dialogue that could have occurred between Microsoft CEO Bill Gates and rapper Eminem. They used a rapper dialogue, along with body movements, to transmit the idea of multiple intelligences. The contrast between the personalities of Gates and Eminem allowed for the incorporation of humour in the presentation. It would be hard to imagine that any member of the audience would not remember the musical interaction or the lesson that was transmitted. On other occasions, class members have used games such as 'Jeopardy' to test the knowledge of class members on topics discussed in the presentation. As you plan your activities, ask yourself which intelligences are required to carry out the activities. If the activities seem to be too linguistically-based, restructure for diversity. For example, if you plan to make a presentation on television reality shows, consider the following kinds of activities:

- Lecturing on the popularity of current reality shows (appeal to linguistic intelligence).
- Asking the class to guess the ratings for five of the top shows (appeal to logical-mathematical intelligence).
- Presenting a graph showing the rise of reality shows over time, concurrent with the fall in popularity of other types of shows (appeal to spatial intelligence).
- Showing a video clip from one of the *Amazing Race* episodes (appeal to naturalist, bodily-kinesthetic, and visual intelligences).
- Asking the class to reflect on whether they would consider trying out for a show such as *Big Brother*, where they would have little privacy, or *Joe Millionaire*, which requires lying and deception (appeal to intrapersonal intelligence).
- Requesting that students act out an episode of a reality show such as *Average Joe*, in which they depict the ways that contestants show empathy for other contestants (interpersonal intelligence).
- Asking the class to create a plot line for a new reality show (linguistic intelligence), to create the spirit of the new reality show through a group painting (visual-spatial intelligence), and to choose the music for the show (musical intelligence).

Taking Audience Adaptation Theories into Account

As noted earlier, audiences should be the starting point for designing the presentation. Examining the demographic and value profiles of the class will enable presenters to create examples with which their audience can identify and to speculate about the level of knowledge present in the group.

Levels of knowledge will vary considerably between men and women on some topics (e.g., the history of the feminist movement or Major League Baseball players). But variations will also occur among members of the same gender. Some women are heavily into baseball history and memorabilia, whereas others have no interest. The meaning of being a feminist has acquired different interpretations over the years; so the knowledge gap between women of different ages may be almost as wide on that topic as the gap between men and women. In the same way, an older audience may know more about environmental disasters that occurred in the 1980s and the work of Ralph Nader and Bruce Cockburn, but a younger audience may know more about recent celebrity crusaders such as Bono.

Concepts and words change their meaning over time. I recall an experience with one student in the early 1980s. The young man had a short crewcut, which I identified with a conservative period in Canadian cultural history—the 1950s. His 'A+' status in the class lent credibility to my diagnosis of his personality as serious and probably conservative in nature. However, the final project submission from the student included lyrics to a song he had written. The lyrics contained many obscenities, not unlike those of Eminem; and I learned that the young man played in a hard rock band. Not only was he *not* conservative, but he was at the vanguard of a movement that soon swept the country, as the military cuts gave way to pink hair and shaved heads. When his uniquely adorned girlfriend came to collect one of his papers at the end of the semester, I became even more convinced of the inaccuracy of my initial perception. In short, I learned that the meanings I had attached to hair conventions and other symbols of behaviour had changed dramatically since the 1950s and even the 1960s. Crewcuts had assumed a very different meaning over the intervening decades between 1950 and 1980.

In the same way, the meaning of symbols changes from one cultural context to the next. In the late 1960s, I lived in the same building as two young men from India. One confided in me, 'I am worried because I have cut my hair, and my father will be very angry.' What an interesting comment, I thought—that his father would be upset with him for cutting his hair! At that moment, across North America, young males were engaged in daily confrontations with their parents because they *refused* to cut their hair. The differences in cultural expectations seemed very tangible to me at that moment. In response to the 2001 Census, the people of Canada listed 28 different ethnic origins. In addition to the two official languages, Canadians speak more than 15 different non-official languages as their mother tongue.[20] Any college or university classroom will likely have a representation of various ethnic groups and national origins; homogeneity in the classroom is rare. So classroom presenters typically face the challenge of appealing to different cultural and ethnic groups.

Sometimes we need to educate our audiences on the contemporary meanings of words and symbols and on their differences across cultures. What is politically correct also changes almost annually, as minority groups seek to define themselves in cultural and political terms. Some Aboriginal groups, for example, do not agree on preferred designations. In the last few years, gays and lesbians have added positive content to words such as *queer*, a term that was politically incorrect in earlier years. An example is the television show *Queer Eye for the Straight Guy*. *The Passionate Eye* (CBC) recently aired a documentary on 'fag hags', a term that refers to women who like gay men. One woman discussed how two negative terms ('fag' and 'hag') have acquired positive connotations for women with strong ties to gay men.[21]

With the trend towards lifetime learning, more professionals and older adults have returned to the classroom. Almost one out of eight Canadians is over 65 years of age. By 2020, one out of every five Canadians will be a senior. The numbers will increase to almost one out of four by 2041. These figures stand in stark opposition to earlier periods. In 1921, for example, only one out of 20 Canadians was a senior, and few pursued a higher education. The situation is quite different today, as older faces appear in graduating classes across the country, pursuing BA, MA, and Ph.D. degrees. People are living longer and enjoying more active lifestyles as they age. In recognition of changing global demographics, the United Nations established 1999 as the Year of Older Persons. In addition, the focus on 'just-in-time' learning sends many professionals back to the classroom to retool and learn new skills.

These older adults and professionals have more experiences and different kinds of experiences from their younger cohorts. Moreover, they may have organized the experiences differently.[22] These seasoned adults almost always prefer an interactive classroom that allows them to share their life and work experiences and to learn from each other. They want to know how they can apply what they learn inside and outside of the classroom. They adhere to a philosophy articulated by noted psychologist Carl Rogers:

> Experience is, for me, the highest authority. The touchstone of validity is my own experience. No other person's ideas, and none of my own ideas, are as authoritative as my experience. It is to experience that I must return again and again.[23]

Thus, presenters need to be sensitive to the diverse groups that make up a typical class. They need to speak in politically correct terms by today's standards. As with the more traditional public-speaking situation, identifying the values, opinions, and beliefs of the audience on any given topic can also help group presenters to achieve their teaching goals. When people do not agree with positions presented by speakers, they tend not to hear, to 'tune out' or to 'forget' the information.

As in the case of audiences with different learning preferences, group presenters may seek to bridge the differences or adopt a 'something-for-everyone' approach in the design of their oral presentations. To appeal to gender differences, for example, they may choose to include an activity such as a fishbowl exercise that allows males and females to respond differentially to a topic—taking turns as speakers and listeners. They can apply the same activity to a topic where the views of different age groups diverge. The next section considers the fishbowl activity, along with other options, in more detail.

Seeking Balance in Learning Activities

In determining the agenda, the presenting group needs to consider the appropriate mix of lecture and other activities. They also need to establish appropriate and realistic timelines for the activities. The following section identifies activities that appeal to different kinds of learners: icebreakers, energizers, guided fantasies, storytelling, gallery exercises, read-arounds, timelines, card sorting, case studies and scenarios, fishbowl exercises, role-plays, and artwork and other visuals. For the purpose of de-emphasizing the role of presenters as 'instructors of learning,' I will use the term *facilitator*. A facilitator frames and guides the process of learning. The role is dynamic, interactive, and two-way.

Icebreakers

The first item on any agenda should be an icebreaker, an activity designed to warm the climate of the group, eliminate inhibitions, and establish a frame of mind conducive to active participation in the presentation. The icebreaker may be tied directly to the theme of the presentation, or it may be unlinked, since the major purpose of the activity is to 'break the ice' and establish a strong group dynamic.

Examples of icebreakers abound. One icebreaker asks members of the audience to remove their shoes and to place one shoe on the floor in the middle of the classroom. Afterwards everyone takes a shoe from the pile and attempts to locate its owner. After identifying the owner, the person collects enough information to introduce the person to the larger group. A second individual, in turn, introduces that person. In another icebreaker, members of the group receive balloons. Inside each balloon is a question that the person must answer after popping the balloon. A favourite icebreaker with students involves asking the class to pull pieces of toilet paper from a roll passed around the group. They are not told how much paper to pull. Afterwards, the members of the class must answer as many questions about themselves as the numbers of articulated paper that they hold. A fourth icebreaker requires class members to describe a favourite childhood game.

Some icebreakers have a largely physical component. They may require group members to tangle and disentangle themselves. The 'Mill Mill' exercise, similar to the floor game Twister®, requires that participants assume difficult body positions that bring them into close physical contact with other group members. The common ingredient to all icebreakers is that they take participants to a higher level of familiarity with other members—either by requiring that they disclose personal information or come into close physical proximity with other members of the group.

One caution is in order. People from cultures that are more reserved, formal, or characterized by strict limits on cross-gender interactions may resist participating in high-contact icebreakers. Older individuals may also feel uncomfortable participating in some of the more physical exercises. One exercise requests that people sit on a balloon. If the balloon bursts, you must answer the question that is inside. Of course, people who feel sensitive about their weight may feel uncomfortable with this exercise. Before selecting an icebreaker, group presenters should assess the appropriateness of the activity and the probable level of acceptance by participants. In last year's class, for example, one icebreaker required students to sit on the laps of other students. I could see that some students were clearly uncomfortable with the exercise, even though no one complained. Still, I could not imagine that an older audience would have agreed to participate. The exercise might have worked well with young children, but it was marginally appropriate in a university classroom.

After placing the icebreaker on the agenda, the presenting group should establish the order of lectures and other activities. They should set limits on the time to be spent on any single lecture or activity. As mentioned earlier, I suggest that presenters adhere to five-minute lecture segments to allow time for a variety of other activities in a one-hour presentation. A sample agenda appears in the PowerPoint presentation, located in the appendix to Chapter 7. This agenda for a longer presentation demonstrates how varied activities can illuminate and expand on the concepts introduced in the lectures.

Depending on their nature, icebreakers hold appeal for many different kinds of learners. The more physical icebreakers appeal to bodily-kinesthetic learners and those who enjoy tactile experiences. Icebreakers that require listing of personal qualities appeal to learners with intrapersonal and linguistic intelligences. People with interpersonal intelligence enjoy icebreakers that require interacting with other people; and people with musical intelligence respond well to icebreakers that require singing, dancing, or chanting.[24]

Energizers

During a presentation of three or more hours, facilitators should make use of energizer activities. Energizers engage a group in some kind of physical activity that allows a break from concentrating on a demanding mental task. A popular energizer is 'shoot the rabbit.' The learners divide into two groups. Among themselves, members of each group decide on the posture that they will assume. They have three choices: wall, rabbit, or arrow. On cue, the two groups show their posture to the other group. The following criteria determine the winner:

- An arrow beats a rabbit, since the arrow can kill a rabbit.
- A wall beats an arrow, since it can stop the arrow.
- A rabbit beats a wall, since it can jump over the wall.

Other energizers require participants to move about the room, talk to other people, sing, or dance. Songs accompanied by actions, such as clapping or stomping, are especially good. Applauding latecomers in the morning or after lunch also provides a way to activate a sleepy group and add a touch of laughter to the room.[25] Balloon games are also popular as energizers. Some games require that people keep the balloons in the air, much as they would do in a volleyball game. To make the exercise more difficult, facilitators can ask participants to sort the balloons into colour clusters as they work to keep them in the air.[26]

Obviously, in a one-hour presentation, energizers have limited use; however, in longer presentations, they can be important. Energizers appeal to learners with bodily-kinesthetic intelligence, as well as those with interpersonal and musical intelligence. Learners who enjoy tactile experiences also enjoy many of the energizers.

Guided Fantasies

Guided fantasies ask participants to relax, close their eyes, and visualize scenes and experiences. The facilitator acts as a guide and talks the group through the visualization experience. In the following example, the facilitator asks the class to imagine the consequences of an environment out of control:

> I want all of you to close your eyes. Think of yourself walking down a dirt road. All around you are valleys and hills, and the sun is shining down upon you. The sky is

blue and the wind blows lightly against your face, whishing your hair back and forth. The sun gets hotter as you walk, and you begin to sweat. You stop by the side of the road to get a drink of water from a nearby stream. As you bend down, you notice that the water is a bright chemical green. You see an oily black substance, almost like gasoline, floating on top of the water. Looking deeper, you notice dead fish floating just beneath the surface. Suddenly you realize that the plant life around you looks twisted and gnarled, and the weeds are coated with the same black substance as the water. Startled, you turn to run back to the road but stumble over something. You realize that a dead cow is just one of many animals and birds strewn about the field. Escaping back to the road, you run until you see a farm. Relieved and still thirsty, you look for some sign of life to remind yourself that you have not been transported to another planet. In the near distance, you see a farmer looking across his fields. You look, too, and see a large truck dumping material into a landfill located about a half-kilometre away. When you reach the farm, you ask the man what the trucks are dumping. He replies, 'Death.'[27]

In a presentation to medical students, a facilitator could ask a group to imagine a day in the life of a medical doctor in 2020:

You get up at your usual time—7:30 a.m. You take a cup of strong black coffee into your office to begin your work day—at home, of course. Your office is bright and cheerful. Large windows overlook a lake, and the sun is arching higher in the morning sky. A few geese light on a nearby pond. You feel comfortable, sitting with a pair of slippers and light robe in a comfortable easy chair. A breeze wafts through the room and rustles a few papers on your large mahogany desk. Checking the calendar, you notice that the date is January 15, 2020. But you don't feel the cold because you are in a 'cocooned' office. Last night, before you went to bed, you programmed your office for mid-April. The computer program set the temperature, images that you see outside the window, and the general ambience. You can hear the flapping of the wings of the geese from time to time. To alert your staff to the fact that you are now on duty, you press a button, embedded in your wrist. Promptly, you receive a mental image of your schedule for the day, set to run until about 5:30 p.m., with an hour for lunch. Before switching to an interactive screen, you program your internal computer for a business day. That means that you will not appear in a robe and slippers to your patients. You will appear in a light grey business suit with a red tie. No need for uniforms in this virtual world! Finally you switch to an interactive screen on your computer, which shows a hologram of your first patient. She sits at a table with her child. Her dress has a pleasant floral pattern. (She was able to discern the fact that your office was set for spring.) You switch the audio to interactive mode. 'Hello there. I see that (oops, need a name, another button to push) Jimmy is having some problems with his (ah, another button, virtual scan of body) throat. I'll order the prescription (push another button). Have a good evening. Must be late in Finland.'

While these two examples concern the future, guided fantasies need not be futuristic. You can imagine any encounter or event. You could, for example, conduct a guided fantasy that leads people through a desired response to an assault or a guided fantasy that asks people to imagine the life of someone who lived in the eighteenth century. Alternatively, you could lead a group through a visualization exercise that would help them to enter a meditative state. Learners with linguistic intelligence, as well as those with visual-spatial intelligence, enjoy guided fantasies. Depending on the nature of the visualization, other intelligences such as the naturalist may also come into play. Those who like auditory experiences and imaginative learners are receptive to guided fantasies.

Storytelling

The facilitator can use a story (real or metaphorical) to generate reflection on a given topic. The following description of a Native protest, for example, could be used to stimulate a discussion on crisis management:

> In 1990 a group of Mohawk Indians erected barricades at Oka, Quebec. They blocked the road leading into an area that had been marked for development as a municipal golf course. The Natives refused to relinquish the land that had been their sacred burial grounds for many centuries. The crisis escalated in July 1990, when the Sureté du Québec sent 250 members of a SWAT team to disperse the Mohawk Warriors. In the confusion, a police officer died in 'friendly' crossfire. Following these events, Mohawks extended their blockade onto a main highway, and Natives from a nearby reserve erected a sympathy barricade on the Mercier Bridge leading into Montreal. This second blockade fuelled the emotions of non-Native townspeople, who faced long commuting times. When several hundred members of the Royal Canadian Mounted Police arrived to assist local police, they confronted 4,000 non-Native rioters, who were throwing Molotov cocktails and burning Mohawk Warriors in effigy. Premier Robert Bourassa appealed to the federal government for military intervention.[28]

Metaphors, fables, folktales, and parables can also be used to stimulate group discussion. The following legend of the dream catcher could lead into a discussion on dreams or mythology or Native culture or any one of a number of topics:

> A long time ago, the clans of the Ojibway nation lived in a place known as Turtle Island. To ensure that the babies of the tribe enjoyed peaceful sleep, Spider Woman wove little dream catchers on the tops of their cradle boards. Bad dreams stuck in the spider-like webs, while the good dreams found their way through the openings. Each morning, with the first rays of dawn, the bad dreams died. In later years, Spider Woman found it hard to make her way to all the cradle boards. So others in the clan—the grandmothers, mothers, and sisters—began to help to weave the magical webs. They used hoops from willow trees, sinew from animals, and cords from plants to make the dream catchers. In honor of ancient traditions, they connected the web to the hoop at seven or eight points. The number 7 represents the Seven Prophecies and the number 8 represents Spider Woman's eight legs.[29]

Storytelling as a teaching strategy offers a way of reaching out to imaginative learners and to those with visual-spatial and linguistic intelligence. People who enjoy auditory experiences also like storytelling.

Gallery Exercises

Gallery exercises use pictures to stimulate discussion on a topic relevant to the theme of the presentation. Assume, for example, that you want to sensitize managers to behaviours that could be construed as sexual harassment. You could include a series of slides in your presentation that depict inappropriate behaviours. One slide could show a manager with a hand on the shoulder of a subordinate. Another slide could show a manager who has invaded the personal space of an employee by leaning over her shoulder as she sits at her desk. A short video clip could depict employee reaction to an off-colour joke by an employer or an invitation to go for drinks at a local bar. You should seek some degree of balance in showing slides and video clips on a topic such as sexual harassment. That is, attempt to show members of both sexes in uncomfortable positions. Gallery exercises appeal, in particular, to learners with visual-spatial intelligence.

Read-Arounds

Read-arounds are similar to tryouts in theatre. Participants take turns reading aloud from material provided by the group facilitators. The material used in a read-around could come from a poem, play, story, travelogue, book, or other material. Imagine that you are making a presentation on superstitious behaviours. The following material from a Japanese Web site would work well for a read-around. Proceeding around the circle or room, each person from the group reads one point. The facilitator prefaces the read-around with the following kind of statement: 'In Japan, you avoid certain actions because they bring bad luck.'

- Avoid the number 4. The number 4 is pronounced the same as *shi*, the word for *death*. Therefore, you should not give presents with four pieces. [first person in read-around]
- Avoid the number 9. The number 9 rhymes with *ku*, the word for *pain*. Some hospitals do not have fourth or ninth floors. [second person in read-around]
- Do not stick your chopsticks upright in a full rice bowl. At funerals, chopsticks are stuck into rice that is placed on the altar. [third person in read-around]
- Do not transfer food from chopstick to chopstick. This practice only occurs at funerals with the bones of the cremated body. [fourth person in read-around]
- Do not sleep towards the north because bodies, in Buddhist funerals, are laid in a northward-facing direction. [fifth person in read-around]
- If a funeral car passes, be sure to hide your thumb. [sixth person in read-around]
- If you cut your nails at night, you will not be with your parents when they die. [seventh person in read-around]
- Do not stare at anyone over your rice bowl, lest you become increasingly ugly in appearance. [eighth person in read-around]
- If you whistle in the night, a snake will come to you. [ninth person in read-around]
- You will have bad luck if you break a comb or a wooden shoe. [tenth person in read-around]
- If your ear itches, you will hear good news. [eleventh person in read-around][30]

Read-arounds appeal to the auditory learner and to the learner with linguistic intelligence.

Timelines

One kind of activity calls on participants to develop a calendar of activities. If you were making a presentation on crisis communication planning, for example, you might ask participants to construct a timeline of when things tend to go wrong in their organization. Afterwards you could discuss their examples. The timeline activity would appeal to learners with logical-mathematical intelligence.

Card Sorting

With card-sorting activities, you ask participating group members to sort and order cards in terms of priorities, time sequence, or some other organizational scheme. The cards may pertain to duties that have to be performed, the component parts of some task, or the distinguishing features of some situation. If you are making a presentation on change management, the card-sorting exercise could involve establishing the order for undertaking various change management activities. The facilitators use this information as a takeoff point for discussion. Card sorting will appeal to tactile learners, as well as logical-mathematical and linguistic learners.

Case Studies and Scenarios

Case studies describe some incident that has occurred in the past. If you are making a presentation on airport security, for example, you could develop a case study that points to inadequacies in the system. Then you ask the class to divide into small groups to review the case and to arrive at solutions to the problems. Afterwards you facilitate a discussion of the findings. Your introduction to the case study could read something like the following:

> Imagine that you have been charged with making recommendations on enhanced airport security. Review the scenario that describes what happened in several recent breaches of airport security. Then identify possible solutions to the problem. Suggest measures that could better ensure the safety of air travellers.

Organizations often develop case studies of best practices and worst practices, from which their members can draw lessons (see Box 13.2).

Box 13.2 Customer Care

Imagine that you have been asked to set up a new customer response policy at your restaurant. Review the problems associated with earlier policies. (See below list of problems identified by previous employees of the restaurant.) Design a new policy that overcomes these problems.

· Failure of employees to solicit feedback from discontented customers.

· Inability of employees to respond to negative customer feedback.
· Lack of support from supervisors, who fear admonishment.
· Response policy seen as way to punish, not reward, employees.
· No monetary incentives for employees.
· No monetary or other incentives for customers.
· Need for fast customer turnover when restaurant is busy.

Whereas case studies concern the past, scenarios offer a glimpse into a possible future. Typically, scenarios depict a situation that could occur at some future date, such as a natural disaster. They ask participants to answer the question 'What if?' What if a Category 3 hurricane hit Newfoundland? What if terrorists attacked the Toronto subway system? What if an ice storm wreaked havoc in western Quebec and eastern Ontario or a computer virus shut down air traffic control at Pearson International Airport in Toronto?

Scenarios offer participants the chance to test their response systems and practise their skills in a simulated environment, thus ensuring a faster and more effective response in an actual threat situation. Public schools conduct fire drills; emergency preparedness teams conduct simulations based on scenarios of potential future disasters. In the late 1980s, for example, the Solicitor General of Canada and federal agencies in the United States acted out a scenario that entailed terrorists overtaking a barge in the Detroit River. In the scenario, the terrorists threatened to release toxic gases into the atmosphere. The toxic gases would have affected both Detroit and Windsor residents. The two governments (Canada and the US) co-ordinated their responses to the simulated threat. A second example, often used in presentations devoted to small-group dynamics or teambuilding, follows:

> You and your companions have just survived the crash of a small plane. Both the pilot and co-pilot were killed in the crash. It is mid-January, and you are in northern Canada. The daily temperature is 25° below zero, and the night time temperature is 40° below zero. The nearest town is 20 miles away. You are all dressed in city clothes appropriate for a business meeting. Your group of survivors managed to salvage the following items: a ball of steel wool; a hunting rifle; a can of Crisco shortening; newspapers (one per person); a cigarette lighter (without fluid); an extra shirt and pants for each survivor; 20 x 20 ft. piece of heavy-duty canvas; a sectional air map made of plastic; one quart of 100-proof whisky; a compass; and family-size chocolate bars (one per person). Your task as a group is to list the above 12 items in order of importance for your survival. List the uses for each. You *must* come to agreement as a group.[31]

Both case studies and scenarios are attractive learning tools for people with logical-mathematical, linguistic, and interpersonal intelligences. The exercise itself appeals to those with logical and linguistic intelligence, whereas the small-group interaction appeals to those with interpersonal intelligence. If you include visuals (maps, photographs, etc.) with the exercise, then you can also appeal to those with visual-spatial intelligence. Tactile learners will also like dealing with objects, papers, or other tangible items.

Case studies and scenarios consume too much time for short classroom presentations; however, a three-hour presentation may be able to employ limited versions of such narratives.

Fishbowl Exercises

A fishbowl is a structured discussion, about 15 minutes in length, which allows class members to rotate between speaking and listening roles. A few participants (fish) take seats in the middle of the larger group. They discuss their views on some assigned topic, while the others listen quietly. Whenever observers are ready to join the fishbowl discussion, they signal their interest by standing at their seats. Once a speaker has finished her turn making a statement and interacting with other members of the fishbowl, she surrenders her seat to a member of the listening audience. The rotational process continues as various members join and leave the fishbowl. Speaking is restricted to the four or five people in the fishbowl at any given time.

Facilitators prepare the group for the exercise by defining any relevant terms, identifying key concepts, and asking for questions about the exercise. Handouts with terms, background information, and questions are helpful in stimulating an organized discussion. The facilitators prepare responses in advance for the large group discussion to follow the fishbowl exercise.

Sometimes facilitators divide groups along gender, occupational, ideological, or other lines to allow for the expression of minority or less popular views. The females in the group, for example, could be asked to conduct a fishbowl discussion of a topic such as division of responsibilities in the home. The males would be asked to listen, without interrupting. Once the females have finished their discussion, they would vacate their seats in the fishbowl and the males would take their places. Then the females would listen, without responding, to the male perspective. Afterwards, the facilitators (who act as note-takers in the discussions) would lead the whole group in a discussion.

Another example of an appropriate topic for a fishbowl discussion is employment equity. Members of the class could be asked to create and join groups that they believe to have experienced some form of discrimination in workplace environments. One group might form to represent the interests of women; another might create a group that reflects the interests of a linguistic minority; still another group might form to represent the views of ethnic or cultural minorities in the workplace. One by one, the members of the various groups would take their places in the fishbowl and express their points of view on the topic of equity in the workplace. The group would rely on discussion guidelines distributed by the facilitators.

Fishbowl activities hold a strong appeal for learners with linguistic, bodily-kinesthetic, and interpersonal intelligences. The activity is also compatible with a bias towards auditory learning. Because the activity requires thoughtful consideration, learners with logical-mathematical and intrapersonal intelligences would respond favourably, as well.

Role-Plays

In 1956, Benjamin Bloom identified three aspects of learning experiences: cognitive (knowledge), psychomotor (skills), and affective (beliefs).[32] Role-playing taps into the *affective* or emotional domain of learning. Role-plays are used to convey concepts related to human interactions such as doctor–patient, management–employee, and business–client. In a presentation on management theories, facilitators could ask participants to assume the role of employees in an organization with a scientific management philosophy or a human relations philosophy. In a presentation on intercultural variables in negotiation, facilitators could ask students to assume the roles of business executives from two different cultures who are trying to negotiate an agreement. With some role-plays, facilitators ask participants to model an effective behaviour, such as assertiveness, or to demonstrate an ineffective response such as aggressiveness or passivity.

Role-plays are attractive to learners with linguistic, bodily-kinesthetic, and interpersonal intelligences.

Artwork and Other Visuals

Facilitators might give finger paints to members of the audience and ask them to create individual or group paintings that illustrate their perceptions of some topic, group, philosophy, or institution. Afterwards, they lead the group in a discussion of the meanings and feelings behind their paintings. Tactile learners and those with visual-spatial, bodily-kinesthetic, and interpersonal intelligences would enjoy this activity. Most groups enjoy presentations that include the use of slides and video and film clips. When the latter are used in presentations, facilitators must limit the time given to the clips. For three-hour presentations, I suggest limiting video clips to five-minute segments. No group should use more than one five-minute video clip or several two-minute clips in a one-hour presentation.

Managing Group Dynamics

Early in the project, the group needs to set regular meeting times, establish ground rules, and allocate tasks. Ground rules for meetings typically require that members inform others if they cannot attend a meeting, arrive on time, come prepared, make constructive suggestions, and treat team members with respect. Ground rules may also set out procedures for dealing with conflict. Some groups write a contract, in which they agree to assume certain responsibilities and to meet deadlines. They may even take a group picture to accompany the signed contract, as a sign of their commitment to the team.

To facilitate the group process, course instructors can use student presentation tools such as Blackboard or WebCT. This computer software program allows students to

Photo Gill Ferguson

upload and share files and create group presentations. All group members are able to access a folder that contains the work of the members, but they cannot access the work of other groups. The software also enables instructors to establish discussion forums for exchange of ideas among group members. The discussions remain in the on-line file so that members can review comments from other group members as time allows. That is, group members are not bound by the time schedules of the other members. They can participate on their own time schedules. The instructor can also monitor the progress of the group. After the group has completed and delivered its presentation, they can allow public access to the file by transferring the information to a Web page. The software enables this transfer process.[33]

A group's success will depend on their ability to work together as a team. While division of tasks works relatively well for the research phase of a group project, members must engage in higher levels of interaction as the work progresses. Ideally, group members will take the roles for which they are best suited. Every group needs a leader, who can assign tasks and ensure that the group meets its deadlines. A person with good writing and editing skills should assume the role of editor for the entire project so that the final product has stylistic integrity. Another group member may be good at interacting with people. That person could be charged with tasks such as interviewing or making telephone calls. Someone with artistic skills could prepare the visuals for the presentation, and the individual with technological skills could prepare the PowerPoint presentation and video or film clips. Someone should be in charge of equipment and ensuring that the group has backup computer disks for the presentation. The person with the best organizational skills could take care of miscellaneous tasks such as purchasing the supplies required for the presentation, making name tags, purchasing refreshments, and locating appropriate music for break periods in the presentation.

A classical study in group dynamics classified common participant behaviours under the categories of group task roles, group building and maintenance roles, and self-centred and dysfunctional roles.[34] According to this study, group members act out one or more of these roles during the course of a group discussion. Awareness can help people to assume more positive roles in group discussions and avoid the more dysfunctional roles.

When members assume *task-oriented roles*, they act as initiators, information givers, information seekers, opinion givers, opinion seekers, elaborators, integrators, orienters, and/or energizers. *Initiators* propose new ideas, directions, and solutions. *Information givers* support their opinions with evidence, whereas *opinion givers* contribute only their personal views on a topic. *Information seekers* look for information and explanations, and *opinion seekers* ask others to provide and explain their ideas. By offering examples, stories, and explanations, *elaborators* clarify and build on ideas presented by others. *Integrators* act as synthesizers of ideas contributed by others. *Orienters* keep groups focused on goals by summarizing and clarifying group contributions at different stages in the process. *Energizers* encourage members to participate more fully in the group process.

Those acting in *maintenance* roles nurture the interpersonal relationships in groups and try to increase group cohesiveness. They act as encouragers, harmonizers, tension relievers, gatekeepers, and/or followers. The *encourager* compliments the contributions of others. The *tension reliever* uses humour to achieve a more informal and relaxed atmosphere, and the *harmonizer* mediates conflicts by proposing compromises to the group.

The *gatekeeper* uses body language and eye contact to encourage balanced participation from group members. The *follower* allows others to decide her stance on issues.

Dysfunctional roles inhibit the achievement of group goals and threaten interpersonal relationships. Members who assume the roles of blockers, aggressors, recognition seekers, 'anecdoters', distracters, dominators, confessors, and special-interest pleaders can derail a discussion or cause friction and disruption. The *blocker* complains and offers negative feedback when others try to move the discussion forward. The *aggressor* insults, criticizes, and points to the mistakes of group members. *Dominators* monopolize proceedings by interrupting or flattering others, whereas *recognition seekers* focus group attention on their own achievements. The '*anecdoter*' takes the group on side trips with irrelevant stories and personal experiences; and the *distracter* (originally labelled as *playboy/playgirl*) uses antics, jokes, and irrelevant comments to divert a group from task-oriented goals. The *confessor* talks about personal problems, revealing fears and perceived inadequacies. The *special-interest pleader* seeks favours for someone who is not present.

If every group has some members operating in maintenance roles, the group will have an easier time negotiating conflict situations. Early in the life of the group, members may want to consciously adopt certain maintenance roles. Not only in group meetings, but also on the day of presentation, the group will need to function as a team. So every group needs to conduct a dry run prior to the day of presentation, preferably in the same physical setting. Those who are responsible for technical matters such as changing slides in the PowerPoint presentation or operating lights and sound will need to co-ordinate their efforts with the presenters. Successful group presentations are team efforts. Videotaping the presentations allows the opportunity for the group members to review their performance after class hours.

Delivering the Presentation

On the day of the presentation, team members should arrive early to prepare the room, check equipment, organize their materials, and share last-minute concerns or information with team mates. Next we will consider the requirements for setting up the room, making an impression through dress, sharing responsibilities for the presentation, interacting with other team members and the audience, communicating 'outside the kite', managing the feedback process, and distributing materials.

Setting up the Room

Presenting group members should always arrive early enough to adjust for unexpected problems—microphones that do not function, missing lecture podiums, cassette players that malfunction, multimedia consoles that become like alien pieces of machinery when you need them the most, or a room in disarray. Whenever possible, the arrangement of seating should be appropriate for the type of presentation you plan to make. If you are in a setting with bolted chairs, flexibility is not possible. Nor are adjustments possible in a room with theatre seating or an auditorium. In other more flexible situations, you may be able to relocate chairs or tables into a U-shaped or more friendly arrangement. Comfortable seating is always a plus. The experts do not agree on whether windows act as a positive or negative force in presentations. People can become more easily distracted, but they are also happier in rooms with windows. Some studies show that turnover rates are much higher in physical settings that lack windows. Presenters should also check the temperature settings and ensure that doors are not locked so that late-comers can enter without major disruptions.

In an earlier chapter, we discussed the fact that intimate settings (small rooms that allow for maximum eye contact and a sense of closeness to others) work best for short presentations. If you are making a half-day or longer presentation to a group, however, you should try to arrange for a room with ample space for milling and talking, stretching, and moving about for small-group work. As a facilitator, you need sufficient space to conduct icebreakers and energizers. Sometimes group presenters are able to relocate the group to another setting more conducive to learning and conducting interactive exercises. If you do relocate to a different room, you need to announce the change and post signs to the new location for those who are not present for the announcement or who arrive late.

If the cost is not prohibitive, group members (involved in a presentation of three or more hours) might consider sharing the cost of refreshments for the break period—coffee, juice, and doughnuts or finger foods that conform to the theme of your presentation. If you are making a presentation on business etiquette in Brazil, for example, you could provide coffee and brigadeiros (a chocolate candy of Swiss origins that is common to Brazil, inexpensive, and easy to prepare). If you are making a presentation on yoga, you might provide fruit and juices or bottled water.

Making an Impression through Dress

The manner of dress will vary from one group presentation to the next. Team members often choose to dress in a more formal manner than they would normally dress. Sometimes they colour co-ordinate their dress to appear more professional, wearing the same colour of shirts, skirts, and/or slacks. The most frequent choices are colours that the students already have in their closets, such as black and white. Occasionally, students choose to wear costumes that reflect the theme of their presentation. If they are speaking on the topic of dealing with difficult customers in a restaurant setting, they might wear waiter/waitress or host/hostess type clothing. If they are talking about cross-cultural communication in a tropical setting like Hawaii, they might wear floral shirts or dresses.

Sharing Responsibilities

Group members should plan to greet their classmates as they enter the room and distribute names tags (if appropriate), a copy of the agenda, and materials required to conduct small-group exercises. Sometimes presenting groups give a copy of the PowerPoint presentation. Many groups like to establish a mood by playing background music as the audience enters the room. If the audience is scattered in a large room, presenters should suggest that they move closer to the front of the room.

The presentation itself should be a co-operative effort, with tasks distributed evenly among the group members. The mantra should be 'different but equal.' One person will act as moderator for the presentation, introducing the other members and introducing each new item on the agenda. The moderator should announce the topics to be covered by each new presenter. The same person should summarize and conclude the discussion to give a sense of continuity to the presentation.

If some members are better at interacting spontaneously with the audience, those members could facilitate question-and-answer sessions or follow-ups to exercises. Members with less ability in impromptu speaking could prepare the lecture portions of the presentation. Sometimes two group members will co-facilitate a part of the presentation, with one fielding questions and the other recording comments on the chalkboard or whiteboard. Facilitators with good interpersonal skills can move among small groups, formed to participate in exercises, to answer questions about assigned exercises, while others use the time to prepare for the next part of the presentation. When one person makes a PowerPoint presentation, an assistant should handle the console, relieving the presenter of the task of technical responsibilities—operating lights, sound, PowerPoint, and other tasks. The focus should always be on the presenter.

Interacting during the Presentation

Interaction between presenting members during the presentation conveys a feeling of co-operation and team spirit. While interruptions during lectures are not recommended, interjections from different team members during discussions or question-and-answer sessions add dynamism to the presentation. They also make the team look knowledgeable and interested and comfortable with each other. To the extent possible, uninvolved team members should avoid looking unoccupied when others are presenting. They should either be listening actively or engaged in some preparatory activity that does not distract the audience. Uninvolved members should sit (as a group) in locations that do not draw attention from the presenters. Their listening postures should convey interest in the presentation. They should not be scanning the room during the presentation or slumping in a bored posture, especially if they are within view of the audience. Speakers should also refer to presenters who came before them and note how their contribution will relate to other topics in the team presentation, including those that will come later on the agenda.

When members of the class are engaged in small-group activities, presenting team members need to circulate among the groups to be sure that they understand the exercise. Leaders will generally emerge from every small group; however, if a group seems to be struggling with an exercise, members of the presenting team should move to their aid to respond to questions and assist in organizing the group.

To ensure good group dynamics and to save class time, you should place people in groups prior to the day of the presentation. If you assign colours, numbers, or names to teams, you can include the team identities in introductory materials that you give to the class. Varying the membership of groups for different activities is a good idea. In that situation, you can present a grid or other visual that depicts the assignments.

Communicating Outside the Kite

In an earlier chapter, we noted that speakers tend to communicate in a diamond- or kite-shaped pattern, ignoring people seated in front and rear corners. So in a theatre-style or straight-row seating arrangement, speakers must take care to maintain eye contact with all of the audience, not just those who are sitting in the 'action zone'. If the audience is large, speakers can create the perception that they are communicating with everyone by catching the eye of some individuals in all parts of the room.

As in other kinds of presentations, extemporaneous delivery works best. When members are delivering a lecture, they should use the PowerPoint slides as their guide and use note cards for supplementary materials. Because PowerPoint is a relatively formal instructional tool, speakers can close some of the psychological distance that separates them from the audience by moving away from the podium. They can rely on a team member or use a remote control to change slides. See Chapter 7 for additional discussion of PowerPoint.

Earlier chapters have discussed the importance for instructors and other speakers of *immediacy* behaviours in stimulating feelings of affinity. Some of those behaviours include use of humour, vocal expressiveness, smiling, relaxed body postures, warmth, sustained eye contact, dynamism in gestures and movement, and high levels of approachability. Most studies have also found a relationship between immediacy behaviours and student learning.[35] In fact, in a review of 81 studies, researchers found a striking relationship between non-verbal immediacy and reported student learning.[36] These findings apply to multicultural classrooms, as well as more homogeneous ones.[37] They also apply to distance learning in televised situations.[38]

Managing the Feedback Process

Managing the feedback process involves knowing how to ask questions, acknowledge and respond to questions and comments, and reframe and redirect questions.

Asking Questions

When asking questions, facilitators should observe certain rules. Questions should be prepared in advance. They should be open-ended, answerable, clearly worded, significant, and thought-provoking. Rhetorical questions do not require a response, only consideration by the audience.

Questions should be *planned in advance*, and they should be *open-ended*. Open-ended questions call for unstructured responses: What are the most important issues in the debate over regulation of the Internet? How do you feel about the new gun control legislation? If I asked you to name the three most important steps that governments could take to ensure international peace, what would you say? Open-ended questions do not anticipate a response. Rather, they give people the freedom to generate their own answers, and they encourage in-depth responses. Open-ended questions can also probe to find out why a person answered in a certain way: 'What did you mean when you said that governments are invading our privacy?' 'Why did you say that the border control policies discriminate against some ethnic groups?'

Unlike open-ended questions, *closed-ended* questions ask respondents to choose from the alternatives provided. Examples of close-ended questions are multiple-choice questions and those that ask for 'yes-no' or 'agree-disagree' answers. Compared to open-ended questions, close-ended questions require little time or effort to answer. The responses, which are often 'top-of-mind', provide little information. If you do choose to ask a close-ended question, you should be prepared to follow with an open-ended probe. An example follows: Do you prefer less directive or more directive styles of leadership? (close-ended question). Why did you choose less directive? (follow-up open-ended question).

Facilitators should ask *questions that the audience can answer*. If you ask questions that are too controversial, too complicated, or too technical, you may get no response. People do not like to give politically incorrect answers, even if their belief structures vary from the accepted social norms of the day. Questions should not have multiple parts. You should not ask two-part or three-part questions such as the following: 'What do you like and dislike about the new company logo? Do you think that the logo represents the mission and mandate of the company? Why do you think people have been protesting against the new design?' If you want to ask multiple questions, you should ask the additional questions as follow-up after people respond to the first question. Alternatively, you can put the three questions on a PowerPoint slide and ask for the group to consider one point at a time. Finally, questions should not require expertise lacking in the audience. If you ask lower-level employees, for example, to respond to a question that requires management experience, they are less likely to provide an appropriate answer. In the same way, questions that call for highly technical expertise are inappropriate in some cases.

Questions should be *clearly framed*, *significant*, and *thought-provoking*. Facilitators should plan alternative ways to ask the same questions in the event that the group does not understand the original question. The questions should be significant enough to demand the consideration and time of the group. When an answer is too obvious or a concern too trivial, people will be reluctant to answer the question.

Some questions are rhetorical, intended only to provoke thought, not to get actual responses. Facilitators might ask the following question, for instance: 'Consider for a moment. What do you think could happen next if we don't change direction—if we don't stop the incremental takeover of our civil liberties? Civil liberties, once lost, can become fugitives from justice.'

Facilitators can direct questions to the entire audience or to specific individuals or subgroups. Or they can go from one to another class member in the manner of a relay. If a group has generated a response to some problem, for example, the facilitator could say the following: 'John, I know that your group has arrived at a pretty creative answer to this problem. Could you share your ideas with the group?' Group presenters must take care, however, not to embarrass people by calling on individuals who may not have an opinion or information on a topic. Usually, when people do not know the answer to a question, they will avoid the eye gaze of the interrogator. When participants close the lines of communication in this way, facilitators should look elsewhere for a respondent.

Acknowledging and Responding to Comments and Questions

Give the group time to respond to questions and do not let silence unnerve you. If you think the group has not understood your question, rephrase it. Do not continue asking the same question, using the same wording. If the same people answer every question (not uncommon), you need to find a way to involve more people. You may want to direct your eye gaze away from the persons who respond quickly and look in the direction of those who have been silent. You might need to say, 'I've received some really interesting responses from some of you, but I would like to know the opinions of others as well.' Then you catch the eye of several people who have not yet responded. If they close the communication channel by looking away, locate other respondents.

In another case, you could say: 'Jennifer has offered one perspective to us. But I would like to get at least three or four other views. I'll give you a couple of minutes to think about the question.' Some people are slower to respond to questions, because they like to give thoughtful, measured responses. If you go consistently to the first person who answers, you may miss the input from people who like to think through problems before answering. Different people have different personalities. Giving that extra time for thought can result in wider involvement among group members.

Always acknowledge the responses of those who answer a question and, whenever possible, find a way to integrate the ideas into summaries and conclusions. Rephrase the thoughts to show that you are listening and understanding. Rephrasing can also help to clarify the responses for the larger group. Try to position the idea within the framework of your discussion. If you do not understand a response, ask for clarification.

If a response reveals lack of understanding, do not put down the respondent. If you undermine the contribution of even one person in a group, others will be reluctant to offer their ideas. Audience members are often as nervous as presenting group members. They fear looking unintelligent or uninformed in front of their peers (class members or work colleagues). In work situations, they often fear that they might be overlooked for a job transfer or promotion if they seem incompetent in a group situation. For that reason, responses from some group members will be timid and tentative. Facilitators must offer encouragement and, when warranted, compliments to those who make themselves vulnerable. If responses are not on target, you can still thank the person for contributing to the discussion or acknowledge points of interest in the remark.

Often a person will raise an idea or ask a question about something that you plan to discuss later in the presentation. In that case, you might want to say: 'That's a really interesting idea, and we will be discussing it later. Perhaps you could hold comments on this point. But you've definitely raised a point of relevance to our topic. You're just a bit ahead of the rest of us.' When you do reach the point where you planned to discuss the topic, make reference back to the question and acknowledge the individual who raised the point. If you decide to respond to a question that takes the discussion off track, take the time after answering to reposition the discussion by giving a brief review of what you had covered to that point. If you do not know the answer to a question, tell the group that you will check and get back to them with the answer. If you need more time to think about the question, you can ask the person to repeat it, or you can say that you will come back to the point later in the presentation. A sample response follows: 'To be honest, I haven't given much thought to that question. But it is an interesting one, and I will get back to you before the end of the period.' You might want to write the question on the board to allow more time to consider it before responding to the person.

Notice the kind of language that one uses in facilitation. Effective facilitation is courteous, sensitive to the feelings of participants, and encouraging in tone. When you employ 'we' language as a facilitator, you assume more of the responsibility for what does not work in the presentation. Mistakes and problems become 'our' mistakes and problems—not 'your mistakes and your confused understanding'. Body language should also be supportive and encouraging. Qualifiers such as 'a bit', 'a little', and 'somewhat' soften the impact of less positive responses. If you say 'There appears to be *some* misunderstanding on this point', you have avoided saying 'You have misunderstood this point.' The first statement is less *bare*. Adding some flesh softens the impact of the statement.

Using the same example, we can note some other points about appropriate language to use in group facilitation. When you use *indirect language*, you soften the impact. If you say, for example, '*There* appears to be some confusion on this point', you have avoided saying '*You* are confused.' This kind of language serves the function of allowing those who are among the confused to 'save face'. In addition, this example illustrates a third point. If you say 'There *appears to be* some misunderstanding', you sound less dogmatic than when you say 'There *is* some misunderstanding.' While you should avoid this kind of indirect and powerless language in speeches, the language is appropriate in group facilitation, where you are encouraging audience participation and offering feedback.

Box 13.3 Tips on Using Visual Aids and Equipment

Presentation Software
· Print should be large. Don't copy from books.
· Don't put more than eight lines on a page or six words per line.
· Use upper- and lower-case instead of all capitals.
· Use dark colours (black, blue, green, red, etc.) rather than light.
· Don't overuse pictures and icons; do use enough to add interest.
· If possible, personalize by using photos of class or local scenes.
· Use short video clip (no more than 30 seconds for a short speech) to add interest to presentation.
· Explain purpose of video or audio clips prior to playing them. If there is anything objectionable in clip, mention it and explain why you chose to use it anyway.

Three-Dimensional Objects
· If you use an object, make it sufficiently large to be seen throughout classroom.
· If the object is too small to be seen, construct a model. Make a poster. Use felt or flannel shapes on the chalkboard. Use magnetic means of attaching materials.

Flip Charts
· Use flip charts to gather information.
· If you plan to use a flip chart, be sure it is available and ready to use, with sufficient paper.
· Put notes on the back of the flip chart and position yourself several feet behind the chart to deliver.
· Use the upper two-thirds of each page; restrict to five lines of no more than five words each.
· Abbreviate long words and use acronyms when possible.
· Tape charts, once torn off, to walls for easy viewing by participants.

Workbooks, Handouts, and Other Reference Materials
· Avoid passing handouts to class during a talk.
· Bind workbooks—cerlox or spiral for maximum appeal.
· Leave room on pages for people to write in workbook or on handouts.
· Ask the group not to look ahead in their workbooks.
· If you refer to a book, have a copy of the book with you to show the group.
· Include bibliographical information on sources used in lectures.
· Give transparencies and markers to groups to record responses.

Box 13.3 continued

Equipment and Lighting

· If you are using equipment, get someone to perform these tasks. The speaker should not run back and forth to VCR or audio player.
· Do the same with lighting. If lights require adjustment during presentation (on, off, or dim), assign this task to a group member. Cues should be noted in a script.
· Don't keep group in the dark for too long.
· If you use music, don't play it too loud.
· When working in a new location, be sure you have an extra extension cable for use with TVs, VCRs, overhead projectors, slide projectors, etc.

Delivery

· Know your material.
· Maintain eye contact with the group.
· With presentation software, look at projected image; don't tie yourself to podium.
· Use remote control to switch slides.
· If necessary, use note cards-not pieces of paper—for additional support.
· Arrange for someone to help you with lights and equipment.
· Avoid clutter; hide any materials that you are not using.

Reframing and Redirecting Questions

Sometimes facilitators redirect questions to the larger group. In a session on retirement planning, someone might ask about the best savings plans. The facilitator could redirect the question to the larger group: 'What are your experiences with some of the savings plans? Which ones would you recommend?' In a presentation on the increasing costs of automobile insurance, an audience member might ask for more information about specific plans. Again the facilitator could say: 'Most of you are in the same age and risk group as the person who asked the question. What do some of you pay for insurance?' At other times, you might want to redirect a question to the person who asked it: 'That is a good question. Do you have any ideas on the topic?'

Handouts and Other Supplementary Materials

Materials provided to the class should be professional in appearance. Handouts should be neatly packaged or bound, preferably with cerlox or spiral binding. As mentioned earlier, these handouts typically include the agenda, materials for group exercises, copies of the PowerPoint presentation, and references. Instead of binding the materials, some groups provide folders to each class member. If the group does not give out name tags as people enter the room, the folders may also include name tags, pens, and small favours. Whenever possible, the facilitators should give transparencies and markers to the groups to record any responses that they will share with the larger group. If flip charts are available, the groups can profit from having individual flip charts at their disposal for collecting and recording ideas. If you make reference to a book, you should have the book with you. Visual aids are highly desirable in long presentations. Box 13.3 provides tips for using visual aids, as discussed in Chapter 7 and in this chapter.

Questions for Discussion

1. Have you ever made a team presentation in a classroom or other context? What problems did your group experience, if any, in preparing and presenting? What were the strengths of your presentation? Do you prefer individual or team presentations? Why?
2. What weaknesses have you observed in team presentations by others?
3. What is the difference between teaching and learning objectives?
4. What is your preferred method of learning (auditory, visual, tactile, or kinesthetic)?
5. Multiple intelligence theory tells us that there are seven to nine pathways to learning. Which pathways work best for you?
6. What are some popular icebreakers? Some popular energizers?
7. What are some of the differences in the priorities of older adults and professionals who return to the classroom? How do their expectations about the learning experience differ from those of their younger and less experienced peers?
8. Analyze the dynamics of some small group in which you have held membership. What were the roles played by different people? Do they conform to the discussion in your text?

CHAPTER FOURTEEN

Speaking in Political and Business Contexts

Goodwill and Other Special Purpose Speeches

Preparing a Special Purpose Speech

The suggested assignment for this chapter is to prepare one of the types of political speeches described in this chapter: apologia, campaign, nomination, acceptance, concession, or condolence. Alternatively, the student may choose to present one of the following speeches, associated with the corporate or business world: sales talk, project proposal, debriefing or postmortem, or motivational speech. (The goodwill speech appears as a suggested assignment for Chapter 15 on ghostwriting.) In marking the assignment, the instructor will look for the quality of the delivery, the extent to which the speaker has conformed to the best practices in the chosen genre, and (in the case of business presentations) the best practices in computer-assisted presentations. Motivational speeches, however, do not require the use of presentation software.

Learning Objectives
- To find out about the major types of political speeches—goodwill, apologia, campaign, nomination, acceptance, concession, and condolence—and the occasions on which they are presented.
- To learn about the various types of business speeches, including goodwill speeches, sales talks, project proposals, debriefings, and motivational talks.
- To discover how to deliver a manuscript speech.

In this chapter we will look at the major categories of political and business speeches and discuss how to deliver manuscript speeches.

Political Contexts

The political speaker delivers a wide range of speeches, including campaign, goodwill, nomination, acceptance or concession, commemoration and condolence, and apologia (speeches defending one's position, often on matters of a highly personal nature).

Goodwill Speeches

The most common political speech event is the goodwill speech. As the name implies, the most obvious purpose of this type of speech is to create goodwill. Whether the position occupied is mayor, municipal councillor, member of Parliament, senator, or even Prime Minister, political figures occupy roles with expectations. An image of the role exists with some level of clarity within the minds of most Canadians. The occupant of a political role, for example, is expected to be sociable, articulate, honest, trustworthy, competent, *and* accessible. The individual must shake hands with innumerable people, respond to telephone calls, approve and sign an endless stream of correspondence, and speak on countless occasions. Whether the politicians act at the municipal, provincial, or federal level, they must meet these public expectations to stay in office. Even if based in Ottawa, federal MPs must make regular trips to their home provinces to meet the public demand for personal contact and accessibility.

The large majority of these speeches involve appearances at dedications, club banquets and awards ceremonies, and convention settings. In the months leading to an elec-

---

Box 14.1 Tips from a Professional: Briefing Your Speaker

by Juline Ranger

Especially in the political world, senior staff and political handlers often negotiate speaking invitations on behalf of their political masters; and in most cases, they inform the actual speakers, almost as an afterthought. Whether you are a press attaché, communication assistant, or media relations specialist, you must ensure that the speaker is well-briefed—not only on the contents of the speech, but also on the event. Omitting a detail as mundane as what to wear (especially for women) can have a devastating effect on the speaker and his or her state of mind prior to delivering the speech. I recall a time when my boss, a politician, showed up for work on the day of an afternoon speaking assignment wearing a golf shirt. He had to return home to change when he learned the event warranted a suit and tie. I don't

have to tell you how unimpressed he was by the 45-minute detour home to change.

Time with your speaker beforehand is crucial and often limited; so make the best of it. Speech rehearsal aside, the spokesperson counts on you to provide the following key details about the event:

· Why am I giving the speech? What is the tone of the event? The format?
· Where am I going? Is it outdoors or indoors? Am I speaking with a microphone? Podium? Will I use a data projector? Audio visuals?
· To whom am I speaking? Are they content experts? How many people will be present?
· Will my audience be hungry, sipping coffee, or waiting to eat?
· Who will introduce me?
· Am I the only speaker? If not, who else? Who speaks before me? After me?
· How much time do I have?
· Are the media invited? Will there be a photo opportunity, scrum or Q&A session?
· What should I wear?

As a communicator, you will need to be prepared for everything! I carried a special 'speaker's emergency kit' with me to events. The kit contained a hodgepodge of items such as mirror, comb/brush, breath mints, cough drops, Tylenol (or your spokesperson's medicine of choice), micro-fibre cloth for cleaning eyeglasses, Kleenex, water, antacids, sewing kit, powder makeup, and of course, an extra copy of the speech! Another helpful tip is to get your spokesperson to keep a few outfits at the office for any last-minute changes. When you are on site, don't forget to check your speaker for lipstick smudges, opened zippers, drippy noses, and other potentially embarrassing physical faux pas. Trust me, it does happen!

While textbooks emphasize the importance of lead time and rehearsing the speech with your speaker, the reality is that there are only 24 hours in a day. Whether it's a scheduled meeting a week before or five minutes in the car on the way to the event, preparation time with your spokesperson is precious. Use it wisely for best results.

Juline Ranger is Director of Communications for Cable Public Affairs Channel (CPAC). She is responsible for the promotion of the national channel to key audiences: viewers, elected officials, media, and affiliate members. She is also the General Manager of Cable in the Classroom, a national program that offers copyright-cleared, commercial-free programming to Canadian teachers as a way to enhance the learning experience for their students. In addition to her experience in the broadcast industry, Juline has worked in the field of politics and municipal affairs.

tion, as well as during the course of an election campaign, politicians may act as speakers at scores of events ranging from fundraising to dedications of buildings to commemoration of people. They appear at gatherings of the Rotary Club, the Lions Club, and an assortment of charities and volunteer organizations. They serve as keynote speakers at major business events and conferences. They do not always announce their intention in accepting these invitations, and their speeches do not always talk about their desire for re-election.

Goodwill speech-making serves three major functions. First, political figures are able to keep their names before the public without actively campaigning for office. In this way, they are also able to reach a sometimes apathetic audience, who may not read newspapers on a regular basis, join political parties, or attend events of a strictly political nature. Some of these audience members serve as opinion leaders for other constituents, who may not be present in the audience on a particular occasion but who may go to the opinion leaders at some later point to ask for impressions or advice on voting. Studies in opinion leadership confirm that the influence of opinion leaders can explain later, unexpected shifts in attitude, long after a message has had a seemingly minimal effect on an audience.[1] People often change their attitudes only after they have talked with others in whom they have confidence. Some researchers have found that the best political persuaders are our close friends and the 'small, permanent social groups' of which we are a part.[2]

Second, goodwill speech-making offers opportunities for constituents to question their representatives in government:

> If his opinion happens to coincide with that of the organized groups in his district, it is not simply because he is controlled by them. It is because he is one of them; he is a Legionnaire; he is close to the farmers and their interests; his roots are in the business class. He knows the leaders of the various organizations.[3]

A politician's goodwill speeches carry him to these people. Many legislators who claim to 'think like' the people of their regions would lose this ability if they did not stay in close personal contact with their constituencies.

Third, occasional speaking events enable politicians and their representatives to convey the major policy messages of their government and to reach the public at large. These messages reflect the strategic mission, vision, and priorities of the government or political party. Within the federal, provincial, and municipal governments, bureaucrats often act as spokespersons for politicians on matters of policy. These government officials seek to publicize their successes, respond to the critics of government policy, and talk about their plans for future undertakings. At the same time, the spokespersons are able to associate their names with reputable organizations.

To cope with the large numbers of goodwill speaking occasions, politicians and governing officials often ask communication staff members and professional speech-writers to assist in writing the speeches. (Chapter 15 discusses this 'ghost-writing' function in some depth. The chapter also discusses the tendency to recycle content in goodwill speeches.)

Many speeches of the goodwill variety will be manuscript speeches, especially those prepared by communication staff members or professional speechwriters. When delivering a manuscript speech, the speaker may bring a full sheaf of pages to the speaker's podium. For televised speeches, speakers use teleprompters. Even when speakers rely on teleprompters, however, they often choose to present the appearance of delivering a manuscript speech (see Box 14.2).

When working from talking points prepared by communication staff members (as opposed to full manuscripts), speakers use a more extemporaneous speaking style. If they want to appear more spontaneous, speakers may choose to speak without note cards. Whatever the choice of delivery styles, communication staff members often prepare politicians for appropriate responses to follow-up questions that could be asked by audience members. In organizations, they refer to these questions and answers as 'Q's and A's'.

Apologia

An apologia is a speech of defence. The genre dates from the time of Socrates, who delivered a speech in 399 BC in defence of his life. His audience consisted of 501 Athenian

---

Box 14.2 Tips for Reading from a Teleprompter

- Practise at least one time (more if possible) with the teleprompter.
- Identify any words that could pose pronunciation problems.
- Make changes in the script, as necessary, for readability.
- Speak in a conversational and energetic manner.
- Imagine that you are speaking to a live person, not the camera.
- Avoid looking at the monitor; it looks unnatural.
- Read the text from the upper third, not the bottom, of the screen.
- Avoid giving the appearance of being a rotating fan.

- When reading ahead, look for idea clusters.
- Use controlled gestures when speaking from a teleprompter.
- Use appropriate facial expressions.
- Employ pauses for attention and emphasis.
- Avoid rushing delivery; the operator will follow your speed.
- Keep your head and chin elevated; don't slouch or slump.
- Keep a glass of water close at hand.
- When you finish, look at the camera until the director yells 'cut'.

---

men, faced with deciding whether Socrates should be condemned to death or, alternatively, be feasted in the president's hall for his contributions to Greek society. In the end, the judges cast 281 votes against Socrates and 220 for him; he was put to death a month after the trial. Modern apologia, however, have more to do with survival of political careers than with survival of individuals. A number of researchers have examined the common elements in apologia involving US politicians and presidents. These studies provide us with the basic material required to understand what happens in apologia.

Accused of financial improprieties in 1952 and faced with the prospect of being dropped from the presidential ticket of Dwight Eisenhower, Richard Nixon delivered his famous 'Checkers' speech. On national television, he laid bare the details of his finances and personal life, including speaking at some length about his family's devotion to their dog Checkers. His strategy succeeded, and running on the Eisenhower ticket, he became the vice-president of the United States.

Senator Edward Kennedy delivered the next prominent apologia, in July 1969. Kennedy went on national television to explain his involvement in the events that resulted in the drowning death of Mary Jo Kopechne, a young staff member with whom he had been partying on the night of her death. On the surface, Kennedy was directing his comments to the voters in his home state of Massachusetts, asking for a mandate to continue in office. But because his audience was national, observers believed that he was also checking the pulse of the larger American public. The Democratic Party had been considering Kennedy as a potential candidate in the next presidential election. Unlike the apologia of Nixon, the address of Kennedy was only partially successful. He did receive a mandate from the Massachusetts people to continue in office, but polls demonstrated that most Americans reacted with great skepticism to the address.[4] The final measure of the apologia's success was Kennedy's failure in later years to move beyond state representation.

The second apologia delivered by Richard Nixon, at the time of Watergate, was far less successful than his 'Checkers' address. And most recently, President Bill Clinton went on national television in August 1998 to respond to allegations of misconduct with regard to his relationship with Monica Lewinsky. The public responded to the address with cynicism, even though polls indicated a lack of public support for proceeding with the case of impeachment against Clinton.

The same kind of cynicism characterized the response of many Canadians to the apologetic discourse of Svend Robinson. On 15 April 2004, the public learned that Robinson—well-known and controversial member of Parliament for the NDP for the Burnaby-Douglas riding in British Columbia at that time—had admitted stealing a $50,000 diamond ring at a public auction house. In the week following this event, he issued a statement at a nationally televised press conference, explaining and seeking to justify his actions. Robinson claimed that severe emotional distress had been the catalyst for his action. He explained that, after an unsuccessful effort to contact the owners by telephone, he had returned the jewellery to the police and given a full account of his actions. He said that he would take medical leave while he underwent psychological counselling and therapy (see Box 14.3).

Box 14.3 Apologia of Svend Robinson

For some time now, I have been suffering from severe stress and emotional pain. While continuing to undertake my responsibilities as the federal Member of Parliament for Burnaby-Douglas, and to serve my constituents with dedication and hard work, I have experienced great inner turmoil. The reasons for this are of course intensely personal, and I am not prepared to discuss them, but among others relate to the cumulative pressures of dealing with the emotional consequences of a nearly fatal hiking accident. The past few months have been particularly difficult and painful.

This accumulated stress culminated last Friday in my engaging in an act that was totally inexplicable and unthinkable. While attending a public jewellery sale, I pocketed a piece of jewellery. I did this despite knowing full well that the employees who were there recognized me and did so in a context where I had provided to them my full name and contact information in writing, and that the entire area was under electronic surveillance.

Something just snapped in this moment of utter irrationality. Immediately upon leaving the premises I realized that I must return the jewellery. Too afraid to go back, and unable to contact the owners by telephone, during the long weekend, I spent a weekend of great anguish, determined to return the jewellery at the first opportunity. On Tuesday morning, I attempted to contact the owners, and not being able to do so directly, I went to the police and gave them a full account of what I had done, and returned the jewellery to them. This matter is now in the hands of the police and Crown Counsel. My legal counsel, Clayton Ruby, has communicated with Crown Counsel and outlined the circumstances fully. I await the decision of Crown Counsel and will not seek to in any way avoid full responsibility for my actions should charges be laid in these circumstances.

I have sought and am receiving professional medical help to understand and deal with these issues. I have commenced a course of therapy with this objective, and I look forward to full healing and recovery with the excellent professional assistance I am receiving. Clearly at this painful and difficult time, while there are outstanding legal and health issues to be addressed, I must devote my full energy and time to recovery and healing.

I will therefore be taking time off for medical leave immediately. My hard-working and experienced staff will certainly continue to serve the needs of my constituents, and I will remain in close contact with them. I am also stepping down at this time as the federal New Democrat candidate for Burnaby-Douglas while these issues remain unresolved. I do this with the full support of my federal

Leader Jack Layton, my riding President, Doug Sigurdson, and my partner Max Riveron. I will be meeting in the near future with my riding executive to discuss the longer-term implications of this decision should an election be called while these issues remain outstanding.

As you can imagine this has been a nightmare. I cannot believe that it has happened, but I am human and I have failed. I have felt such a sense of privilege and honour to serve my constituents in Burnaby and indeed people across Canada, and feel an equally powerful sense of sadness that I have let them down. As I deal with this issue, I hope I will have their understanding and support.

In light of the very personal nature of this statement, and the outstanding legal issues, I will not be able to take any questions. Thank you for your understanding.

Svend J. Robinson, MP, Statement to the press,
Burnaby, BC, 15 Apr. 2004

Reprinted by permission of Svend Robinson.

What goes into a successful apologia? How do you create such a rhetorical product? After examining media apologia over a 17-year period (1981–98), James Aucoin and Melva Kearney found that the basic ingredients of successful apologia are 'sincerely admitting mistakes, showing regret for them, and correcting them because it is the right thing to do, and announcing long-term corrective actions to prevent reoccurrences.'[5] Others agree that the ability to make a personal connection with the audience is extremely important with apologia. A study of a later apologia that Clinton delivered to a White House prayer breakfast on 11 September 1998 found that a focus on the personal and the contrite in this second address accomplished far more than the attack on special prosecutor Kenneth Starr in the August apologia.[6]

Nonetheless, some studies have found that successful apologia go beyond defensive argumentation. A 1968 study of apologia delivered by Richard Nixon and former US President Harry Truman, for example, found that both men included attacks on their opponents.[7] Researcher Lawrence E. Rosenfeld also discovered that a preponderance of facts appeared in the second third of the discourses by these two men.[8] In a 1971 study of Edward Kennedy's apologia, I found that the same structural pattern prevailed, although the outcome was not so favourable for Kennedy. Source credibility appeals occurred early in the speech, followed by argumentation and reasoning. An appeal to emotion concluded the speech.[9] Karolyn Kohrs Campbell and Kathleen Jamieson, for their part, found that most political apologia end with an appeal to put aside the present concerns and to look to the future.[10] The apologist asks the audience to consider the bigger picture.

Since the structural elements were the same in the successful and unsuccessful apologia, I looked for other reasons to explain the failure of the Kennedy speech to achieve its ultimate purpose (support for Kennedy's presidential bid). Eventually I concluded that the failure of this apologia derived not from speech elements, but from characteristics of the viewing audience. American audiences had become increasingly sophisticated since the time of the Truman and Nixon addresses, and they were no longer prepared to accept discourse of the soap opera genre. They would have been as likely to laugh at Nixon's crybaby 'Checkers' speech as they were to look with cynical eyes at Kennedy's lament. The fact that Kennedy's discourse was sandwiched between Kal Kan dog food and Brut cologne commercials did not do anything to add credibility to his rhetorical efforts.[11]

The prediction that future apologists would have difficulty establishing credibility with the American public has been borne out by Nixon's Watergate *mea culpa* and the 1998 television address of Bill Clinton, proclaiming his innocence in the Monica Lewinsky affair.

Box 14.4 Media Scrums—Avoiding the 'Deer in the Headlights'

by Laura Peck

You have just emerged from a televised committee appearance on a critical issue of public importance, and feeling good about how it went, you see a crush of reporters, cameras, and technicians in front of you. A 'fight or flight' feeling in the pit of your stomach triggers a glistening sweat on your forehead and your palms start to sweat.

If you feel this way, you certainly wouldn't be alone in your feelings towards the 'media scrum' (as it is called in Canada) or the 'ambush' (the more popular American term). Thinking of the scrum in 'ambush' terms, however, may not do justice to the opportunities that a media encounter can offer.

First, the speaker must reduce the downside risk of the 'sound bite from hell,' which most people fear. How to prevent such a career-limiting opportunity? You should realize that the reporters are looking for a usable sound bite to use in 'clip city', not a detailed explanation. So give them what they came for—a seven-second sound bite that cuts to the heart of your point. Second, use the scrum to drive your messages, rather than merely letting it become a Q&A session, in which you react to all the questions without any attempt to steer the interview to what you want to say. Finally, avoid the 'deer in the headlight' look by fixing your gaze on some chosen spot during the questions—either down or at a place just slightly to one side or beyond the reporters, who are immediately in front of you. By focusing on that spot, you can gain a few seconds to think before beginning your response. That will reduce the pressure—and temptation—to blurt out a response without the time to think. When you are ready to speak, you can look more directly towards the reporter or the camera.

So, even if you never grow to love the 'scrum' or 'ambush', you can at least learn to survive the experience—and in media interviews, that is absolutely essential.

Laura Peck, Vice-President and co-founder of McLoughlin Media in 1984, has conducted thousands of communication skills programs for senior executives globally. Laura is a graduate of Dalhousie University with a BA and B.Ed. Laura also completed the Executive Leadership Program at the John F. Kennedy School of Government at Harvard University.

Campaign Speeches

Campaign speakers have a very specific purpose: to secure their own election or re-election or to promote the election of another candidate for office. As such, the key to understanding campaign speeches is the word *promises*—promises of a better future, a cleaner city, safer and more prosperous communities. The speeches tend to be ritualistic in nature, including a mix of the following ingredients: why the candidate has chosen to run for office, record of service, platform, the benefits of voting for the candidate, the qualities that separate the candidate from the other contenders for office, an expression of gratitude to supporters, and a statement of confidence in the outcome of the election. Politicians usually pursue a central theme, with supporting messages. The theme might be reducing the deficit, modernizing government, or protecting the principle of a one-tiered health-care system. (Chapter 15 provides more information on the function of themes and messages.) Those who do not have access to professional speechwriters must develop a core speech that they can shorten or lengthen to respond to the occasion.

Nomination, Acceptance, and Concession Speeches

Speeches of nomination and acceptance share many elements in common with campaign speeches. In the speech of nomination, the speaker must state the requirements for the office or post. Then the speaker relates the qualifications of the candidate to those requirements.

Whereas the speech of nomination focuses on the past accomplishments of the candidate, the speech of acceptance focuses on what the candidate will do for the organization or community in the future. The candidate should talk about his pride in representing the organization or community and his dedication to its values and principles. A speech of acceptance also includes statements of appreciation for those who have offered support—professionals and colleagues, friends, and family members.

Candidates for political office often prepare two speeches—a speech of acceptance and a speech of concession. In a speech of concession, the speaker attempts to accomplish four goals: publicly acknowledge the victory of the other person, wish the person well, thank all of her supporters, and look to the future. In looking to the future, the defeated candidate attempts to establish a positive climate within which to view the loss. Values such as generosity of spirit, co-operation, and optimism are manifested in speeches of concessions. Canadian audiences expect people to be gracious losers.

Condolence

Political figures must speak on sad, as well as happy, occasions. Presidents and prime ministers around the world take the podium when an earthquake shakes the mountains of Pakistan and India, a space shuttle plummets to Earth in flames, a tsunami washes away the lives of hundreds of thousands of people in South Asia, or a hurricane devastates Gulf states in the US South. Although the words may be ritualistic, the public expects the leaders of countries to become their voice in such moments. Like the eulogy, the words are often religious in tone, sympathetic in nature, and inspirational in quality. The speaker attempts to offer hope to the victims and their families. As with many other types of political discourse, at some point in the speech the focus shifts to the future. Sometimes the speakers talk about the importance of taking corrective measures to avoid future catastrophes. In situations involving terrorism, the political figure may promise to bring the guilty parties to justice and exact retribution.

Like federal politicians, local and provincial representatives must act as voices for their constituents when events occur at a local level. In crisis situations involving human error, such as discovery of a contaminated water supply, spokespersons will state their personal commitment to identify and work to correct the sources of the problem. Government representatives often offer support to victims in the way of human, financial, and organizational resources. Legal experts almost always vet the messages of speakers in situations where the organization may bear blame for the event.

Business Contexts

Several types of speeches are specific to business contexts, including the sales talk, project proposal, post-mortem or debriefing, motivational talk, and goodwill speech (mostly delivered by top business executives).

Sales Talks

Sales talks generally include an attention-getting device, reason to listen, details on desirable characteristics of the product or service, benefits to be accrued through purchase, responses to questions and objections, and the steps to be taken in acquiring the product or service. The inclusion of concrete details and specifics about the product is extremely important. The ability to convey enthusiasm and belief in the product is critical to completing a sale. As with all speech situations, ethical considerations should place limits on claims related to the product. No salesperson should make unrealistic or exaggerated claims about a product.

Some organizations insist that salespersons use 'canned' spiels, but most salespersons resent demands to adhere to formulaic presentations. Many years ago I taught dance for one of the national dance studios. All of the instructors were asked to use prepared materials when they interacted with clients or closed sales with customers. One of the

Photo Gill Ferguson

lines from the sales manual, intended to compliment the customer, was the following: 'You are so light and buoyant.' This line was the opposite of the reality for a large number of our clients, who took dance lessons because they were insecure about their abilities. Not only I, but also a number of other instructors, felt uncomfortable using lines that sounded so unnatural and patronizing. Commenting more on the organization's sales policies than on the abilities of our clients, another young instructor and I used to joke, 'Boy oh boy, is he buoyant!' That example typifies the response of many salespersons to the stock sales talk. They believe that a spontaneous interaction between salesperson and client is far more productive—that their own personalities should be able to surface in the interaction and that the audience for their sales pitches should govern decisions on presentation style and content. The more sophisticated the client, the more likely that the client will also recognize and resent formulaic presentations.

Box 14.5 A Question of Ethics

Is lying ever justified? Should truth be a relative commodity? Consider the following examples. *Example #1*. You are a political figure. Someone asks, 'Have you had an affair with Susie Smith?' You consider the impact of admitting the affair and the likelihood that your marriage will be destroyed. Moreover, you have never put Susie Smith on payroll or done anything to favour her with regard to your official duties as a politician. You answer, 'No, I don't know Susie Smith.' Later you go on national television and deny having had an affair. *Example #2*. Your friend asks if you like her new hairstyle. You think it is extremely unattractive, but you respond, 'Yes, it's really nice.' *Example #3*. You live in a military state. A soldier arrives at your home in the middle of the night. He demands, 'Is anyone else in the house?' You know that your brother is sleeping in the other room and he will be at risk if you say 'yes'. You respond, 'No, no one is here.'

What is the difference, if any, in these three situations? Can you suggest criteria for determining when (if ever) lying is acceptable? Should the criteria vary from situation to situation—public versus private, number of people affected, level of harm, or other?

Is omission the same thing as lying? If an audience member questions a speaker on some point and she avoids responding or answers a different question, has she behaved in an unethical way? If a persuasive speaker gives only the positive attributes of a facial cream and ignores the negative, has the person committed an unethical act? Is it reasonable to expect salespersons to talk about the weaknesses of their products? What if the product is prescription medication? Advertising rules now require that drug companies list all of the potential side effects of medications, in addition to telling about the benefits?

Do speakers have the same obligation to give complete information, even if it harms their cases? In answering that question, should we consider the potential costs of using the products in determining ethical criteria for speech-making? Alternatively, should we apply the same criteria to promotion of all products?

Despite the above cautions, most people would agree that the standard ingredients, outlined in the first paragraph of this section, should be present in most sales talks. Potential customers do not want salespersons to waste their time with a disorganized and rambling presentation. New salespersons often benefit from a 'canned' presentation, whereas more experienced salespersons are able to adapt the presentation to the client in a more convincing way.

A number of options exist in relationship to organizational formats. Speakers may, for example, order their speeches according to claims made about a product or service. In business and professional situations, some audience members must leave before the end of the presentation. Ordering the claims from most important to least important ensures that a maximum number of audience members will receive the most critical information. A second option entails presenting the strongest claims at the beginning and end of the presentation. A number of studies have shown that audiences pay the greatest attention to information that appears in the early and latter parts of a presentation.

Project Proposals

Individuals or teams may present proposals to members of an organization. The presenters may be members of the organization to whom they are delivering the talk, or they may come from outside. If employed by the organization, the presenters are often speaking to those in higher-level positions. Many such presentations aim to convince higher management to adopt a new business strategy, venture, or practice. These proposals may argue, for example, for upper management to invest more money in research and development, to involve more partners in a business venture, or to adopt a new organizational approach.

In the same situation, outside consultants or entrepreneurs may argue for the organization to use their training services, adopt a new management procedure or product to which they hold the rights, or accept an idea for an advertising strategy. Within government, proposals often take the form of argumentation briefs, where presenters ask for additional funding for projects, advocate the extension of programs, or explain the ramifications of proposed policy changes.

The presentations are typically extemporaneous in nature, where the speakers work from bullets on overhead transparencies or PowerPoint, commonly called 'decks'. Within larger organizations, communication groups often prepare the decks for management

Photo Gill Ferguson

presentations. Presenters must respect time limitations and pay attention to group dynamics. Adequate audience research can help speakers to select examples to which the group can relate, to understand the reservations that the audience may hold, and to direct extra attention to key decision-makers in the audience (opinion leaders to whom others may turn).

Knowledge of the organizational culture can be critical to the success of a presenter. In one instance, for example, a workshop presenter demanded that her audience commit themselves to specific actions. She did not understand that, in the military culture she was addressing, officers of lower rank could not commit to initiatives unapproved by their superiors. Consequently, in the question-and-answer session that followed her talk, the audience remained totally silent. No one volunteered to participate in the activities. Not understanding the situation, the speaker grew frustrated and chided the members for their lack of interest in volunteering. Her tone became patronizing and non-professional. At the conclusion of the presentation, several audience members spoke privately with the woman about the inappropriate nature of her request; but other audience members left the meeting, annoyed with a speaker who had lost all credibility in their eyes.

As noted earlier, audience members often enjoy a higher status or at least more power than the speakers. In that situation, the speaker may tend to feel more anxious than would be the case in other circumstances. As we discussed in Chapter 2, being well-prepared is the key to coping with this kind of communication anxiety. In most organizational contexts, audiences expect a highly polished presentation, which employs presentation aids such as PowerPoint and visual supports.

No one format is appropriate for all presentations of this nature. The speaker may choose to use one of the organizational formats described in an earlier chapter, such as problem-solution or motivated sequence. In the case of the problem-solution format, the speaker will present the problem, followed by a proposed solution. At that point, the speaker may talk about the benefits of adopting the solution or a plan of action for realizing the solution. If the speaker uses the motivated sequence, she will present the problem, alternative solutions, the best solution, visualization of the future with or without this solution, and an action step.

Alternatively, the speaker may describe the proposal and defend it through a series of *claims*, backed up by supporting evidence. These claims or assertions may relate to the value of the proposal or the risks that will be incurred if the organization does not adopt the proposal. The organizational format would be as follows: introduction with attention step, thesis statement, claims, and supporting details.

The *comparative advantage* approach is similar to what Thomas H. Neale calls the 'this-or-nothing' proposal. After presenting a proposal or policy option, the speaker refutes alternatives as lacking in substance or quality. He bolsters his case by comparing the strengths of his proposal with the weaknesses of other options.[12] With the *criteria satisfaction* format, the speaker presents a set of criteria by which to evaluate the proposal. Then he describes how his proposal will meet those criteria.

Debriefings or Post-Mortems

The post-mortem or the speech that debriefs offers a summary of the results of some study or undertaking of the organization. The focus on learning is a defining characteristic of this speech. What has the researcher learned from the exercise? Sometimes responsible members of the organization present these speeches. On other occasions, outside consultants deliver the results of a study commissioned by the organization. Consider the following example. The organization has asked an outside consultant to conduct a series of focus groups to determine employee experiences with customer service. At the conclusion of the study, the consultant may be expected to present the report to the management team. (Presentation requirements are often written into consulting contracts.) Alternatively, the middle or senior manager who commissioned the work may decide to present the results to the executive team. If the results are contentious, the outside consultant will often be the person to present the findings. If the results are interesting and innovative, with sufficient positive content, the organizational member will typically present the results, especially if he has made a significant contribution to the design of the study and final look of the report.

The structure of the debriefing speech will conform to that of a report. Early in the speech, the presenter will introduce the purpose of the project or undertaking, the rationale for undertaking the study, participants in the study, the procedures followed, the results achieved, and lessons learned. The speaker may conclude the presentation with a discussion of an appropriate organizational response to the findings. These reports will often take the form of a PowerPoint presentation, where the speaker delivers in an extemporaneous fashion. A question-and-answer session may engage a number of people, including those who commissioned the study and other research team members. The consultant will rarely be the only person who defends the study or responds to questions.

Motivational Talks

Motivational speakers play an important role in the business world. Their speaking engagements range from corporate training environments to engagements on cruise ships. Colleges, convention planners, non-profit organizations, and trade shows hire motivational speakers. Corporations enlist motivational speakers to prepare employees for structural changes, mergers, and acquisitions. When you go to the Web sites of motivational speakers, you will find the following topics among their repertoire of offerings: creative problem-solving, goal-setting, change management, time management, customer satisfaction, team-building, stress management, and diversity training. Most motivational speakers choose a 'niche' area upon which to concentrate their marketing efforts. Their speech topics relate to this niche market. When motivational speakers have management and leadership training and experience, for example, they often select topics such as leadership and motivation as their niches.

Motivational speakers use some standard ploys when developing their speeches. They rely heavily on stories, parables, and personal experiences that carry a moral. They focus on lessons learned from their experiences and the positive aspects of seemingly negative experiences. They define ambiguous and abstract terms such as *love*, *dedication*, *commitment*, *work ethic*, and *success* in terms of these experiences. Many motivational speeches conclude by asking the audience to take specified actions and to visualize the kind of future that will materialize from these actions.

Most successful motivational speakers have a grab bag of activities designed to get the audience on their feet and participating in the presentations—singing, dancing, and interacting with each other. Many (but not all) popular motivational speakers also rely heavily on gimmicks. They engage in highly theatrical performances, rarely staying for any length of time behind the speaker's podium. They pace the floor, join the audience in activities, and act as cheerleaders. The audience often feels 'charged' after they leave such a presentation, but the effects may be extremely short term. Asked the following week about what was said, the audience members may recall a story or two.

Outside of business settings, the most common motivational speeches dwell on personal relationships, fulfillment of personal goals, and financial gain. The latter tend to focus on the materialistic, offering ways to achieve an easy fortune, success in the stock market, or upward mobility in the organization. The speeches that address personal relationships and goals may leave the audience with an inspired thought, a story, or a moral that they carry with them for a week. As stories proliferate on the Internet, it becomes increasingly difficult for the motivational speaker to offer original content.

Many 'retired' athletes and politicians also earn large incomes as motivational speakers. The Canadian Olympic Committee has established a national speakers' bureau called the Olympic Voice, which co-ordinates requests for motivational and keynote speakers. The names of about 3,300 Canadian Olympians appear on the current list, including two-time Olympic gold medallist Catriona Le May Doan (speed skating), two-time Olympic medallist Mathieu Turcotte (speed skating), and Olympic bronze medallist Deidra Dionne (freestyle skiing).

Like evangelists, motivational speakers spread a sort of gospel; and many sound like preachers, both in content and cadence of delivery. Some audience members react negatively to this style of delivery, as well as to the overall concept of sermons delivered in lay settings. Some also react negatively to requests to participate in activities that make them feel foolish. The most credible motivational speakers have earned a reputation by performing altruistic deeds or contributing to society in some fashion beyond the rhetorical. This person might have overcome significant physical challenges to achieve personal goals, worked as an advocate for social justice causes, worked with a group like Doctors without Borders to help impoverished children in developing countries, or made some significant contribution to world peace. We are inspired by the person. When we listen to the person speak, we know that the words are not empty shells. These are the motivational speakers who command the greatest respect from audiences.

When preparing to advertise your work as a motivational speaker, you need to create a portfolio with the following materials: letter of introduction with contact information and Web site, resumé of qualifications and prior experience, photograph (optional), quotations or letters from satisfied clients, sample speech topics, rates, and business card. In addition to sending materials through the post, you can telephone, fax, or e-mail potential clients. Speakers' bureaus often help motivational speakers to locate job opportunities. Most motivational speakers also do extensive networking, gain visibility by presenting some unpaid speeches to community organizations, offer communication training services, arrange media interviews, and contribute articles to community and local newspapers.

Goodwill Speeches

Like politicians and bureaucrats, CEOs deliver goodwill speeches in which they attempt to publicize the mission, mandate, and messages of their organization. Local businesses are able to show their commitment to the community by appearing at major gatherings and events. Within the larger corporate world, the goodwill speech often takes the form of a keynote address, delivered by senior management or executive officers, to a convention or association meeting. At other times, the organizational representatives speak to community organizations about sponsored events or contributions. Sometimes they present awards on behalf of their organizations. More specific details on goodwill speaking appear in Chapter 15 on ghostwriting, and additional advice on award presentations appears in Chapter 12.

Delivering the Manuscript Speech

The following advice applies to anyone delivering a manuscript speech, whether written by oneself or by a ghost writer.

When delivering from a manuscript, the speaker should place a folder containing the papers on the podium. She should open the folder before beginning to speak. The podium should be high enough to allow the speaker to maintain an erect head as she reads the words, but low enough to allow the audience to see her face. She slides the papers from one side of the folder to the other as she progresses through the speech. If the speaker chooses not to use a podium, she should hold the folder (containing the manuscript) with one hand, somewhat above waist level.

Whichever approach (podium or free-standing delivery) is selected, the speaker should assume a posture that enables her to maintain eye contact with the audience. She should lower her eyes, not her head, as she scans the manuscript for meaning. She should decide, in advance, the points at which she will want to refer to the manuscript. No ghostwriter can identify those points for the speaker. Adequate practice enables a speaker to refer less often to the manuscript. A general rule of thumb is that a speaker should be able to look at her audience at least 80 per cent of the time. In other words, she should have eye contact with the audience for eight minutes of a 10-minute speech.

In reading the manuscript speech, speakers should look for thought clusters—focusing on meaning and ideas rather than individual words. Some pauses will be shorter and others longer. Prior marking of the manuscript (see Chapter 15) will tell the speaker *where* to pause, but, in my experience, will rarely tell the speaker *how long* to pause. So speakers should adhere to the following advice when delivering the manuscript. Pause briefly when ideas in different word clusters are linked to each other. Take a longer pause after an introduction, the conclusion of a major thought sequence, and when you want to achieve dramatic effect.

The goal of all manuscript speaking is to sound as if you are engaged in direct conversation. The speaker needs to be keenly aware of what she is saying and to be very much 'in the moment', cognizant of the audience and their reactions to the speech. Adding spontaneous introductory comments that give the impression of immediate engagement is often appropriate. Speakers should build the feeling that they are talking with this audience at this time. Using pauses effectively helps to transmit the impression of spontaneity. Moving too rapidly through material gives the impression of reading the speech. By speaking too fast, less skilful readers almost always give their audience little time to react to thoughts. The only real formula for delivering an excellent manuscript speech, however, involves practising the speech multiple times and visualizing oneself in the situation of actual delivery.

Speakers often make last-minute changes to manuscripts written by others. In that situation, the person delivering the speech should review the manuscript sufficiently in advance to ask for typewritten changes. Last-minute changes entered between the lines or in the margins can clutter the manuscript to the point that the text becomes unreadable. Speakers should also avoid crossing out words. The exception to this rule involves the addition of impromptu references to the audience, occasion, or context that may not have been known at the time of writing the speech.

Conclusion

The above discussion on speech-making within political and business contexts is not exhaustive. Politicians, bureaucrats, and representatives of business and non-profit organizations speak in a multitude of environments. They promote charities, engage in civic activities, and argue for causes. They speak at conferences, and sometimes they defend their organizations before parliamentary committees of inquiry. They are active participants in their communities, where they gain visibility on speakers' platforms. This chapter has sought to offer examples of some of the most common speech purposes, but the illustrations do not represent the full continuum of speech-making performed by these community members and leaders.

Questions for Discussion

1. A successful apologia wins back the trust of the public. Describe the characteristics of an apologia that would accomplish this end.
2. Suggest some common venues for goodwill speaking in your community. Which organizations tend to host these events?
3. What does the term *sales talk* call to mind? A formal presentation in an organization? A door-to-door salesperson? Someone selling you a television in a department store? Does the format of sales talks vary greatly from one situation to another, or only the style of delivery?

CHAPTER FIFTEEN

Professional Speechwriting

SUGGESTED ASSIGNMENT

Preparing a Ghost-written Speech

Prepare a 10-minute goodwill speech for delivery as a manu- script speech. Identify a second party (local politician, corpo- rate executive, or bureaucrat) who would be interested in a free speech by a novice writer. A member of the organization, charged with speechwriting tasks, should be willing to hold at least one meeting with the writer and to offer feedback at the end of the process. Writers should apply the principles learned in this chapter to their speechwriting efforts. They should also prepare the manuscript for delivery, using the guidelines pre- scribed in this chapter. In evaluating this assignment, instruc- tors should consider the extent to which the writer has adapted the speech to the audience and the occasion, conveyed the messages of the organization, and made appropriate choices in the use of humour (if applicable). The instructor will also assess the speechwriter on the preparation of the manuscript for delivery.

Learning Objectives
- To learn about the steps required to produce a ghost-written speech.
- To understand the techniques for preparing a manuscript for delivery.
- To discover the importance of relinquishing ownership.
- To find out how to evaluate your efforts as a speechwriter.
- To learn about finding work as a speechwriter.
- To gain an appreciation of the debate over the ethics of ghost-writing.

Because of the multitude of occasions at which politicians, bureaucrats, and CEOs must speak, they often call upon professional speechwriters and staff members to write speeches on their behalf. Ghost-writing occurs equally frequently within politics and business in Canada. Canadian legislatures sponsor parliamentary internship programs that engage young Canadian scholars in tasks such as speechwriting, among other duties. Assigned to individual members of Parliament, 10 interns serve each year as spe- cial assistants in the House of Commons. Four provinces have similar programs.[1] Fed- eral and provincial governments employ professional communicators whose duties include the preparation of speech manuscripts. Within government, these communica-

tion staff members serve whatever government is in power—Liberal, Conservative, or other.

Although ministers' offices have the final say on all speeches, they rarely produce the initial drafts of the speeches. The communication officers have this responsibility. They, in turn, contract out many of the speeches to freelance speechwriters. A large number of outside contractors perform these services for government officials. Although few government offices would go to the Yellow Pages or the Internet to select a speechwriter, advertisements abound on these media.

At one point in time, these speechwriters were anonymous, unknown to the public. In fact, their anonymity resulted in their being titled *ghost writers*. For many years, politicians protected the names of their speechwriters, concerned that they could appear less sincere if the public knew for certain that someone else was putting the words in their mouths. As late as 1952, for example, US presidential candidate Adlai Stevenson worried about admitting that he hired speechwriters. On one occasion, Stevenson restricted speechwriter John Kenneth Galbraith to his hotel room for an entire day before allowing the noted economist to emerge and join Arthur M. Schlesinger Jr as a visible member of his team of advisers.[2]

This chapter will examine (1) steps in producing a ghost-written speech, (2) techniques for preparing a manuscript for delivery, (3) the importance of relinquishing ownership of the speech, (4) evaluating your efforts, (5) getting work as a speechwriter, and (5) the debate over the ethics of ghost-writing.

Steps in Producing a Ghost-written Speech

As noted in Chapter 14, the large majority of speeches delivered by government and business leaders fall into the category of goodwill speeches, those speeches that allow the speakers to build rapport with the audience and transmit the strategic messages of the organization. In a guide prepared for the US Congress, Thomas H. Neale described the role of the goodwill speech in the following way:

> [These] speeches may be solemn in nature, such as a Memorial Day address or celebratory, at the opening of a new school, library, or child-care facility. They remind citizens of their joint identity as members of a community; these events, seemingly everyday, or even trite, are actually vital expressions of civic life. The Member's role as a community leader and spokesperson on these occasions should not be underestimated; it is a great honour for him or her to deliver remarks at these community rites; and a congressional speechwriter should devote talent and originality to them.[3]

The work of crafting the speech involves gathering background materials, structuring and developing the speech, recycling content, and making choices on language.

Gathering Background Materials

If the speechwriter is not a member of the organization, the person will usually meet with some organizational member (often a staff assistant, press secretary, or communication officer) to discuss the requirements for the speech. Within the Canadian government, speechwriting is a function of the communication group; however, as noted earlier, lack of time often means that communication directors consign the work to outside contractors. Even so, the communication representative will oversee the development of the speech by setting up meetings with staff members, providing background material, responding to questions from the speechwriter, setting deadlines for speech drafts, circulating the drafts for comments from relevant policy executives, and editing and approving the final product.

Background material, usually acquired from the organization, will include information on the speaker and the organization, speech purpose, occasion, audience, and messages to be conveyed.

Researching the Speaker and the Organization

If you are not personally acquainted with the person for whom you are writing the speech, your job will be much more difficult. You can, however, take steps to learn more about the speaker. Ask to meet and interview the person. If the speaker is not available to you, interview other individuals within the organization who have an intimate knowledge of the speaker. Ask for a biographical statement on the speaker if one is not available on the organization's Web site. Most politicians will have these kinds of statements. If they do not, their chiefs of staff or other close associates will have the information. Does the organization have a videotape of an earlier speaking engagement? Transcripts of what the person has said on the topic in radio or television interviews?

Gather information on the speaker's background—where the person was raised and has resided, cultural and travel experiences, knowledge of languages, education, and family. The best speakers will often make references to their own background and experiences as a means of identifying and cultivating a relationship with their audiences. If you are writing the speech, you should be able to draw on the background of the speaker to add colour to the speech and to personalize it.

Learn as much as you can about the person's attitude towards speaking—stylistic preferences, commonplaces that the person likes to use in speeches (for example, references to certain experiences or affiliations), and words that he or she might have difficulty pronouncing. Attend a press conference or other occasion where the speaker is interacting with a group. Note patterns of speech and preferred expressions. Review press clippings on the speaker to learn more about the person and audience reactions to previous speaking experiences.

Ask for copies of previous speeches that the speaker felt comfortable giving. Study the speeches for content, style, and other cues to understanding the speaker. If you do not meet the speaker in person, these speeches will be especially valuable in identifying the linguistic style preferred by the speaker. On some occasions I was told, for example, 'This is a speech that the person liked.' Organizations often tell speechwriters to use excerpts from the speeches or to use the speeches as models. Again, you can find examples of speeches on the Web sites of many organizations. Many speakers discard speeches that do not fit their style and personality. This action may have nothing to do with the inherent quality of the speech, but it may have everything to do with the fact that the person writing the speech was a stranger to the person delivering it. Box 15.1 reviews what you should do in researching the speaker.

Box 15.1 Researching the Speaker

· Ask to meet and interview the speaker.
· If the speaker is not available, interview close associates.
· Request copies of previous speeches.

· Attend a speech or press conference.
· Ask for a biographical statement.
· Locate information on the Internet and in newspapers and other media—bio, speeches, and articles.

You also need to know as much as possible about the organization. The mission, mandate, and priorities of most organizations—as well as current and archived press releases—are available on the Web. The strategic plans of many public institutions appear on their Web sites. The communication plans (in which messages appear), however, are not usually available. Speechwriters must request those documents from organizational representatives.

Researching the Speech Purpose

Find out what motivated the speaker to accept this particular occasion. What does he/she wish to accomplish with the speech? The best way to think of purpose is to think of the *response* that the speaker wants from the audience. What does the speaker want the audience to think, to understand, to say, to feel, to know, to value, to dislike?

The three most commonly acknowledged purposes of speeches follow: (1) to inform (increase the knowledge or awareness of the audience on a particular topic), (2) to persuade (reinforce or change opinions and attitudes held by the audience or to encourage the audience to think, believe, feel, or act in a certain way), (3) to entertain (amuse or give pleasure, with no particular concern that the audience learn a great deal or adopt a definite attitude or belief), and (4) to inspire (encourage the audience to set lofty goals).

The most common speech crafted for government officials and CEOs will 'look like' a speech to inform. The ostensible purpose of the speech will be to tell the audience what the organization is doing in the way of programs, services, and research. The unspoken purposes of the speech will be to create goodwill, to leave a favourable impression of the speaker and his/her organization, and to transmit the strategic messages and themes of the organization. The speaker will probably be seeking support not only for himself as an individual but also for the organization. The person who made the initial contact will probably be able to respond to your questions on purposes of the speech.

Researching the Occasion

Occasion governs the content and style of a speech. Remembrance Day calls for serious and sombre speeches, which dwell on themes of 'commemoration, service, and sacrifice'.[4] Similar speeches are presented on the anniversaries of tragedies (the Montreal massacre, the Swissair plane crash just off the coast of Nova Scotia) and important or costly battles (the Dieppe Raid of 19 August 1942). Other occasions call for motivational or informative speeches.

Every occasion is unique. The physical environment can place constraints on the speaker or can contribute to the ability of the speaker to achieve his or her purposes. Settings can also diminish or enhance the status of the speaker. As a means of adaptation, speakers will often make references to the region, city, or building in which they are speaking. This is especially the case if the building has historical or other significance. Sometimes a speaker is dedicating a building or participating in opening ceremonies. As a speechwriter, you should learn as much as possible about where the speaker will be delivering the speech.

Some useful questions to ask are the following:

- Is the occasion formal or informal? Just as speakers wear different types of clothing for different speaking occasions, they will use a different kind of language for different occasions.
- Are you writing a keynote speech? Or are you preparing a panel presentation for the speaker, a situation where different individuals address different aspects of a topic? Again, the style and content of speeches will vary, depending on the answers to these questions.
- Will someone else introduce your speaker? If so, he/she may need to acknowledge the introductory comments.
- Will your speaker be the only speaker? If not, how many other speakers are involved in the event? In the event of multiple speakers, will your speaker begin or end the session? What time of the day will the speech be delivered? Will the speech precede or follow a dinner? What are the time limits for the speeches? The attention span of audiences will vary from the first to the last speaker, from the beginning to the end of the day, and before and after dinner. Audiences become restless when speakers exceed their time limits, and the last speakers pay for failure of the first speakers to observe time requirements. Humour or other strong attention-getting devices may be critical if your speaker is coming later on the agenda.

- Who will precede and follow your speaker? If your speaker comes after other prominent speakers, you may wish to insert references to the earlier speeches. If the other speakers come from the same organization, you may want to find out what they are saying to avoid overlap and repetition. Try to complement rather than reiterate what other speakers have said. Work with the other speechwriters to negotiate content areas.
- Has a period been set aside for questions during or after the speech? Additional briefing notes may be necessary if questions are expected.
- Will the speech be televised? If so, who will be the first audience—the live audience or the television audience? References to the immediate occasion and audience may be inappropriate in some situations. Language style and content may have to change if the speech is to be broadcast.

Most of the time, event or conference organizers will give specific instructions on time requirements for speaking; the decision regarding the length of the speech will not reside with the speaker. The more prestigious the speaker, however, the higher the level of control. Event planners may suggest a time, but they are likely to be flexible if a high-status speaker asks for more or less time. In the latter case, it can be useful to the ghost writer to understand the expectations of audiences. Whatever time is allotted, you may decide to adjust the length of the speech to accommodate the realities of audience attention spans. According to the congressional speechwriting guide (and my own experience), few speeches exceed 20 minutes in length in today's environment.[5] The appropriate time for speaking at many events ranges from five to 10 minutes.

Researching the Audience

The ultimate success of a speaker will depend, at least in part, on his/her ability to achieve empathy with the audience—that is, to be able to project himself or herself into the position of the other person. To achieve empathy, a speaker must be familiar with the audience and their situation.

Factors such as age, gender, ethnicity, education and income level, occupation, and regional and political affiliations influence the receptivity of the audience to the message. What is their level of knowledge on the topic under discussion? Will the audience know a great deal or little about the topic? What are their affiliations in terms of associations and reference groups? What are their religious, economic, and political biases? What beliefs, attitudes, and values bring this audience together as a group? Does the audience meet on a regular basis, or will they be gathering for a special occasion? Will the audience perceive your speaker as an insider or an outsider? What is the anticipated size of the group? What are their goals and purposes in attending the meeting? Will they consider the topic to be important and relevant to their special needs and preoccupations or peripheral and inconsequential? Will audience members be friendly, interested, hostile, or apathetic? What are possible sensitivities of this audience? Should the speaker avoid some subjects or take particular care in wording some parts of the speech? How open is the audience to change? Research can provide you with the answer to many of these questions.

Speechwriters must tailor their messages to take these and other variables into account. Knowing whether the speech will be delivered to members of a large heterogeneous audience, a small group of business leaders or municipal officials, a seniors' organization, or an activist group is very important. The references and examples must be appropriate to the audience. More knowledgeable publics require less explanation than less knowledgeable publics. You can use professional jargon with specialists that you cannot use with the lay public. Educated listeners look for balanced presentations, where the speaker acknowledges more than one point of view on controversial topics. Apathetic audiences will not listen unless you give them a reason to listen. You must stress the take-away value of the speech. If the audience sees the speaker as an insider, you can employ humour that would be inappropriate if the person is perceived as an outsider. When viewed as an outsider, the speaker must point to areas of commonality—shared experiences, values, and/or acquaintances. Where audiences know each other in advance, the atmosphere is likely to be warmer and more social. Speakers can use that kind of climate to their benefit.

To obtain information of this nature, speechwriters need to make direct contact with the host organization or request the information from the organization that commissioned the speech. Local ridings can obtain this information for political speeches. In government, ministers' offices have a wealth of information on grassroots organizations. Many voluntary groups, professional associations, and charitable organizations have Web sites.

Identifying the Strategic Messages of the Organization

Does the organization want to highlight some areas more than others? Do they want to give an overview of activities undertaken in recent weeks or months? Or do they simply have several messages that they want to convey? Most speeches have a central overriding theme, as well as a series of organizational 'messages', that speechwriters build into the speech. Higher-level executives or bureaucrats agree on the messages prior to giving them to speechwriters and public relations specialists. In the case of government, the messages must reflect the actual policies and directions of government. Otherwise, the government will be held accountable for not fulfilling its promises. Businesses can also lose credibility if they make promises that they cannot fulfill or do not want to fulfill.

In my experience, ghost writers do not conduct a great deal of original research in preparing speeches for government. Typically, communication and political staff prepare a package of material for use by the speechwriter. Governments employ large numbers of people in policy areas who do nothing but research the issues of the organization. The demand for original research is greater, however, in corporate and business environments.

When asked to conduct original research, speechwriters increase their fees significantly to accommodate the increased time demands. Most other kinds of supporting materials, such as collections of quotations, encyclopedias, and dictionaries, are available on-line, although professional speechwriters will also have their own small reference collections. Box 15.2 lists a number of on-line resources for speechwriters. Useful books of quotations include *Colombo's All Time Great Canadian Quotations* (Toronto: Stoddart, 1994), *The Dictionary of Canadian Quotations & Phrases*, revised and enlarged edition (Toronto: McClelland & Stewart, 1979), and *Dictionary of Political Quotations*, by Lewis D. Eigen, Lewis D. Siegel, and Jonathan P. Siegel (London: Hale Ltd, 1994). Undertaking research can be far more time-consuming than writing the speech.

Box 15.2   On-line Resources for Speechwriters

Periodicals and professional publications for speechwriters: www.executive-speaker.com/res_peri.html

> Resources for speechwriters, including references to such publications as *Executive Speeches* and *Canadian Speeches: A National Forum of Diverse Views*.

On Speechwriting: www.thespeechwriter.com/

> Free Internet newsletter with tips on speechwriting.

TheSpeechWriters.com: http://thespeechwriters.com/

> Web site of Canadian speechwriter Garrett Patterson, with tips on professional speechwriting.

The Executive Speaker: www.executive-speaker.com/lib_spch.html

> Resources for speechwriters.

Speechwriting tools: www.gov.mb.ca/chc/leg-lib/vrd/speech.html

> On-line resources for speechwriters.

Washington Speechwriters Roundtable: www.washingtonspeechwriters.com/

> Articles and exchanges about speechwriting experiences.

SpeechTips.Com: www.speechtips.com/

> Guide to speechwriting and delivery.

Dave's Guide to Speechwriting: http://davegustafson.com/speech/

> Tips on writing a variety of special occasion and other speeches, as well as PowerPoint presentations.

Public speaking and communications resources: www.danieljanssen.com/MainPagePublicSpeaking CommunicationResources.shtml

> Tips for speechwriting, sample speeches, and links to other resources.

Structuring and Developing the Goodwill Speech

Thomas H. Neale explained the importance of preparing an initial outline for speeches, striving to maintain a central theme throughout the speech, and having a clear three-part structure (introduction, body, and conclusion). He urges speechwriters to save these outlines for future reference.[6]

Like other kinds of speeches, goodwill speeches require clear thesis and purpose statements. The thesis statement reveals the dominant theme of the speech, and the purpose statement usually has an informative component. A statement of structural progression should introduce the main points to be covered in the speech. Within the first minute or two of the speech, for example, the audience should know the organizational scheme of the speech.

Most goodwill speeches begin with a fairly predictable opening. The speaker mentions the names of specific individuals who hold a place of status within the group or who have contributed to the planning of the event. Remarks by former Prime Minister Brian Mulroney at the signing ceremony for the Saskatchewan Treaty Land Entitlement Agreement in 1992 illustrate this technique:

> There are many whose names should be on the honour roll. But the first should be that of Chief Roland Crowe, President of the Federation of Saskatchewan Indian

Nations. Chief Crowe was instrumental in setting up the treaty commission; without his dedication and perseverance, we would not be here today. I would also like to recognize the work of his vice-chief, Dan Bellegarde. Special congratulations and gratitude must also go to Cliff Wright, a highly respected former mayor of Saskatoon, who as treaty commissioner for Saskatchewan, developed the concepts and formulae which form the basis for this agreement. I would like to salute the three negotiators who developed the agreement—Lloyd Barber of the Federation of Saskatchewan Indian Nations; Al Gross, the federal negotiator; and Ron Hewitt, the negotiator for the province of Saskatchewan.[7]

Any attempts at humour will appear early in the goodwill speech, along with other attention strategies that the speaker may choose to use such as stories, parables, or personal instances.

The strategic messages typically govern the organization of business and political speeches. If a politician speaks to an audience of poultry farmers, for example, the theme of the speech might be government actions to control the avian flu virus. The supporting messages might be the following: (1) My government is undertaking research to find a vaccine capable of immunizing humans against the avian flu. (2) The depopulation of birds in the western provinces will help to control the spread of avian flu. (3) Measures will be put in place to test immigrants from affected countries if the virus continues to spread among humans. (4) The government is offering subsidies to poultry farmers affected by the controls that have been put in place in western Canada.

If the politician speaks to an audience of educators, he might talk about what the government is doing in the area of educational reform. In that case, the major messages could be the following: (1) Educational reform is long overdue. (2) Educational reform implies finding new and better ways to provide quality education to our youth. (3) Educational reform does not imply throwing more money at an outdated system. (4) This government is committed to supporting the provinces in their efforts to undertake meaningful reform. (5) In partnership with the provinces and institutions of higher learning, the federal government is supporting a number of research initiatives, designed to assist in finding solutions to the challenges faced by higher education institutions across Canada.

On a topic such as mad cow disease, the messages of the Canadian Food Inspection Agency could be the following: (1) The government has implemented procedures to spot check feed supplies in affected regions of Canada. (2) The threat to human life posed by BSE is much less serious than originally perceived. (3) The government is working to open the US–Canada border to beef exports.

The messages for a fitness club might be the following: (1) Our equipment is state of the art. (2) Our club provides affordable rates to its members. (3) The cost of annual membership is less than the cost of staying home from work for one minor illness. (4) We are a certified member of the Fitness Clubs of Canada.

When politicians, bureaucrats, and CEOs deliver goodwill speeches, they always talk about what they are doing to help their constituencies and stakeholders and to meet the challenges they confront. Business and corporate leaders stress the positive aspects of their environment—their innovations, growing client base, competitive edge, and/or commitment to customers and employees or the community. In a goodwill speech, messages focus on accomplishments, not failures, and speakers stress their efforts to achieve solutions to problems.

As discussed above, goodwill speeches have an organizational structure different from that of other kinds of speeches. Speechwriters will be wise to put the most important messages of the speech early. In the event of time overruns by other presenters, the speaker may decide (or be confronted with the need) at the last minute to shorten the speech. Speakers should avoid trying to cover too much territory. Audiences will be bored by speeches that are too broad and general in focus. The speechwriter should narrow the focus to allow more specificity and concreteness in the development of the topic. Instead of writing about economic trends in the new century, the speechwriter could focus on the buying patterns of older people or the trend towards private investments by young people.

Obviously, the time available for speaking will influence the amount of content you can include in the speech. Speaker variables will also influence the length of a manuscript. Different people speak at different rates. When engaged in ghost-writing for politicians and bureaucrats, I found that most speakers take two minutes to cover one typewritten page, double-spaced, 12 point Times New Roman font (i.e., approximately 250 words). That calculation translates into an average of 125 words per minute. Studies have found, however, that speaker rate can vary considerably, ranging up to 180 words or more per minute.[8] We speak more slowly when we deliver a speech in a second or third language. We speak faster when we are nervous. Some cultures are more ponderous in their speaking rhythms. Sometimes speechwriters may have to prepare shorter or longer speeches for the allocated time slot, depending on the personality, culture, and language of the client who will be delivering the speech. The writer must assume that a slower speech rate will translate into less content.

The conclusion of a goodwill speech has familiar elements—usually a summary statement, a challenge or request for support, or an inspirational thought. The speaker might conclude with a quotation, poem, story, or some other memorable idea.

Recycling Content

Politicians and executives with frequent speaking engagements tend to recycle content, using commonplaces that appear in multiple speeches. Since the messages of some organizations remain relatively constant, this recycling of content makes sense. If you write a speech for a politician or executive, the person may ask you to use excerpts from favourite passages in other speeches. Veteran speechwriter Frederick J.O. Blachly recounted one of his experiences with this kind of recyling:

> When Thomas W. Wilson . . . and I were working for Averell Harriman, in the Executive Office of the President, we were asked to prepare a speech. We did. He gave the speech, not once, but over and over again. No matter what the occasion, or what the audience, he gave the same speech. However, since Harriman's usual style of delivery was a barely audible mumble, perhaps it didn't make any difference.[9]

Arthur M. Schlesinger Jr—speechwriter and special assistant to President John F. Kennedy—explained that people used to prepare different speeches for different occasions. However, over time, presidents (and others) began to give the same speech over and over again.[10] Given the number of speeches that must be presented in a year by members of Parliament, cabinet ministers, and some CEOs, this practice should not be surprising. Ironically, the issues of plagiarism that plague university students do not apply in the context of professional speechwriting. If you pay for a speech, you typically acquire the rights to use that speech in whatever circumstances you wish—for that occasion or future occasions.

Despite this tendency to be most comfortable with commonplaces (favourite passages used in multiple speeches), speakers usually want their writers to tailor the speech (at least to some extent) to specific audiences and occasions. So humour, acknowledgements, and linguistic style may vary even when the main body of the speech remains constant. The more important the speaking event, the higher the level of customization. Also, the more important the speaking event, the more people will look at the speech and the higher the likelihood that the speaker himself or herself will take a personal interest in the final speech product. Organizations with larger communication budgets will often invest more in original speeches than smaller organizations with smaller budgets. Most presentations will have some elements of uniqueness, but the amount of original material will vary from presentation to presentation.

Making Choices on Language

In making choices on language, you must consider the speaker, the audience, and the occasion.

Speaker

The words should sound natural for the person for whom you are penning the speech. As mentioned earlier, you should study speeches given on earlier occasions by the speaker (and, if possible, videos of speaking occasions) to become acquainted with the person's style. Before writing her first speech for Maryland Governor Parris Glendening, speechwriter Samantha Kappalman spent her 'first few weeks going to events . . . and watching the way the governor spoke, what his hand movements were and writing down phrases he liked to say.'[11]

The speechwriter must consider the linguistic profile of the speaker. If the person does not speak English or French as a first language, the writer may need to consider the possibility that some words or phrases will be more difficult to pronounce.

If you choose to include humour in the speech, you should ascertain the comfort level of the speaker with delivering jokes. Unlike their male counterparts, female speakers are often uncomfortable delivering stock jokes; they prefer humour that comes from the telling of personal experiences.[12]

Audience

As with other kinds of speeches, writers must write for the ear of the listener. The best way to ensure that you are writing for the ear is to read the speech aloud as you write—to make adjustments whenever a sentence or cluster of ideas does not allow for the taking of a breath. Some experts say that the average length of sentences, written for the ear, should be eight to 10 words in length.[13] However, I have found that the structure of ideas within the sentence (not the *number of words*) determines the comprehensibility of the speech. Consider the following statement: *The sound of the rain, the rush of the wind, the silence of the forest—all speak to us of the eloquence of nature.* This sentence has 24 words; however, a speaker could easily deliver the sentence, and audiences could just as easily grasp the meaning. In delivering the above statement, the speaker pauses for effect after each phrase. Varying the length of sentences, inverting the order of words, and speaking in sentence fragments can also add variation and interest to speeches. Speechwriters often ask rhetorical questions, to which the speaker does not expect an audible response.

Writers should paint pictures by using concrete language and extended metaphors. They should listen for the sound of words and aim for cadence and lyricism in passages that they would like to be eloquent. The guide to congressional speechwriting, mentioned earlier, urges writers to use devices such as repetition (with variation), antithesis, alliteration, parallelism, and rhythmic triads (groups of three words, phrases, or clauses).[14] (See Chapter 10 for a detailed discussion of these linguistic strategies.) If you are not well-schooled in literature and history, you may wish to purchase a few standard poetry, literature, and history books. Quotations are readily available on the Internet. Most of the other material is also available on the Web, but you may not find what you need if you do not have a reference framework. Historical references are often interesting additions to speeches.

As noted earlier, speechwriting involves preparing a speech, not an essay. Admittedly, many of the same rules apply to both genres in terms of attention-getting strategies, thesis and purpose statements, summaries, and the need for clarity of organization and vivid concrete language. Because the writer of speeches must write for the ear, not the eye, he will sometimes write in incomplete sentences. Meaning is more important than grammar, although most 'great' speeches are also grammatically correct.

To involve the audience, the speechwriter should use first-person collective (*we, us, our*) and second person (*you*) more often than *they, people, a person, the author*. Sometimes the use of first person *I* can be important, if the speaker wants to take responsibility for some decision or action. When talking about a third person, speechwriters should make the person real to the audience. They should call the person by name (real or fictitious) and talk about the situation in concrete terms.

Political correctness is extremely important—whether writing for oneself or for a second party. Audiences will hold the speaker accountable for whatever is said, but the speechwriter will ultimately pay as great a price in loss of reputation and income. As noted in an earlier chapter, speechwriters need to research the current terms used to refer to older people, those with disabilities, and ethnic and minority groups. In government, some terms are considered totally inappropriate, even when they are politically correct. Politicians and bureaucrats, for example, never include the word *problem* in any speech. Instead, they substitute the term *challenge*. So governments face 'challenges', never 'problems'. Examine any text by a political figure to confirm this point. An upbeat and optimistic style characterizes the goodwill speech.

At the same time that political correctness is important, speechwriters should avoid professional jargon when writing for lay audiences. They should avoid terms such as *portfolio, downsizing, rightsizing, prioritizing, branding, customer-calibrated, benchmarking, value-driven, memorandum to cabinet, contingency planning, need-to-know, stakeholders, reputation management, per-share growth, leveraging, facilitation, strategy, at-risk publics, buy-in, promise management, knowledge management, human capital performance, outcomes, paradigms, sunset clause, risk management,* and *balanced scorecard.*

Speakers should also avoid the use of acronyms such as OD (organizational development), ADM (assistant deputy minister), IT (Internet technology), MOU (memorandum of understanding), SAP (simplified acquisition procedures), WOSB (women-owned small business), RFP or RFQ (request for proposal or quotation), and LB (large business), which only serve to confuse lay audiences.

Speechwriters should define terms that may be unfamiliar to the audience and explain concepts that may be alien to audience experiences, but they should avoid condescending language. *Uneducated* does not mean *unintelligent* or even *unlearned*. My father had a tenth grade education, but he never missed the nightly news reports. My husband did not return to school until he was 40, but he knew all the major historical and classical works and could recite Shakespeare and other favourites by heart. If the audience cannot understand what you are saying, it is probably because you are not saying it very well.

Sometimes writers must consider not only the immediate audience, but also remote audiences who may view the speech on television or listen to a radio broadcast. The speechwriter must take both audiences into account.

When making choices on the inclusion of humour in a speech, you should note some basic facts about how men and women respond to humour. Long anecdotal jokes tend to be popular with both men and women, but jokes with a punch line (as noted earlier) are less popular with women.[15] Women, on the other hand, enjoy humour that makes fun of the affectations and hypocrisies of people and pokes fun at the powerful in society. Many female humorists rely almost exclusively on self-deprecating humour—that is, humour that occurs at their own expense:

> The self-deprecating joke is considered to be the most 'traditional' form of women's humor. This is what comediennes in the fifties and early sixties relied on for their standard fare. When Jean Kerr writes that she bought an expensive brown dress only to realize that it makes her look like a large bran muffin, she's relying on self-deprecation. Or when Erma Bombeck points out that 'one-size-fits-all' is an incomplete sentence, the implication is that the garment doesn't fit her, and her humor is directed against herself. In domestic humor it has traditionally been okay for a woman to make fun of her home, her children, and her husband, because she was seen as responsible for them. Therefore, if Bombeck says 'In general my children refused to eat anything that hadn't danced on TV', we see this as a sort of extended self-deprecation, because we see children as an extension of their mother.[16]

Occasion

Simplicity and clarity are the keys to a good speech. The direct and low-key approach, characterized by a casual and conversational quality, is the most acceptable style in contemporary North American rhetoric.[17] The more formal the occasion, however, the more formal the language should be. You must adapt your language to the nature of the event—a dedication or commemorative event, an after-dinner speech, a keynote address, or other.

Techniques for Preparing a Manuscript for Delivery

Many government, political, and business figures read their speeches from manuscripts. They rely on a written script to ensure the accuracy and specificity of statements. Public figures can incur high risks for the organization when they speak loosely. In most cases, their words are not a personal statement. They are an organizational statement. And the organization can become politically, financially, or legally responsible for promises made in public speeches or inaccurate presentation of facts. For that reason, governments in particular require multiple levels of approval for speeches with policy content.

To deal with the excessive number of speeches that must be given by governing politicians and bureaucrats, some organizations commission the creation of speech modules for use by departmental or agency representatives. A speech module contains prepared and approved statements on a specified topic, with paragraphs that can be cut and pasted together for different speaking occasions. These modules serve the same function as the canned statements used by correspondence units to respond to public inquiries. The more important the speaking event, however, the more likely the speech will have been written or customized for that particular occasion.

Communication staff members also prepare speaker notes or talking points for top-level government officials and CEOs. These talking points allow the speakers to sound more spontaneous in their style of delivery. But important speaking occasions will almost always necessitate the preparation of a full manuscript. The speakers will want to take care in making assertions and promises. Some communication staff members have told me that they cringe when political figures move away from their manuscripts, because they not infrequently make claims that do not reflect existing government policies. At that point, communication staff members have to lurch into damage control to recover the situation.

Appropriate formatting of manuscript speeches can facilitate the reading of the manuscript. The speechwriter should *triple-space* the manuscript and *put markings* between the phrases, as in the following example:

> Jenny was tall / lean in build / and muscular and athletic in body type. / She gave every appearance of being healthy / free of disease / and the most unlikely candidate for cancer. / But cancer does not put broad markers on its early victims. / No / cancer is a silent stalker / moving easily among all classes and occupations. /

When marking the manuscript, the ghost writer will want to make some word clusters shorter and others longer. Commas are unnecessary, since the slashes define where pauses should occur. Reading the speech aloud will facilitate the process of marking the manuscript. When I write speeches, I read the words aloud as I write. Only in that way can I obtain a true feeling for the lyricism of phrases and some idea of how to phrase the ideas for readability.

A large font (14 to 16 points) creates a more readable manuscript, but the use of all capital letters creates a less readable manuscript. Other markings in the speech can be personal ones, intended to assist the speaker in delivering the speech. The ghost writer may choose, for example, to underline or highlight places of emphasis or to indicate length of pauses. She may want to leave a good deal of white space on the first page so that the speaker can add last-minute references to audience members or other impromptu remarks about the occasion.

The manuscript should be typed on one side of the page only. The pages should be numbered in case the speaker drops them. The weight of the paper should be sufficiently heavy that the pages will not rustle or bend when the speaker turns them.

Relinquishing Ownership

Those who choose to make a career of writing speeches for others must learn to relinquish ownership of the speech at some point. Relinquishing ownership means forfeiting authorship. Obviously, when a writer pens a speech for money, the person will not deliver the speech, hear the applause, or receive compliments from the audience. In the majority of cases, the client will never acknowledge the writer; and in my experience, the ghost writer rarely receives feedback on the speech event. The client has purchased the speech, and the writer has received compensation of a monetary nature for his work. In the eyes of the organization, nothing more is required.

For many speechwriters, however, the most difficult aspect of relinquishing ownership does not relate to the forfeiting of recognition. Most writers accept that they are being paid in money, not in accolades; however, they find it more difficult to accept perceived assaults on the aesthetics of the work. In government, in particular, large numbers of policy and program experts analyze every word that appears in major addresses. The higher the status of the person delivering the speech, the greater the level of scrutiny to which the organization subjects the speech. Legal experts pore over the manuscript, carefully replacing objectionable passages with legalese. Policy experts often change the content or wording, without regard for the need to write for the ear. In cases where the speaker is talking about government programs, program experts will have their say on what to include or exclude from the speech. These writers may have limited abilities (or interest) in producing a document that is 'sayable'. And as Clinton speechwriter Carolyn Curiel observed, 'Everyone thinks that they can write.'[18] Ironically, scientific and research organizations are the worst offenders, because their highly educated members often think that they have better writing skills than communication staffers or outside consultants. They certainly possess the knowledge, but they are often unable to communicate their ideas to a lay audience.

Most writers place a great value on the written and spoken word. Many are English, French, or linguistic majors; or they have specialized in speech or journalism. They appreciate language. Yet in their chosen profession of speechwriting, they must learn to accept critiques from those who may know little to nothing about speechwriting; and they cannot become defensive or argumentative. They must respond to the concerns of individuals who are more worried about the legal ramifications of the wrong phrase than the quality of the language. When enough different people edit a speech, it often loses its coherence and stylistic consistency; and the requested changes may destroy the cadence of the speech or the flow of ideas.

In the end, the product may bear little resemblance to the original draft, which can be a source of professional concern to speechwriters. They may fear that a poorly edited product will reflect on their abilities, since the speaker may unfairly attribute problems of flow or quality of language to the speechwriter. But experienced speechwriters know that the client has the right to make the changes that he or she desires.

In August 2000, John Podhoretz wrote that the 'pride of every speechwriter in the world is deeply wounded today' because Democrat presidential nominee Al Gore had claimed to be writing his acceptance speech himself.[19] In the view of most professional writers, this 'wounded pride' would be out of place. Clinton speechwriter Terry Edmonds said that 'unless the president credits us, we don't publicize what we've done. . . . You have to bury your ego entirely.'[20] As reporter Jan Tracy noted, speechwriters 'live by deadlines but do not write for bylines or public praise.'[21]

Evaluating Your Efforts

Speechwriters require feedback to improve their ability to meet the needs of clients. *People within the organization* require feedback to discover if they have met their objectives with the speech. To improve, the *speaker* requires feedback on the performance. In concluding comments, I discuss the grounds on which you can base these evaluations.

Feedback to the Speechwriter

Organizational representatives should inform speechwriters of any changes made to the speech, either before or after the speech is given. Not uncommonly, advisers and staff members will make changes in content and style. Ideally, the speechwriter should be involved in these changes. The changes may disrupt the style and flow of the speech. A speech should appear to be the product of one person; it should not have the look or feel of a patchwork quilt. Input by many people makes the speech less coherent as a unit and less fluid.

The reality of bureaucracies, however, is that changes may occur at any stage of a speech's journey through the many layers of the organization that must approve it. All too often, the speechwriter will be excluded from any say in the finalizing of speech content and form. The speech suffers, and the individual slated to give the speech may blame the resulting non-fluencies on the speechwriter. Those who make their living as speechwriters will occasionally (but not usually) put clauses in their contracts, insisting that they be consulted when changes are made in content and wording. Some writers have been known to quit when such consultations do not occur. The reason for their concern is easy to understand, given the fact that the speaker (often an executive with influence) may not realize that the speechwriter lost ownership of the speech at some point before the final draft. Where teams of writers produce speeches, the speechwriters do not feel so much personal responsibility; however, they confront equally great challenges in producing a coherent final draft.

Where the writer is excluded from the editing process, he should secure copies of the different drafts of the speech to learn who made what changes. Sometimes, the changes reflect organizational sensitivities; and if a speechwriter does not see the revised copy, he will continue to make the same mistakes in future writing assignments. In other cases, the speaker will be uncomfortable with the content or language of the speech. Sometimes, organizational priorities will change at the last minute and involve shifts in emphasis or content. If the language of the speech is not the first language of the speaker, the person may have difficulty pronouncing certain words. Those whose first language is French, for example, sometimes have difficulty with the word *focus*, which can be a source of embarrassment! Again, it is important to learn from each speech effort. In that way, speechwriters can avoid making the same mistake a second or third time.

Feedback to Speech Organizers

Organizations should try to evaluate the results of their speech-making efforts. The following discussion suggests questions that can be asked to determine whether a speech achieved its purposes. The discussion also identifies methods to carry out this evaluation.

Strategic Considerations

Did the audience demonstrate enhanced levels of awareness or knowledge of the topic as a result of the speech? Did their understanding of the organization's policies, priorities, and programs improve as a result of attending this speaking engagement? Did listeners leave with a better understanding of the organization's mandate and mission? Entrance and exit interviews can help the organization to respond to these questions.

Have opinions regarding policies, priorities, and programs changed as a result of the speech? Was the audience moved to action after attending the speech? Is the organization getting more requests for information or services, increased business, or fewer complaints in the period following a speaking tour? Entrance and exit interviews can solicit the answers to some of these questions. Follow-up reports by inquiry units, publication departments, and human resources personnel can assess the nature and content of subsequent relations with clients. On issues of particular importance, political parties, governments, and large corporations may hire polling firms to measure 'before' and 'after' public opinion.

Did the audience react favourably to the speaker at the time of the speech? Was the applause generous? Did audience questions demonstrate interest in the presentation? Did their non-verbal reactions suggest positive attitudes towards the speech and speaker? Did audience members make favourable comments to the speaker, other audience members, or organizational representatives following the speech? Did other organizations make follow-up requests for the speaker? What was the nature of media comment on the speech? Observation, interviews, logs of telephone calls and other inquiries, and analysis of media clippings and transcripts can assist the organization in responding to these questions.

Could the information in this speech have been better conveyed by some other vehicle? Did the attendance figures justify the time and money expended by the organization and the speaker? Were the 'right' people in the audience (that is, the people that the organization wanted to reach, elite opinion leaders, or others)? Could the target audience have been reached in some other way—a press release, brochure, talk show, or public service announcement?

Should this forum be regarded as a suitable vehicle for future efforts to carry the organization's messages? Would a failure to provide a speaker for future meetings of this group undermine the organization's ability to achieve its strategic objectives with respect to this target audience? Did the speaking engagement generate further opportunities for meeting this target public or produce other benefits (for example, new contacts, partnerships, or sources of information)? Will this target audience be more likely to co-operate with the organization in the future as a consequence of this engagement?

Was the environment of the speech event conducive to getting across the ideas? Was it noisy or chaotic? Did hostile groups disrupt the proceedings? What was the effect of these influences on achievement of the speech purposes?

Follow-up interviews with advisers and bureaucrats who attended the speech event provide a way to gain insights into questions unanswered by other methodologies.

Tactical Considerations

The next questions deal with practical matters related to the planning and implementation of the speech event. Were arrangements for pre-event and post-event publicity adequate? Did other communication products (e.g., press releases, backgrounders, and advance interviews with the media) give adequate support to the event? Follow-up interviews with members of media organizations, analysis of media coverage, and the calculation of attendance can help the organization to respond to these questions.

Were the room arrangements satisfactory from the perspective of the speaker, the audience, and the media? Were the acoustics acceptable? Were the facilities adequate for recording the event? Did the events proceed on time? Observation and interviews provide appropriate ways to answer these questions.

Were sufficient numbers of the speech available for distribution to the media, interested audience members, consumers of media coverage of the event, regional and branch offices, elite opinion leaders, associations interested in the topic area, and other stakeholders? Attendance at the speech event yields the opportunity to observe the distribution of speeches, and the units that handle follow-up requests for information can provide further insights.

Were publishing and distribution deadlines respected? Were budgetary restrictions respected? If appropriate, did the organization follow up with other activities to maximize the impact of this event? The organization's communication plans should contain the information necessary to answer these questions, since they identify ways to sustain messages and allocate funding to different communication activities.

Feedback to the Speaker

The speaker should receive some of the same feedback as the organization. In addition, someone in the organization (probably a speech adviser or chief of staff) should sit down with the speaker after the occasion to discuss strengths and weaknesses of the performance. While this feedback may require some diplomacy, many organizations put their executives through speech and interview training. So the executives are not unacquainted with this kind of feedback.

Evaluation of the speaker's performance entails looking at the following areas: Did the speaker use his/her voice (including volume, pitch, rate, and diction) to the best advantage? How effectively did the speaker use pauses and emphasis? Did gestures and movement add to—or detract from—the speech? Were these movements motivated? There is no magic formula for an appropriate number of gestures or movements, but unnecessary movements (especially repetitive ones) distract from the content of the speech. Did the speaker maintain (or appear to maintain, in the case of a large auditorium group) eye contact with the audience? Did the speaker have a natural and relaxed posture? Were visual aids used effectively? Was the speaker composed and articulate in responding to questions that followed the delivery of the speech? Did the speaker reinforce the organization's messages and themes in responding to questions?

Grounds for Judging Success

Like rhetorical critics, audiences judge speeches on many grounds. They may reach their judgements on the basis of the artistic merit of the speech, quality of the delivery, value of the information, ethics of the speech, or whether they agreed with the speaker at the end of the speech. (See Chapter 16 for further consideration of these points.) If you are to evaluate the success of your speaker's efforts and your own speechwriting efforts, you must take these points into consideration. You should also take the nature of the occasion and cultural differences into account. Different audiences have different expectations of speakers.

Employment Opportunities as a Freelance Writer

Getting work as a freelance writer involves gaining experience, advertising your work, negotiating a contract and professional fees, and establishing a schedule for completing the work. The following discussion considers each point in more depth.

Gaining Experience

When securing work as a speechwriter within organizations, communication specialists often have to pass writing tests. Within the Canadian government, public service examinations test writing abilities, along with other communication skills. Communication specialists enter the ranks of 'information service' officers. The communication officers progress from level to level. They have to pass tests of knowledge and skill, along with language tests, to move to the next level.

Would-be speechwriters can gain experience in a number of different ways. Many freelance writers begin their careers in public relations capacities. Speechwriting is one job duty of most PR practitioners or public affairs officers in government. Other speechwriters have journalism degrees or experience writing for newspapers or magazines. If you have published some of your work, you will have enhanced credibility when you apply for work as a speechwriter.

Another source of experience is delivering your own speeches to a variety of organizations. Most social clubs, libraries, and community organizations welcome speakers who volunteer their services. Local chapters of Toastmasters International also help speakers to gain experience in writing and delivering speeches.

Advertising Your Work

Getting work as a freelance writer is not unlike getting work of any kind. You need to create business cards, brochures, and a portfolio of your work. Even if Web sites do not generate that much work, they give you a place to direct potential clients, where they can view your portfolio, read your biography, and learn more about your speechwriting services and fees.

Markets vary greatly, depending on where you live. If you live in Ottawa or Toronto, the demand is large. In small locales, the writer must reach beyond his or her own community to find more than the occasional writing assignment. With the growth of the Internet and the possibility for writers to work with clients who are geographically dispersed, these kinds of possibilities grow larger. In my experience, however, organizations still like that one-on-one contact with their writers. Municipal governments, large business enterprises, and chambers of commerce offer possibilities for speechwriting assignments in smaller towns.

Negotiating a Contract and Professional Fees

An organization may employ a speechwriter on a full-time regular basis or hire the person on a contract basis. In some cases, speechwriters have a standing offer with an organization, where they are on 'call-by' status. This kind of arrangement eliminates the necessity to write a new contract each time the organization requires the writer's services. At other times, the organization contracts for speechwriting services on a speech-by-speech basis.

Often writers get less for their services than more specialized communication consultants. The numbers of freelance writers are significantly greater than the numbers of strategic planners, organizational development (OD) consultants, or crisis management experts. Nonetheless, the quality of writing services varies greatly, and the better writers can command higher rates than their weaker colleagues.

Rates also vary greatly from one community to another. Working in the nation's capital, writers have a more lively market than those working in smaller locales. If you write for non-profit organizations, you will make less than you make when you write for government. Governments, on the other hand, pay less than big business; but you never have to worry about being paid. You may prefer to ask lower rates and get more business or ask higher rates and obtain a more select clientele of those who are prepared to pay for quality.

Not all writers advertise their fees, because some do not want to be locked into a rate. Many prefer to negotiate their fees with clients on a job-by-job basis. If you have any measure of flexibility with your rates, you may not want to advertise them. Some writers, for example, offer better rates to voluntary organizations than they offer to businesses and governments. Many Canadian government departments, however, have a policy that requires consultants and contractors to sell similar services to all clients at the same rate. You are not allowed to vary your rate from job to job and department to department.

Internet advertisements indicate that the going rate for speechwriters varies significantly. Some writers advertise their services at $100 per minute or $100 per double-spaced page. Although speechwriters typically triple-space manuscripts for delivery, rates are based on double-spaced pages. (In my experience, these rates do not make sense, since most speakers take about two minutes—not one minute—to cover a double-spaced page. Therefore, the writer is charging twice as much with one rate structure as the other.) Without specifying particulars, another writer advertised a minimum of $750 for a speech. Some writers charge by the word. One advertisement, for example, indicated a rate of $1 per word or $250 per page. Since manuscripts typed in Times Roman font, double-spaced with one-inch margins, have about 250 words on the page, these two figures match. In my experience, this latter rate makes sense for a writer who is reasonably experienced, with some track record.

Some writers advertise hourly rates. One experienced writer indicated, for example, that he had obtained $5,000 for 40 hours work ($125 per hour or $1,000 per diem). Another writer advertised an hourly rate of $75. *Writer's Market* lists current rates in its 'How Much Should I Charge?' section.

Since speechwriting is often done on short deadlines, involving late-night and weekend work, freelance writers should avoid billing on an hourly basis. A writer should not get less for a speech that she has only three hours or a weekend to prepare. The mental effort will be similar and the stress factor will be significantly greater, given the compressed time frame for writing the speech. Nor should experienced writers be penalized for taking a shorter period of time to produce a speech. If billing on a per diem or hourly basis, the beginning speechwriter could conceivably make more than the experienced writer. Professional speechwriters often bill according to the length of the speech (so much per page of text or minute of speaking time). In that regard, their practices are like the translator, who bills by the word or page.

Contracts should include a description of the writing project, specifics on deliverables (a term used by contractors to talk about the final products they will deliver to the client), deadlines, milestones, number of drafts for which the writer will be responsible, and amounts and terms of payment. When you produce a speech for the Canadian government, they rarely ask for more than one draft, occasionally two drafts. Government contracts typically demand rights of ownership to all materials generated under the agreement (unless otherwise specified).

Establishing a Schedule for Completing the Work

Speechwriters often work on very tight deadlines. Samantha Kappalman said that she had two hours, for example, to prepare Maryland Governor Parris Glendening's victory speech.[22] When politicians are unsure of the likely election results, they must prepare two speeches—a victory speech and a speech of concession.

In the case of major speech events (known and anticipated), speechwriters may receive a briefing several weeks in advance of the occasion. However, political communicators often find themselves in the situation of writing a speech in the course of a short afternoon or evening. Most governments and many large organizations perceive themselves in an ongoing state of crisis, and crisis calls for personal statements by organizational leaders.

To the extent possible, speechwriters attempt to establish schedules for working on speeches. Professional writers may be working on multiple communication products at the same time. They cannot afford to book only one contract at a time. See Figure 15.1 for an example of a schedule sheet for completing work on a paid speech assignment.

The Debate over the Ethics of Ghost Writing

Speechwriter Terry Edmonds has said that writers must commit themselves to articulating the philosophy of the person for whom they are writing. She explained that the job of a speechwriter is 'not to push our own personal agenda . . . but to articulate a policy for someone else.'[23] Carolyn Curiel, former editor at the *New York Times* and the *Washington Post*, agreed that speechwriters must be able to put on 'someone else's thinking cap'.[24] According to defenders of ghost-writing, conformity to this norm will exonerate the ghost writer from charges of unethical undertakings. They further assert that organizations, including the Prime Minister's Office, are aggregates of individuals or corporate entities. According to this view, individual spokespersons (whether Prime Minister or CEO) do not speak for themselves. They speak for the corporation or government they were chosen to represent. So speeches reflecting the views of the corporate body do not need to originate with one person.[25] Others argue that, so long as the public understands that the words are the creation of a second party, the speaker has not violated an ethical convention. Responding to criticisms of Bill Clinton, John Scalzi said:

Figure 15.1

TheSpeechWriters.com Checklist

Source: Speechwriters.com, from Garrett Patterson.

Date _____

Client: Name: Mr/Ms _____

Phone, e-mail _____

Title, Organization: _____

Address: suite no., street address _____

City, State/Province, zip/postal code _____

Speaker: Name, title: _____

Event: Organization/Audience_____

Date, Occasion, Venue _____

Topic, Length: _____

Objective: _____

Points to cover: _____

1. _____

2. _____

3. _____

4. _____

Contacts:

1. Name, title, phone, e-mail _____

2. Name, title, phone, e-mail _____

3. Name, title, phone, e-mail _____

Research sources—documents (locations), Web sites:

1._____   4._____

2._____   5._____

3._____   6._____

Schedule: Enter nine production schedule dates for client (C) and speechwriter (SW) onto a calendar in reverse order:

*Speaking date _____   *Final draft—SW to C (1 week earlier) _____

*Rev of 2nd—C to SW _____   *2nd draft—SW to C (1 week earlier) _____

*Rev of 1st—C to SW _____   *First draft—SW to C (1 week earlier) _____

*Rev of outline—C to SW _____   *Outline—SW to C (1 week earlier) _____

*Assignment—C to SW_____

With politicians there's the accepted fact that their words are written for them all of the time—they have speechwriters. When a president goes up and gives a State of the Union address, no one in his right mind believes that he's written that speech himself. . . . However, news reports don't say 'Tonight, President Bush, as written by David Frum, announced sweeping new tax proposals.' The words are attributed to Bush [or Paul Martin, in the case of the contemporary Canadian scene].[26]

In presenting her perspectives on the issue, Patricia J. Parsons points to the definition of plagiarism as 'the unauthorized use or close imitation of the language and thoughts of another author and the representation of them as one's original work'.[27] Using this definition, she says that only unauthorized words qualify as plagiarism. If the professional speechwriter is hired to produce speeches, then the speaker is clearly authorized to use the words.

Not everyone agrees, however, with these perspectives. Some say that the public grows cynical when they realize they are being misled about authorship of speeches: 'When politicians pay writers to tell their stories, they generate a perception of insincerity that dilutes the public trust so that citizens greet even the most upstanding politician with cynicism.'[28] Others say that the average person does not realize the extent to which politicians and CEOs rely on communication staff and speechwriters to generate their communication products.[29]

Politicians place themselves at risk when they use ghost writers they do not know well. In 1987, Delaware Senator Joseph Biden withdrew from the Democratic presidential primary after critics disclosed that 'large portions of his closing statement at a debate were nearly identical to portions of speeches delivered earlier by a leader of Britain's Labour Party.'[30] Massachusetts Senator John Kerry also faced charges of plagiarism from critics in 2004. One researcher claimed to have found 11 instances of passages from other people's work, used without attribution, in Kerry's published writings.[31] Even if ghost writers penned the problematic passages (a likely scenario), ultimately the speaker or apparent author had to bear the responsibility for the words.

Responses to ghost-writing practices may also vary across countries and cultures. In countries that recognize group (as opposed to individual) efforts, people are unlikely to question the legitimacy of ghost-writing practices.

In the same way that the speaker faces the risk of unconscious plagiarism in an environment where words are regularly recycled, speechwriters face the same problem. As mentioned earlier, communication or political staff members give copies of archived speeches to ghost writers. They anticipate that the speechwriters will draw passages from these earlier speeches and use the speeches as models. Yet these archived speeches may contain instances of plagiarism, unknown to the current writer. Sometimes the speeches may even come from an earlier holder of an office, who delivered the policy address on behalf of the organization. So the situation is very complex when both speakers and writers work in an environment of 'institutionalized plagiarism'—a situation where people are accustomed to using words purchased from paid writers.[32]

Since many ghost writers are journalists, the 'plagiarized' passages could even come from their own work. Speakers could scarcely say to their publics, however, 'I didn't actually plagiarize the words. They belong to my speechwriter, who just happened to have written an article last year on the same topic.' A humorous example of one speech-

Box 15.3 A Question of Ethics

A professional speechwriter, Jeremy Smith, received about $2,500 for a 10-minute speech and $5,000 for a 20-minute speech. Last-minute requests or jobs involving evening and weekend work were more expensive. His speechwriting duties involved meeting with a representative of the organization to learn more about the speaker, audience, and occasion; receiving instruction on the messages that should appear in the speech; reviewing materials provided by the organization, including previous speeches on the same or similar topics; producing a first draft of the speech; and making the requested changes for a final draft. At the first meeting, Jeremy usually outlined his own expectations in regard to the desired client-consultant relationship.

After being contracted to write a speech for the CEO of a large home office firm, Jeremy met with Susan, head of public relations; Joe, the special events planner; and Hannah, the CEO's personal assistant. The three could not agree on the messages for the speech. Jeremy concluded that politics were at work in the situation, and eventually he followed the suggestions of Hannah, the personal assistant. When Hannah gave a set of former speeches to Jeremy, she asked him to use highlighted passages intact in the new speech. This request was not unusual, and

Jeremy complied. He delivered the first draft of the speech to Hannah.

When Jeremy received a call a week later, it came from Susan (head of public relations), who was displeased by his failure to follow her advice. She demanded that he completely rewrite the speech, using the ideas that she had contributed. Moreover, she gave him 24 hours to produce a second draft. She told him that several drafts might be necessary. Susan also told him that the ghost writer for the other speeches would be upset by the inclusion of his material. This speechwriter was known for demanding that the organization acknowledge his contribution if they used his material in a second speech. Given the conflicting instructions, Jeremy felt that he had done the best he could. Also, recycling content was common; and speechwriters did not typically demand acknowledgement. He found the requests unreasonable and asked for an additional $1,000 to revise the speech. Susan balked at the demand. She said that she would revise the speech herself and dismissed Jeremy, cutting his pay by half since he would not be producing a final draft. Discuss the ethics in this situation from the point of view of the organization, Jeremy, and the earlier ghost writer whose materials were being used without his explicit consent.

writer's effort to secure the 'original' words and views of his client comes from the account of Frederick J.O. Blachly:

> I decided to use the President's own words to put together a [UN] proclamation. Using sentences from various speeches by the former Representative, Senator, Vice-President, and now President Nixon, I stitched together a suitable text and submitted it to the front office. The text came back marked 'Too liberal!' Try again. I resubmitted the same text, but after each sentence I gave the [original speech] source. . . . So there I was, a ghost living off the work of other ghosts! The text went to the White House and appeared over the President's signature just the way I had put it together.[33]

Conclusion

Unlike earlier years when poet, journalist, and politician D'Arcy McGee delivered eloquent, spell-binding speeches of his own making, the ghost-writing function in government has become institutionalized. Speechwriters occupy prominent staff positions and write books about their careers. Although corporate speechwriters enjoy a less publicly acknowledged role, they are also highly visible within their organizations. And many thousands of freelance writers make a living by putting words in the mouths of others.

Those interested in making a career in the field of speechwriting have a host of possibilities from which to choose. The large majority will, however, combine a speechwriting career with other forms of writing. Within the organization, for example, speechwriters produce a multitude of public relations products. Most freelance speechwriters also ghost other kinds of products, including books, brochures, and magazine articles.

Questions for Discussion

1. How do you feel about the ethics of ghost-writing? Did you realize that most prominent politicians, including prime ministers, employ speechwriters?
2. Some people say that representatives of governments and business are not really espousing their own views, but rather the views of their organizations—that their views represent the stance of the organization on issues. Therefore, the organization is justified in paying a ghost writer to create the speeches. Do you agree or disagree? Explain your point of view.
3. Should speakers publicly acknowledge those who write their speeches?
4. To what extent should speakers be involved in the final editing of speeches written by a paid speechwriter?
5. Is it important for the speechwriter to get to know the person for whom she is writing the speeches? To what extent should a ghost writer attempt to emulate the style of the speaker? (Not all speakers have a natural eloquence.)
6. Is it ethical to 'recycle' content from one speech to another? Is it ethical for an organization to ask a speechwriter to incorporate passages from a speech written by a different speechwriter? Who 'owns' the rights to the speech—the speechwriter, the organization that paid for the speech, or the speaker who delivers the speech?

CHAPTER SIXTEEN

The Nature and Function of Rhetorical Criticism

Preparing a Rhetorical Analysis

Prepare a rhetorical analysis of a speech event. Look at speaker purposes, environment, audience, speaker credibility, message, outcomes, and costs of achieving outcomes. A detailed description of the assignment accompanies this chapter. The emphasis in the marking of this assignment will be on the extent to which the paper reflects speech theory, thematic coherence, creativity of approach, clarity of organization, clarity of writing style, adequacy of background research, and appropriate use of excerpts from the speech to support your arguments.

Learning Objectives
- To understand the bases on which speeches should be judged.
- To learn about the role of the critic in undertaking an analysis.
- To appreciate the importance of knowing about the historical, social, and political contexts in analyzing speeches of the past.

In an academic sense, criticism implies trying to understand or pass judgement on some work. Rhetorical criticism refers to an attempt to understand and pass reasoned judgement on written or oral discourse.[1] In the process of making this judgement, the critic seeks to discriminate between what is better or worse in the discourse. Sometimes the judgements will be negative in tone and content; at other times, they will be positive.

In many regards, analysts are like forensic detectives. In their quest to understand the rhetorical event, they look for evidence—evidence of speaker motives and purposes in delivering the speech, environment or context for the speech, primary and secondary audiences for the speech, initial speaker credibility, message strategies and supporting materials used to achieve purposes (logical, emotional, and source credibility appeals), impact, and cost of achieving impact in ethical terms. And any search for answers must begin with the framing of questions.[2] For that reason, the following discussion often suggests questions that can lead to better understanding of the rhetorical event. This chapter applies the framework from the Critical Communication Model (described in Chapter 1) to the discussion of rhetorical analysis.

Box 16.1 Areas Addressed in Rhetorical Analysis

· Speaker motives and purposes
· Environment or context
· Primary and secondary audiences
· Speaker credibility

· Message strategies
· Supporting materials (ethos, logos, pathos)
· Impact
· Cost of achieving impact in ethical terms.

Speaker Motives

When trying to analyze speeches, we talk about the 'rhetorical imperative' or the driving force behind the speech. Did the speaker articulate some purpose in giving the speech? If not, is there an unstated purpose? Is the real purpose different from the stated purpose? When a politician comes to your local Rotary Club meeting to talk about what he has been doing lately, is he really seeking to inform you or is he hoping that you will vote for him in the upcoming election? What does he or she have to gain by giving the speech?

Speaker purposes could be 'to convince an audience to support social security reforms', 'to inspire an audience to put aside their fears of failure when they tackle new challenges', 'to encourage the audience to give financial support to flood victims', 'to pay tribute to the veterans of foreign wars', or 'to entertain the audience with stories of strange places and people'. Examples of unspoken purposes could be 'to rebuild personal credibility after allegations of misconduct', 'to persuade the audience to vote for me in the next election', or 'to reinforce my image as a family man after voting for the legalization of same-sex marriage'.

In a rhetorical analysis, you should seek to identify stated and unstated speaker purposes. Some speaker purposes will be ethical; others may be unethical. The rhetorical analyst attempts to identify and sometimes to judge speaker motives. Like any other researcher, you must support your ideas with evidence. That is, you must select passages from the speech and secondary sources to support your assessment of speech purpose(s). Examples of secondary sources are newspaper accounts of the speech event, media or personal interviews with the speaker, correspondence, or other supporting data. In other words, you should give evidence to back up your assertions.

Environment

It has been said that the task of a rhetorical critic is the 'reconstruction of public consciousness'.[3] The rhetorical critic must identify the broader context within which a speech occurred—the political, economic, cultural, social, technological, and legal factors that gave rise to the rhetorical event; the conventions that govern the speech occasion; and the immediate physical setting. Many disciplines—including 'history, politics, law, religion, sociology, psychology, cultural studies, [and] literature'—have insights to offer the rhetorical critic.[4]

In writing the context statement for your rhetorical analysis, for example, you can go to historical accounts of the speech—books that talk about the speech, newspaper or magazine accounts, and Web sites that describe the setting and context. You should cite any sources that you use at the end of your analysis (as well as giving a reference within the text of your paper). A good print source for Canadian speeches is Dennis Gruending, ed., *Great Canadian Speeches* (Calgary: Fifth House, 2004), which includes speeches by both historical and contemporary figures, including John A. Macdonald, Nellie McClung, John Polanyi, David Suzuki, Pierre Trudeau, Louis Riel, and Norman Bethune.

You must place yourself in the period and place in history in which the rhetorical event occurred. To analyze a speech about feminist rhetoric in the 1960s, for example, you must understand what was happening in that decade. Much has happened since the sexual revolution and the activism of women's rights advocates such as Betty Friedan and Germaine Greer.

To understand the rhetoric surrounding AIDS in the 1980s, you have to place yourself within the fabric of the society at that time. People were gripped with fear and lack of understanding of the threat. Members of the New York and San Francisco gay communities attended funerals on an almost weekly basis. The public looked with wonder and surprise at celebrities like Princess Diana, who dared to put themselves in close contact with those who had contracted AIDS. Certainly an audience in the 1980s would have reacted differently from present-day audiences to public discourse on the topic of AIDS. Their level of knowledge would have been dramatically lower, as well. The environment statement should reflect the knowledge of the day.

When writing an environment statement about public discourse in the days leading to the invasion of Iraq, you must disregard the fact that no one ever uncovered weapons of mass destruction after that invasion. You must erase the images of statues of Saddam Hussein being pulled down in public squares. You are obliged to blank out the numbers of soldiers and Iraqi civilians who have died since the US occupation of Iraq. For the purposes of understanding speaker motives and strategies and audience responses to the rhetoric, you must return to the period before 20 March 2003 when the first bombs fell on Baghdad.

This idea—that you must place yourself in the virtual moment of the speech event in order to write an environment statement—dominates all other considerations. If you are looking at religious discourse from the 1950s, for example, you should not bring discussion of scandals involving Roman Catholic priests in Newfoundland into your environment statement. In the 1950s, most audiences were deferential towards priests. Although abuses were occurring, they were not public knowledge. No scandals had been unearthed. So your consideration of the religious rhetoric of the 1950s must omit consideration of these later events.

In other words, to create your environment statements, you must be a time traveller. You must move backward in time, identifying the spirit and climate of the times that generated the speech. You have to don the mindset of audiences in that day and place, taking relevant political, economic, cultural, social, technological, legal, and ethical contexts into account. The rhetorical conventions of the day also influence the unfolding of the speech event. Some of these contextual matters will be more important than others in any given situation.

Political Context

The rhetoric surrounding the invasion and occupation of Iraq and the war against terrorism, for example, takes place within the broader political context of the events of 11 September 2001. In later years, rhetorical critics will not be able to divorce an understanding of the political rhetoric of the early part of this century from those events.

To analyze the 30 October 1995 speech by Jacques Parizeau, following the failed Quebec referendum, you must understand the events leading to the referendum. You would need to talk about the political climate, the politicians who occupied prominent positions of leadership in Quebec, and the efforts by federal politicians and other Canadians to influence the vote through speeches, rallies, and travels to Quebec. You would need to talk about the historical events that gave rise to the speech.

Martin Luther King Jr delivered his historical speech 'I Have a Dream' at a time of great civil unrest in the US, with marches in the streets of Washington and Selma, Alabama, and non-violent sit-ins in cities such as Nashville, Tennessee. Some of the more aggressive of the black leaders, such as Malcolm X and Stokely Carmichael, had denounced the non-violent nature of King's approach. So the black community was divided in the 1960s. These political factors are important to understanding King's motivations, his rhetorical strategies, and audience response.

Economic Context

Economic factors can be important. Periods of heavy layoffs, economic recession, and unemployment generate many issues to which speakers respond. The end of the new technology boom, the soaring costs of health care and insurance, the rise of China as a major economic power, and the high cost of oil have created the economic backdrop for much of the rhetoric of this century. A rhetorical analyst must identify relevant factors in the economic environment likely to influence speaker motives, as well as audience reactions to the public discourse. The factors must, of course, be relevant to the particular speech event that you have chosen to analyze.

Cultural Context

The rhetorical critic must place herself, as well, in the cultural context in which the speech event occurred. How would that particular audience have judged the reasoning or the moral position of the speaker? Would the speech have achieved its purposes with that particular group? Taking culture and ethnicity into account, would the audience have accepted the presentation style of the speaker? Would a Japanese audience, for example, have appreciated a highly animated and dynamic mode of delivery, or would they have expected a more dignified and quiet presence in a speaker?

Social Context

The response of television audiences to comedienne Ellen DeGeneres illustrates the fluid nature of the social environment within which communication events occur. In 1997, ABC yanked the television series *Ellen* from the air after both Ellen DeGeneres and her character 'came out of the closet'. Low audience ratings had followed on the heels of the episode where Ellen's character proclaimed her sexual preferences. By

2003, however, DeGeneres was able to launch a new syndicated daytime talk show, which won four Emmy awards in its first season. With 12 daytime Emmy nominations, the show bested all other talk show ratings.

Social factors inevitably influence the character of speech events and responses to speakers. When the University of Western Ontario awarded an honorary Doctor of Law in June 2005 to abortion pioneer Dr Henry Morgentaler, many Canadians protested the award. To understand the polarized responses to Morgentaler's award and commencement address, you need to understand not only the history of the abortion debate in Canada, but also the larger set of social issues within which that debate has been set—the growing divide, for example, between liberal and conservative views of marriage, the family, and morality.

Technological Context

Technological factors govern the options available to speakers in terms of channels. Speakers have a choice of delivering face-to-face, without technical interventions. Alternatively, they may choose to present their messages over the radio or on television. Speakers may also present live addresses over the Internet or archive their addresses on Web sites. (Box 16.2 offers a variety of on-line sources for speech texts.) These new and old technologies place some restraints on the speakers, who must conform to the conventions of the medium of communication. Television requires a close personal style of delivery, for example, whereas auditorium situations may demand larger gestures, broader movements, and a more public persona. The use of microphones, on the other hand, allows the speaker to adopt a more personal style of delivery. A rhetorical critic must look for the potential influence of technology on the situation, as well as the extent to which the speaker recognizes and adapts to these conventions.

Box 16.2 On-line Speech Sources

Selected Canadian Sites

http://collections.ic.gc.ca/canspeak/
  Bilingual collection of speeches by Canadian prime ministers.

www.canadahistory.com/sections/documents/speeches_1875_-_1920.htm
  Speeches delivered by Canadian political figures, 1875-1920.

www.canadahistory.com/sections/documents/speeches_1921_-_1950.htm
  Speeches delivered by Canadian political figures, 1921-50.

www.historychannel.com/speeches/
  World speeches.

www.lt.gov.on.ca/sections_english/history/history_middle_frame/history_speeches.html
  Archived speeches by recent lieutenant-governors of Ontario.

http://cbc.radio-canada.ca/speeches/index.asp
  Index to speeches broadcast over CBC radio and television in Canada.

www.collectionscanada.ca/primeministers/
  Biographical information on and speeches by prime ministers of Canada, via Library and Archives Canada.

http://archives.cbc.ca/
  CBC site provides clips from speeches broadcast over radio or television.

Box 16.2 continued

www.empireclubfoundation.com/
This Empire Club of Canada site provides collections of speeches by many prominent Canadians, especially politicians.

http://canada.gc.ca/
The Canadian government site has links to all government departments. Keyword searches will bring you to speeches at these sites.

http://pm.gc.ca/
The PMO site includes speeches by the Prime Minister.

www.gg.ca/media/
Speeches by the Governor-General of Canada of a ceremonial nature.

www.ceocouncil.ca/
Speeches by CEOs of Canada at the Canadian Council of Chief Executives site.

http://artsandscience.concordia.ca/comm
Concordia University collection of historical and recent speeches on issues pertaining to Canada.

www.royal.gov.uk/output/
British monarchy Web site with speeches and press releases.

www.canadacouncil.ca/
Speeches on arts topics from the Canada Council of the Arts.

www.liberal.ca/
Speeches by Liberal Party politicians.

www.conservative.ca/
Speeches by Conservative Party politicians.

www.ndp.ca/
Speeches of NDP politicians.

www.uni.ca/pq.html
Speeches by members of the Parti Québécois.

www.ltgov.bc.ca/
Ceremonial speeches by the Lieutenant-Governor of British Columbia.

www.healthcoalition.ca/tommy2.html
Speeches by Tommy Douglas on health care at the Canadian Health Coalition site.

Selected American Sites

www.americanrhetoric.com/
Index to and database for 5,000+ audio and video (streaming) versions of public speeches, sermons, lectures, and other rhetoric.

www.americanrhetoric.com/top100speechesall.html
Top-ranked 100 speeches.

http://gos.sbc.edu/byyears/old.html
Collection at Sweet Briar College, Virginia.

www.historicaldocuments.com/Top100American Speeches.htm
Top 100 American speeches.

www.udayton.edu/~dss/past_speakers.htm
Archived speeches at the University of Dayton.

Legal Context

Recognition of legal constraints can also be important. Speakers are not always able to say exactly what they want to say. They may be forced, on the advice of lawyers, to talk around points, to be deliberately vague or ambiguous. We live in litigious days, when a cup of spilled coffee or a fall in someone's front yard can be grounds for a legal suit. Spokespersons for organizations pay serious attention to these legal threats.

Rhetorical Conventions

The rhetorical conventions of a given period also exert an influence on the speech event. If you are judging a speaker from an earlier period, you must understand the requirements for delivering a speech in that period of time. If you judge a parliamentary speaker, you must understand the norms that govern rhetoric in the House of Commons or Senate. Are the speakers allowed to make caustic comments? Are personal attacks allowed? Are there time limits? Are interruptions tolerated? Are speakers typically low-key in their delivery style or dramatic and accusatory?

Cultural and religious norms also influence rhetorical conventions. Some religious groups expect to be highly engaged in church ceremonies. They expect the preacher to shout and exhort them to come to the front of the church and repent their sins. They may clap and stomp their feet as they become highly engaged in the church rituals. Other congregations may have quite different expectations of what should happen in a church setting. They may expect to remain quiet in their seats, while their ministers speak in a conversational manner, telling stories and using humour to impart their messages.

Ethical Context

The ethical norms and moral tenor of any period also influence the rhetoric of political and social actors, as well as reactions of audiences to the speeches. Until relatively recently, for example, Roman Catholics saw their priests as infallible representatives of God. Recent revelations of wrongdoing, however, have produced a new climate and a new rhetoric. When you write an environment statement, you must ask yourself how the people of a particular historical period (not your period) would have judged the speech. What were the ethical norms of that period? What were the moral taboos?

Physical Setting

Rhetorical analysts also need to understand the *immediate* context within which the speech occurs—the location, time, and other relevant characteristics of the setting. These settings greatly influence the mode of delivery, the content of speeches, and the expectations of the audience. The settings influence our expectations of speaker and occasion.

In some political settings such as the House of Commons, the seating arrangements place the speakers within a particular context, setting limits on the interactions that can occur within that context. Conflict is often ritualistic. The presence of television cameras within a setting also can influence interactions between speakers and audience members. With the televising of the parliamentary sessions, speakers had to learn how to be humorous to appeal to the enlarged audience.

In the same way, the introduction of television cameras to the courtroom has had a dramatic effect on speaking styles. Lawyers in some instances have felt a need to become more theatrical in their presentations, like the leading characters in television courtroom dramas. They have to dress and act the role, as Marcia Clarke (lead prosecutor in the O.J. Simpson trial) discovered.[5]

A speech may take place in a large auditorium or a small meeting room. The acoustics may be good or bad, and the general ambience may be friendly or cold and intimidating. The audience may have expectations of what should happen in this setting. Therefore, as rhetorical analysts, we must ask ourselves the following kinds of questions: Was the occasion formal and ceremonial or informal and personal? Was the seating comfortable? Were audience members sitting in close proximity to each other or widely dispersed in an auditorium? Did an overheated room encourage listeners to become sleepy and inattentive, or did activity in the outside hallway serve as a distraction? Could the audience hear the speaker?

Audience

All good or successful speeches will have been adapted to their audiences. You must identify all of the audiences targeted by the speech if you want to understand its possible impact. You may have one audience or multiple audiences when you speak. Your audience may be immediate or remote in time and space, domestic or international in nature. Some audiences will be more important to the speaker than others. The task of a rhetorical critic is to identify these audiences.

Politicians and celebrities often have many different audiences when they speak. Possible audiences for a Prime Minister may be the general public, lobby or other interest groups, legislators, foreign governments, or international organizations, among others. At an awards ceremony such as the Genies or Academy Awards, a celebrity might be speaking to an auditorium full of directors, fellow actors, and producers. But the most important audience may be the fans sitting before their television sets at home, watching the event.

Some audiences are more important to speakers than others. The rhetorical critic must identify and prioritize the different audiences of a speaker, judging which ones the speaker was trying hardest to reach. On whom did the speaker want to have the greatest impact? The remote television viewing audiences are often the largest and most important audiences to speakers.

The audience may also be present in 'real' time or 'virtual' time. An increasingly large number of people are going to the Internet to hear all or parts of speeches delivered by political and celebrity figures. You can listen to inaugural speeches delivered decades ago or to graduation speeches delivered last month. Excerpts from the Throne Speech can be heard for weeks after the event, as pundits ponder the words, dissect the meaning, and speculate about the significance of the event.

Sometimes the immediate audience becomes 'wallpaper' for the televised speaking event—a backdrop against which the speaker delivers his address. There will be clues in the speech as to whom the speaker regards to be his audience. As a rhetorical analyst, you must find these clues and use them to support your assertions about audiences.

Other audiences are remote, not only in physical terms, but also in generational terms. As noted in an earlier chapter, Nelson Mandela spoke to future generations of South Africans when he delivered his famous courtroom address in the 1960s. Knowing that he could not achieve his speech purposes at that point in time, he wrote his speech for those who would follow. Similarly, an audience may be domestic or international in scope. When Prime Minister Paul Martin delivers a speech on foreign policy, he has domestic audiences, but he also has international audiences. Some audience members may be located in Africa, Asia, or Russia.

Rhetorical critics need to respond to the following questions about audiences: Who are the primary or most important audiences for this speech? Who are the secondary audiences that the speaker hopes to reach? What do audience members know about the subject, and how do they feel about it? Would the audience have had any experiences that could have influenced their reactions? With what reference groups does the audience identify? How would these reference groups feel about the topic? Would the reference groups have an official stance on issues discussed in the speech? Would the age, gender, ethnicity, or other demographic variables have influenced the reaction of the audience to the speech? In what way would the values of the audience have influenced their reactions?

While historians are concerned with what actually happened, rhetorical critics are concerned with *perceptions* of what happened. The perceptions may or may not be correct. As a rhetorical critic, you want to understand how audiences reacted to speeches. Sometimes, when you cannot know for certain how they responded, you can only speculate about how they *might* have reacted, based on your knowledge of the period in which the rhetoric occurred, audience composition, and other variables. So you make statements such as, 'It is *likely* that . . .' or 'The audience *probably* reacted with some skepticism. . . .' Again you could say, 'The loud clapping *suggested* that the audience supported the views of the speaker.' In situations where you cannot have absolute knowledge of audience reactions, you should be tentative in your statements. You should avoid making comments such as, 'The audience did not like the speaker's approach' or 'The audience would have wanted to leave almost immediately.' Instead say, 'The audience *probably* was anxious to leave, given the length of the speech and the time of day.' The wording in the second case is speculative rather than dogmatic, and the writer offers some support for her reasoning on the matter. Words such as *could*, *might be*, *perhaps*, *sometimes*, and *often* qualify and soften assertions.

Speaker

As discussed in previous chapters, audiences judge speakers on the basis of the source credibility factors such as perceived dynamism, trustworthiness, expertise, composure, status, and sociability. When we talk about source credibility, however, we are talking about *perceptions*, which may or may not be valid. An audience may believe that a dishonest speaker is honest; or they may arrive falsely at the conclusion that an expert has no real knowledge of a situation. Their perceptions may be totally erroneous.

The idea of initial and terminal credibility is also relevant to this discussion. Speakers arrive at the podium or speaker's platform with an existing persona and image. That is their initial credibility. During the course of the speech, speakers can improve or worsen this image. *Terminal credibility* refers to the last impression made by the speaker.

Dynamism

North American audiences expect speakers to be energetic and dynamic in their choice of words and style of delivery. They perceive speakers to be dynamic when they use forceful and assertive language, when they portray themselves as active and involved in the social and political life of the community, and when they are progressive and innovative in their ideas. When speakers talk about the future, rather than the past, audiences see them as more dynamic. They also see speakers as more dynamic when they advocate change and when they appear in settings with young people. Box 16.3 lists video sources for historical and important speeches and speakers.

Box 16.3 Selected Video Recordings of Speeches

Bring the Troops Home (1991), produced and distributed by Paper Tiger Television. Includes speeches by conscientious objectors and other protests against US military presence in the Persian Gulf during the crisis.

Buffalo Soldiers (1998). Speeches by General Colin Powell and other high-ranking black officers in the US Armed Forces. Copy held at York University.

Building the CPR: with a recording of John A. Macdonald's speeches by John Diefenbaker (1968), written and compiled by Douglas Stuebing (London: Jackdaw Publications).

Canadian Great Speeches (1997), vols 1 and 2, narrated by Jill Tomassen Goodwin and Scott Spidell; executive producer and director, Roger Cook; co-product of the Educational Video Group, Montreal, and the Canadian Broadcasting Company. Distributed by the CBC. Historical speeches by Canadian politicians from Mackenzie King to René Lévesque.

Canadian Unity and Quebec Nationalism (1995), produced by CTV and distributed by Magic Lantern Communications. Speeches by and interviews with major political figures from Canada and France.

Honorary Doctorate Ceremony for Nelson Mandela and Graca Machel, 17 November 2001, Ryerson University. Broadcast live across Canada on CBC Newsworld. Copy held at Ryerson University, Toronto.

James Baldwin: The Price of the Ticket (1990), produced by Nobody Knows Productions and distributed by California Newsreel. Includes civil rights speeches of noted author and black, gay activist James Baldwin.

Legacy of a Dream: Martin Luther King (1974), produced by Richard Kaplan Productions. Includes clips from King's best-known addresses.

Martin Luther King: Commemorative Collection (1988). Features all of King's major speeches.

In Remembrance of Martin (1986), produced by Idanha Films and distributed by VEC. Celebration of first federal holiday commemorating Martin Luther King Jr. Includes a number of speeches by King and comments by friends, family, and advisers.

The Speeches Collection, produced by Darrell Moore and Joy Conley; distributed by SMA Distribution. Individual recordings of speeches by Adolph Hitler (with subtitles); Douglas McArthur; Dwight D. Eisenhower; Franklin Roosevelt; Harry S. Truman; John F. Kennedy; Martin Luther King Jr; Richard Nixon; Robert F. Kennedy; Winston Churchill; and others. Volume 1 is now available on DVD, sold by Amazon and other booksellers.

The Speeches of Famous Women: From Suffragette to Senator (1995), produced by Dennis Mueller and distributed by SMA. Includes speeches by Elizabeth Stanton, Eleanor Roosevelt, Betty Ford, Betty Friedan, and others.

Trustworthiness

Audiences expect speakers to be trustworthy. They perceive speakers to be trustworthy when they are willing to take a position on issues, even when they stand to lose from taking that position. They expect speakers to believe in what they say and to say what they believe. Audiences do not like speakers who vacillate or change sides on issues. Audiences expect speakers to be dedicated to their families and jobs. They also expect them to be socially responsible and to support laudable causes. When speakers share a common fate with the audience (meaning that the speaker will suffer the same consequences as the audience), audiences are more likely to trust and accept the proposals of the speaker. They are also likely to feel safer with speakers who have similar backgrounds and goals.

Expertise

Audiences expect speakers to be qualified to speak on a topic. Audiences perceive speakers to be competent when they demonstrate a good knowledge of the subject matter and have relevant experience. Speakers should be able to argue their positions in a logical fashion and cite statistics and evidence in support of their arguments.

Composure

Audiences expect speakers to be relatively composed. They perceive speakers to be composed when they appear confident, articulate, and in control. North American audiences tend to view direct eye contact as a sign of both honesty and confidence. Speakers show control when they do not stumble over their words or stammer or behave in a confused fashion when someone questions their ideas. Audiences look for such verbal and non-verbal signs of composure. North American audiences are willing, however, to tolerate occasional blips in composure, because these occasional mistakes suggest that the speaker is human, 'one of us'. They also admire a speaker who recovers, with some degree of panache, from a difficult situation.

Status

Audiences tend to accord more credibility to speakers who enjoy a prominent status. Different audiences, of course, have different standards for interpreting status. To an audience of Wall Street brokers, status could derive from success in the business world, whereas members of Amnesty International might accord more status to someone who has earned a reputation as a peacemaker. In either case, the person enjoys a privileged position in the minds of the audience. Association with a prestigious occupation, an influential authority figure, or a prominent family may give status to a speaker. Some speakers gain status by wearing designer clothing or executive suits. Some speakers position themselves for major addresses before respected authority symbols (the national or provincial flag, a crest or coat of arms, or parliamentary insignia) in an attempt to draw credibility from their status as office-holders. Prime ministers and presidents often seek photo opportunities with respected leaders and charismatic figures as a means of enhancing their status. An introduction by another person with status can also increase the status of the speaker.

Sometimes, of course, these associations backfire. Paul Martin's affiliation with rock star and global social activist Bono soured when the Martin government failed to commit 0.7 per cent of gross domestic product to foreign aid, one of the Millennium Development Goals of the United Nations to assist less-developed countries.

Sociability

Audiences expect speakers to be sociable. They perceive speakers as sociable when they are friendly in demeanour and when they adopt a warm personal style of delivery. They also perceive them as sociable when they attend community meetings, speak at social gatherings, and make personal references to members of the audience. Audiences like speakers who share their values and aspirations, who are 'one of us'.

Message

The next step in a rhetorical critique is analysis of message or text. At this point, the critic looks strictly at the words of the speaker—the written or spoken text. (When speakers abandon their manuscripts or add spontaneous comments, the spoken text will diverge from the written script.) The analyst looks for strategies used by the speaker to achieve his purposes, dominant themes in the speech, and choice of supporting materials.

First, the analyst identifies the strategies used to achieve the speech purposes. What was the speaker's plan for persuading or informing the audience? How does she attempt to get past the objections of her audience? How does she enhance her credibility without diminishing the credibility of her opponent? What are the major arguments that she uses to convince her audience? In achieving speech purposes, for example, the speaker may pursue a strategy that relies heavily on logic and reasoning. Alternatively, the speaker may appeal almost exclusively to the emotions of the audience in achieving her purposes. Eloquent or divisive language may characterize the speech.

In a short analysis, you cannot cover everything. As a consequence, you may want to identify an area on which to concentrate—in other words, a theme.[6] A thematic approach can look at how a speech reflects attitudes towards women in a particular time period, how the speaker uses the language of hip-hop culture to get across his message to youthful audiences, or how a Native speaker establishes credibility by connecting with the spiritual traditions of his people. Another approach involves looking at the kinds of examples used to bolster a political position or the aesthetics of a particular speech—how the speaker uses metaphorical language to paint images in the minds of the audience.

The title of a rhetorical analysis often hints at the themes identified in a speech: 'The Logical Fallacies of Bill Smith', 'Failing Credibility: The Speaker's Downhill Run', 'Grabbing Attention: The Antics of Speaker X', 'Eloquence in Shorthand', or 'Testing the Tolerance of the Audience: A Question of Ethics'. The following titles, drawn from analyses conducted by first- and second-year communication students, illustrate how themes can help to focus an analysis: 'The Rhetoric of Today with a Message for Tomorrow: The Final Farewell of William Lyon Mackenzie King', 'Reverend Churchill: Listening to God', 'This is Our Finest Hour: Churchill's Finest Speech', 'Emotion through Eloquence: Earl Spencer's Eulogy at Princess Diana's Funeral', 'The Five Audiences of John F. Kennedy's Commencement Address', 'The Use of Humour in Prince Charles' Address to the Invensys Conference on Tall Buildings', 'Poised Passion: The Moving Eulogy of Justin Trudeau', 'Second to No Other: Paul Martin's Use of Language to Inspire Patriotism', 'A Nation Divided: Unification Strategies in President Bush's Acceptance Speech', 'Wading in the Deep End: The Politics of Hip Hop with K-OS', and 'The Power of One: A Rhetorical Analysis of Motivational Speaker Erin Brockovich'. The rhetorical critic must allow the content of the speech to inform on the strategies of the speaker.

After identifying the speaker's strategies and limiting the analysis of the message to one thematic area, the critic looks for support of these ideas. How has the speaker supported his or her claims or assertions? With examples? Statistics? Personal experience? To review logical, emotional, and credibility supports, refer to Chapter 9. Give specific examples from the speech to back up your claims.

Outcomes

The rhetorical analyst can look at the outcomes of a speech in terms of the extent to which the speaker achieved his purposes (a pragmatic perspective), made a contribution to the knowledge of the audience (a socially responsible perspective), or stimulated positive change in the audience and/or the larger environment (an ethical perspective). What were the effects of the speech? In pragmatic terms, did the speech achieve its purposes? Did the audience react favourably to the speaker? Did they vote as the speaker asked that they vote, buy the product advocated, or change buying habits in the direction suggested by the speaker? Did the speaker increase the knowledge or understanding of the audience? Or did the person deal in superficial terms with the subject matter, address a trivial subject, or tell the audience something they already knew? Did the speaker act with integrity and effect positive changes in the environment?[7]

Many speeches succeed on some points and fail on others. Some of the most beautifully written speeches have failed to achieve their goals. The speaker has lost the election, failed to win a court victory, or eloquently championed a lost cause. Abraham Lincoln's two-minute Gettysburg Address got scant mention in the papers of the day, while Edward Everett's less memorable speech on the same occasion made headlines. If you judge the speeches on immediate impact, you would have to say that Everett's speech was more effective at achieving its goals. But if you judge the speeches on long-term impact, Lincoln's was certainly more successful.

At other times, a speaker may be highly successful in achieving his purposes, but society condemns and laments the ethics of the person's discourse and actions. The rhetoric of Adolf Hitler comes quickly to mind on this point. At the other extreme, a completely inarticulate speaker may make a significant contribution to the knowledge of her audience and adhere to the highest of ethical standards. So, judged on aesthetic or artistic standards of a particular time and place, the speaker may fail dramatically. But judged on criteria such as contribution and ethics, the speech may be considered a 'good' one.

Cost of Achieving Outcomes

A rhetorical critic can also ask, 'What was the cost of achieving the desired outcomes?' Is the speaker telling the truth as he or she knows it? Has the speaker assumed a position that is 'morally right' by some standards of society? Are the argumentation and reasoning legitimate and honest? Was anyone hurt by the outcomes of the speaking event?

Questions for Discussion

1. Do most speakers have unstated and multiple purposes in delivering speeches? Give some examples to illustrate your position.
2. Can you think of any speaking occasions where the immediate audience was less important than a remote audience? Can you think of any examples of speakers talking to future generations more than to the present generation?
3. When researching contemporary rhetorical events, the analyst goes to different kinds of sources than when analyzing rhetorical events from other time periods. Why would you use different kinds of sources?
4. Explain the following statement: While historians are concerned with what actually happened, rhetorical critics are concerned with *perceptions* of what happened.

Justin Trudeau at his father's casket after reading the eulogy during the state funeral for former Prime Minister Pierre Trudeau on 3 October, 2000 in Montreal. (CP PHOTO/Paul Chaisson)

Appendix: Sample Rhetorical Analysis

Justin Trudeau's Eulogy: A Touching Tribute from Son to Father

by Diana Aird

On September 28, 2000, former Prime Minister of Canada Pierre Elliott Trudeau died of prostate cancer. Five days later, the country gathered around their television screens to watch his memorial service. With so many seasoned politicians and distinguished guests present in the cathedral that day, no one would have guessed that the most memorable tribute would come from Trudeau's eldest son, Justin.

A eulogy is never an easy speech to give. The speaker is not only under immense pressure to honour and do justice to the deceased, but he must also deal with the sorrow, loss, and despair that accompany a death. According to McKerrow and colleagues, the purpose of a eulogy is 'to renew and reinforce the audience's adherence to ideals possessed by the deceased and worthy of emulation by the community'.[1]

In Justin Trudeau's eulogy, he sought to honour and pay respect to the memory of his father. The analysis of how he achieved this purpose will include a consideration of context, speaker, rhetorical strategies, and audience reactions to the eulogy.

Context

Justin is the son of 'political royalty',[2] the progeny of Canada's most flamboyant and charismatic (albeit controversial) prime minister. Pierre Elliott Trudeau had incited 'Trudeaumania' in the late 1960s and early 1970s, when he drove the streets of Montreal in his Mercedes Benz convertible, dated celebrities such as Barbra Streisand and Bianca Jagger, canoed in the whitewaters of the Canadian wilderness, slid down banisters in Buckingham Palace, and did pirouettes behind the back of Queen Elizabeth. With a trademark rose in his lapel, a floppy hat on his head, and a cape around his shoulders, Pierre Trudeau acquired the status of 'political pop star'.[3]

A constitutional lawyer and the son of a French-Canadian millionaire businessman, he was brilliant, cosmopolitan, bilingual, and irreverent. In later years, Trudeau wore sandals to Parliament, gave the finger to protestors, and won a reputation for unbridled arrogance. His most famous comment came at the time of the 1970 October Crisis, when a terrorist organization abducted a British diplomat and murdered a Quebec minister. The Front de libération du Québec had carried out over 200 violent acts, including the bombing of the Montreal Stock Exchange. To deal with the threat, Trudeau invoked the War Measures Act, which put tanks and soldiers in full battle gear on the streets of Montreal, Quebec. Critics attacked Trudeau for suspending civil liberties and establishing the outward manifestations of a police state. When asked how far he would go, he returned without pause, 'Just watch me!'

Setting and Audience

The eulogy took place in Notre Dame Basilica, Montreal's largest and grandest cathedral. The vaults of the ceiling were deep Prussian blue and studded with a vast firmament of gilt stars and gold fleurs-de-lys, once the symbol of French colonialism and today the standard of separatism. There were 7,000 pipes in the organ. The pulpits and confessionals (12) and altars (at least four) and back pieces and vestry and side chapels were hand carved. . . . [The cathedral floor was] a bright light-blue linoleum with French-vanilla borders. . . . Walking into the Notre Dame Cathedral was like walking into a vast spiritual bazaar.[4]

The funeral followed days of mourning, in which Canadians had waited in long lines to pay homage to Trudeau, who lay in state in the Palais de Justice in Old Montreal. Many had travelled from across Canada to pay tribute to a man who had captured the hearts of many and the imaginations of others. Some just wanted to participate in history.

In attendance at the funeral were almost 3000 people, including family and friends, politicians, business associates, and dignitaries from other countries. Cuban president Fidel Castro and former US President Jimmy Carter were among the familiar faces from the world of politics. Celebrities such as actress Margot Kidder and singer/poet Leonard Cohen represented the arts at the event. Former wife Margaret Sinclair Trudeau sat in the audience with her son Alexandre (Sasha). Trudeau's youngest child, Sarah, sat next to Sasha. For many Canadians, this was their first acquaintance with Sarah, a child conceived when Trudeau was 71 years old and kept out of the media spotlight prior to this occasion. Sarah sat with her mother, Deborah Coyne, a constitutional lawyer and author.

Between 30,000 and 50,000 Canadians, unable to obtain a place in the cathedral, waited outside.[5] The crowds had begun to gather before dawn, hoping to secure seats at the historical event. For days prior to the state funeral, many thousands more had waited in long lines to pay homage to their former leader, who lay in state at the Palais de Justice in Old Montreal. The millions of Canadians who watched the televised speech from their homes constituted a secondary—but very important—audience for the eulogy.

Speaker

When Justin Trudeau rose to pay tribute to his famous father, he faced an empathetic audience. Canadians knew and liked him. He had grown up in the spotlight of his father's celebrity. Canadians remembered the young boy, scurried through airports by Margaret and Pierre Trudeau. They also remembered the loss of his brother, Michel, in 1998. While skiing in the back country of British Colum-

bia, Michel had been swept by an avalanche into the frigid waters of a glacial lake. In the months that followed Michel's death, Justin had taken time from his job as English teacher to become a spokesperson for wilderness safety and avalanche awareness groups. At 28 years of age, Justin Trudeau now faced his second major loss; and Canadians shared his grief. When the attractive young man rose to speak, the audience responded with warmth.

Rhetorical Strategies

In this speech, Justin Trudeau sought to honour his father by focusing on the lessons that his father had imparted to him—lessons that demonstrated Pierre Trudeau's unqualified commitment to family, his love of country, and his respect for humankind.

He sought to accomplish this purpose by appealing to multiple audiences, adopting an intimate approach in which he shared private moments with his audience, and relying on lyrical and poetic language to evoke emotion.

Adapting to Multiple Audiences

Unlike the case of most eulogies, the audience for eulogies involving a former head of a state is the population of the entire country, as well as citizens in other countries. To adapt to such a diverse audience, which held many sworn political enemies, Justin Trudeau took a three-pronged approach. First, he recognized that his father represented different things to different people: 'Pierre Elliott Trudeau. The very words convey so many things to so many people. Statesman, intellectual, professor, adversary, outdoorsman, lawyer, journalist, author, prime minister.'

The opening greeting 'Friends, Romans, Countrymen', taken from a eulogy delivered by Marc Antony in *Julius Caesar*, took the audience by surprise. No one quite knew how to interpret the enigmatic salutation. But the greeting could be interpreted as recognition that not everyone viewed his father's accomplishments in the same positive light. Like Julius Caesar, Pierre Trudeau had supporters and detractors; and both groups were in attendance at his funeral. Trudeau removed the edge from the irony of this greeting when he smiled at his audience, a non-verbal acceptance of the reality of politics and a possible statement that he did not hold grudges toward his father's enemies.

Third, Justin Trudeau acknowledged his television audience, who were also grieving the loss of his father; and he thanked Canadians for their support:

We have gathered from coast to coast, from one ocean to another, united in our grief, to say goodbye.

. . . Over the past few days, with every card, every rose, every tear, every wave and every pirouette, you returned his love. It means the world to Sacha and me. Thank you.

Finally, while Trudeau delivered the majority of the speech in English, he included French passages, as well. This bilingual content conveyed the message that francophone and anglophone Canadians were equally important members of the immediate and remote audiences. Furthermore, given its dominant place in the legacy of Pierre Elliott Trudeau, bilingual content was imperative.

Sharing of Intimacies

Audience adaptation was certainly important to the success of Justin Trudeau's eulogy. But his success also came from the highly personal quality of his address, which centred on the love and respect of a son for his father. The stories in the speech were not about a prime minister. They were about the relationship of two men—father and son—and the lessons passed from one to the other. As Justin Trudeau stated, 'More than anything to me, he was dad.'

Trudeau recounted how excited he was to accompany his father on a 'special top secret mission' to see Santa Claus at the North Pole. Hearing his description of the events, the listeners can envision six-year-old Justin peering through the window as he describes his adventure with his father:

So I clambered over the snowbank, was boosted up to the window, rubbed my sleeve against the frosty glass to see inside, and as my eyes adjusted to the gloom, I saw a figure, hunched over one of many work tables that seemed very cluttered. He was wearing a red suit with that furry white trim. And that's when I understood just how powerful and wonderful my father was.

Justin also recounted another instance when he tried to impress his father by telling a mean joke about his father's political rival. In response, Pierre Trudeau chastised his eight-year-old son, telling him that he should never 'attack the individual.' His father explained that a person 'can be in total disagreement with someone without denigrating him.' Justin explained that his father then took him by the hand and led him to his opponent's table, where he introduced him to the person whom we assume to be former Prime Minister Joe Clark and his young daughter. As listeners, we feel that we are privy to a very personal moment in the life of Justin Trudeau; and like Justin, we are able to learn something of significance from the account.

The best speeches of tribute focus, as did Trudeau's, on a select number of traits and/or accomplishments of the person who is being remembered.[6] Justin Trudeau could have spoken about his father's career or his status as a world leader. Instead he focused on the personal values of his father and his dedication to family and country. Tacked onto every story and anecdote were the life lessons that the father passed to his son:

He encouraged us to push ourselves, to test limits, to challenge anyone and anything. . . . Because mere tolerance is not enough: we must have true and deep respect for every human being, regardless of his beliefs, his origins and his values. That is what my father demanded of his sons and that is what he demanded of his country. . . . My father's fundamental belief stemmed from his deep love for and faith in all Canadians.

Pierre Elliott Trudeau relayed these lessons to his son, who in turn conveyed them to his audience. For the many Canadians who admired and respected Pierre Elliott Trudeau, the words had a ring of truth. They recalled Trudeau's personal vision of a united, bilingual, and multicultural Canada—a vision to which he devoted his political career.

Relying on Lyrical and Poetic Language to Evoke Emotion

The success of the eulogy also derived from its lyrical and poetic qualities. Trudeau opened and closed the eulogy with a quotation. As noted earlier, his opening line was borrowed from the eulogy of Shakespeare's Marc Antony. In the conclusion of the speech, he referenced the following passage from Robert Frost's poem 'Stopping by the Woods on a Snowy Evening':

The woods are lovely, dark and deep,
But I have promises to keep,
And miles to go before I sleep,
And miles to go before I sleep.

In the passage that concluded his speech, Trudeau used the linguistic device of repetition and referred back to Robert Frost's poem:

He left politics in '84. But he came back for Meech. He came back for Charlottetown. He came back to remind us of who we are and what we're all capable of. But he won't be coming back anymore. It's all up to us now. The woods are lovely, dark and deep. He has kept his promises and earned his sleep. Je t'aime, Papa.

Justin changed the last line of Frost's poem to reflect the fact that his father had fulfilled his promises to Canadians, coming back to politics again and again when his country needed his involvement. Only after pronouncing these final words and issuing the challenge to Canadians to pursue the ideals of his father did Justin Trudeau allow himself to demonstrate emotion. In a poignant and powerful moment, he rested his head on his father's casket and cried.

Audience Reactions

The reaction to the speech was unambiguous. At the end of the eulogy, the audience in the church stood and applauded—a strange reaction to a eulogy. According to newspaper accounts, there was not a dry eye in the cathedral. CTV news talked about a 'transfixed' audience.[7] A journalist wrote:

> In his absence, Justin stepped into the void in a way that uncannily reminded the public, and the pundits, of the Trudeau magic. For a country looking for some sense of the man he had become, the moving eulogy he delivered for his father was seen as a defining moment.[8]

In the week following the funeral, newspapers across Canada carried copies of the eulogy, which was also broadcast on evening news. One writer noted that even those Canadians who disagreed with the political beliefs of Pierre Trudeau could not help but be moved by the eulogy.[9] This ability to unite people in a common emotion has to be an important marker of a successful speech.

Conclusion

Using effective audience adaptation strategies, a highly personal approach, and lyrical and poetic language, Trudeau accomplished his major goal: to paint a picture of a man whose commitments to family matched his dedication to country and whose humanistic values governed his behavior in both roles. While the eulogies of others focused on the accomplishments of 'Pierre Elliott Trudeau, statesman', the eulogy of Justin Trudeau successfully centred on the legacy of 'Pierre Elliott Trudeau, family man'.

And on that day in early October 2000, Justin Trudeau acquired the status in Canada of John Kennedy Jr in the United States and Prince William in England. He became Canada's son. Today Justin Trudeau drives along Saint Catherine's Street in Montreal in his father's old Mercedes Benz, argues for environmental causes, and canoes in the Canadian Rockies, where his brother Michel died in 1998. He chairs the Board of Directors of Katimavik, a program begun by his father in 1977, and attends a program in mechanical engineering at Ecole Polytechnique. Many predict the inevitability of a political future for Justin Trudeau, a future born on the day that a grieving young man rested his head beside a single red rose on his father's casket.[10]

Notes

[1] Raymie E. McKerrow et al., *Principles and Types of Speech Communication* (New York: Prentice-Hall Longman, 2000): 391.

[2] Dorothy Bartoszewski, 'Justin Trudeau's Unity Strategy', February 23, 2005, http://www.thetyee.ca/Views/2005/02/23/Justin TrudeauUnity/. Accessed March 22, 2005.

[3] CBC archives, 'A Swinger for Prime Minister', http://archives.cbc.ca/IDD-1-74-73/people/trudeaumania/. Accessed March 19, 2005.

[4] Ian Brown, 'Love in a Cold Climate', *Globe and Mail*, October 7, 2000, http://www.theglobeandmail.comseries/trudeau/ibrownlov_oct07.html. Accessed March 21, 2005.

[5] Ibid.

[6] McKerrow et al., p. 392.

[7] CTV news staff, 'Justin Trudeau: Raising Awareness about Avalanches', April 11, 2003, http://www.ctv.ca/servlet/ArticleNews/story/CTVNews/. Accessed March 21, 2005.

[8] Ibid.

[9] Eli Schuster, 'The Purpose of Teaching: Justin Trudeau Seems to Echo One of the World's Great Christian Apologists', *Report: Canada's Independent News Magazine* (May 28, 2001). http://report.ca/archive/report/20010528/p59i010528f.html.

[10] For an audio version of the complete text, go to Justin Trudeau's eulogy at CBC archives: http://archives.cbc.ca.

Additional references

Donna Kurt, Wilds of Manitoba. http://www.wilds.mb.ca/womb. Accessed October 3, 2000.

Appendix:

A Selection of Speeches

Dr Martin Luther King Jr
'I Have a Dream'
March on Washington
Lincoln Memorial, Washington, DC
28 August 1963

I am happy to join with you today in what will go down in history as the greatest demonstration for freedom in the history of our nation.

Five score years ago, a great American, in whose symbolic shadow we stand today, signed the Emancipation Proclamation. This momentous decree came as a great beacon light of hope to millions of Negro slaves who had been seared in the flames of withering injustice. It came as a joyous daybreak to end the long night of their captivity.

But one hundred years later, the Negro still is not free. One hundred years later, the life of the Negro is still sadly crippled by the manacles of segregation and the chains of discrimination. One hundred years later, the Negro lives on a lonely island of poverty in the midst of a vast ocean of material prosperity. One hundred years later, the Negro is still languished in the corners of American society and finds himself an exile in his own land. And so we've come here today to dramatize a shameful condition.

In a sense we've come to our nation's capital to cash a check. When the architects of our republic wrote the magnificent words of the Constitution and the Declaration of Independence, they were signing a promissory note to which every American was to fall heir. This note was a promise that all men, yes, black men as well as white men, would be guaranteed the 'unalienable Rights' of 'Life, Liberty and the pursuit of Happiness'. It is obvious today that America has defaulted on this promissory note, insofar as her citizens of color are concerned. Instead of honoring this sacred obligation, America has given the Negro people a bad check, a check which has come back marked 'insufficient funds'.

But we refuse to believe that the bank of justice is bankrupt. We refuse to believe that there are insufficient funds in the great vaults of opportunity of this nation. And so, we've come to cash this check, a check that will give us upon demand the riches of freedom and the security of justice.

We have also come to this hallowed spot to remind America of the fierce urgency of Now. This is no time to engage in the luxury of cooling off or to take the tranquilizing drug of gradualism. Now is the time to make real the promises of democracy. Now is the time to rise from the dark and desolate valley of segregation to the sunlit path of racial justice. Now is the time to lift our nation from the quicksands of racial injustice to the solid rock of brotherhood. Now is the time to make justice a reality for all of God's children.

It would be fatal for the nation to overlook the urgency of the moment. This sweltering summer of the Negro's legitimate discontent will not pass until there is an invigorating autumn of freedom and equality. Nineteen sixty-three is not an end, but a beginning. And those who hope that the Negro needed to blow off steam and will now be content will have a rude awakening if the nation returns to business as usual. And there will be neither rest nor tranquility in America until the Negro is granted his citizenship rights. The whirlwinds of revolt will continue to shake the foundations of our nation until the bright day of justice emerges.

But there is something that I must say to my people, who stand on the warm threshold which leads into the palace of justice: In the process of gaining our rightful place, we must not be guilty of wrongful deeds. Let us not seek to satisfy our thirst for freedom by drinking from the cup of bitterness and hatred. We must forever conduct our struggle on the high plane of dignity and discipline. We must not allow our creative protest to degenerate into physical violence. Again and again, we must rise to the majestic heights of meeting physical force with soul force.

The marvelous new militancy which has engulfed the Negro community must not lead us to a distrust of all white people, for many of our white brothers, as evidenced by their presence here today, have come to realize that their destiny is tied up with our destiny. And they have come to realize that their freedom is inextricably bound to our freedom.

We cannot walk alone.

And as we walk, we must make the pledge that we shall always march ahead.

We cannot turn back.

There are those who are asking the devotees of civil rights, 'When will you be satisfied?' We can never be satisfied as long as the Negro is the victim of the unspeakable horrors of police brutality. We can never be satisfied as long as our bodies, heavy with the fatigue of travel, cannot gain lodging in the motels of the highways and the hotels of the cities. We cannot be satisfied as long as a Negro in Mississippi cannot vote and a Negro in New York believes he has nothing for which to vote. No, no, we are not satisfied, and we will not be satisfied until 'justice rolls down like waters, and righteousness like a mighty stream.'[1]

I am not unmindful that some of you have come here out of great trials and tribulations. Some of you have come fresh from narrow jail cells. And some of you have come from areas where your quest—quest for freedom left you battered by the storms of persecution and staggered by the winds of police brutality. You have been the veterans of creative suffering. Continue to work with the faith that unearned suffering is redemptive. Go back to Mississippi, go back to Alabama, go back to South Carolina, go back to Georgia, go back to Louisiana, go back to the slums and ghettos of our northern cities, knowing that somehow this situation can and will be changed.

Let us not wallow in the valley of despair, I say to you today, my friends.

And so even though we face the difficulties of today and tomorrow, I still have a dream. It is a dream deeply rooted in the American dream.

I have a dream that one day this nation will rise up and live out the true meaning of its creed: 'We hold these truths to be self-evident, that all men are created equal.'

I have a dream that one day on the red hills of Georgia, the sons of former slaves and the sons of former slave owners will be able to sit down together at the table of brotherhood.

I have a dream that one day even the state of Mississippi, a state sweltering with the heat of injustice, sweltering with the heat of oppression, will be transformed into an oasis of freedom and justice.

I have a dream that my four little children will one day live in a nation where they will not be judged by the color of their skin but by the content of their character.

I have a *dream* today!

I have a dream that one day, down in Alabama, with its vicious racists, with its governor having his lips dripping with the words of 'interposition' and 'nullification'—one day right there in Alabama little black boys and black girls will be able to join hands with little white boys and white girls as sisters and brothers.

I have a *dream* today!

I have a dream that one day every valley shall be exalted, and every hill and mountain shall be made low, the rough places will be made plain, and the crooked places will be made straight; 'and the glory of the Lord shall be revealed and all flesh shall see it together.'[2]

This is our hope, and this is the faith that I go back to the South with.

With this faith, we will be able to hew out of the mountain of despair a stone of hope. With this faith, we will be able to transform the jangling discords of our nation into a beautiful symphony of brotherhood. With this faith, we will be able to work together, to pray together, to struggle together, to go to jail together, to stand up for freedom together, knowing that we will be free one day.

And this will be the day—this will be the day when all of God's children will be able to sing with new meaning:

My country 'tis of thee, sweet land of liberty, of thee I sing.
Land where my fathers died, land of the Pilgrim's pride,
From every mountainside, let freedom ring!

And if America is to be a great nation, this must become true.

And so let freedom ring from the prodigious hilltops of New Hampshire.

Let freedom ring from the mighty mountains of New York.

Let freedom ring from the heightening Alleghenies of Pennsylvania.

Let freedom ring from the snow-capped Rockies of Colorado.

Let freedom ring from the curvaceous slopes of California.

But not only that:

Let freedom ring from Stone Mountain of Georgia.

Let freedom ring from Lookout Mountain of Tennessee.

Let freedom ring from every hill and molehill of Mississippi.

From every mountainside, let freedom ring.

And when this happens, when we allow freedom ring, when we let it ring from every village and every hamlet, from every state and every city, we will be able to speed up that day when all of God's children, black men and white men, Jews and Gentiles, Protestants and Catholics, will be able to join hands and sing in the words of the old Negro spiritual:

Free at last! free at last!
Thank God Almighty, we are free at last!

---

[1] Amos 5:24 (rendered precisely in The American Standard Version of the Holy Bible).

[2] Isaiah 40:4-5 (King James Version of the Holy Bible).

Prime Minister Joe Clark
Eulogy at the Burial of the Right Honourable John G. Diefenbaker
Saskatoon, Saskatchewan
22 August 1979

John Diefenbaker is home—at the end of a life which started in another century, and embraced most of the history of our Canada. He came to this West when it was raw and young, in the year Saskatchewan became a province. As a child, he talked with the buffalo hunters. As a man, he led his country and dominated its Parliament. Along the way, he touched the lives of his fellow Canadians as no one ever will again.

It is easier to change laws than to change lives. John Diefenbaker changed both. His Bill of Rights, his social programs, his resource and regional development policies, changed permanently the laws of Canada. But, more fundamental than that, he changed our vision of our country. He opened the nation to itself, and let us see our possibilities. It is fitting that his last work, from which death took him, was to prepare a speech to open the Dempster, his highway to our Northern Sea.

We are not here to pass judgement on John Diefenbaker. We are here to celebrate the frontier strength and spirit of an indomitable man, born to a minority group, raised in a minority region, leader of a minority party, who went on to change the very nature of his country—and to change it permanently. When any man dies, after nearly 84 full years, there is a mixture of memories. With this man, there is the certain knowledge that he leaves his country better, broader, prouder than he found it.

He was the great populist of Canadian politics. John Diefenbaker opened the politics of our country to those to whom it had always been closed. He gave politics a lively reality to those to whom it had seemed remote. He brought daylight to a process too long obscured in shadow and mystery.

He was a man of passion. Whatever the issue, whomever the person, he had a view—strongly held—forcefully offered—vigorously defended. John Diefenbaker did not tiptoe through the public life of Canada; he strode through—and, as he offered passion to his fellow Canadians, he drew passion in return. John Diefenbaker attracted every reaction from the people of this country, except indifference.

He was a patriot. To John Diefenbaker patriotism was never out of fashion; it was the essence of his life. Not every Canadian shared his view of Canada, but all knew and were touched by his devotion to his view. His faith shaped and formed all his other beliefs. His belief in Canada as a land of equality for all its citizens is in his Bill of Rights. His awareness of the full breadth of this land is in the northern development he spurred and in the regional development he fostered. His abiding commitment to social justice and human dignity is in the health care system he initiated, and in the programs he sponsored to help the disadvantaged.

He was much more than a statesman. Statesmen are strangers, and John Diefenbaker was personal to most of the people of Canada. He mainstreamed through life. And in those last days, the mourners, who lined the train's long route, who came at midnight to say farewell, who sang and applauded as he left—they were not remembering a Bill of Rights, or a debate in Parliament, or a particular cause or party. Their homage was to a singular man, who entered and enlarged our lives and whom we wanted to see home.

In a very real sense, his life, was Canada. Over eight decades, he spanned our history, from the ox cart on the Prairies to the satellite in space. He shaped much of that history, all of it shaped him.

Now that life—that sweep of history—has ended. And we are here today to see John Diefenbaker to his final place of rest.

It is appropriate that it be here. For, while John Diefenbaker was of all of Canada, he was, above all else, a man of the Prairies. His populism was inspired in this open land. His deep feelings for the needs of individuals were shaped by what he saw and felt during the Depression years. The South Saskatchewan dam—one of his physical legacies—reflected his determination that farmers in the region never again suffer dust when there should be grass. It was from Prince Albert that he looked North and caught the vision with which he stirred the minds and hearts of all of us.

And so we commit his mortal remains to the Prairie soil, here, on the campus where he studied and was chancellor, above the river which was a route of our first westward pioneers, in the province which formed him. He showed what one man can do in a country like Canada.

As we commit his body to the land he loved, we commit his soul to the Creator he sought to serve. And we—each of us—commit our memories of him to all of our hearts.

Eternal rest grant unto him, Oh Lord, and let Perpetual Light shine upon him.

God bless and keep John Diefenbaker.

Prime Minister Pierre Elliott Trudeau
On Quebec's Sovereignty-Association Referendum
Paul Sauvé Arena
Montreal, Quebec
14 May 1980

(TRANSLATION)

Mr Chairman . . .

Thank you. Thank you very much. Thank you very much. No, no. Thank you very much.

Mr Chairman, fellow Canadians.

First of all, I want to thank you for this warm welcome. I think it is obvious by this immense gathering—it is obvious that these are historic moments.

There are very few examples in the history of democracy of one part of a country choosing to decide, for itself and by itself, whether, YES or NO, it wants to be part of the country to which it has always belonged. There are very few occasions when this has happened in the history of democracy. And I believe that all those here this evening, all those who have worked for the NO in this province for over a month, will be proud to reply when . . . when our children and perhaps, if we are lucky our grandchildren, ask us in twenty or thirty years:

You were there in May 1980. You were there when the people of Quebec were asked to decide freely on their future. You were there when Quebec had the option to stay in Canada or to leave. What did you do in May 1980—'No, that was our answer.'

(Applause)

I should like to ask you this evening to reflect on the question that is asked of us, and on the consequences of the answers we may give to these questions.

Allow me—perhaps for the last time before going to the polls—allow me to remind you of the essence of the question. There are two issues involved:

The first is the sovereignty of Quebec, and that is defined in the question itself as: the exclusive power to make its laws, levy its taxes and establish relations abroad . . . in other words, sovereignty.

And while we in this room answer NO, in other rooms in other parts of the province, there are people who answer YES; who truly and honestly want sovereignty.

I share your opinion: this is the false option; an option that means, as Jean Chrétien said, that we will no longer send Quebec MPs to govern us in Canada; an option that means independence; an option that means the separation of Quebec from the rest of the country.

To this our answer is NO.

But it is not to those who are for or against sovereignty that I wish to address my remarks this evening.

After the referendum, I hope we will continue to respect one another's differences; that we will respect the option which has been freely chosen by those who are for or against independence for Quebec.

(Applause)

In this question, therefore, there is sovereignty and there is everything else.

Everything else is a new agreement. It is equality of nations. It is at the same time economic association. It is a common currency. It is change through another referendum. It is a mandate to negotiate.

And we know very well what they are doing, these hucksters of the YES vote.

They are trying to appeal to everyone who would say YES to a new agreement. YES to equality of nations. YES at the same time to association. YES at the same time to a common currency. YES to a second referendum. YES to a simple mandate to negotiate.

It is those who say YES through pride of because they do not understand the question, or because they want to increase their bargaining power, and to those among the undecided who are on the brink of voting YES, to whom I am addressing myself this evening, because what we have to ask ourselves is what would happen in the case of a YES vote, as in the case of a NO vote.

And it is the undecided, those who are on the YES side through pride, or because they are tired and fed up, who, in these last few days, must be addressed.

So let us consider this. The Government of Canada and all the provincial governments have made themselves perfectly clear.

If the answer to the referendum question is NO, we have all said that this NO will be interpreted as a mandate to change the Constitution, to renew federalism.

(Applause)

I am not the only person saying this. Nor is Mr Clark. Nor is Mr Broadbent. It is not only the nine premiers of the other provinces saying this. It is also the seventy-five MPs

elected by Quebecers to represent them in Ottawa . . .

(Applause)

. . . who are saying that a NO means change. And because I spoke to these MPs this morning, I know that I can make a most solemn commitment that following a NO vote, we will immediately take action to renew the Constitution and we will not stop until we have done that.

And I make a solemn declaration to all Canadians in the other provinces, we, the Quebec MPs, are laying ourselves on the line, because we are telling Quebecers to vote NO and telling you in the other provinces that we will not agree to your interpreting a NO vote as an indication that everything is fine and can remain as it was before.

We want change and we are willing to lay our seats in the House on the line to have change.

This would be our attitude in the case of a NO vote.

Mr Lévesque has asked me what my attitude would be if the majority of Quebecers voted YES.

I have already answered this question. I did so in Parliament. I did so in Montreal and in Quebec City. And I say it again this evening: if the answer to the referendum is YES— I have said it clearly in the House of Commons—Mr Lévesque will be welcome to come to Ottawa, where I will receive politely, as he has always received me in Quebec City, and I will tell him that there are two doors. If you knock on the sovereignty-association door, there is no negotiation possible.

Mr Lévesque continues to repeat, 'But what about democracy—what would you do if a majority of the Quebec people voted YES? Would you not be obliged, by the principle of democracy, to negotiate?'

No indeed!

It is like saying to Mr Lévesque, 'The people of Newfoundland have just voted 100 per cent in favour of renegotiating the electricity contract with Quebec. You are obliged, the name of democracy, to respect the will of Newfoundland, are you not?'

It is obvious that this sort of logic does not work.

The wishes of Quebecers may be expressed through democratic process, but that cannot bind others—those in other provinces who did not vote to act as Quebec decides.

So by that reasoning, Mr Lévesque, there will be no association. Now, if you want to speak, if you want to speak of sovereignty, let me say that you have no mandate to negotiate that, because you did not ask Quebecers if they wanted sovereignty pure and simple.

You said: Do you want sovereignty on the condition that there is also association?

So, with no association, you have no mandate to negotiate sovereignty; you do not have the key to open that door, and neither do I.

I do not have that mandate either, because we were elected on February 18, scarcely a couple of months ago—for the specific purpose of making laws for the province of Quebec.

So don't ask me not to make any, don't ask me to give full powers to Quebec.

On the other hand, if Mr Lévesque, by some miracle, and it truly would be a miracle, knocked on the other door, saying: I have a mandate to negotiate, and would like to negotiate renewed federalism then the door would be wide open to him, and I would say: you did not have to go to the trouble of holding a referendum for that; if it is renewed federalism you want, if that is what you wish to negotiate, then you are welcome.

But is it really possible that Mr Lévesque would say that, because what are the YES supporters saying?

The YES supporters are saying—and I asked Mr Lévesque this a couple of weeks ago: What will you do if the majority votes NO? What will you say then? Will you respect the will of the people, or will you claim that a NO vote does not mean as much as a YES vote, and that a NO does not count for the moment, but that another referendum needs to be held?

I asked Mr Lévesque that, and this was his answer: We will not refuse a few crumbs of autonomy for Quebec, but we will still be going around in circles.

Mr Lévesque, if the people of Quebec vote NO, as I believe they will . . .

. . . won't you say that since the people have rejected sovereignty-association, it is your duty to be a good government and put an end to the status quo on which you place so much blame, and to join us in changing the Constitution.

Mr Lévesque told us: we will still be going around in circles.

Well, that should enlighten all those who intend to vote YES in order to increase Quebec's bargaining power, all those who intend to vote YES out of pride, and all those who intend to vote YES because they are fed up.

If Mr Lévesque does not want renewed federalism even if the people note NO, then, clearly, if the people vote YES, he is going to say:

'Renewed federalism is out of the question.'

For my part, I will say: Sovereignty-Association is out of the question.

(Applause)

Which means that we have reached an impasse and those who vote YES must realize right now that a YES vote will result in either independence, pure and simple, or the status quo—that is what the YES option boils down to: the independence of Quebec, the separation of Quebec, or else the status quo, no change, because Mr Lévesque refuses to negotiate.

That's what we have to say to the YES side: if you want independence, if you vote YES, you won't get independence because you made it conditional on there being an Association, an Association being achieved along with independence.

If you want Association, your YES vote doesn't mean anything because it is not binding on the other provinces, which refuse to join in an association with you. And if you vote YES for a renewed federalism, your vote will be lost as well, because Mr Lévesque will still be going around in circles.

So you see, that is the impasse that this ambiguous, equivocal question has led us into, and that is what the people who are going to vote YES out of pride, that is what they should think about.

Voting YES out of pride means that we are putting our fate in the hands of the other provinces, which are going to say NO, no association, and then we will have to swallow our pride and our YES vote.

And those who are saying YES in order to get it over with, YES to break away, YES to get negotiations started, they read in the question itself that there will be a second referendum, and then maybe a third, and then maybe a fourth. And that, my friends, that is precisely what we are criticizing the Parti Québécois government for; not for having wanted independence—that is an option we reject and we're fighting it openly.

But what we are criticizing the Parti Québécois for is for not having the courage to ask: INDEPENDENCE, YES or NO?

YES or NO?

You, the supporters of the NO side, you know the divisions this referendum has caused. You have seen the divisions it has caused with families. You have seen the hatred it has created between neighbours. You know it has widened the generation gap. You know that the deep suspicion and mistrust between supporters of the YES side and those of the NO side will last for a long time to come.

You know what kind of trial the referendum is. Well, you have been told by the Parti Québécois government that there will be other referendums and you know that the hatred, the differences, the enormous waste of energy in Quebec will go on and on. Well, we are saying NO to that. NO, it will not go on.

Here is a party whose goal was separation, then independence, then sovereignty, then Sovereignty-Association, and then they even said that Sovereignty-Association was only for the purposes of negotiation. Here is a party that, in the name of pride, said to Quebecers: Stand up, we are going to move on to the world stage and assert ourselves.

And now, this party, on the point of entering the world stage, gets frightened and stays in the wings. Is that pride? Should we use that as a reason to vote for a party that tells us it will start all over again if the answer is YES, that there will be another referendum?

Well, that is what we are criticizing the Parti Québécois for—not having the courage to ask a clear question, a question a mature people would have been able to answer, really a simple question: DO YOU WANT TO LEAVE CANADA, YES OR NO?

NO:

Well, it's because the Parti Québécois knew how the vast majority of Quebecers would answer the question: DO YOU want to stop being Canadians. The answer would have been NO and that is why it has failed to enter the world stage.

Well, we know there is a clear answer, there is an unambiguous answer and that answer is NO. That answer is NO to those who want, as Camil Samson, I think said, to take our heritage away from us and from our children.

The answer is NO to those who advocate separation rather than sharing, to those who advocate isolation rather than fellowship, to those who—basically—advocate pride rather than love, because love involves challenges coming together and meeting others halfway, and working with them to build a better world.

So then, one must say, leaving that whole convoluted question aside, one must say NO to ambiguity. One must say NO to tricks. One must say NO to contempt, because they have come to that.

I was told that no more than two days ago Mr Lévesque

was saying that part of my name was Elliott and, since Elliott was an English name, it was perfectly understandable that I was for the NO side, because, really, you see, I was not as much of a Quebecer as those who are going to vote YES.

That, my dear friends, is what contempt is. It means saying that there are different kinds of Quebecers. It means that saying that the Quebecers on the NO side are not as good Quebecers as the others and perhaps they have a drop or two of foreign blood, while the people on the YES side have pure blood in their veins. That is what contempt is and that is the kind of division which builds up within a people, and that is what we are saying NO to.

Of course my name is Pierre Elliott Trudeau. Yes, Elliott was my mother's name. It was the name borne by the Elliotts who came to Canada more than two hundred years ago. It is the name of the Elliotts who, more than one hundred years ago, settled in Saint-Gabriel de Brandon, where you can still see their graves in the cemetery. That is what the Elliotts are.

My name is a Quebec name, but my name is a Canadian name also, and that's the story of my name.

Since Mr Lévesque has chosen to analyze my name, but let me show you how ridiculous it is to use that kind of contemptuous argument.

Mr Pierre-Marc Johnson is a Minister. Now, I ask you, is Johnson an English name or a French name?

And Louis O'Neill—a former Minister of Mr Lévesque's, and Robert Burns, and Daniel Johnson, I ask you, are they Quebecers, yes or no?

And, if we are looking at names, I saw in yesterday's newspaper that the leader of Quebec's Inuit, the Eskimos, they are going to vote NO. Do you know what the leader's name is? His name is Charlie Watt. Is Charlie Watt not a Quebecer? These people have lived in Quebec since the Stone Age; they have been here since time immemorial. And Mr Watt is not a Quebecer?

And, according to yesterday's newspaper, the chief of the Micmac Band, at Restigouche, the chief of fifteen hundred Indians—what is his name? Ron Maloney. Is he not a Quebecer? The Indians have been there for a good two thousand years. And their chief is not a Quebecer?

My dear friends, Laurier said something in 1889, nearly one hundred years ago now, and it's worth taking the time to read these lines: 'My Countrymen', said Laurier, 'are not only those in whose veins runs the blood of France. My countrymen are all those people—no matter what their race or language—whom the fortunes of war, the twists and turns of fate, or their own choice, have brought among us.'

All Quebecers have the right to vote YES or NO, as Mrs De Santis said. And all those Nos are as valid as any YES, regardless of the name of the person voting, or the colour of his skin.

My friends, Péquistes often tell us: the world is watching us, hold our heads high; the world is watching us, the whole world is watching what is happening in our democracy. Let's show them we are proud.

Well, I just received what is apparently the last pamphlet that will be put out by the YES committee. Go pick it up somewhere. I recommend it. It's a historic document.

It's a historic document because we find, all through this pamphlet, expressions such as NEGOTIATE SERI-OUSLY—A QUEBEC PROJECT—A BETTER CON-TRACT WITH THE REST OF CANADA—AN ASSOCIATION BETWEEN EQUALS—NEGOTIA-TIONS—ANOTHER REFERENDUM.

We don't once find the word SEPARATISM. We don't find the word INDEPENDENCE, either. We don't find the word SOVEREIGNTY. We don't find, not even once, the term SOVEREIGNTY-ASSOCIATION.

That's what pride is!

That's what deceiving the public is. And I don't know what historians will say about those who lacked courage at this historic turning point, but I know that they will be hard on those who sought to deceive the public and who say, in this last pamphlet—who say this: Some would have you believe that the question deals with separation. That's false.

That's false. Your question is about SOVEREIGNTY. Take a stand, you PQ supporters. Show us your true colours. Are you for independence?

(From the floor: NO)

No. We are against independence. Of course the world is watching us. The world will be a bit astonished by what it sees, I admit, because in today's world . . .

. . . you see, things are unstable, to say the least. The parameters are changing, to use a big word. And that means that there is fire and blood in the Middle East, in

Afghanistan, in Iran, in Vietnam, that means that there is inflation which is crippling the free economy; that means that there is division in the world; that means there is per-haps a third of the human race which goes to bed hungry every night, because there is not enough food and not enough medicine to keep the children in good health.

And that world is looking at Canada, the second largest country in the world, one of the richest, perhaps the second richest country in the world . . .

. . . a country which is composed of the meeting of the two most outstanding cultures of the Western world: the French and the English, added to by all the other cultures coming from every corner of Europe and every corner of the world. And this is what the world is looking at with astonishment, saying: These people think they might split up today when the whole world is interdependent? When Europe is trying to seek some kind of political union? These people in Quebec and in Canada want to split it up?

(From the floor: NO)

. . . they want to take it away from their children . . .

(From the floor: NO)

. . . they want to break it down? NO. That's what I am answering.

(NO, NO, NO)

I quoted Laurier, and let me quote a father of Confeder-ation who was an illustrious Quebecer: Thomas D'Arcy McGee: The new nationality—he was saying—is thought-ful and true; nationalist in its preference, but universal in its sympathies; a nationality of the spirit, for there is a new duty which especially belongs to Canada to create a state and to originate a history which the world will not willingly let die.

Well, we won't let it die. Our answer is: NO, to those who would kill it.

(Prime Minister repeats in French last part of D'Arcy McGee quotation)

We won't let this country die, this Canada, our home and native land, this Canada which really is, as our national anthem says, our home and native land. We are going to say to those who want us to stop being Canadians, we are going to say a resounding, an overwhelming NO.

(NO)

Prime Minister Kim Campbell
Vancouver, British Columbia
Canada Day, 1 July 1993

This morning at 5:30 a.m. (1 a.m. Vancouver time), I watched the sun rise on Signal Hill in St John's, Newfoundland. A few hours later, I participated in Canada Day celebrations on Parliament Hill in Ottawa and in Hull, Quebec. Now, about 19 hours and more than 7,000 kilometres later, I have come home to Vancouver to share with you the pride and enthusiasm that our national birthday inspires in all of us.

I cannot begin to tell what pride and what exhilaration I felt while I was flying across the country during most of today. From the silvery shores of the Atlantic to the familiar shimmering sheen of the Pacific, beneath me was the country that was lovingly carved out of a forbidding but fabulous wilderness by generations and generations of Canadians using the simple but strong instruments called faith, determination and tolerance.

I felt that same sense of purpose and of faith in the future everywhere I went today. In St John's, Ottawa, Hull, and now in Vancouver, I met Canadians of all ages, from all walks of life, who wanted to share their joy in their common citizenship. And, as Canada's first woman Prime Minister, Canada's first Prime Minister from British Columbia, I am indeed very proud, so very proud, to be in your company on this special evening in the life of our country.

The sun is about to set on our 126th anniversary year. A page has been turned. I invite you today to join with me and begin preparing another 126 years of peace and prosperity, of success through solidarity and of unity through understanding.

Let us set out together to meet the challenges of the twenty-first century that are just beyond the horizon. The government has already started taking the tough decisions that a difficult economic situation calls for. And I strongly believe that we are on the right course to maintain and enhance our position at the forefront of industrialized nations and as one of the best places to live in the world. But much remains to be done. We have to renew our commitment to excellence, quicken our pace on the path to prosperity and fortify our faith in social justice and equality.

Let us start building today for the next generation the same strong prosperous and united Canada that our parents worked so hard to give us. In the 126 years of our common history, anglophones and francophones, Aboriginal peoples and new Canadians have shown that our political system, founded on the profound respect of differences and the sharing of fundamental values, is our most powerful tool of development.

As we lay the groundwork for our future, I invite all my fellow Canadians, on this 126th birthday of our country, to firmly take hold of this tool and help build an even greater, even more united and even more prosperous Canada.

Today is not a day for long speeches. It is a day of celebration and solidarity, a day to express our pride in our past and our faith in our future. From the bottom of my heart, I thank you for your warm welcome and your kind encouragement. It feels so good to be back in Vancouver. And it feels especially good, this evening, to say, Happy birthday Canada! Bone fête Canada!

Earl Charles Spencer
Eulogy at the Funeral of Diana Princess of Wales
Westminster Abbey
London, England
6 September 1997

I stand before you today, the representative of a family in grief, in a country in mourning, before a world in shock.

We are all united, not only in our desire to pay our respects to Diana but rather in our need to do so.

For such was her extraordinary appeal that the tens of millions of people taking part in this service all over the world, via television and radio, who never actually met her, feel that they, too, lost someone close to them in the early hours of Sunday morning. It is a more remarkable tribute to Diana than I can ever hope to offer her today.

Diana was the very essence of compassion, of duty, of style, of beauty. All over the world, she was a symbol of selfless humanity. All over the world, a standard bearer for the rights of the truly downtrodden, a very British girl who transcended nationality. Someone with a natural nobility who was classless and who proved in the last year that she needed no royal title to continue to generate her particular brand of magic.

Today is our chance to say thank you for the way you brightened our lives, even though God granted you but half a life. We will all feel cheated, always, that you were taken from us so young, and yet we must learn to be grateful that you came along at all. Only now that you are gone do we truly appreciate what we are now without and we want you to know that life without you is very, very difficult.

We have all despaired at our loss over the past week and only the strength of the message you gave us through your years of giving has afforded us the strength to move forward.

There is a temptation to rush to canonize your memory; there is no need to do so. You stand tall enough as a human being of unique qualities not to need to be seen as a saint. Indeed, to sanctify your memory would be to miss out on the very core of your being, your wonderfully mischievous sense of humour, with a laugh that bent you double.

Your joy for life, transmitted wherever you took your smile and the sparkle in those unforgettable eyes. Your boundless energy which you could barely contain.

But your greatest gift was your intuition and it was a gift you used wisely. This is what underpinned all your other wonderful attributes, and if we look to analyze what it was about you that had such a wide appeal, we find it in your instinctive feel for what was really important in all our lives.

Without your God-given sensitivity, we would be immersed in greater ignorance at the anguish of AIDS and HIV sufferers, the plight of the homeless, the isolation of lepers, the random destruction of land mines. Diana explained to me once that it was her innermost feelings of suffering that made it possible for her to connect with her constituency of the rejected.

And here we come to another truth about her. For all the status, the glamour, the applause, Diana remained throughout a very insecure person at heart, almost childlike in her desire to do good for others so she could release herself from deep feelings of unworthiness, of which her eating disorders were merely a symptom.

The world sensed this part of her character and cherished her for her vulnerability, while admiring her for her honesty.

The last time I saw Diana was on July 1, her birthday in London, when, typically, she was not taking time to celebrate her special day with friends but was guest of honour at a special charity fundraising evening. She sparkled, of course, but I would rather cherish the days I spent with her in March when she came to visit me and my children in our home in South Africa.

I am proud of the fact, apart from when she was on display meeting President Mandela, we managed to contrive to stop the ever-present paparazzi from getting a single picture of her—that meant a lot to her.

These were days I will always treasure. It was as if we had been transported back to our childhood, when we spent such an enormous amount of time together—the two youngest in the family.

Fundamentally, she had not changed at all from the big sister who mothered me as a baby, fought with me at school and endured those long train journeys between our parents' homes with me at weekends. It is a tribute to her level-headedness and strength that despite the most bizarre-like life imaginable after her childhood, she remained intact, true to herself.

There is no doubt that she was looking for a new direction in her life at this time. She talked endlessly of getting away from England, mainly because of the treatment that she received at the hands of the newspapers.

I don't think she ever understood why her genuinely good intentions were sneered at by the media, why there appeared to be a permanent quest on their behalf to bring her down. It is baffling.

My own and only explanation is that genuine goodness is threatening to those at the opposite end of the moral spectrum.

It is a point to remember that of all the ironies about Diana, perhaps the greatest was this—a girl given the name of the ancient goddess of hunting was, in the end, the most hunted person of the modern age.

She would want us today to pledge ourselves to protecting her beloved boys William and Harry from a similar fate, and I do this here, Diana, on your behalf. We will not allow them to suffer the anguish that was used regularly to drive you to tearful despair.

And, beyond that, on behalf of your mother and sisters, I pledge that we, your blood family, will do all we can to continue the imaginative way in which you were steering these two exceptional young men, so that their souls are not simply immersed by duty and tradition but can sing openly, as you planned.

We fully respect the heritage into which they have both been born and will always respect and encourage them in their royal role, but we, like you, recognize the need for them to experience as many different aspects of life as possible to arm them spiritually and emotionally for the years ahead. I know you would have expected nothing less from us.

William and Harry, we all care desperately for you today. We are all chewed up with the sadness at the loss of a woman who was not even our mother. How great your suffering is, we cannot even imagine.

I would like to end by thanking God for the small mercies he has shown us at this dreadful time. For taking Diana at her most beautiful and radiant and when she had joy in her private life.

Above all, we give thanks for the life of a woman I am so proud to be able to call my sister—the unique, the complex, the extraordinary and irreplaceable Diana, whose beauty, both internal and external, will never be extinguished from our minds.

Reprinted by permission of Althorp.

Adrienne Clarkson
Governor-General of Canada
Eulogy for Canada's Unknown Soldier
Ottawa, Ontario
28 May 2000

Wars are as old as history. Over two thousand years ago, Herodotus wrote, 'In peace, sons bury their fathers; in war, fathers bury their sons.' Today, we are gathered together as one, to bury someone's son. The only certainty about him is that he was young. If death is a debt we all must pay, he paid before he owed it.

We do not know whose son he was. We do not know his name. We do not know if he was a MacPherson or a Chartrand. He could have been a Kaminski or a Swiftarrow. We do not know if he was a father himself. We do not know if his mother or wife received that telegram with the words 'Missing In Action' typed with electrifying clarity on the anonymous piece of paper. We do not know whether he had begun truly to live his life as a truck driver or a scientist, a miner or a teacher, a farmer or a student. We do not know where he came from.

Was it the Prairies whose rolling sinuous curves recall a certain kind of eternity?

Was he someone who loved our lakes and knew them from a canoe?

Was he someone who saw the whales at the mouth of the Saguenay?

Was he someone who hiked in the Rockies or went sailing in the Atlantic or in the Gulf Islands?

Did he have brown eyes?

Did he know what it was to love someone and be loved back?

Was he a father who had not seen his child?

Did he love hockey? Did he play defence?

Did he play football? Could he kick a field goal?

Did he like to fix cars? Did he dream of owning a Buick?

Did he read poetry?

Did he get into fights?

Did he have freckles?

Did he think nobody understood him?

Did he just want to go out and have a good time with the boys?

We will never know the answers to these questions. We will never know him. But we come today to do him honour as someone who could have been all these things and now is no more. We who are left have all kinds of questions that only he could answer. And we, by this act today, are admitting with terrible finality that we will never know those answers.

We cannot know him. And no honour we do him can give him the future that was destroyed when he was killed. Whatever life he could have led, whatever choices he could have made are all shuttered. They are over. We are honouring that unacceptable thing—a life stopped by doing one's duty. The end of a future, the death of dreams.

Yet we give thanks for those who were willing to sacrifice themselves and who gave their youth and their future so that we could live in peace. With their lives they ransomed our future.

We have a wealth of witnesses in Canada to describe to us the unspeakable horror and frightening maelstrom that war brings. What that First World War was like has been described in our poetry, novels and paintings. Some of our greatest artists came out of that conflict, able to create beauty out of the hell that they had seen. The renowned member of the Group of Seven, F.H. Varley, was one of those artists. Writing in April 1918 he said,

You in Canada . . . cannot realize at all what war is like. You must see it and live it. You must see the barren deserts war has made of once fertile country . . . see the turned-up graves, see the dead on the field, freakishly mutilated—headless, legless, stomachless, a perfect body and a passive face and a broken empty skull—see your own countrymen, unidentified, thrown into a cart, their coats over them, boys digging a grave in a land of yellow slimy mud and green pools of water under a weeping sky. You must have heard the screeching shells and have the shrapnel fall around you, whistling by you—seen the results of it, seen scores of horses, bits of horses lying around in the open—in the street and soldiers marching by these scenes as if they never knew of their presence. Until you've lived this . . . you cannot know.

It is a frightening thing for human beings to think that we could die and that no one would know to mark our grave, to say where we had come from, to say when we had been born and when exactly we died. In honouring this unknown soldier today, through this funeral and this burial, we are embracing the fact of the anonymity and saying that because we do not know him and we do not know what he could have become, he has become more than one body, more than one grave. He is an ideal. He is a symbol of all sacrifice. He is every soldier in all our wars.

Our veterans, who are here with us today, know what it is to have been in battle and to have seen their friends cut down in their youth. That is why remembrance is so necessary and yet so difficult. It is necessary because we must not forget and it is difficult because the pain is never forgotten.

And the sense of loss, what this soldier's family must have felt is captured in a poem by Jacques Brault, the Quebec poet who lost his brother in Sicily in the Second World War, and wrote 'Suite Fraternelle',

I remember you my brother Gilles lying forgotten in
   the earth of Sicily . . .
I know now that you are dead, a cold, hard lump in
   your throat fear lying heavy in your belly I still hear
   your twenty years swaying in the blasted July weeds . . .
There is only one name on my lips, and it is yours
   Gilles
You did not die in vain Gilles and you carry on
   through our changing seasons
And we, we carry on as well, like the laughter of waves
   that sweep across each tearful cove . . .
Your death gives off light Gilles and illuminates a
   brother's memories . . .
The grass grows on your tomb Gilles and the sand
   creeps up
And the nearby sea feels the pull of your death
You live on in us as you never could in yourself
You are where we will be you open the road for us.
          [interpretation of original French poem]

When a word like Sicily is heard, it reverberates with all the far countries where our youth died. When we hear Normandy, Vimy, Hong Kong, we know that what happened so far away, paradoxically, made our country and the future of our society. These young people and soldiers bought our future for us. And for that, we are eternally grateful.

Whatever dreams we have, they were shared in some measure by this man who is only unknown by name but who is known in the hearts of all Canadians by all the virtues that we respect—selflessness, honour, courage and commitment.

We are now able to understand what was written in 1916 by the grandson of Louis Joseph Papineau, Major Talbot Papineau, who was killed two years later: 'Is their sacrifice to go for nothing or will it not cement a foundation for a true Canadian nation, a Canadian nation independent in thought, independent in action, independent even in its political organization—but in spirit united for high international and humane purposes . . . .'

The wars fought by Canadians in the twentieth century were not fought for the purpose of uniting Canada, but the country that emerged was forged in the smithy of sacrifice. We will not forget that.

This unknown soldier was not able to live out his allotted span of life to contribute to his country. But in giving himself totally through duty, commitment, love and honour he has become part of us forever. As we are part of him.

Dr Leslie Tutty, Faculty of Social Work
Eleventh Anniversary Memorial Service for Women Murdered at Montreal's École
    Polytechnique
Nickle Arts Museum, University of Calgary
Calgary, Alberta
6 December 2000

It has been a trying year for those of us working in the field of violence against women. If we are not yet experiencing a full-blown backlash, we are perhaps on the cusp of one. In Edmonton, a men's group won a challenge under the Alberta Human Rights Legislation against a family service agency because their brochures for support groups for abused women did not mention that women partners may also abuse men.

Throughout the year, the results of sociological studies on violence between intimate partners have repeatedly been misrepresented in the media as proving that women are equally as violent as men. This ignores the experiences of front-line workers such as police and shelter staff who know that the many seriously abused women they see does, indeed, constitute 'gendered violence'.

A woman who phoned into a radio show I was speaking on in Ottawa, who coincidentally was herself abused and is now homeless, had visited the December 6th memorial and queried whether the monument should not also be dedicated to men who are murdered.

In a conversation about today's memorial, one individual was overheard questioning the need to have a ceremony after all these years, commenting, 'Can't they just get over it?'

So, an appropriate question 11 years later is, 'Why do we remember the 14 young women murdered in Montreal?'

We remember because they might have been our daughters, sisters, friends. This was the first incident in Canadian history, perhaps in recent world history, when a group of people were targeted and murdered simply because they were women. This must not happen again.

We remember, not to punish men for the violence that other men perpetrate against women, but to appreciate the men who do advocate for women's rights—the men who create white ribbon campaigns and join us today in memoriam. These men have an essential place in changing societal attitudes, especially the attitudes of other men.

We remember, because of the seldom-heard voices of other Canadian women who live every day with the threat of violence and even of death. Here are comments from several Alberta women abused by partners. These women participated in research I completed last year for Justice Canada on domestic violence involving firearms.

'He threatened my daughter. He put his finger right to her forehead and said, "I'll kill you, I'll kill your mother, I'll kill your baby brother, and I'll kill myself." To see my kids screaming and crying and scared, and my oldest daughter didn't want to go to school anymore because she was scared to leave me alone with the little ones. I couldn't handle that.'

'He went downstairs to where he had a gun, got bullets and loaded it, and stood at the end of the bed screaming that I'd ruined his family. He'd kill me first and I'd never leave. I said, "Are you going to shoot me now?" He said, "Yes I am", and he fired it. It was close. I thought he'd shot me. It went through the wall probably two inches from my head.'

Any of the 41 women I interviewed could have been killed with the firearms with which their partners threatened them. All of them lived in fear.

And so, we remember the 14 young women because it reminds us that countless Canadian women live with violence every day and we need to do something to address this sad fact.

We remember, so we can channel today's grief into action, to read, do research, advocate and protest any act of violence against others, but for today, especially, violence against women. Talk to your friends, your partners, your daughters, and especially your sons. Send a cheque to the Herald's Christmas fund that today highlighted the essential work of the Calgary Women's Emergency Shelter. Or give to the United Way, specifying that the funds be sent to agencies that address domestic abuse. In some small way, let's extend December 6th into the rest of the year.

Finally, we remember, because it would be dishonourable to the memory of the 14 young women killed in the Montreal Massacre, to forget.

Reprinted by permission of Leslie M. Tutty, Ph.D., Faculty of Social Work, University of Calgary.

Prime Minister Jean Chrétien
Ottawa Central Mosque
Ottawa, Ontario
21 September 2001

I want to thank you for meeting with me today.

I have come here, as your Prime Minister, to bring a message of reassurance and tolerance.

I know that the days since September 11, 2001, have been ones of great sadness and anxiety for Muslims across Canada. Because the cold-blooded killers who committed the atrocities in New York and Washington invoked the name and words of Islam as justification.

Many of your faith have felt constrained when expressing your sympathy and solidarity with the victims. This despite the fact that many Muslims also perished in the attacks. Worse. Some have been singled out for denunciation and violence. Acts that have no place in Canada or any civilized nation. And which have made me feel shame as Prime Minister.

I wanted to stand by your side today. And to reaffirm with you that Islam has nothing to do with the mass murder that was planned and carried out by the terrorists and their masters.

Like all faiths Islam is about peace. About justice. And about harmony among all people. And I sense your sadness at the way that a great world religion has been unjustly smeared by this evil.

Above all I want to stand by your side to condemn the acts of intolerance and hatred that have been committed against your community since the attack. Let me say that I turn my back on the people who have done this. I have no time for them. And I call on our police and courts to apply the full force of our laws against them.

As a sign of the importance our government attaches to this issue, we have amended the criminal code to provide for tougher sentences for those who are convicted of hate crimes.

While they may feel a righteous motivation for such conduct, nothing could be further from the truth. By giving into hate and an unreasoned thirst for vengeance, they are doing the work of the terrorists, who win when they export their hatred. They are, in my judgement, a disgrace to the memory of the victims.

As I have said, this is a struggle against terrorism, not against any faith or community. And Canada will not use the justification of national security to abandon our cherished values of freedom and tolerance. We will not fall into the trap of exclusion as we have in past.

I say today, once again, that we are all Canadians. We stand together as one against this evil. We grieve together as a family. As one nation we defy the twisted philosophy of the terrorists. And shoulder to shoulder we will pursue the struggle for justice.

Patrick Brazeau, Vice-Chief, Congress of Aboriginal Peoples
Native Women's Association of Canada Launch: Sisters in Spirit
Parliament Hill
Ottawa, Ontario
22 March 2004

Kwey, Bonjour and Hello.

My name is Patrick Brazeau and I am the Vice-Chief of the Congress of Aboriginal Peoples, which is a National Organization that advocates for the rights and interests of off-reserve Aboriginal people throughout Canada.

I would like to recognize my people, the Algonquin and the territory on which we stand.

I would also like to acknowledge the Elders in attendance and offer condolences to the friends and family, who have been affected by the unfortunate issues that unite us here today.

Since the last 15 years or so, approximately 500 Aboriginal women have gone missing, of which many have been murdered.

These incidents, which are growing by the day, demand our immediate attention. A recent example stems from Winnipeg. A 16-year-old female by the name of Sunshine Woods has gone missing since February 20, 2004.

It angers me that these types of incidents receive modest attention from the Canadian media and both Provincial and Federal Governments seem [to] do very little in terms of investigations, prevention and support for the victims and their families.

We must not forget that the women we are speaking on behalf of here today are our mothers, our sisters and our daughters.

I am a proud husband and father to my three-year-old daughter. My Native culture has taught me to respect women.

Traditionally, women played a central role in the family. They were responsible for domestic relationships and were viewed both as life-givers and caretakers of life.

Little has changed in my culture.

These women who have passed on or have gone missing were leaders, academics, some were addicts, some were prostitutes, but the end result is the same for all.

They were all victims of marginalization.

The ongoing marginalization of Aboriginal women has made them one of the most vulnerable groups in Canadian society.

It is necessary to acknowledge that these women were targeted victims by their attackers—not because of how these women lived, what they did or whom they knew.

These women were targeted because crimes against our Aboriginal mothers, sisters and daughters are trivialized—where individual blame is placed on the victim and the violence that these women experienced [was] dismissed as insignificant in mainstream society.

One might ask, why are Aboriginal women victims?

It is no great secret that dislocation into urban settings has contributed to high rates of unemployment, suicide, alcoholism, domestic violence and other social problems.

It has been very well documented that the residential school system has played a major role in the victimization of women. The development of parenting skills, important to Aboriginal women, was denied to them.

These effects have lasted for several generations. In addition to the physical and sexual abuse that Canadians are now hearing took place in those schools, emotional abuse was and is most prevalent and severe.

Discriminatory and unfair treatment to Aboriginal women throughout Canadian history has made them vulnerable targets.

How do we improve these situations?

The answer is not easily achievable because it seems that no one is listening.

Reprinted by permission of the author.

The federal government has generally restricted its provision of services to Indians living on reserve. Once an Aboriginal person leaves the reserve, federal services are no longer available. Once an Aboriginal person relocates to a city, they become under provincial jurisdiction but the reality is that they end up falling in between the cracks because of the jurisdictional backlashing between the levels of government.

In order to properly address the issues and implement the needed social services that these women need, financial resources must be allocated directly into Aboriginal control in the urban, rural and remote areas, as the case may be. Without this actual transfer, the status quo will remain.

From an Aboriginal perspective and from personal experience, racial discrimination and misogyny (or hate for women) is unfortunately prevalent in this country and it must come to an end.

The UN Special Rapporteur on Human Rights visited Canada last fall and his recent report notes, 'the lack of any intellectual strategy is a serious handicap in Canada's undoubted efforts to combat racism, racial discrimination and xenophobia.'

He further calls on the Government of Canada to add credibility, trust and recognition to its political commitment to combat racism, while recognizing that such evils persist, despite the efforts accomplished.

It is time for us to work together. It is time for our Aboriginal women to get their fair justice. The time for action is long overdue.

On behalf of the National Chief, Dwight Dorey and I, the Congress of Aboriginal Peoples supports the initiative of the Native Women's Association of Canada and we will contribute in any way we can for the betterment of Aboriginal women.

It is time for jurisdictional barriers to fall between the different organizations to work together for the common purpose.

Let us be more than just Sisters in Spirit, let us act in solidarity with our sisters in research, public education, outreach, and change.

Let 500 missing and murdered women be more than just a statistic used to catch media attention. Let our solidarity appreciate these women, as valued members of our communities who were lost but definitely not forgotten because in the end, their absence is a loss for all Canadians.

Meegwetch, Merci and Thank you!

Senator Vivienne Poy
'The Gender Gap'
Zonta Club, Hong Kong
24 November 2004

Today, I will address the topic of the gender gap within the Canadian context—the real and perceived gap between men and women in 2004.

Over the last two decades, we've seen a lot of changes in Canada for both women and men. No longer are individuals governed by the strict roles which limited their participation in society. Today, many more women are working outside the home, and we are proving to be very successful in business, in politics, and in the professions. In fact, Canada has one of the highest levels of participation of women in the workforce of any developed country.

At the same time, we also have many more men who are staying home to care for their children, and taking their role as fathers very seriously. However, a gap still exists between men and women's aspirations to participate in all aspects of life, and the actual opportunities available to them.

Having said that, men continue to be more revered than women. I know that in some instances, awards given to women are also given to their husbands because society dictates that it is wrong to leave them out. The same does not apply to women, because we are still perceived to be less important than men.

So, the big problem is one of perception. After 30 odd years of progress, Canadian women are still perceived to be unworthy of the kind of recognition that is afforded men. You may say to me, well, you've made it, so what's the problem? The problem is that, I am more of an exception than the rule, and all Canadian women need to have the same opportunities. And besides, I do encounter the same problem with perception.

At the University of Toronto, I am only the fourth woman Chancellor in its 177-year history, and we still have not had a woman President at the university yet. And in the Senate of Canada, even though over 30 per cent of the senators are women, the public still think that senators are old white males. When I introduce myself to strangers around Parliament Hill, I am asked which Senator I work for. Well, I am female, and a visible minority at that, so I must be staff!

Recently, CBC had a program called 'The Greatest Canadian'. The public was asked to identify 100 great Canadians. Guess what? A list was produced without one woman in the Top 10. To add insult to injury, the top woman on the list of 100 was a country music singer with a pretty face and a great body. In fact, of the 19 women who made the list of the top 100 greatest Canadians, six of them were pop singers, and another was an actress. What does this say about the way women are perceived in Canadian society? In reference to this CBC program, the November 1st issue of *Maclean's* magazine, wrote, '. . . sorry ladies. Seems some people take HIStory literally.'

Because of this perception, many women who might deserve the label of greatness do not make it into our history books. One of these women, who I have become familiar with in my research, is Dr Elsie MacGill. She was a woman who overcame society's prejudice, and a nasty bout of polio, to become the first aeronautical engineer in North America, and the first woman aircraft designer in the world. She led a staff of 4,500 to create a fleet of more than 1,400 Hawker Hurricane fighter aircraft, which contributed enormously to Canada's war effort during World War II. She was, without a doubt, a great Canadian! But, was she ever mentioned as a great Canadian on the CBC?

On the other side of the coin are the men who have found it difficult to take on new roles. In a recent study by the Radcliffe Public Policy Centre, young men indicated that they wanted to take an active role in raising their children, and that they are willing to make the time and effort, even sacrificing promotions in their careers, if necessary. And, in the case of marriage breakdown, many men are now involved in joint custody arrangements. In Canada, the figure stood at 42 per cent in 2002, an increase from 30 per cent in 1998. Women are now awarded custody in less than 50 per cent of court decisions.

Many men are willing to take on the responsibility of caring for their families so why does society still think women are the primary caregivers?

I want to stress that equal opportunity does not mean that women and men are the same—nor would we want to be. What it means is that we can be both equal and different. It is a matter of being open-minded to the possibility of changing roles. Thirty years ago, we couldn't have imagined that women and men would be where we are today in

Canada. As women, we have entered the workforce in large numbers, and many men have gravitated towards the home, but Canadian perceptions remain outdated.

One of the real areas where the gender gap is great is in Canadian politics. About 20 per cent of the MPs in the House of Commons are women, and this level has not changed for a decade. In the Senate, which is an appointed body, we are doing a little better at over 30 per cent. But we are still well behind Rwanda and the Nordic countries. (Rwanda is now number one for representation in the lower house at 48.8 per cent. Among Nordic countries, such as Sweden and Norway, the regional average for representation stands at 39.7 per cent!)

With so many women in the workplace in Canada, why are we so far behind in politics? Is it because women just aren't interested? Or is it like the former Governor of Texas, Ann Richards, said, 'Being a woman in politics is like being Ginger Rogers. You have to do all the same dance steps as Fred Astaire, but you have to do them backwards and in high heels.'

The situation is similar in the business arena. Women held just over 11 per cent of board director positions in the Financial Post 500 in 2001. More than half of these corporate boards had no women at all, and only three were chaired by women. Interestingly, our Crown corporations, where board members are politically appointed, had the highest percentage of women (over 23 per cent). This means that the Canadian government is trying to close the gender gap.

The fact is, most women still work in pink-collar jobs, and some traditionally male professions are still employing mostly men. And, the average wage for women is only about 73 per cent of that of men's. We need to correct that.

Understanding why there are few women in politics, on corporate boards, and in the professions is not a simple matter, and I don't have enough time today to go into it. However, we can discuss a couple of ways this can be corrected. We know that both children and adults tend to look for mentors and role models, so, the few women who have attained high positions have the responsibility to pave the way for others to follow.

To prove my point, I'd like to tell you a story about Dr Gro Harlem Brundtland, former Prime Minister of Norway. As the first woman ever elected as Prime Minister, everyone said she wouldn't last, but she was Prime Minister for 10 years. During her tenure, a group of boys and girls were playing in a schoolyard. A boy boasted to his friends

that he would like to be Prime Minister when he grew up, but the girls laughed at him and said, 'Don't be silly! A man can't be Prime Minister. It has to be a woman.'

Another way to correct the gender gap is that progressive leaders in the community, with an understanding of the principles of merit and equity, nominate suitable candidates for awards, for political parties, Crown corporations, as well as membership on corporate boards. In my case, I am doing my part, by helping individuals who I believe in, male or female, to advance the agenda of equity based on merit.

Today, in Canadian universities, 60 per cent of the graduates are women. Taking the University of Toronto as an example, as of 2002, women comprised more than 56 per cent of the full-time undergraduate program, and over 54 per cent of the graduate program. The percentage is even higher in the part-time program. Realizing that these numbers have been gradually increasing, it is puzzling that less than 30 per cent (28 per cent) of full-time tenured and tenured-stream faculty are women. We know that this gender gap needs to be closed so that our investment in education is realized.

Incidentally, just as girls are catching up in education, boys are falling behind. According to Canadian testing on literacy between 1994 and 2002, girls maintained a significant advantage over boys in reading and writing. In recent figures, at age 16, girls scored one-fifth higher in reading, and over 16 per cent higher in writing, over boys. There are also fewer boys than girls graduating from our high schools. Canadian society needs to address this phenomenon before the education gap becomes even wider. While we move the women's agenda forward, we need to be mindful not to forget the boys in our schools.

In Canada, we have two laws that help make equity possible. The first is the Employment Equity Act which requires that employers set goals to move towards achieving equity for minority groups that include women, persons with disabilities, visible minorities, and aboriginals.

The second Act is the Canadian Charter of Rights and Freedoms in which there is an equality provision which reads:

'Every individual is equal before and under the law and has the right to the equal protection and equal benefit of the law without discrimination and, in particular, without discrimination based on race, national or ethnic origin, colour, religion, sex, age or mental or physical ability.'

This Charter shapes our character as Canadians, and has formed the basis of our values over the past two decades. In

Canadian society, we are continuously striving towards equity, where individuals will be judged on merit and merit alone. We are not there yet, but we have these two pieces of legislation as our best tools to move our agenda forward.

As a woman, I am well aware that I am much better off in Canada than in most nations in the world. Still, I look forward to changes over the next decades, when Canadian society recognizes that men and women are equal—in rights as well as in recognition of our contributions to our country.

Personally, I look forward to the day when strangers address me instead of my husband as 'Senator', and as 'Dr' Poy instead of 'Mrs' Poy. The day will come when credit card companies no longer request the approval of major purchases by my husband, nor send refunds, owed to me, to him. Believe me, all this is still happening today. Frustrating, isn't it? Despite our achievements, we are still sometimes perceived to be dependants of men. We all need to work towards closing that gender gap.

Vivienne Poy is the first Canadian of Asian descent appointed to the Senate of Canada. She often speaks on issues pertaining to gender, multiculturalism, and human rights. Reprinted by permission of Senator Poy.

Notes

Chapter 1

1. K. Viner, 'Hand-to-Brand Combat: A Profile of Naomi Klein', *The Guardian*, 23 Sept. 2000, at: <www.common dreams.org/views/092300-103.htm>. Accessed 24 July 2004.
2. E. Potter, 'Anarchy Makes a Comeback', in S.D. Ferguson and L.R. Shade, eds, *Civic Discourse and Cultural Politics in Canada: A Cacophony of Voices* (Westport, Conn.: Ablex Publishing, 2002), 91–108.
3. N. Nevitte, *The Decline of Deference* (Peterborough, Ont.: Broadview Press, 1996), cited ibid., 106.
4. See N. Chomsky and E.S. Herman, *The Manufacturing of Consent* (New York: Pantheon Books, 1988).
5. N. Klein, *No Logo* (Toronto, Ont.: Knopf Canada, 2000).
6. 'Exhibition, Performers: Raging Grannies', April 2001, at: <http://library.usask.ca/herstory/granni.html>. Accessed 30 Sept. 2001.
7. K. Luniman, 'Canadians Less Trusting Now, Poll Finds', *Globe and Mail*, 25 June 2003, A8.
8. D. Taras, 'The Winds of Right-wing Change in Canadian Journalism', *Canadian Journal of Communication* 21 (1996): 103–25.
9. Canadian Security Intelligence Service, Government of Canada, 'Perspectives', at: <www.csis-scrs.gc.ca/eng/misc docs/200008_e.html>. Accessed 23 July 2004.
10. 'CEO Pay Hikes Double', 28 July 2004, at: <http://money.cnn.com/2004/07/28/news/economy/ceo_pay/index.htm>. Accessed 28 July 2004.
11. The Netherlands (2001) and Belgium (2003) finalized their laws while petitions to recognize Canada's same-sex marriages wended their way through the country's legal system. However, once recognized, the marriages in Canada predated the first same-sex marriages registered elsewhere in the world.
12. Statistics Canada, 'The Daily', 21 Jan. 2003, at: <www.statcan.ca/Daily/English/030121/d030121a.htm>. Accessed 15 Oct. 2004.
13. N. Stone, 'The Role of Social Values in Communicating Programs and Policies to Canadians'. Research undertaken by Communication Canada, PowerPoint presentation to Professional Marketing Research Society at National Press Club, Ottawa, 29 Jan. 2003.
14. D. Dasko, 'A Survey of Canadian Values and Attitudes', Environics research poll, presented at Citizenship Conference, Montreal, Oct. 2000.
15. E. Anderssen, 'On Canada's Campuses, Women are Almost in a Class by Themselves', *Globe and Mail*, on-line edition, 31 July 2004, at: <www.theglobeandmail.com/servlet/story/RTGAM.20040731.wxstude0731/BNStory/Front/>. Accessed 31 July 2004.
16. Statistics Canada, 2001 Census, reported on the Canada Unity Council Web site, at: <www.cric.ca>.
17. Anderssen, 'On Canada's Campuses'.
18. Versna Chuop, communication student, University of Ottawa, 2002.
19. C. Clemmensen, 'A Guide for Determining the Ethos of Online Brand Mascots', Nov. 1999–May 2000, at: <www.filmtracks.com/home/mascots_thesis/index.html>. Accessed 24 July 2004.
20. N. Postman, *Amusing Ourselves to Death: Public Discourse in the Age of Show Business* (New York: Penguin Books, 1985).
21. In the same way, today's students expect and want higher levels of engagement in the classroom situation. See P. Smagorinsky and P.K. Fly, 'The Social Environment of the Classroom: A Vygotskian Perspective on Small Group Process', *Communication Education* 42 (1993): 157–71.
22. A.N. Miller, 'An Exploration of Kenyan Public Speaking Patterns with Implications for the American Introductory Public Speaking Course', *Communication Education* 51 (2002): 179.
23. S.D. Ferguson, 'Robespierre: High Priest of the Jacobins', *Central States Speech Journal* (1972): 246–53.
24. F.J. Macke, 'Communication Left Speechless: A Critical Examination of the Evolution of Speech Communication as an Academic Discipline', *Communication Education* 40 (1991): 125–43. Macke cites several articles that appeared in a classical collection by K.R. Wallace, ed., *History of Speech Education in America* (New York: Appleton, 1954): W. Guthrie, 'Rhetorical Theory in Colonial America', 48–59; M. Hochmuth and R. Murphy, 'Rhetorical and Elocutionary Training in Nineteenth Century Colleges', 153–77; and M.M. Robb, 'The Elocutionary Movement and its Main Figures', 178–201.
25. J. Walker, 'The Elements of Gesture', in W. Scott, *Scott's New Lessons in Reading and Writing* (Philadelphia: A.

Walker, 1816); G. Austin, *Chironomia, or a Treatise on Rhetorical Delivery* (London: T. Cadell and W. Davies, 1806), reprinted in M.M. Robb and L. Thonssen, eds, *Chironomia, or a Treatise on Rhetorical Delivery* (Carbondale, Ill.: University of Illinois Press, 1966).

26. M.L. Clarke, *Rhetoric at Rome: A Historical Survey* (New York: Barnes & Noble, 1968).

27. 'Traveling Culture: What is Chataqua?', at: <http://sdrc.lib.uiowa.edu/traveling-culture/essay.htm>, p. 2. Accessed 18 June 2004.

28. Ibid.

29. 'Chautauqua', *The Canadian Encyclopedia* (2004), at: <www.thecanadianencyclopedia.com/index>, p. 1. Accessed 18 June 2004.

30. 'Sheridan', *The 1911 Edition Encyclopedia*, at: <http://26.1911encyclopedia.org/S/SH/SHERIDAN.htm>. Accessed 18 June 2004.

31. *This is Marshall McLuhan: The Medium is the Massage*, film produced by Ernest Pintoff and Guy Fraumini and aired on NBC, 19 Mar. 1967.

32. S. Ferguson and S.D. Ferguson, 'Proxemics and Television: The Politician's Dilemma', *Canadian Journal of Communication* 4 (1978): 26–35.

33. K. Jamieson, *Eloquence in an Electronic Age: The Transformation of Political Speechmaking* (New York: Oxford University Press, 1988). See D. Schwartz, 'Interdisciplinary and Pedagogical Implications of Rhetorical Theory', *Communication Studies* 46 (1995): 130–9; T.S. Frobish, 'Jamieson Meets Lucas: Eloquence and Pedagogical Model(s) in *The Art of Public Speaking*', *Communication Education* 49 (2000): 239–52; G. Sorensen, 'The Relationships among Teachers' Self-Disclosive Statements, Students' Perceptions, and Affective Learning', *Communication Education* 38 (1989): 259–76; M. Javidi, V.C. Downs, and J.F. Nussbaum, 'A Comparative Analysis of Teachers' Use of Dramatic Style Behaviors at Higher and Secondary Educational Levels', *Communication Education* 37 (1988): 278–88.

34. S. Waxman, 'The Oscar Acceptance Speech: By and Large, it's a Lost Art', *Washington Post*, 21 Mar. 1999, at: <www.littlereview.com/>. Accessed 15 Oct. 2004.

35. 'Putin Pledges to Fight Back', *Globe and Mail*, on-line edition, 4 Sept. 2004, at: <www.theglobeandmail.com>. Accessed September 4, 2004.

36. Cicero, *De Oratore*, ii.43.

Chapter 2

1. J. Tang, 'Cracking under Pressure', *The Varsity Online*, University of Toronto student newspaper, 21 June 2004, at: <www.thevarsity.ca/news/2003/03/11/Science/Cracking.Under.Pressure-391211.shtml>. Accessed 17 July 2004.

2. 'Famous People, Funny Stories', at: <www.anecdotage.com/index.php?aid=12880>. Accessed 18 July 2004.

3. 'Famous People, Funny Stories', from <www.videoeta.com>.

4. S. Schaefer, 'On and Offstage on Oscar's Big Night', 23 Mar. 1998, at: <http://movies.go.com/news/1998/3/032398oscarnews.html>. Accessed 18 July 2004.

5. 'Famous People, Funny Stories', from G. Brandreth, *Great Theatrical Disasters* (New York: St Martin's Press, 1983).

6. J.C. McCroskey, 'The Communication Apprehension Perspective', in J.C. McCroskey and J.A. Daly, eds, *Avoiding Communication: Shyness, Reticence, and Communication Apprehension* (London: Sage, 1984), 13–38.

7. J.C. McCroskey, 'Measures of Communication-Bound Anxiety', *Speech Monographs* 37 (1970): 269–77.

8. Tang, 'Cracking under Pressure'.

9. T.E. Robinson, 'Communication Apprehension and the Basic Public Speaking Course: A National Survey of In-class Treatment Techniques', *Communication Education* 46 (1997): 188–97.

10. D.W. Moore, 'Firefighters Top Gallup's Honesty and Ethics List', *The Gallup Poll Monthly*, 5 Dec. 2001, 46–8.

11. R.H. Bruskin, 'Fears', *Spectra* 9 (1973): 4. Also D. Wallechinsky, I. Wallace, and A. Wallace, *The Book of Lists* (New York: Bantam Books, 1977), 469. A.C. Baird and F.H. Knower, *Essentials of General Speech* (New York: McGraw-Hill, 1968) found that beginning speech students experience the same high levels of communication anxiety as the general population.

12. Jerry Seinfeld, monologue, *Seinfeld*, episode 61.

13. National Alliance for the Mentally Ill (NAMI), 'Panic Disorder', at: <www.nami.org/Content/ContentGroups/Helpline1/Panic_Disorder_htm>. Accessed 1 Aug. 2005.

14. R.R. Behnke and C.R. Sawyer, 'Anticipatory Anxiety Patterns for Male and Female Public Speakers', *Communication Education* 49 (2000): 187–95.

15. J.C. Hahner, M.A. Sokoloff, and S.L. Salisch, *Speaking Clearly: Improving Voice and Diction*, 5th edn (New York: McGraw-Hill, 1997), 362.

16. P.A. Broughton, 'Communication Apprehension—Implications for a Communication Instructor: Twenty Years of Communication Research Published in Communication Education', paper presented at the National Communication Association, Miami, Fla, Nov. 2003.

17. McCroskey, 'The Communication Apprehension Perspective'.

18. <www.starswelcome.com/>. Accessed 13 Nov. 2003.

19. 'Famous People, Funny Stories'.

20. McCroskey, 'The Communication Apprehension Perspective'.

21. Ibid.

22. S. Bochner, 'Culture Shock due to Contact with Unfamiliar Cultures', in W.J. Lonner, D.L. Dinnel, S.A. Hayes, and D.N. Sattler, eds, *Online Readings in Psychology and Culture* (Unit 8, Chapter 7), Center for Cross-Cultural Research, Western Washington University, 2003, at: <www.wwu.edu/~culture>. Accessed 18 July 2004.

23. McCroskey, 'The Communication Apprehension Perspective'.

24. J.L. Duda and L. Gano-Overway, 'Anxiety in Elite Young Gymnasts: Part II—Sources of Stress', *Technique* (Mar. 1996), at: <www.usa-gymnastics.org/publications/technique/1996/6/anxiety.html>. Accessed 17 July 2004.

25. 'Famous People, Funny Stories', from *Esquire*, Jan. 2001.

26. McCroskey, 'The Communication Apprehension Perspective'.

27. P.D. MacIntyre and R.C. Gardner, 'Language Anxiety: Its Relation to Other Anxieties and to Processing in Native and Second Language', *Language Learning* 41 (1991): 513–34. Also see N.F. Burroughs, V. Marie, and J.C. McCroskey, 'Relationships of Self-Perceived Communication Competence and Communication Apprehension with Willingness to Communicate: A Comparison with First and Second Languages', *Communication Research Reports* 20 (2003): 230–9.

28. J.W. Chesebro, J.C. McCroskey, D.F. Atwater, R.M. Bahrenfuss, G. Cawleti, and J.L. Gaudino, 'Communication Apprehension and Self-Perceived Communication Competence of At-Risk Students', *Communication Education* 41 (1992): 345–60; J. Ayres, 'Perceptions of Speaking Ability: An Explanation for Stage Fright', *Communication Education* 35 (1986): 275–87.

29. 'Bridget Fonda', at: <www.actressgallery.com/bridgetfonda/>. Accessed 18 July 2004.

30. P.D. McIntyre, K.A. Thivierge, and J.R. MacDonald, 'The Effects of Audience Interest, Responsiveness, and Evaluation on Public Speaking Anxiety and Related Variables', *Communication Research Reports* 14 (1997): 157–68.

31. McCroskey, 'The Communication Apprehension Perspective'.

32. Ibid.

33. Ibid.

34. A. Mehrabian, *Silent Messages*, 2nd edn (Belmont, Calif.: Wadsworth, 1981), 47–8, 61–2.

35. McCroskey, 'The Communication Apprehension Perspective'.

36. J.A. Keaton and L. Kelly, 'Disposition versus Situation: Neurocommunicology and the Influence of Trait Apprehension across Situational Factors on State Public Speaking Anxiety', *Communication Research Reports* 21 (2004): 273–83.

37. R. Tattenbaum, 'Want to Beef up Your Performance? Forget the Pantyhose!', Inner Act Peak Performance and Training, 1, at: <www.inner-act.com>. Accessed 10 Nov. 2003.

38. There appears to be no agreement on who first made this comment: Edwin Newman, Edward R. Murrow, or Walter Cronkite. It is possible the three news anchors used variations on the same idea.

39. W. Thompson, *Quantitative Research in Public Address and Communication* (New York: Random House, 1967), 175–6.

40. R.R. Rubin, A.M. Rubin, and F.F. Jordan, 'Effects of Instruction on Communication Apprehension and Communication Competence', *Communication Education* 46 (1997): 104–14; W.S. Zabava Ford and A.D. Wolvin, 'The Differential Impact of a Basic Communication Course on Perceived Communication Competencies in Class, Work, and Social Contexts', *Communication Education* 42 (1993): 215–23.

41. A. Mulac and A.R. Sherman, 'Behavioral Assessment of Speech Anxiety', *Quarterly Journal of Speech* 60 (1974): 134–43.

42. M.T. Motley, 'Taking the Terror Out of Talk', *Psychology Today* (Jan. 1988): 47.

43. J. Ayres, T. Hopf, and D.M. Ayres, 'Visualization and Performance Visualization: Applications, Evidence, and Speculation', in J.A. Daly, J.C. McCroskey, J. Ayres, T. Hopf, and D.M. Ayres, eds, *Avoiding Communication: Shyness, Reticence, and Communication Apprehension*, 2nd edn (Cresskill, NJ: Hampton Press, 1997), 401–22; J. Ayres and T.S. Hopf, 'Visualization: Is it More than Extra-Attention?', *Communication Education* 38 (1989): 1–3; J. Ayres, 'Coping with Speech Anxiety: The Power of Positive Thinking', *Communication Education* 37 (1988): 289–96.

44. T. Orlick and J. Partington, 'Mental Links to Excellence', *Sport Psychologist* 2 (1988): 105–30.

45. J. Bauman, 'The Gold Medal Mind', *Psychology Today* (May/June 2000): 1, at: <www.psychologytoday.com>. Accessed 10 Nov. 2003.

46. M.N. Nazzaro, 'Interview with Peter Jensen—Sports Psychologist', at: <http://members.aol.com/garhun/elvis/pjen.htm>, p. 4. Accessed 10 Nov. 2003.

47. T. Orlick and J. Partington, 'Psyched: Inner Views of Winning', 1988, 112, at: <www.zoneofexcellence.com/Articles/psyched.htm>. Accessed 1 Aug. 2005.

48. Ibid.

49. Ibid.

50. A.M. Bippus and J.A. Daly, 'What Do People Think Causes Stage Fright? Naïve Assumptions about the Reasons for Public Speaking Anxiety', *Communication Education* 48 (1999): 63–72.

51. Bauman, 'The Gold Medal Mind', 5.

52. Nazzaro, 'Interview with Peter Jensen', 1.

53. F.G. De Lacerda, 'Applied Sport Psychology: Peak Perfor-

mance', 2, at: <http://airsports.fai.org/sep98/sept9803 .html>. Accessed 10 Nov. 2003.

54. Bauman, 'The Gold Medal Mind', 2.

55. See M. Martini, R.R. Behnke, and P.E. King, 'The Communication of Public Speaking Anxiety: Perceptions of Asian and American Speakers', *Communication Quarterly* 40 (1992): 279–88.

56. 'Famous People, Funny Stories'.

57. Ibid.

58. 'Sports Performance: Tiger Woods', at: <www.sports-performance.biz/tiger.htm>. Accessed 10 Nov. 2003.

59. For additional insights on how visuals aids can increase speaker confidence, see J. Ayres, 'Using Visual Aids to Reduce Speech Anxiety', *Communication Research Reports* (June/Dec. 1991): 73–9.

60. T.S. Frobish, 'Jamieson Meets Lucas: Eloquence and Pedagogical Model(s) in *The Art of Public Speaking*', *Communication Education* 49 (2000): 239–52.

61. For further discussion of this technique, see W.J. Fremouw and M.D. Scott, 'Cognitive Restructuring: An Alternative Method for the Treatment of Communication Apprehension', *Communication Education* 28 (1979): 129–33.

62. Orlick and Partington, 'Psyched: Inner Views of Winning', 112.

63. Bauman, 'The Gold Medal Mind', 5.

64. J.L. Van Raalte, B.W. Brewer, P.M. Riviera, and A.J. Petitpas, 'The Relationship between Observable Self-Talk and Competitive Junior Tennis Players' Match Performances', *Journal of Exercise Psychology* 16 (1994): 400–15.

65. L.A. Samovar, R.B. Adler, and G. Rodman, *Understanding Human Communication*, 5th edn (New York: Harcourt Brace, 1994), 38.

66. M. Imhof, 'The Social Construction of the Listener: Listening Behavior across Situations, Perceived Listener Status, and Cultures', *Communication Research Reports* 20 (2003): 357–66.

67. Nazzaro, 'Interview with Peter Jensen', 2.

68. R.B. Adler, N. Towne, and R.F. Proctor, *Looking Out, Looking In* (Belmont, Calif.: Wadsworth Thomson Learning, 2004).

Chapter 3

1. R.F. Verderber, *The Challenge of Effective Speaking*, 11th edn (Belmont, Calif.: Wadsworth Thomson Learning, 2000), 36.

2. *The Power of Listening* [motion picture] (Scarborough, Ont.: CRM McGraw-Hill, 1978).

3. F. Wolff, *Perspective Listening* (New York: Holt, Rinehart and Winston, 1983).

4. G. Levoy, 'Is Anyone Listening?', *Toronto Star*, 10 Dec. 1987.

5. S. Hite, *Women and Love* (New York: Alfred Knopf, 1987).

6. K.F. Muenzinger, *The Psychology of Behavior* (New York: Harper, 1942).

7. R.E. Crable, *One to Another: A Guidebook for Interpersonal Communication* (New York: Harper & Row, 1981).

8. C. Rogers and R.E. Farson, 'Active Listening', in S.D. Ferguson and S. Ferguson, *Organizational Communication* (New Brunswick, NJ: Transaction Publishers, 1988), 319–34.

9. R.G. Nichols and L.A. Stevens, 'Six Bad Listening Habits', in Nichols and Stevens, eds, *Are You Listening?* (New York: McGraw-Hill, 1957).

10. Lance Armstrong, quoted in 'Olympic's Perfect Ten', at: <www.sportinglife.com/olympics/perfect_ten/story _get.dor?STORY_NAME=others/00/08/31/manual_ 083643.html>. Accessed 15 July 2004.

11. S. Ferguson and S. Ferguson, 'High Resolution Vision Prosthesis Systems: Research after 15 Years', *Journal of Visual Impairment and Blindness* (1986): 523–7.

12. Moody Institute of Science, *Sense Perception* [video recording], 2nd edn (Whittier, Calif.: Science Institute, 1968).

13. B.A. Wright and M.B. Fitzgerald, 'Sound-Discrimination Learning and Auditory Displays', *Proceedings of the 2003 International Conference on Auditory Display*, Boston, July 2003.

14. A. Koestler, *The Act of Creation* (New York: Macmillan, 1964).

15. W.E. Hill, *Puck* (London, UK), 6 Nov. 1915.

16. E.F. Loftus, *Eyewitness Testimony*, rev. edn (Cambridge, Mass.: Harvard University Press, 1996).

17. ABC News, 9 July 2004, at: <http://abcnews.go.com/ wire/US/ap20040625_1908.html>. Accessed 9 July 2004.

18. L.J. Postman, J.S. Bruner, and E. McGinnies, 'Personal Values as Selective Factors in Perception', *Journal of Abnormal and Social Psychology* 43 (1948): 142–54.

19. J. Senger, 'Seeing Eye to Eye: Practical Problems of Perception', in S. Ferguson and S.D. Ferguson, eds, *Intercom: Readings in Organizational Communication* (Hasbrouck Heights, NJ: Hayden Book Company, 1980), 144–5.

20. N.C. Schaeffer, 'Hardly Ever or Constantly: Group Comparisons Using Vague Qualifiers', *Public Opinion Quarterly* 55 (1991): 395.

21. R.D. Wimmer and J.R. Dominick, *Mass Media Research: An Introduction*, 5th edn (Belmont, Calif.: Wadsworth, 1997), 356–7.

22. E.M. Rogers and R. Agarwala-Rogers, *Communication in Organizations* (New York: Free Press, 1976), 91.

23. 'The Good Times are Killing Me', TVTV production (California and New York), funded by Ford and Rockefeller foundations, aired on PBS in 1975.

24. 'Mardi Gras', at: <www.folkstreams.net/context,43>. Accessed 7 July 2004.

25. G.A. Miller, 'The Magical Number Seven, Plus or Minus Two: Some Limits on Our Capacity for Processing Information', in R.C. Anderson and D.P. Ausubel, eds, *Readings in the Psychology of Cognition* (New York: Holt, Rinehart and Winston, 1965), 241–67.

26. D.B. Orr, 'Time-Compressed Speech—A Perspective', *Journal of Communication* 17 (1967): 223.

27. R.G. Nichols, 'Do We Know How to Listen? Practical Helps in a Modern Age', *Speech Teacher* 10 (Mar. 1961): 118–24.

28. A.D. Wolvin and C.G. Coakley, *Listening*, 2nd edn (Dubuque, Iowa: William C. Brown, 1985), 15.

29. D. Grant, 'Blind Students "Speed Listen"', *Globe and Mail*, 10 Jan. 1983, 14.

30. E. Cohen and A. Cohen, *Planning the Electronic Office* (New York: McGraw-Hill, 1983), 183.

31. A.H. Maslow and N.L. Mintz, 'Effects of Esthetic Surroundings: I. Initial Effects of Three Esthetic Conditions upon Perceiving "Energy" and "Well-Being" in Faces', *Journal of Psychology* 41 (1956): 253. Also see N.L. Mintz, 'Effects of Esthetic Surroundings: II. Prolonged and Repeated Experience in a "Beautiful" and "Ugly" Room', *Journal of Psychology* 41 (1956): 465–6.

32. W. Griffitt and R. Veitch, 'Hot and Crowded: Influences of Population Density and Temperature on Interpersonal Affective Behavior', *Journal of Personality and Social Psychology* 17 (1971): 92–8.

33. Wolff, *Perspective Listening*.

34. R.B. Adler and G. Rodman, *Understanding Human Communication*, 5th edn (New York: Harcourt Brace College Publishers, 1994), 186.

35. R.S. Adams and B. Biddle, *Realities of Teaching: Explorations with Video Tape* (New York: Holt, Rinehart and Winston, 1970).

36. L.B. Rosenfeld and J.M. Civikly, *With Words Unspoken: The Nonverbal Experience* (New York: Holt, Rinehart and Winston, 1976).

37. R. Sommer, *Personal Space: The Behavioral Basis of Design* (Englewood Cliffs, NJ: Prentice-Hall, 1969).

38. Ibid.

39. J.C. McCroskey and R.W. McVetta, 'Classroom Seating Arrangements: Instructional Communication Theory versus Student Preferences', paper presented at the annual meeting of the International Communication Association, Chicago, ERIC 154460, 1978, at: <www.jamesc mccroskey.com/publications/82.htm>. Accessed 15 July 2004.

40. Cited in R.H. Bolton, *People Skills: How to Assert Yourself, Listen to Others and Resolve Conflicts* (New York: Simon & Schuster, 1986).

Chapter 4

1. A.N. Miller, 'An Exploration of Kenyan Public Speaking Patterns with Implications for the American Introductory Public Speaking Course', *Communication Education* 51 (2002): 168–82.

2. T.S. Frobish, 'Jamieson Meets Lucas: Eloquence and Pedagogical Model(s) in *The Art of Public Speaking*', *Communication Education* 49 (2000): 239–52; M. Javidi, V.C. Downs, and J.F. Nussbaum, 'A Comparative Analysis of Teachers' Use of Dramatic Style Behaviors at Higher and Secondary Educational Levels', *Communication Education* 37 (1988): 278–88; K. Jamieson, *Eloquence in an Electronic Age: The Transformation of Political Speechmaking* (New York: Oxford University Press, 1988).

3. W.B. Pillsbury, *Attention* (New York: Macmillan, 1908). See also M. Billings, 'Duration of Attention', *Psychological Review* 21 (1914): 124–35.

4. W.D. Scott, *Psychology of Public Speaking* (New York: Noble and Noble, 1925).

5. B.E. Bradley, *Fundamentals of Speech Communication*, 3rd edn (Dubuque, Iowa: W.C. Brown, 1981), 205–6.

6. D.B. Orr, 'Time-Compressed Speech—A Perspective', *Journal of Communication* 17 (1967): 223. An even wider gap is identified in studies cited by A.D. Wolvin and C. Gwynn Coakley, *Listening*, 2nd edn (Dubuque, Iowa: William C. Brown, 1985), 15.

7. Speech by Alex Himelfarb, Clerk of the Privy Council, Secretary to the Cabinet and Head of the Public Service, Apex Symposium 2002, 'The Intermestic Challenge', Ottawa, 5 June 2002.

8. Speech by Hilary M. Weston, 'His Honour is a Woman', Canadian Club, 8 Dec. 1997.

9. Speech by Kristen Pidduck, communication student, University of Ottawa, 2004.

10. Speech by Alyssa Jacobs, communication student, University of Ottawa, 2004.

11. 'How Pornography Harms Children', excerpted from D.R. Hughes, 'Kids Online: Protecting Your Children in Cyberspace', *Revell* (Sept. 1998), at: <www.protect kids.com/effects/harms.htm>. Accessed 10 July 2004.

12. The statistics, which form the basis for this example, were discussed on the Oprah Winfrey show, 15 July 2004.

13. Speech by Erin Priddle, communication student, University of Ottawa, 2004.

14. Some sources attribute this quotation to Randall G. Leighton; however, the large majority of sources cite Satchel Paige, well-known for his memorable and pithy statements.

15. Speech by Mary Kathryn Roberts, communication student, University of Ottawa, 2004.

16. D. Nimmo and J.E. Combs, *Mediated Political Realities*, 2nd edn (New York: Longman, 1990), 56.

17. Andrew Gowing, communication student, University of Ottawa, 2003.

18. The quotation appears frequently on the Internet, but without attribution.

19. B.W. Jenkins and R.G. Eakins, *Sex Differences in Human Communication* (Boston: Houghton Mifflin, 1978), 75–6.

20. Versna Chuop, communication student, University of Ottawa, 2002.

21. Excerpt from speech by Joanna Mennie, communication student, University of Ottawa, 2004.

22. Excerpt from speech by Mary Kathryn Roberts, communication student, University of Ottawa, 2004.

23. K.E. Menzel and L.J. Carrell, 'The Relationship between Preparation and Performance in Public Speaking', *Communication Education* 43 (1994): 17–26.

24. Ibid.

Chapter 5

1. W.L. Schramm, 'How Communication Works', in Schramm, ed., *The Process and Effects of Communication* (Urbana: University of Illinois Press, 1954): 3–26.

2. T. Striphas, 'A Dialectic with the Everyday: Communication and Cultural Politics on Oprah Winfrey's Book Club', *Critical Studies in Media Communication* 20 (2003): 297.

3. N. Stone, 'The Role of Social Values in Communicating Programs and Policies to Canadians', PowerPoint presentation to Professional Marketing Research Society at National Press Club, Ottawa, 29 Jan. 2003.

4. D. Dasko, Environics Research Group (Toronto), presentation to the Conference on Citizenship, McGill University, 2001.

5. A.H. Maslow, *Motivation and Personality*, 2nd edn (New York: Harper & Row, 1954), 80–92.

6. E.M. Rogers and F.F. Shoemaker, *Communication of Innovations* (New York: Free Press, 1971).

7. See the following discussions of the relationship between esteem and persuasibility: J. Brockner and M. Elkind, 'Self-Esteem and Reactance: Further Evidence of Attitudinal and Motivational Consequences', *Journal of Experimental Social Psychology* 21 (1990): 346–61; E.P. Bettinghaus and M.J. Cody, *Persuasive Communication*, 5th edn (Fort Worth, Texas: Harcourt Brace College, 1994); H. Leventhal and S.I. Perloe, 'A Relationship between Self-Esteem and Persuasibility', *Journal of Abnormal and Social Psychology* 64 (1962): 385–88.

8. J.C. Nunnally and H.M. Bobren, 'Variables Governing the Willingness to Receive Communications on Mental Health', *Journal of Personality* 27 (1959): 275–90.

9. M. Rokeach, *The Open and Closed Mind* (New York: Basic Books, 1960).

10. Bettinghaus and Cody, *Persuasive Communication*.

11. Speech by Heidi Shelton, communication student, University of Ottawa, 2004.

12. C. Hovland and M. Sherif, *Social Judgment Assimilation and Contrast Effects in Communication and Attitude Change* (New Haven: Yale University Press, 1961). Also see C. Sherif, M. Sherif, and R. Nebergall, *Attitudes and Attitude Change: The Social Judgment Approach* (Philadelphia: W.B. Saunders, 1965).

13. G.J.S. Wilde, 'Effects of Mass Media Communications on Health and Safety Habits: An Overview of Issues and Evidence', *Addiction* 88 (7): 983–96.

14. M. Rokeach, *The Nature of Human Values* (New York: Free Press, 1973).

15. E. Griffin, *A First Look at Communication Theory*, 4th edn (Boston: McGraw-Hill, 2000).

16. K. Burke, *A Rhetoric of Motives* (Englewood Cliffs, NJ: Prentice-Hall, 1950), 20–46.

17. Jean Chrétien, speech delivered at the Ottawa Central Mosque, Ottawa, 21 Sept. 2001.

18. John McCallum, speech delivered to the Toronto Board of Trade, 28 Apr. 2005, at: <www.cra-arc.gc.ca/agency/minister/speeches/0428mccallum-e.html>. Accessed 16 June 2005.

19. Matthew Coon Come, speech delivered to Canada Seminar, Harvard Center for International Affairs and the Kennedy School of Government, Harvard University, Boston, 28 Oct. 1996, at: <www.thepeoplespaths.net/articles/spchcome.htm>. Accessed 2 Aug. 2005.

20. George H.W. Bush, address to the nation announcing allied military action in the Persian Gulf, 16 Jan. 1991.

21. Hillary Rodham Clinton, speech to the United Nations Fourth World Conference on Women, 5 Sept. 1995, Beijing.

22. Sarah Johnson, personal experience, e-mail correspondence, 24 May 2004.

23. E. Van Donkersgoed, 'F for Environmental Stewardship', AG Net, 12 Oct. 2001, at: <http://131.104.232.9/agnet/2001/10-2001/agnet_october_16.htm>. Accessed 20 June 2002.

24. I. Mayers, 'A Burning Topic: Tobacco and Death', *Canadian Respiratory Journal* 9 (2002), President's page, at: <www.pulsus.com/Respir/09_02/pree_ed.htm>. Accessed 14 Feb. 2003.

25. A. Picard, 'Medical Mistakes Kill: Why Don't Officials Act?', *Globe and Mail*, 20 Jan. 2005, A23, at: <www.theglobeandmail.com>. Accessed 8 June 2005.

26. This latter figure is fictitious, generated to illustrate the point.

27. Milton Himsl, personal experience, e-mail correspondence, 24 May 2004.

28. A. Ballard, 'Mandela: The Man, the Legend, the Hero', at: <http://wblsi.com/blk_history/mandela.htm>. Accessed 2 June 2002.

29. John F. Kennedy, Inaugural Address to the nation, 20 Jan. 1961, Washington.

30. Joe Clark, eulogy to Pierre Elliott Trudeau, delivered in the House of Commons, Ottawa, 29 Sept. 2000.

31. Pierre Elliott Trudeau, speech delivered at the proclamation ceremony, Ottawa, 17 Apr. 1982.

32. K. Lunman, 'Canadians Less Trusting Now, Poll Finds', *Globe and Mail*, 25 June 2003, A8.

Chapter 6

1. A.H. Monroe, 'Measurement and Analysis of Audience Reaction to Student Speakers' Studies in Attitude Changes', *Bulletin of Purdue University Studies in Higher Education* 22 (1937).

2. J.C. McCroskey and R.S. Mehrley, 'The Effects of Disorganization and Nonfluency on Attitude Change and Source Credibility', *Speech Monographs* 36 (1969): 13–21. Also K.K. Sereno and G.J. Hawkins, 'The Effects of Variations on Speakers' Nonfluency upon Audience Ratings of Attitude toward the Speech Topic and Speakers' Credibility', *Speech Monographs* 34 (1967): 58–64.

3. 'Why My Brain Hates Your Mistakes', Reuters, 26 Apr. 2004, Washington, DC, at Yahoo on-line news service: <www.yahoo.com>. Accessed 3 June 2005.

4. P. Ekman and W.V. Friesen, 'Nonverbal Behavior and Psychopsychology', in R.J. Friedman and M.N. Katz, eds, *The Psychology of Depression: Contemporary Theory and Research* (Washington: J. Winston, 1974).

5. J.K. Burgoon, T. Birk, and M. Pfau, 'Nonverbal Behaviors, Persuasion, and Credibility', *Human Communication Research* 17 (1990): 140–69.

6. J. Mulholland, *The Language of Negotiation* (London: Routledge, 1991), 78.

7. J.A. DeVito, *Human Communication: The Basic Course*, 3rd edn (New York: Harper & Row, 1985).

8. J.C. McCroskey, T. Jensen, and C. Valencia, 'Measurement of the Credibility of Peers and Spouses', paper presented at the International Communication Association Convention, Montreal, 1973. Also J.L. Whitehead Jr, 'Factors of Source Credibility', *Quarterly Journal of Speech* 54 (Feb. 1968): 59–63.

9. S.W. Littlejohn, 'A Bibliography of Studies related to Variables of Source Credibility', in N.A. Shearer, ed., *Bibliographic Annual in Speech Communication* (New York: Speech Communication Association, 1972).

10. P. Ekman, *Telling Lies: Clues to Deceit in the Marketplace, Politics, and Marriage* (New York: Norton, 1985), 107.

11. *Bridging the Culture Gap* (video recording). San Francisco: Copeland Griggs Productions, 1983.

12. Interview with Edwin Edwards, New Orleans, 20 Feb. 1970. Reported in 'Edwin Edwards: A Study in Ethos', MA thesis (University of Houston, 1971).

13. D. Diamond, commencement speech, University College of the Fraser Valley, at: <www.headlinestheatre.com/honourdoc.html>. Accessed 5 Nov. 2003.

14. Monroe, 'Measurement and Analysis of Audience Reaction'.

15. *Webster's Dictionary* (1913), at: <www.webster-dictionary.org/definition/rhythm>. Accessed 22 June 2004.

16. Mulholland, *The Language of Negotiation*, 89.

17. G.R. Miller and M.A. Hewgill, 'The Effect of Variations in Nonfluency on Audience Ratings of Source Credibility', *Quarterly Journal of Speech* 50 (1984): 36–44.

18. S.E. Lucas, *The Art of Public Speaking*, 6th edn (Boston: McGraw-Hill, 2003), 298.

19. L.B. Rosenfeld and J.M. Civikly, *With Words Unspoken: The Nonverbal Experience* (New York: Holt, Rinehart and Winston, 1976).

20. R.D. Albert and G.L. Nelson, 'Hispanic/Anglo-American Differences in Attributions to Paralinguistic Behavior', *International Journal of Intercultural Relations* 17 (1993): 19–40.

21. Lucas, *The Art of Public Speaking*, 298.

22. E. Haley, 'Organization as Source: Consumers' Understandings of Organizational Sponsorship of Advocacy Advertising', *Journal of Advertising* 25 (1996): 19–36. Also see Whitehead, 'Factors of Source Credibility'.

23. E.T. Hall, *The Hidden Dimension* (Garden City, NY: Anchor Books, 1969).

24. A. Mehrabian, *Nonverbal Communication* (Hawthorne, NY: Aldine, 1972).

25. M.L. Knapp, *Nonverbal Communication in Human Interaction* (New York: Holt, Rinehart and Winston, 1972), 5.

26. E.M. Rogers and D.K. Bhowmik, 'Homophily-Heterophily: Relational Concepts for Communication Research', *Public Opinion Quarterly* 34 (1970): 523–38. Also E.M. Rogers and F.F. Shoemaker, *Communication of Innovations* (New York: Free Press, 1971); J.C. McCroskey, V.P. Richmond, and J.A. Daly, 'Toward the Measurement of Perceived Homophily in Interpersonal Communication', paper presented to the International Communication Association Convention, New Orleans, Apr. 1974; V.P. Richmond, J.C. McCroskey, and J.A. Daly, 'The Generalizability of a Measure of Perceived Homophily in Interpersonal Communication', paper presented to the International Communication Association Convention,

Chicago, Apr. 1975; R.L. Atkinson, R.C. Atkinson, E.E. Smith, and D.J. Bem, *Introduction to Psychology*, 10th edn (San Diego: Harcourt Brace Jovanovich, 1990), 713.

27. See J.F. Andersen, 'Teacher Immediacy as a Moderator of Teaching Effectiveness', in D. Nimmo, ed., *Communication Yearbook* (New Brunswick, NJ: Transaction Books, 1979), 543–59. Also Jane Gorham, 'The Relationship between Verbal Teacher Immediacy Behaviors and Student Learning', *Communication Education* 37 (1988): 40–53.

28. C.I. Hovland, I.L. Janis, and H.H. Kelley, *Communication and Persuasion* (New Haven: Yale University Press, 1953).

29. E. Stack, 'Dressing Marcia: The Construction of Gender in the 1990s', at: <http://collection.nlc-bnc.ca/100/202/300/mediatribe95/marcia.html>. Accessed 26 June 2004.

30. J.T. Molloy, *The New Woman's Dress for Success Book* (New York: Warner Books, 1996).

31. R.R. Douglass, 'A Study of the Effect of the Introduction of Visual Communication Devices in a Sermon', Ph.D. dissertation (Grace Theological Seminary, 1997). Cited by K. Bickel, 'Preaching to Listeners: Communicating with Contemporary Listeners', Evangelical Homiletics Society, 2002, at: <www.evangelicalhomiletics.com/Papers2002/Bickel.htm>. Accessed 11 July 2004.

32. R.B. Adler and L.B. Rosenfeld, *Interplay*, 4th edn (New York: Holt, Rinehart and Winston, 1989), 163.

33. L.S. Harms, 'Listener Judgments of Status Cues in Content Free Speech', *Quarterly Journal of Speech* 47 (1961): 164–8.

34. For more information on the importance of personal appearance in speechmaking, see R.M. Perloff, *The Dynamics of Persuasion* (Hillsdale, NJ: Erlbaum, 1993), 149–52. Also see McCroskey, Richmond, and Daly, 'Toward the Measurement of Perceived Homophily'; P.N. Hamid, 'Style of Dress as a Perceptual Cue in Impression Formation', *Perceptual and Motor Skills* 26 (1968): 904–6.

35. J. Mills and E. Aronson, 'Opinion Change as a Function of the Communicator's Attractiveness and Desire to Influence', *Journal of Personality and Social Psychology* 1 (1965): 73–7.

36. H.I. Douty, 'Influence of Clothing on Perception of Persons', *Journal of Home Economics* 55 (1963): 197–202, cited in Rosenfeld and Civikly, *With Words Unspoken*, 73. Also see R.E. Bassett, 'Effects of Source Attire on Judgments of Credibility', *Central States Speech Journal* 30 (1979): 282–5; and J.K. Burgoon, D.B. Buller, and W.G. Woodall, *Nonverbal Communication: The Unspoken Dialogue* (New York: McGraw-Hill, 1996).

37. M.J. Horn, *The Second Skin: An Interdisciplinary Study of Clothing* (Boston: Houghton Mifflin, 1968).

38. E.J. Natalle and F. Bodenheimer, 'Prop-er Attire', Presenters University, sponsored by InFocus, at: <www.presentersuniversity.com/delivery_Attire.php>. Accessed 11 July 2005.

39. V.P. Richmond, J.C. McCroskey, and S.K. Payne, *Nonverbal Behavior in Interpersonal Relations* (Englewood Cliffs, NJ: Prentice-Hall, 1991), 211.

40. N. Carr-Ruffino, *The Promotable Woman* (Franklin Lakes, NJ: Career Press, 1992), 251.

41. Ibid.

42. Study by L. Malandro and L. Barker, reported in Ronald B. Adler and Neil Towne, *Looking Out/Looking In: Interpersonal Communication*, 5th edn (New York: Holt, Rinehart and Winston, 1987), 199.

43. M.B. Myers, D. Templer, and R. Brown, 'Coping Ability of Women Who Become Victims of Rape', *Journal of Consulting and Clinical Psychology* 52 (1984): 73–8.

44. Hovland, Janis, and Kelley, *Communication and Persuasion*; Whitehead, 'Factors of Source Credibility'.

45. Richmond, McCroskey, and Payne, *Nonverbal Behavior in Interpersonal Relations*, 226.

46. Burgoon, Birk, and Pfau, 'Nonverbal Behaviors, Persuasion, and Credibility'.

47. Mulholland, *The Language of Negotiation*, 89.

48. W.J. Seiler, 'The Conjunctive Influence of Source Credibility and the Use of Visual Materials on Communication Effectiveness', *Southern Speech Communication Journal* 37 (Winter 1971): 174–85.

49. Whitehead, 'Factors of Source Credibility'.

50. 'First Peoples and the Fourth Estate', a media conference on Aboriginal issues sponsored by the Carleton University School of Journalism and Communications, Barry McLoughlin Associates, and the Canada Communications Group (Government of Canada), 10 Dec. 1998, Carleton University, Ottawa.

51. R.B. Adler and N. Towne, *Looking Out, Looking In* (New York: Holt, Rinehart and Winston, 1990).

52. E.J. Kempf, 'Abraham Lincoln's Organic and Emotional Neuroses', *A.M.A. Archives of Neurology and Psychiatry* 67 (1952): 419–33.

Chapter 7

1. See, for example, W.J. Ong, *Orality and Literacy: The Technologizing of the Word*, 2nd edn (New York: Routledge, 2002).

2. H. Gardner, *Frames of Mind: The Theory of Multiple Intelligences* (New York: Basic Books, 1983). See also E. Dale, *Audiovisual Methods in Teaching*, 3rd edn (New York: Holt, Rinehart and Winston, 1969).

3. Pictographs collected on a site by E. Brunner, at: <www.csc.calpoly.edu/~ebrunner/ExcelPictographs.html>. Accessed 2 Oct. 2004. The examples come from other sites, such as <www.baddogcomputer.com/unidial/assoc.htm> (dollar bill example); ClarisWorks Tutorial, at <www.rialto.k12.ca.us/frisbie/pictogram.html> (chili

pepper example); USDA studies reported in *Journal of Agricultural and Food Chemistry* 44 (1996): 701–5 and 3426–43; and USDA studies reported in *Journal of Agricultural and Food Chemistry* 46 (1998): 2686–93 (fruit and vegetable pictograph).

4. J. Downing and C. Garmon, 'Teaching Students in the Basic Course How to Use Presentation Software', *Communication Education* 50 (2001): 218–29.

5. D.R. Vogel, G.W. Dickson, and J.A. Lehman, *Persuasion and the Role of Visual Presentation Support: The UM/3M Study* (St Paul, Minn.: 3M General Offices, 1986).

Chapter 8

1. Alyssa Jacobs, communication student, University of Ottawa, 2004.

2. Data from the Computer Industry Almanac and other Internet research companies is reported at: <www.clickz.com/stats/big_picture/geographics/article.php/5911_151151>. Accessed 12 Aug. 2004.

3. Data from the Nielsen/Net Ratings and other Internet research companies is reported at: <www.clickz.com/stats/big_picture/geographics/article.php/5911_151151>. Accessed 12 Aug. 2004. The figures on active users are based on research conducted in June 2004.

4. K.E. Rowan, 'A New Pedagogy for Explanatory Public Speaking: Why Arrangement Should Not Substitute for Invention', *Communication Education* 44 (1995): 236–50.

5. Ibid.

6. M. Nissani, 'Retrospective Reflections on Atoms and Stars: The Counter-Intuitive Nature of Science', at: <www.is.wayne.edu/mnissani/a&s/LESSONS.htm>.

7. Rowan, 'A New Pedagogy'.

8. Ibid.

9. Ibid.

10. E.P. Bettinghaus and M.J. Cody, *Persuasive Communication*, 5th edn (Fort Worth, Texas: Harcourt Brace College, 1994). See also J.C. Jahnke, 'Serial Position Effects in Immediate Serial Recall', *Journal of Verbal Learning and Verbal Behavior* 2 (1963): 284–7.

11. David Bowie, commencement address, Berklee College of Music, 8 May 1999, at: <www.berklee.edu/html>. Accessed 20 Sept. 2002.

12. Excerpted from speech by Magdalen Dabrowski, communication student, University of Ottawa, 2004.

13. Excerpt from speech by Anne Clairmont, communication student, University of Ottawa, 2004.

14. Editorial, 'In the Richest Nation in World, 33 Million Live in Poverty', *Emmitsburg Dispatch* 7 (July 2003): 1, at: <www.emmitsburgdispatch.com/2003/July/editorial.shtml>. Accessed 8 July 2004.

15. Ray Bradbury, commencement speech, California Institute of Technology, 2000, at: <http://pr.caltech.edu/commencement/00/c2kbradburyspeech.html>. Accessed 20 Sept. 2002. Copyright © 2000 by Ray Bradbury. This exerpt and the one appearing on p. 221 are reprinted by permission of Don Congdon Associates, Inc.

16. Based on account by I. Peritz, 'School Turns Tail, Lets Man and Dog into Class', *Globe and Mail*, on-line edition, 8 July 2004, at: <www.theglobeandmail.com>. Accessed 8 July 2004.

17. Excerpted from a speech by Andrea Ball, communication student, University of Ottawa, 2004.

18. One Internet source attributed this quotation to author Stuart Wilde. The others listed the quotation as anonymous.

19. Bradbury, commencement speech.

20. J.C. McCroskey and R.S. Mehrley, 'The Effects of Disorganization and Nonfluency on Attitude Change and Source Credibility', *Speech Monographs* 36 (1969): 13–21. Also K.K. Sereno and G.J. Hawkins, 'The Effects of Variations on Speakers' Nonfluency upon Audience Ratings of Attitude toward the Speech Topic and Speakers' Credibility', *Speech Monographs* 34 (1967): 58–64.

21. Story contributed by Christine Vallières, e-mail communication, 18 May 2004. Reprinted by permission of the author.

22. 'History of the Croissant', *Healthy Home News* (Chelsea, Que.) 8 (2004): 3.

23. Doug Lewis, Solicitor General of Canada, speech delivered at the opening ceremonies of the 60th annual general meeting of the Police Association of Ontario, unpublished manuscript, Ottawa, 10 Aug. 1992, 1.

24. Ibid.

25. B. Malinowski, cited in 'Famous People, Funny Stories', at: <www.anecdotage.com/index.php?aid=12880>. Accessed 18 July 2004. M. Kranes, F. Worth, S. Tremarius, M. Driscoll, M. Kuanes, and F.L. Worth, eds, *5087 Trivia Questions and Answers*.

26. D. Meissner, 'Luna to Stay in Adopted Home', CP wire story, *Globe and Mail*, on-line edition, 29 July 2004, at: <www.theglobeandmail.com>. Accessed 30 July 2004.

27. M. Javidi, V.C. Downs, and J.F. Nussbaum, 'A Comparative Analysis of Teachers' Use of Dramatic Style Behaviors at Higher and Secondary Educational Levels', *Communication Education* 37 (1988): 278–88; also R.W. Norton, *Communicator Style: Theory, Application, and Measures* (Beverly Hills, Calif.: Sage, 1983), 238; K. Jamieson, *Eloquence in an Electronic Age: The Transformation of Political Speechmaking* (New York: Oxford University Press, 1988); T.S. Frobish, 'Jamieson Meets Lucas: Eloquence and Pedagogical Model(s) in *The Art of Public Speaking*', *Communication Education* 49 (2000): 239–52.

28. WordNet Dictionary, at: <www.hyperdictionary.com/dictionary/fable>. Accessed 14 Aug. 2004.

29. <http://encyclopedia.thefreedictionary.com/Parable>. Accessed 14 Aug. 2004.

30. Excerpt from speech by Erin Priddle, communication student, University of Ottawa, 2004.

31. *Engineering Statistics Handbook*, at: <www.itl.nist.gov/div898/handbook/eda/section3/eda35f.htm>. Accessed 16 Aug. 2004.

32. Matthew Breakey (Edmonton), 'Letters to the Editor: The Mail', *Maclean's* (2 May 2005): 2.

33. William J. Kunstler, speech delivered at Indiana University, Bloomington, *Indiana Daily Student* (8 Oct. 1970): 8.

34. Billy Joel, commencement address, Berklee College of Music, May 1993, at: <www.berklee.edu/html>. Accessed 20 Sept. 2002.

35. Excerpt from speech by Erin Priddle, communication student, University of Ottawa, 2004.

36. B. Martin, 'Defamation Law and Free Speech', at: <www.uow.edu.au/arts/sts/bmartin/dissent/documents/defamation.html>. Accessed 16 Aug. 2004.

37. Excerpted from speech by Kristen Pidduck, communication student, University of Ottawa, 2004.

38. Alan Alda, 'A Reel Doctor's Advice to Some Real Doctors', commencement address, Columbia College of Physicians, May 1979.

Chapter 9

1. Aristotle, *Rhetoric*, trans. W.R. Roberts, II.1 (New York: Modern Library, 1954), 90–1. The term *ethos* refers to the credibility or character of a speaker.

2. Cicero, *De Oratore*, ii.43.

3. Prentice A. Meador Jr, 'Speech Education at Rome', *Western Speech* 31 (1967): 14.

4. Quintilian, *The Institutio Oratoria*, 12.1.

5. C.I. Hovland, I.L. Janis, and H.H. Kelley, *Communication and Persuasion* (New Haven: Yale University Press, 1953).

6. K.E. Anderson, 'An Experimental Study of the Interaction of Artistic and Non-Artistic Ethos in Persuasion', Ph.D. dissertation (University of Wisconsin, 1961).

7. K. Anderson and T. Clevenger Jr, 'A Summary of Experimental Research in Ethos', *Speech Monographs* 30 (1963): 59–78.

8. J.C. McCroskey, 'Scales for the Measurement of Ethos', *Speech Monographs* 33 (1966): 65–72.

9. D.K. Berlo, J.B. Lemert, and R.L. Mertz, 'Evaluating the Acceptability of Message Sources', *Public Opinion Quarterly* 33 (1969): 563–76. An earlier representation of their research appeared in *Research Monograph*, Department of Communication, Michigan State University, 1966.

10. McCroskey, 'Scales for the Measurement of Ethos'.

11. Berlo, Lemert, and Mertz, 'Evaluating the Acceptability of Message Sources'.

12. R.G. Smith, 'Source Credibility Context Effects', *Speech Monographs* 40 (1973): 303–9; Jack R. Whitehead, 'Factors of Source Credibility', *Quarterly Journal of Speech* 54 (1968): 61–3.

13. S.W. Littlejohn, 'A Bibliography of Studies related to Variables of Source Credibility', in N.A. Shearer, ed., *Bibliographic Annual in Speech Communication* (New York: Speech Communication Association, 1972).

14. Smith, 'Source Credibility Context Effects'.

15. 'Teresa Heinz Promotes "Women's Voices"', 27 July 2004, Democratic National Convention, Boston, at: <www.cnn.com/2004/ALLPOLITICS/07/27/dems.teresa/index.html>. Accessed 28 July 2004.

16. E.M. Rogers and D.K. Bhowmik, 'Homophily-Heterophily: Relational Concepts for Communication Research', *Public Opinion Quarterly* 34 (1970): 523–38; E.M. Rogers and F.F. Shoemaker, *Communication of Innovations* (New York: Free Press, 1971); J.C. McCroskey, V.P. Richmond, and J.A. Daly, 'Toward the Measurement of Perceived Homophily in Interpersonal Communication', paper presented to the International Communication Association Convention, New Orleans, Apr. 1974; V.P. Richmond, J.C. McCroskey, and J.A. Daly, 'The Generalizability of a Measure of Perceived Homophily in Interpersonal Communication', paper presented to the International Communication Association Convention, Chicago, Apr. 1975; R.L. Atkinson, R.C. Atkinson, E.E. Smith, and D.J. Bem, *Introduction to Psychology*, 10th edn (San Diego: Harcourt Brace Jovanovich, 1990), 713.

17. Tony Blair, British Prime Minister, speech to the Irish Parliament, 26 Nov. 1998, at: <http://mitglied.lycos.de/FrankGemkow/laku/gb/speeches/blair.htm>. Accessed 31 Oct. 2003.

18. Hilary M. Weston, 'Stories and Reflections: My Five Years as Lieutenant Governor', The Canadian Club, Toronto, 10 Dec. 2001, at: <www.lt.gov.on.ca/sections_english/history_middle_frame/hweston_speeches/>. Accessed 5 Nov. 2003.

19. K.S. Thweatt and J.C. McCroskey, 'The Impact of Teacher Immediacy and Misbehaviors on Teacher Credibility', *Communication Education* 47 (1998): 348–58.

20. E. Haley, 'Organization as Source: Consumers' Understandings of Organizational Sponsorship of Advocacy Advertising', *Journal of Advertising* 25 (1996): 19–36.

21. F.S. Haiman, 'The Effects of Ethos in Public Speaking', *Speech Monographs* 16 (1949): 192; C.I. Hovland and W. Weiss, 'The Influence of Source Credibility on Communication Effectiveness', *Public Opinion Quarterly* 16 (1961): 635–50.

22. Margaret Newall, convocation speech, University of Manitoba, 18 Oct. 2001, at: <www.prairieactionfoundation.ca/main/speeches.htm>. Accessed 26 Jan. 2003.

23. Alan Alda, commencement speech, University of Columbia, College of Physicians and Surgeons, New York, 25 May 1979, reprinted in *Physicians and Surgeons Journal* (Summer 1979).

24. B.E. Enochs, comp. and ed., 'Columbia-Presbyterian Medical Center 1928–2004: 75 People, Events, and Contributions Worth Remembering', at: <http://cumc.columbia.edu/news/journal/journal-o/fall-2003/75years_2650.html>. Accessed 25 Sept. 2004.

25. Alda, commencement address at University of Columbia, 25 May 1979, reprinted by permission of Mayflower Productions (Montana Dodel, In-house publicity for Alan Alda).

26. Enochs, comp. and ed., 'Columbia-Presbyterian Medical Center'.

27. E.P. Bettinghaus, *Persuasive Communication*, 2nd edn (New York: Holt, Rinehart, and Winston, 1968).

28. S. Milgram, *Obedience to Authority* (New York: Harper & Row, 1974). See also M. Karlins and H. Abelson, *Persuasion: How Opinions and Attitudes Are Changed* (New York: Springer, 1970).

29. See discussions by B.W. Eakins and R.G. Eakins, *Sex Differences in Communication* (Boston: Houghton Mifflin, 1978), 38–49; P. Bradley, 'The Folklinguistics of Women's Speech: An Empirical Examination,' *Communication Monographs* 48 (1981): 73-90.

30. See discussions by Eakins and Eakins, *Sex Differences*, 38–49; Bradley, 'The Folklinguistics of Women's Speech'.

31. B.R. Sandler, 'Women Faculty at Work in the Classroom, or, Why it Still Hurts to Be a Woman in Labor', *Communication Education* 40 (1991): 6–15.

32. See discussions by Eakins and Eakins, *Sex Differences*, 38-49; Bradley, 'The Folklinguistics of Women's Speech'.

33. R.B. Cialdini, *Influence: Science and Practice*, 4th edn (New York: HarperCollins, 2002).

34. P. Raymont, 'History on the Run—the Media and the '79 Election'.

35. 'Elections: Text of Obama's Address at Convention', AP Wire, *Seattle-Post Intelligencer*, 27 July 2004, at: <http://seattlepi.nwsource.com/national/apelection_story>, 2. Accessed 15 Aug. 2004.

36. A. Mehrabian, 'Attitudes Inferred from Non-immediacy of Verbal Communication', *Journal of Verbal Learning and Verbal Behavior* 6 (1967): 294–5.

37. See, for example, M.L. Houser, 'Are We Violating Their Expectations? Instructor Communication Expectations of Traditional and Nontraditional Students', *Communication Quarterly* 53 (2005): 213–28; W.J. Potter and R. Emanuel, 'Students' Preferences for Communication Styles and Their Relationship to Achievement', *Communication Education* 39 (1990): 234–49; G. Sorensen, 'The Relationships among Teachers' Self-Disclosive Statements, Students' Perceptions, and Affective Learning', *Communication Education* 38 (1989): 259–76; J. Gorham, 'The Relationship between Verbal Teacher Immediacy Behaviors and Student Learning', *Communication Education* 37 (1988): 40–53; V. Downs, M. Javidi, and J. Nussbaum, 'An Analysis of Teachers' Verbal Communication within the College Classroom: Use of Humor, Self-Disclosure, and Narratives', *Communication Education* 37 (1988): 127–41; L.R. Wheeless, 'Self-Disclosure and Interpersonal Solidarity: Measurement, Validation, and Relationships', *Human Communication Research* 3 (1976): 47–61.

38. Alex Himelfarb, Clerk of the Privy Council and Secretary to Cabinet, 'The Intermestic Challenge', APEX symposium, Ottawa, 5 June 2002.

39. Whitehead, 'Factors of Source Credibility'.

40. J. McCroskey, *An Introduction to Rhetorical Communication*, 7th edn (Boston: Allyn and Bacon, 1997), 91–101.

41. Interview with J. Baronet, Channel 10 Television, Lafayette, Louisiana, 26 Mar. 1970.

42. Cited by M. Goldman, interview, Lafayette, Louisiana, 24 Mar. 1970.

43. Interview with M. Goldman, Channel 3 television studio, Lafayette, Louisiana, 24 Mar. 1970.

44. W.C. Minnick, *The Art of Persuasion* (Boston: Houghton Mifflin, 1957).

45. See, for example, B. Reeves, J. Newhagen, E. Maibach, M. Basil, and K. Kurz, 'Negative and Positive Television Messages: Effects of Message Type and Context on Attention and Memory', *American Behavioral Scientist* 34 (1991): 679–94. See also Minnick, *The Art of Persuasion*.

46. 'The Third Man', at: <http://encyclopedia.thefreedictionary.com/The%20Third%20Man>. Accessed 31 Aug. 2004. Some claim that even the cuckoo clock is an invention of the Germans!

47. George W. Bush, excerpt from speech delivered from the Oval Office, Washington, DC, 11 Sept. 2004.

48. Andrew Gowing, speech on the rising costs of snowmobile insurance, 2003.

49. See G.J.S. Wilde, 'Effects of Mass Media Communications on Health and Safety Habits: An Overview of Issues and Evidence', *Addiction* 88 (1993): 983–96; T.E. Backer, E.M. Rogers, and P. Sopory, eds, *Designing Health Communication Campaigns: What Works?* (Newbury Park, Calif.: Sage, 1992); D.J. O'Keefe, *Persuasion: Theory and Research* (Newbury Park, Calif.: Sage, 2002).

50. F.J. Boster and P. Mongeau, 'Fear-Arousing Persuasive Messages', in R.N. Bostrom and B.H. Westley, eds, *Com-*

munication Yearbook 8 (Beverly Hills, Calif.: Sage, 1984), 330–75. See also S. Sutton, 'Fear-Arousing Communications: A Critical Examination of Theory and Research', in J.R. Eiser, ed., *Social Psychology and Behavioral Medicine* (New York: John Wiley, 1982), 303–37.

51. See F. Cope and D. Richardson, 'The Effects of Reassuring Recommendations in a Fear-Arousing Speech', *Speech Monographs* 39 (1972): 148–50; B.J. Fine, 'Conclusion-Drawing, Communicator Credibility, and Anxiety as Factors in Opinion Change', *Journal of Abnormal and Social Psychology* 54 (1957): 369–74; H. Leventhal, J.C. Watts, and F. Pagano, 'Effects of Fear and Instructions on How to Cope with Danger', *Journal of Personality and Social Psychology* 6 (1967): 313–21; K. Witte, 'Fear Control and Danger Control: A Test of the Extended Parallel Process Model', *Communication Monographs* 61 (1994): 113–34; R.E. Petty and J.T. Cacioppo, *Attitudes and Persuasion: Classic and Contemporary Approaches* (Dubuque, Iowa: William C. Brown, 1981); J.B. Stiff, *Persuasive Communication* (New York: Guilford, 1994).

52. Franklin D. Roosevelt, speech delivered on 8 Dec. 1941, to the United States Congress, Washington, DC.

53. Franklin D. Roosevelt, 'Fireside Chat', national radio, 9 Dec. 1941, broadcast from Washington, DC.

54 Hillary Rodham Clinton, 'Women's Rights are Human Rights', address to the UN Fourth World Conference on Women, Beijing, 5 Sept. 1995.

Chapter 10

1. J. Dewey, *How We Think: A Restatement of the Relation of Reflective Thinking to the Educative Process* (New York: D.C. Heath, 1933).

2. S. Strauss, 'How Long Will You Live? What Month Were You Born In?', *Globe and Mail*, on-line edition, 4 Sept. 2004, at: <www.theglobeandmail.com>. Accessed 4 Sept. 2004.

3. A.H. Monroe, *Principles and Types of Speech* (Glenview, Ill.: Scott Foresman, 1945).

4. J.G. Barber, R. Bradshaw, and C. Walsh, 'Reducing Alcohol Consumption through Television Advertising', *Journal of Consulting and Clinical Psychology* 57 (1989): 613–18. See also F. Cope and D. Richardson, 'The Effects of Reassuring Recommendations in a Fear-Arousing Speech', *Speech Monographs* 39 (1972): 148–50; B.J. Fine, 'Conclusion-Drawing, Communicator Credibility, and Anxiety as Factors in Opinion Change', *Journal of Abnormal and Social Psychology* 54 (1957): 369–74; H. Leventhal, J.C. Watts, and F. Pagano, 'Effects of Fear and Instructions on How to Cope with Danger', *Journal of Personality and Social Psychology* 6 (1967): 313–21.

5. S. Jackson and M. Allen, 'Meta-Analysis of the Effectiveness of One-Sided and Two-Sided Argumentation', paper presented at the annual meeting of the International Communication Association, Montreal, May 1987.

6. C.J. Hovland, I.L. Janis, and H.H. Kelley, *Communication and Persuasion* (New Haven: Yale University Press, 1953).

7. Jackson and Allen, 'Meta-Analysis'. Also K.W.E. Anatol, 'Fundamentals of Persuasive Speaking', *MODCOM (Modules in Speech Communication)* (Chicago: Science Research Associates, 1976), 19.

8. W.J. McGuire, 'The Effectiveness of Supportive and Refutational Defenses in Immunizing and Restoring Beliefs against Persuasion', *Sociometry* 24 (1961): 184–97.

9. D.D. Johnston, *The Art and Science of Persuasion* (Madison, Wis.: William C. Brown/Benchmark, 1994), 141–2.

10. K.K. Reardon, *Persuasion in Practice* (Newbury Park, Calif.: Sage, 1991).

11. E.P. Bettinghaus and M.J. Cody, *Persuasive Communication*, 5th edn (Fort Worth, Texas: Harcourt Brace College, 1994); J.C. Jahnke, 'Serial Position Effects in Immediate Serial Recall', *Journal of Verbal Learning and Verbal Behavior* 2 (1963): 284–7.

12. H. Gilkinson, S.F. Paulson, and D.E. Sikkink, 'Effects of Order and Authority in an Argumentative Speech', *Quarterly Journal of Speech* 40 (1954): 183–92; H. Sponberg, 'A Study of the Relative Effectiveness of Climax and Anti-Climax Order in an Argumentative Speech', *Speech Monographs* 13 (1946): 35–44.

13. Bettinghaus and Cody, *Persuasive Communication*; R.N. Bostrom, *Persuasion* (Englewood Cliffs, NJ: Prentice-Hall, 1983).

14. Anatol, 'Fundamentals of Persuasive Speaking', 19.

15. R.S. Ross, *Understanding Persuasion*, 4th edn (Englewood Cliffs, NJ: Prentice-Hall, 1994).

16. Monroe, *Principles and Types of Speech*.

17. Sonia Genovesi, communication student, University of Ottawa, 2003.

18. Royal Commission on the Status of Women, 1970.

19. Excerpted from a speech by Leslie Revere, communication student, University of Ottawa, 2004.

20. S.E. Taylor and S.C. Thompson, 'Stalking the Elusive "Vividness" Effect', *Psychological Review* 89 (1982): 155–81.

21. T.R. Koballa Jr, 'Persuading Teachers to Re-examine the Innovative Elementary Science Programs of Yesterday: The Effect of Anecdotal versus Data-Summary Communications', *Journal of Research in Science Teaching* 23 (1986): 437–49.

22. A.N. Miller, 'An Exploration of Kenyan Public Speaking Patterns with Implications for the American Introductory Public Speaking Course', *Communication Education* 51 (2002): 168–82.

23. K. Jamieson, *Eloquence in an Electronic Age: The Transformation of Political Speechmaking* (New York: Oxford University Press, 1988). Also see T.S. Frobish, 'Jamieson Meets Lucas: Eloquence and Pedagogical Model(s) in *The Art of Public*

Speaking', *Communication Education* 49 (2000): 239–52; M. Javidi, V.C. Downs, and J.F. Nussbaum, 'A Comparative Analysis of Teachers' Use of Dramatic Style Behaviors at Higher and Secondary Educational Levels', *Communication Education* 37 (1988): 278–88.

24. Kim Campbell, address to the Confederation Club of Kitchener, Ont., 16 Aug. 1993, at: <www.nlc-bnc.ca/primeministers/h4-4044-e.html>. Accessed 31 Oct. 2003.

25. *Student*, 8 Oct. 1970, 8.

26. Tony Blair, British Prime Minister, speech to the Irish Parliament, 26 Nov. 1998, at: <http://mitglied.lycos.de/FrankGemkow/laku/gb/speeches/blair.htm>. Accessed 31 Oct. 2003.

27. Hilary M. Weston, 'Stories and Reflections: My Five Years as Lieutenant Governor', The Canadian Club, Toronto, 10 Dec. 2001, at: <www.lt.gov.on.ca/sections_english/history_middle_frame/hweston_speeches/>. Accessed 5 Nov. 2003.

28. Audrey McLaughlin, response to the Prime Minister's statement, speech on the commencement of the Persian Gulf War, House of Commons, Ottawa, 16 Jan. 1991.

29. Mary Fisher, 'The Whisper of AIDS', Republican National Convention address, Houston, 19 Aug. 1992, at: <www.pbs.org/greatspeeches/timeline/m_fisher_s1.html>. Accessed 14 Sept. 2003.

30. Inaugural address of John F. Kennedy, Washington, DC, 20 Jan. 1961, at: <www.yale.edu/lawweb/avalon/presiden/inaug/kennedy.htm>. Accessed 7 Sept. 2004.

31. R. Caldwell, 'Where Have All the Orators Gone?', *Globe and Mail*, 23 Jan. 2002, at: <www.theglobeandmail.com>. Accessed 23 Jan. 2002.

32. J.M. Bumsted and L. Kuffert, eds, *Interpreting Canada's Past: A Pre-Confederation Reader* (Toronto: Oxford University Press, 2004), 303.

33. Leslie Tutty, speech commemorating the 11th anniversary of the Montreal massacre, Nickle Arts Museum, University of Calgary, 6 Dec. 2000.

34. Speech by Winston Churchill, 'We Shall Fight on the Beaches', 4 June 1940, at: <www.winstonchurchill.org/beaches.htm>. Accessed 10 Oct. 2001.

35. Kim Campbell, address to the Confederation Club of Kitchener, Ont., 16 Aug. 1993, at: <www.nlc-bnc.ca/primeministers/h4-4044-e.html>. Accessed 31 Oct. 2003.

36. Andrew Gowing, speech on rising costs of snowmobile insurance, 2003.

37. H.E. Fosdick, sermon delivered at the Riverside Church, New York City, 12 Nov. 1933. Reprinted in *Riverside Sermons* (New York: Harper & Brothers, 1958).

38. John F. Kennedy, farewell address to the people of Massachusetts, 'History Will Be My Judge', 1961.

39. Kennedy, inaugural address.

40. Campbell, speech to the Confederation Club, Kitchener, Ont..

41. Weston, 'Stories and Reflections'.

42. Margaret Newall, convocation speech, University of Manitoba, 18 Oct. 2001, at: <www.prairieactionfoundation.ca/main/speeches.htm>. Accessed 26 Jan. 2003.

43. Matthew Coon Come, National Chief of the Assembly of First Nations, opening remarks at the Indigenous Leaders Summit of the Americas, 29 Mar. 2001, at: <www.turtle-tracks-for-kids.org/Inspiration-/Indig.%20Leaders%20Summit-Matthe>. Accessed 31 Oct. 2003.

44. Nelson Mandela, 'I am Prepared to Die', Rivonia trial, Pretoria Supreme Court, 20 Apr. 1964, at: <www.anc.org.za/ancdocs/history/rivonia.html>. Accessed 11 Nov. 2002.

45. Caldwell, 'Where Have All the Orators Gone?'

46. Jean Chrétien, tribute to Pierre Elliott Trudeau, House of Commons, Ottawa, 29 Sept. 2000, at: <www.nlc-bnc.ca/primeministers/h4-4082-e.html>. Accessed 31 Oct. 2003.

47. Weston, 'Stories and Reflections'.

48. Adrienne Clarkson, 'Decorations for Bravery', speech delivered at Rideau Hall, Ottawa, 9 Dec. 2002, at: <www.gg.ca/media/speeches/archive-2002/20021209_e.asp>. Accessed 28 Jan. 2003.

49. Coon Come, opening remarks at the Indigenous Leaders Summit of the Americas.

50. Winston Churchill, speech to the Canadian Parliament, 30 Dec. 1941, at: <www.nebridge.org/varrieur/Other%20Events/churchill.htm>. Accessed 31 Oct. 2003.

51. Joe Clark, eulogy to Pierre Trudeau, delivered in the House of Commons, 29 Sept. 2000, at: <www.canoe.ca/CNEWSTrudeauNews/000929_clarktribute-cp.html>. Accessed 17 Oct. 2004.

52. Hilary M. Weston, speech to the Ireland Fund of Canada's Emerald Ball 2001, Toronto, 19 Oct. 2001.

53. Weston, 'Stories and Reflections'.

54. Campbell, address to the Confederation Club, Kitchener, Ont.

55. Winston Churchill, 'This was their Finest Hour', 18 June 1940, at: <http://mitglied.lycos.de/FrankGemkow/laku/gb/speeches/churchill-hour.htm>. Accessed 31 Oct. 2003.

56. Winston Churchill, speech to the British House of Commons, 22 Jan. 1941, at: <http://mitglied.lycos.de/FrankGemkow/laku/gb/speeches/churchill-hour.htm>. Accessed 31 Oct. 2003.

57. Clark, eulogy to Pierre Trudeau.

58. Martin Luther King, 'I've Been to the Mountaintop', speech delivered at Mason Temple in Memphis, Tennessee, 3 Apr. 1968. Reprinted by arrangement with the Estate of Martin Luther King Jr, c/o Writers House as agent for the proprietor New York, NY. Copyright 1968 Martin Luther King Jr, copyright renewed 1996 Coretta Scott King.

59. 'Protesters, Police Gear up for Bush Visit', *Globe and Mail*, on-line edition, 29 Nov. 2004, at: <www.theglobeand mail.com/servlet/story/RTGAM.20041129.w2bush1129 a/BNStory/National/>. Accessed 29 Nov. 2004.

60. Campbell Clark, 'PM Poised to Counter Gomery "Outrage"', on-line edition, 11 Apr. 2005, at: <www.theglobe andmail.com/servlet/story/RTGAM.20050411.wxgomer y11/BNStory/National/>. Accessed 11 Apr. 2005.

61. Churchill, 'This was their Finest Hour'.

62. Martin Luther King Jr, 'I Have a Dream', delivered in Washington, DC, on the steps of the Lincoln Memorial, 28 Aug. 1963. Reprinted by arrangement with the Estate of Martin Luther King Jr, c/o Writers House as agent for the proprietor New York, NY. Copyright 1963 Martin Luther King Jr, copyright renewed 1991 Coretta Scott King. The full text of the speech can be found in the Appendix.

63. Ronald Reagan, televised speech to the nation, 28 Jan. 1986.

64. George W. Bush, televised speech to the nation, 1 Feb. 2003.

65. Anatol, 'Fundamentals of Persuasive Speaking', 19.

66. D.R. Roskos-Ewoldsen, H.J. Yu, and N. Rhodes, 'Fear Appeal Messages Affect Accessibility of Attitudes toward Threat and Adaptive Behaviors', *Communication Monographs* 71 (2004): 49–69. Also F.J. Boster and P. Mongeau, 'Fear-arousing Persuasive Messages', in R.N. Bostrom and B.H. Westley, eds, *Communication Yearbook* 8 (Newbury Park, Calif.: Sage, 1984), 330–75.

67. See the following discussions of the relationship between esteem and persuasibility: J. Brockner and M. Elkind, 'Self-Esteem and Reactance: Further Evidence of Attitudinal and Motivational Consequences', *Journal of Experimental Social Psychology* 21 (1990): 346–61; Bettinghaus and Cody, *Persuasive Communication*; H. Leventhal and S.I. Perloe, 'A Relationship between Self-Esteem and Persuasibility', *Journal of Abnormal and Social Psychology* 64 (1962): 385–8.

68. Bettinghaus and Cody. *Persuasive Communication*.

Chapter 11

1. G.S. Jowett and V. O'Donnell, *Propaganda and Persuasion*, 2nd edn (Newbury Park, Calif.: Sage, 1992), 54.

2. Ibid., 185–99.

3. J. Ellul, *Propaganda: The Formation of Men's Attitudes* (New York: Vintage, 1973).

4. Hermann Göring, interview with Gustave M. Gilbert, 18 Apr. 1946, reported in G.M. Gilbert, *The Nuremberg Diary* (New York: Da Capo Press, 1995).

5. *WordNet Dictionary*, at: <www.hyperdictionary.com/ dictionary/demagogue>. Accessed 17 Sept. 2004.

6. *Webster's Dictionary* (1913), at: <www.hyperdictionary .com/dictionary/demagogue>. Accessed 17 Sept. 2004.

7. Ellul, *Propaganda*.

8. K. Witte, 'The Manipulative Nature of Health Communication Research: Ethical Issues and Guidelines', *American Behavioral Scientist* 38 (1994): 285.

9. Jowett and O'Donnell, *Propaganda and Persuasion*, 4.

10. W.L. Brembeck and W.S. Howell, *Persuasion: A Means of Social Control* (Englewood Cliffs, NJ: Prentice-Hall, 1952).

11. S.L. Hayakawa, *Language in Thought and Action* (New York: Harcourt, Brace and Company, 1949).

12. Jowett and O'Donnell, *Propaganda and Persuasion*, 186.

13. A. Hitler, *Mein Kampf*, vol. 1, trans. J. Murphy (Germany, 1925), ch. 12.

14. Phillip Knightley, 'The Disinformation Campaign', *The Guardian*, 4 Oct. 2001, at: <www.guardian.co.uk/Archive/ Article/0,4273,4270014,00.html>. Accessed 20 Sept. 2004. Reprinted by permission.

15. G. Orwell, 'Politics and the English Language', *Horizon* (Apr. 1946). Also Orwell, *Shooting an Elephant and Other Essays* (London: Secker and Warburg, 1950).

16. W. Lutz, *Doublespeak: From ROM Revenue Enhancement to Terminal Living: How Government, Business, Advertisers, and Others Use the Language to Deceive* (New York: Harper-Collins, 1990). Also W.D. Lutz, *Doublespeak Defined: Cut through the Bull**** and Get to the Point* (New York: HarperResource, 1999).

17. R. Weaver, 'Ultimate Terms in Contemporary Rhetoric', in R.L. Johannessen, R. Strickland, and R.T. Eubanks, eds, *Language is Sermonic: Richard M. Weaver on the Nature of Rhetoric* (Baton Rouge: Louisiana State University Press, 1970), 87–112.

18. Hitler, *Mein Kampf*, vol. 1, ch. 11.

19. M.H. Prosser, 'Introduction', in *Sow the Wind, Reap the Whirlwind*, vol. 1 (New York: William Morrow, 1970).

20. 'Abu Ghraib General Blames Conspiracy', *Globe and Mail*, on-line edition, 3 Aug. 2004, 1, at: <www.theglobeand mail.com>. Accessed 3 Aug. 2004.

21. Kim Witte, 'Putting the Fear Back into Fear Appeals: The Extended Parallel Process Model', *Communication Monographs* 59 (1992): 329–49.

22. D.D. Johnston, *The Art and Science of Persuasion* (Madison, Wis.: W.C. Brown & Benchmark, 1994).

23. D.J. O'Keefe, *Persuasion: Theory and Research* (Newbury Park, Calif.: Sage, 1990).

24. E.B. Arkin, 'Interview', in T.E. Backer, E.M. Rogers, and P. Sopory, eds, *Designing Health Communication Campaigns: What Works?* (Newbury Park, Calif.: Sage, 1992), 36–40.

25. Brian Mulroney, speech in the House of Commons, Ottawa, 15 Jan. 1991.

26. Ibid.

27. Audrey McLaughlin, speech in the House of Commons, Ottawa, 15 Jan. 1991.

28. 'Haiti on the Brink of Famine', at: <www.poe-news.com/stories.php?poeurlid=34916>. Accessed 26 Sept. 2004.

29. L. Taylor, 'Confusing Statistics', 22 July 2004, at: <www.channel4.com/news/2004/07/week_4/22_crime_t.html>. Accessed 16 Aug. 2004.

30. Mel Cappe, 'Canada's Unique Presence in North America: Why Better than Ever is Not Good Enough', notes for an address by the Clerk of the Privy Council and Secretary to the Cabinet, opening plenary session of canada@theworld.ca, Ottawa, 30 Nov. 2000.

31. K. McRoberts, *Quebec: Social Change and Political Crisis*, 3rd edn (Toronto: McClelland & Stewart, 1993), 94–5; B.D. Palmer, *Working-Class Experience: Rethinking the History of Canadian Labour, 1800–1991* (Toronto: McClelland & Stewart, 1992), 256, 308–11.

Chapter 12

1. By collectivist cultures, I mean those that stress the group over the individual. A.N. Miller, 'An Exploration of Kenyan Public Speaking Patterns with Implications for the American Introductory Public Speaking Course', *Communication Education* 51 (2002): 168–82.

2. 'Princeton University Confers 1,806 Degrees at 252nd Commencement', Office of Communications, Princeton press release, 1 June 1999, at: <www.princeton.edu/pr/news/99/q2/0601-stats.htm>. Accessed 13 Feb. 2005.

3. 'Schwarzenegger Hits the Cruz Control', *The Insider*, 9 Jan. 2005, at: <www.sacunion.com/pages/columns/articles/1633/>. Accessed 14 Feb. 2005.

4. R. Williams, 'BrainyQuote', at: <www.brainyquote.com/quotes/authors/r/robin_williams.html>. Accessed on June 18, 2005.

5. J. Rivers, Biography Channel, A & E Television Networks, at: <www.thebiographychannel.co.uk/new_site/biography.php?id=1208&view=4>. Accessed 18 June 2005.

6. M. Smith, 'Timeless Quotes', at: <www.timelessquotes.com/author/Margaret_Smith.html>. Accessed 18 June 2005.

7. Williams, 'BrainyQuote'.

8. C. Rock, 'DFR: Daily Fashion Report', lookonline.com, 1 Apr. 2003, at: <www.lookonline.com/2003_04_01_archive.html>. Accessed 18 June 2005.

9. 'Linda Ross, Reptile at Law', Canoe, CN News, 16 Dec. 1999, at: <www.canoe.ca/CNEWSHeyMartha9912/16_two.html>. Accessed 11 Feb. 2005.

10. C. Leifer, 'Quote of the Day', at: <http://listserver.themacintoshguy.com/pipermail/x-apps/2003-June.txt>. Accessed 18 June 2005.

11. D. Russell, 'Self-Deprecatory Humour and the Female Comic: Self-Destruction or Comedic Construction', *Third Space* 2 (Nov. 2002), at: <www.thirdspace.ca/articles/druss.htm>. Accessed 21 June 2005. Also R. Jenkins, *Subversive Laughter: The Liberating Power of Comedy* (New York: Free Press, 1994).

12. 'The Battle of the N-Word', *The Observer*, 20 Jan. 2002, at: <http://education.guardian.co.uk/racism/comment/0,10795,636886,00.html>. Accessed 10 July 2004.

13. R. Barreca, *They Used to Call Me Snow White . . . But I Drifted: Women's Strategic Use of Humor* (New York: Penguin Books, 1991). Also T. Lundell, 'An Experimental Exploration of Why Men and Women Laugh', *Humor* 6, 3 (1993): 301.

14. B.W. Eakins and R.G. Eakins, *Sex Differences in Human Communication* (Boston: Houghton Mifflin, 1978), 75–7. Also M. Crawford, 'Just Kidding: Gender and Conversational Humor', in R. Barreca, ed., *New Perspectives on Women and Comedy* (Philadelphia: Gordon and Breach, 1992), 24.

15. 'Gender Differences in Comfort with Communication Situations is Evident in Poll Results (NCA/Roper Starch Poll)', *Spectra*, National Communication Association newsletter (Feb. 2000): 5.

16. Barreca, *They Used to Call Me Snow White*.

Chapter 13

1. Little agreement exists in the management literature on the differentiation between 'goals' and 'objectives'. Some use 'goals' to suggest a broader focus and 'objectives' to suggest a more narrow focus; others use the terms in the opposite way. See P.G. Bergeron, *Modern Management in Canada: Concepts and Practices* (Scarborough, Ont.: Nelson Canada, 1989), 254.

2. J.E. Brooks-Harris and S.R. Stock-Ward, *Workshops: Designing and Facilitating Experiential Learning* (Thousand Oaks, Calif.: Sage, 1999), 55–6. See also P.N. Blanchard and J.W. Thacker, *Effective Training: Systems, Strategies, and Practices*, 2nd edn (Upper Saddle River, NJ: Pearson Education, 2004), 122–4.

3. L. Stoneall, 'The Case for More Flexible Objectives', *Training and Development* (Aug. 1992): 67–9.

4. See the following: J. Colquitt and J. Lepine, 'Toward an Integrative Theory of Training Motivation: A Meta-analytic Path Analysis of 20 years of Research', *Journal of Applied Psychology* 85 (2000): 678–707; Blanchard and Thacker, *Effective Training*, 126; J. Lewis, 'Answers to Twenty Questions on Behavioral Objectives', *Educational Technology* (Mar. 1981): 27–31.

5. Blanchard and Thacker, *Effective Training*, 193.

6. Lewis, 'Answers to Twenty Questions'.

7. See, for example, D.A. Kolb, *Experiential Learning: Experience as the Source of Learning and Development* (Englewood Cliffs, NJ: Prentice-Hall, 1984).

8. A study completed by the US Department of Health, Education, and Welfare is referenced in W.E. Arnold and L. McClure, *Communication Training and Development*, 2nd edn (Prospect Heights, Ill.: Waveland Press, 1995), 38.

9. *The Power of Listening* [motion picture] (Scarborough, Ont.: CRM McGraw-Hill, 1978).

10. S.S. Wulff and D.H. Wulff, 'Of Course I'm Communicating; I Lecture Every Day: Enhancing Teaching and Learning in Introductory Statistics', *Communication Education* 53 (2004): 92–102; also P. Smagorinsky and P.K. Fly, 'The Social Environment of the Classroom: A Vygotskian Perspective on Small Group Process', *Communication Education* 42 (1993): 157–71.

11. J. Middendorf and A. Kalish, 'The Change-up in Lectures', unpublished manuscript, Indiana University (1995), 6, cited in P.H. Andrews, J.R. Andrews, and G. Williams, *Public Speaking: Connecting You and Your Audience*, 2nd edn (Boston: Houghton Mifflin, 2003), 54.

12. R. Dunn and K. Dunn, *Teaching Secondary Students through Their Individual Learning Styles: Practical Approaches for Grades 7-12* (Boston: Allyn & Bacon, 1993).

13. H. Gardner, *Frames of Mind: The Theory of Multiple Intelligences* (New York: Basic Books, 1983).

14. Dunn and Dunn, *Teaching Secondary Students*.

15. Brooks-Harris and Stock-Ward, *Workshops*, 30–1.

16. K.K. Dwyer, 'Communication Apprehension and Learning Style Preference: Correlations and Implications for Teaching', *Communication Education* 47 (1998): 137–50.

17. J.A. Daly and C.A. Diesel, 'Measures of Communication-Related Personality Variables', *Communication Education* 41 (1992): 405–14.

18. Brooks-Harris and Stock-Ward, *Workshops*, 29.

19. Arnold and McClure, *Communication Training and Development*, 21.

20. Statistics Canada, 2001 Census.

21. 'Fag Hags: Women Who Love Men', *The Passionate Eye*, 29 Sept. 2005.

22. J.R. Kidd, *How Adults Learn* (New York: Association Press, 1955), 44.

23. C.R. Rogers, *On Becoming a Person: A Therapist's View of Psychotherapy* (Boston: Houghton Mifflin, 1995); cited by K.H. Dover, 'Carl Rogers and Experiential Learning', at: <http://adulted.about.com/cs/adultlearningthe/a/carl_rogers.htm>. Accessed 28 July 2004.

24. For more information on the function of icebreakers, energizers, and other educational strategies that involve the student on a kinesthetic level, please refer to material developed by the Ontario Institute for Studies in Education, University of Toronto. Joan Vanden Hazel, Ontario Institute for Studies in Education, University of Toronto, at: <www.educationalconsulting.ca/ice break.htm>.

25. 'Methodology: Energizers', at: <www.isodec.org.gh/work shop-cd/workshops/methodology/energiser/Energisers .htm>. Accessed 2 Mar. 2003.

26. J. Neill, 'Games and Activities with Balloons', at: <www .wilderdom.com/games/descriptions/gamesballoons.html>. Accessed 28 July 2004.

27. Christina Kirkey, communication student, 2004.

28. S.D. Ferguson, 'Standoff at Oka: Take Me to Your Leader', in Ferguson and L.R. Shade, *Civic Discourse and Cultural Politics in Canada: A Cacophony of Voices* (Westport, Conn.: Ablex, 2002).

29. This passage is a paraphrased version of 'The Legend of the Dream Catcher', at: <www.y-indianguides.com/pfm_st_dreamcatacher.html>. Accessed 26 July 2004.

30. This information was drawn from: <http://lokrin.net/nynees/superstitions.php> and <www.japan-guide.com/e/e2209.html>. Accessed 27 July 2004.

31. 'Survival: A Simulation Game', at: <http://scouting web.com/scoutingweb/SubPages/SurvivalGame.htm>. Accessed 28 July 2004.

32. B.S. Bloom, ed., *Taxonomy of Educational Objectives: Book 1, Cognitive Domain* (New York: Longman, 1956).

33. *The Ultimate WebCT Handbook: A Practical and Pedagogical Guide to WebCT*, at: <www.ultimatehandbooks.net/excerpts/presentations.html>. Accessed 2 Oct. 2004.

34. M. Burgoon, J.K. Heston, and J. McCroskey, 'Communication Roles in Small Group Interaction', in S.D. Ferguson, *Organizational Communication*, 2nd edn (New Brunswick, NJ: Transaction, 1990), 386–90. Also K. Benne and P. Sheats, 'Functional Roles of Group Members', *Journal of Social Issues* 4 (1948): 41–9.

35. J.L. Chesebro and J.C. McCroskey, 'The Relationship of Teacher Clarity and Immediacy with Student State Receiver Apprehension, Affect, and Cognitive Learning', *Communication Education* 50 (2001): 59–68; B.S. Titsworth, 'An Experiment Testing the Effects of Teacher Immediacy, Use of Organizational Lecture Cues, and Students' Note-taking on Cognitive Learning', *Communication Education* 50 (2001): 283–97; M.B. Wanzer and A.B. Frymier, 'The Relationship between Student Perceptions of Instructor Humor and Students' Reports of Learning', *Communication Education* 48 (1999): 48–62; L.J. Christensen and K.E. Menzel, 'The Linear Relationship between Student Reports of Immediacy Behaviors and Perceptions of State

Motivation, and of Cognitive, Affective, and Behavioral Learning', *Communication Education* 47 (1998): 82–90; A. Moore, J.T. Masterson, D.M. Christophel, and K.A. Shea, 'College Teacher Immediacy and Student Ratings of Instruction', *Communication Education* 45 (1996): 29–39; J.I. Rodriguez, T.G. Plax, and P. Kearney, 'Clarifying the Relationship between Teacher Nonverbal Immediacy and Student Cognitive Learning: Affective Learning as the Central Causal Mediator', *Communication Education* 45 (1996): 293–305; J. Comstock, E. Rowell, and J.W. Bowers, 'Food for Thought: Teacher Nonverbal Immediacy, Student Learning, and Curvilinearity', *Communication Education* 44 (1995): 251–66; D. Christophel, 'The Relationships among Teacher Immediacy Behaviors, Student Motivation, and Learning', *Communication Education* 39 (1990): 323–40; ; J. Gorham and D. Christophel, 'The Relationship of Teachers' Use of Humor in the Classroom to Immediacy and Student Learning', *Communication Education* 39 (1990): 46–62; J.L. Allen and D.H. Shaw, 'Teachers' Communication Behaviors and Supervisors' Evaluation of Instruction in Elementary and Secondary Classrooms', *Communication Education* 39 (1990): 308–22; J. Gorham and W.R. Zakahi, 'A Comparison of Teacher and Student Perceptions of Immediacy and Learning: Monitoring Process and Product', *Communication Education* 39 (1990): 354–68; J.S. Gorham, "The Relationship between Verbal Teacher Immediacy Behaviors and Student Learning', *Communication Education* 37 (1988): 40–53; D.H. Kelley and J. Gorham, 'Effects of Immediacy on Recall of Information', *Communication Education* 37 (1988): 198–207; V.P. Richmond, J. Gorham, and J.C. McCroskey, 'The Relationship between Selected Immediacy Behaviors and Cognitive Learning', in M.A. McLaughlin, ed., *Communication Yearbook* 10 (Newbury Park, Calif.: Sage, 1987), 574–90; P. Andersen and J. Andersen, 'Nonverbal Immediacy in Instruction', in L. Barker, ed., *Communication in the Classroom* (Englewood Cliffs, NJ: Prentice-Hall, 1982), 98–120.

36. P.L. Witt, L.R. Wheeless, and M. Allen, 'A Meta-Analytical Review of the Relationship between Teacher Immediacy and Student Learning', *Communication Monographs* 71 (2004): 184–207.

37. Q. Zhang, 'Immediacy, Humor, Power, Distance, and Classroom Communication Apprehension in Chinese College Classrooms', *Communication Quarterly* 53 (2005): 87–108; J.C. McCroskey, A. Sallinen, J.M. Fayer, and R.A. Barraclough, 'Nonverbal Immediacy and Cognitive Learning: A Cross-Cultural Investigation', *Communication Education* 45 (1996): 200–11; J.C. McCroskey, A. Sallinen, J.M. Fayer, and R.A. Barraclough, 'A Cross-Cultural and Multi-Behavioral Analysis of the Relationship between Nonver-

bal Immediacy and Teacher Evaluation', *Communication Education* 44 (1995): 281–91; R.G. Powell and B. Harville, 'The Effects of Teacher Immediacy and Clarity on Instructional Outcomes: An Intercultural Assessment', *Communication Education* 39 (1990): 369–79; J.A. Sanders and R.L. Wiseman, 'The Effects of Verbal and Nonverbal Teacher Immediacy on Perceived Cognitive, Affective, and Behavioral Learning in the Multicultural Classroom', *Communication Education* 39 (1990): 341–53; P. Kearney, T.G. Plax, and N.J. Wendt-Wasco, 'Teacher Immediacy for Affective Learning in Divergent College Classes', *Communication Quarterly* 33 (1985): 61–74.

38. See, for example, M.Z. Hackman and Kim B. Walker, 'Instructional Communication in the Televised Classroom: The Effects of System Design and Teacher Immediacy on Student Learning and Satisfaction', *Communication Education* 39 (1990): 196–206.

Chapter 14

1. E. Katz and P.F. Lazarsfeld, *Personal Influence* (New York: Free Press of Glencoe, 1955).

2. W.L. Brembeck and W.S. Howell, *Persuasion: A Means of Social Control* (Englewood Cliffs, NJ: Prentice-Hall, 1952).

3. E.P. Bettinghaus, *Persuasive Communication* (New York: Holt, Rinehart and Winston, 1968), 112.

4. S.D. Butler, 'The Apologia, 1971 Genre', *Southern Speech Communication Journal* 37 (1972): 281–9.

5. J. Aucoin and M. Kearney, 'Saying They're Sorry: News Media Apologia Strategies', *AEJMC*, submitted to Critical and Cultural Studies Division, 2003, cited at: <http://list.msu.edu/cgi-bin/>. Accessed 1 Feb. 2005.

6. A.R. Cline, 'There's "Something" about "It" in the Political Apologia', cited at: <http://rhetorica.net/docs/apologia.pdf>. Accessed 1 Feb. 2005.

7. L.E. Rosenfield, 'A Case Study in Speech Criticism: The Nixon-Truman Analog', *Communication Monographs* 35 (1968): 435–50.

8. Ibid.

9. Butler, 'The Apologia, 1971 Genre'.

10. K.K. Campbell and K.H. Jamieson, *Deeds Done in Words: Presidential Rhetoric and the Genre of Governance* (Chicago: University of Chicago Press, 1990).

11. Butler, 'The Apologia, 1971 Genre'.

12. T.H. Neale, CRS Report for Congress, *Speechwriting in Perspective: A Brief Guide to Effective and Persuasive Communication*, Congressional Research Service, Library of Congress, Washington, DC, 25 Feb. 1998, cited at: <http://countingcalifornia.cdlib.org/crs/ascii/98-170>. Accessed 21 Jan. 2005.

Chapter 15

1. D. Mitchell, 'A Most Important Experiment: Parliamentary Internship Programs in Canada', *Canadian Parliamentary Review* 5 (1982), at: <www.parl.gc.ca/infoparl/english/issue.htm>. Accessed 23 Jan. 2005.

2. 'John Harvard's Journal', *Harvard Magazine*, at: <www.harvard magazine.com/issues/so96/jhj.friends.html>. Accessed 22 Jan. 2005.

3. T.H. Neale, CRS Report for Congress, *Speechwriting in Perspective: A Brief Guide to Effective and Persuasive Communication*, Congressional Research Service, Library of Congress, Washington, DC, 25 Feb. 1998, cited at: <http://counting california.cdlib.org/crs/ascii/98-170>. Accessed 21 Jan. 2005.

4. Ibid.

5. Ibid.

6. Ibid.

7. Speaking notes for Brian Mulroney, Prime Minister, at the signing ceremony for the Saskatchewan Treaty Land Entitlement Final Framework Agreement, 1992.

8. See S.E. Lucas, *The Art of Public Speaking*, 6th edn (Boston: McGraw-Hill, 1998), 298.

9. F.J.O. Blachly, 'Ghost Stories', at: <www.cosmos-club.org/journals/1999/blachly.html>. Accessed 21 Jan. 2005.

10. 'John Harvard's Journal'.

11. 'D.C. Gator Writing Campaign Speeches', at: <www.jou.ufl.edu/pubs/communigator/Archives/S99/pages/alumni/kappalman.htm>. Accessed 18 Jan. 2005.

12. B.W. Eakins and R.G. Eakins, *Sex Differences in Human Communication* (Boston: Houghton Mifflin, 1978), 75–7. Also M. Crawford, 'Just Kidding: Gender and Conversational Humor', in R. Barreca, ed., *New Perspectives on Women and Comedy* (Philadelphia: Gordon and Breach, 1992), 24.

13. Neale, *Speechwriting in Perspective*.

14. Ibid.

15. T. Lundell, 'An Experiential Exploration of Why Men and Women Laugh', *Humor* 6 (1993): 301.

16. R. Barreca, *They Used to Call Me Snow White . . . But I Drifted: Women's Strategic Use of Humor* (New York: Penguin, 1991), 1–37, cited at: <http://condor.depaul.edu/~mwilson/extra/humor/snowedt1.html>. Accessed 18 Jan. 2005.

17. Neale, *Speechwriting in Perspective*.

18. T. Jan, reporter for the American Society of Newspaper Editors, 'Presidential Speechwriters Don Thinking Caps and Beepers', 2 Apr. 2000, cited at: <www.asne.org/>. Accessed 21 Jan. 2005.

19. J. Podhoretz, 'The Breakfast Table: John Podhoretz and Michael Waldman', 14 Aug. 2000, cited at: <http://slate.msn.com/id/2000191/entry/1005882/>. Accessed 26 Jan. 2005.

20. Jan, 'Presidential Speechwriters Don Thinking Caps and Beepers'.

21. Ibid.

22. 'D.C. Gator Writing Campaign Speeches'.

23. Jan, 'Presidential Speechwriters Don Thinking Caps and Beepers'.

24. Ibid.

25. 'Presidential Genres', summarized from K.K. Campbell and K.H. Jamieson, *Deeds Done in Words: Presidential Rhetoric and the Genres of Governance* (Chicago: University of Chicago Press, 1990), 11, cited at: www.janda.org/politxts/methods &links/genres.html>. Accessed 23 Jan. 2005.

26. J. Scalzi, 'Whatever: The Stupidest Criticism of a Clinton, This Week', 12 June 2003, cited at: <www.scalzi.com/whatever/002465.html>. Accessed 21 Jan. 2005.

27. P.J. Parsons, 'Ethics: PR and Plagiarism', *PR Canada* (Apr. 2003), cited at: <www.prcanada.ca/ETHIX/PLAGT.HTM>. Accessed 25 Jan. 2004.

28. Joel Deshaye, 'The English Department's (Anti-) Plagiarism Road Show, Part II', *Teaching and Learning Bridges* (University of Saskatchewan) 2 (Mar. 2004), cited at: <www.usask.ca/tlc/bridges_journal/v2n5_mar_04/v2n5_anti-plagiarism.html>. Accessed 23 Jan. 2005.

29. Parsons, 'Ethics: PR and Plagiarism'.

30. J. Gerstein, 'Researcher Alleges Potential Plagiarism in 11 Passages of Kerry's Writings', *New York Sun*, 26 Oct. 2004, cited at: <http://daily.nysun.com>. Accessed 21 Jan. 2005.

31. Ibid.

32. B. Martin, 'Plagiarism: A Misplaced Emphasis', *Journal of Information Ethics* 3 (Fall 1994): 36-47, at: <www.uow.edu.au/arts/sts/bmartin/pubs/94jie.html>. Accessed 21 Jan. 2005.

33. Blachly, 'Ghost Stories'.

Chapter 16

1. M.J. Medhurst, 'Teaching Rhetorical Criticism to Undergraduates: Special Editor's Introduction', *Communication Education* 38 (1989): 175–90.

2. S.K. Foss, 'Rhetorical Criticism as the Asking of Questions', *Communication Education* 38 (1989): 191–6.

3 J. Andrews, *The Practice of Rhetorical Criticism* (New York: Macmillan, 1983).

4. Medhurst, 'Teaching Rhetorical Criticism'.

5. E. Stack, 'Dressing Marcia: The Construction of Gender in the 1990s', at: <http://collection.nlc-bnc.ca/100/202/300/mediatribe/mtribe95/marcia.html>.

6. See D. Henry and H. Sharp Jr, 'Thematic Approaches to Teaching Rhetorical Criticism', *Communication Education* 38 (1989): 197–204.

7. W.A. Linsley, classroom handout, University of Houston, 1968. Later published in W.A. Linsley, ed., *Speech Criticism: Methods and Materials* (Dubuque, Iowa: William C. Brown, 1968).

Index

accents: status and, 132
acceptance: latitudes of, 98–9
accountability, 1, 13, 18
acronyms, 378–9
action step, 245
activity: as attention strategy, 73–4, 186–7, 251
Adams, Raymond S., and Bruce J. Biddle, 51
advertising: speechwriters and, 385
agenda: team presentations and, 325–9
Alda, Alan, 217
alliteration, 257–8
'ambush', 357
amplification: as support, 199–200
analogies, 192, 262–3
Anderson, Kenneth E., 210–11
Aniston, Jennifer, 21–2
antithesis, 255–6
anxiety, 20–37; causes of, 23–7; coping strategies
    for, 28–36; physical manifestations of, 27–8;
    situational, 21–4; trait, 21, 22
apologia, 353–7
apprehensiveness, communication, 20–37
arguments: 'bandwagon', 291; one-sided v. two-
    sided, 247; ordering of, 247–8; strength of,
    247–8
Aristotle, 210, 222–3
Armstrong, Lance, 41
artwork: in learning activities, 339
assertiveness, 133–4
assimilation, 48, 49–50
attention strategies, 67–75, 122–3, 183–9,
    248–52
Aucoin, James, and Melva Kearney, 356
audience: analyzing, 89–95; appropriate
    language and, 106–8; attitudes of, 92–3,
    102–3; beliefs of, 92; common perspective
    with, 100–1; complimenting, 102;
    demographic profile of, 90–1; ethical and
    critical concerns and, 111–12; knowledge
    level of, 108; model of public speaking and,
    16–17; multiple, 108–10; needs of, 94–5,
    105–6; occasion and place and, 110–11;
    personal connections with, 99–100;
    personality profile of, 95, 266; principles of,
    103–5; purposes and, 98–9; psychographic
    profile of, 91–5; reason to listen and, 189;
    recognizing, 99–110; reference groups and,
    101–2; researching, 89–95; rhetorical
    criticism and, 399–400; team presentations
    and, 329–30; topics and, 96–8; values of,
    93–4, 103–5
audience adaptation, 88–114
audiotapes: as aid, 147–8

Banderas, Antonio, 24

Baronet, Jim, 222
Barrault, Jean-Louis, 24
Basinger, Kim, 22
Bauman, James, 32
Berlo, David K., 211
Bible: references to, 263–4
Bickel, Kenneth E., 130
Blachly, Frederick J.O., 376, 390
Blair, Tony, 212, 214–15
Blondin, Ethel, 120–1
Bloom, Benjamin, 338
Boucher, Gaetan, 30
Bowie, David, 183
Bradbury, Ray, 188, 221
Brando, Marlon, 305
Branson, Richard, 25
Brazeau, Patrick, 422–3
Brembeck, Winston, and William Howell, 284–5
Broughton, Paul A., 24
Brown, Beuenia, 212
Bryan, William Jennings, 11
Burke, Kenneth, 100
Burns, George, 73
Busby, John, 75, 107
Bush, George H.W., 103, 126
Bush, George W., 126–7, 223–4, 264, 289

Campbell, Karolyn Kohrs, and Kathleen
    Jamieson, 356
Campbell, Kim, 196, 220, 254, 255, 257, 261,
    417
Cappe, Mel, 298
card sorting, 336
case studies, 336–7
cases, parallel, 227, 296
chalkboards, 144–5
channel: model of public speaking and, 16
character, 211
Charleson, Mary, 81
charts: flip, 145, 347; pie, 148
Chautauqua movement, 10–11
Chomsky, Noam, 2
Chrétien, Jean, 11, 100–1, 110, 220, 255, 257,
    258, 259, 260, 263, 290, 422
Churchill, Winston, 116, 257, 259–60, 261, 262
Cialdini, Robert B., 219
Cicero, 14, 210
Clark, Joe, 111, 255, 260, 261; Diefenbaker
    eulogy, 411–12
Clark, Marcia, 129
Clarkson, Adrienne, 219, 259, 419–20
Clausen, Curt, 29
Clevinger, Theodore Jr, 211
Clinton, Bill, 264, 354–5, 356, 357
Clinton, Hillary, 103–4, 225–6

commonplaces, 116, 376–7
communication breakdown: reasons for, 52
comparisons, 260, 307
competence, 133–4, 211, 213–18
composure, 118–21, 211, 402
computer-generated presentations, 143, 151–62,
    339–40, 343–4, 347; see also PowerPoint
    presentations
conclusions, 77–8, 203–4, 268–9
conflict: as attention strategy, 73–4, 186–7, 251
contracts: speechwriters and, 386–7
contrast, 260
conventions, rhetorical, 9–10, 398
Coon Come, Matthew, 101, 102, 259
Cooper, Tommy, 33
Creamer, Brian, 213–14
credibility: delivery and, 118–35; derived, 222;
    informative speeches and, 189–90; initial,
    222; shifts in, 222; source, 14, 210–22;
    terminal, 222, 400
Critical Communication Model, 12–18, 393;
    ethics and, 299
critical society, 2–3
criticism, rhetorical; see rhetorical criticism
Cronkite, Walter, 28
Crosby, John, 212
culture: clashes of, 125–6
Curiel, Carolyn, 381, 387

databases, 171
data projectors, 146–7
debate, 209
delivery: conversational, 68–9, 127–9; ethics
    and, 138; humour and, 310; persuasive
    speech and, 269–70; principles of, 115–39;
    significance of, 137–8; team presentations
    and, 341–8
demagoguery, 280, 282, 283
demographics, audience, 264–5
description: audience attention and, 187–8; as
    support, 191–2
Devereaux, Desirée, 125, 152
Dewey, John, 239
dialects: status and, 132
disclaimers, 219
dogmatism, 95
drama: as attention strategy, 73–4, 186–7, 251
dramatism, 100
dress, 129–30, 130–2, 342
Dunkin, Christopher, 256
Duplessis, Maurice, 299
dynamism, 121–5, 211, 220, 400–1

Edmonds, Terry, 381, 387
Edwards, Edwin, 222

Elbert, Steve, 73
Ellul, Jacques, 281
emotions: appeals to, 222–4, 284–6; control of, 120–1
energizers, 332
environments, speaking, 16, 95–6, 124, 133, 135; team presentations and, 341–2
equipment, 95–6, 124, 135, 152; team presentations and, 348
ethics, 18, 22, 55, 71–2, 97; academic freedom and, 323; delivery and, 138; free speech and, 15; lying and, 360; persuasive speech and, 267; propaganda and, 283; purpose and, 216; research and, 174; rhetorical criticism and, 396; social occasion speeches and, 308; visual aids and, 142
ethos, 209–22
eulogies, 305–6
euphemisms, 287
exaggeration, 307
examples: hypothetical, 198–9; reasoning and, 224–5, 293–4; as support, 197–9
expertise, 134, 211, 213, 402
expert testimony: as support, 200–1
expressions: audience attention and, 188; as support, 199–20
extroversion, 211
eye contact: trustworthiness and, 125–6

fables: as support, 194–5
facilitators: feedback and, 344–7; team presentations and, 331–48
facts: as support, 191
fallacies, 292–7
fear: appeals to, 224, 290
feedback: negative, 53–4; professional speechwriting and, 382–5; supportive, 52–4; team presentations and, 344–7
feedback options: model of public speaking and, 17–18
fees: speechwriters and, 386–7
Field, Sally, 12
field of experience, 88–9
fishbowl exercises, 337–8
Fisher, Mary, 256
flannel boards, 145
fluency: credibility and, 119–20
Fontaine, Phil, 135
Fosdick, Harry, 258
fours: rule of, 259–60
Fox, Michael J., 309
frames: listening, 46, 49–50; perceptual, 49–50
framing theory, 46
Frost, Robert, 73

gallery exercises, 335
Gardner, Howard, 326
Gelinas, Johanne, 105
generalities, 288–9
generalization: reasoning and, 225–6, 294–5
Genovesi, Sonia, 250

gestures: credibility and, 119, 121–2, 126–7
ghost-written speeches: ethics of, 387, 389–90; researching, 369–73; steps in, 368–79
gimmicks: as attention strategy, 75
Gooding, Cuba Jr, 12
Göring, Hermann, 281
Gossage, Patrick, 259
Graham, Laurie, 29
graphs: bar, 148–51; line, 149–50
group dynamics, 339–41
guided fantasies, 332–4

Haiman, Frank S., 210
handouts, 145–6, 347–8
Hayakawa, S.L., 285
Herman, Edward S., 2
Hermann, Andrew, 32
hesitations, 219
Hill, W.E., 44
Hill & Knowlton, 286
Himelfarb, Alex, 68, 74, 221
Himsl, Milton, 108
Hite, Shere, 39
Hitler, Adolf, 285–6, 289
Hodgins, Jamie, 125–6
Holloway, Sue, 34
Hovland, Carl I., 210
Huff, Daryl, 142
humour: as attention strategy, 74, 188–9; cautions in using, 309–10; female and male response to, 379; social occasion speeches and, 307–10

icebreakers, 331–2
illustrators, 127
imaging, internal, 29–31
immediacy strategies, 68–70, 127–30, 183–5, 221, 248–9
indexes, 171
inflection: dynamism and, 123
information: processing of, 50–1; propaganda and, 282–3
informative speeches, 163–208; introduction of, 182–90; organization of, 175–81; outlines for, 181–2; purpose statement for, 166; researching, 167–74; samples of, 204–8; supporting materials and, 191–201; thesis statement for, 166–7; topics for, 165–6; types of, 164–5
intelligences, 'multiple', 326–7
intensifiers, 219
Internet: research and, 170–4, 374; search engines, 172–4; speechwriting and, 374
internship, parliamentary, 367
interviews, 168–70
introduction(s), 67–75; informative speeches and, 182–90; persuasive speech and, 248–52; speech of, 57–87, 306–7
irony, 309

Jamieson, Kathleen, 12

Janis, Irving L., 210
jargon, 378
Jensen, Peter, 29, 32, 36
'Joe Canadian rant', 195
Joel, Billy, 197–8
Johnson, Sarah, 104–5

Kappalman, Samantha, 377, 387
Karpinski, Janis, 289
Katzman, Martin, 21, 23
Kelley, Harold H., 210
Kennedy, Edward, 354, 356
Kennedy, John F., 109–10, 256, 258, 261
Kerry, John, 212
Kilgour, David, 262
King, Martin Luther Jr, 124, 137, 261–2, 263; 'I Have a Dream', 409–11
Klein, Bonnie, 2–3
Klein, Naomi, 2–3
Koestler, Arthur, 44
Kunstler, William J., 197, 254
'Kuwaiti babies incident', 286–7

labelling by association, 291–2
La Guardia, Fiorello, 127
language: concrete and vivid, 253–4; evocative, 253–64; level of, 107; politically correct, 106–8, 378; professional speechwriting and, 377–9
latitudes of acceptance, 98–9
Layton, Jack, 262
learning: auditory, 326; kinesthetic, 326; tactile, 326; types of, 326–7; visual, 326
learning activities, 325–9; types of, 328, 330–9
learning theories, 325–8
legends: as support, 193–4
Leifer, Carol, 309
Lemert, James B., 211
levelling, 48, 49
Lévesque, René, 11
libraries, 170–2
likeability, 211
Lincoln, Abraham, 137
linguistic strategies, 72–3
listening, 38–56; deliberative, 40; empathic, 40; good attitudes and behaviours for, 53; perception and, 41–52; purposeful, 39–41; responsibilities of, 52–4
listening frames, 46; inadequate, 49–50
Littlefeather, Sacheen, 305
logic: appeals to, 224–7; see also reasoning
logos, 209–10, 224–7
Lutz, William, 288

McCallum, John, 102, 104
McCroskey, James C., 22, 211
McCroskey, James, and Rod McVetta, 52
McLaughlin, Audrey, 111, 256–7, 293
McLuhan, Marshall, 11
Malandro, Loretta, and Larry Barker, 133
Malinowksi, Bronislaw, 193

Mandela, Nelson, 109, 258–9
manipulators, 119
manuscripts, preparing, 379–80
Mardi Gras, film about, 47–50
Martin, Paul, 215
Maslow, Abraham, 94, 249
Maslow, Abraham, and Robert Mintz, 51
Matthews, Alfred Edward, 22
media scrums, 357
memorization, 81
men: dress and, 129, 131
Mertz, Robert J., 211
messages: model of public speaking and, 14–16; rhetorical criticism and, 403; strategic, 373, 375
metaphors, 261–2
Milgram, Stanley, 218–19
misconceptions, 175, 179
modules, speech, 116, 380
Molloy, John T., 131
Monroe, Alan H., 116, 243
Moore, Michael, 305
movements: credibility and, 119, 132–3; *see also* gesture; posture
Mulroney, Brian, 11, 135, 293, 374–5
myth response, 179

name-calling, 291–2
Neale, Thomas H., 369, 374
Newall, Margaret, 216
Nissani, Moti, 175
Nixon, Richard, 354, 356, 357
noise, 16, 17
note cards, 79–82, 270
novel: as attention strategy, 70–1, 185–6, 251

Obama, Barack, 220
objectives: learning, 324–5; teaching, 324–5
objectivity, 134–5, 211, 221
objects: as visual aid, 143–4, 347
O'Neill, Susie, 25
organization, 60–6; informative speeches and, 175–81; team presentations and, 326; *see also* patterns, organizational
Orwell, George, 287
outcomes: persuasive speech and, 237–8; rhetorical criticism and, 404
outlines: 62–6; informative speeches and, 181–2; parallel construction in, 63; phrases in, 65–6; sentences in, 64–5; subheadings in, 62
oversimplification, 289
oxymoron, 309

Paige, Satchel, 73
panic disorders, 23
parables: as support, 194–5
Parizeau, Jacques, 11
Parson, Patricia J., 389
pathos, 209–10, 222–4
patriotism, 288–9

patterns, organizational, 175–81; causal, 241–2; chronological, 60, 176; claims, 243; comparative advantages, 242; comparative, 61, 177–8; criteria-satisfaction, 243; motivated sequence, 243–7; narrative, 61, 179; problem and solution, 238–9; reflective thinking, 239–41; spatial, 60–1, 176–7; topical, 61, 177; transformative, 179–81
Peck, Laura, 357
perception: attitudinal issues and, 46–8; backward-looking, 43–4; culture-bound, 42–3; frames of, 49–50; influence of, 46–8; learned, 42–3; message reception and, 41–52; nature of, 41–6; relative, 45–6; selective, 39, 44–5; value-laden, 45
periodicals, 170–2
personalization, persuasive, 249–50
Personal Report of Communication Apprehension (PRCA), 22
Personal Report of Public Speaking Anxiety (PRPSA), 22
personification, 262
persuasive speech, 209–28, 229–79; audiences and, 236, 264–8; conclusions and, 268–9; delivery of, 269–70; introductions and, 248–52; organization of, 238–48; outcome and, 237–8; position statement for, 235; propaganda and, 282–3; purposes of, 230, 236–7; samples of, 271–9; thesis statement for, 236; topics for, 230–5
phobia, social, 20–1, 23
pictographs, 149
pitch: dynamism, and, 123
plagiarism, 389–90
'plain folks': pretending to be, 290–1
Podhoretz, John, 381
poems: as support, 195
polarization, 289
posters, 146
Postman, Leo, Jerome Bruner, and Elliott McGinnies, 45
posture, 119, 132–3; *see also* gestures; movement
PowerPoint presentations, 143, 151–7; sample presentation, 158–62; team presentations and, 343–4
Poy, Vivienne, 424–6
practice, 79–82
presentations: computer-generated, 143, 151–62, 339–40; mixed media, 152–3; team, 321–49
primacy effect, 182, 247–8
professional speechwriting, 367–91; checklist for, 388; employment opportunities in, 385–7; evaluation of, 382–5
projectors, overhead, 146–7
proofs: emotional/ethical/logical, 16
propaganda, 280–300; definition of, 280–4; modern context of, 282–4; strategies of, 284–92; World War II context of, 281–2
proposals, project, 361–2
proverbs: as support, 192–3

proximity, physical, 130
psychographics, audience, 265
puns, 308
purpose, 59–60, 166, 236–7

qualification, 211
questions: 'Q's and A's', 117; responding to, 270; rhetorical, 69–70, 263; tag, 219; team presentations and, 344–7
Quintilian, 210
quotations: as attention strategy, 73, 188; books of, 373; persuasive speech and, 251–2; as support, 192–3

Ranger, Juline, 351–2
rate, speech: dynamism and, 123–4
read-arounds, 335
Reagan, Ronald, 188, 263
reasoning, 224–7; causal, 295–6; circular, 292; fallacies of, 292–7; slippery slope, 292–3
recency effect, 182, 248
red herrings, 296–7
repetition, 256–7
research: credibility and, 173; Internet, 170–4, 374; interviewing for, 168–70; personal experience, 167; persuasive speech and, 252–3; sources for, 167–74
resolution, 209
resources: on-line, 170–2, 374; on-site, 170–2; *see also* sources
responses: signal, 284–6; symbol, 284–5
responsiveness: competence and, 133–4
rhetorical criticism, 392–408; audience and, 399–400; cultural context and, 395; economic context and, 395; environment and, 393–9; ethical context of, 396; legal context of, 397; message and, 403; outcomes and, 404; physical setting of, 396–7; political context and, 395; sample of, 405–8; social context and, 395–6; speaker and, 400–3; speaker motives and, 393; technological context and, 396
'rhetorical imperative', 393
rhythm: dynamism and, 123
Richmond, Virginia P., James C. McCroskey, and Steven K. Payne, 131
Rivers, Joan, 307
roasts, 302
Robertson, Kathleen, 131
Robespierre, Maximilien, 9
Robinson, Svend, 355–6
Rock, Chris, 308
Rogers, Carl, 330
Rokeach, Milton, 99, 231
role-plays, 338
roles: team presentation and, 340–1, 342–3
Roosevelt, Franklin D., 224–5
Rosenfeld, Lawrence E., 356

safety, 211
sales talks, 359–61

Scalzi, John, 387, 389
scenarios, 336–7
schedules: speechwriters and, 387, 388
Schlesinger, Arthur M. Jr, 376
Schramm, Wilbur, 88–9
Scott, Walter Dill, 67
Seinfeld, Jerry, 23
self-esteem: audience and, 95
sharpening, 48, 49
Sheridan, Richard, 9, 11
shock: as attention strategy, 71, 186, 251
sign: reasoning and, 226–7, 295
signposts, 76–7, 202, 268
silence: control of, 120
similes, 262
sincerity, 213–14
slides, 147
Smith, F.E., 116
Smith, Murray, 125–6
sociability, 127–30, 211, 220–1, 402–3
social occasion speeches, 301–20; samples of,
    311–20; types of, 302–7
Socrates, 353–4
software, presentation, 143, 151–62, 339–40,
    343–4, 347; see also PowerPoint
    presentations
Sommer, Robert, 52
songs: as support, 195
sources: research, 167–74; secondary, 170; see also
    resources
speakers: briefing, 251–2; model of public
    speaking and, 14; responsibilities of, 52–3;
    rhetorical criticism and, 400–3
speeches: acceptance, 304–5, 358; after-dinner,
    302; apologia, 353–7; award, 304–5;
    business, 359–65; campaign, 357–8;
    commencement, 303–4; concession, 358;
    condolence, 358–9; debriefings, 362–3;
    ghost-written, 367–91; goodwill, 351–2,
    364–5, 367–91; graduation, 303–4;
    impromptu, 115–18; informative, 163–208;
    introduction, 57–87, 306–7; keynote, 303–4;
    manuscript, 353, 365–6; motivational,

363–4; nomination, 358; one-point, 115;
    on-line sources of, 396–7; persuasive,
    229–79; political, 351–9; post-mortems,
    362–3; project proposals, 361–2; sales talks,
    359–61; salutatory, 304; social occasion,
    310–20; special purpose, 350–66; tribute,
    305; valedictory, 304; welcome, 88, 113–14
speechwriting: on-line resources for, 374;
    professional, 367–91
Spencer, Charles, 417–19
statements: context, 394; environment, 394;
    position, 235; preview, 66–7, 182; purpose,
    166; thesis, 60, 166–7, 236
statistics: as support, 195–7; visual aids and, 142,
    148–51, 297–8
status, 130–3, 211, 218–20, 402
stereotypes, 308
Stojko, Elvis, 35
stories: as support, 193–4
storytelling: team presentation and, 334
structure, parallel, 63, 154–5, 182, 254–5
summaries, internal, 77, 202, 268
support materials, 191–201, 252–3
suspense: as attention strategy, 71, 186, 251

tables, breakdown, 148
talking points, 380
Taras, David, 4
Tattenbaum, Rae, 27
team presentations, 321–49; delivery of, 341–8;
    group dynamics and, 339–41; learning
    activities and, 325–39; objectives and,
    324–5; roles in, 340–1, 342–3
teleprompter, 354
'10-year rule', 36
theme: choosing, 58–9; team presentations and,
    324
third person, 289–90
threes: rule of, 259–60
timelines, 336
topics: audiences and, 96–8; informative
    speeches and, 165–6; persuasive speech and,
    230–5

Tracy, Jan, 381
transfer, 287
transitions, 75–6, 201–2, 268
tributes, 305
Trudeau, Pierre, 11, 111, 220; on Quebec
    Referendum, 412–17
Truman, Harry, 356
trustworthiness, 125–7, 211, 212–15, 401–2
truth: manipulation of, 286–7; softening of,
    287–8
Turner, John, 101–2
Tutty, Leslie, 256, 421

Underhill, Barbara, 30
understatement, 307

values, 231; audience, 93–4, 103–5
versatility: competence and, 133–4
videotapes: selected, 139, 401; as visual aids,
    147–8
visual aids, 58–9, 82, 140–62, 339; ethics and,
    142; general principles of, 141–3;
    informative speeches and, 202–3; kinds of,
    143–8; purposes of, 140–1; statistics and,
    298; team presentations and, 347–8
visualization, 29–31, 244–5
voice: first and second, 258–9
volume: dynamism and, 123–4

Walker, John, 9, 10
war: terminology of, 287–8
Weaver, Richard, 289
wedding toasts, 303
Weston, Hilary M., 68–9, 100, 101, 215, 255,
    259, 260
whiteboards, 144–5
Whittier, John Greenleaf, 73
Williams, Robin, 307, 308
Williams, Vic, 142
Winfrey, Oprah, 88–9, 90–1, 93–4, 221
women: dress and, 129, 131
Woods, Tiger, 33–4
workbooks, 347